THINGS I DO IN DETROIT

A Guidebook to the Coolest Places

by the

Nain Rouge

Written and Photographed by Dave Krieger

Things I Do in Detroit
A Guidebook to the Coolest Places by the Nain Rouge
www. thenainrouge.net

First Edition, 2017
Published and designed by KMW studio publishing, New York
www.kmwstudio.com

For information: contact@kmwstudio.com

ISBN: 978-0-9973916-0-2

Printed in Italy

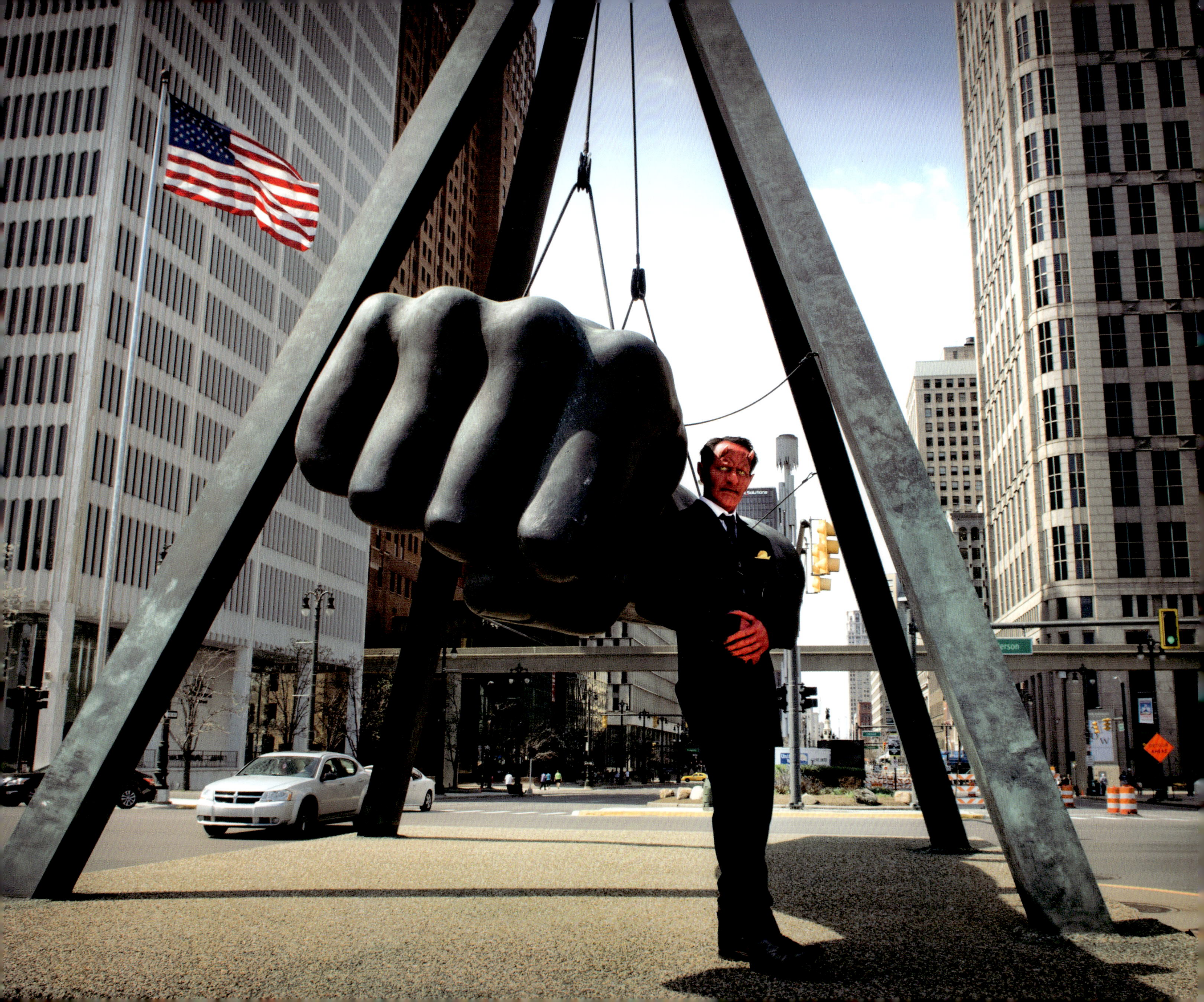

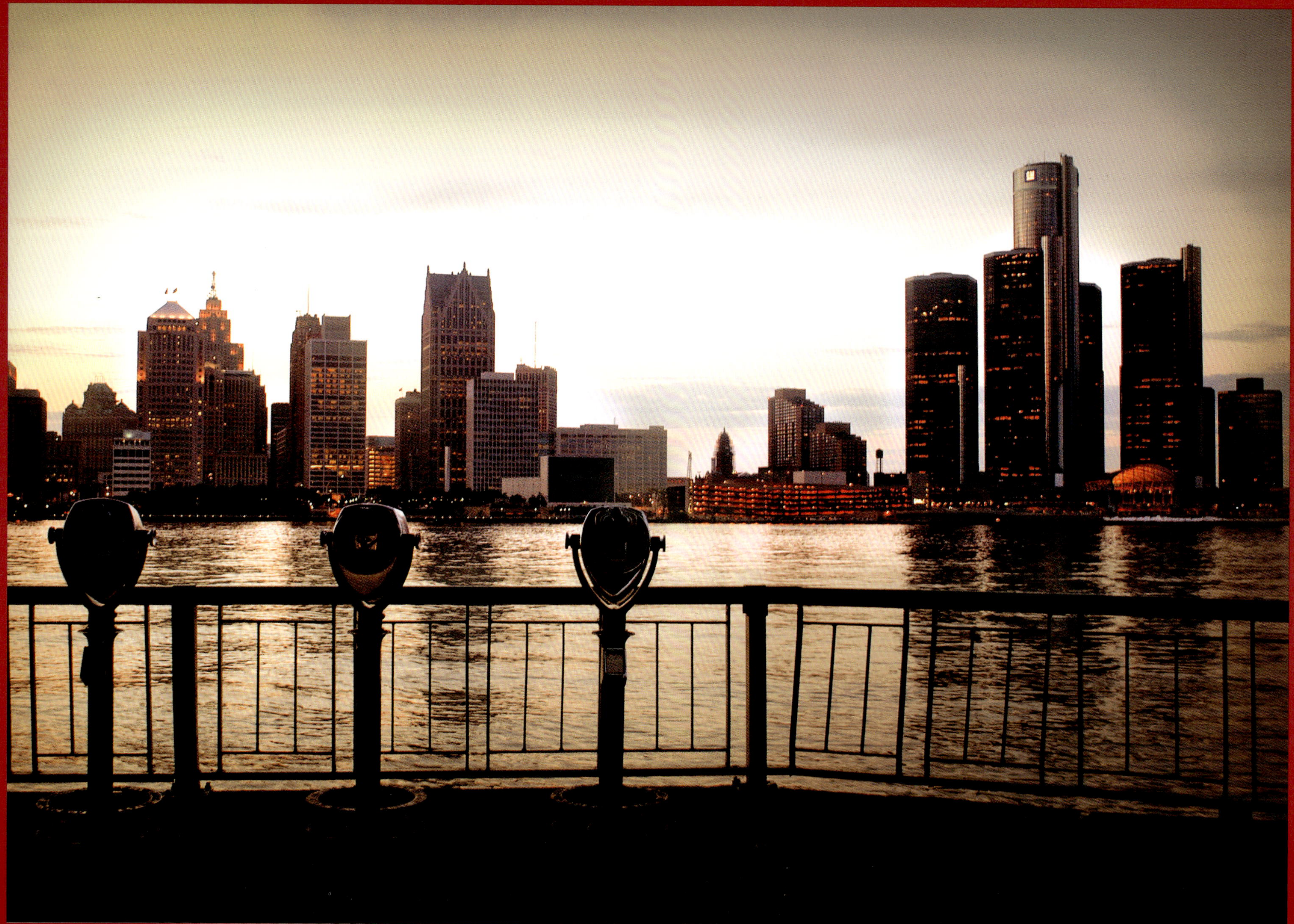

CONTENTS

PREFACE

I learned about the Nain Rouge from my father when I was nine years old. It was a fascinating tale of history and mystery. His story in Detroit begins with Cadillac arriving in 1701 and continues throughout moments in the city's history, including the fire at St. Anne's church, Pontiac's siege of Detroit, the 1805 fire that destroyed the city, and the '67 riots. He's been blamed for any disaster or misfortune that happens in Detroit. His purported malevolence is famous, and his appearance only adds to the mistrust and scorn he has withstood.

Growing up in Detroit during "white flight" and manufacturing contraction, and amid the growing disdain for anything "Detroit" by former residents and national media, I used to wonder what made Detroit so powerful and why it provoked such strong feelings. Once regarded as the "Arsenal of Democracy," the birthplace of automation and the automobile, and the "Paris of the Midwest," over the last five decades, as a million residents left, the city became the symbol of post-industrial failure.

As Detroit was derided and belittled, I sought out stories of Detroit's innovative prowess and its contributions to the world, never losing confidence in its historic importance and creative energy. For those of us who stayed during the decline, as we were battered by jokes and feared, our pride grew greater, becoming a badge of honor.

I have had the luxury of hanging out with the Nain Rouge, and his explanations of events are quite different than the popular historical narrative. He is misunderstood and has been maligned for centuries. He stands accused for Detroit's most catastrophic events. During all this time he has never been recognized for, or sought praise for, the many acts of philanthropy he performs. Under these circumstances, if he didn't love Detroit, why would he make this his home for more than three centuries? He is the ultimate Detroiter. From its founding he has continually participated in Detroit's affairs, always working behind the scenes to make it a better, richer city.

Like the Nain Rouge, Detroiters don't give a damn about you or your cities' problems or successes. We do things our way because we have been forced to. In Detroit, there is a freedom in creating your own identity, following your own dreams, and knowing that you alone are responsible for who you become. Detroiters have had to overcome more obstacles than most, teaching us resilience when faced with adversity. If you are from Detroit, it is in your blood. Detroiters are proud of their history, their toughness, and most importantly, their hometown.

Dozens of books and articles have exploited the "ruins" of Detroit's collapsed economy and crumbling buildings. I was never able to fetishize or celebrate these great "ruins." These buildings were part of my home, my memories, and my past or, more to my point, our past, our history, and our collective identity.

The following list, assembled by the Nain Rouge, illustrates just some of the things that make Detroit an amazing place to live. This is where he goes to enjoy Detroit and what he would recommend to any new visitor, tourist, or neighbor.

Dave Krieger

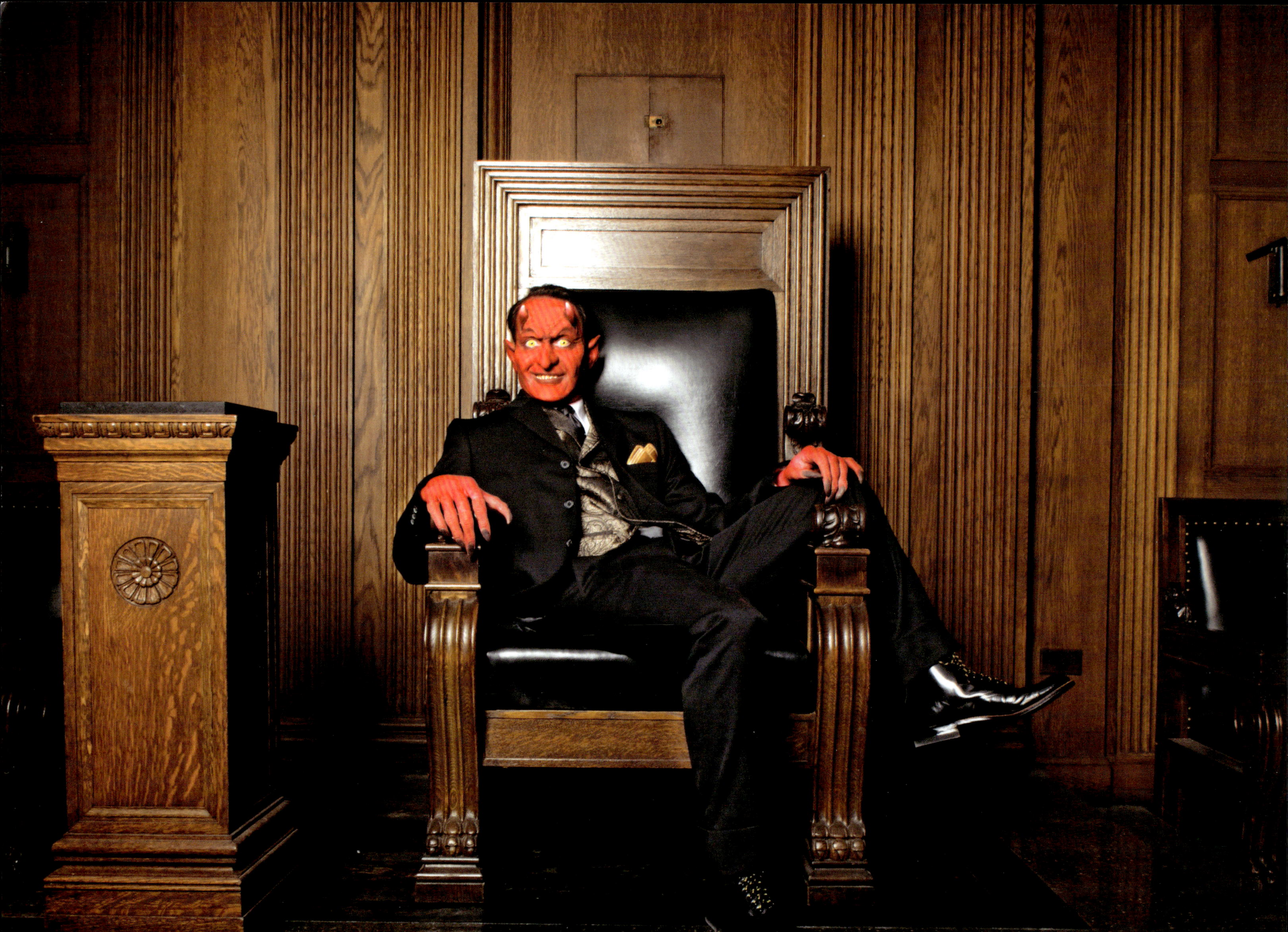

A WORD FROM THE NAIN ROUGE

For those of you unaware, I'm called the Nain Rouge. I am a gnome, or imp. Some call gnomes, dwarves, imps and fairies mythological creatures, but I'm living proof that we exist.

According to the popular narrative, I am a malevolent creature, determined to create havoc whenever possible. As the consummate outsider – continually shunned for my physical differences, dismissed because I do not assimilate easily, and resented due to others' insecurities – I have been accused, disparaged, and misrepresented by those who fear the unfamiliar.

Not giving a shit what people thought of me was my policy for years – for centuries, actually. If my contribution to the growth and advancement of Detroit over the years went unrecognized, okay. My self-regard does not require accolades. If folks wanted to blame me for a fire or a riot, fine. I could take it. My red skin is pretty thick.

But then people started marching around insisting that I needed to be chased out of town. You don't have to like the way I look or my irreverent attitude, but that's taking things too far. So now I want to set the record straight. Realizing the importance of this moment in Detroit's history, I have decided to reveal myself to the public for the first time.

Sure, I was there when a lot of things went down, but it doesn't take a genius to see that I didn't cause the problems that plagued Detroit from the beginning. Did I burn down buildings belonging to my friends? Did I bulldoze neighborhoods to build the freeways that eased the exit of those who preferred suburban living? Did I implement segregation in schools and housing? Did I close factories which employed my neighbors? Don't be absurd. All of those were the acts committed by many, many people, not one single imp. Blaming them all on me means failing to take responsibility or come up with real solutions. Making me a scapegoat fixes nothing.

I've watched good people lose jobs, homes, and self-esteem because of intolerance, racism, and fear. I've become distraught that, under the guise of progress and capitalism, a great city was left to rot. I am tired after decades of witnessing Detroit's slow, painful demise.

At the same time, I've come to love Detroit's people and the city's place in history. To show my affection for the place where I've opted to remain for more than 300 years, I took my buddy Dave around town to take pictures of some of my favorite things. The places that follow are the reasons why I feel Detroit is a beautiful city, filled with dedicated, energized, and talented people. I've added (in appropriately red ink) some of my memories and opinions about each and every one of them, including that silly anti-me parade (which is, in fact, rather fun).

If, after looking through these pages, you still want to blame me for the city's ills, then you're just an idiot. And remember: I'll still be here, living it up, long after you're gone.

Enjoy!

Nain Rouge

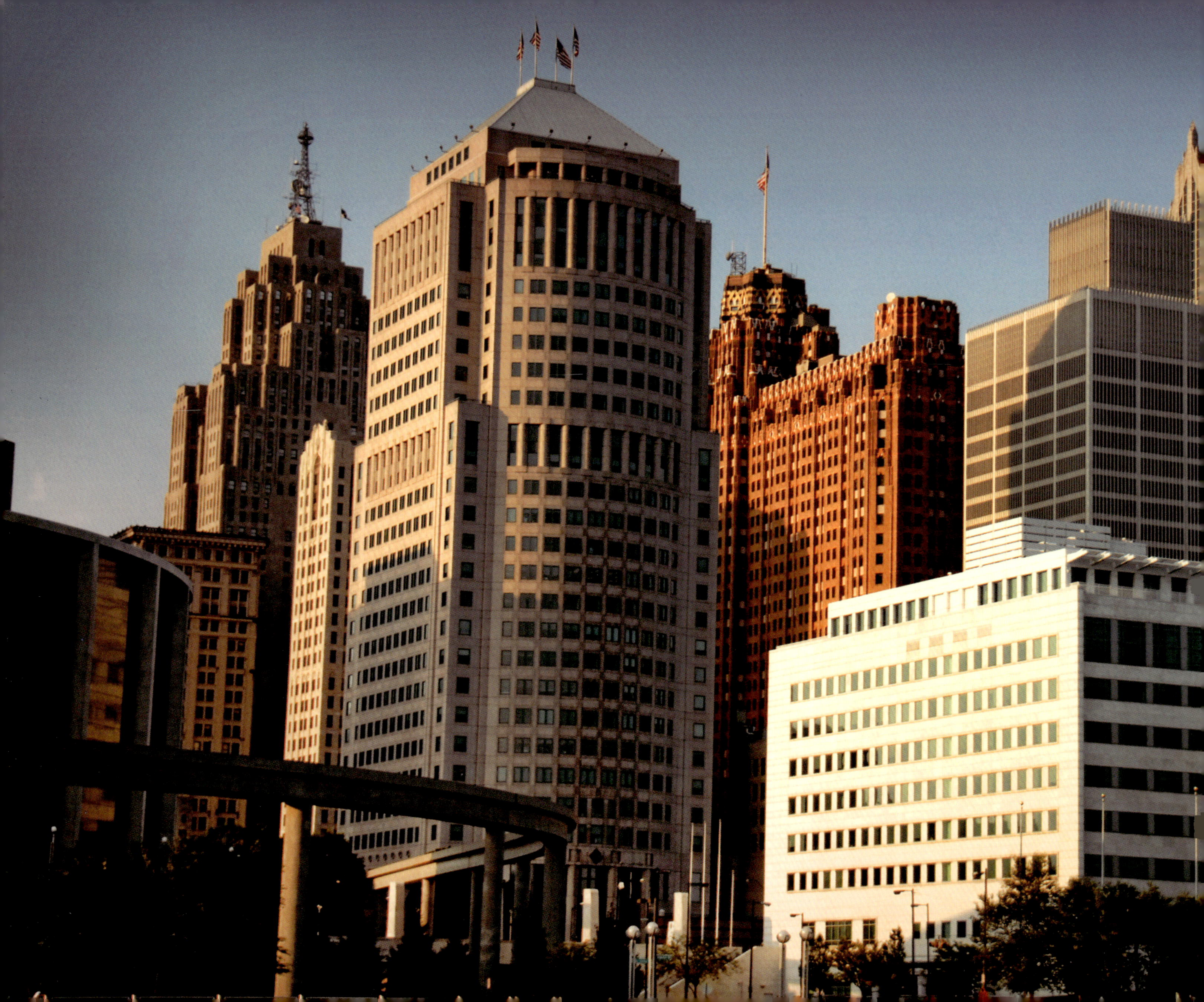

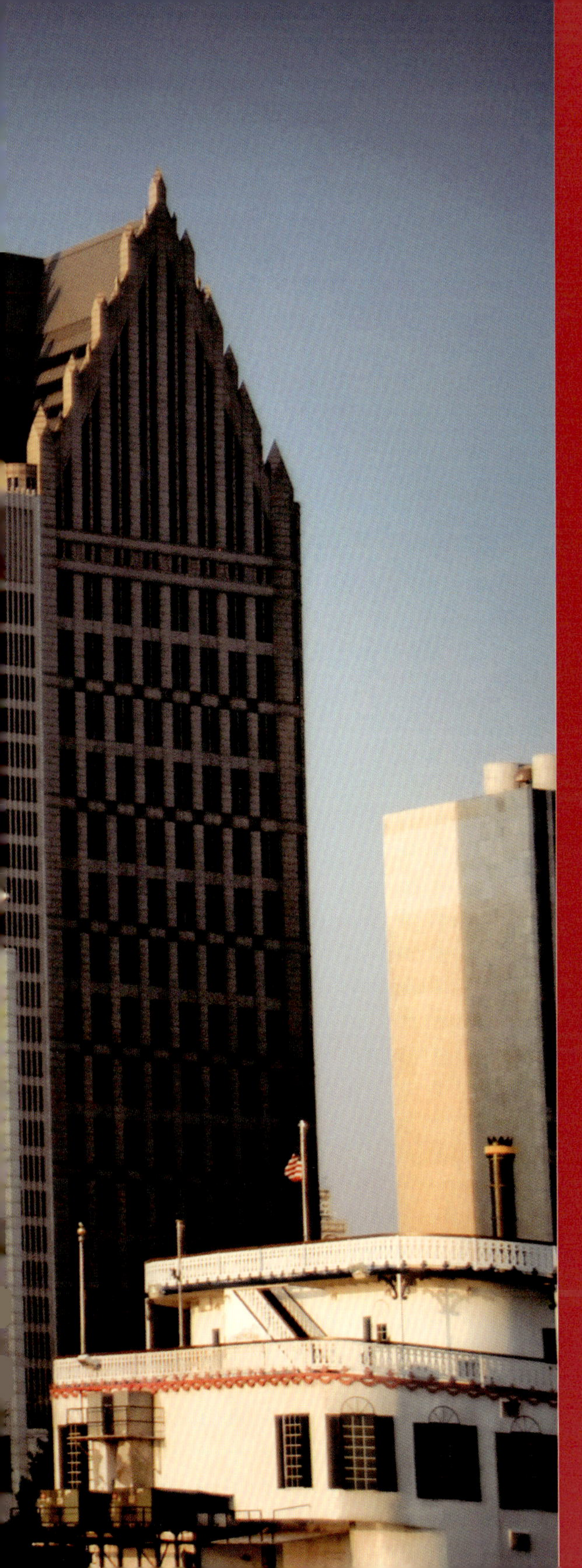

ARCHITECTURE

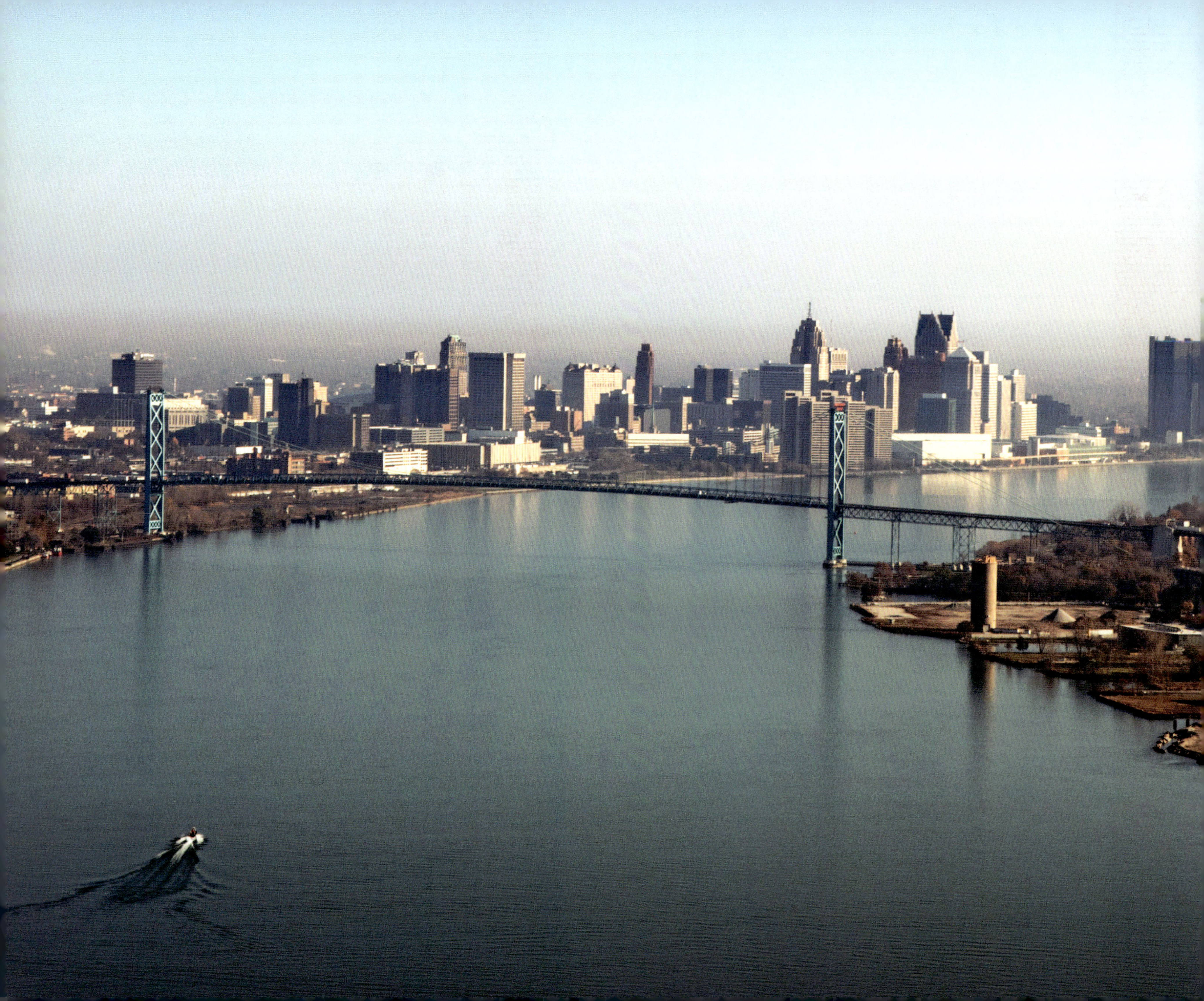

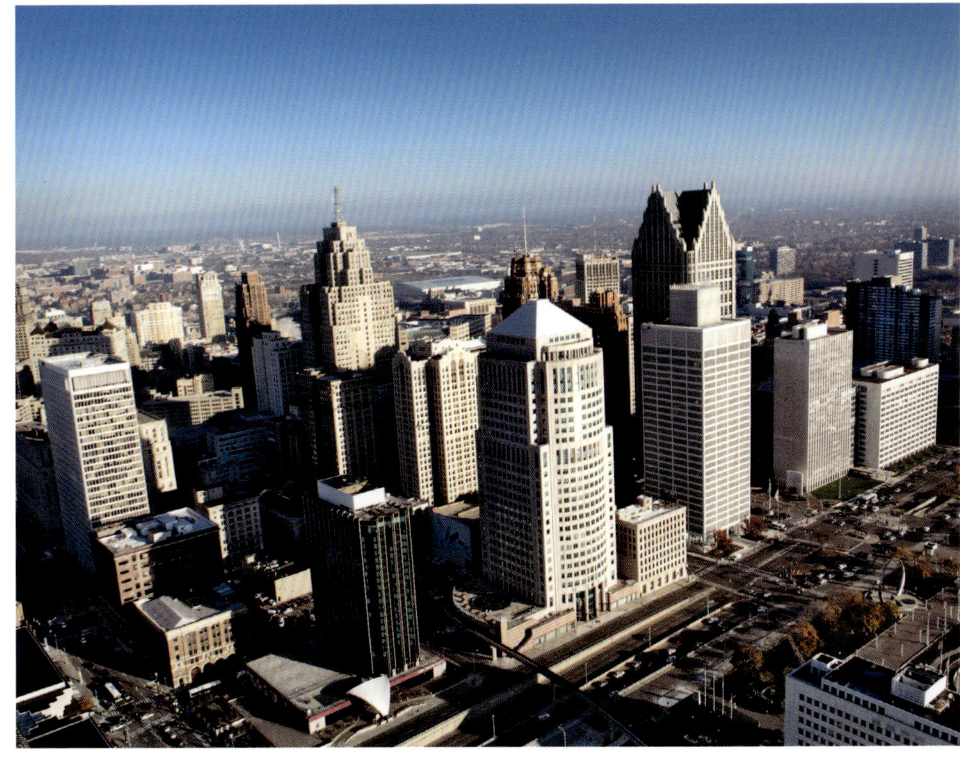

AERIAL DETROIT

Downtown Detroit
www.detroitexperiencefactory.org

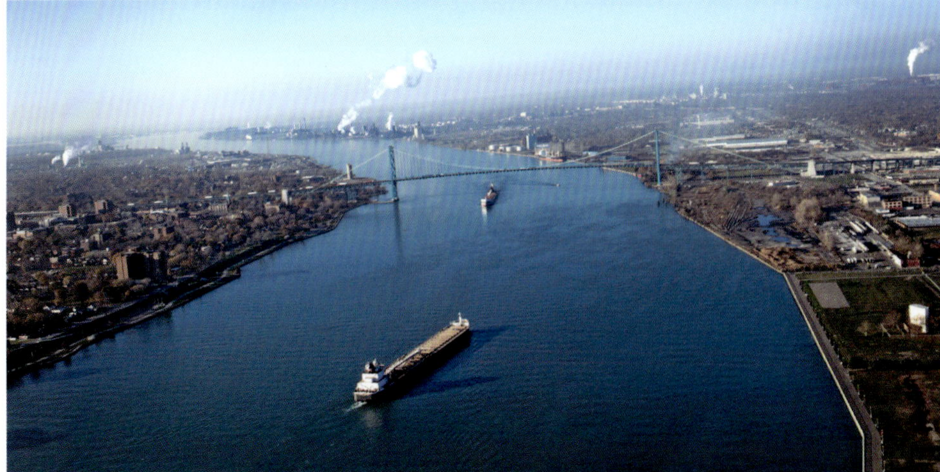

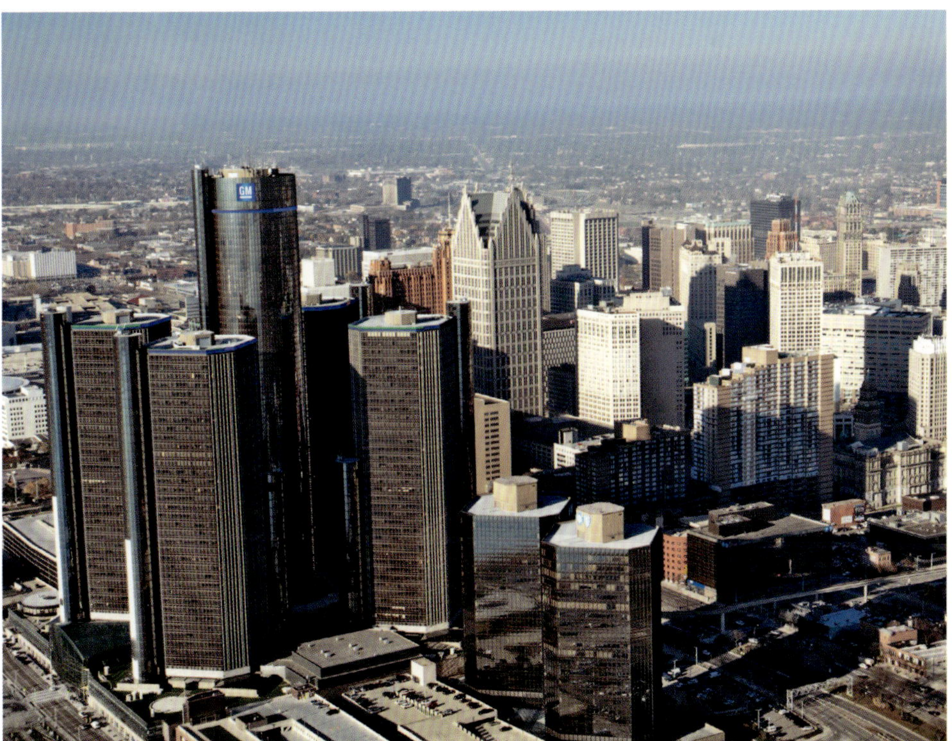

Designated the Automotive Capital of the World, Paris of the Midwest, the Arsenal of Democracy, and Motown, Detroit is huge, covering 139 square miles. The city expanded exponentially in the early 20th century, increasing its population from 200,000 to almost 2 million in the 1950s. In 1957, Detroit had 153% of the median income, offering the middle class the best opportunities in the world. Detroit's citizens had the largest percentage of per capita single-family homes with a garage and car on a tree-lined street. Since the 1960s, Detroit has since seen a steady decline of population and economic force, resulting in today's 650,000 hard-living, dedicated Detroiters. At more than 80% of the city's total, our African American population has become the largest, most concentrated, and most influential in the country. Throughout its history, Detroit has been, at one time or another, a leader in shipbuilding, stove and automotive production, aeronautics, agricultural seeds, pharmaceuticals, and music.

There is nothing more beautiful to me than seeing Detroit from the air. You can see miles down the river, Belle Isle, the neighborhoods spread for miles, the great concentration of mid-1920s architecture, and the riverfront parks. Perhaps it's a bit perverse to include these pictures in a guide like this, since not everyone gets to see our city from this perspective. Then again, perhaps what would have been perverse would have been to deny folks such glimpses of majestic Detroit. - NR

BEAUX ARTS & ART DECO ARCHITECTURE

Central Business District, Detroit, 48226

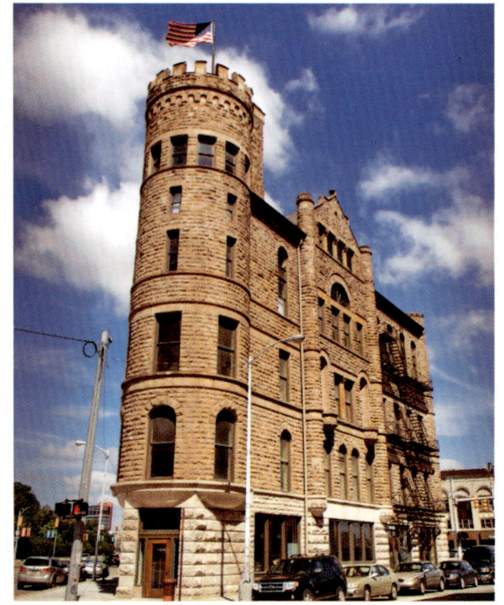

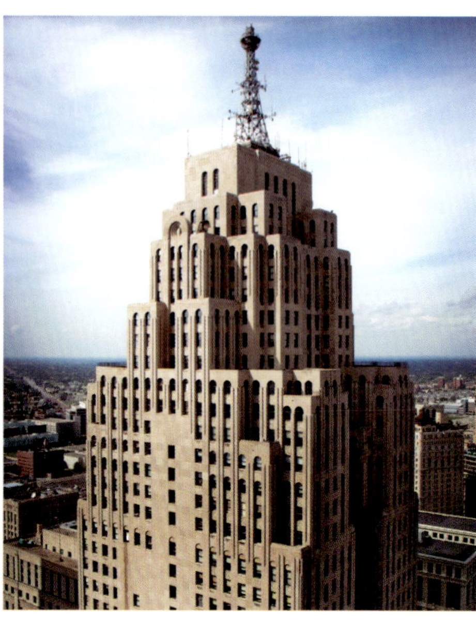

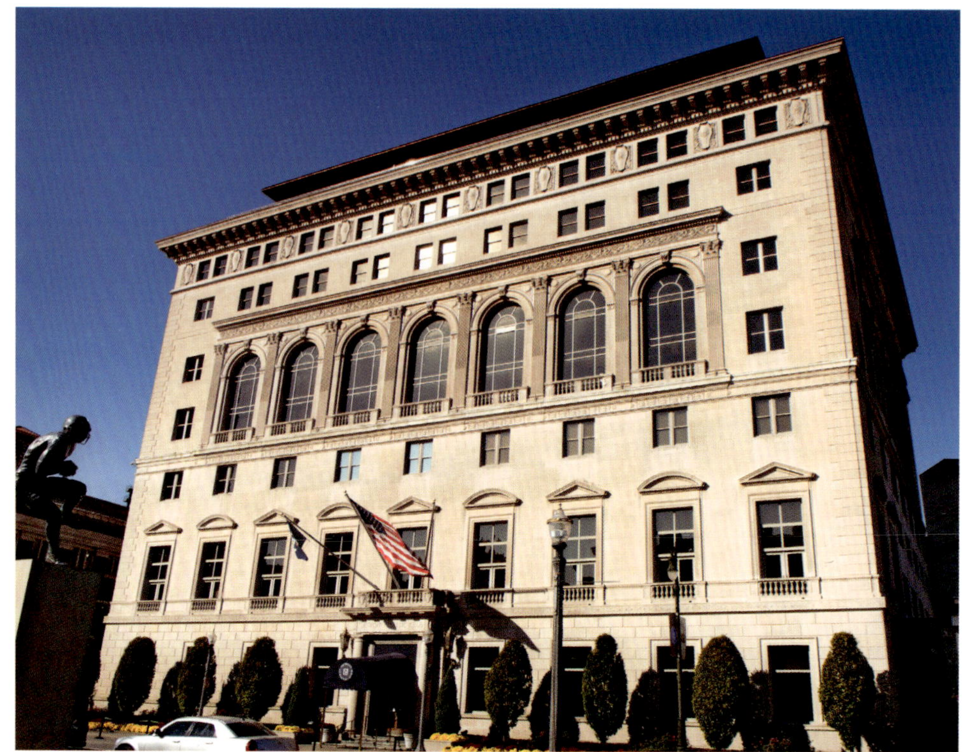

Glorious buildings from the roaring 20s adorn Detroit's skyline. Wirt Rowland designed art deco gems including the Guardian, Penobscot, and Buhl buildings. Daniel Burnham designed the Chrysler House, while Louis Kamper's designs include the David Broderick, Water Board Building, the Beaux Arts Book Tower and the neo-Renaissance Book Cadillac Hotel, which opened in 1924 as the world's tallest. The rapid development of the growing skyline abruptly ended during the Great Depression. After World War II, as downtown grew less influential, many beautiful buildings were lost due to suburban relocation or were neglected. Yet the wealth of our remaining architectural diversity and design has now become our greatest asset as these early architectural wonders, refurbished, inspire a new generation.

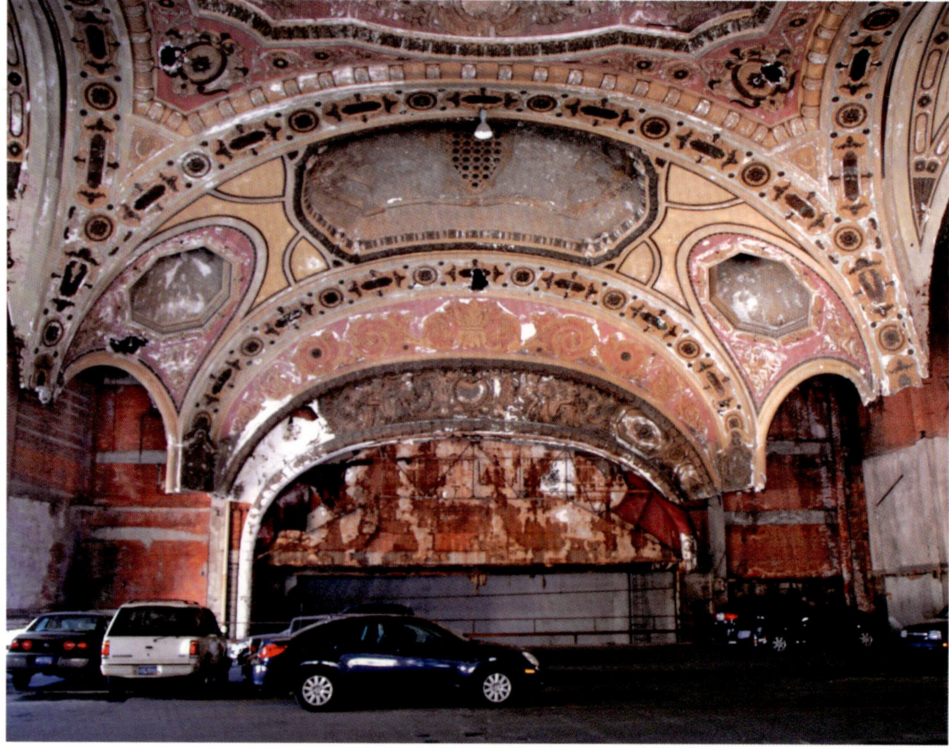

I sometimes think of Detroit as stuck in time. The downtown skyline was transformed, within the decade of the 1920s, from a comfortable little town into one of America's great cities. It has remained great, for the most part. The post-war modern skyscraper never manifested here. Because of that, Detroit has one of the great collections of early 20th century architecture in the world.

- NR

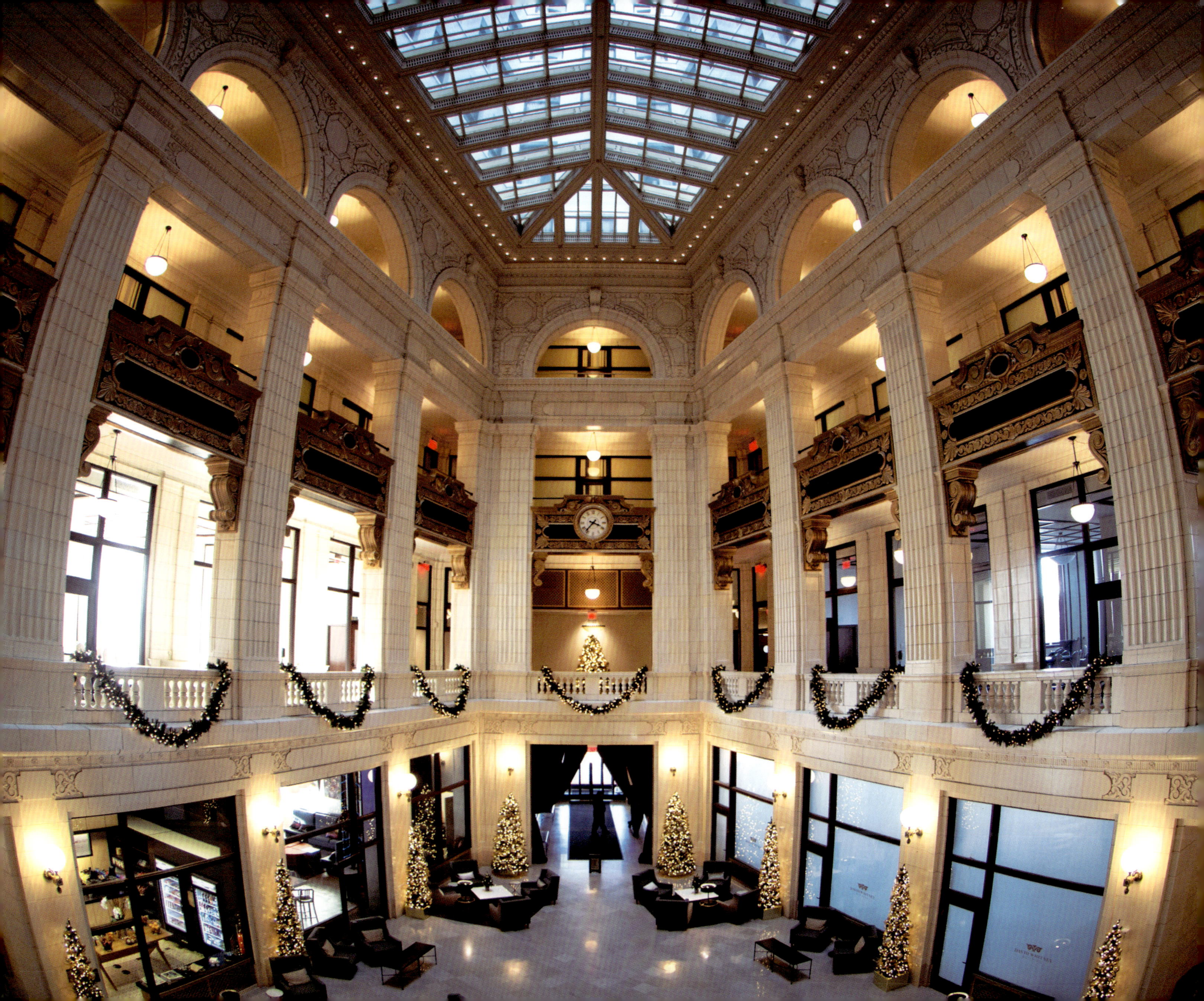

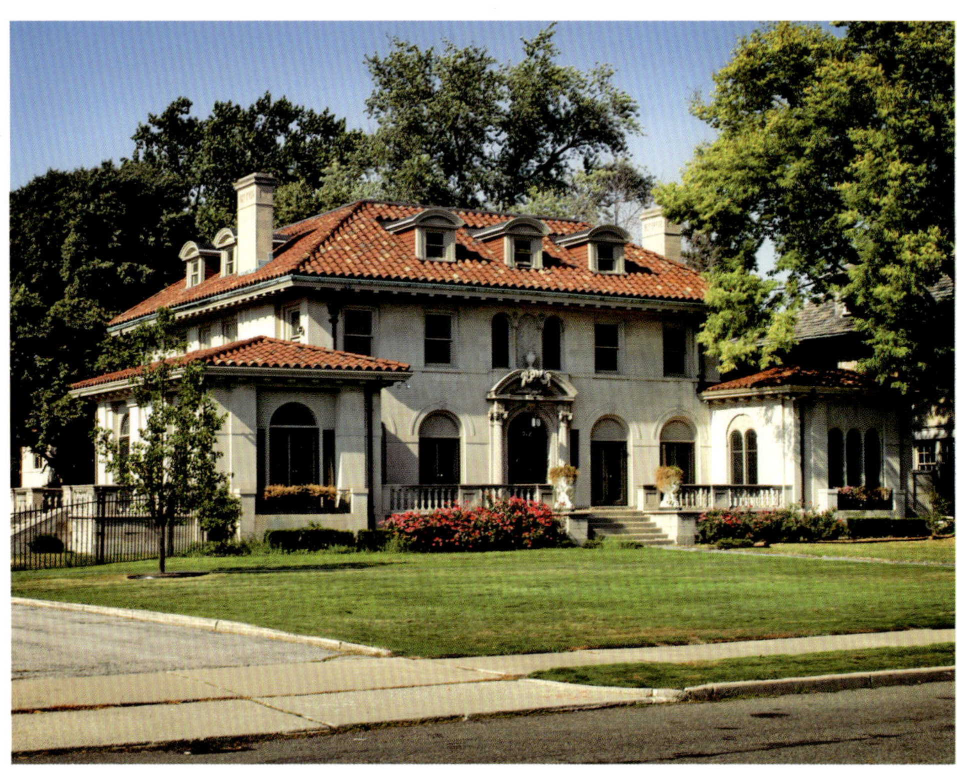

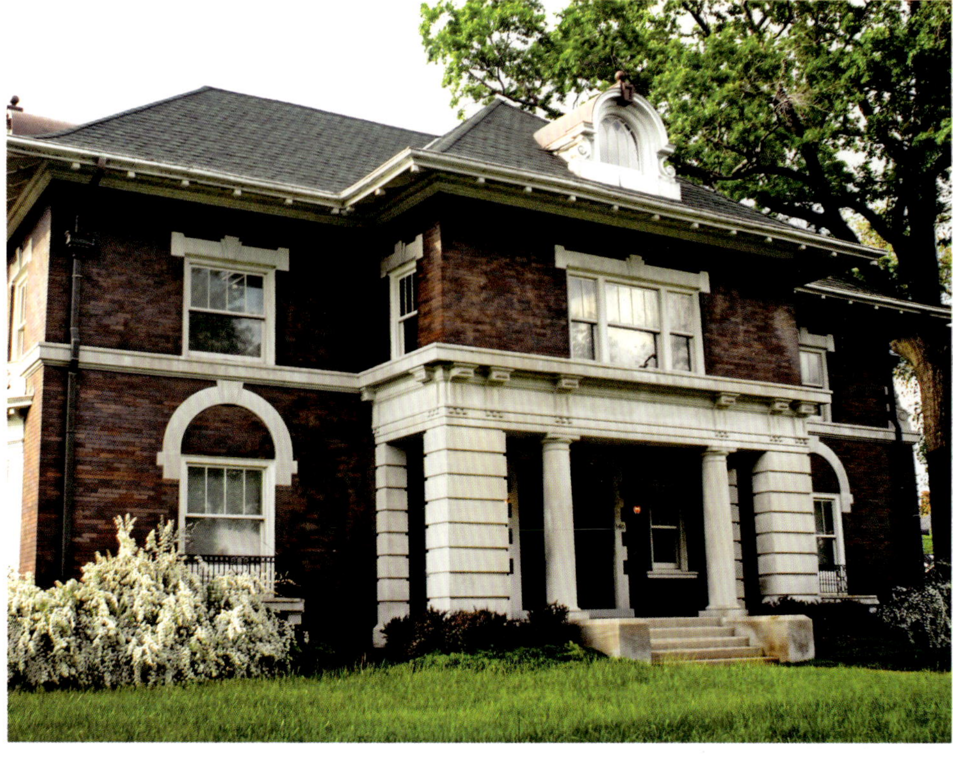

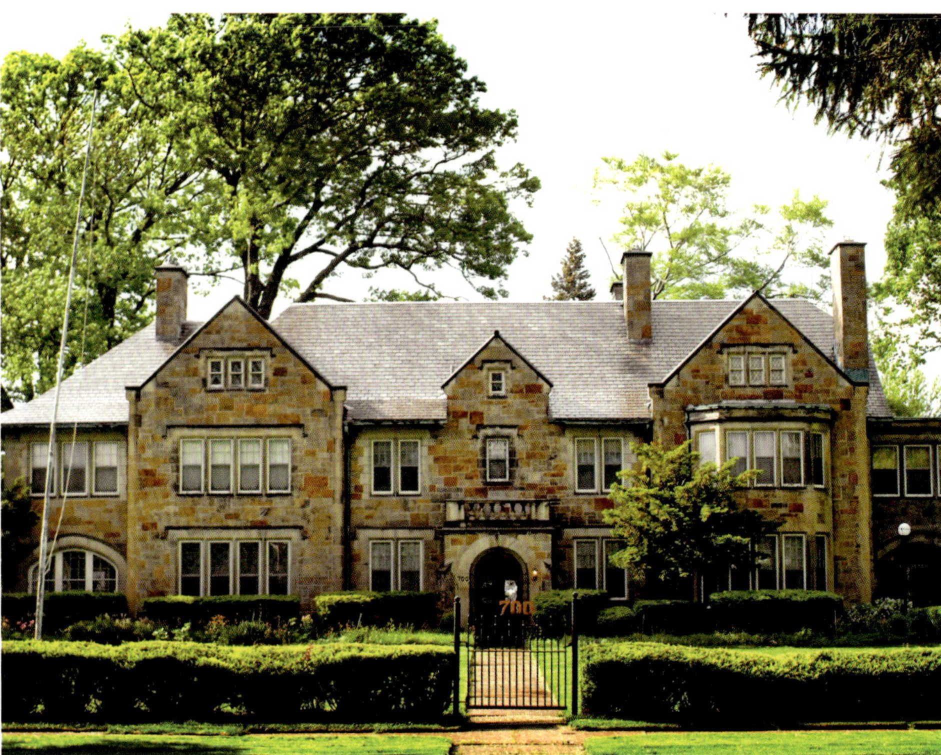

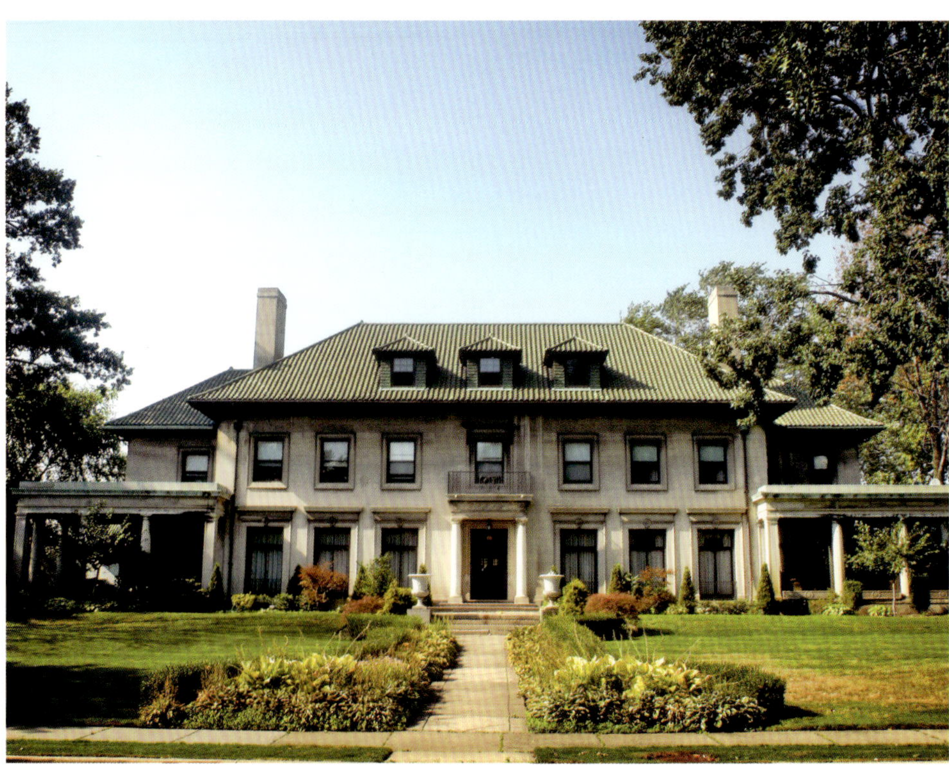

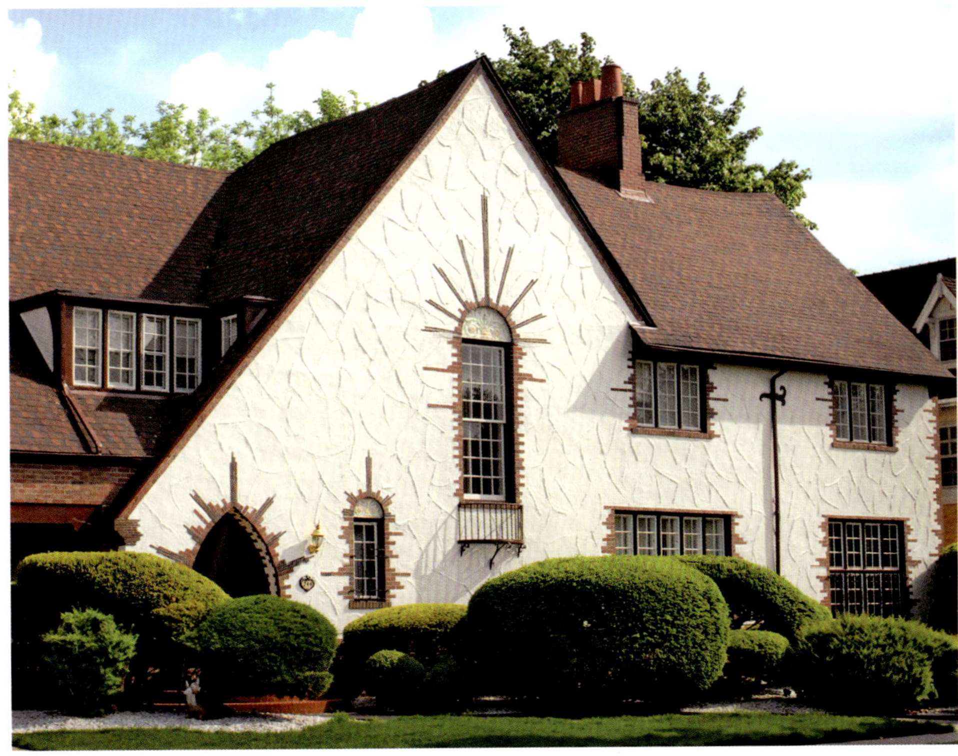

BOSTON EDISON NEIGHBORHOOD

Boston Ave. South to Atkinson St., Oakland Ave. West to 14th St.
www.historicbostonedison.org

Boston Edison, so named after the two streets which mark the district's northern and southern borders, contains 900 turn-of-the-20th century mansions and homes for Detroit's wealthy and elite. Similar in style and exquisite detail to its Indian Village counterpart, Boston Edison is a much larger neighborhood. Henry Ford built his first mansion, along a with two-story carriage house, designed as a laboratory and shop for his son Edsel. Famous residents of the neighborhood through the years include Ty Cobb, Joe Louis, four of the Fisher brothers, Sebastian Kresge, Clara Clemens (Mark Twain's daughter), Berry Gordy, Walter Briggs, JL Hudson, Walter Reuther, Horace Dodge, and many other early auto barons.

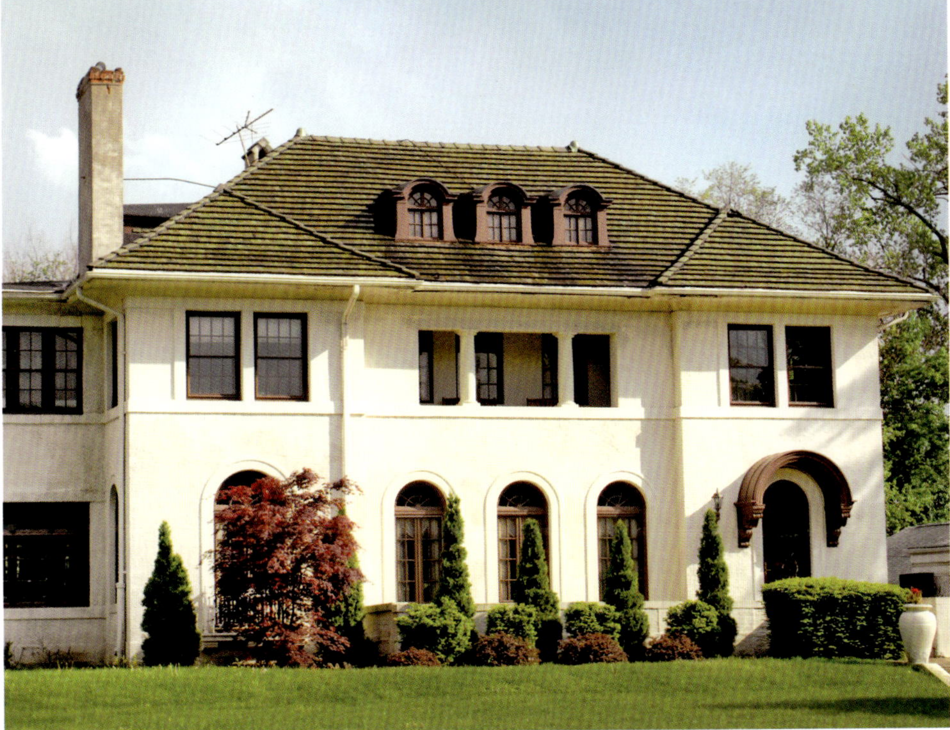

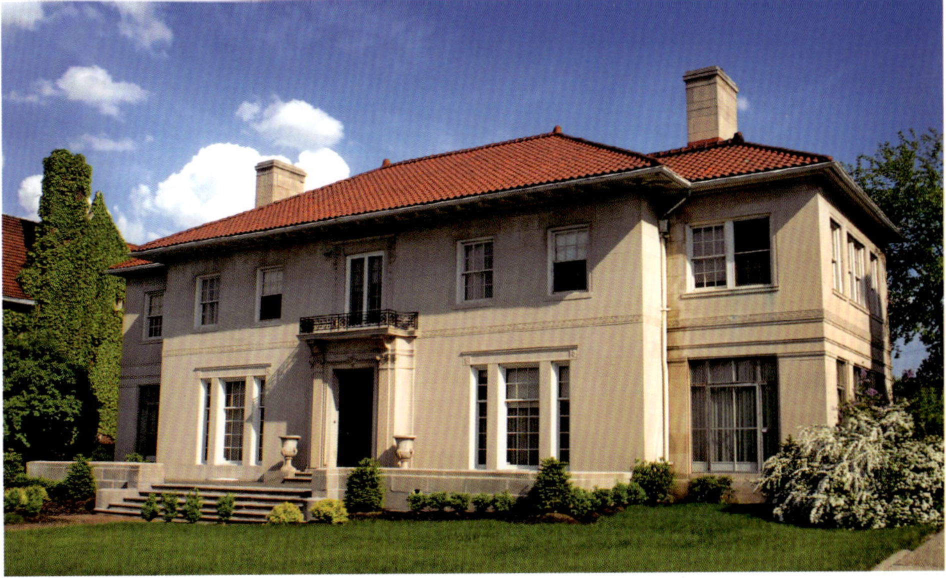

Once the premier neighborhood in Detroit, Boston Edison, and its mansion lined streets, continues to impress visitors with its elegant and historic homes. I have so many memories here: playing pickup baseball in Voight Park with Ty Cobb and the neighborhood kids; going to Motown parties at Berry Gordy's pool house, where most of us hung out, and which was linked by tunnel to the main house; talking about worker rights with Walter Reuther; and tinkering with young Edsel in his shop over the garage. - NR

ELMWOOD CEMETERY

1200 Elmwood St., Detroit, 48207
www.elmwoodhistoriccemetery.org

Elmwood was established by the city's elite in 1846 in what was then the suburb of Hamtramck. It is the oldest nondenominational, continuously operating cemetery in Michigan. The cemetery is situated on the site of the famous Indian insurgency led by Pontiac in 1763 at Parent's Creek, renamed the Battle of Bloody Run due to the overflow of blood into the creek as the British were massacred in a surprise attack. Renowned landscape architect Frederick Law Olmsted enhanced the design and natural beauty in 1890. Among the prominent people interred are famed abolitionists George DeBaptiste, William Lambert, and Zachariah Chandler; brewer families Stroh and Goebel; and a host of politicians including Lewis Cass, Coleman Young and Russell A. Alger.

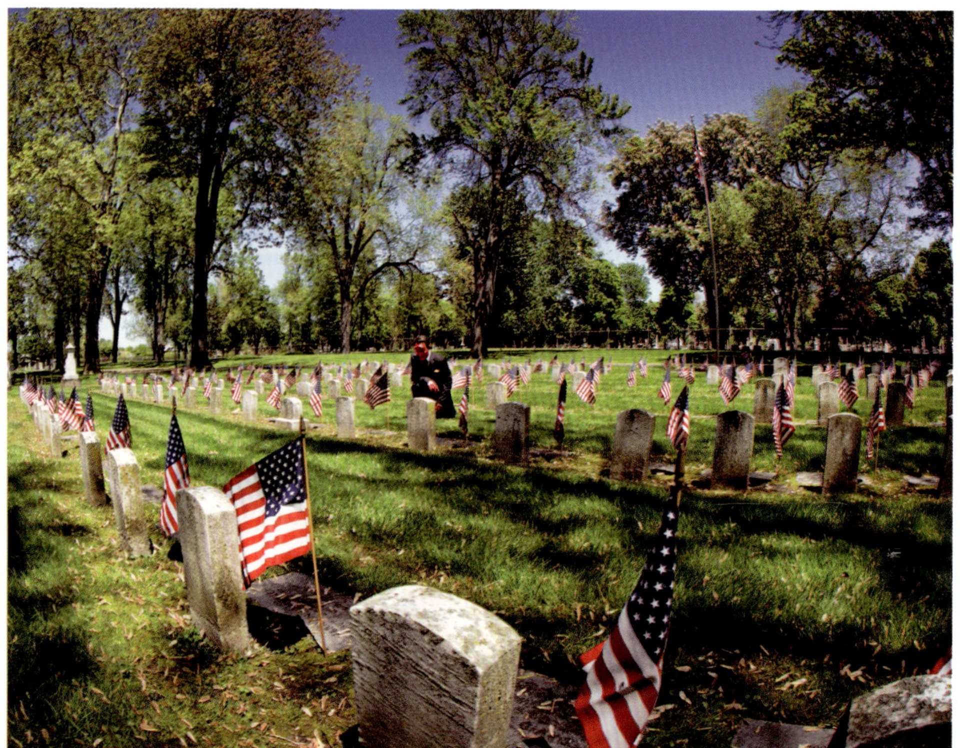

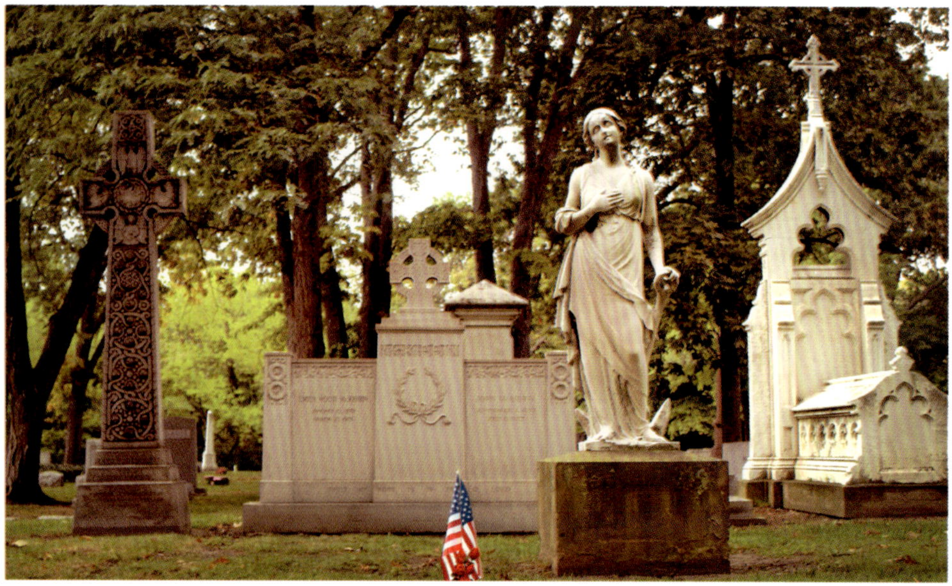

When I stroll through the grounds of Elmwood or ride my bike through the twisty turns and rolling hills, I am reminded of the way to Detroit used to look. Back in 1763, Chief Pontiac camped around here when he laid siege to Detroit. I was there when the Indians routed the British, turning Parent's Creek blood red. Now a lot of my old friends (and some folks I merely tolerated) are buried here. - NR

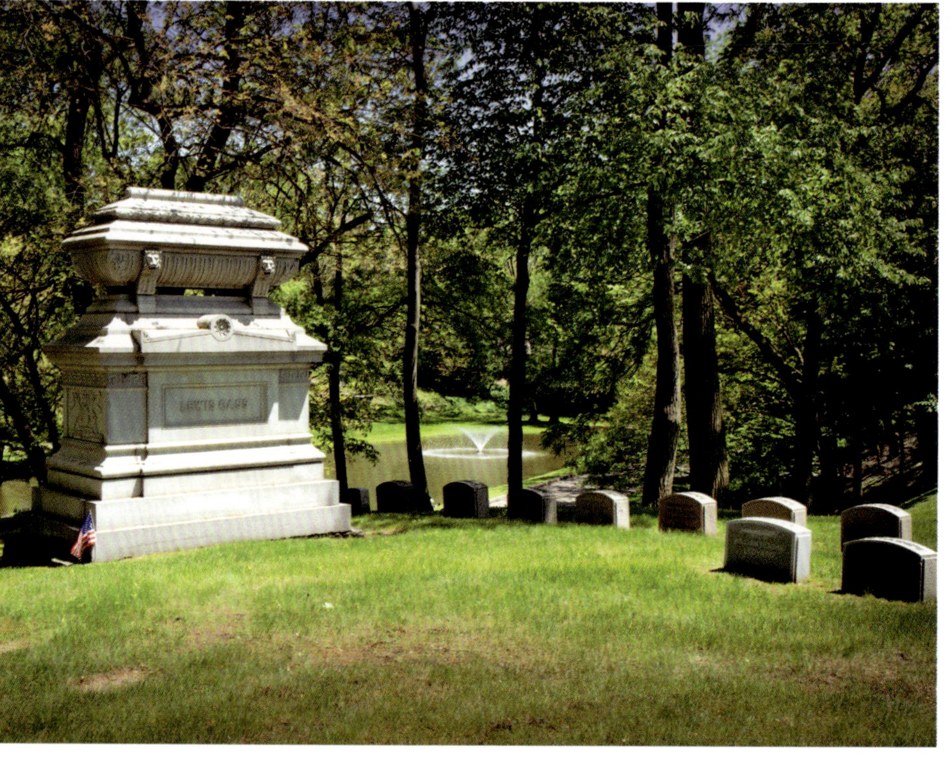

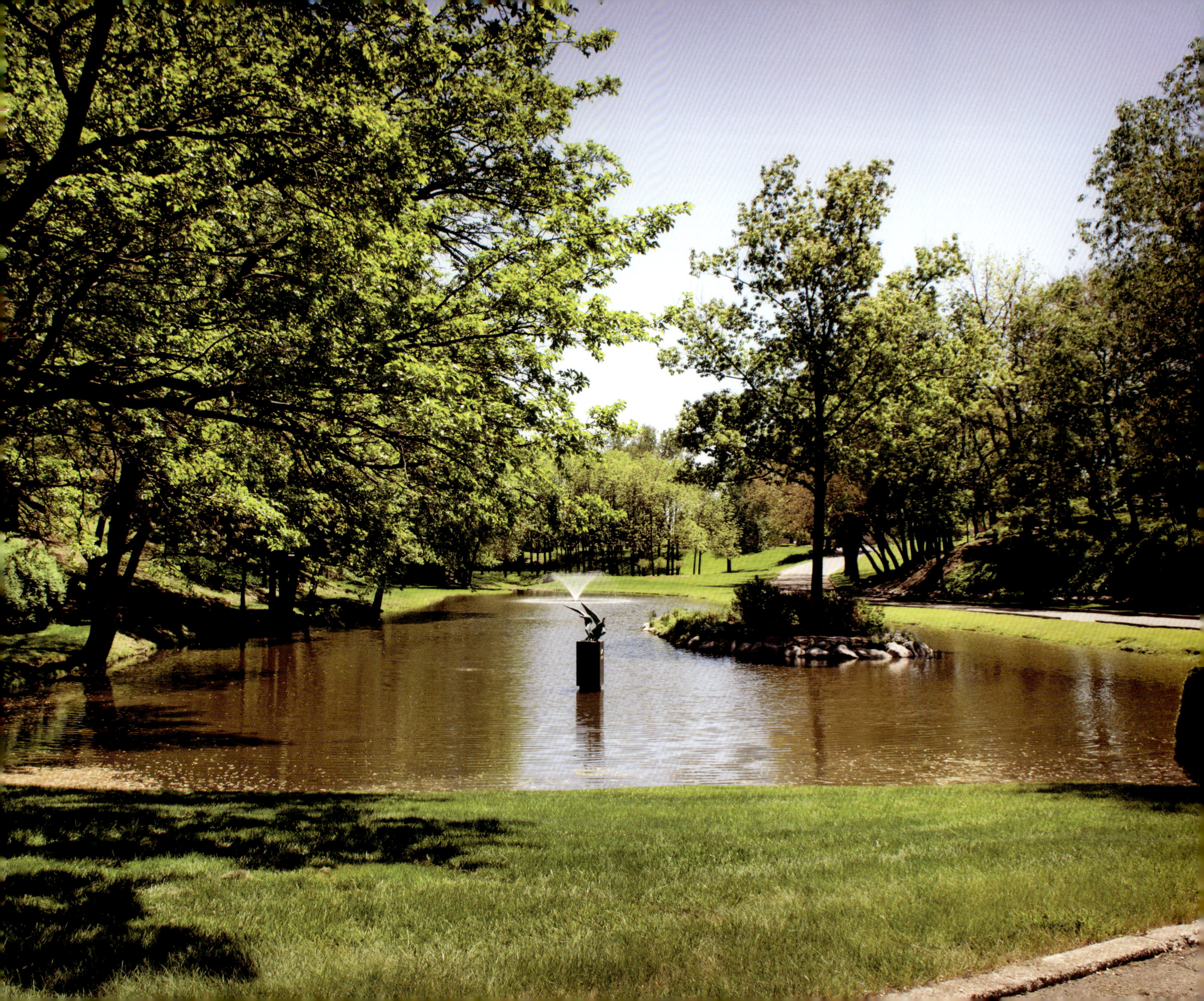

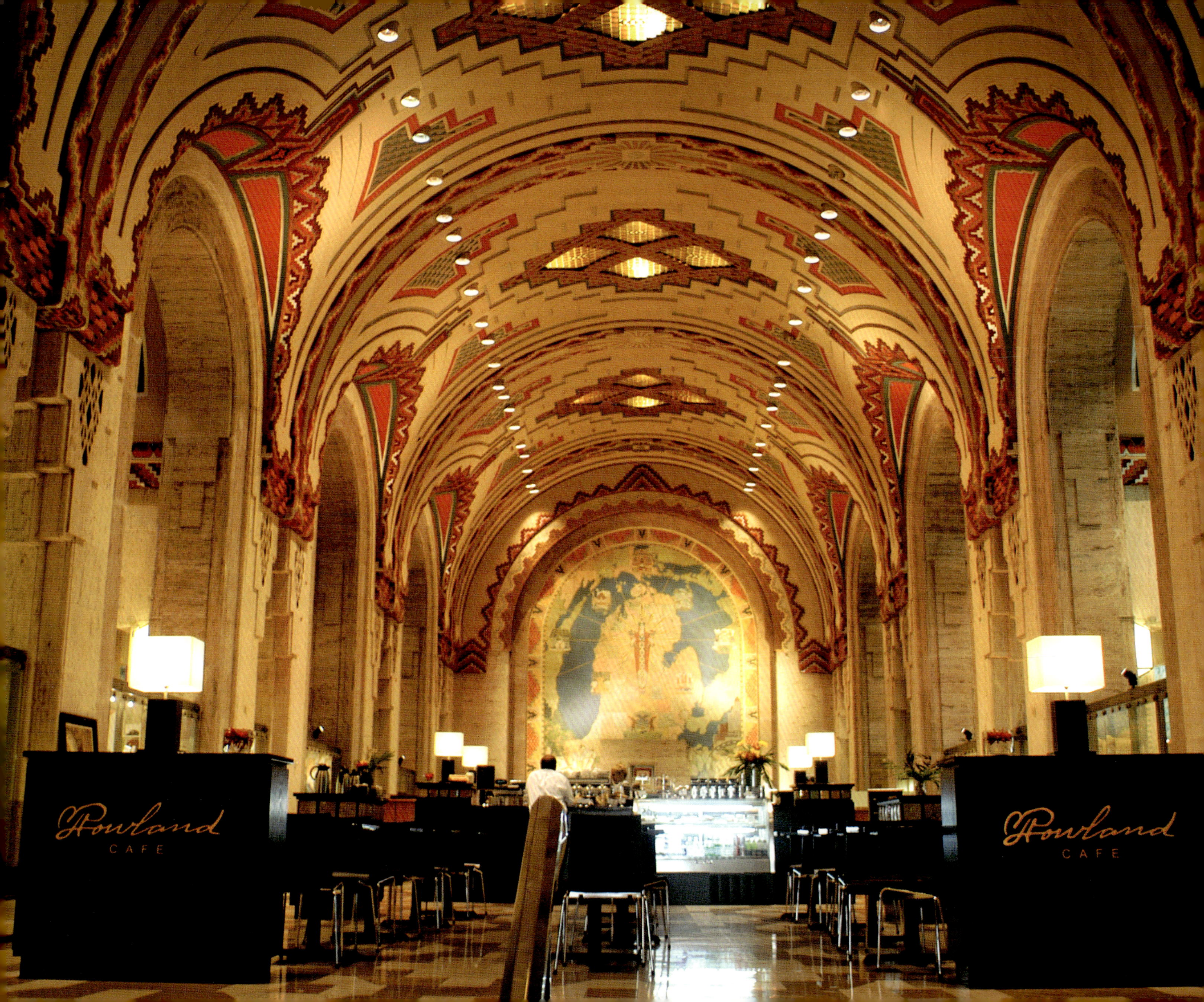
Rowland
CAFE
Rowland
CAFE

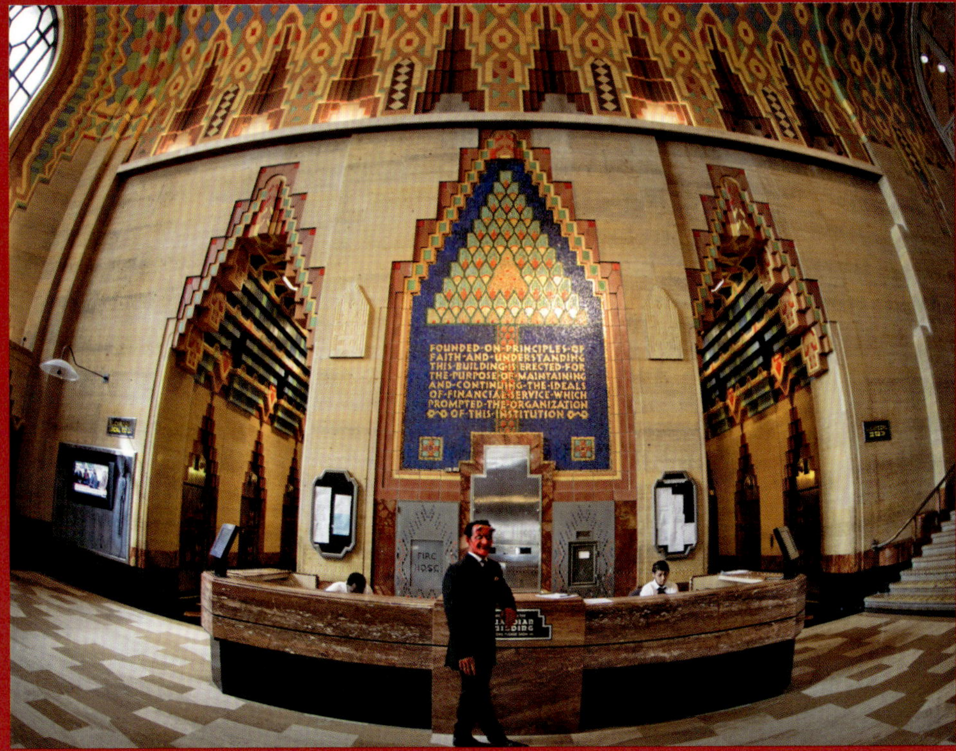

GUARDIAN BUILDING

500 Griswold St., Detroit, 48226
www.guardianbuilding.com

Nicknamed the "Cathedral of Finance," the Guardian Building is a 36-story Art Deco masterpiece, originally built as the Union Trust Building. Inspired by native American design, the opulent interior is decorated with Pewabic tiles throughout. The vaulted interior lobby towers over the shops below. Facing the lobby is a mural of Michigan by Ezra Winter. Meticulously designed by Wirt Rowland, the building's every detail was supervised and approved by him. The exterior brick was specifically created for the building and became so popular it was offered by the manufacturer as "Union Trust Brick." The Guardian Building is now home to Wayne County's administration offices.

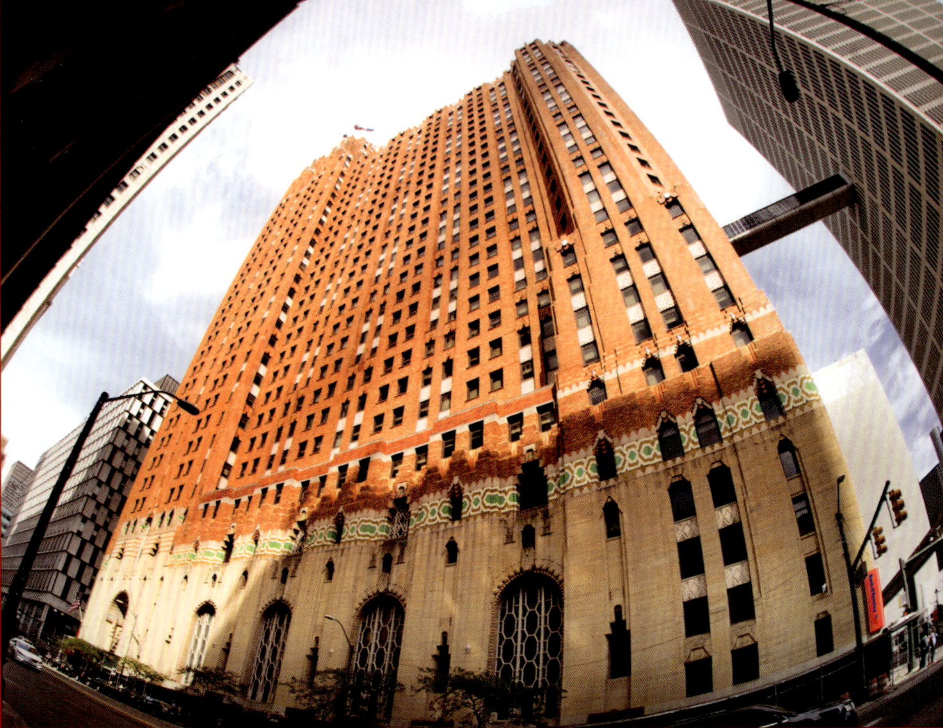

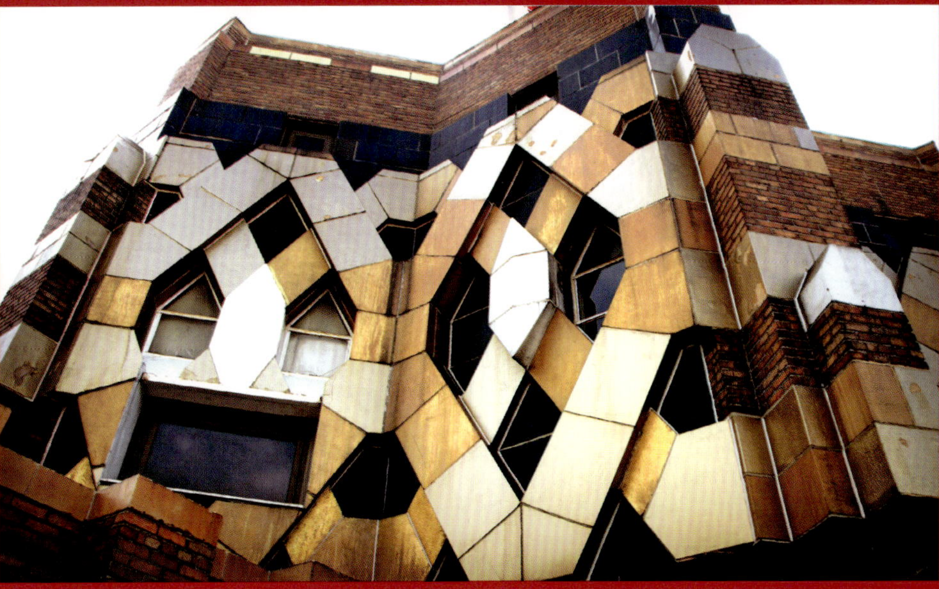

The Guardian stands as testament to the extravagant and resplendent skyscraper building boom of the 1920s. It was a tremendous time in Detroit as the city grew skyward. Distinctive and unique, the Guardian is Detroit's most spectacular art deco tower. Every morning, on my way about town, I stop in and grab a coffee, each time mesmerized by the stunning details. - NR

INDIAN VILLAGE NEIGHBORHOOD

Seminole, Iroquois, and Burns Sts., North of E. Jefferson Ave., Detroit, 48214
www.historicindianvillage.org

Situated on Detroit's near east side and encompassing three blocks each about a mile long, Indian Village is home to great turn-of-the-20th century mansions designed for those prosperous Detroiters with newfound auto money. Annual home and garden tours offer visitors the opportunity to see the glamorous interiors of these massive homes with incredible plaster detailing, fine woodworking, and lavishly decorated Pewabic pottery. The mansions include the "Honeymoon Cottage" (designed for Edsel and Eleanor Ford), the Goebel House (built for the prominent brewing family), the Henry Leland House (founder of Cadillac and Lincoln), and the Robert Hupp House (founder of the Huppmobile).

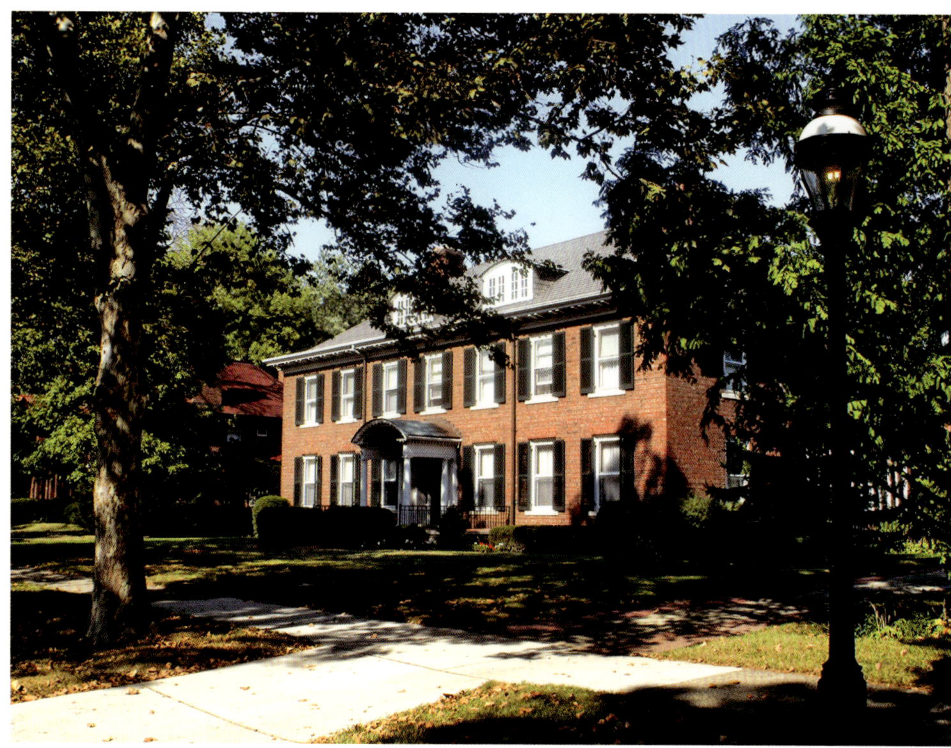

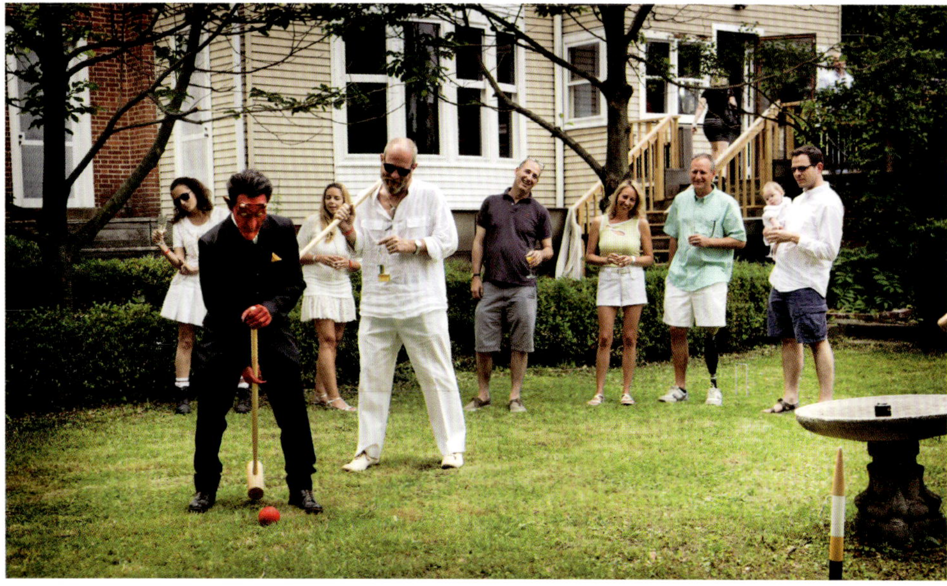

With the explosion of wealth during the first years of the auto industry, Indian Village became the place to be for the newly minted millionaires. Over the years, I have been to some wicked parties. During the Prohibition days, we would import the booze from Canada and dance in the massive ballrooms out of sight from the authorities. In the past few years, the neighborhood's residents have gotten younger, yet the parties continue. - NR

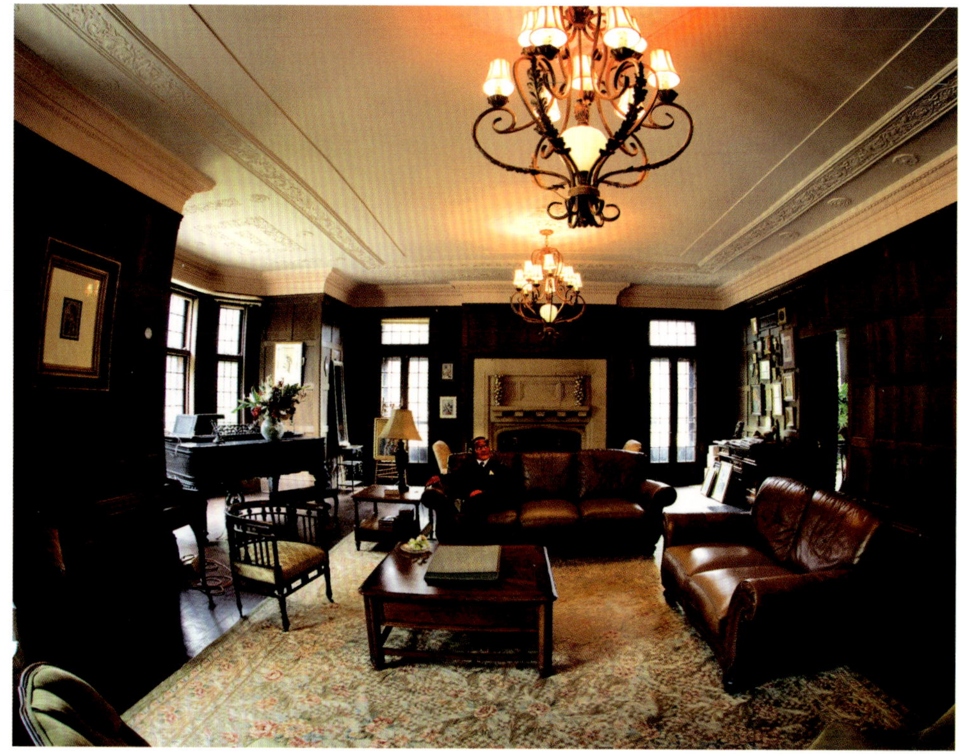

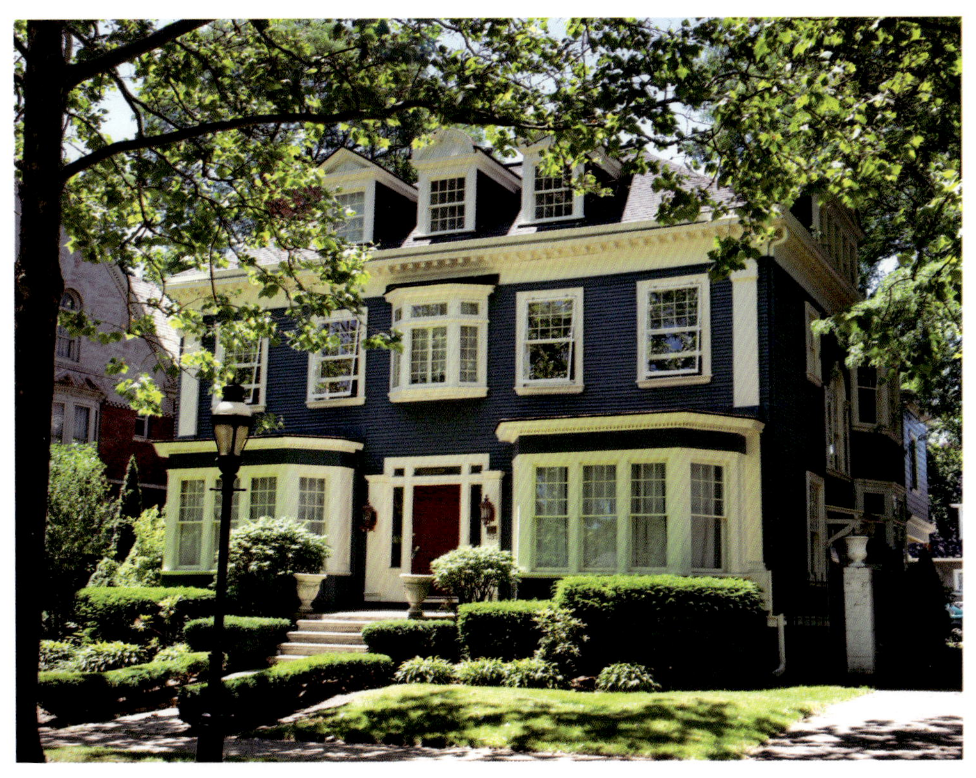

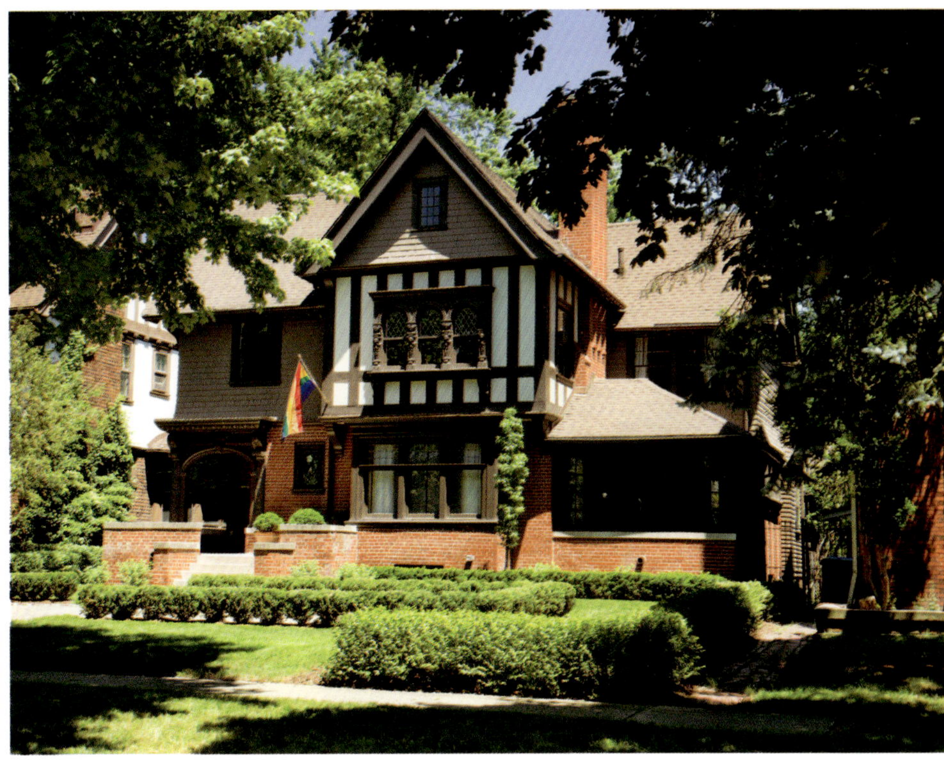

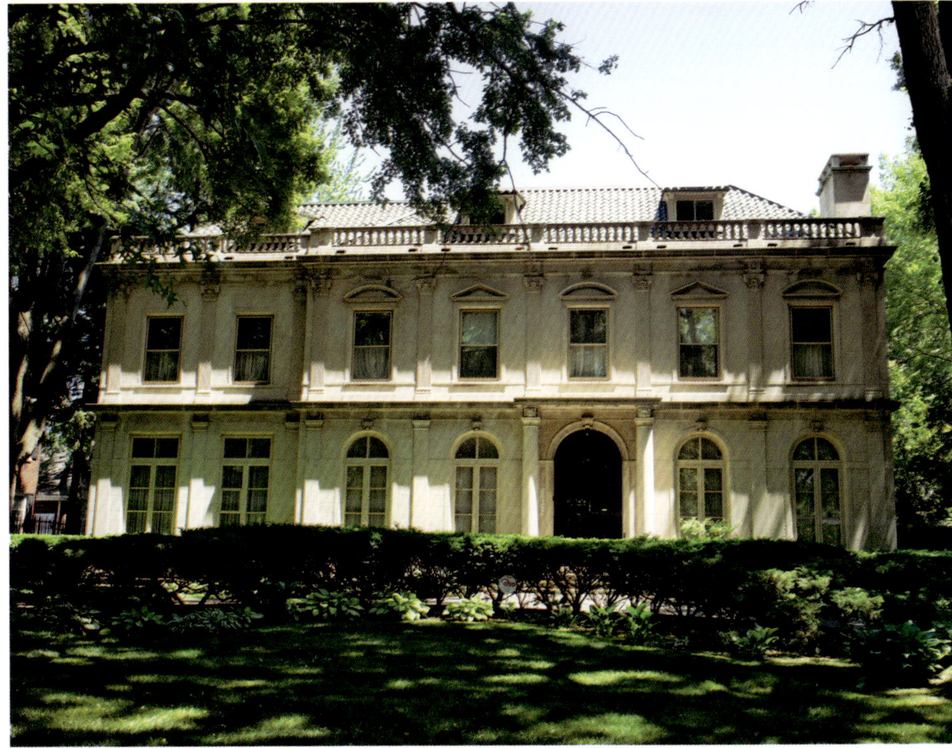

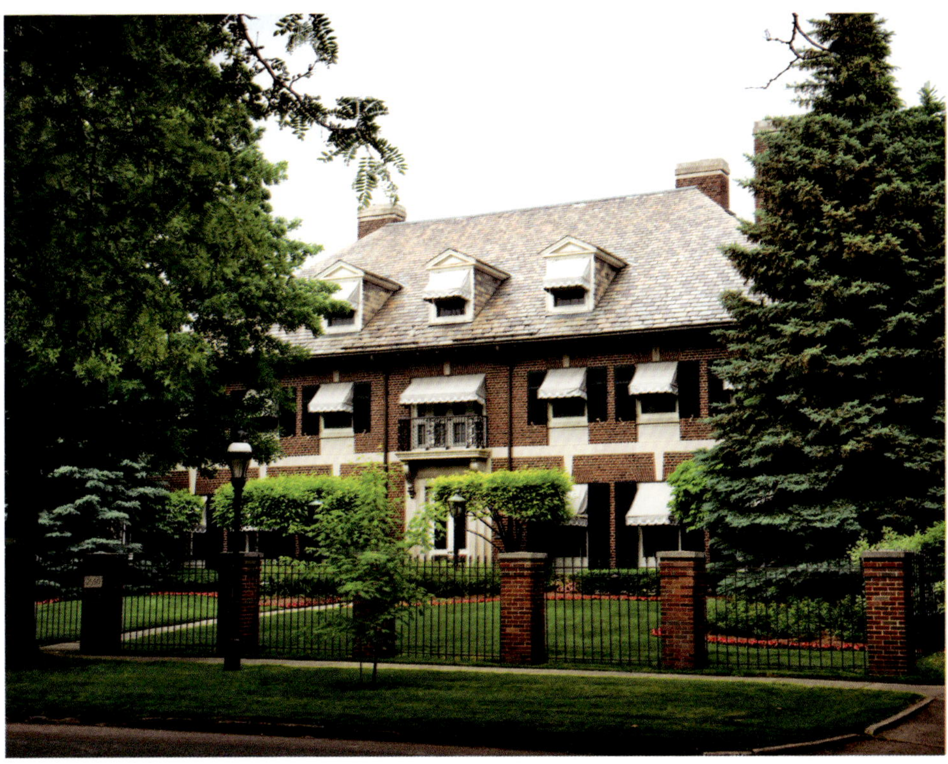

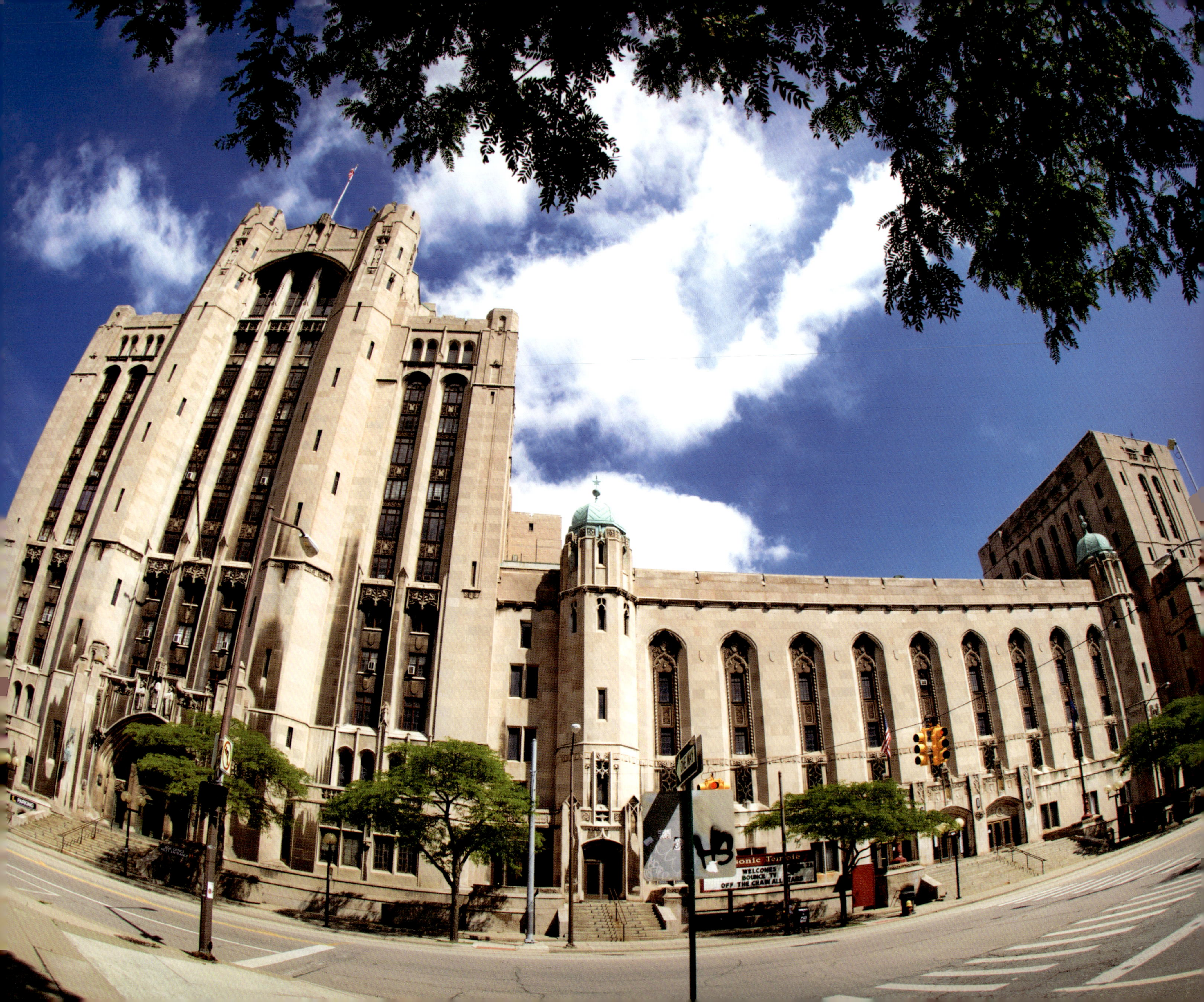
WELCOMES
BOUNCE TV
OFF THE CHAIN ALL

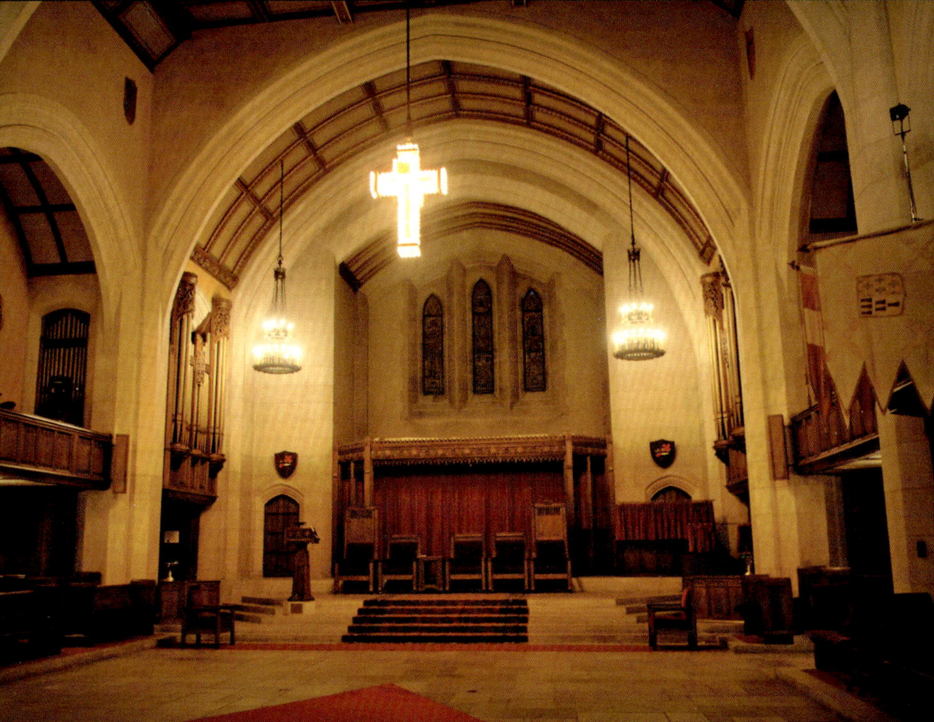

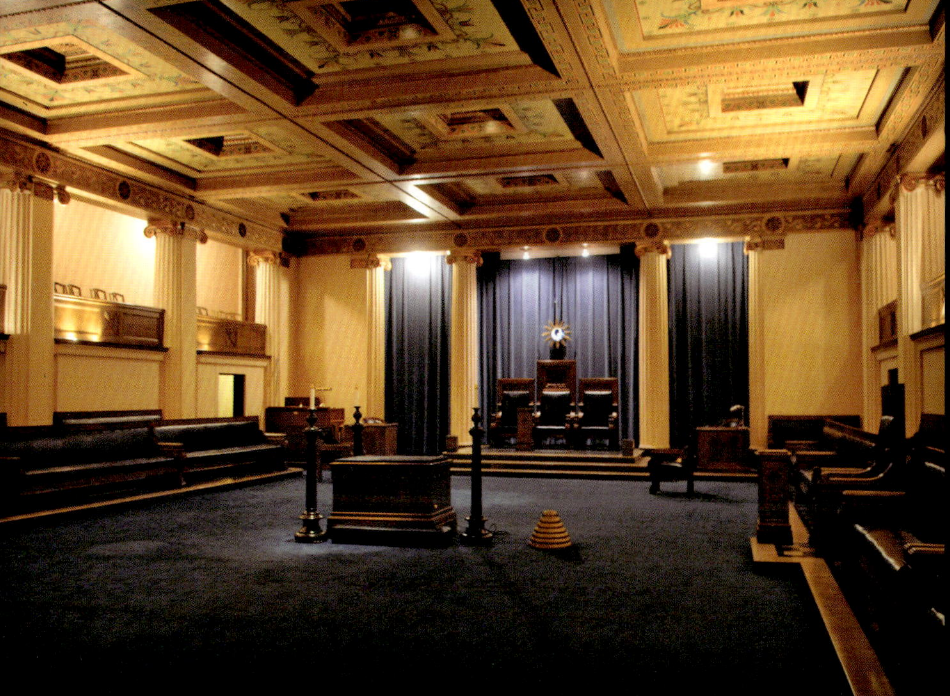

MASONIC TEMPLE

500 Temple St., Detroit, 48201
www.themasonic.com

The largest Masonic Temple in the world resides off Cass Park just north of downtown. The 14-story Ritualistic Building includes two auditoriums, ten lodge rooms, a drill hall, two ballrooms, and a total of 1,037 rooms. Detroit's first Masonic first chapter, Zion #1, began in 1764. The cornerstone was laid in 1922, using the same tools George Washington used to lay the U.S. Capitol cornerstone in Washington DC. The architect George Mason chose a Gothic style, which he thought expressed the best traditions of masonry. Notable members included Lewis Cass, Judge Augustus Brevoort Woodward, Henry Ford, and Stanley Kresge, along with thousands of other Detroiters.

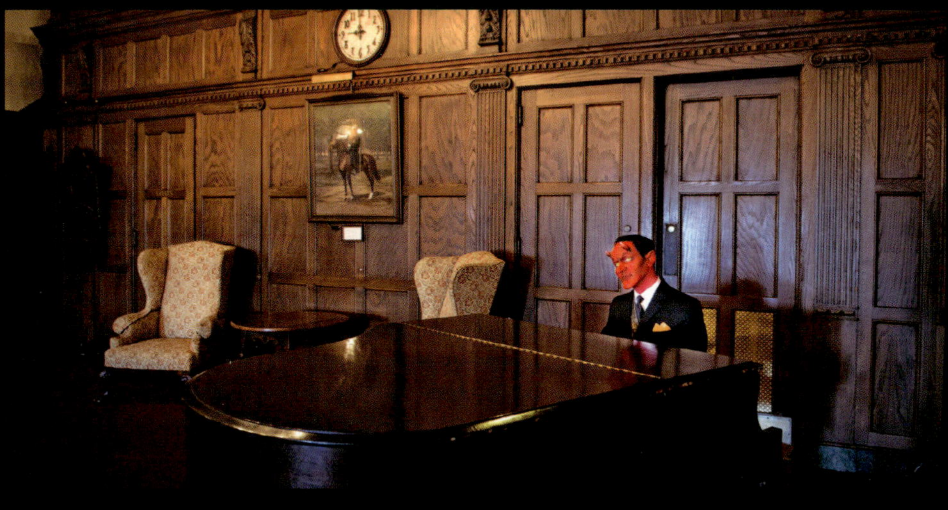

Masons? Who the hell are they? And why do they want to control the world? A secret society? I'm all in. Unfortunately, although these guys do have some crazy secret rituals, most members are just average Joes, doing their thing. Mainly focused on civic pride and spiritual giving, Masons are just really about trying to enlighten themselves. Although I was never a member, I have participated in many events over the years. I come here occasionally to enjoy the company of old friends, learn more about the Masonic way, or crash a wedding. - NR

MICHIGAN CENTRAL TRAIN STATION

2001 15th St., Detroit, 48216

Michigan Central continues to rise above the Corktown neighborhood, withstanding years of neglect and looting. Before symbolizing Detroit's urban decay, it originally served as Detroit's main train station, with more than 200 trains arriving daily. Its spiritual sister, Grand Central Station in New York City, was built in 1914 in the same Beaux-Arts Classical style by the same architectural firms, Warren & Wetmore and Reed and Stem, as flagship stations for the Vanderbilt line. The waiting room in the Detroit depot, modeled after the public baths of ancient Rome, stretches the length of the building. Decorated with ornate marble and bronze chandeliers, the 78 foot Corinthian columns and 65 foot arched ceilings dwarfed the station's passengers. The last train left the station in 1988, marking the beginning of the station's long, slow demise.

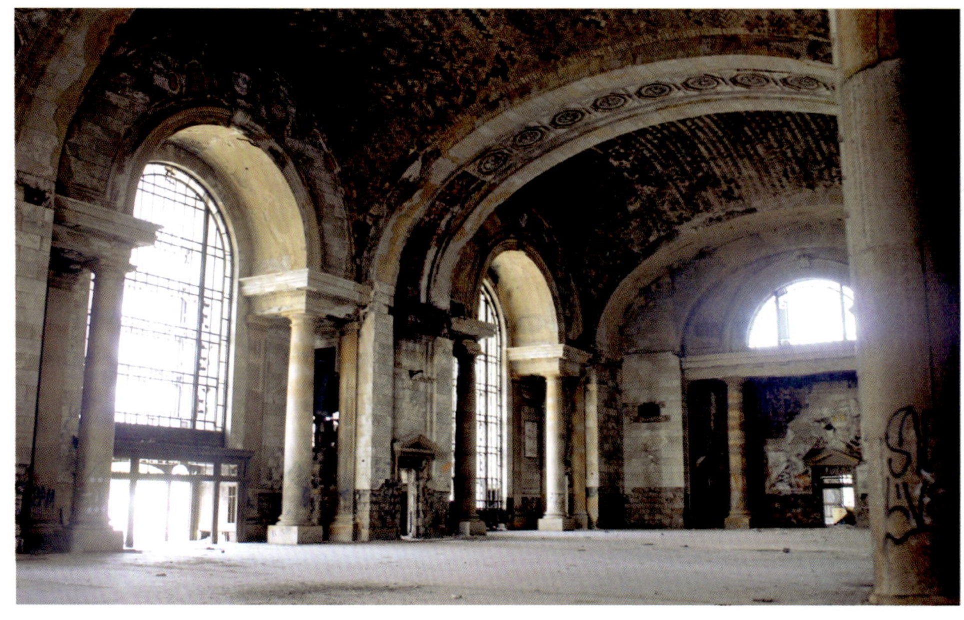

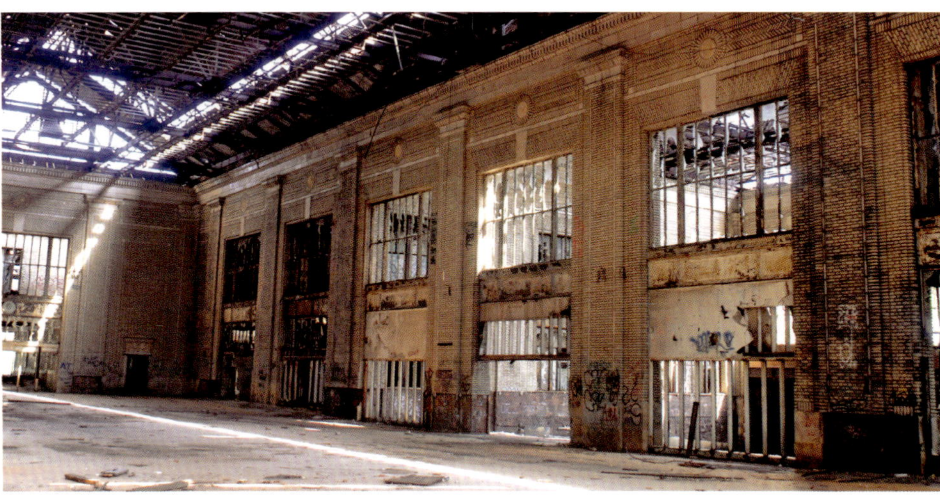

Under two glorious barrel vaulted ceilings, echoes of passengers greeting loved ones resonated throughout the building. For years, it witnessed both homecomings and travelers leaving on new adventures. After its last departure, we used to have art shows in the lobby. Dripping with architectural details, like most of the city, it was neglected by its owner and stripped of its beauty. After years of neglect, which prompted call for demolition, the owner finally boarded it up, replaced the roof and windows, and sealed it from the elements. From what I've been told, it would cost more to tear down then seal up. I consider it our Parthenon. Someday it'll shine again. - NR

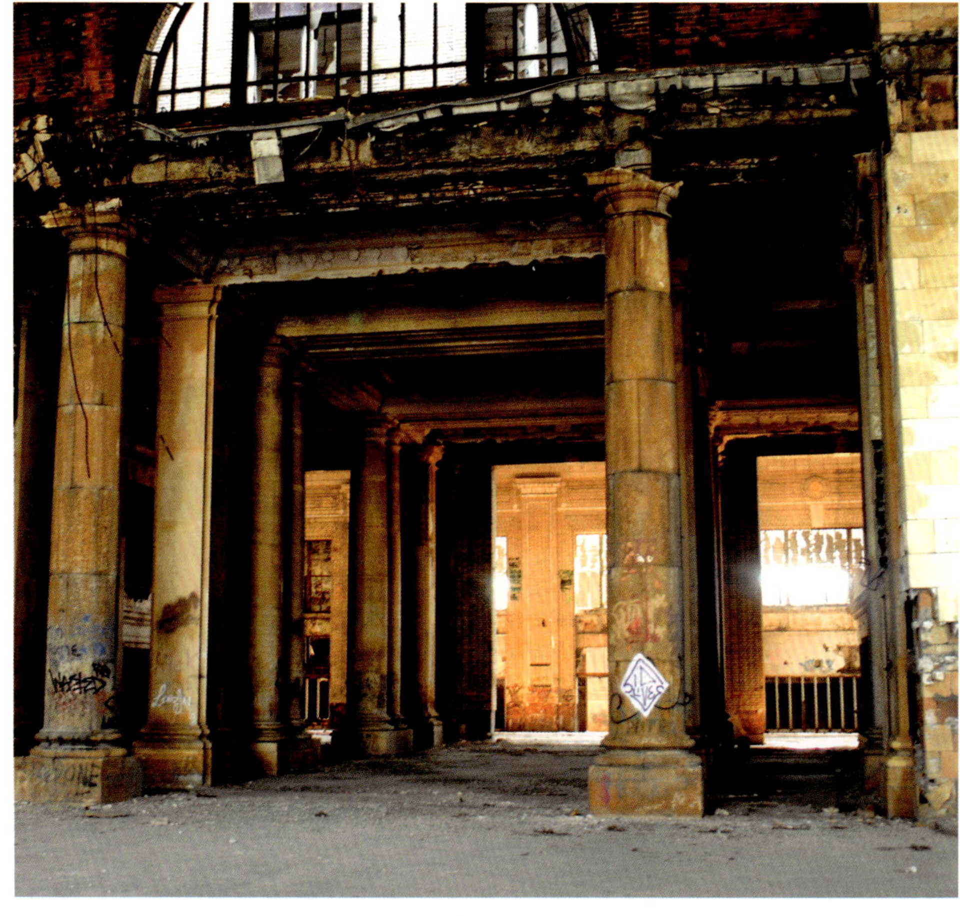

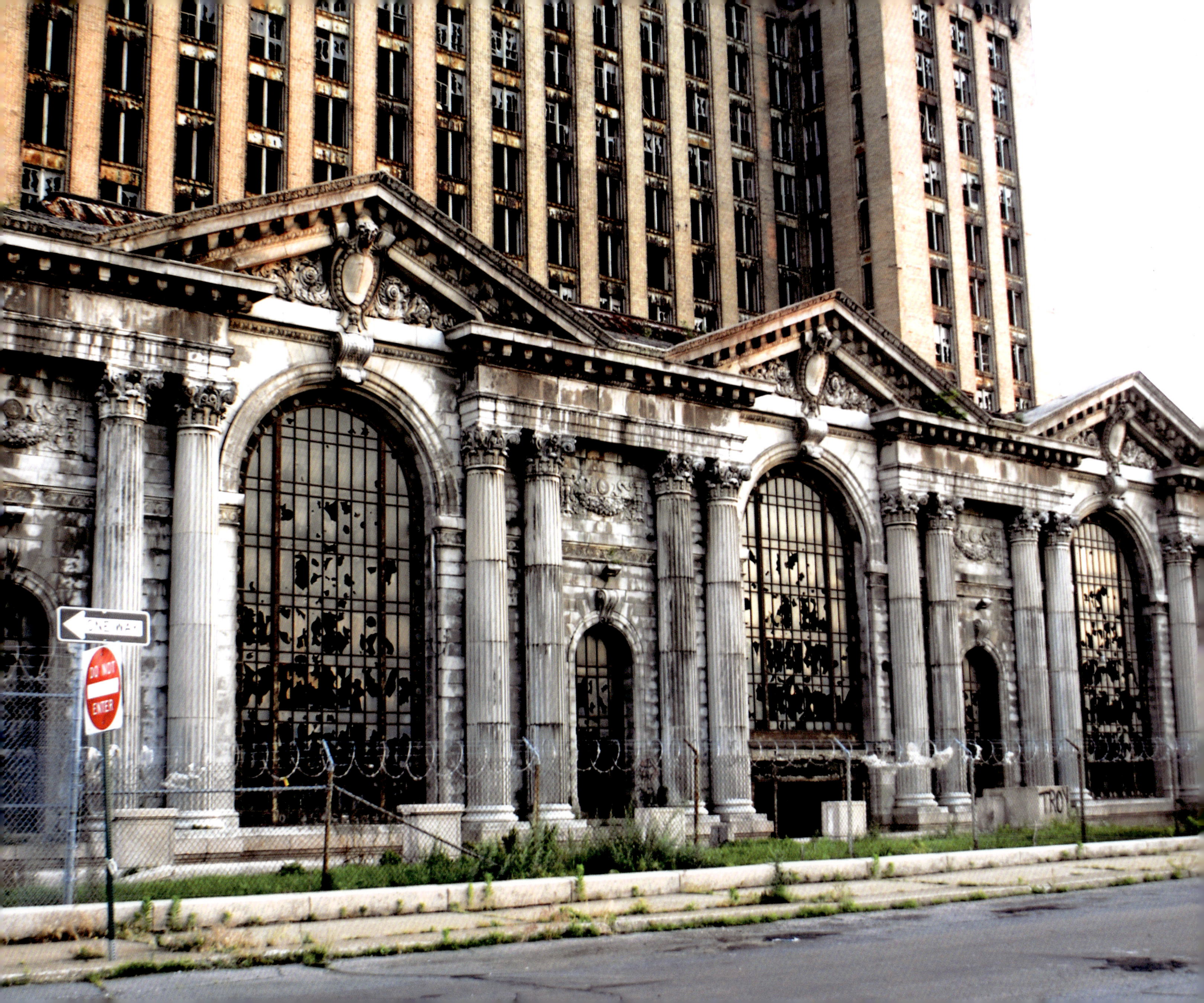
ONE WAY
DO NOT
ENTER
TROY

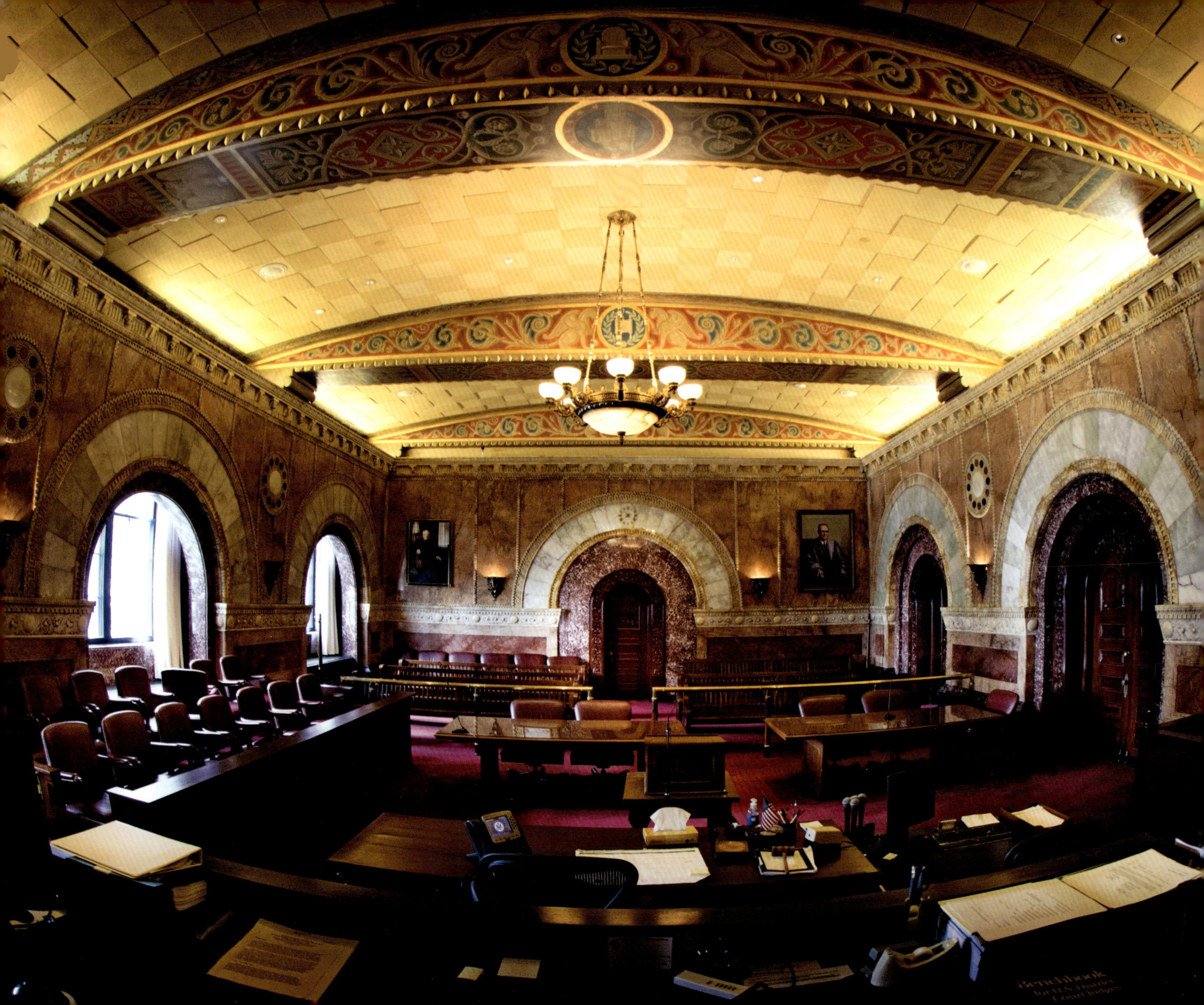
Benchbook

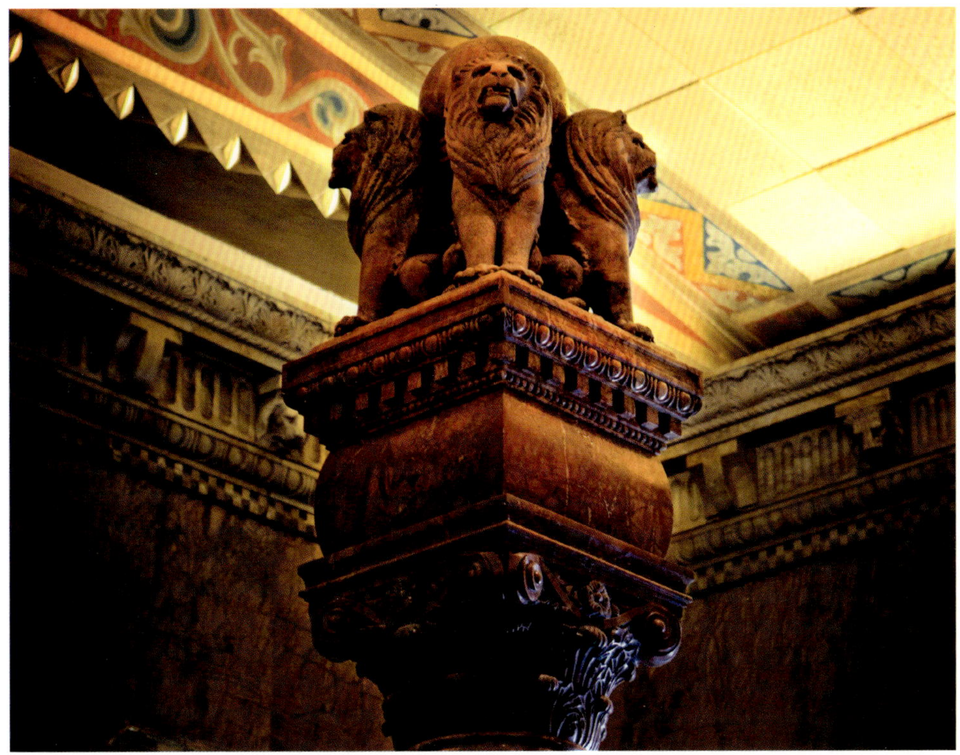

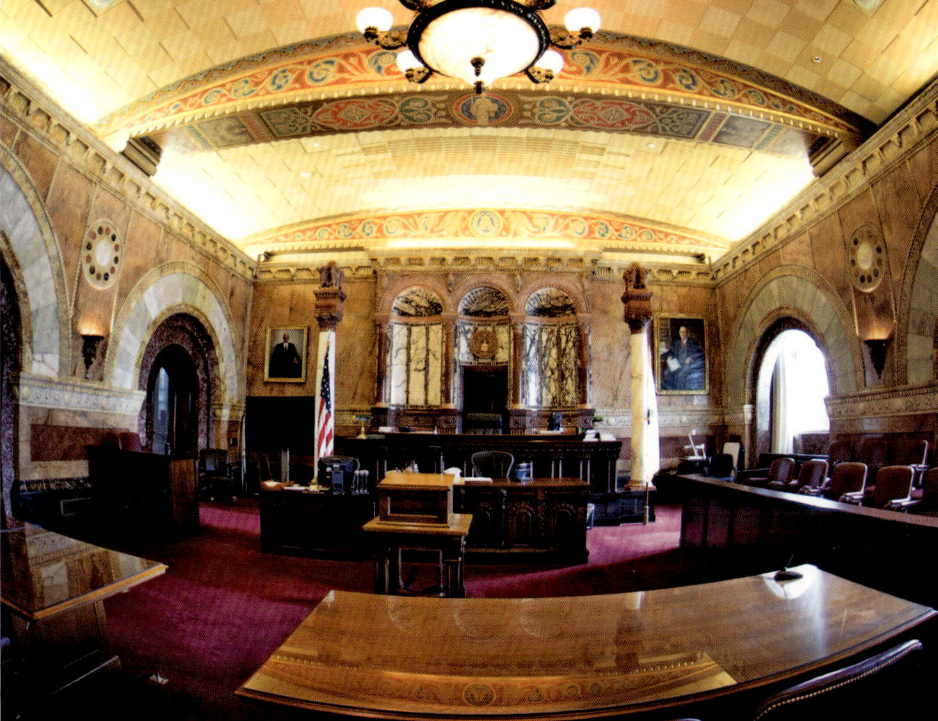

MILLION DOLLAR COURTROOM

Theodore Levin US Courthouse
231 W. Lafayette Blvd., Detroit, 48226

During the height of the Depression, the government undertook massive infrastructure improvements to reduce unemployment. Beginning construction in 1932 and finishing in 1934, Detroit replaced its castle-like Victorian court house with a modern Federal building. Chief Judge Arthur Tuttle refused to allow the demolition of his courtroom. The courtroom was dismantled, saved, and rebuilt in the new complex at a cost of $1 million. The courtroom incorporates more than 30 different types of marble with an East Indian mahogany bench flanked by two columns of marble, each topped by four lions holding a globe. Behind the bench is a frieze of ten female figures depicting the purity of justice. More than 100 lion heads surround the courtroom at the ceiling. The Romanesque style is a dramatic contrast to the neo classical architecture of the present courthouse.

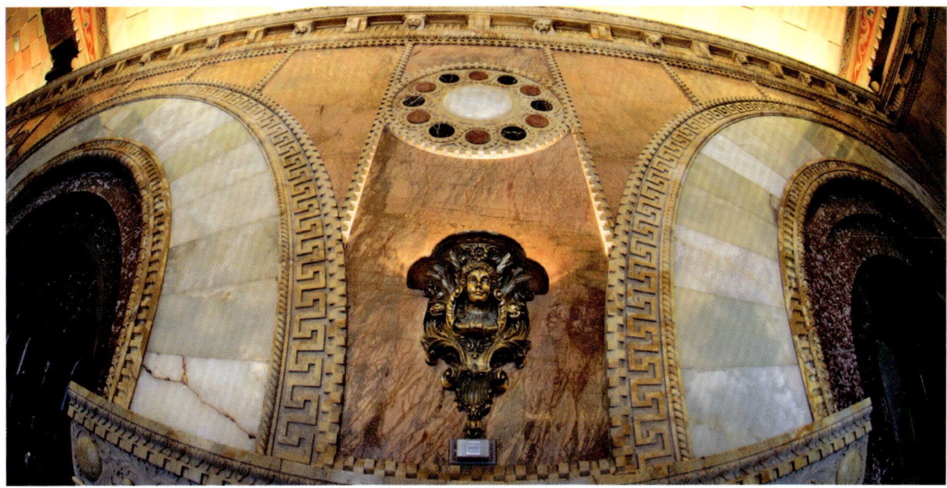

This story for me is one of sadness and misguided intentions. Despite Judge Tuttle's victory, the Million Dollar Courtroom is an early example of us discarding extraordinary architecture in Detroit in the name of progress. Architecture tells our story through design and history. It connects generations. I could list dozens of buildings that we have lost to time, poor judgment, and the wrecking ball. Detroit needs more advocates for preserving our architectural history or, before we know it, it will be lost forever. - NR

MODERN ARCHITECTURE

Central Business District, Detroit, 48226

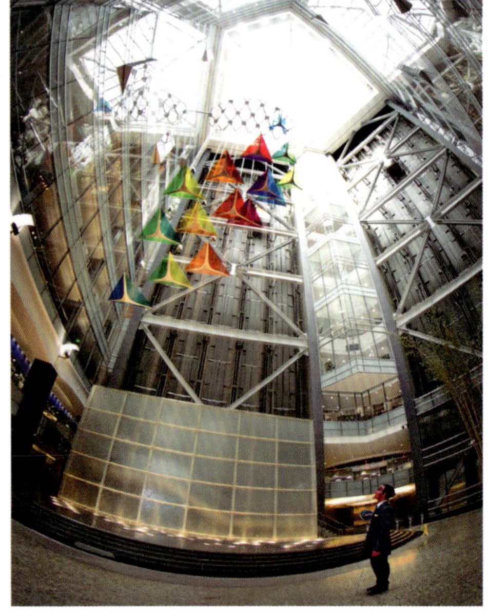

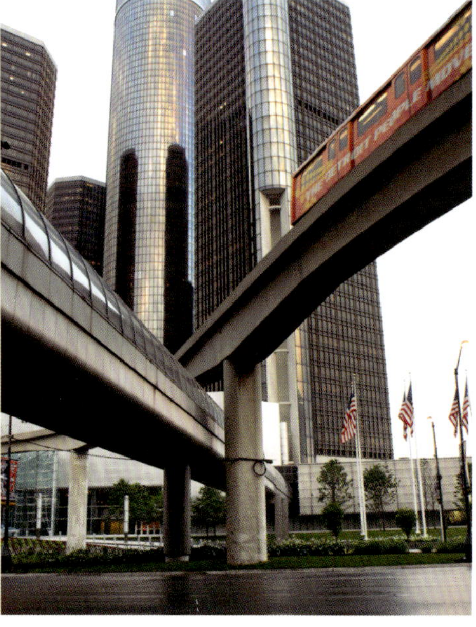

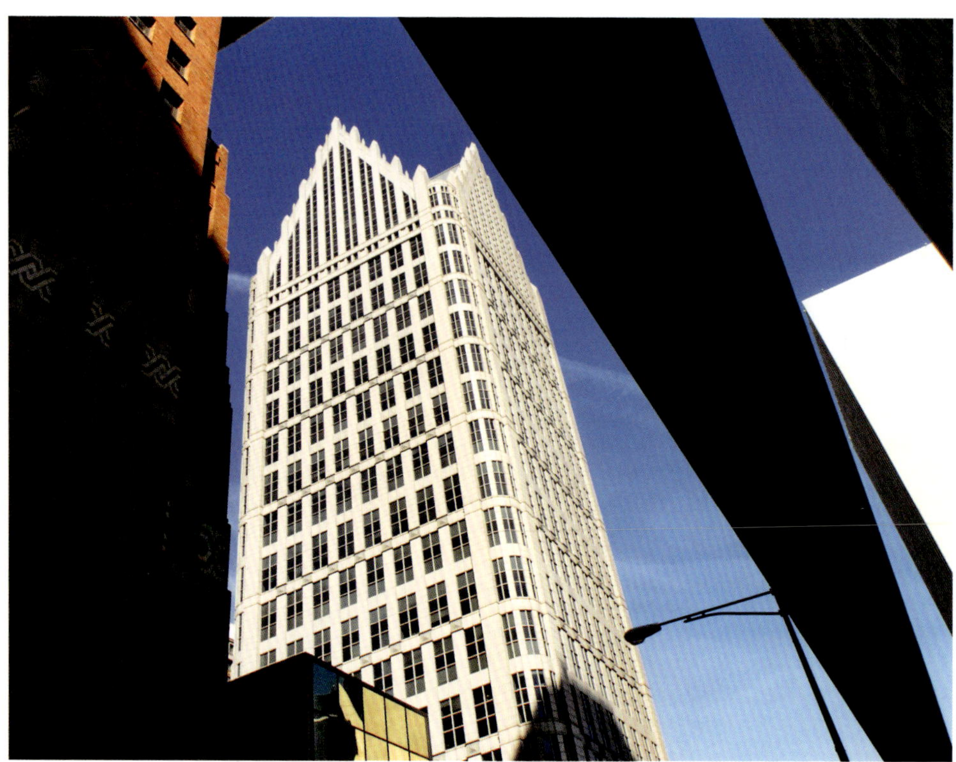

In 1951, the City County Building, now named the Coleman A. Young Center, initiated a surge of modern architecture in Detroit. Inspired by the new international-styled United Nations building in New York City, the building was the anchor for a series of others, including Cobo Center and Ford Auditorium, which were conceived to revitalize and modernize the riverfront. Development of 1001 Woodward, 211 Fort Street, and the Federal Reserve followed, bringing modern architecture to downtown. One of the best representations of this era is the American Natural Resources building, designed by the renowned Detroit architect Minoru Yamasaki. Using elements based on this design, he went onto develop New York's World Trade Center.

I believe that one of the reasons Detroit didn't experience the post-war modern skyscraper boom that swept through Manhattan and Chicago is that it was never essential for manufacturing companies to establish a presence in our downtown. Most auto companies located their office staff alongside their assembly or parts plants. Despite this, there have been some modern additions to downtown. Indeed, every decade brings a new addition, and I'm guessing the Hudson site will be this decade's contribution. - NR

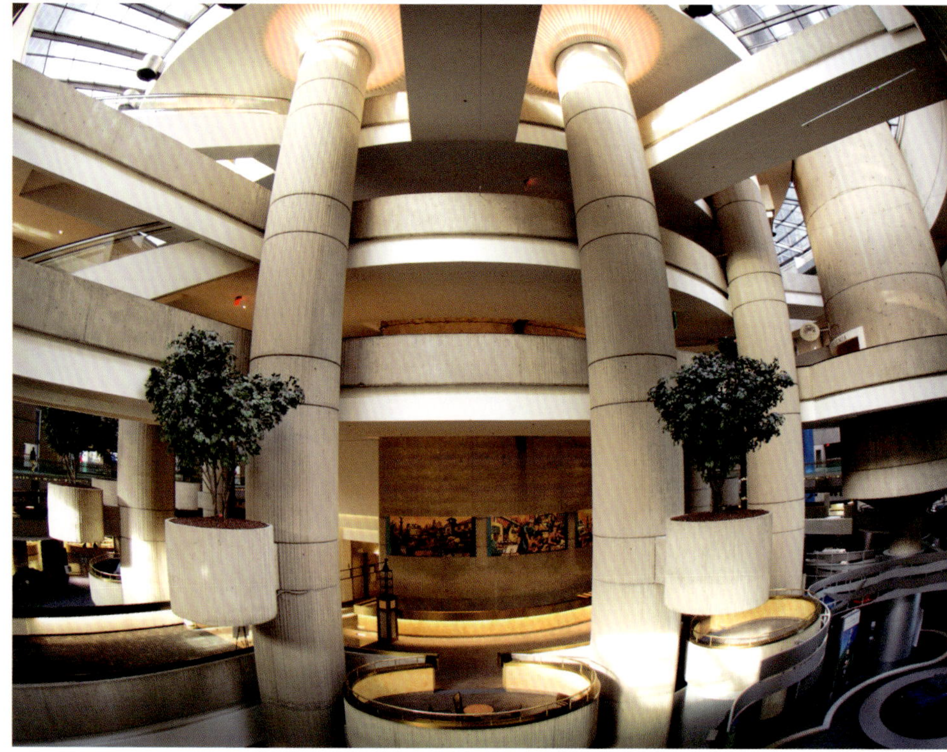

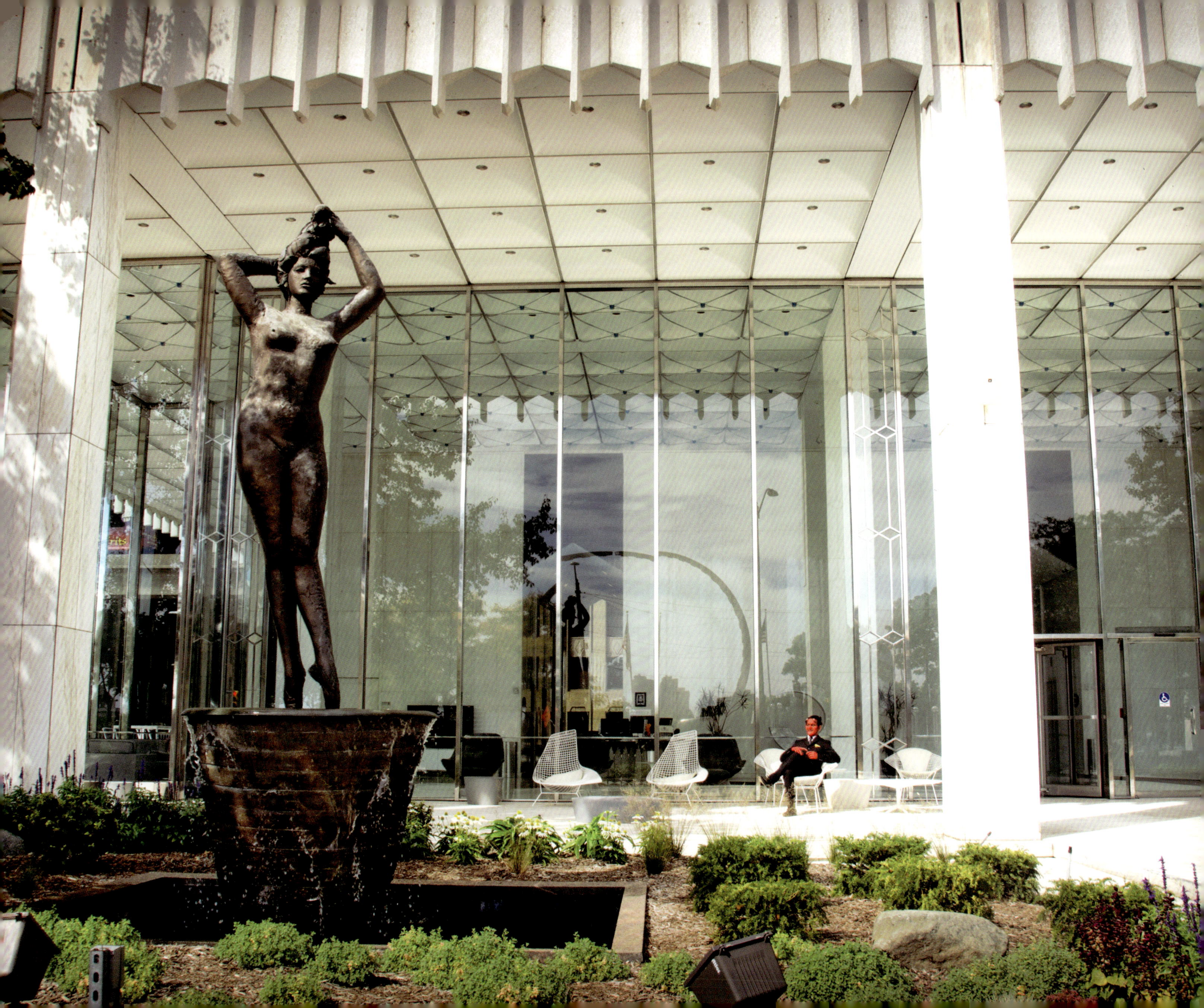

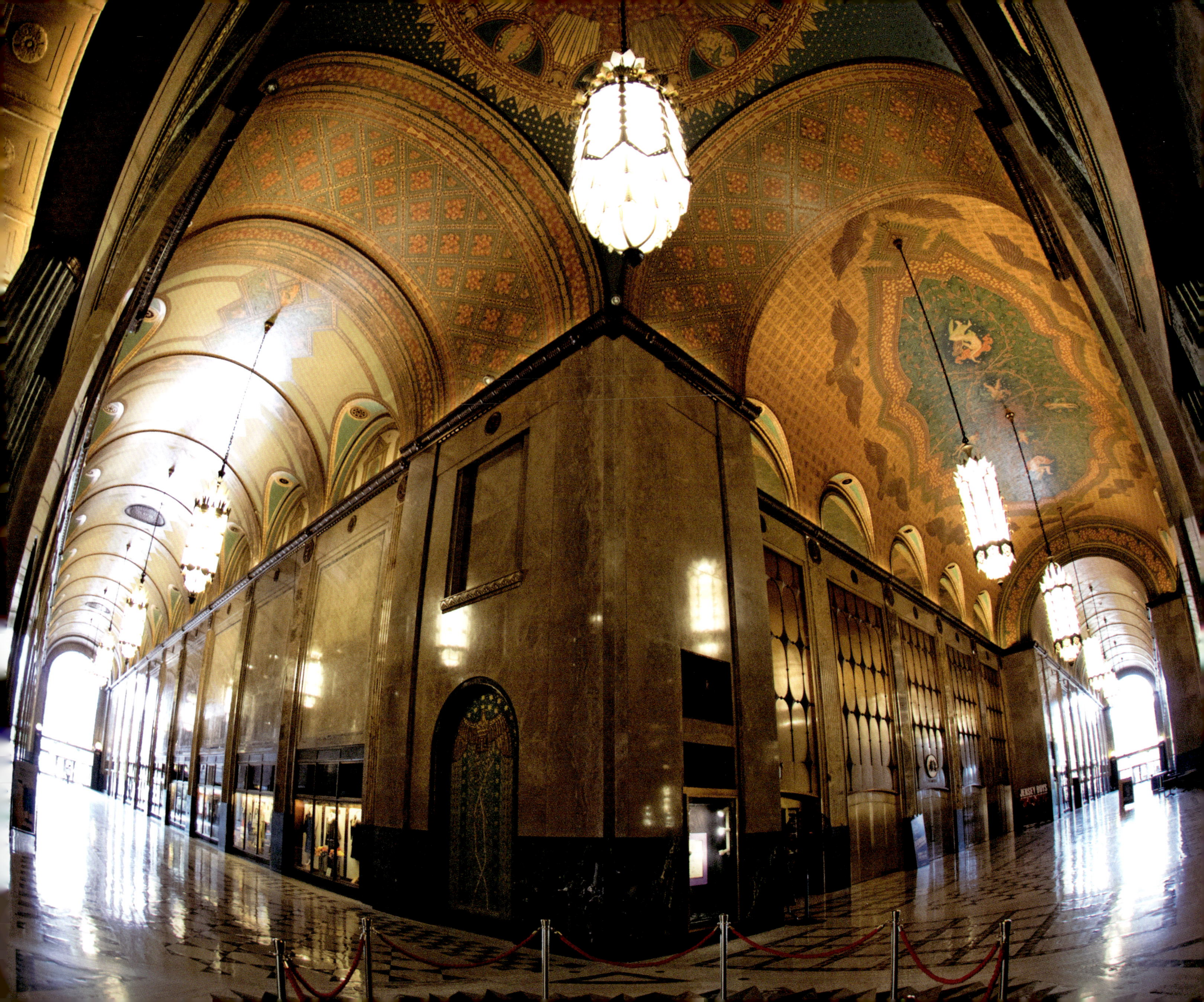

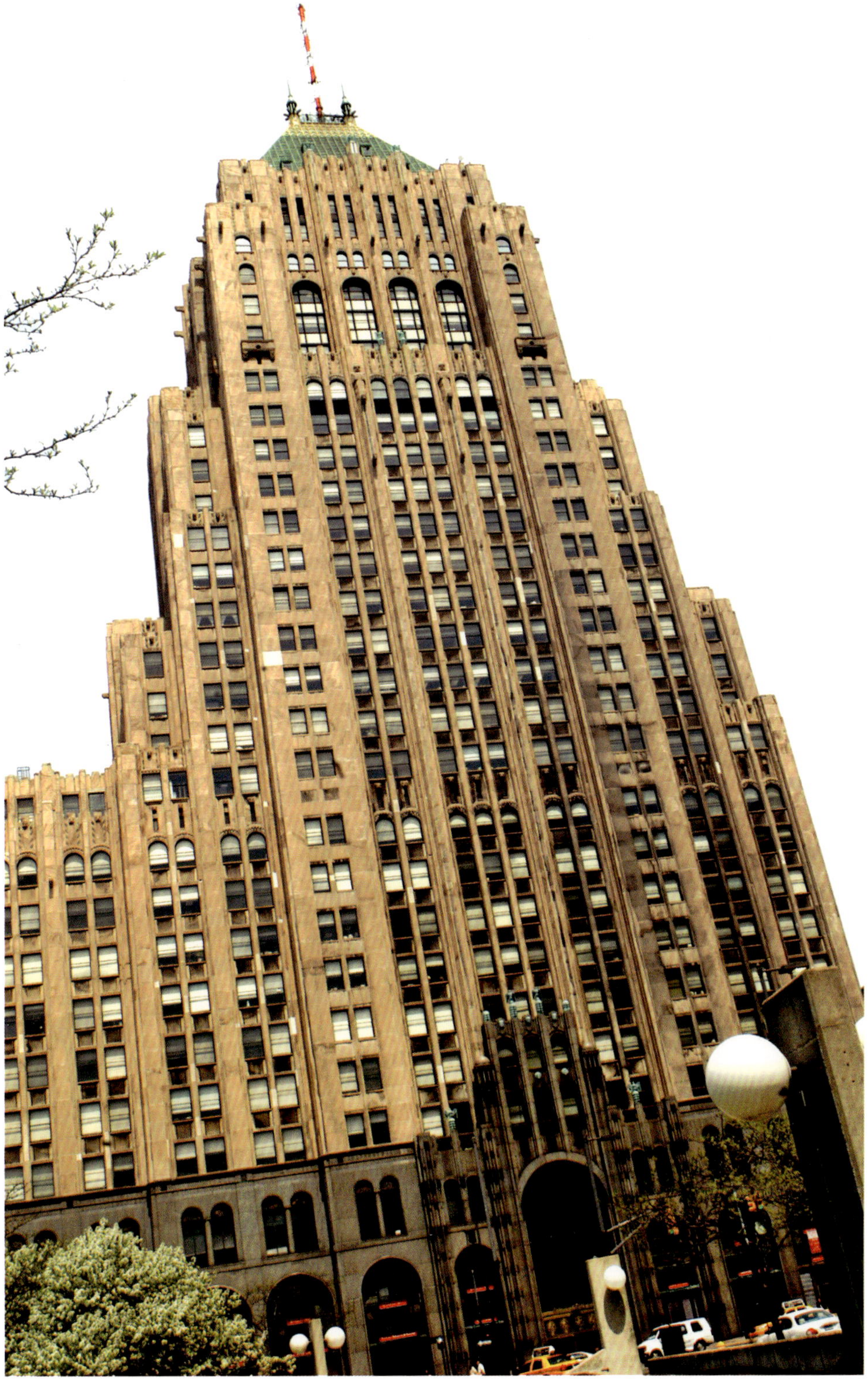

NEW CENTER

West Grand Blvd. and Second Ave., Detroit, 48202
www.newcenterpark.com

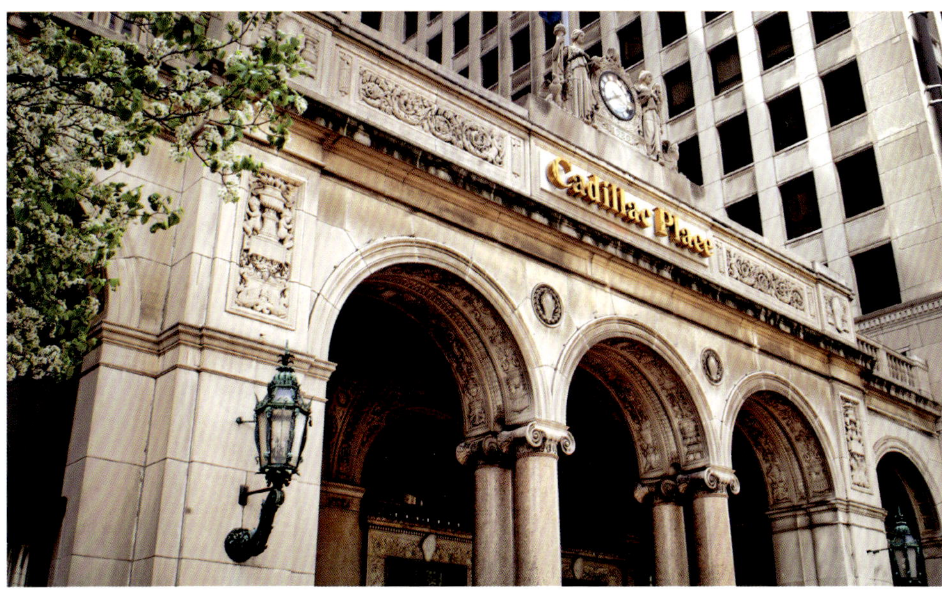

Three miles north of downtown, and once considered the outskirts of the city, New Center began as a business hub as Detroit's growth outpaced its available space. The General Motors Corporation built its world headquarters in 1922. Across Grand Blvd., the Fisher brothers, a major supplier to GM, built their incredible art deco tower. The initial tower was one of three planned until the Great Depression curtailed their vision for a complex of buildings. WJR, one of the nation's oldest radio stations, continues to broadcast from the "Golden Tower of the Fisher Building."

Once the center of the automobile industry, the New Center area teemed with fledgling auto companies. After WWII, GM dominated the industry, becoming the largest company in the world. The Eisenhower administration declared, "What's good for General Motors is good for the country." You can argue about that if you want, but once you see GM's grand former headquarters (now called Cadillac Place, formally at least), you might agree that there was something to it.
- NR

PACKARD PLANT

1800 E. Grand Blvd., Detroit, 48211
www.packardplantproject.com

Moving to Detroit from Ohio in 1903, Packard offered the ultimate luxury vehicle. The complex of buildings comprises almost 3.5 million square feet of space, spread over 40 acres. A symbol of wealth and power, the Packard was desired by kings of industry, Hollywood stars and European royalty. The Japanese Royal Family owned ten, and the Packard was the Russian Imperial state limousine. The Great Depression and, subsequently, World War II ended Packard's dominance as a luxury auto maker. During the war, the plant was retooled to build engines for the P51 Mustang and PT boats. The plant produced more than 55,000 combat engines by the end of the war. The last Packard rolled off the line in 1958, and over the last decade, the factory has been stripped by scrappers, exposed to the weather, and suffered multiple fires by arsonists.

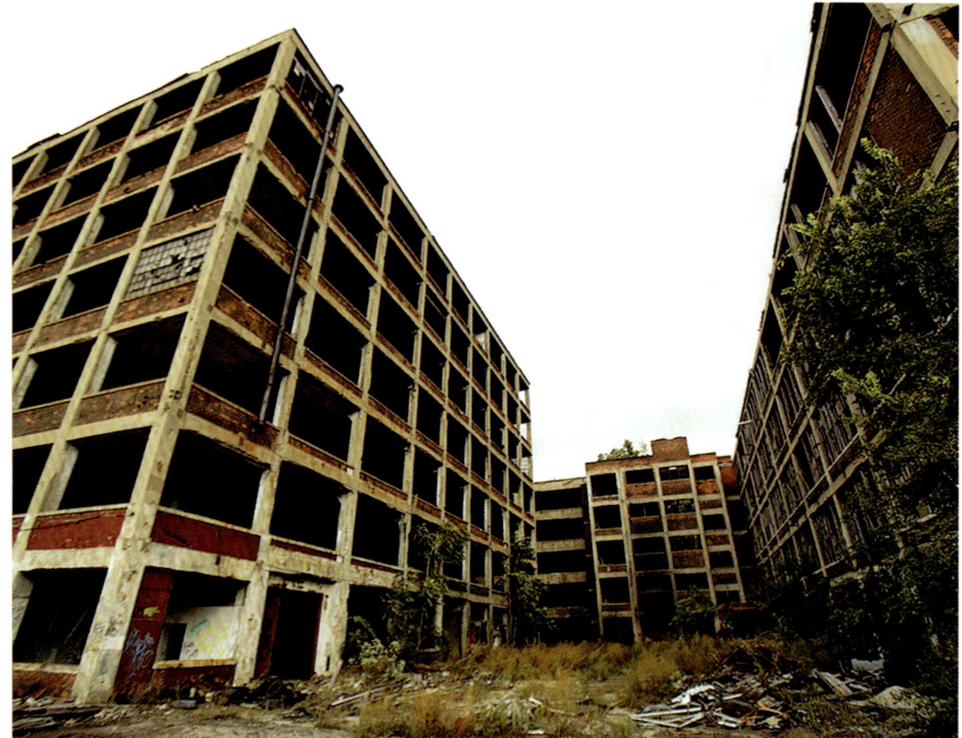

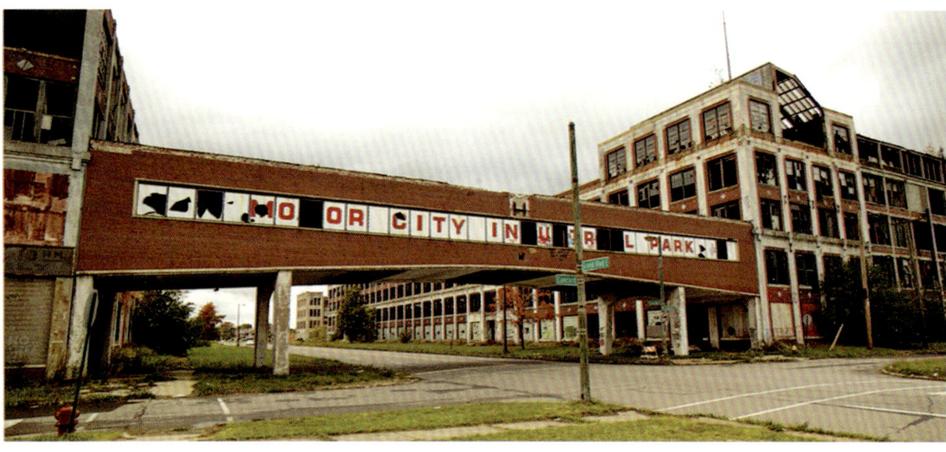

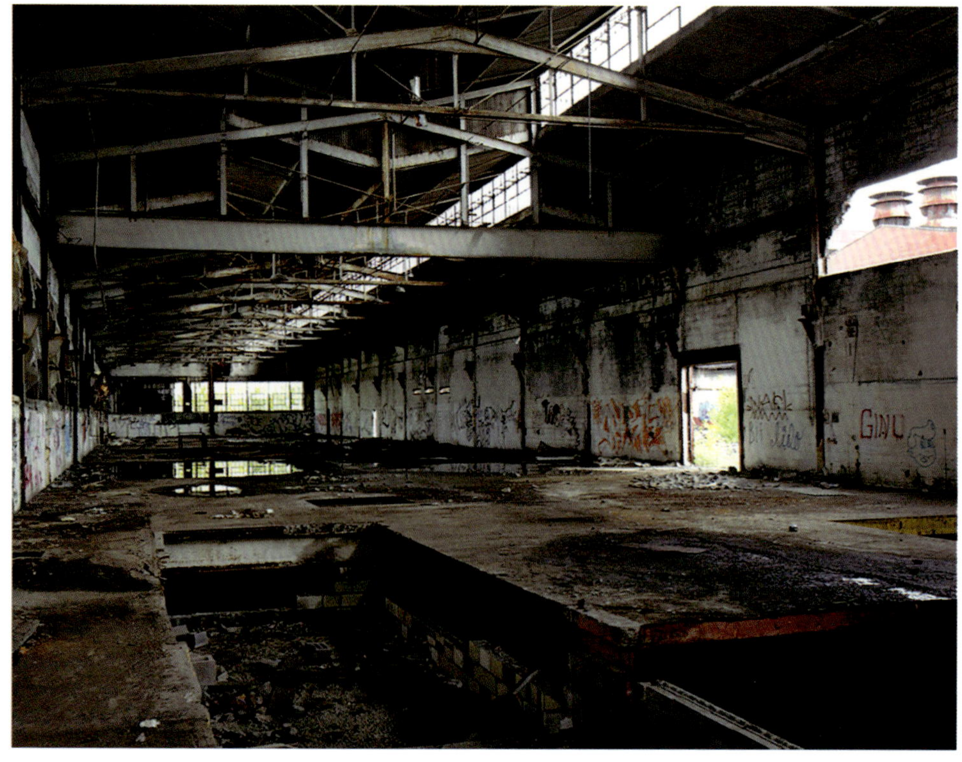

Henry Bourne Joy, an old friend, purchased a Packard in 1902. We had a tremendous time riding through the city and along Lake St. Clair. I persuaded him, Russell Alger, and Truman Newberry to buy the company from the Packard brothers and move it to Detroit. Packard was the luxury car of its day, becoming the number-one designer and producer of luxury automobiles in the United States and coining the phrase, "Ask the Man Who Owns One." In 1952, despite my objections, Packard merged with Studebaker, which was the end of the line for Packard. I continue to visit the old factory, now and then, recalling its glory days and sadly I am reminded of how our city has lost its manufacturing superiority. - NR

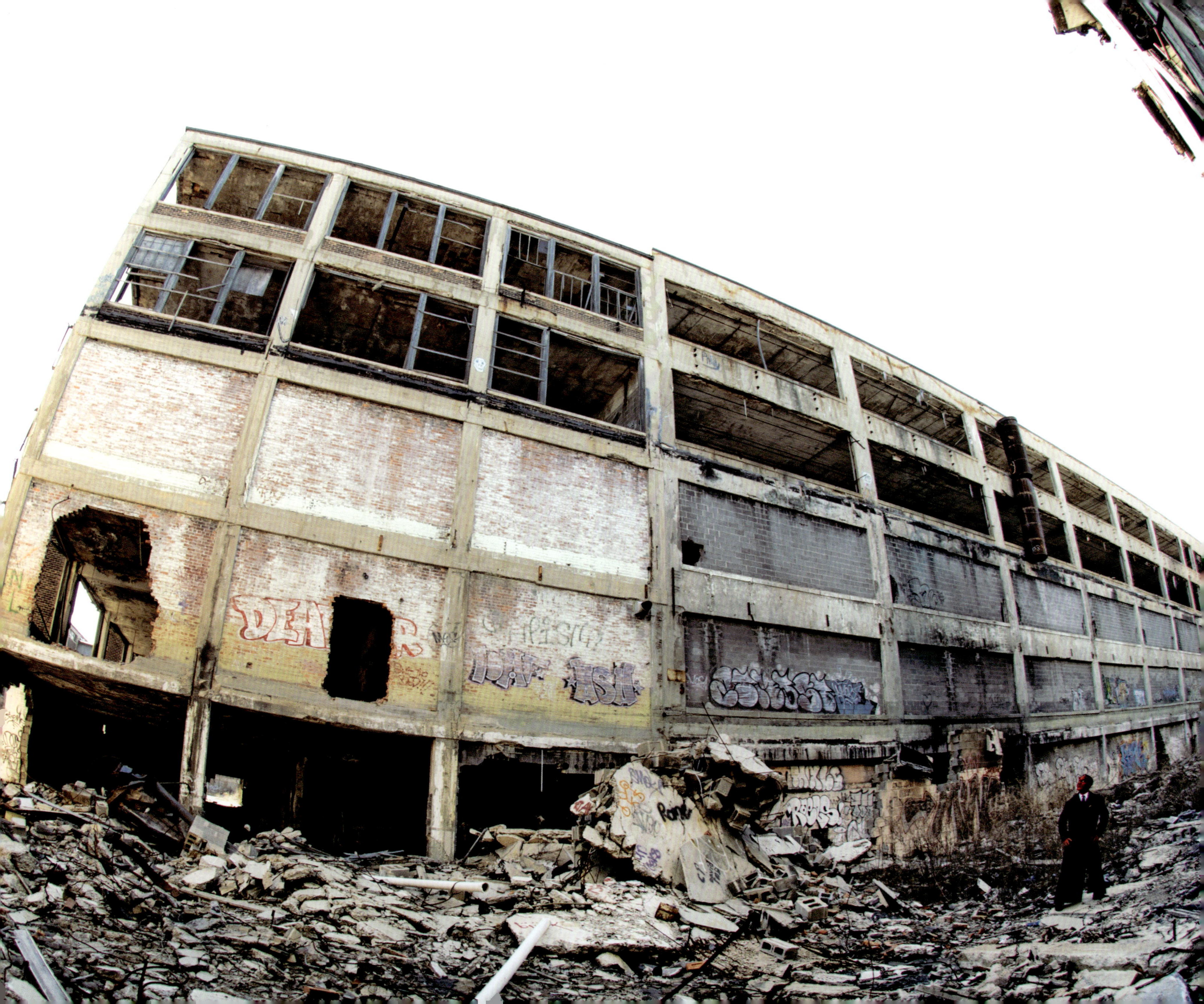

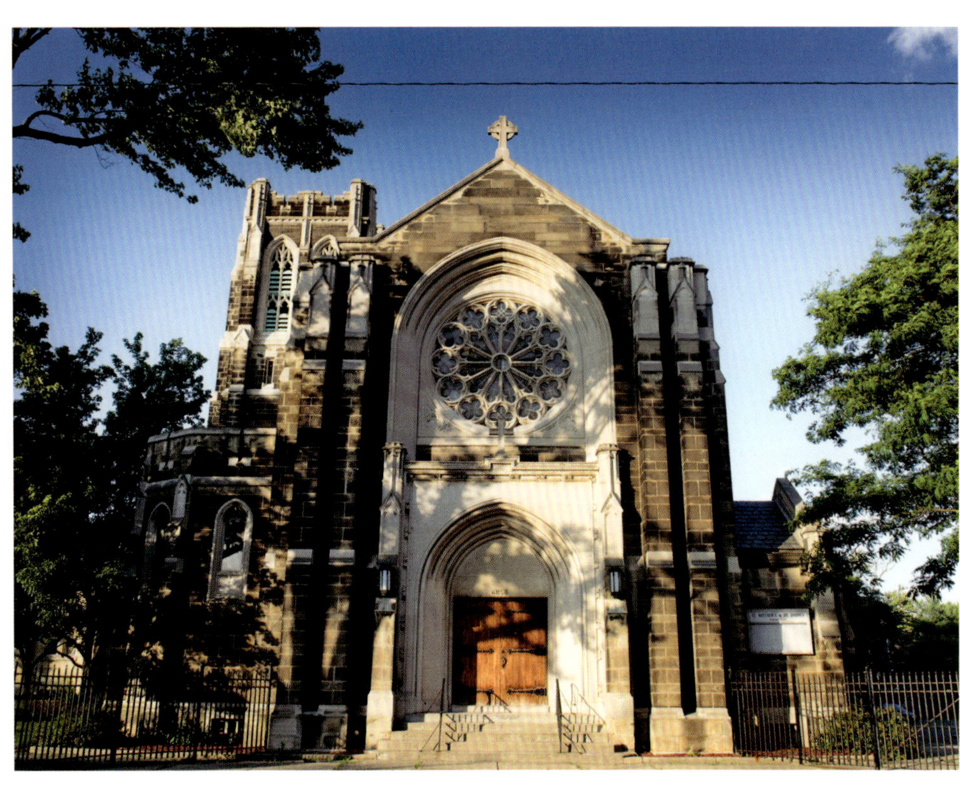

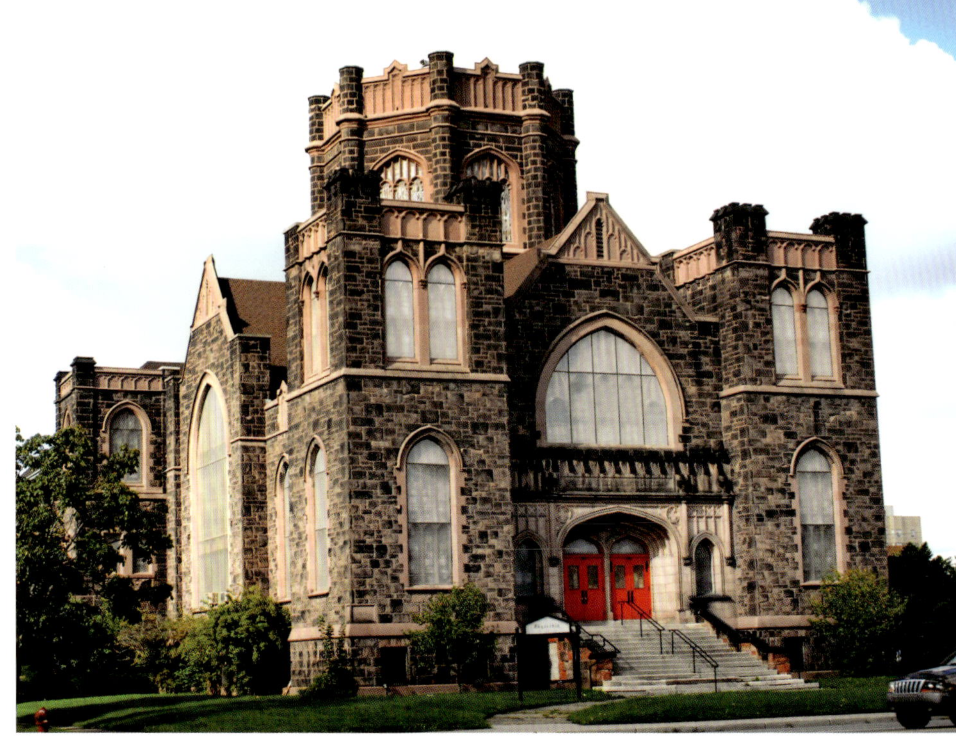

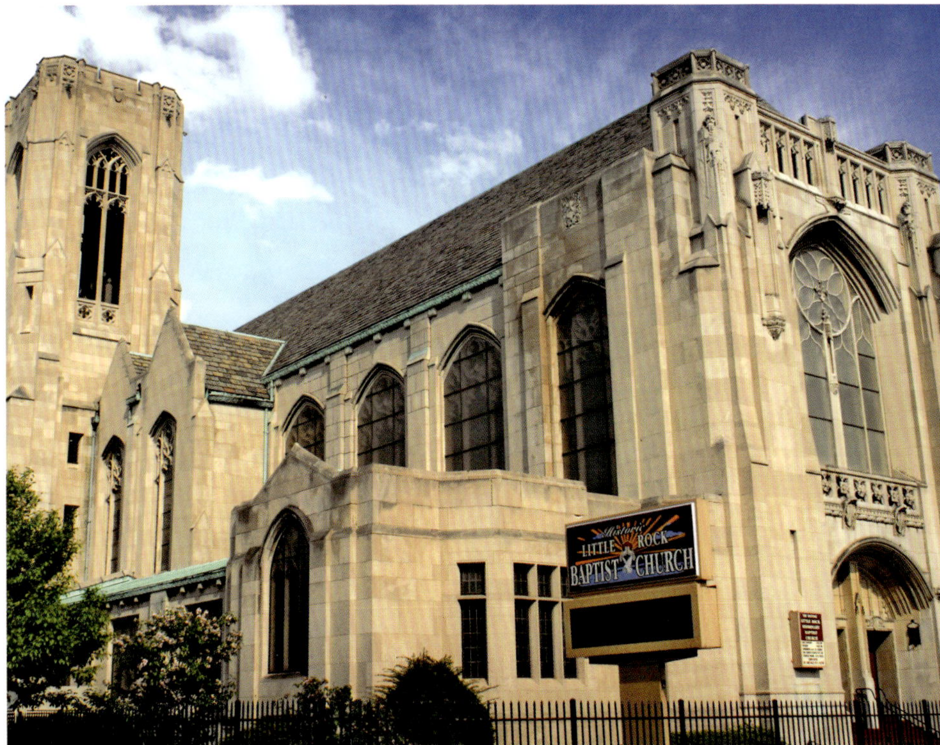
Historic
LITTLE ROCK
BAPTIST CHURCH

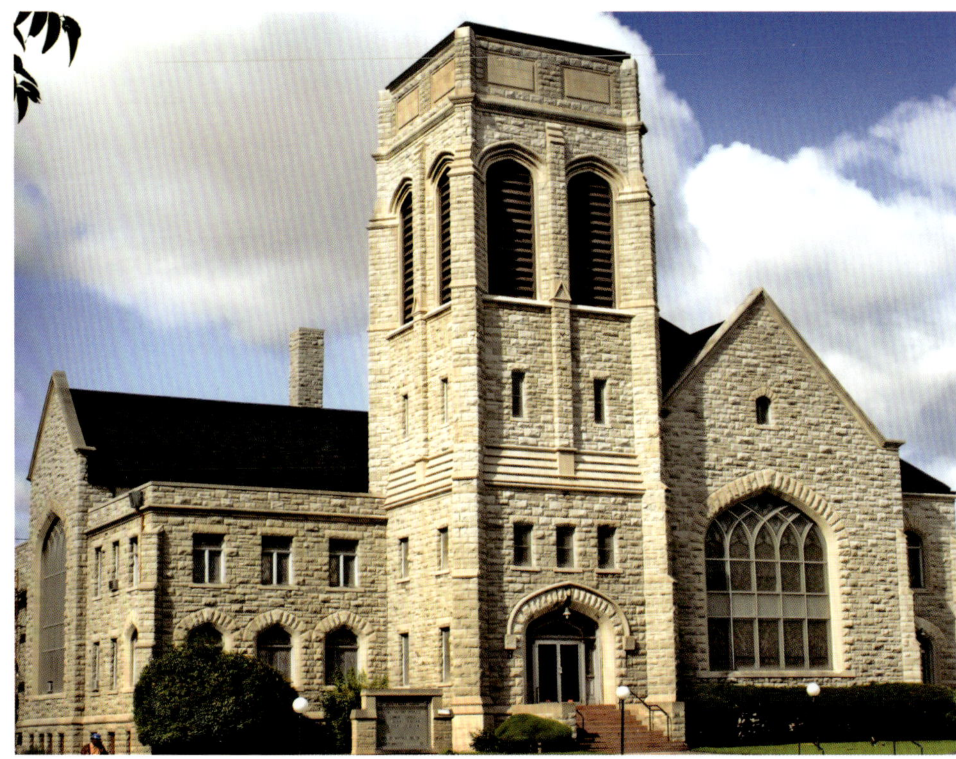

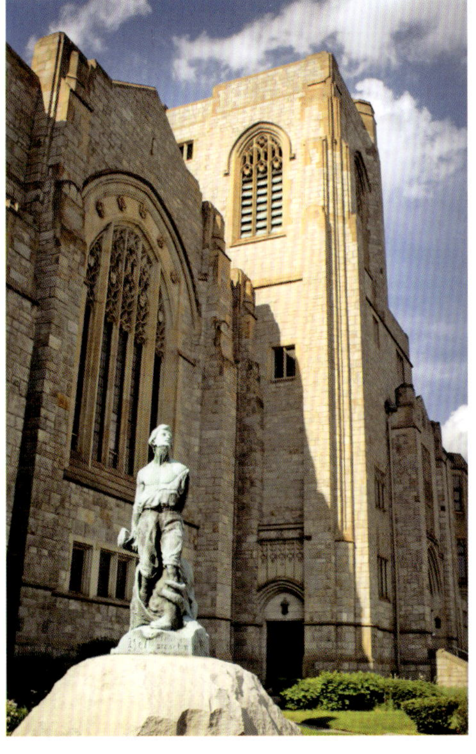

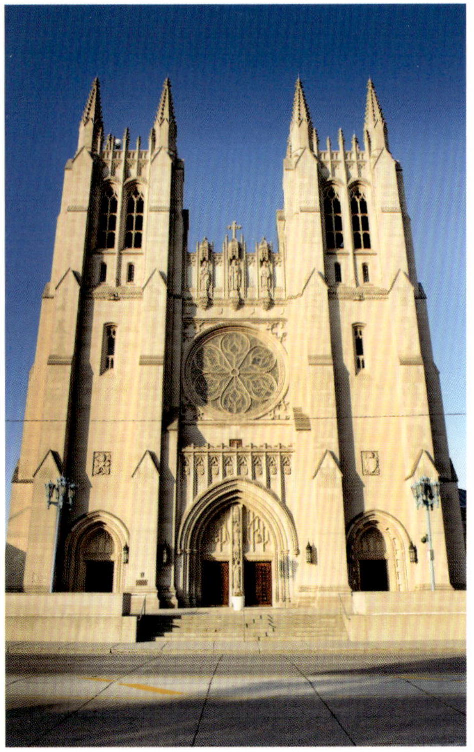

PIETY HILL

Woodward Ave., North of Grand Blvd., Detroit, 48202

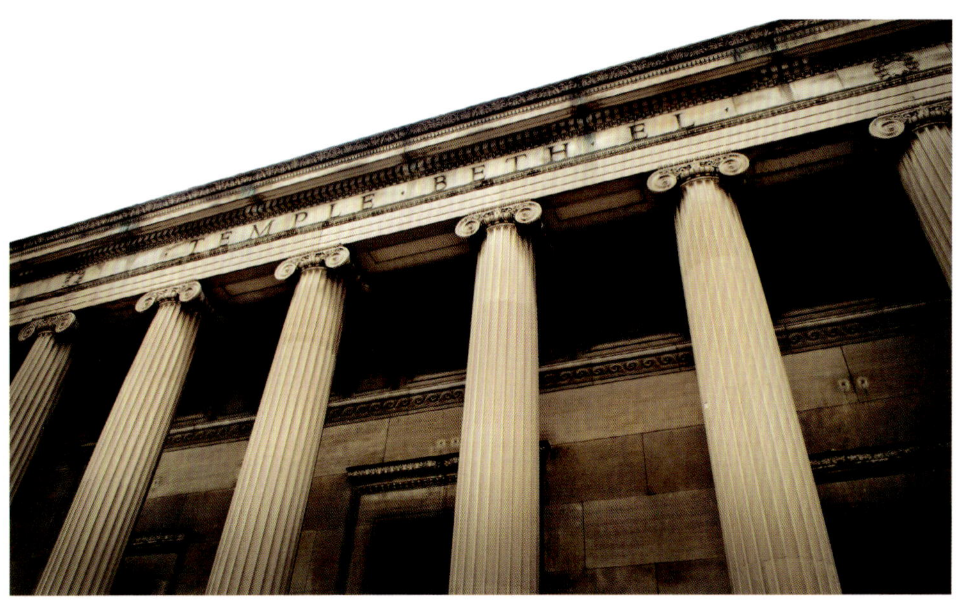

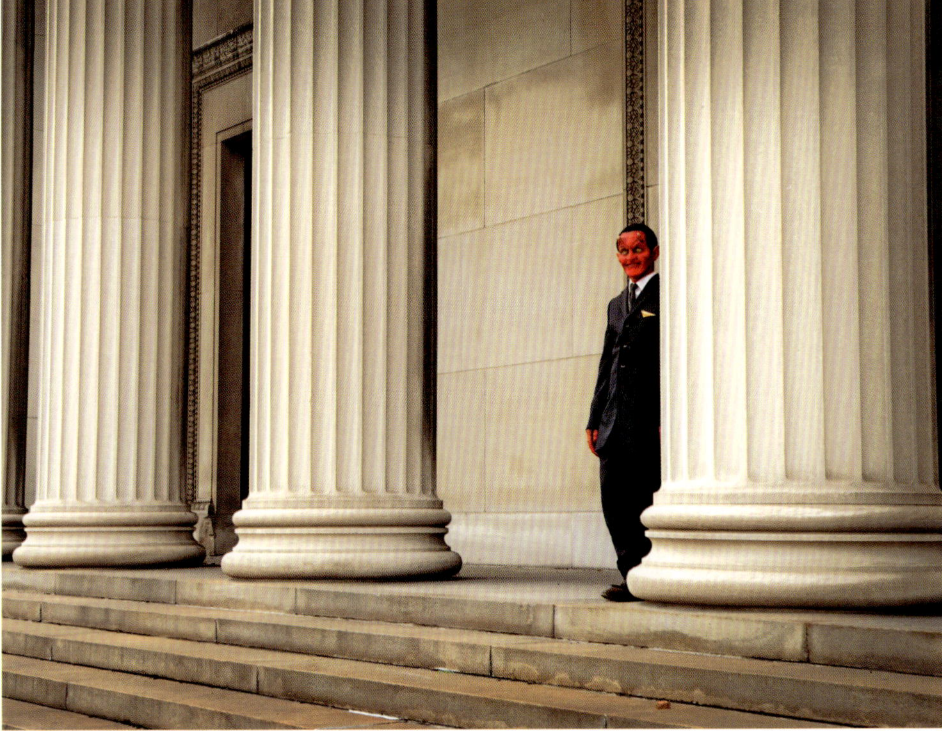

As the wealthy moved north up Woodward Avenue in the golden age of the automobile industry, their houses of worship followed. Massive new cathedrals representing every denomination were constructed in stone and granite, adorned with Pewabic tiling and dramatic stained glass. The Cathedral of the Most Blessed Sacrament was dedicated in 1930 and in 1938 became the seat of the archdiocese. Metropolitan Methodist Church anchors the southern end of the strip. Detroit's oldest synagogue, Temple Beth El, moved farther north, and the oldest Black Episcopal congregation, St. Joseph's, merged with St. Matthew's.

More spiritual than religious, I can still appreciate one's devotion to a belief or cause. Churches, mosques, and synagogues became important social centers for assimilating immigrants. Devoted congregants built massive edifices, replicating the cathedrals of their homelands. Every denomination built ever more impressive places for worship, trying to eclipse each other. As the city's population declined, these architectural wonders have become endangered. In response, traveling mass mobs rally worshippers to support struggling parishes, wonderstruck by the ornate interiors. - NR

WAYNE COUNTY BUILDING

600 Randolph St., Detroit, 48226

Founded in 1796 and named after Revolutionary War hero "Mad" Anthony Wayne, Wayne County is the most populous county in Michigan, and this building served as its offices from 1904 until 2008. One of the nation's finest surviving examples of Roman Baroque Revival architecture, and built with buff Berea sandstone, the structure boasts an interior finished with a variety of marbles and mosaics. Its sister building, similarly designed, was the old Detroit City Hall, demolished in 1961. The two building faced each other, bookending Campus Martius and Cadillac Square.

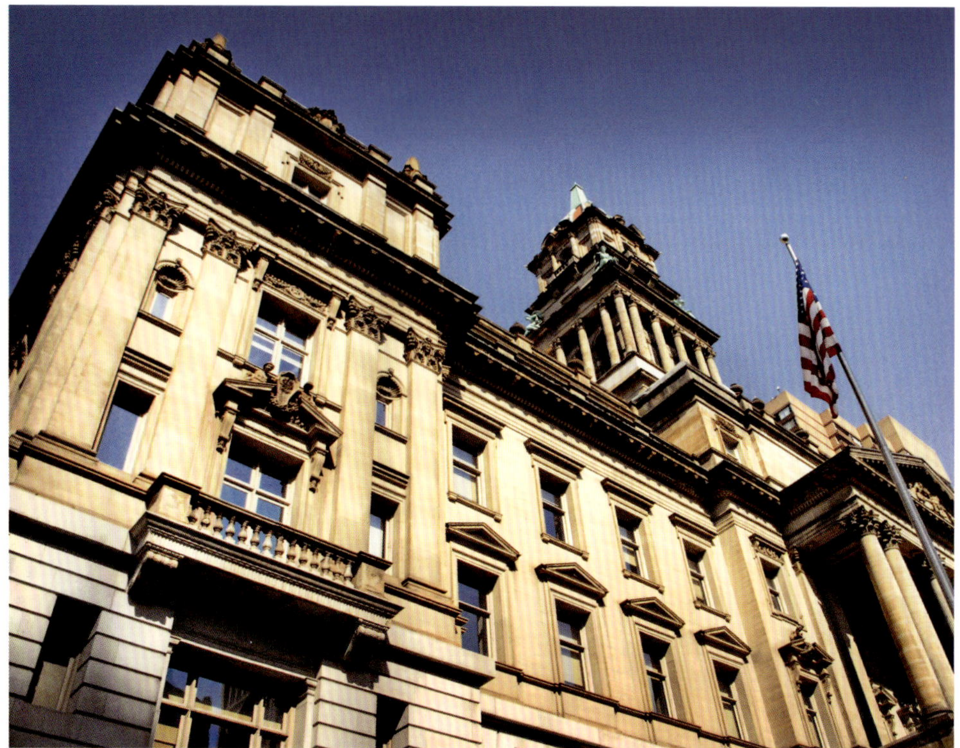

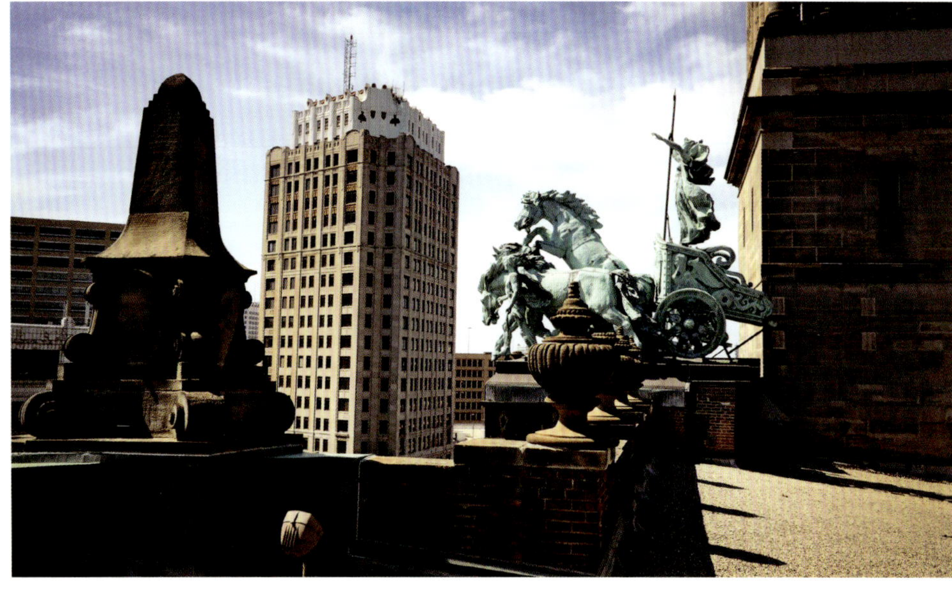

"Mad" Anthony Wayne was a tough SOB and Revolutionary War hero. Nicknamed "Mad" after he led a resounding victory, he was sent to Detroit to establish American sovereignty from the British in 1796. Just like Tony, we're tough as nails and a little bit crazy, continuing his legacy in the county named after him. The Old Wayne County building was constructed with the finest details, representing the prominence of the growing city. To this day, I am shocked that it escaped the wrecking ball of progress. - NR

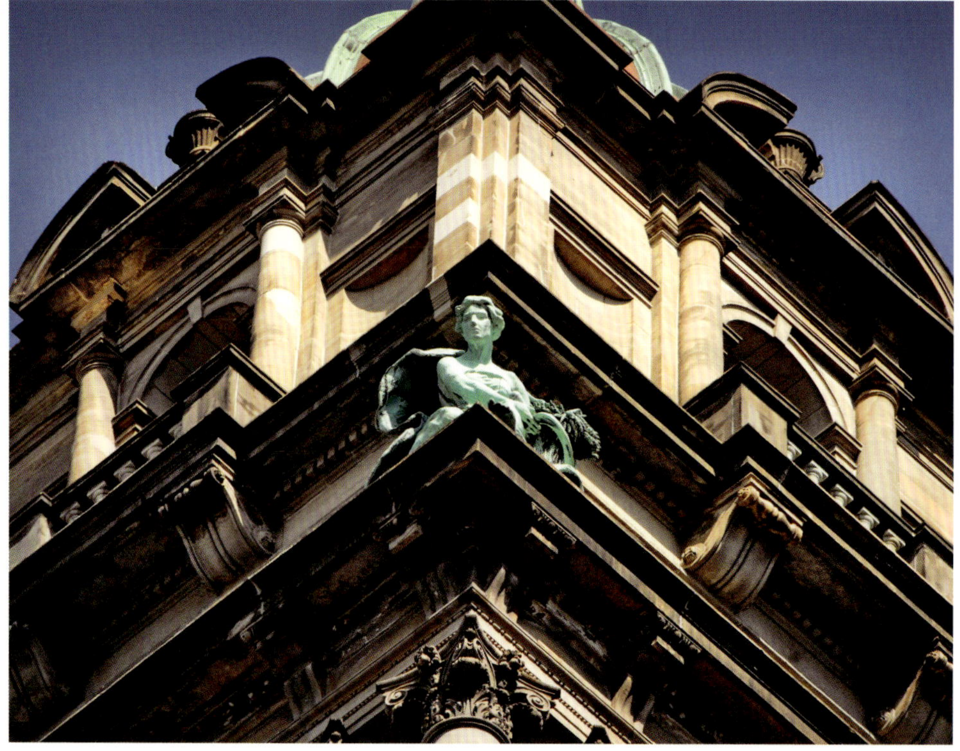

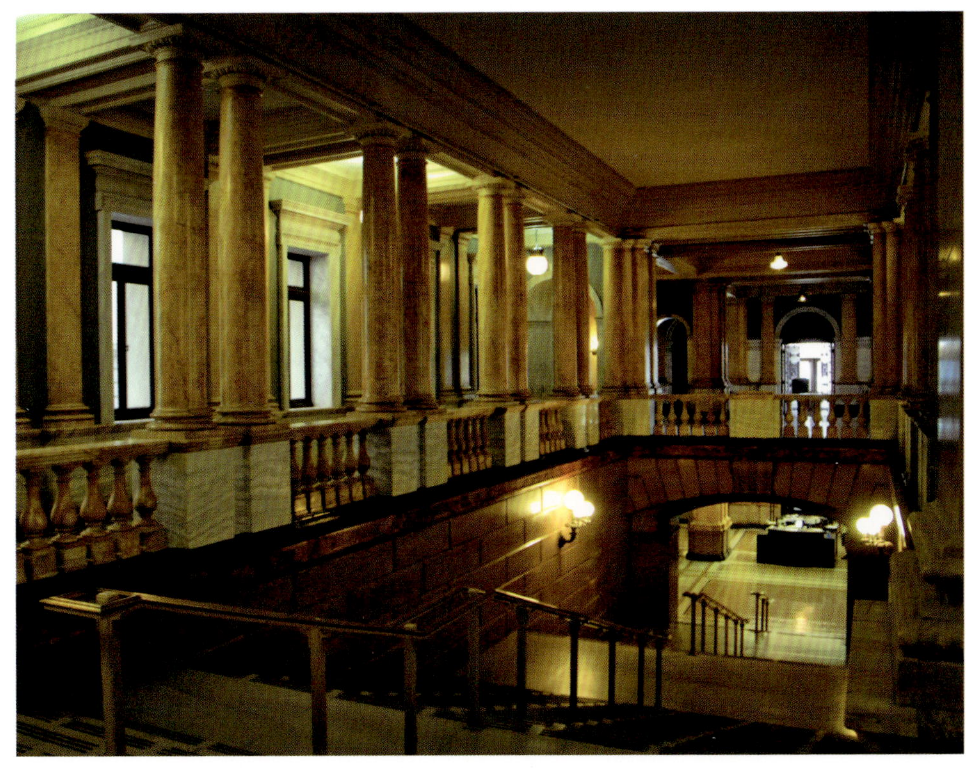

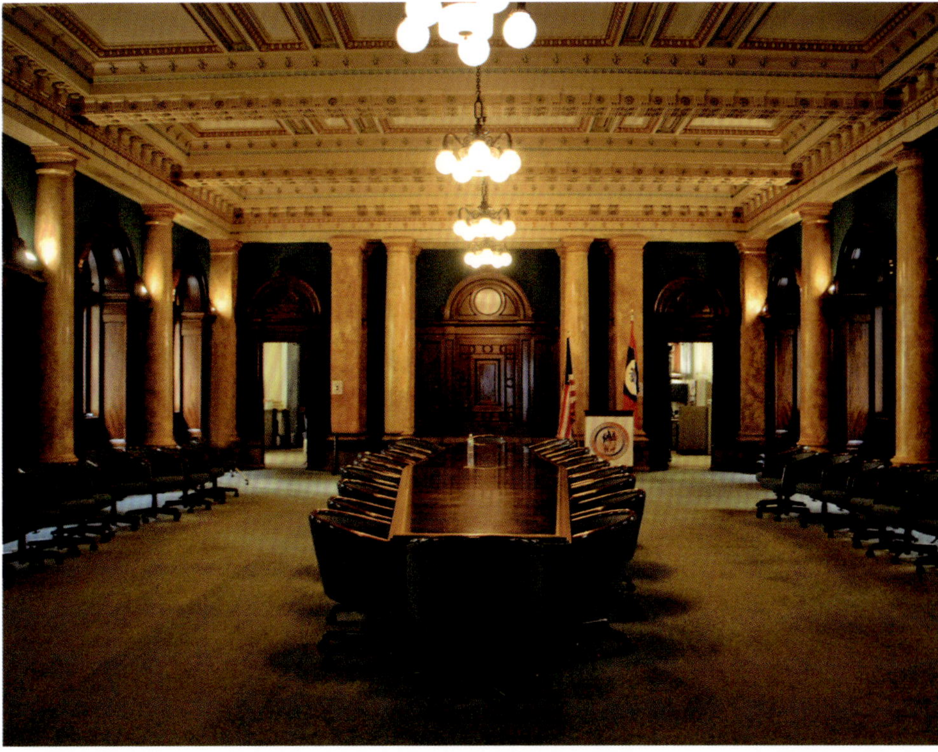

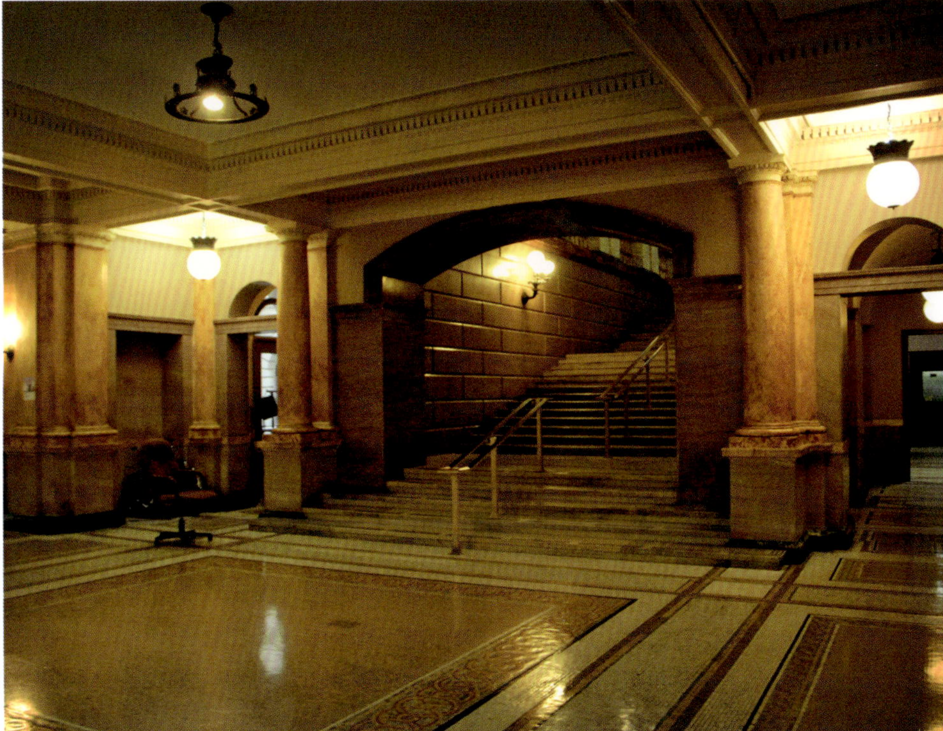

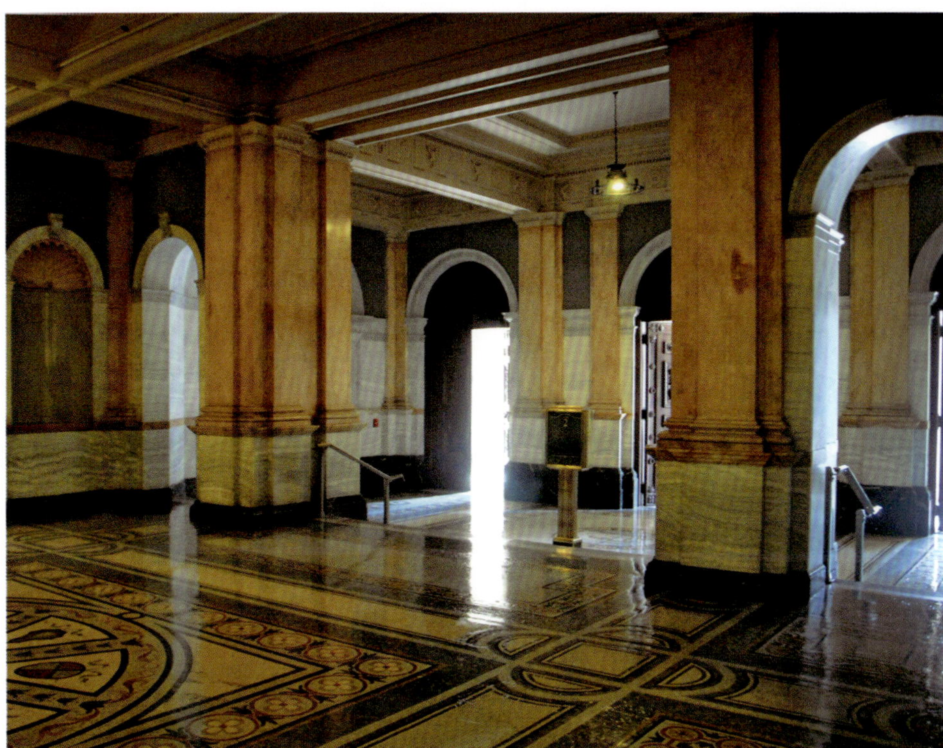

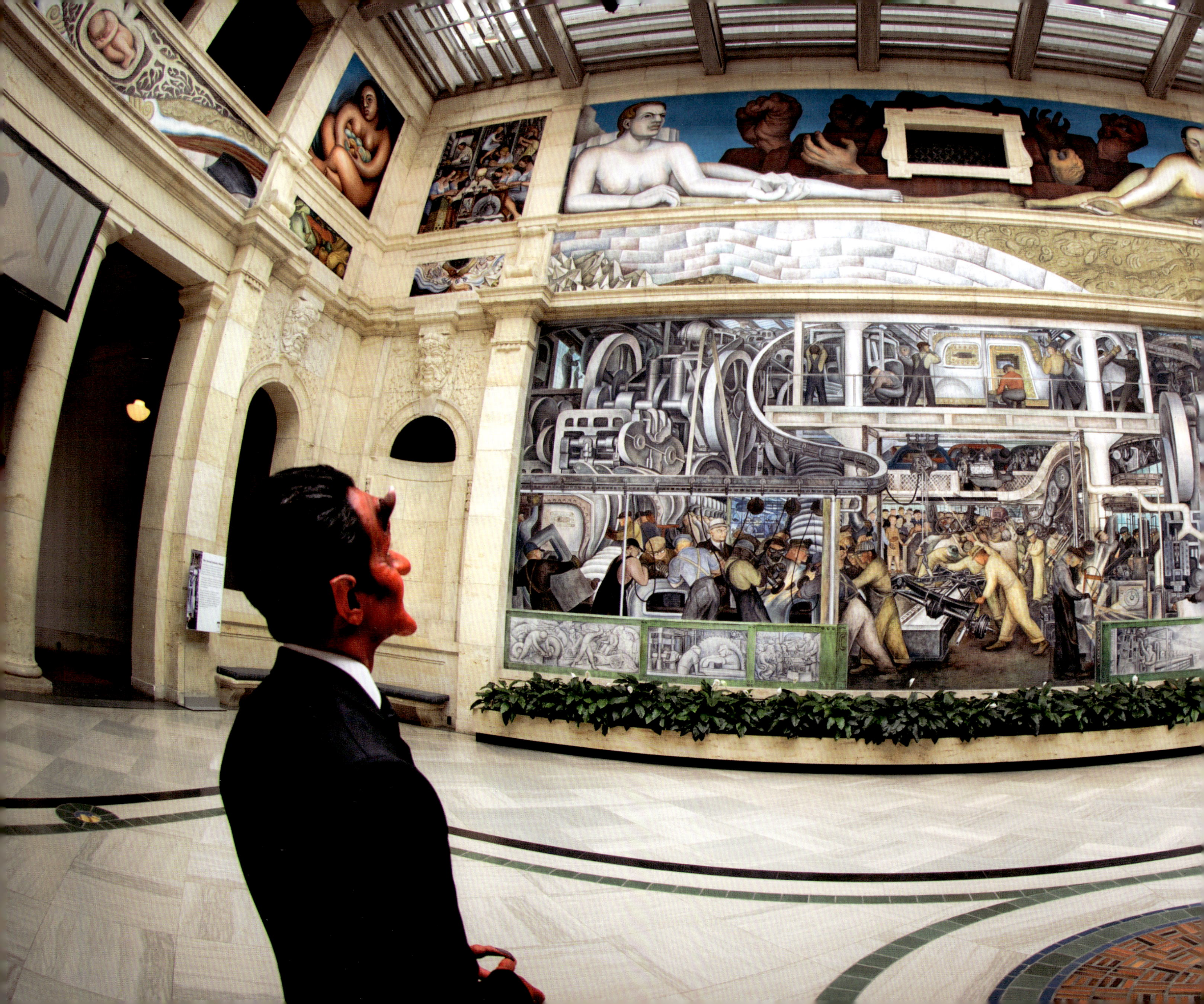

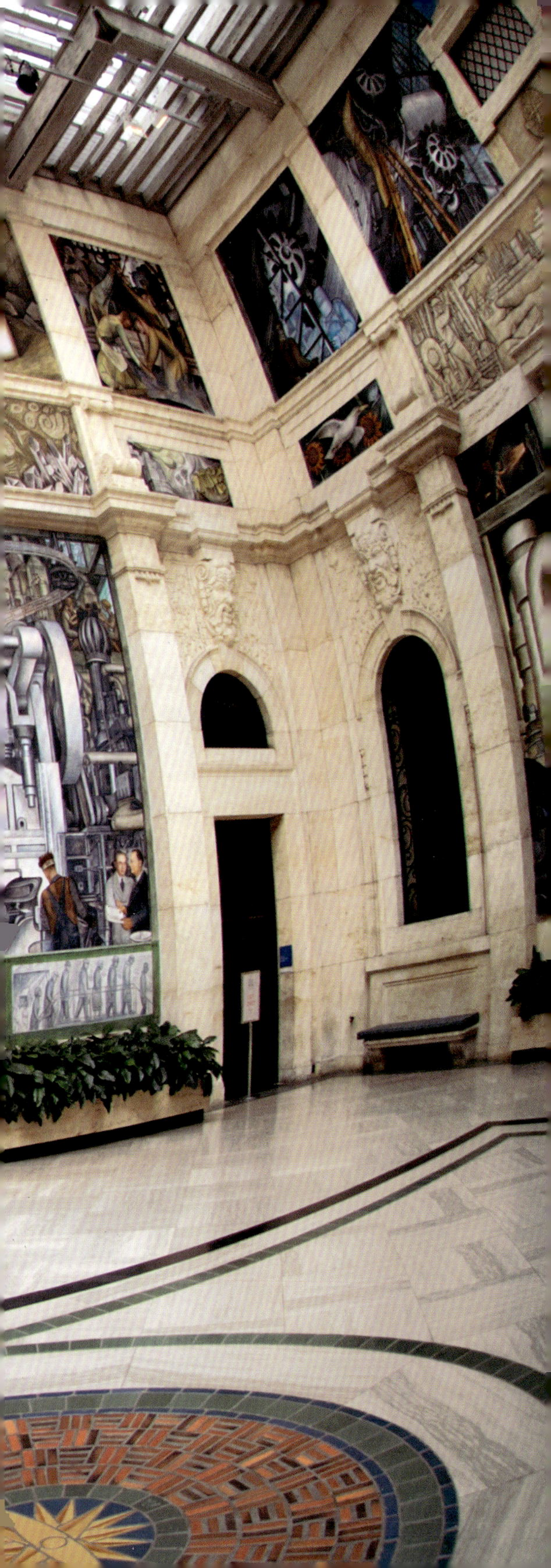

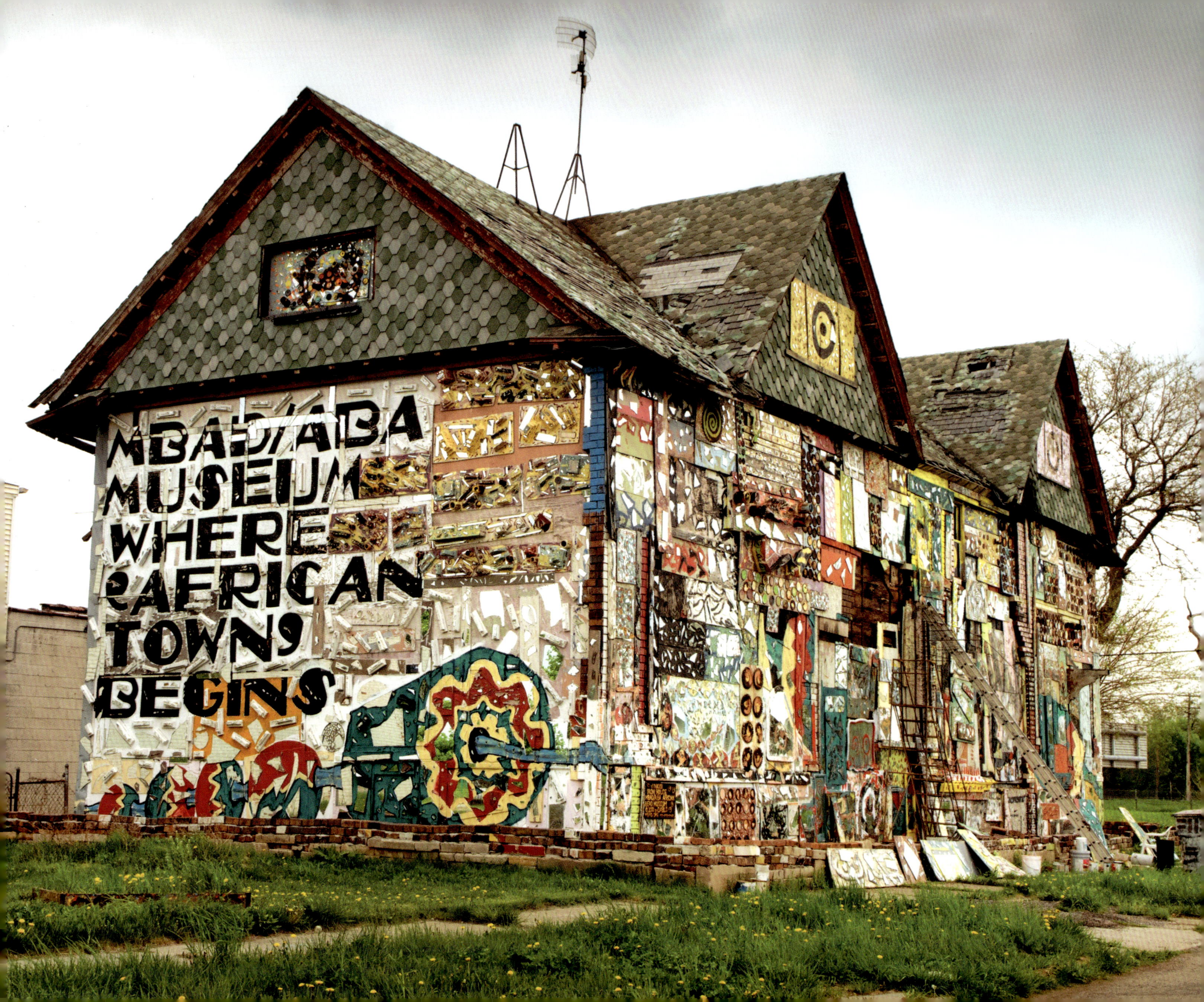
MBAD/ABA
MUSEUM
WHERE
AFRICAN
TOWNS
BEGINS

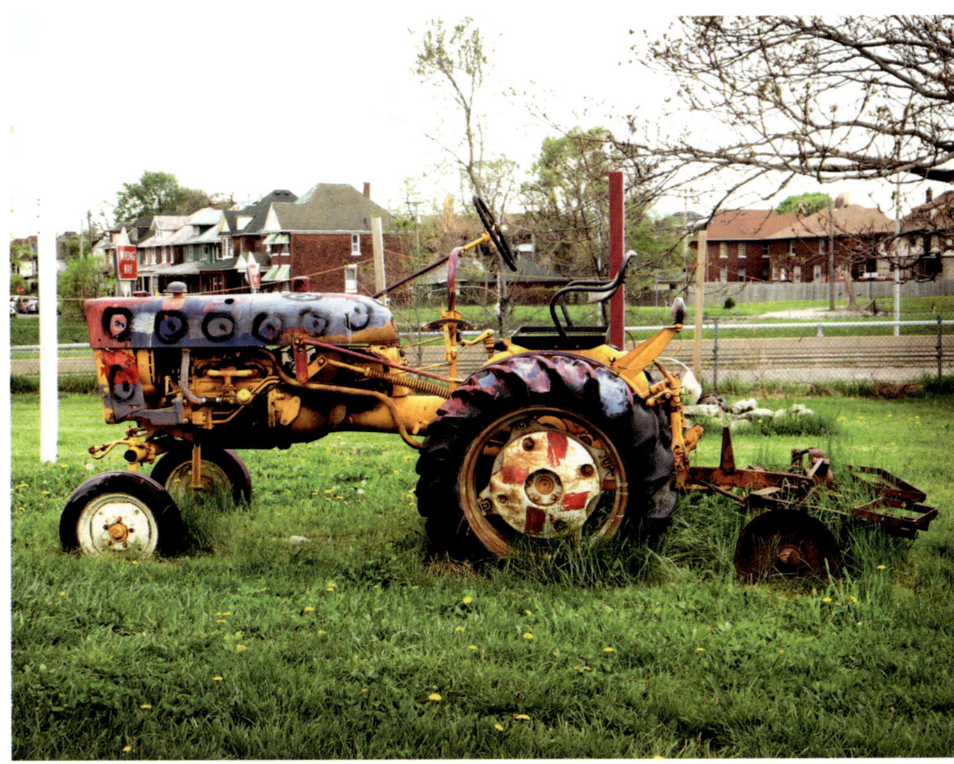

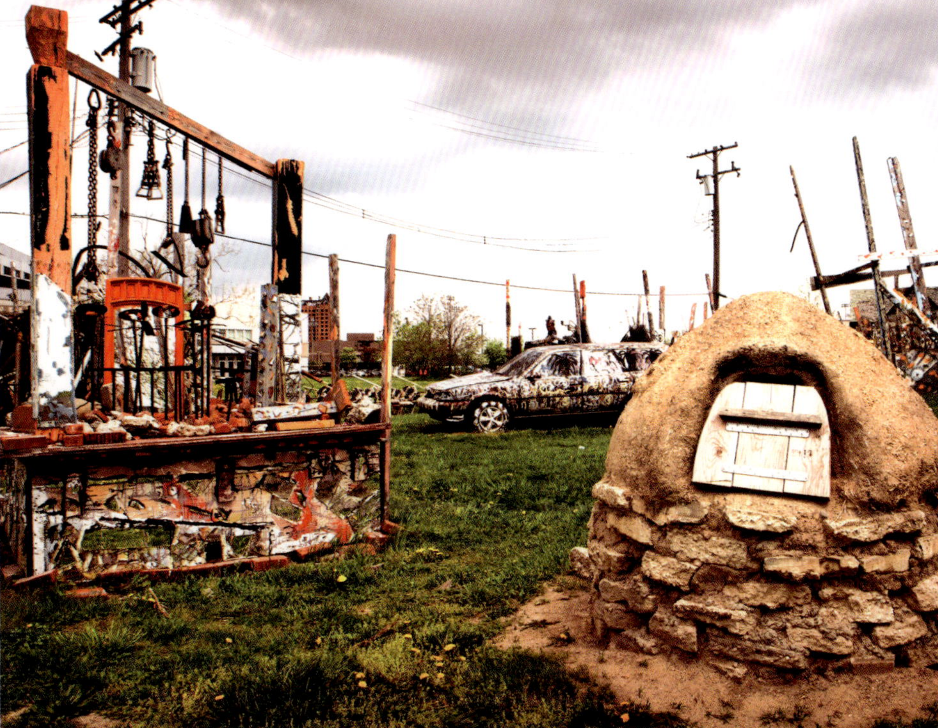

DABL'S AFRICAN BEAD GALLERY

6559 Grand River, Detroit, 48208
www.mbad.org

Artist, curator, and historian Olayami Dabls has amassed a huge, wondrous collection of African beads. His mission is to maintain and promote African artisanal beadwork. In addition, his own artwork decorates buildings throughout his compound off Grand River, which includes a vast sculpture garden. His work demonstrates his passion for color and takes inspiration from African culture.

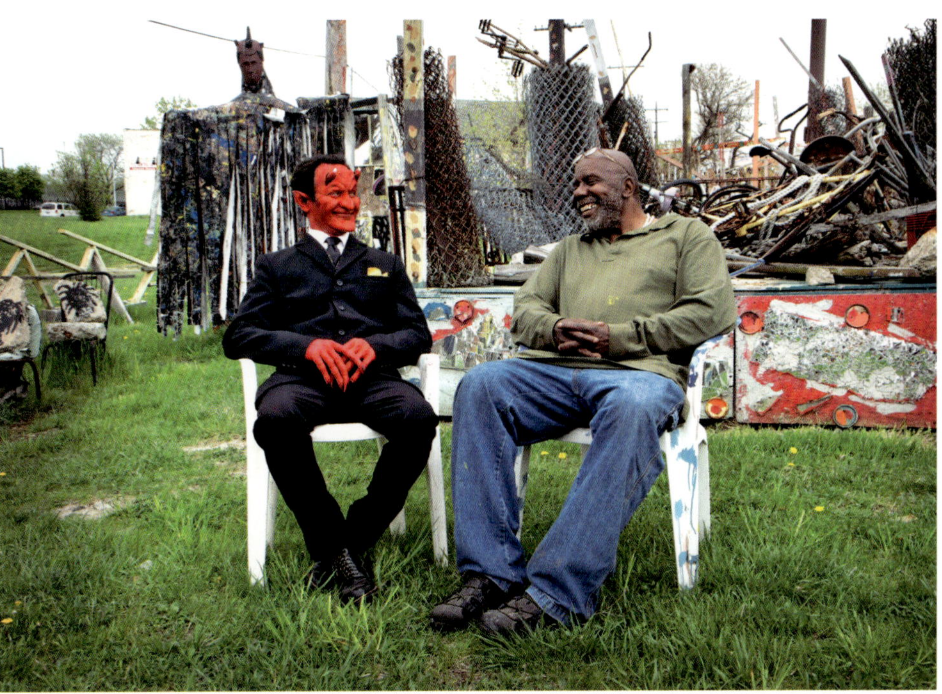

There's really no place like this place. Legendary folk artist Olayami Dabls has created his own world, filled with African cultural references, on two city blocks. Using four fundamental materials – iron, rock, wood, and mirrors – in his work, he encourages people to understand and value African culture. Be sure to check out his immense collection of African beads. - NR

DETROIT ARTIST MARKET

4719 Woodward Ave., Detroit, 48201
www.detroitartistsmarket.org

A contemporary art gallery founded by local artists during the Great Depression in 1932, the Detroit Artists Market provides artists with an opportunity to exhibit new works. Located in Midtown, near the Detroit Institute of Arts, it endures as the oldest continuously running nonprofit gallery in the Midwest, following its mandate as a promoter of emerging Detroit-area artists and educating the public about contemporary art.

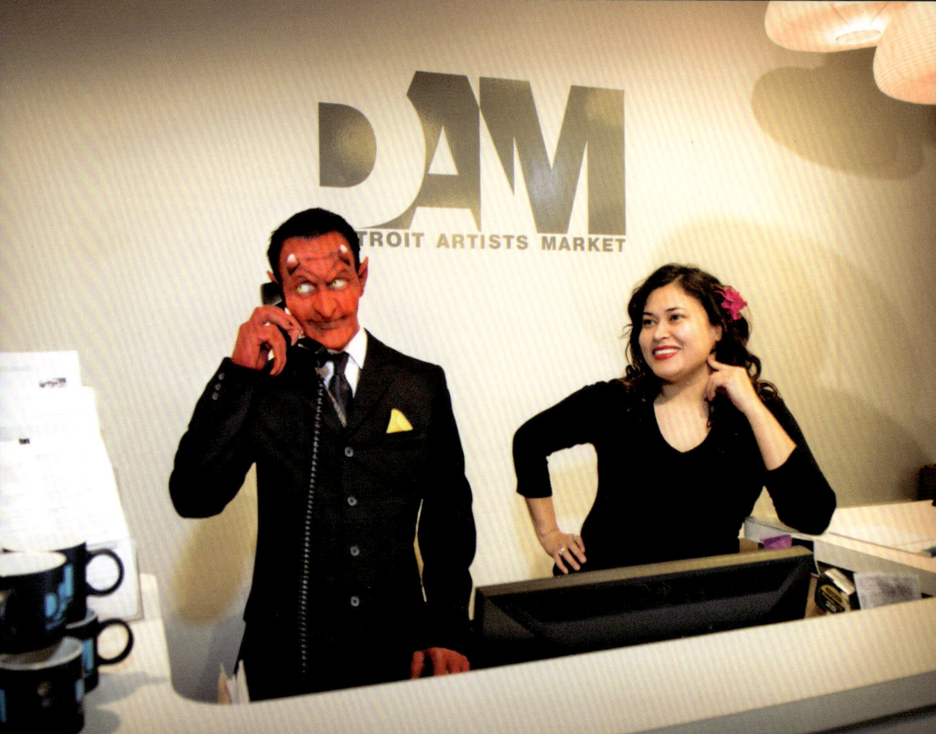

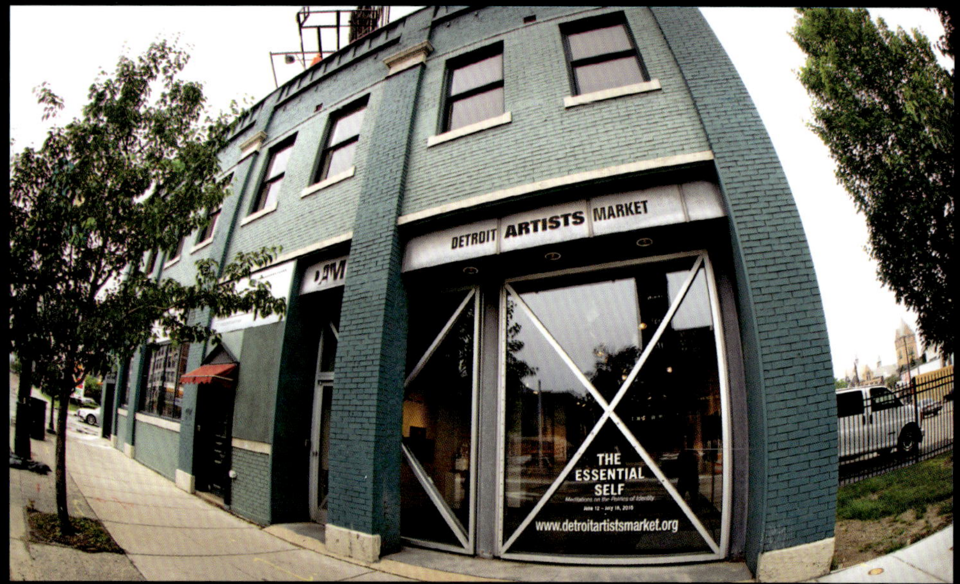

Every other month or so, on a Friday evening, free wine is poured, art is exhibited, and people congregate. This worthy exercise has been going on for more than 80 years. Fortunately, at DAM, where their colleagues curate exhibits, artists are given a warm reception. DAM offers a revolving schedule of group shows and recognizes individuals, especially local artist, for their breadth of works.

- NR

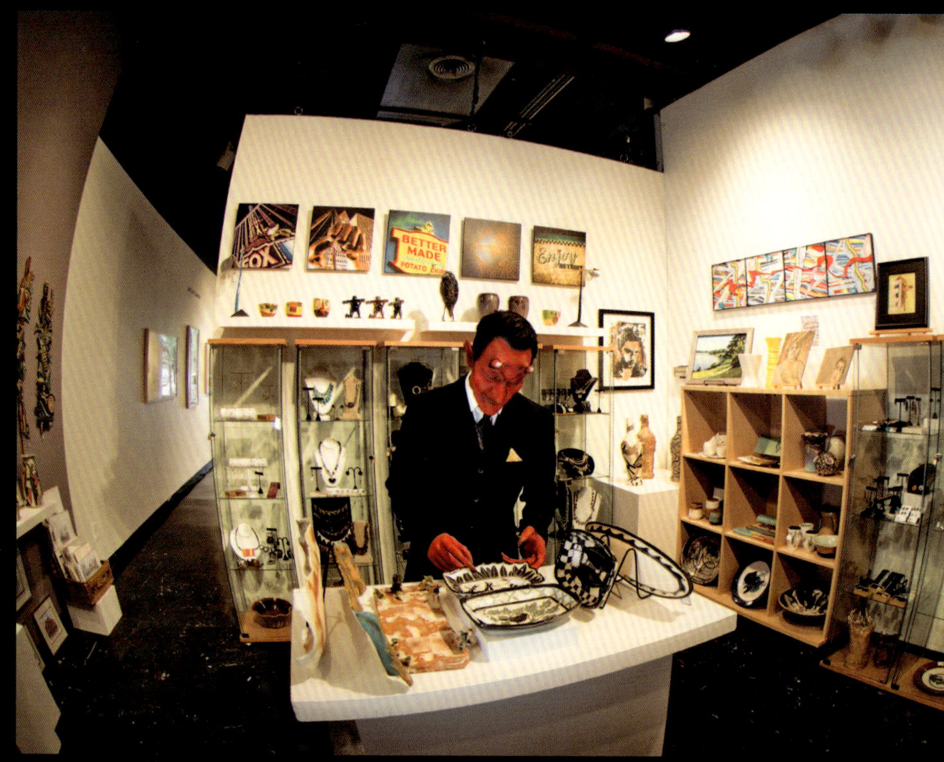

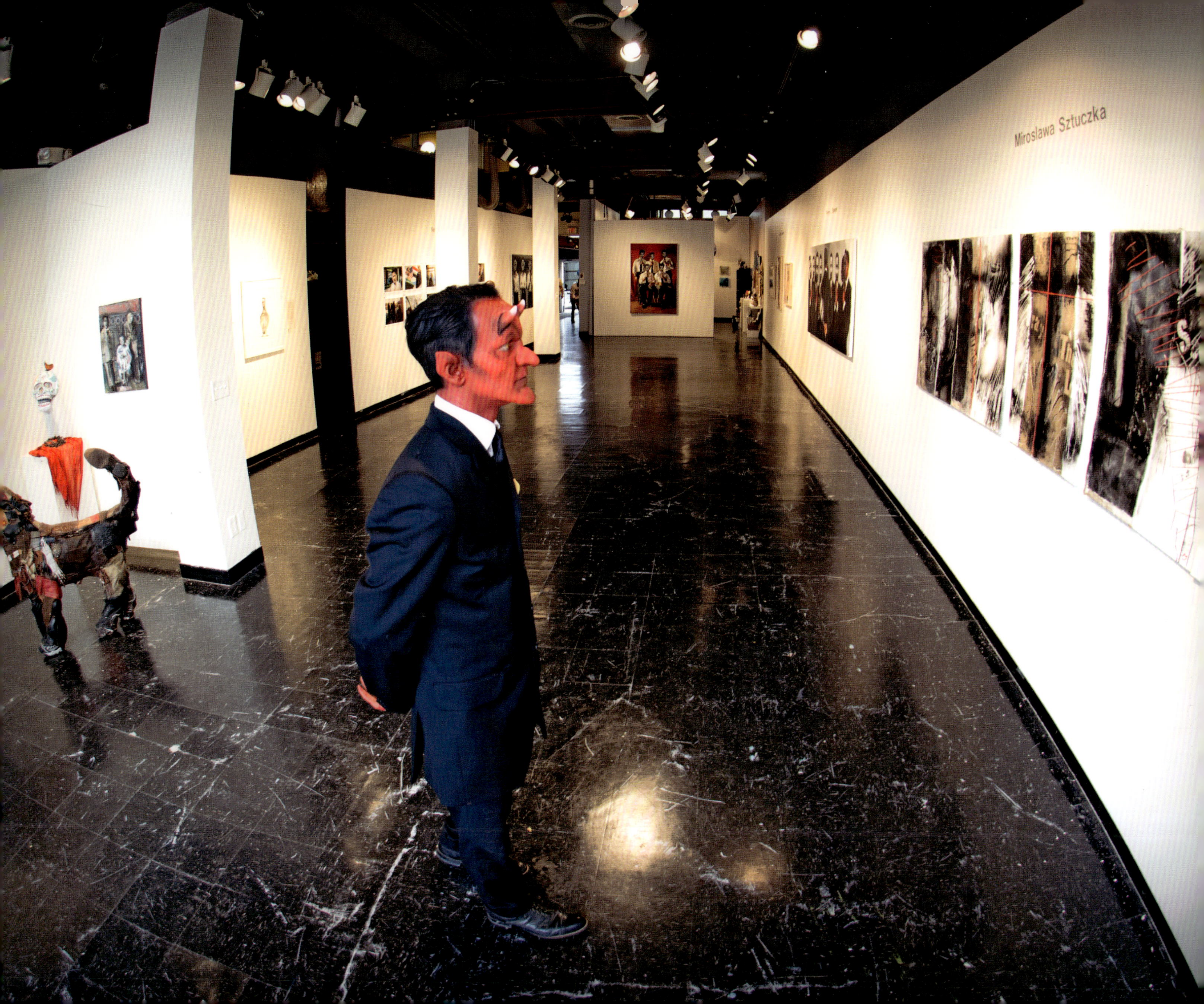
Miroslawa Sztuczka

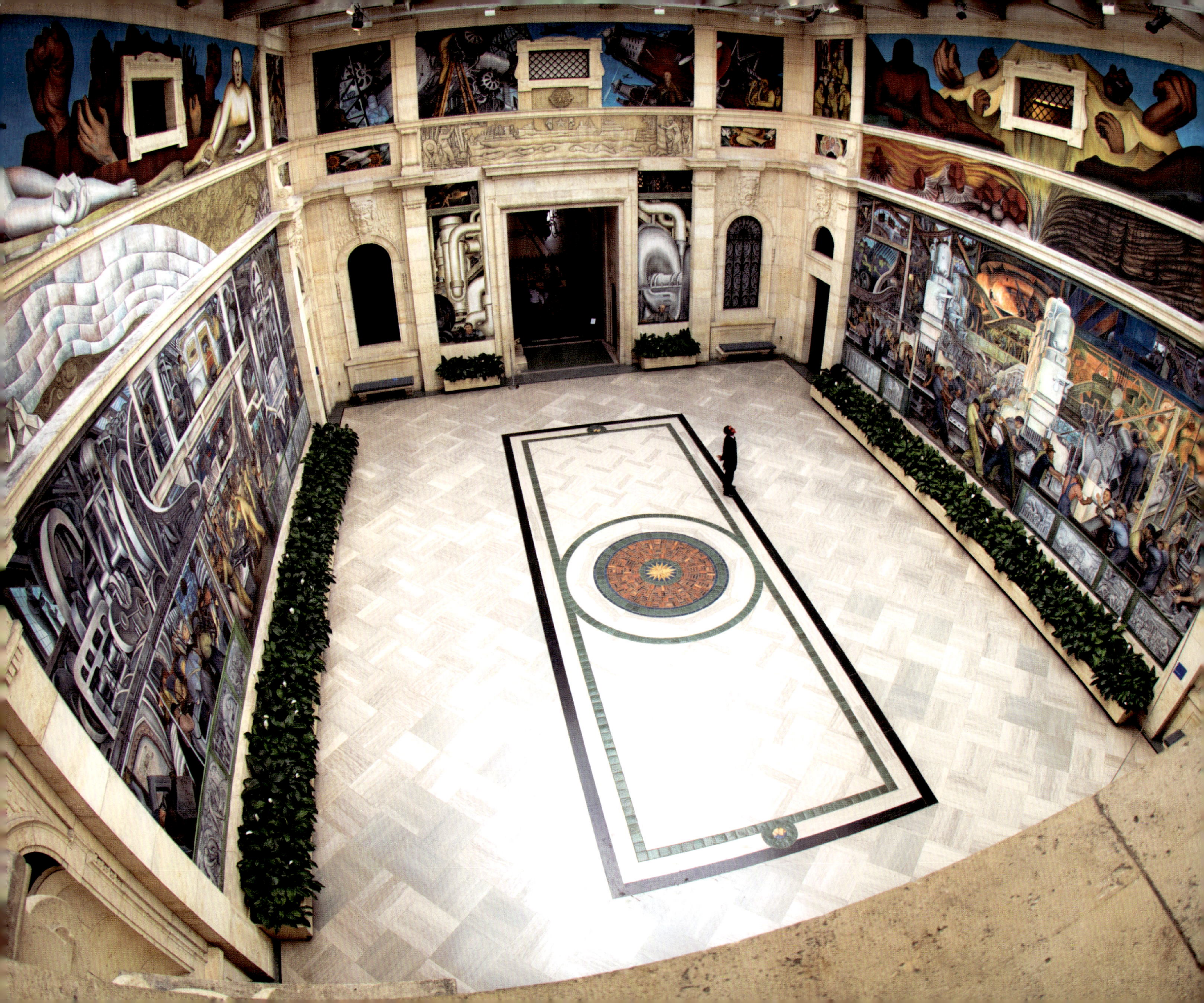

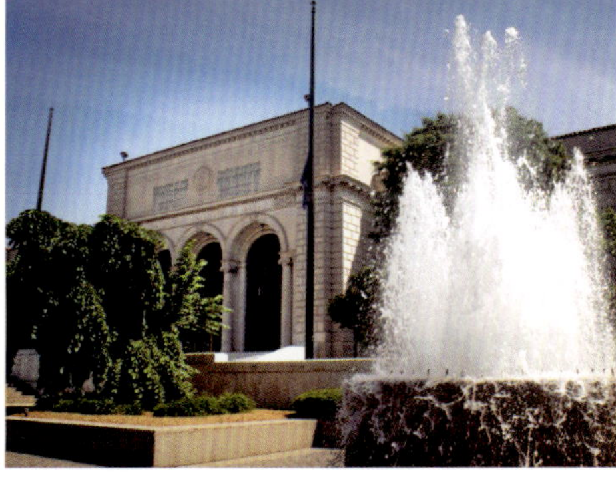

DETROIT INSTITUTE OF ARTS

5200 Woodward Ave., Detroit, 48202
www.dia.org

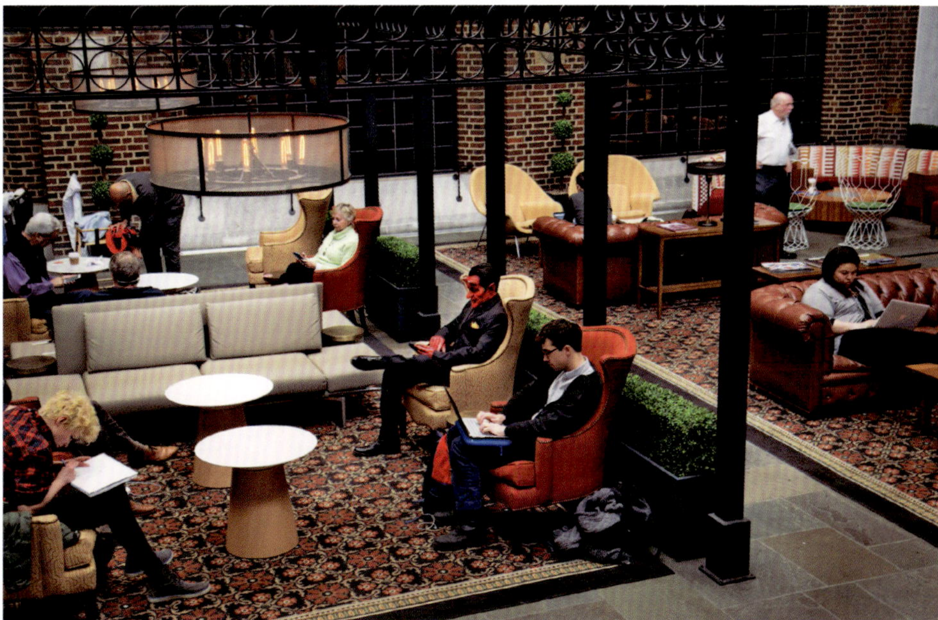

Considered one of the country's top-five art museums, the Detroit Institute of Arts was founded in 1885. The collection includes more than 62,000 works of art within its 100 galleries. The American, German Expressionist, and African art collections are considered some of the best in the country. The masterpiece of the museum, Diego Rivera's *Detroit Industry, or Man and Machine* murals, illustrates Detroit's auto industrial might. The expanding African American art collection is becoming one of the most important new contributions to Detroit.

I remember like it was yesterday when Diego Rivera, accompanied by Frida Kahlo, arrived to paint his masterwork. While Diego was painting, I befriended a young couple on their first date. They continued to court while they watched his progress. Inspired by his artistry, Irving and Harriet Berg, who were married for more than 60 years, became important artists and teachers to many Detroiters. Irving led the vaunted Cass Tech Art Department for decades, and Harriet was instrumental in bringing modern dance to Wayne State University. - NR

HAMTRAMCK DISNEYLAND

12087 Klinger St., alley, Hamtramck, 48212
www.hatchart.org/hamtramck-disneyland/

Hamtramck, a small enclave surrounded by Detroit, was a tightly knit, mostly Polish and Eastern European immigrant community. A GM factory worker for 32 years, Dmytro Szylak began his art project in 1992 using Christmas lights, mechanical fans, plastic horses, and American flags. It soon became a notable folk art installation, visited by many who knew the obscure alley where it's located. Handcrafted and lovingly painted soldiers, helicopters, and an aircraft overwhelmed the yard becoming an international fascination.

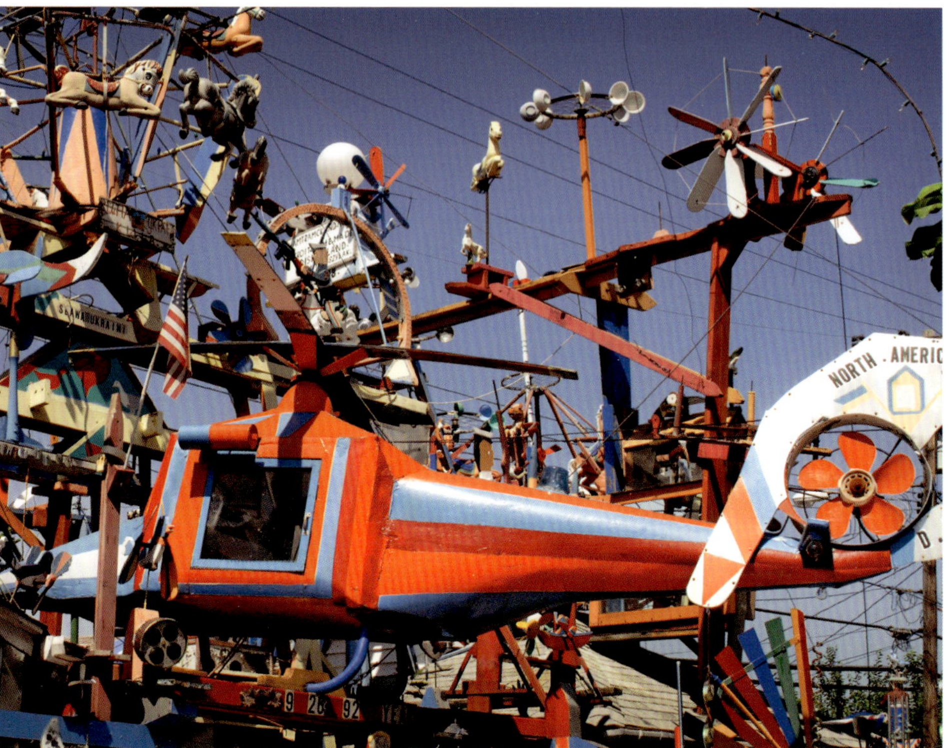

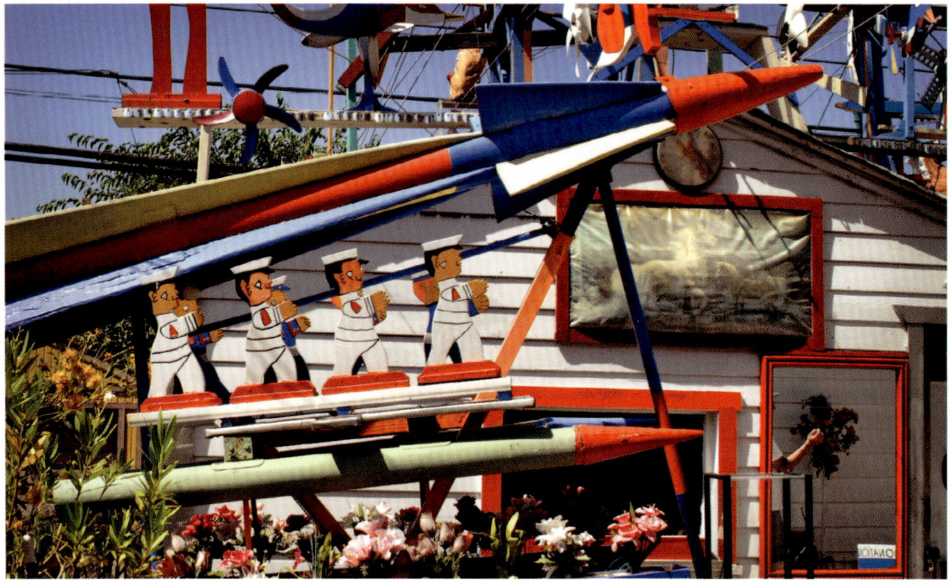

Most people in the neighborhood thought my friend Dmytro was either crazy or eccentric. He was a bit of both but also a fascinating man devoted to his ever-expanding chaotic sculptural collage. His imagination continually fed him until the project, which first started in his backyard, took over the entire yard and two garages. Word on the street soon made him a folk art sensation. Undeterred by his detractors in the city, and with his charm and the growing popularity of his work, the project was allowed to remain. After his death in 2015, the arts collective Hatch Art became custodians committed to preserve his work. - NR

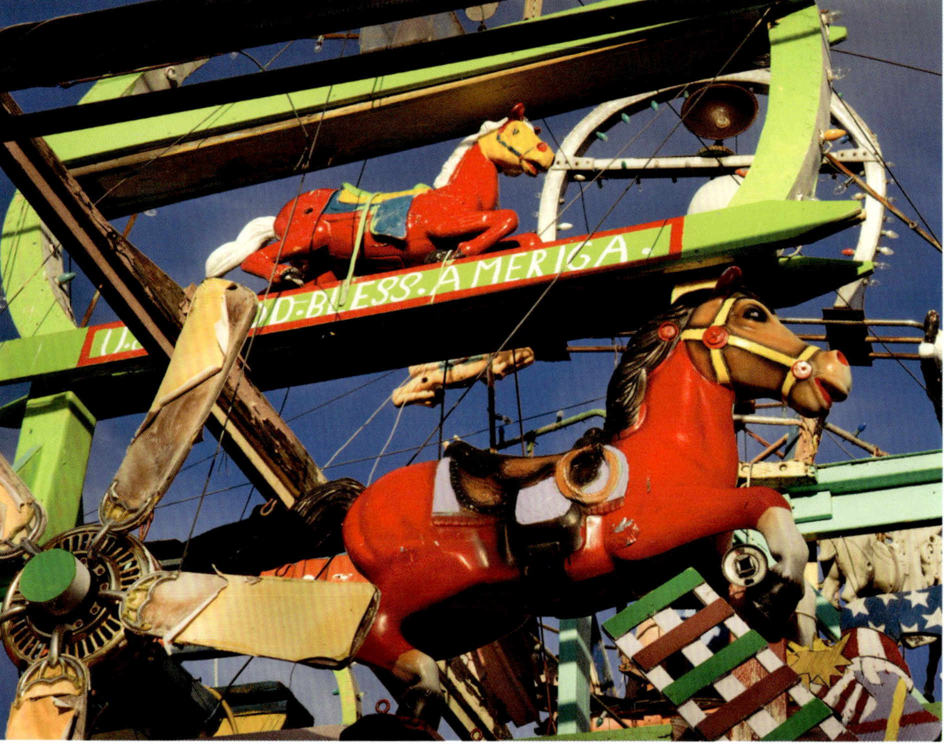

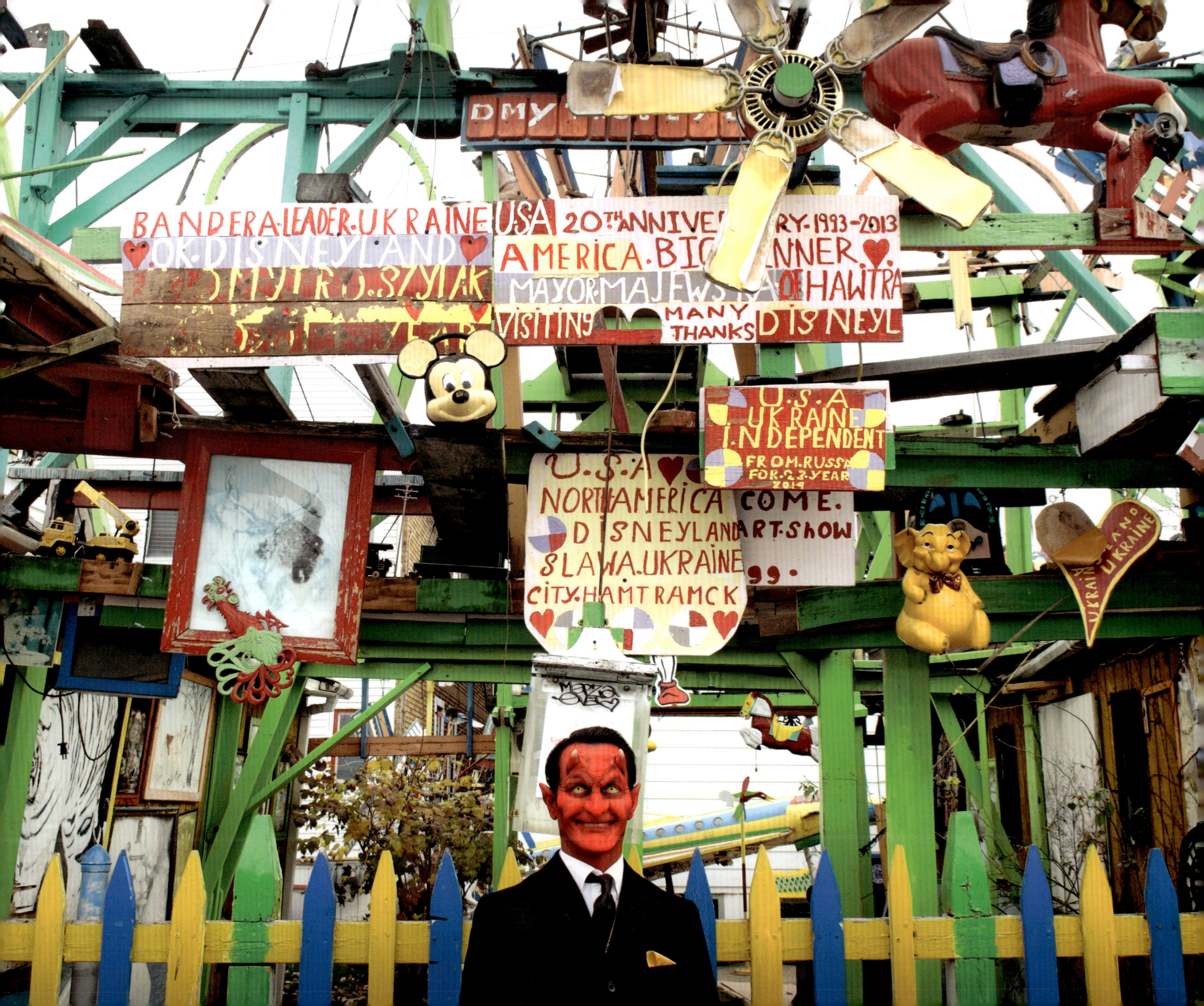
BANDERA-LEADER-UKRAINE
OK.DISNEYLAND
DMYTRO.SZYLAK
1993-2013
VISITING
MANY THANKS
U.S.A
UKRAINE
INDEPENDENT
FROM.RUSSA
U.S.A
NORTHAMERICA
DISNEYLAND
SLAWA.UKRAINE
CITY.HAMTRAMCK
COME.
ART.SHOW
99.

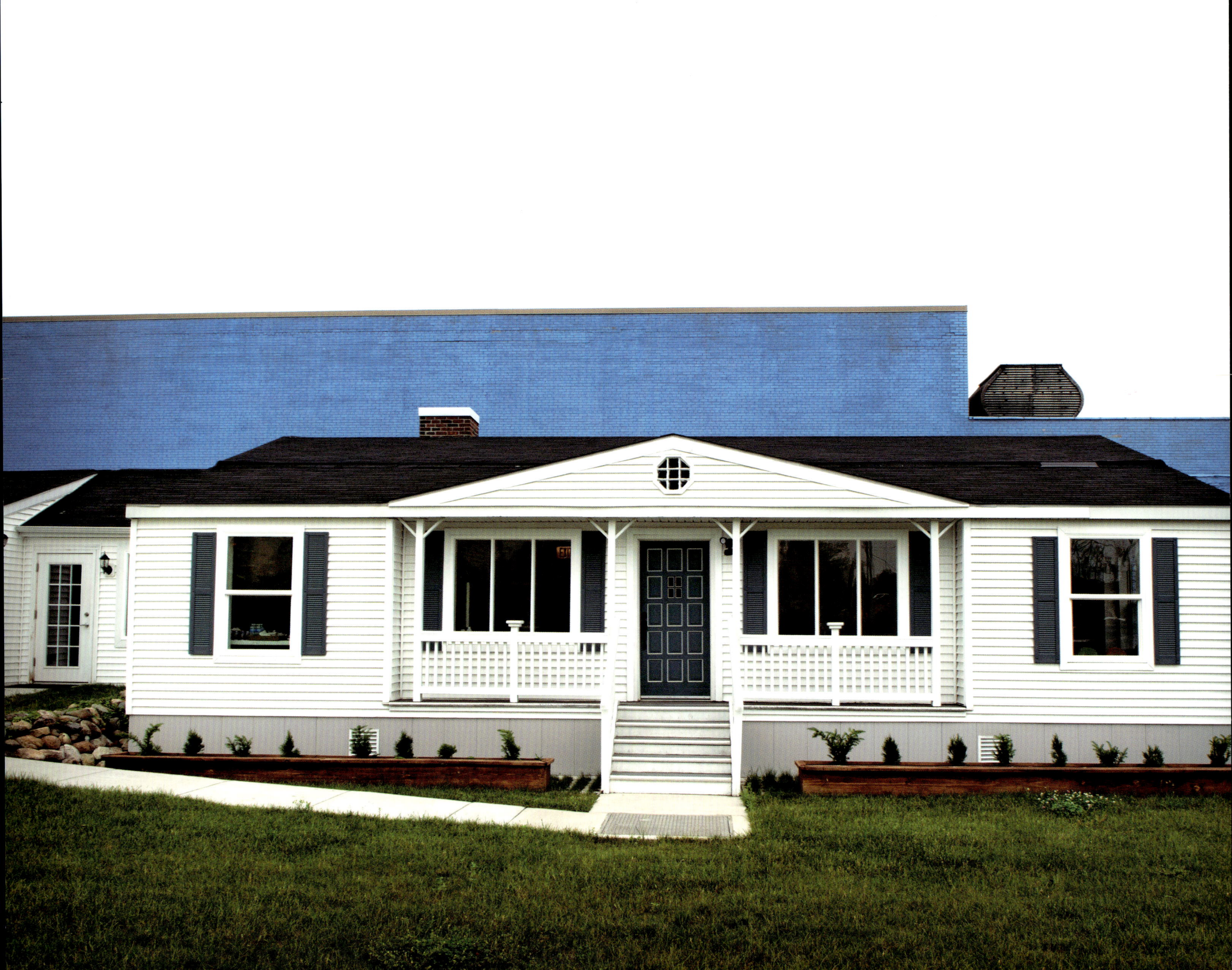

MUSEUM OF CONTEMPORARY ART DETROIT

4454 Woodward Ave., Detroit, 48201
www.mocadetroit.org

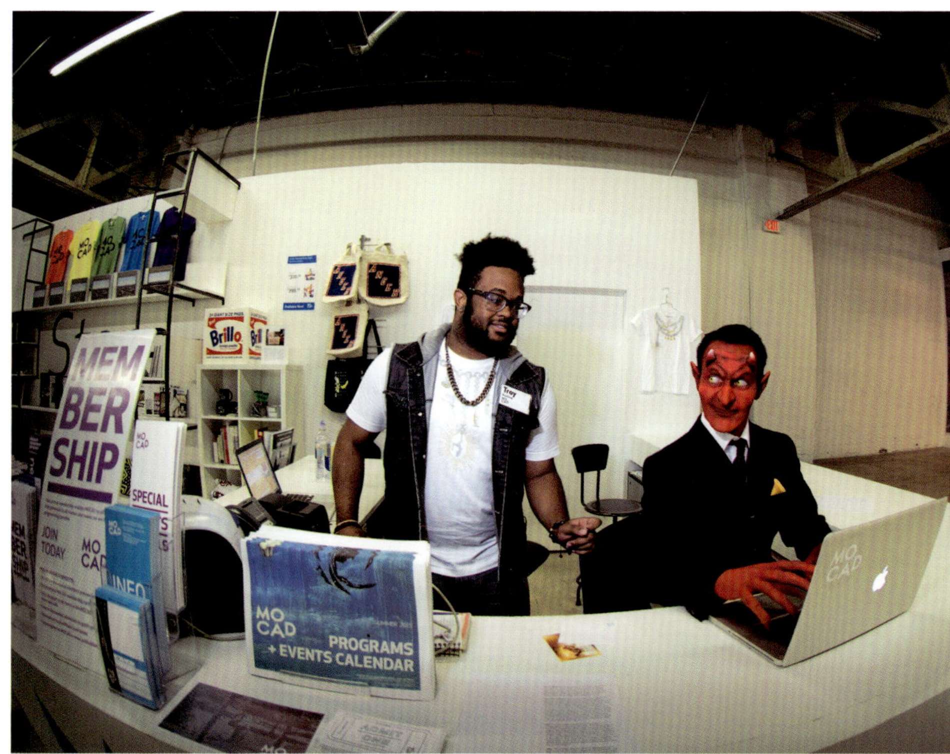

The most recent addition to Detroit's arts community, MOCAD has established its place as the heart of modern art. It was created to present and introduce works at the forefront of contemporary culture. Embracing all varieties of artistic explorations, including dance performance, music, and film, the museum hosts an eclectic array of exhibitions. The transient nature of the exhibits entices visitors to continually return for a new experience or event.

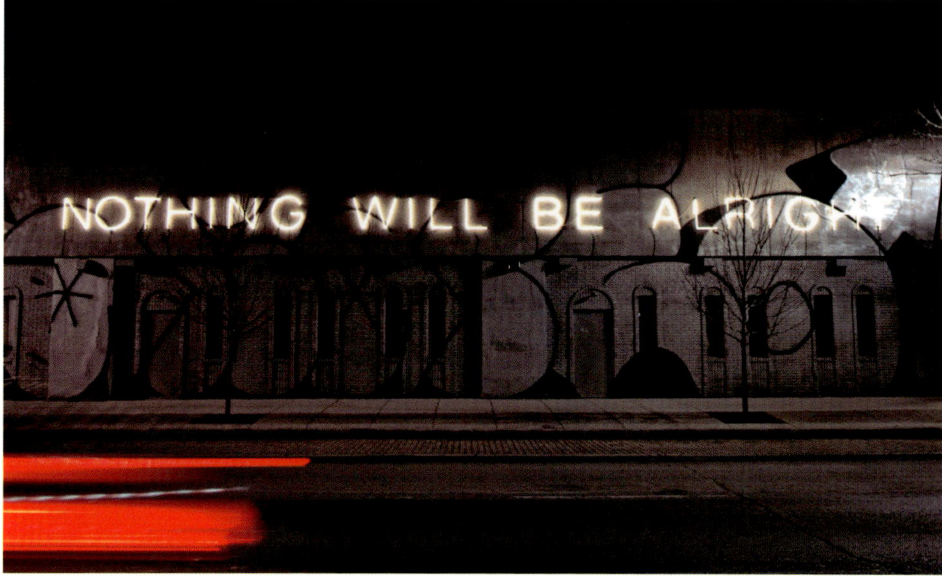

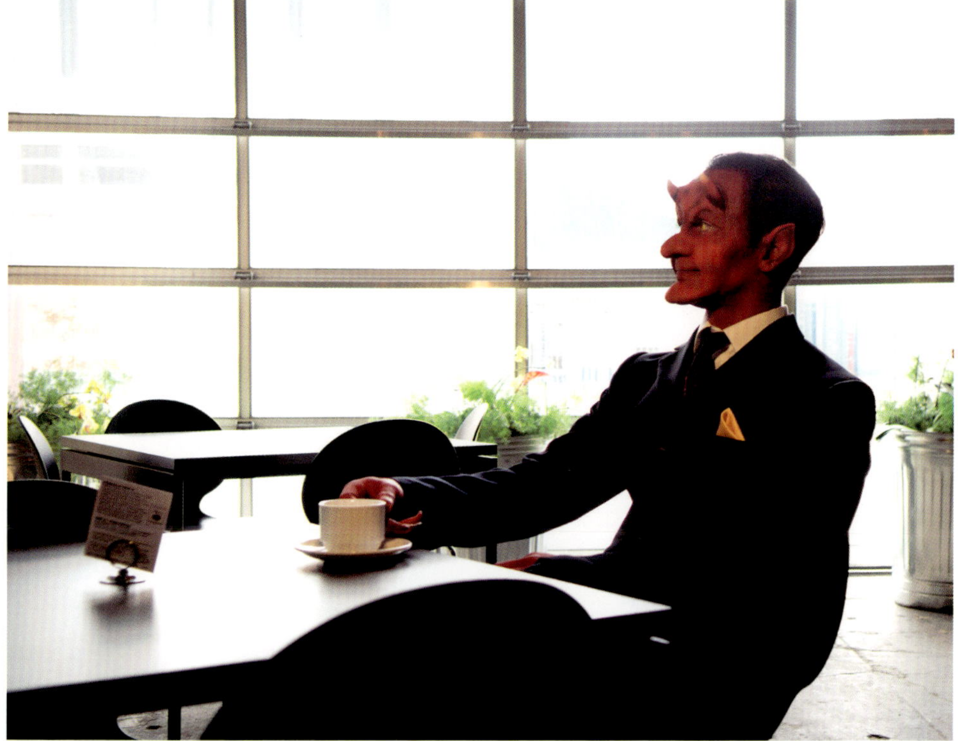

Like any decent art museum, MOCAD offers cleverly curated exhibits, artist talks and workshops, and even the occasional music performance. But MOCAD also boasts Mike Kelly's Mobile Homestead, a traveling house (made to look like the artist's childhood home) that's used to take art programs to communities outside the city's cultural district. When it's not on the road, the Mobile Homestead, which has inspired a multi-year project with artists active in participatory and socially transformative art, is showcased off Canfield Street. Oh, and MOCAD hosts booming dance parties too. - NR

PEWABIC POTTERY

10125 E. Jefferson Ave., Detroit, 48214
www.pewabic.org

Mary Chase Perry Stratton and Horace James Caulkins opened their studio in 1903, becoming important contributors to the International Arts and Crafts movement. Known for their distinct iridescent glazes, Pewabic tiles have been used in architectural accents throughout the United States, including the Shedd Aquarium in Chicago, Herald Square in New York and throughout many mansions and churches in Detroit. *Pewabic* is derived from the Ojibwa word *wabic*, which means metal. Pewabic Pottery continues its tradition of fine pottery while offering classes for novices and studio space to artists.

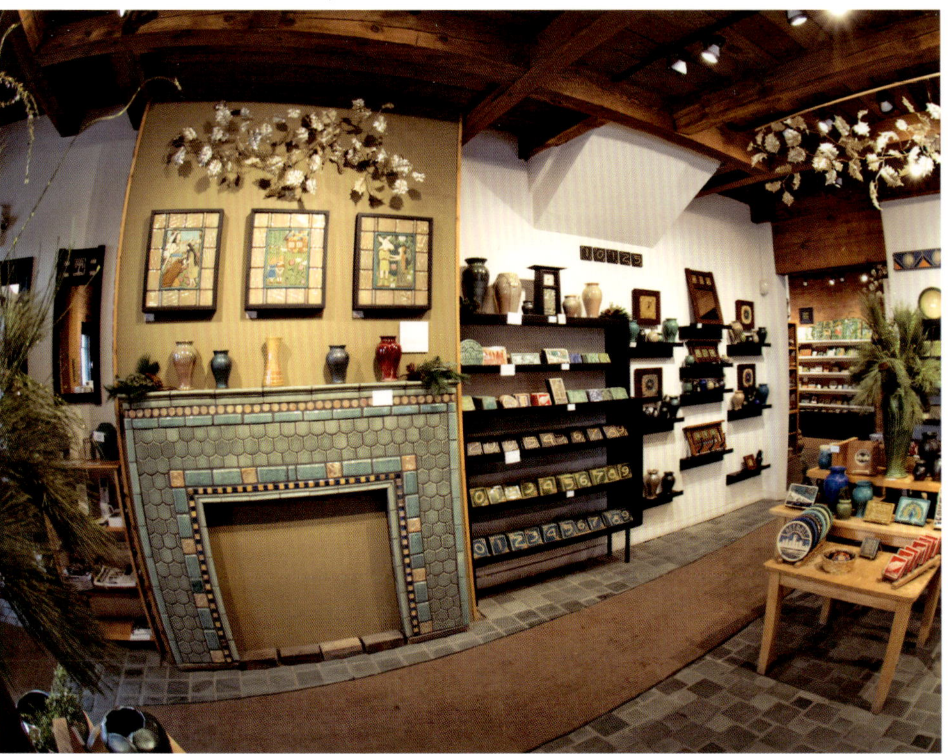

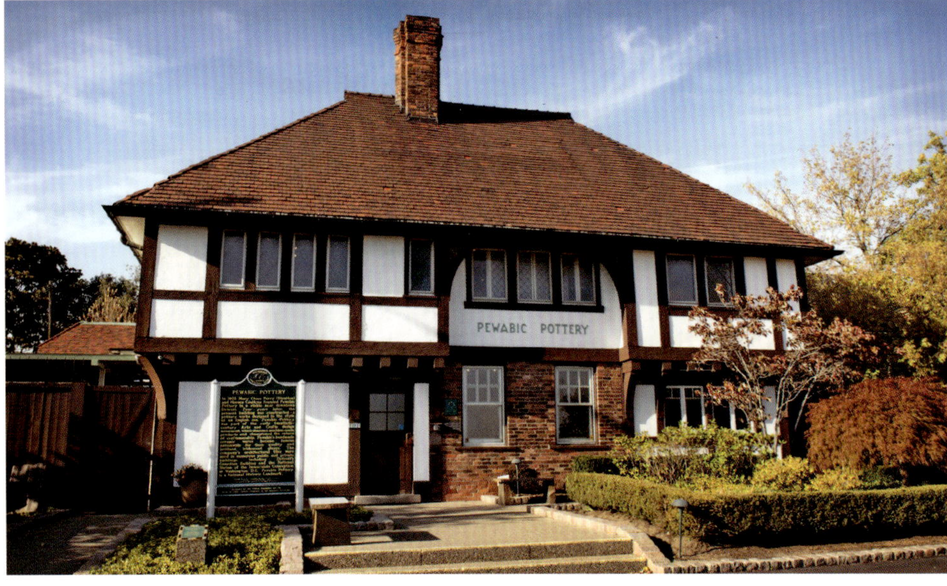

Every year, I take a class to refine my skills and make a mug for my Mom on Mother's Day. When Mary and Horace started their studio, I used to come by and help mix glazes. Their talents for designing and glazing clay tiles were exceptional and eventually their work appeared in just about every mansion or architecturally significant building in Detroit. There is a rumor that Mary's famous iridescent glaze recipe was lost upon her death, but I have it written down somewhere, though I just can't seem to find it... - NR

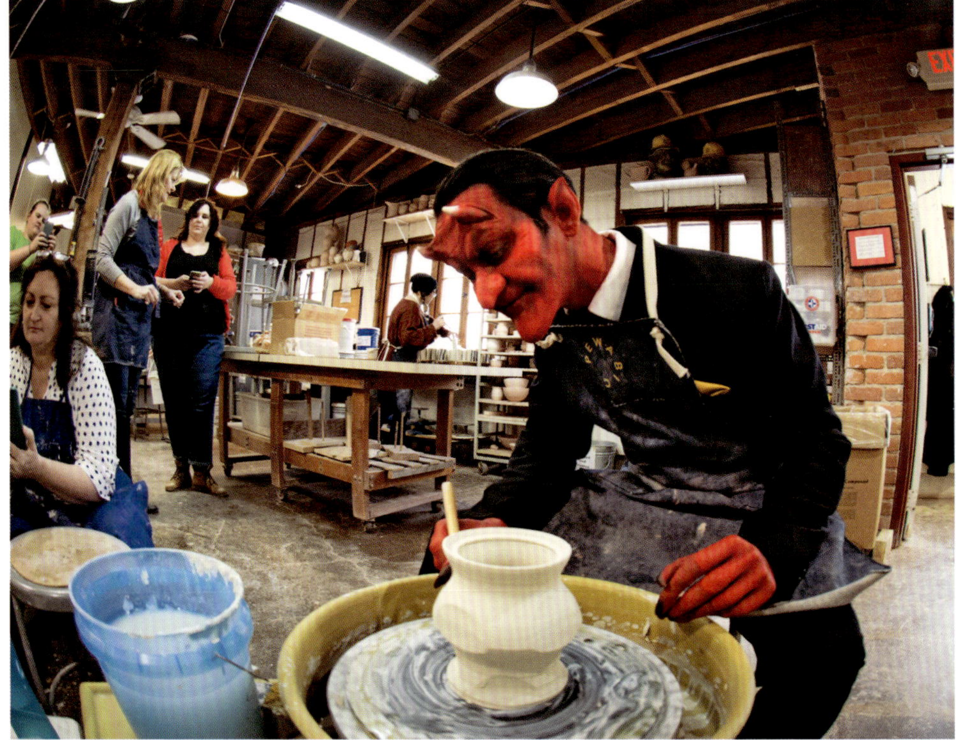

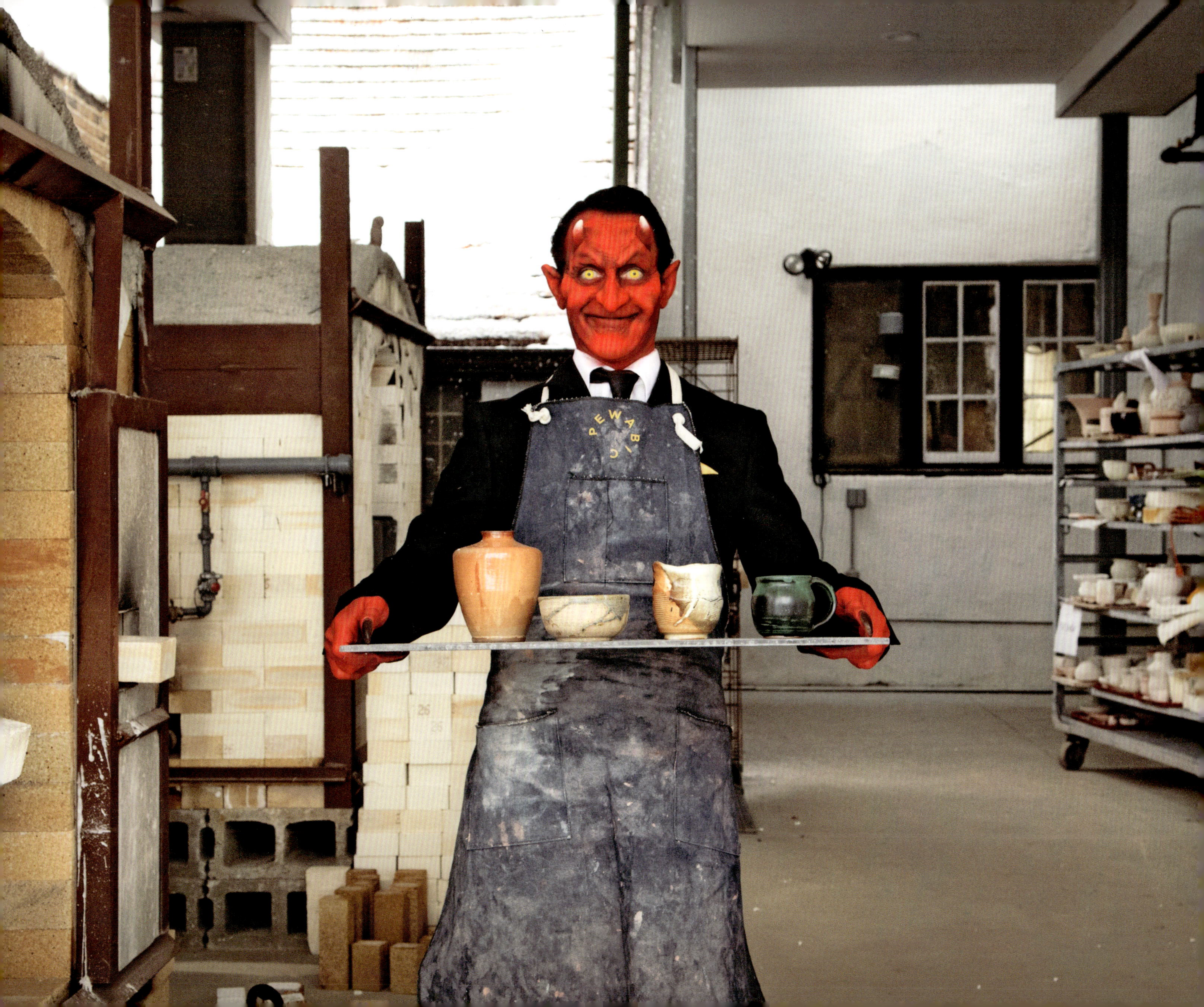
PEWABIC

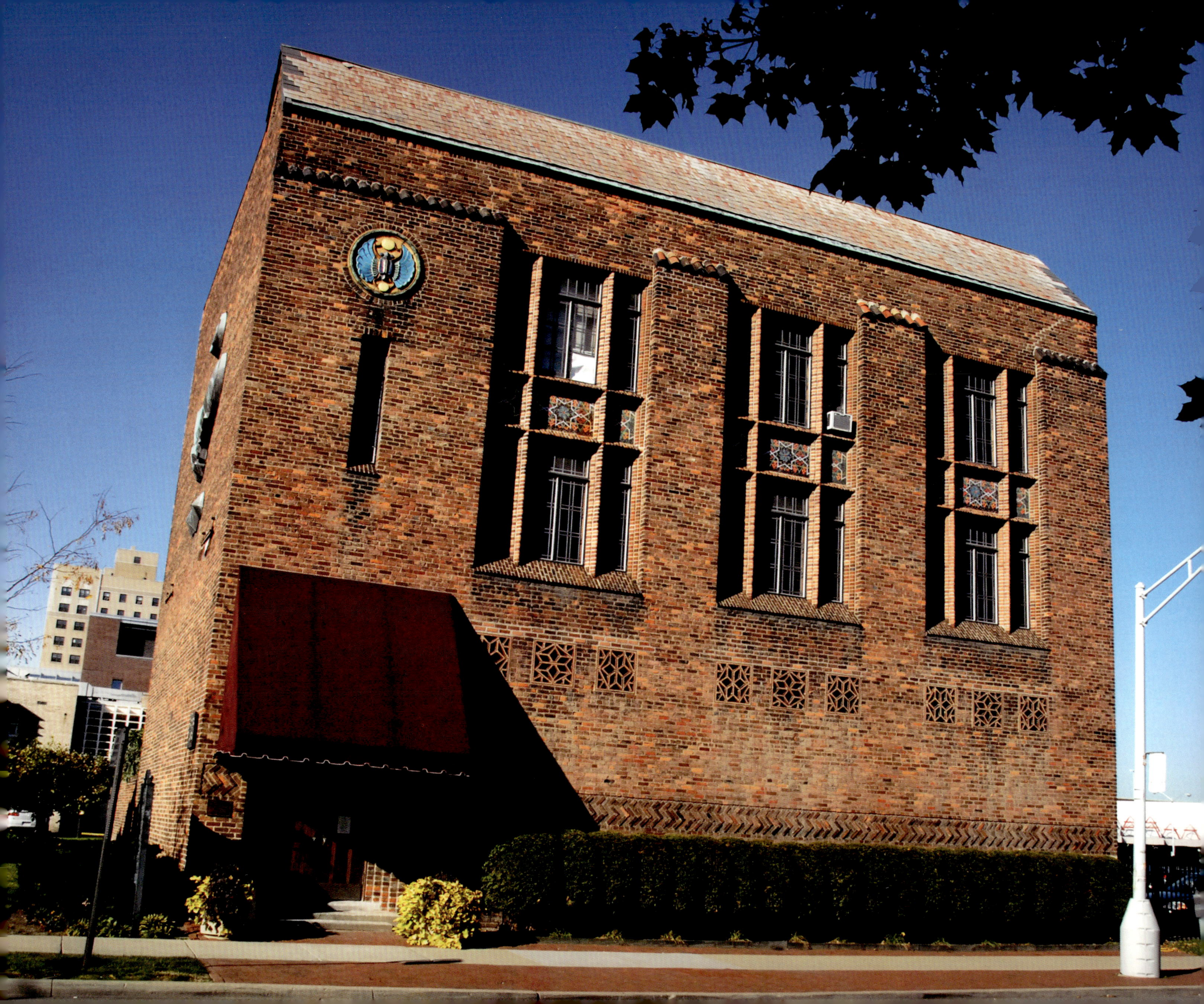

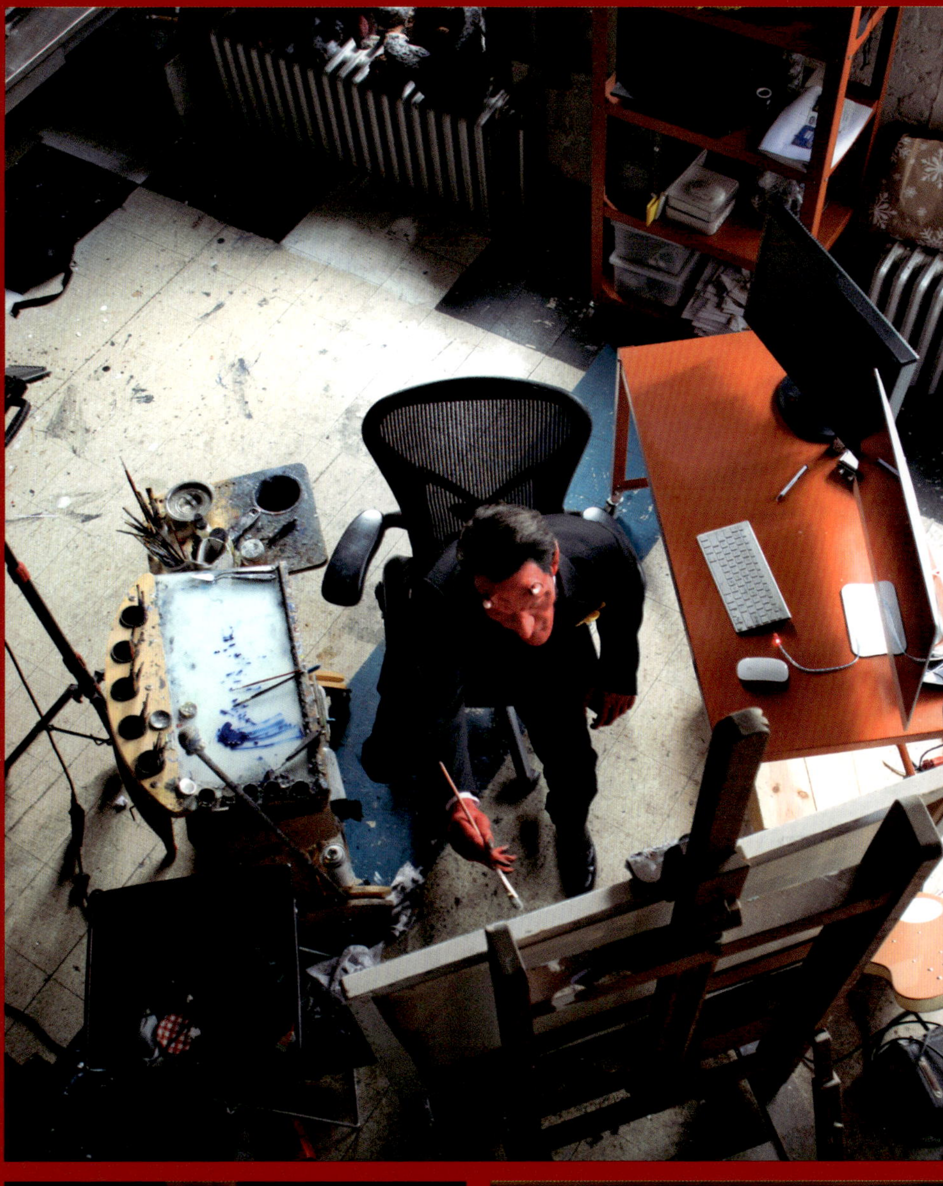

SCARAB CLUB

217 Farnsworth St., Detroit, 48202
www.scarabclub.org

Originally formed in 1907 as the Hopkin Club, after founder Robert Hopkin, the Scarab Club is an informal arts association created by artists to offer mutual support, discuss art, and critique members' works. The club continues "to promote the mutual acquaintance of art lovers and art workers; to stimulate and guide toward practical expression the artistic sense of the people of Detroit; to advance the knowledge and love of the fine arts in every possible manner; and to maintain a clubhouse for entertainment and social purposes as well as to provide working and exhibit facilities for artist members." The club has several galleries and six artist studios. Ceiling beams on the second floor serve as the club's guest book, and signing them has become a ceremonial honor for visiting artists. Artists Pablo Picasso, Marcel DuChamp, Diego Rivera, and Norman Rockwell's signatures are mixed along with local Detroiters who have had the honor of showing their works in the galleries.

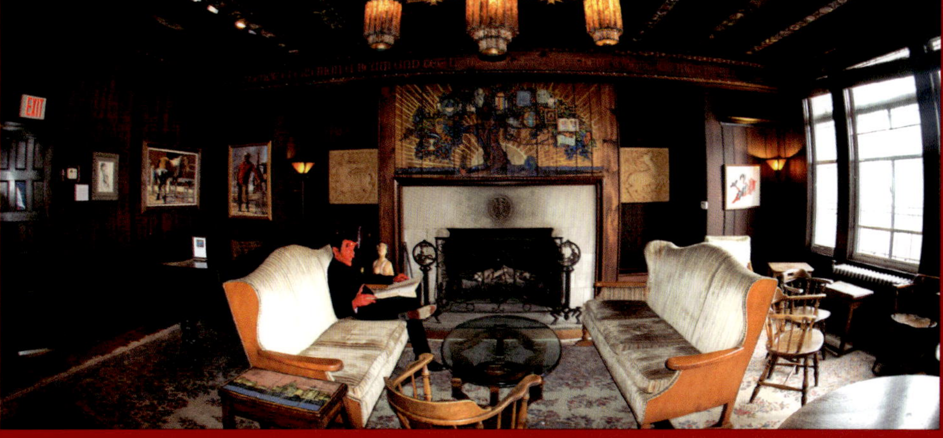

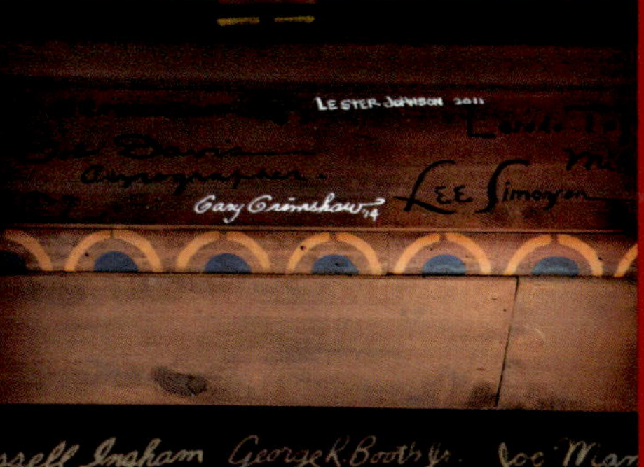

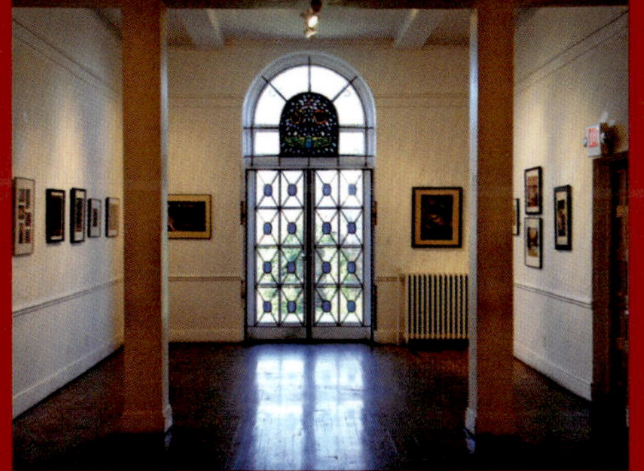

In a city which regards most artists with a shrug of indifference, the Scarab Club is unique in celebrating and elevating those of us who have chosen "artist" as our occupation. It is an oasis for artists to show their works within the community. Though I may not be as accomplished as most members, I have shared studio space with other artists since the Scarab Club opened. Visiting artists or notable locals who have shown their works in the gallery are invited to sign the ceiling beams as a permanent reminder of their attendance. (Alas, I have not yet been asked to add my name...)

- NR

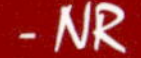

SIGNAL-RETURN

1345 Division St., #102, Detroit, 48207
www.signalreturnpress.org

Signal-Return is determined to preserve, advance, and teach the art of the letterpress printing. Open since 2011, it offers classes and equipment to the novice or professional artist. With thousands of typestyles in its collection, Signal-Return keeps current the centuries-old letterpress printing methods and techniques that Guttenberg used to produce his first book. Located in Eastern Market, Signal-Return promotes and sells many of the artist-designed works it produces.

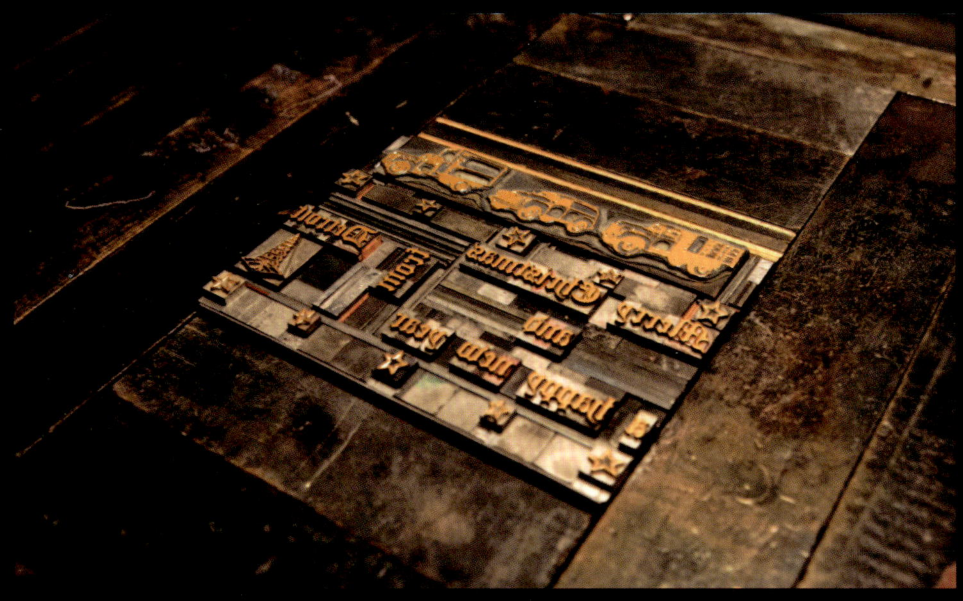

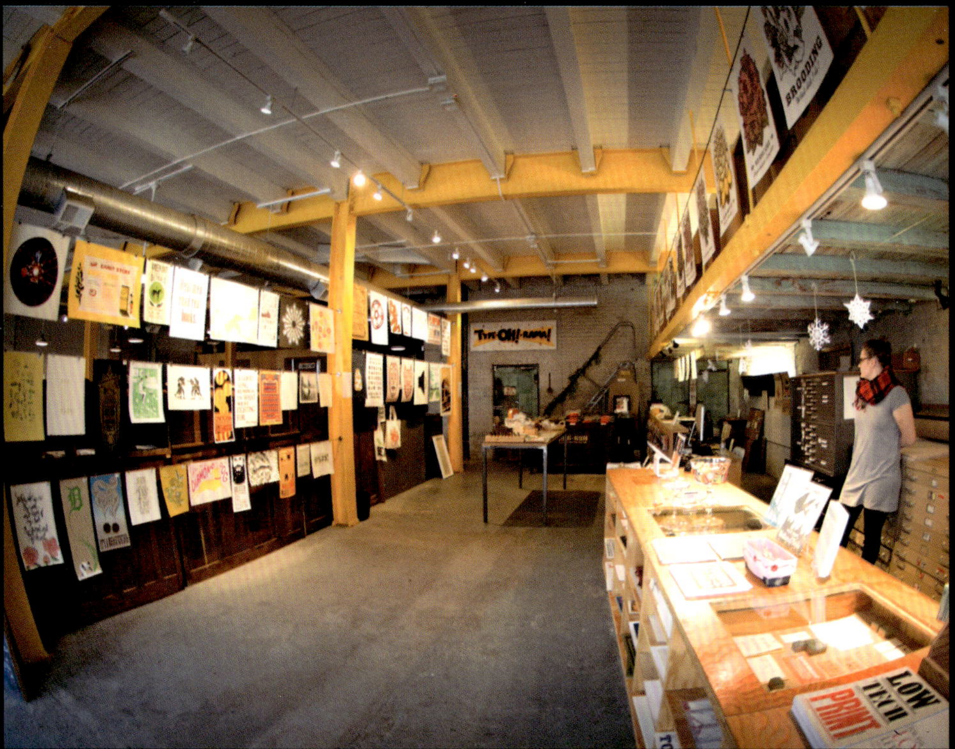

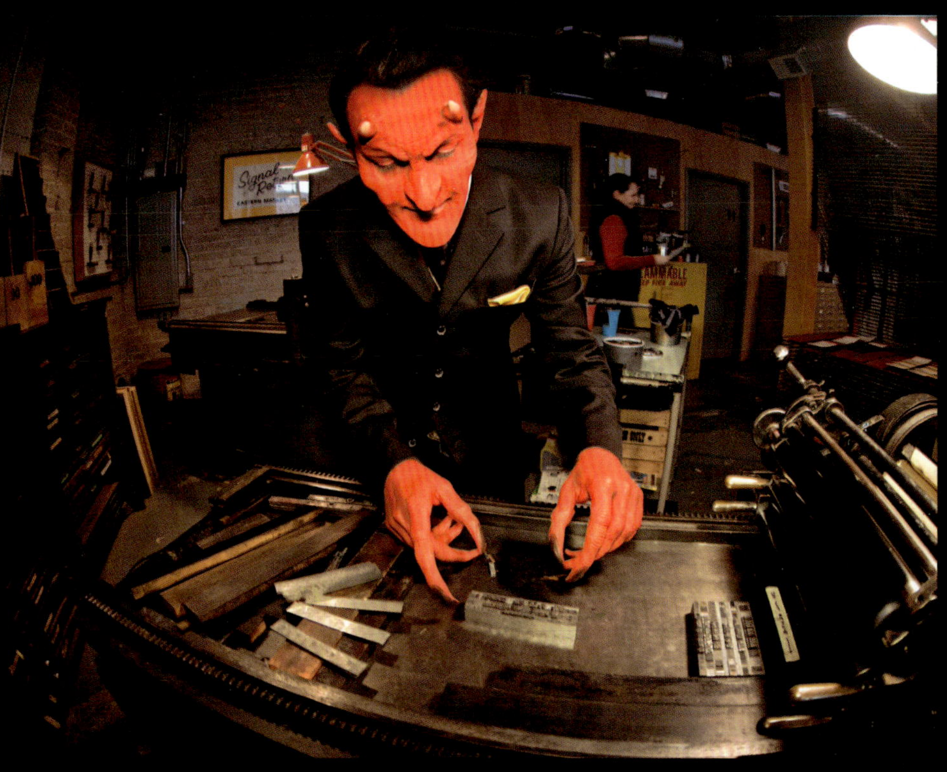

The art of typesetting is about as old as me. I do have a particular skill for it though, based on decades of experience. There is an inherent beauty to typesetting that a computer font doesn't possess. Maybe it's something in the creator's eyes as he is the one who assembles and inks the type, presses the paper and hangs the finished piece to dry. The process makes the appreciation for the result that much more special. - NR

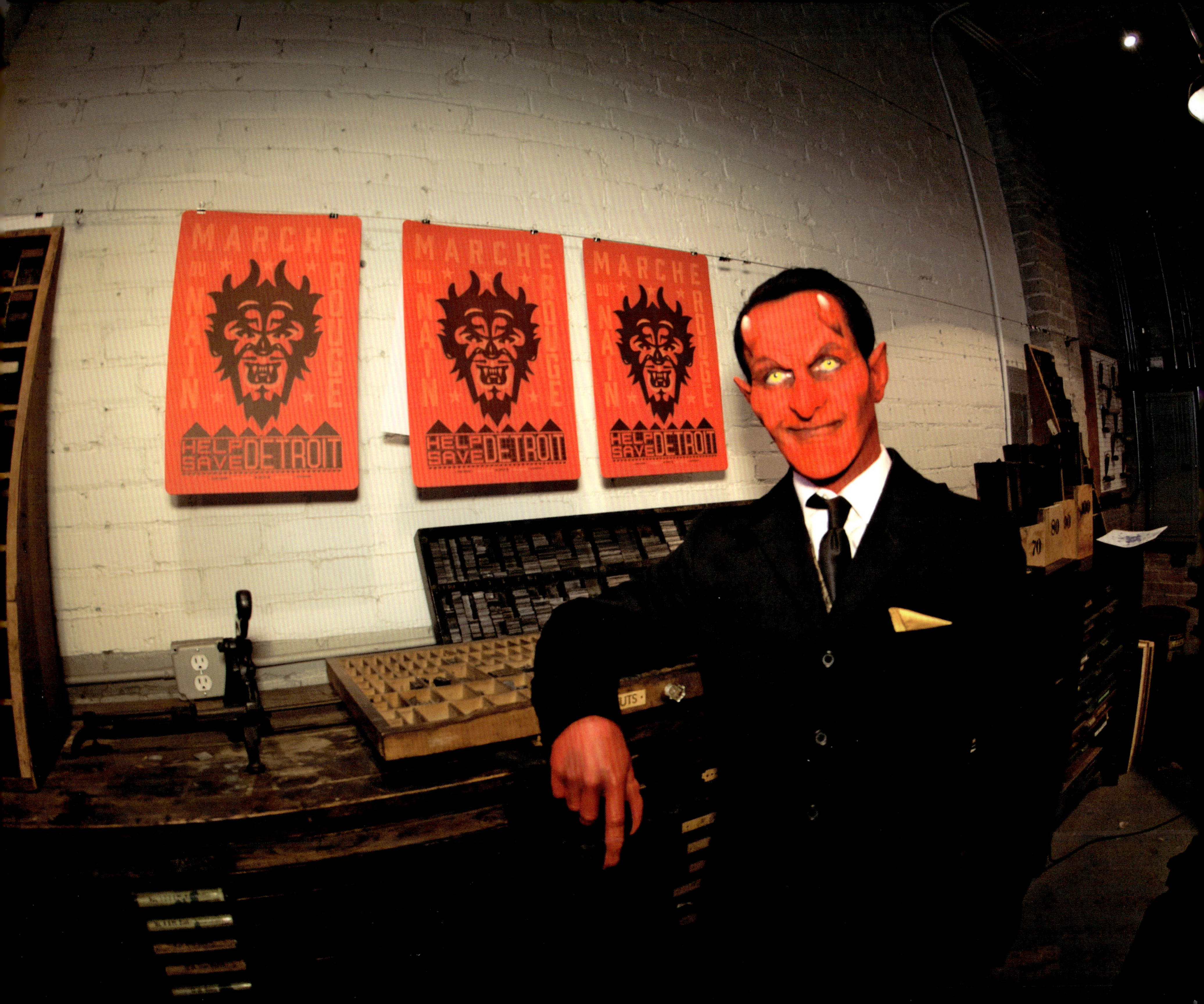
MARCHE
DU
NAIN
ROUGE
HELP SAVE DETROIT
MARCHE
DU
NAIN
ROUGE
HELP SAVE DETROIT
MARCHE
DU
NAIN
ROUGE
HELP SAVE DETROIT

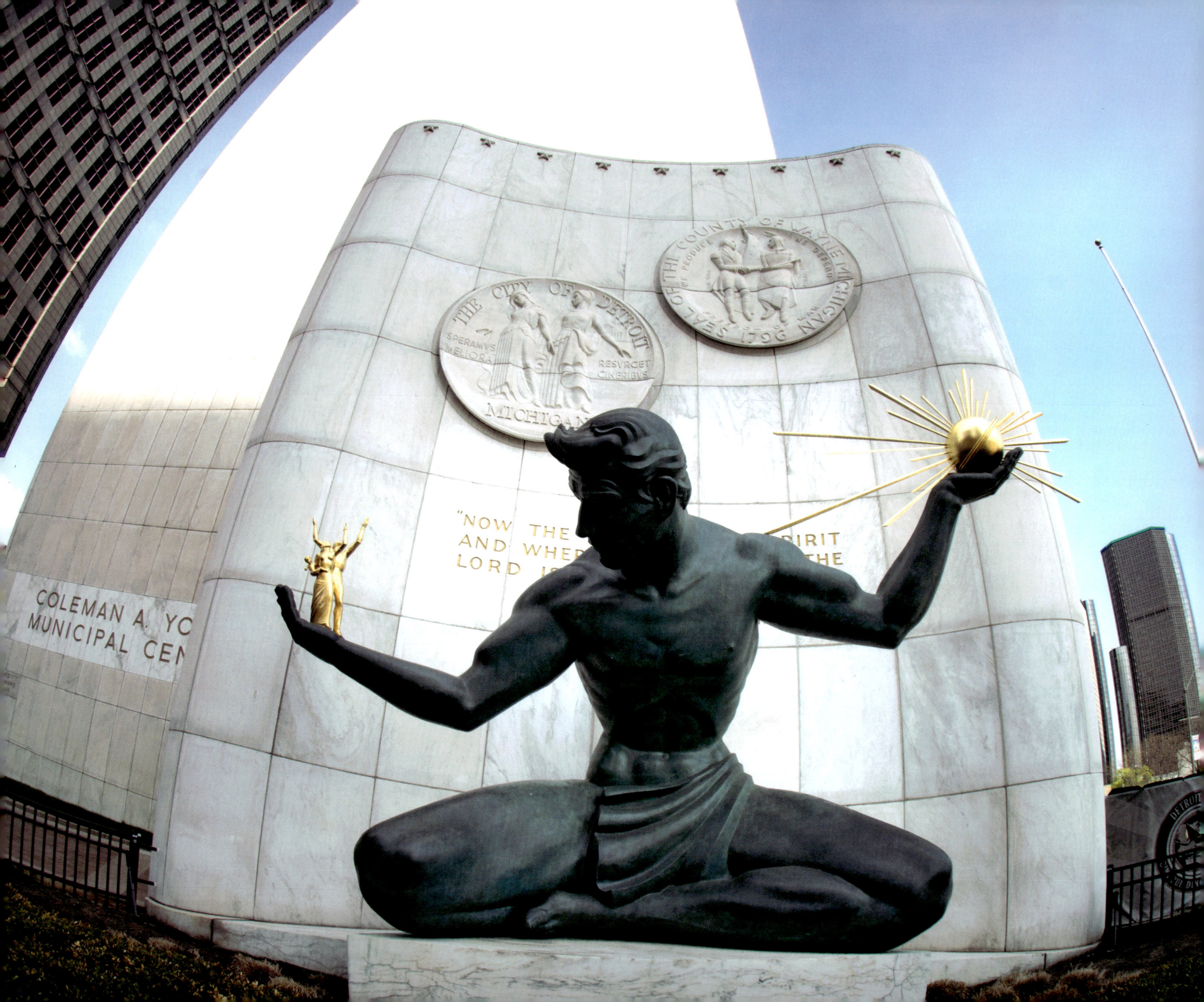

THE CITY OF DETROIT
SPERAMVS MELIORA
RESVRGET CINERIBVS
MICHIGAN
SEAL OF THE COUNTY OF WAYNE MICHIGAN
1796
"NOW THE
AND WHER
LORD IS
IRIT
THE
COLEMAN A. YO
MUNICIPAL CEN

SPIRIT OF DETROIT

2 Woodward Ave., Detroit, 48226
www.detroitmi.gov

Located at the base of the Coleman Young Center, Detroit's city hall, the Spirit of Detroit is a large bronze statue designed by Marshall Fredericks, a world renowned local artist. Dedicated in 1955, it quickly became an iconic Detroit character. A plaque in front reveals the artist's ideals for Detroit: "The artist expresses the concept that God, through the spirit of man is manifested in the family, the noblest human relationship." Nearby, the Joe Louis "Fist" celebrates his accomplishments as a boxer and his efforts at attaining racial equality. Designed by Robert Graham, the "Fist" represents a battering ram at racial injustice.

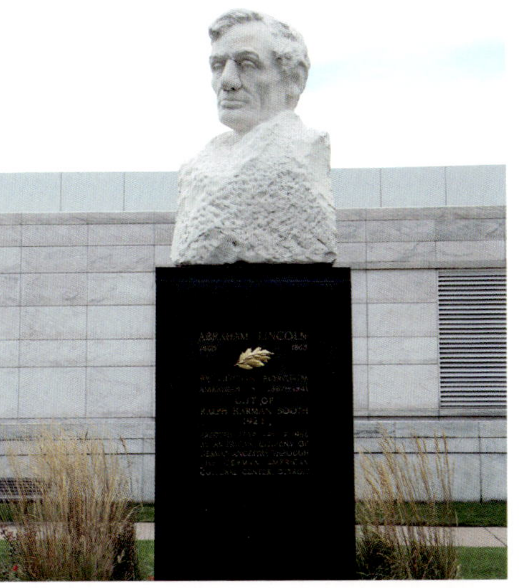

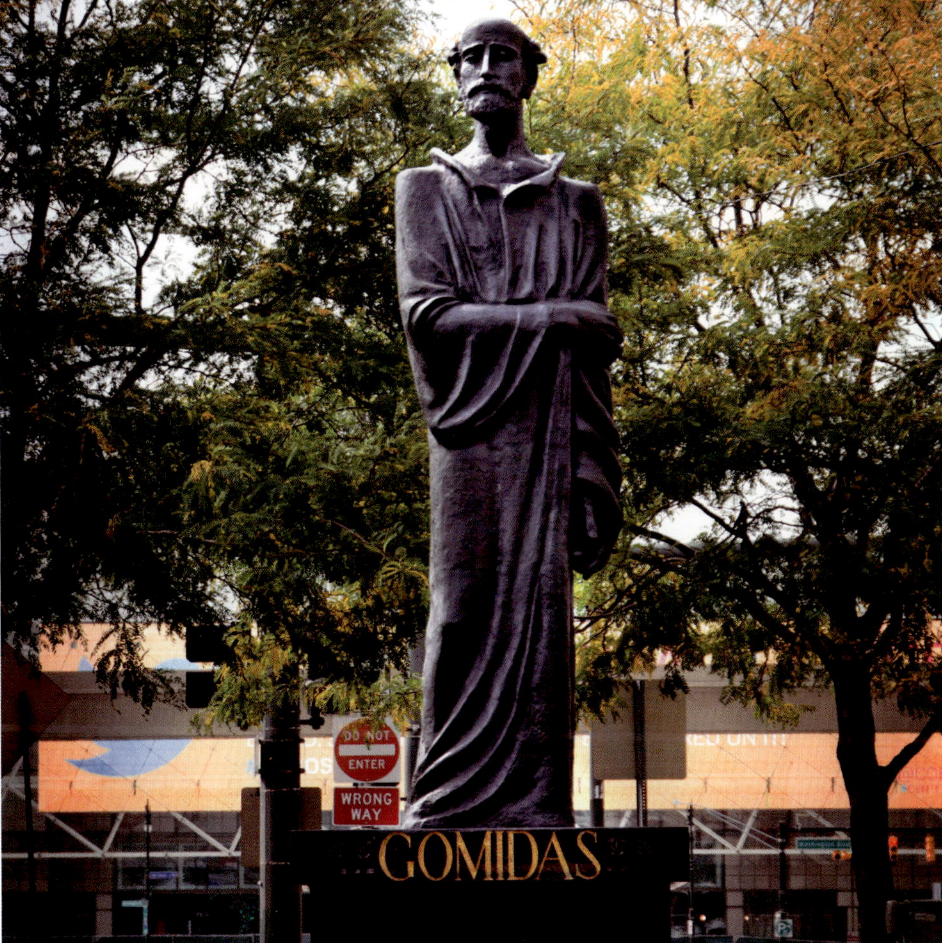

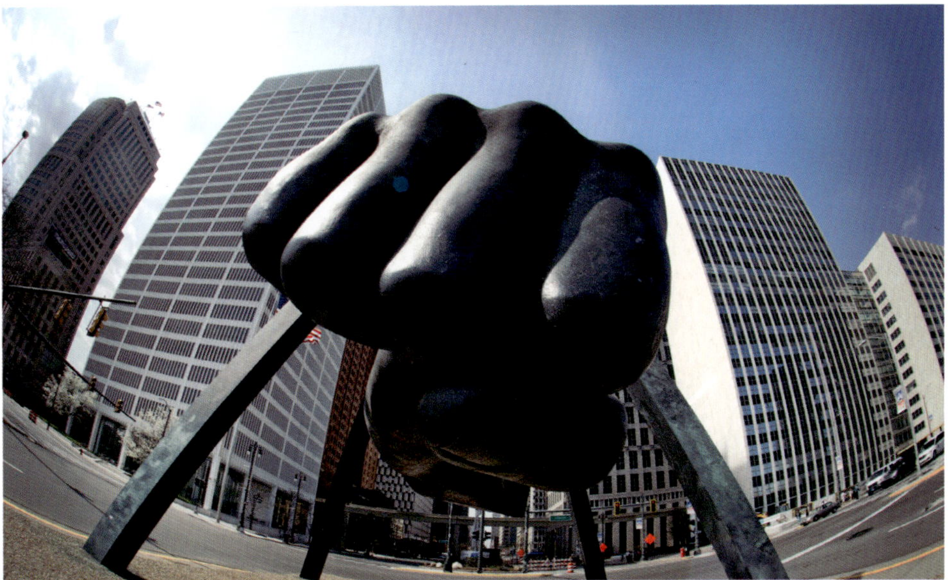

Once, as a prank, a few friends and I painted green footprints from the Spirit of Detroit over to Giacomo Manzù's "Passo di Danza" or "Step of the Dance," a bronze nude of a woman, located across the street at Yamasaki's ANR building. It seemed to us that he had been staring at her for years. Nearby, at the foot of Woodward, is the "Fist" monument to Joe Louis. Derided and misunderstood at its dedication, it has now come to symbolize Detroit's toughness and resolve. My city is packed with some powerful public sculptures.

- NR

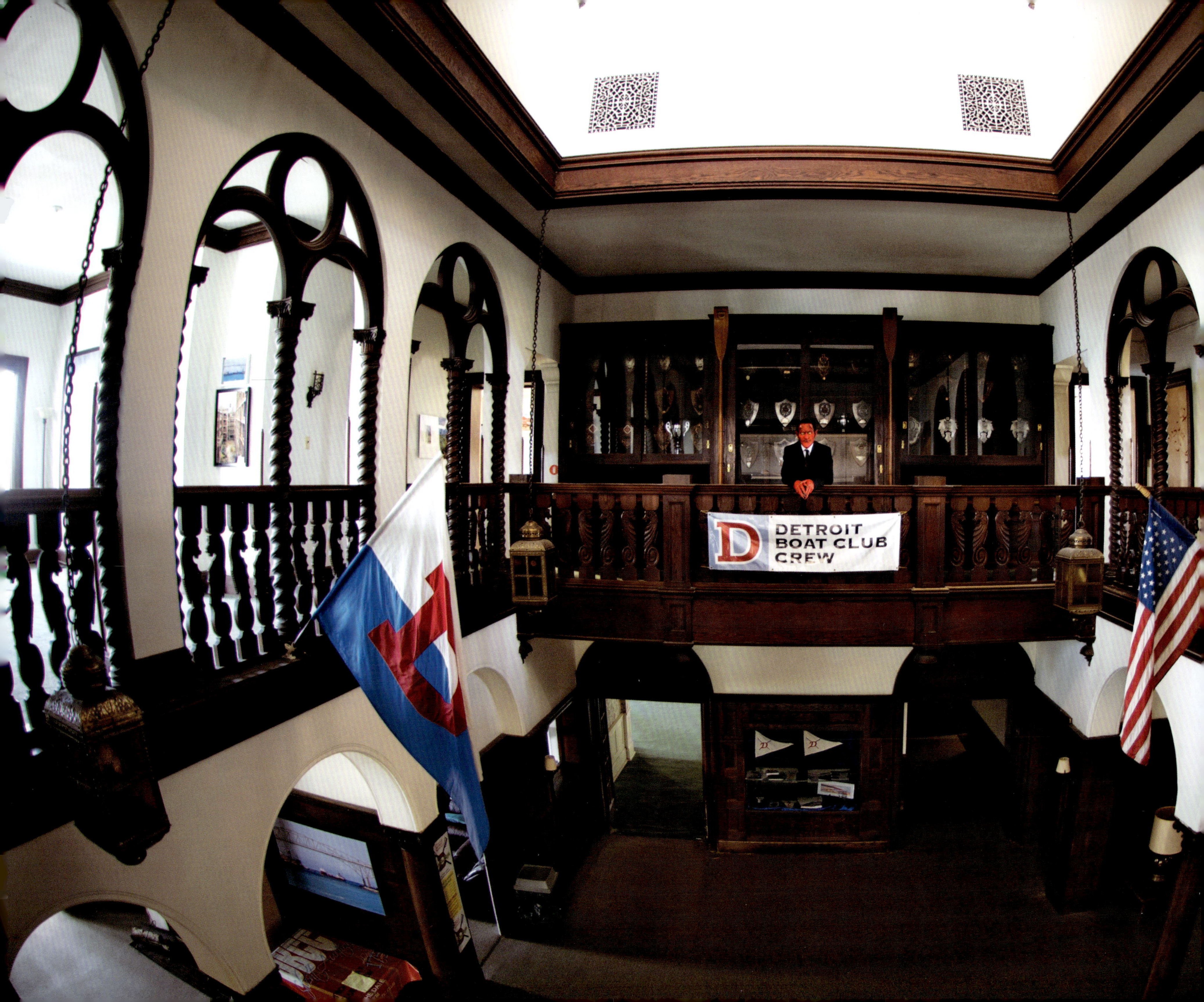
D
DETROIT
BOAT CLUB
CREW

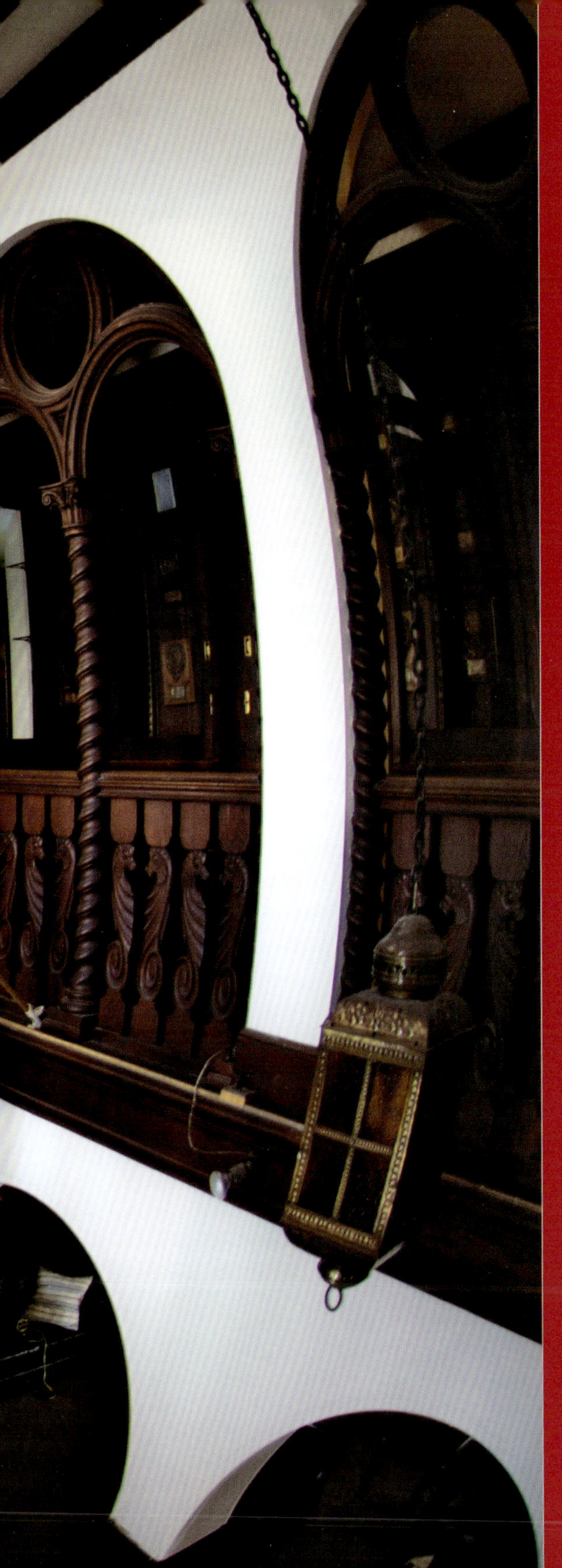

CLUBS

BAYVIEW YACHT CLUB

100 Clairpointe St., Detroit, 48215
www.byc.com

Host to the annual Port Huron to Mackinac sailboat race since 1925, the Bayview Yacht Club, founded in 1915, is recognized worldwide as a premier sail club and as the Midwest's "Shrine to Nautical Culture." Sailors from Bayview have competed internationally since its inception. Bayview members participate in regional regattas throughout the season. After a day of sailing, it is customary for members to congregate at the clubhouse bar, manned by Jerome Adams since 1967, and known the world over as the creator of the "Hummer" cocktail. Bayview's Junior Sailing Program, considered one of the best, competes with clubs across the country and offers summer classes for aspiring sailors to be.

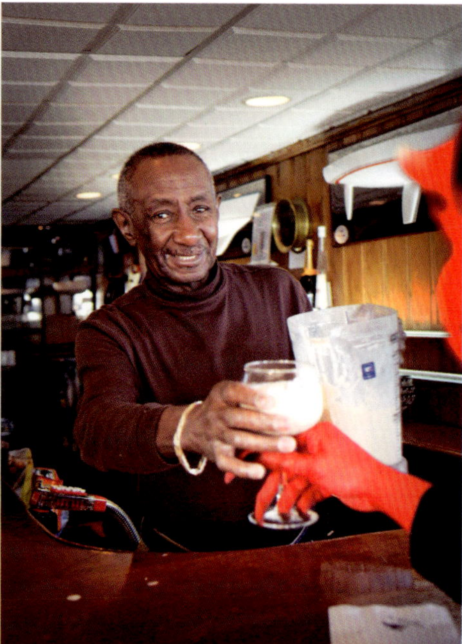

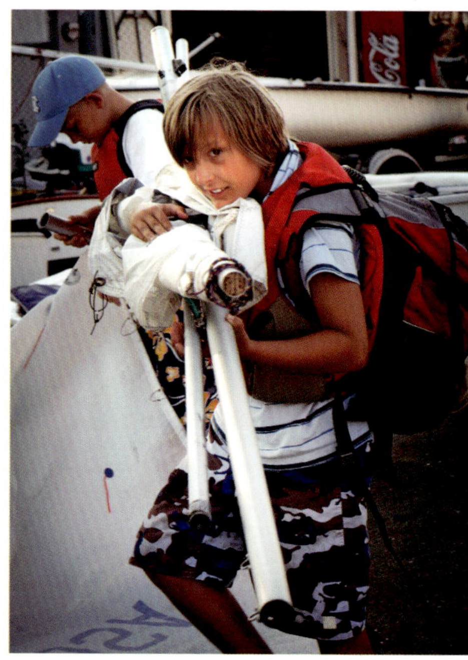

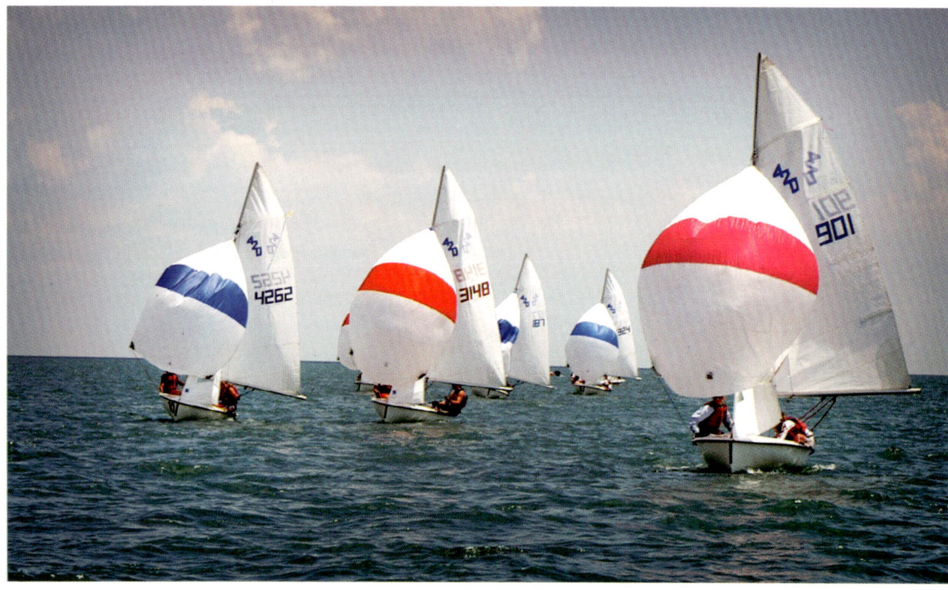

Here they take sailing seriously. Unlike most clubs, with their attitudes and fussy social norms, Bayview is about sailing. Every Tuesday evening, members race on Lake St. Clair, honing their skills and preparing for the Port Huron to Mackinac Race. Occasionally, I am invited to crew on one of the boats, which means that post-race, I get to head to the bar and enjoy a Hummer mixed by one of the best bartenders I have ever known. - NR

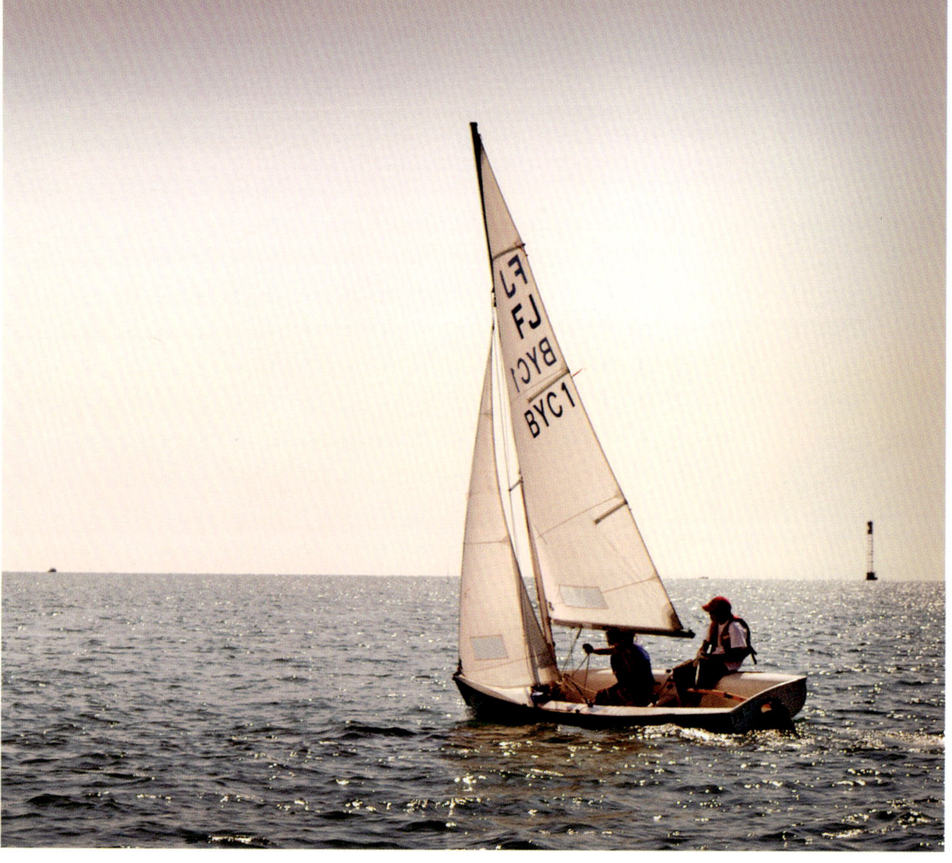

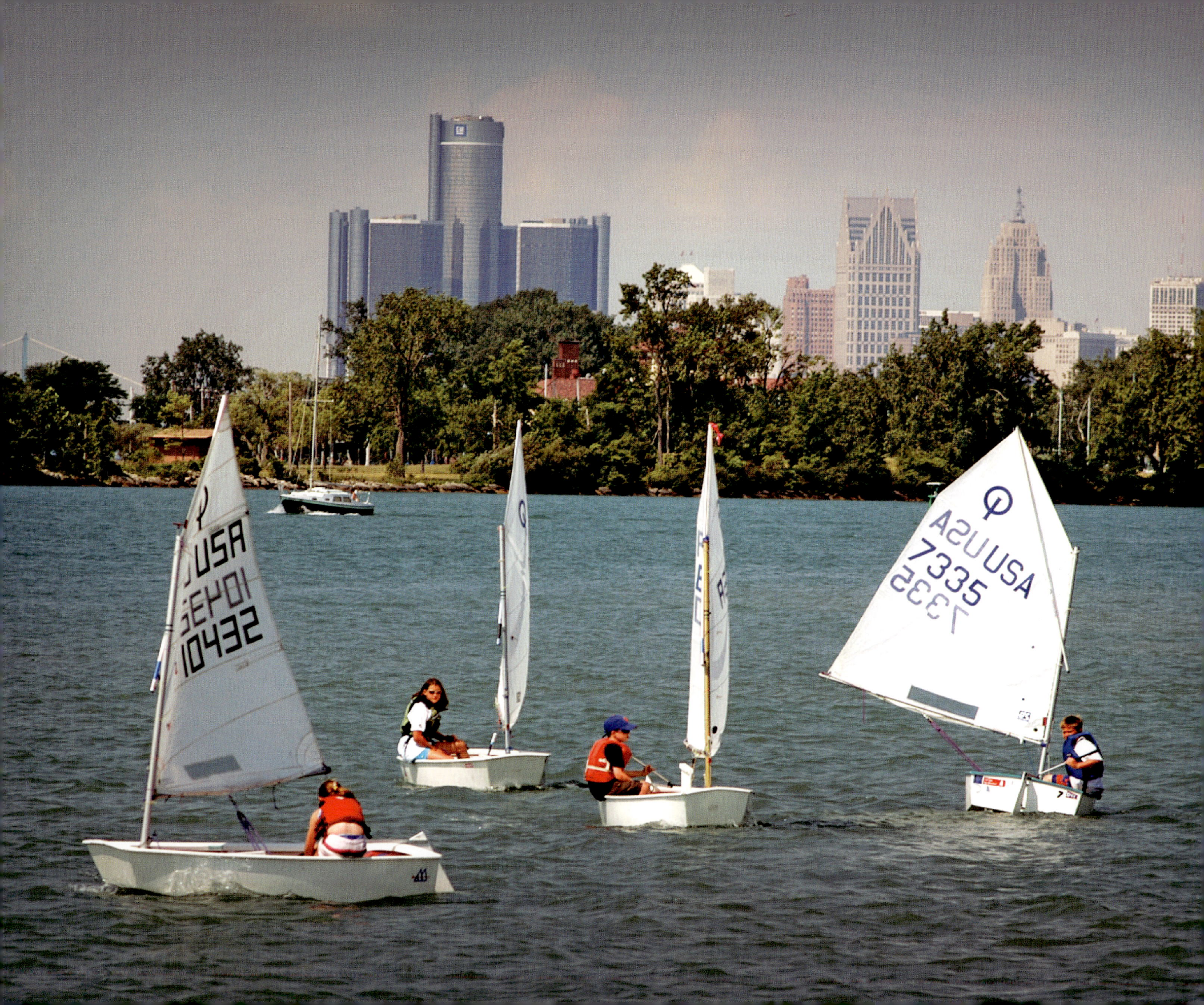
USA
10432
USA
7335

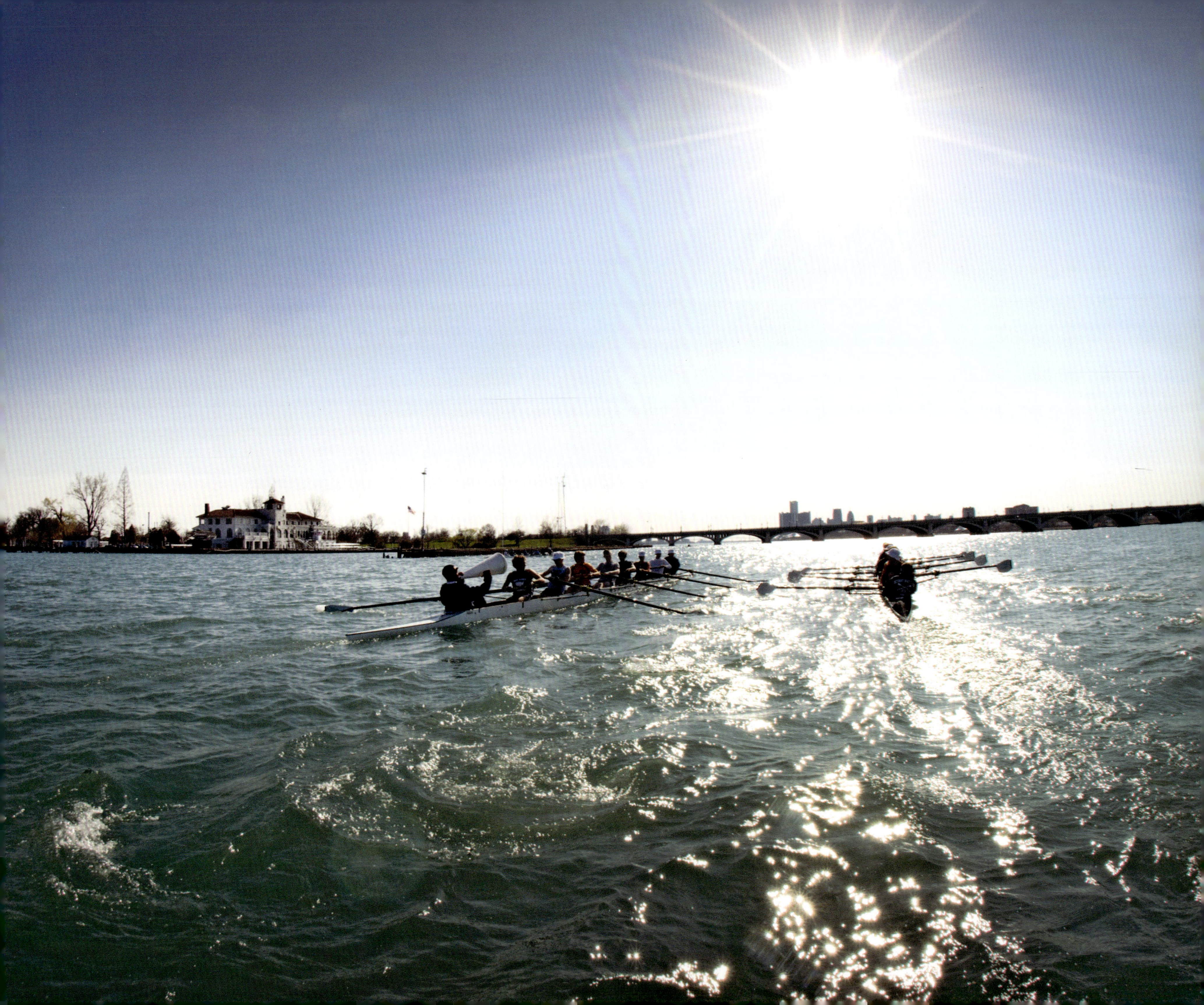

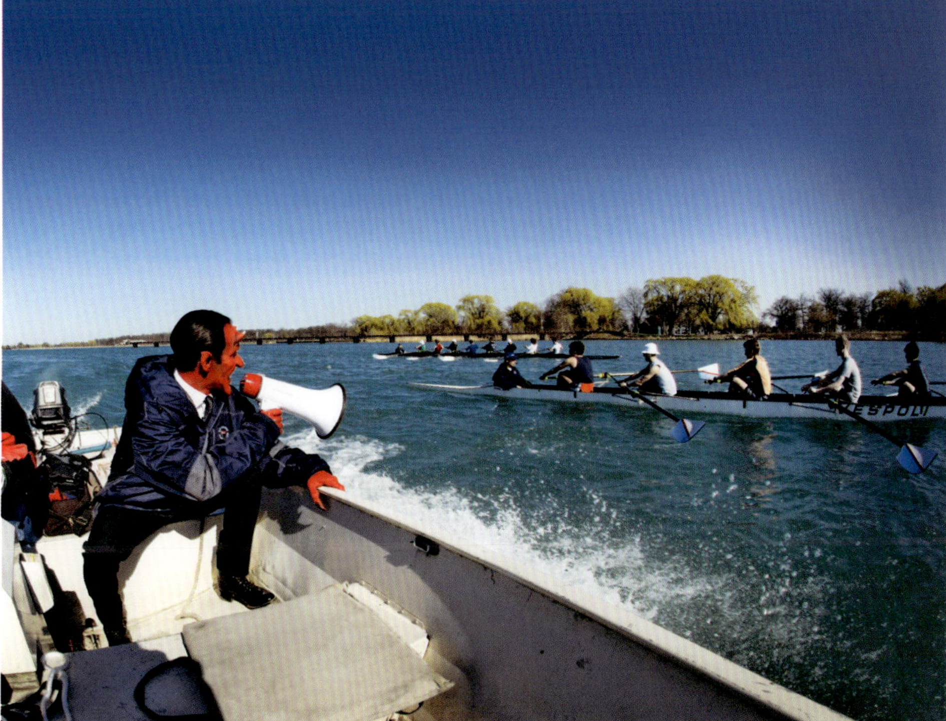

DETROIT BOAT CLUB

Belle Isle Boathouse, E. Riverbank Dr., Detroit, 48207
www.detroitboatclubcrew.com

Established in 1839, the Detroit Boat Club is the second oldest sport rowing club in the United States. The club moved to its present location in 1889, and the current building was built in 1902 using reinforced concrete, a relatively new material at the time. Since 1873, DBC oarsmen have won 54 events, including eight national team championships. In the 1956 Olympics, seven members represented the United States and brought home two silver medals. Although the social club left in 1996, the Friends of Detroit Rowing continues to operate rowing programs for all ages.

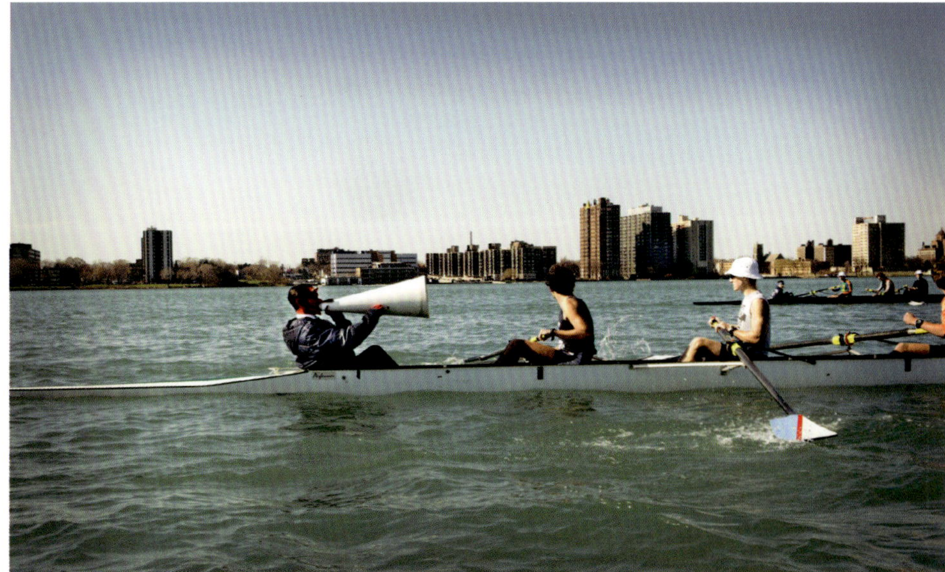

At the foot of the MacArthur Bridge on Belle Isle, what looks like an abandoned building is home to the Detroit Boat Club. Although a bit shabby on the outside, the interior remains intact. Burdened with the loss of the social club, the Rowing Club continues to offer classes and practice time to its members. As for me, I enjoy working with the younger students, coaching their techniques or serving as a coxswain calling out instructions. - NR

DETROIT YACHT CLUB

1 Riverbank Dr., Detroit, 48207
www.dyc.com

The Detroit Yacht Club, founded in 1868, moved to the north shore of Belle Isle in 1881. The present Mediterranean-style clubhouse was built in 1923 and is the largest in the United States. During the roaring 20s, the DYC reached national and international prominence as Club Commodore Gar Wood set world speed records in hydroplanes and brought home numerous Gold Cup victories. Rows of docks are filled with yachts and sailboats of all sizes. Members can enjoy cocktails poolside in the summer and dancing in the grand ballroom year-round. The Flying Scots offers sailing lessons and complimentary access to a fleet of sailboats. Family friendly, the Club has many programs for youngsters including a summer camp and swim team.

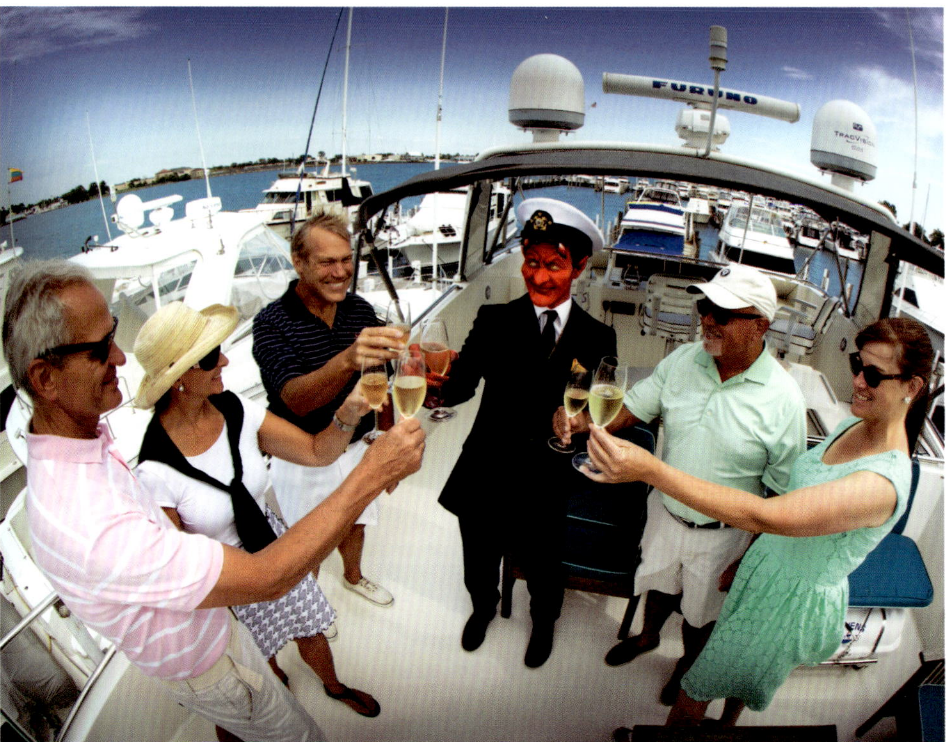

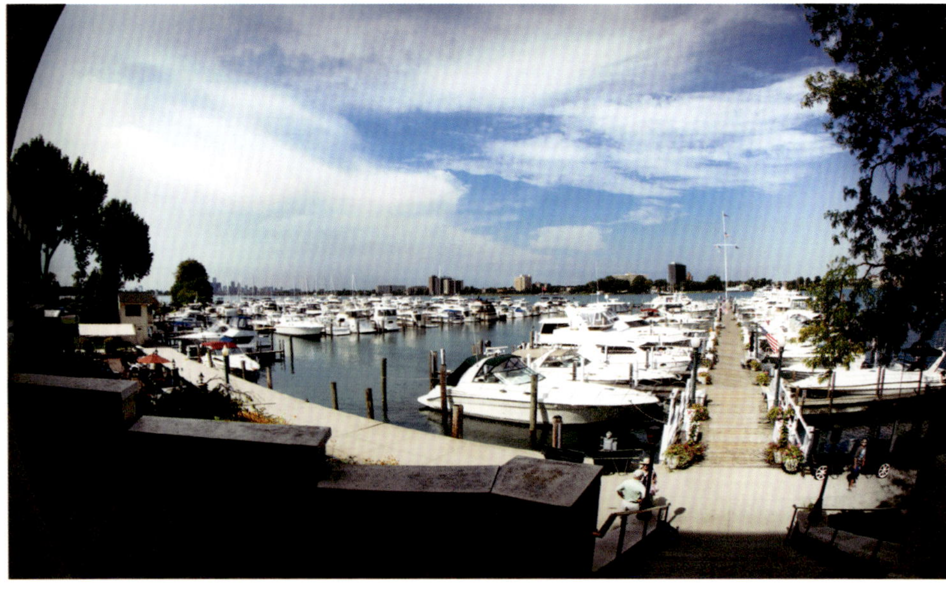

A fantastic summertime escape, the Yacht Club is a getaway without going anywhere. As an honorary member since its inception, I have been able to cruise the river with some of Detroit's elite, including Edsel Ford and Horace Dodge. I swear there is not a better view of Detroit than sitting on the veranda as the late summer sun sets while you're drinking a mojito and smoking a cigar with friends. And when you're too bombed to leave, you avail yourself of the club apartment in the tower. - NR

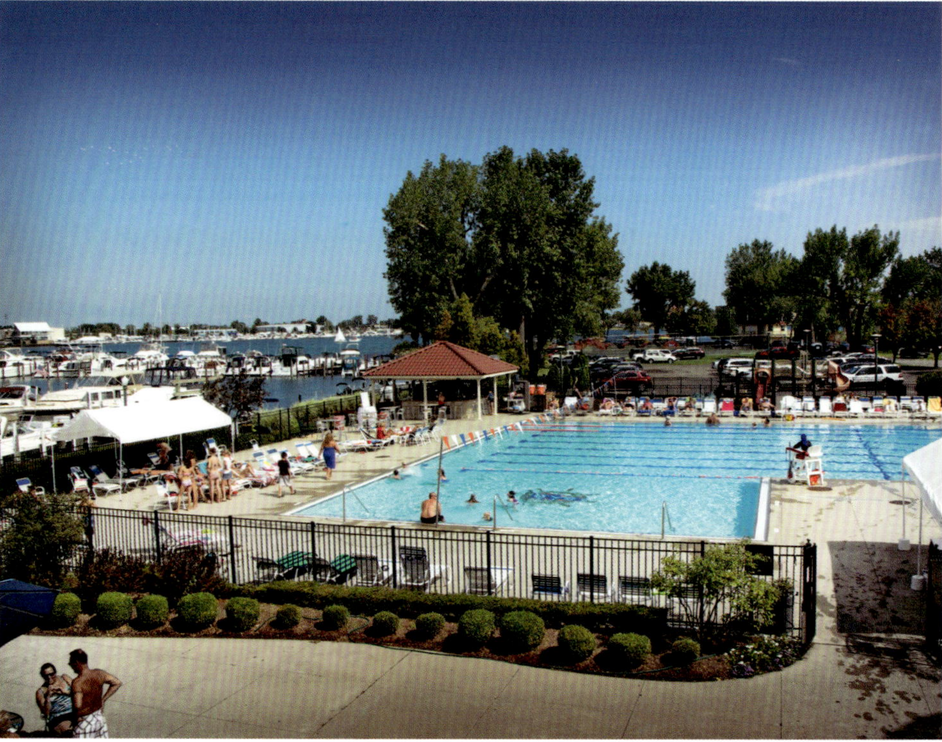

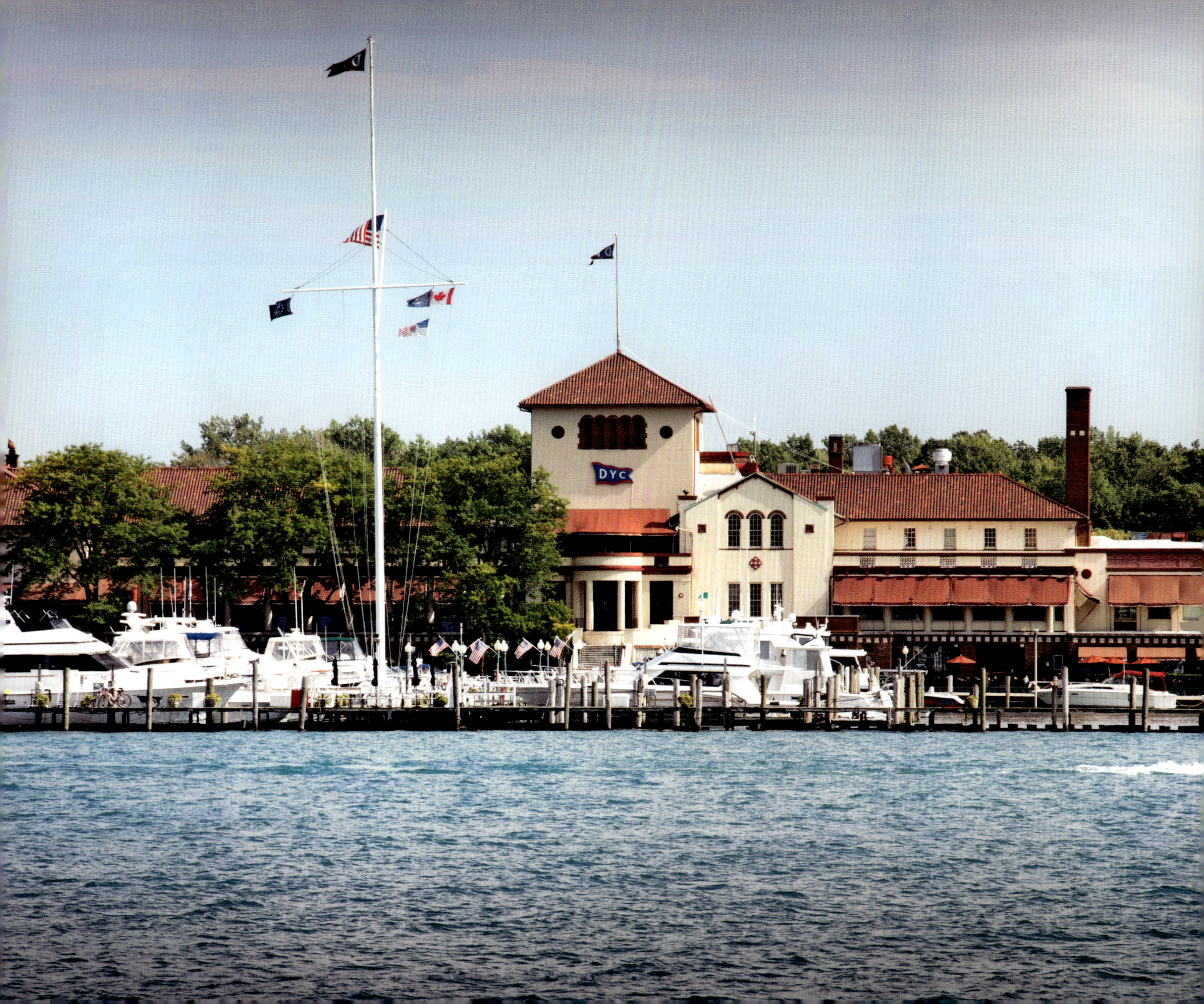
DYC

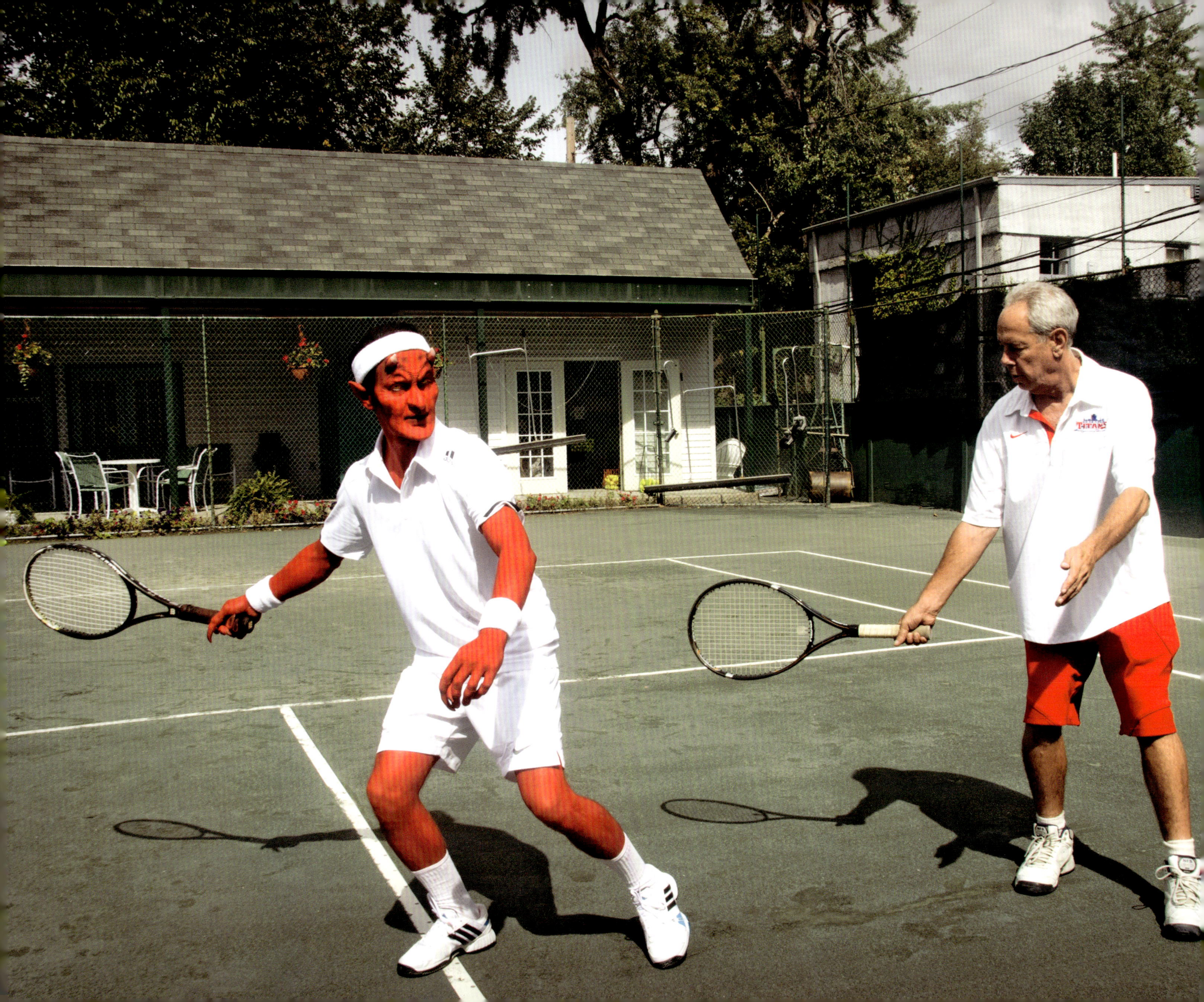
TITANS

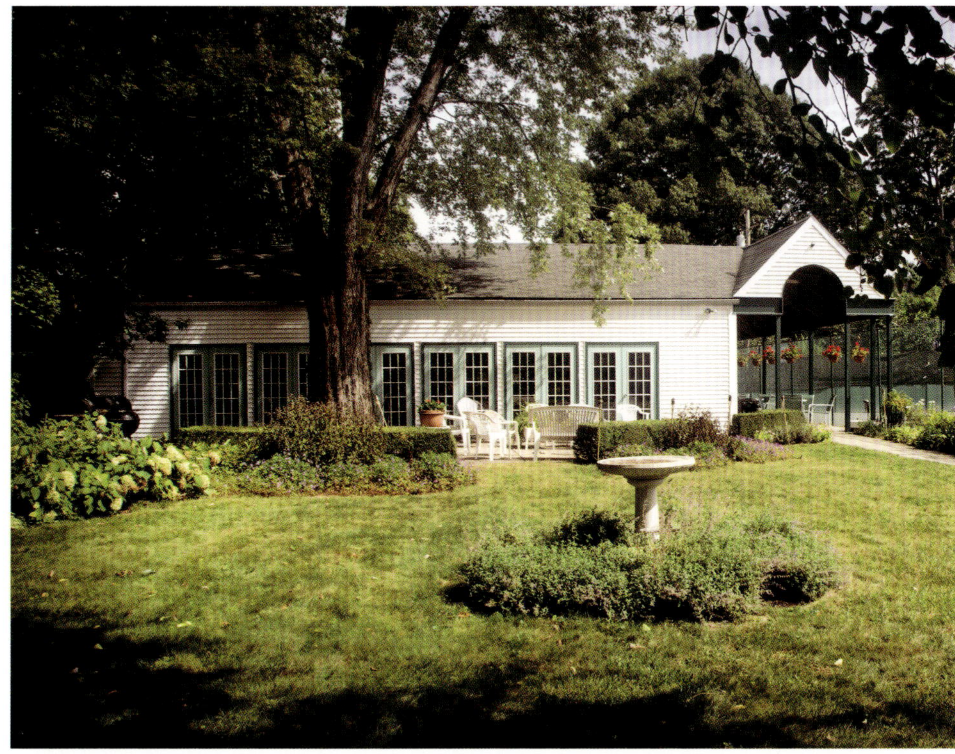

INDIAN VILLAGE TENNIS CLUB

1502 Parker St., Detroit, 48214
www.indianvillagetennis.com

With some of the only clay courts around, the Indian Village Tennis club has discreetly coexisted between homes in the Indian Village neighborhood since 1912. Barely identifiable from the street, it has a bronze sign above the door as the only clue that you've found it. With three courts, a clubhouse, and an open patio, it is peacefully quaint. Members set up their own times and participate in the many club tournaments.

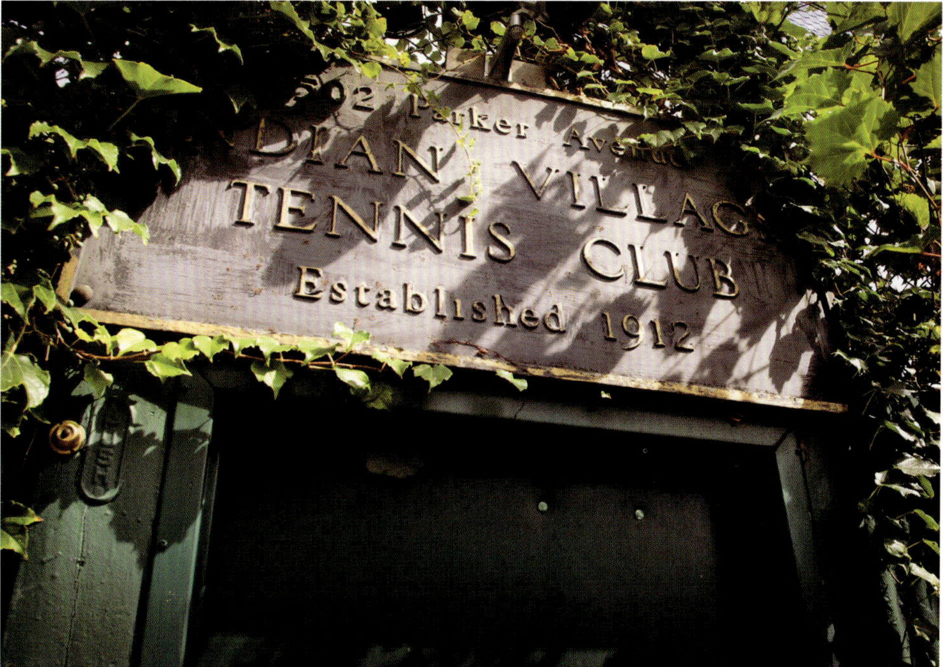

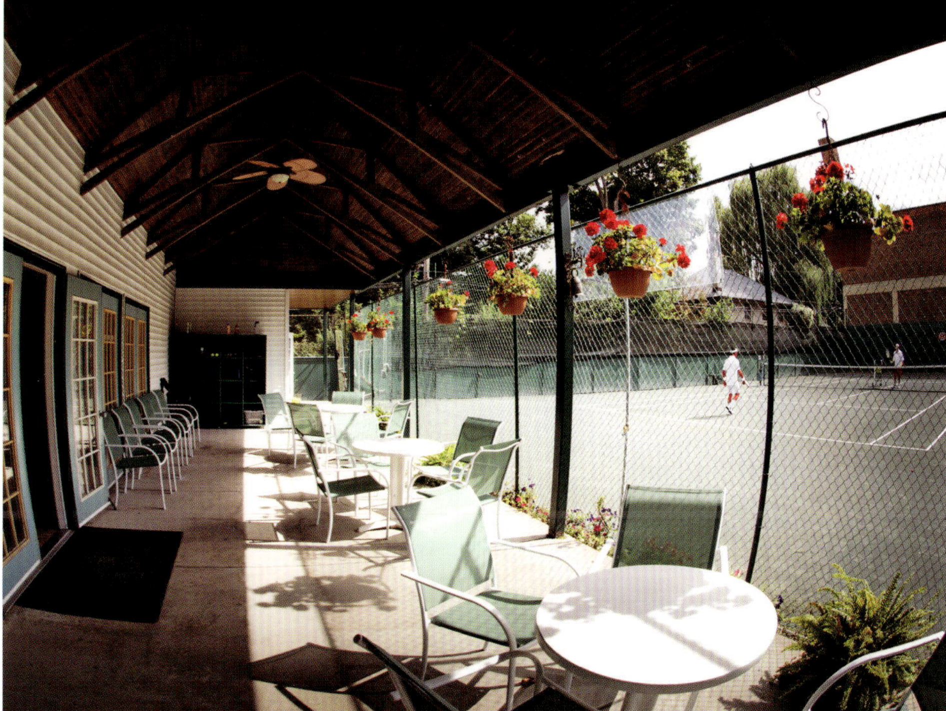

Although I have been a guest for decades, I only recently decided to join and learn how to play tennis. My instructor, David Lee, is one of my longtime friends. A club professional, he played on scholarship at U of D Mercy. Testing his patience, I have slowly improved my game. The next step is entering a tournament. - NR

THE PLAYERS CLUB

3321 E. Jefferson Ave., Detroit, 48207
playersdetroit.azurewebsites.net

As times change, the Players Club continues as one of the last "men's only" clubs in Detroit. The Club has been home to theatre aficionados, having performed live theatre since 1910. Every month, selected members organize and produce a three-act play or "frolic," followed by a dinner, hosted by the actors for the entertainment of the other members and their guests. The performances revolve through the membership, offering all members the opportunity to participate. The playhouse, built in 1925, is actually home to three clubs, the Players Club, the Fine Arts Society, and the Theatre Arts Club.

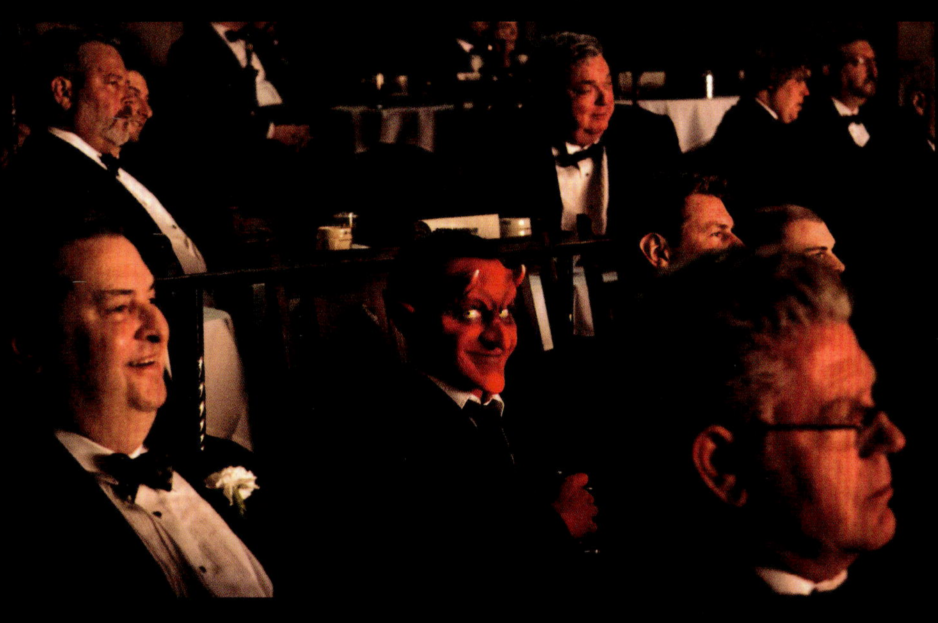

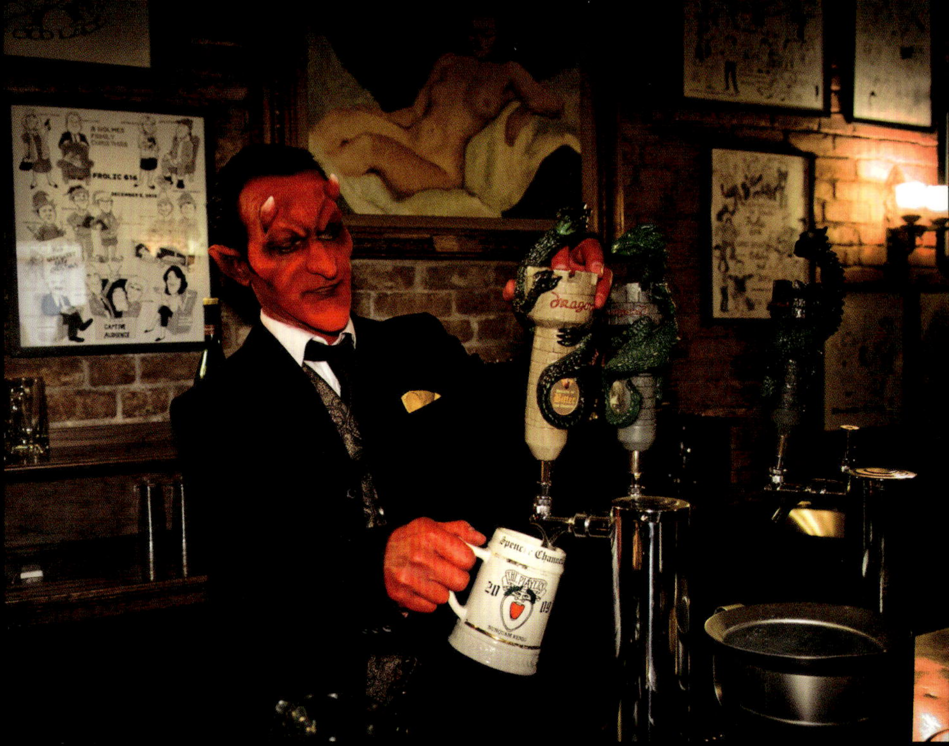

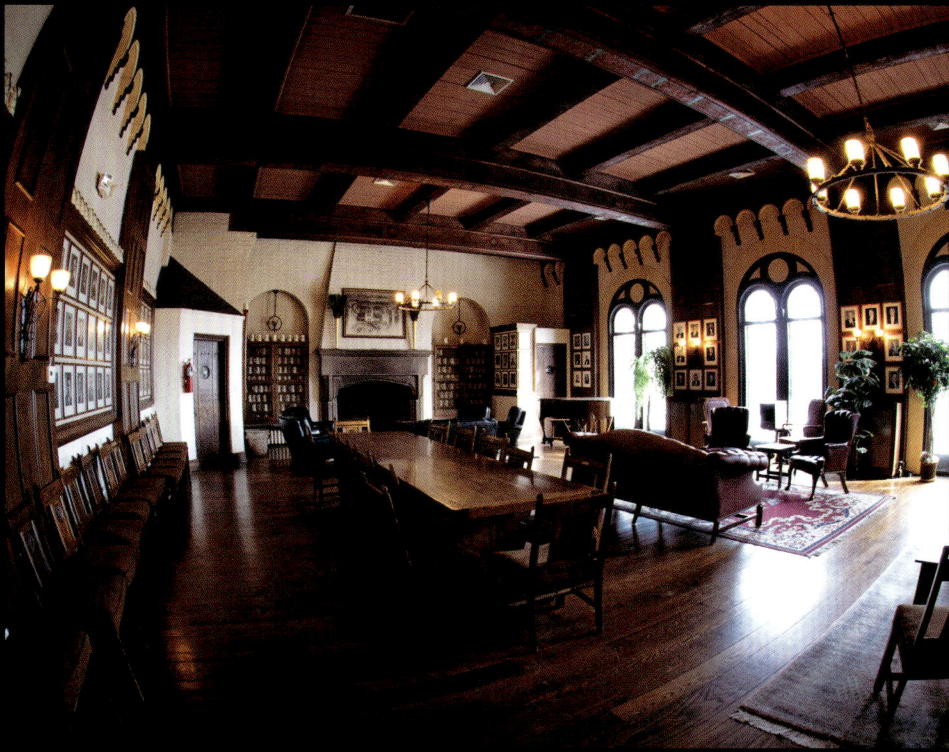

The Players Club provides an outlet for those of us who dreamt of the stage and becoming famous actors but ended up in less creative careers. The monthly "frolics" are black tie only, which I appreciate. It seems much more sophisticated when men are dressed in tuxedos. I attend a performance every now and then, but my real joy is when I am asked on stage. As a men's only club, the parts of women are played by the men. Intermissions are for drinking and, by the end of the night, the audience can become a little raucous. - NR

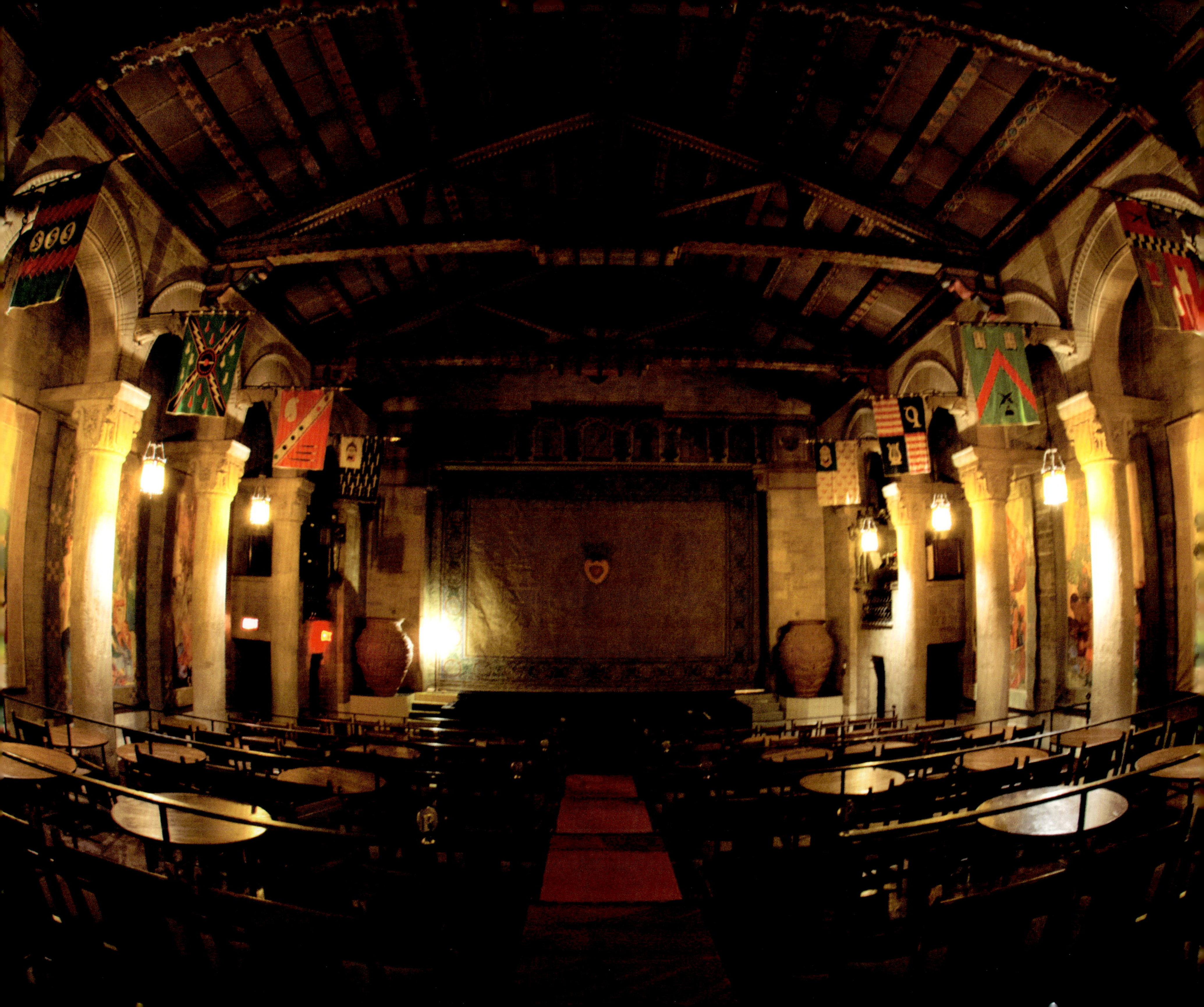

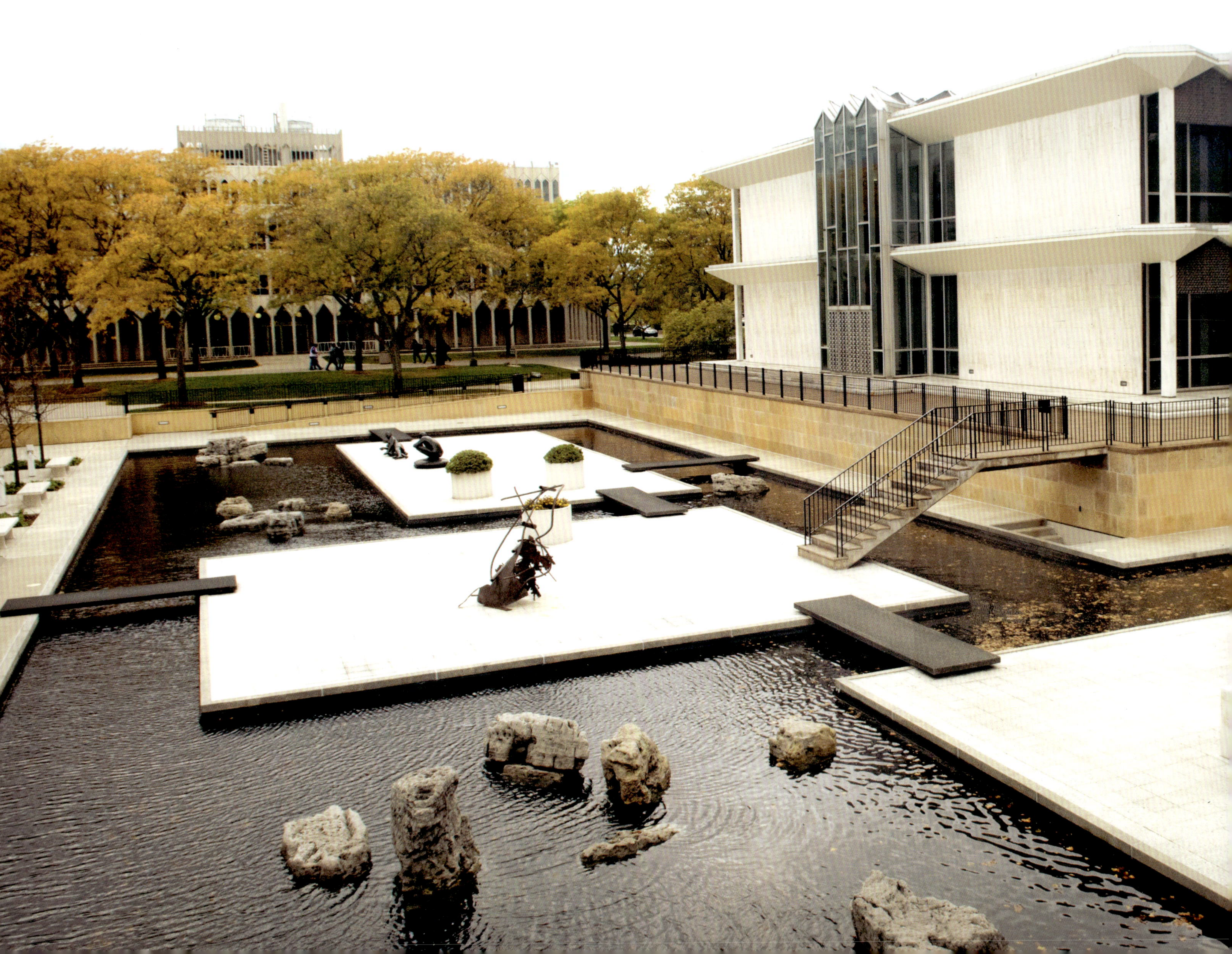

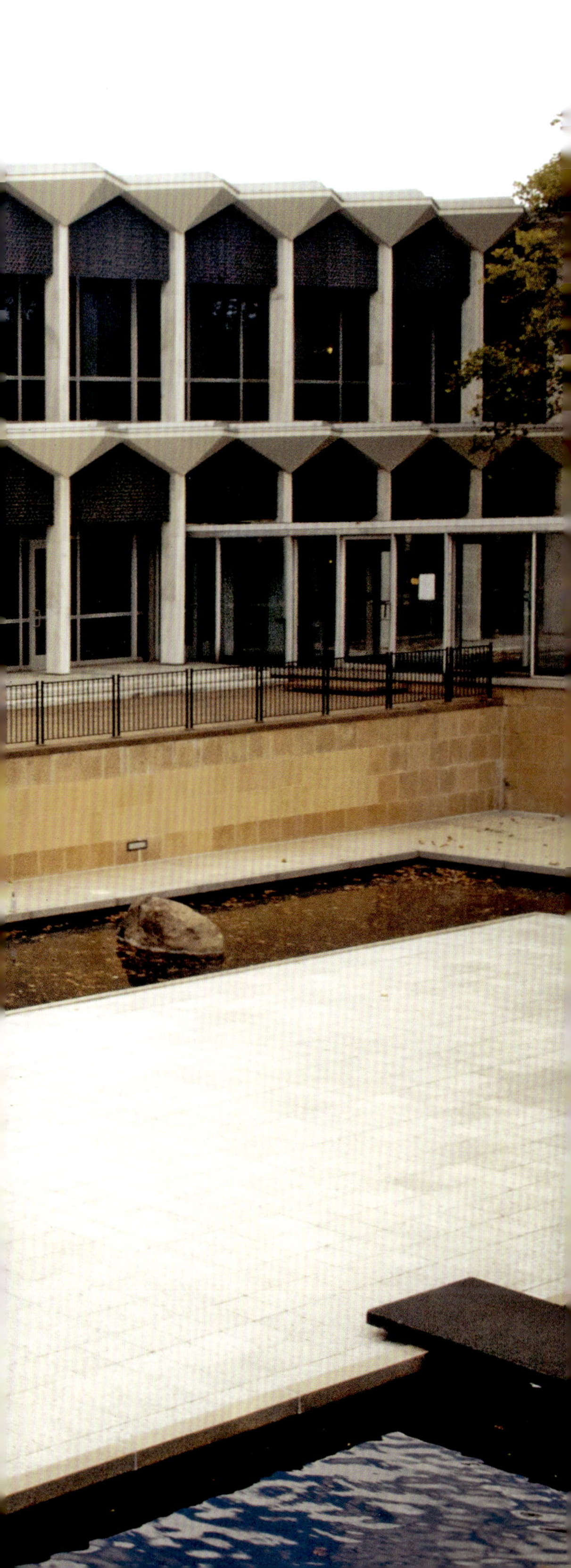

COLLEGE FOR CREATIVE STUDIES

201 E. Kirby St., Detroit, 48202
www.collegeforcreativestudies.edu

In response to rapid industrialization, the Detroit Society of Arts and Crafts was formed in 1906 to preserve artistic craftsmanship. It evolved into the College for Creative Studies, becoming one of the best design schools in the world, noted for its industrial and transportation curriculums. Many CCS students transition into automotive design, continuing Detroit's tradition as a leader in the field. Sculptures from the Detroit Institute of Arts grace the campus grounds. The annual graduate exhibit showcases the works of Detroit's up and coming new artists.

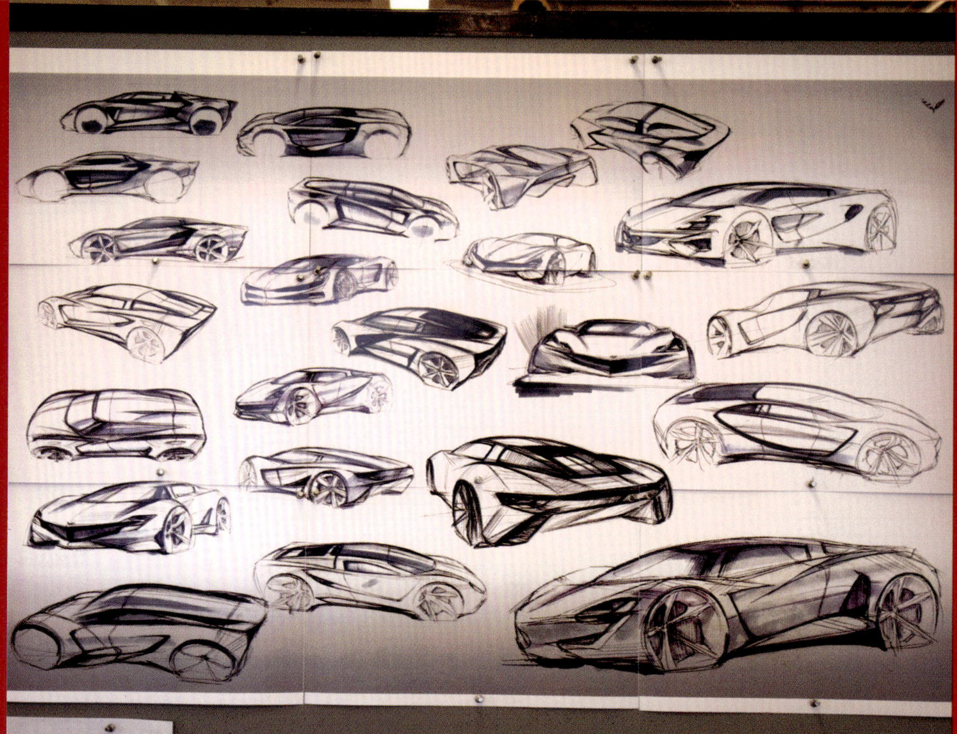

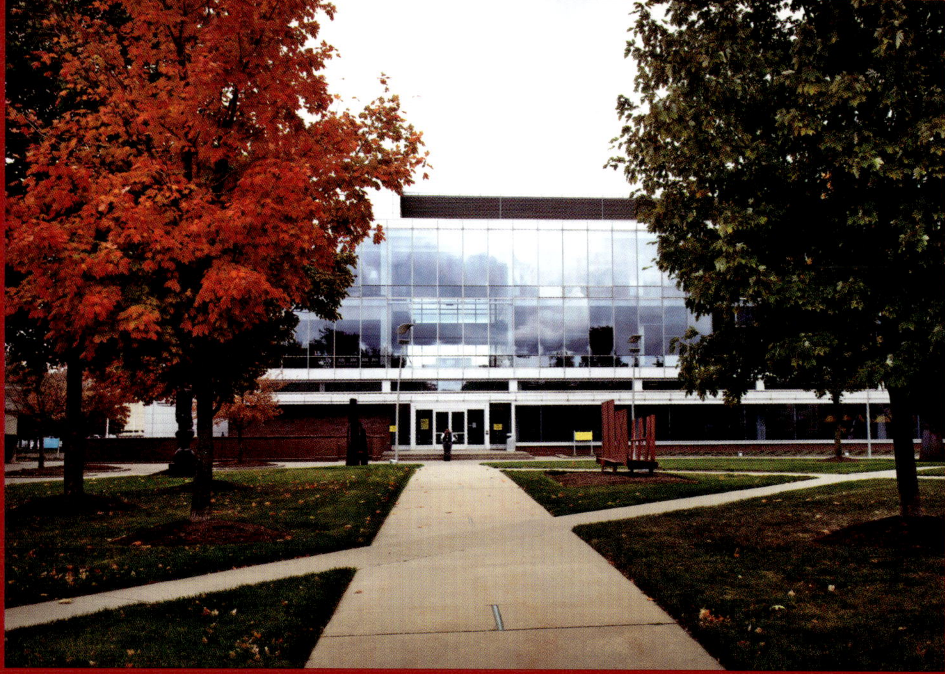

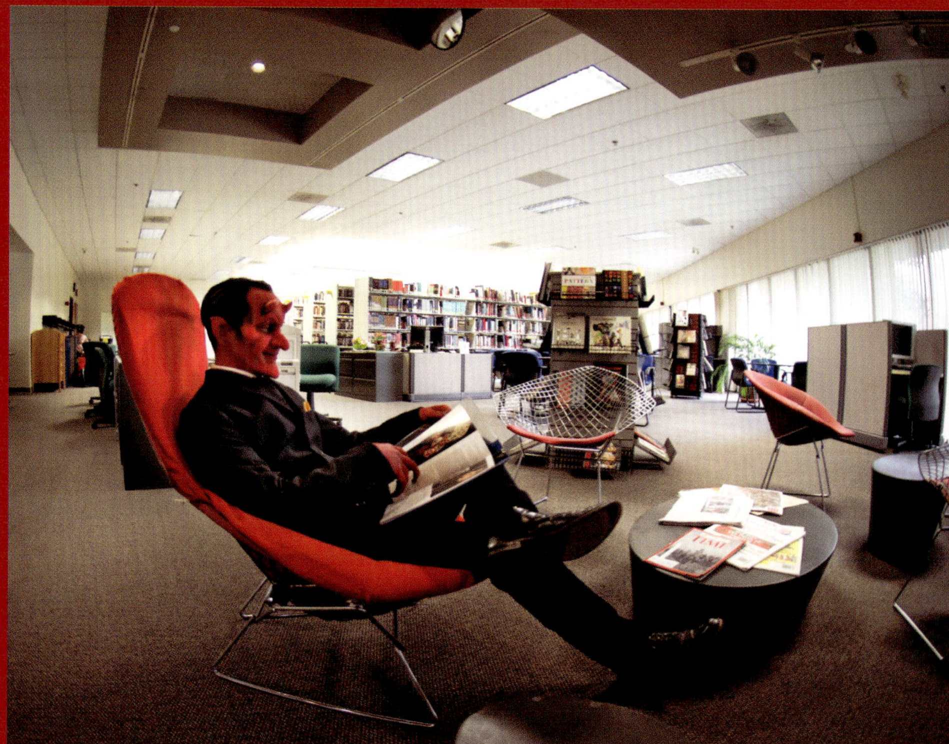

Despite my artistic shortcomings, I attend CCS classes once in a while, if for no other reason than to surround myself with the creative energy generated by the students here. So many of my more talented friends have gone on from CCS to design the latest automobiles or to become renowned artists. - NR

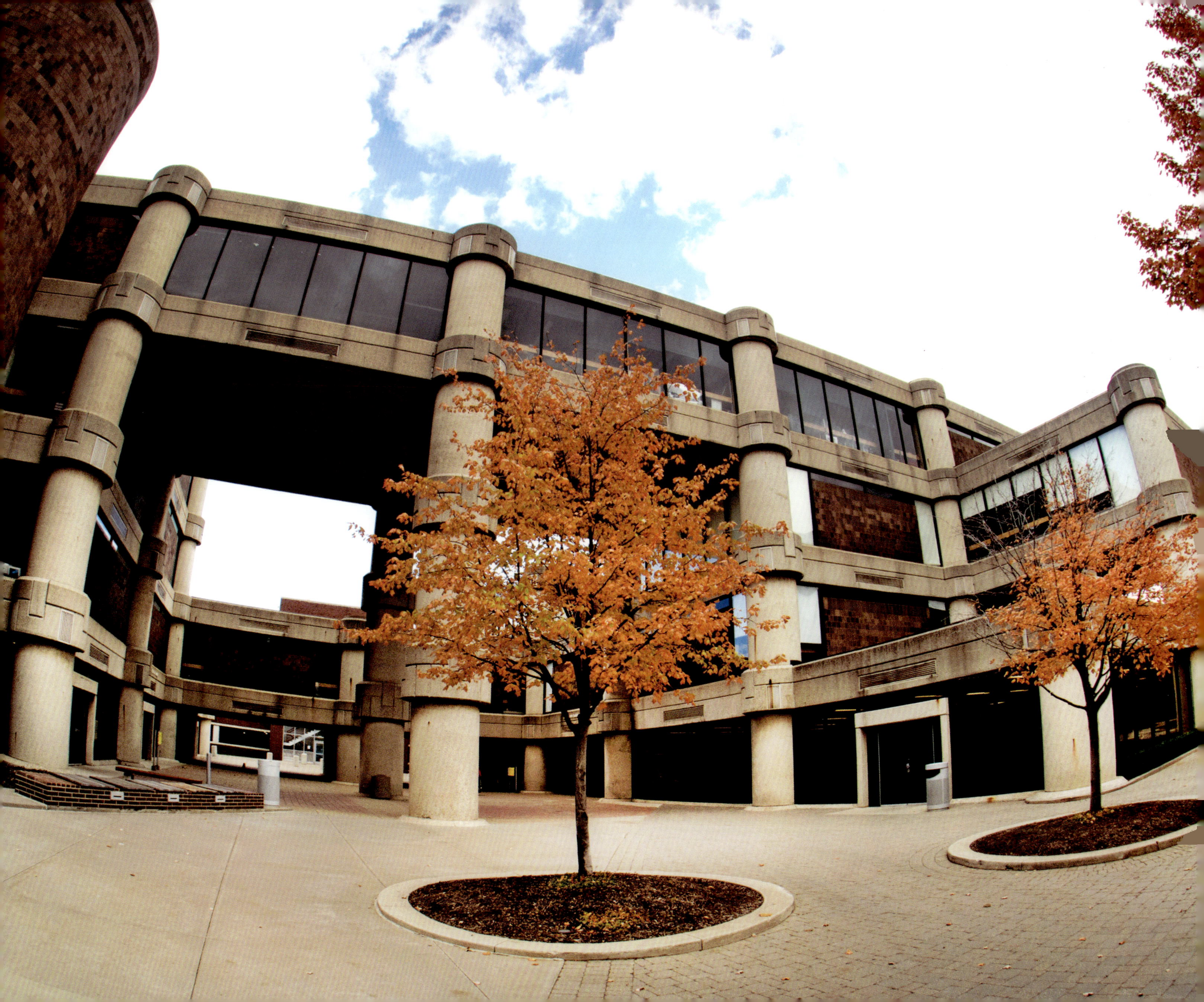

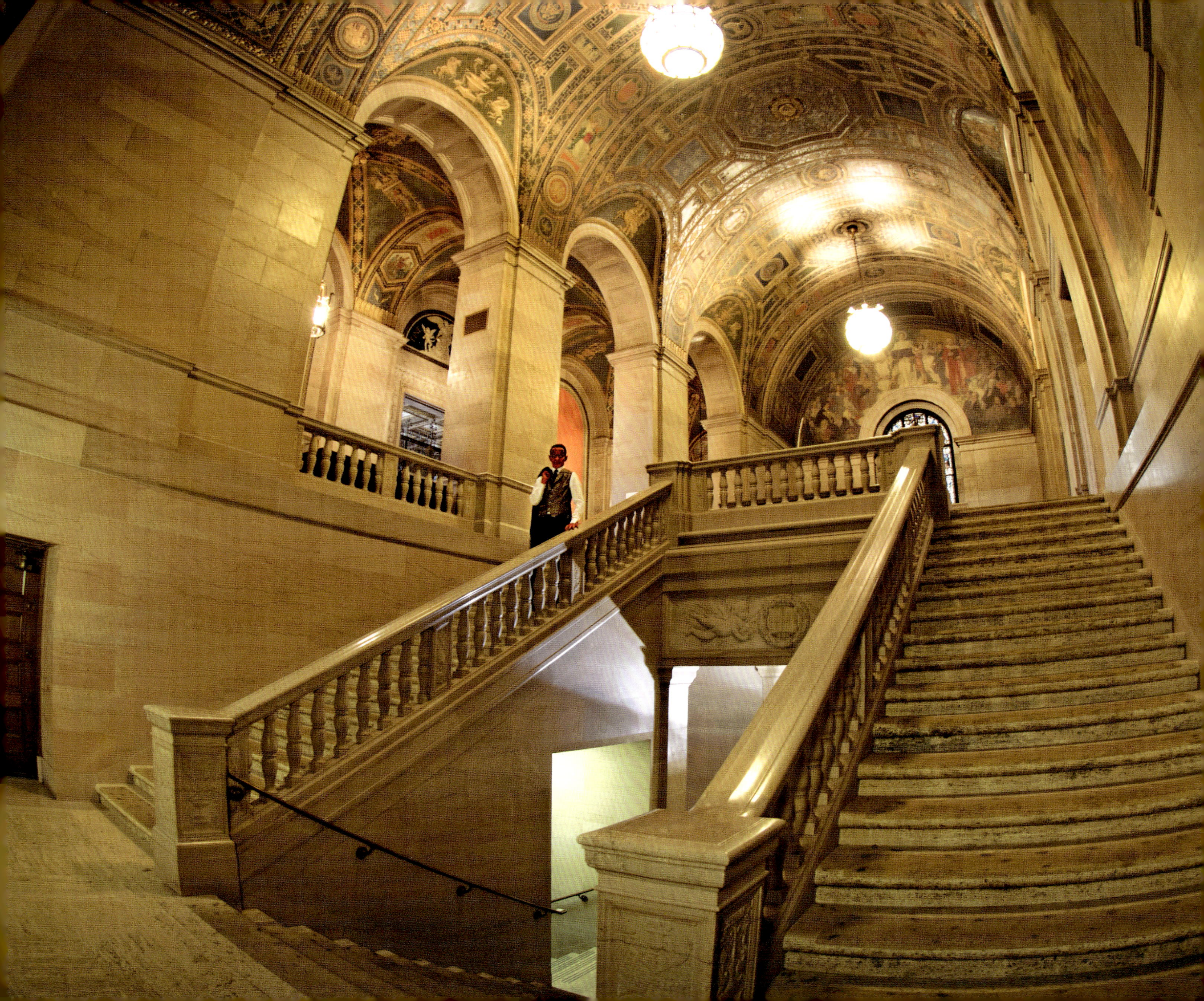

DETROIT PUBLIC LIBRARY

5201 Woodward Ave., Detroit, 48202
www.detroitpubliclibrary.org

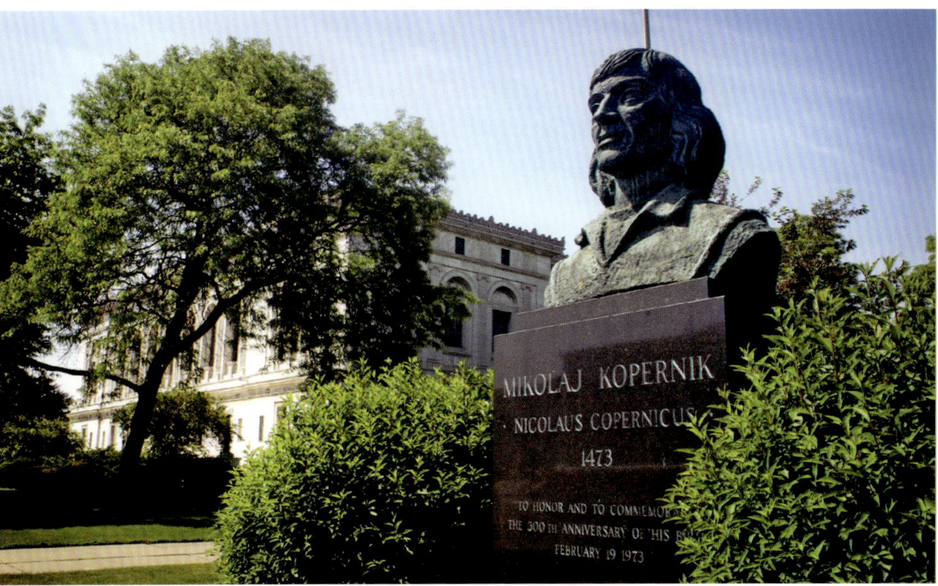

The Main Library in Detroit is a monument to the pursuit of knowledge and education. It says so right over the front doors: "Knowledge is power." The city's library system was founded on March 25, 1865, becoming the fourth largest library system in the United States with more than a dozen branches serving outlying neighborhoods. Within the Main Library, the Burton Historical Collection contains images, maps and manuscripts of Detroit history, the Ernie Harwell Collection, an array of sports memorabilia, and the E. Azalia Hackley Collection of African Americans in the Performing Arts, specializing in black music history. The Rare Book collection includes the original manuscript of Mark Twain's unfinished *Huck Finn and Tom Sawyer among the Indians*.

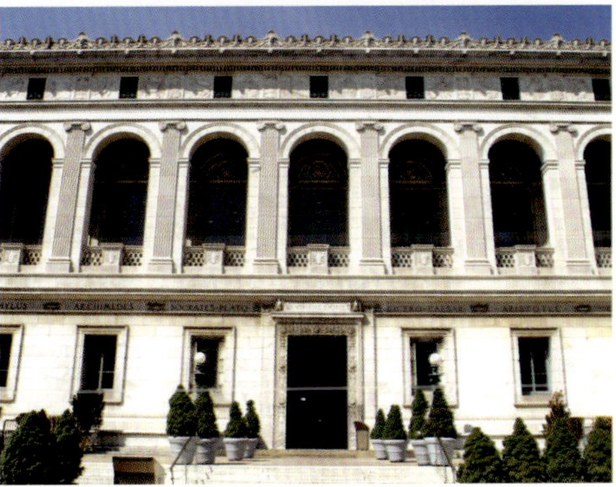

Those words carved above the doors are so damn true. Realizing the importance of information and the power it bestows, Detroit built amazing libraries throughout the city. I'm a regular at the Main Library; the librarians know me by name. You can usually find me reading in Strohm Hall, under John Stephens Coppin's "Man's Mobility," one of my favorite murals. - NR

MARYGROVE COLLEGE

8325 W. McNichols Ave., Detroit, 48221
www.marygrove.edu

St. Mary's Academy was founded in 1899, as a Catholic women's college, in Monroe, Michigan. Upon its relocation to Detroit in 1927, it was renamed Marygrove College. Always a leader in progressive social action, the school encouraged women to look beyond the prospect of marriage and to find their own place in the world. In 1970, it became co-educational. The 53-acre campus is located in northwest Detroit and adorned with large trees and lush lawns surrounding two main Tudor Gothic structures.

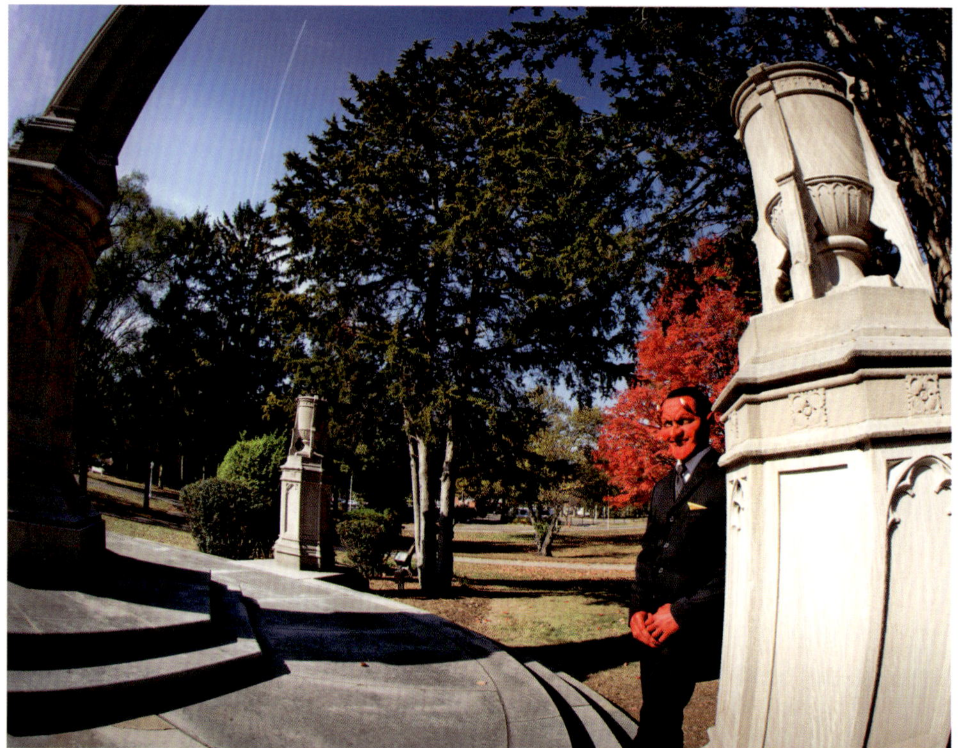

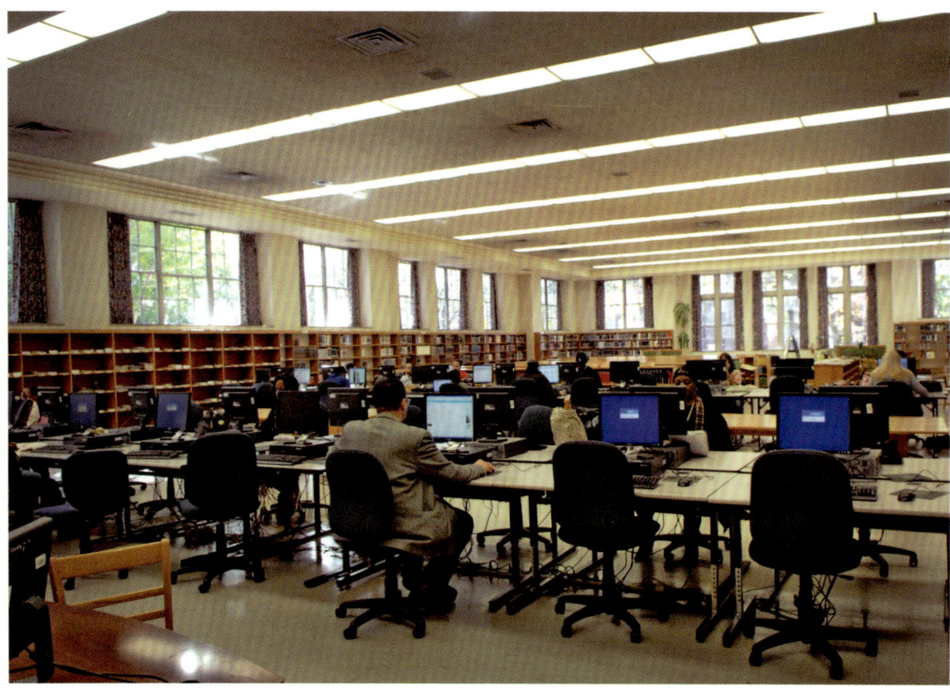

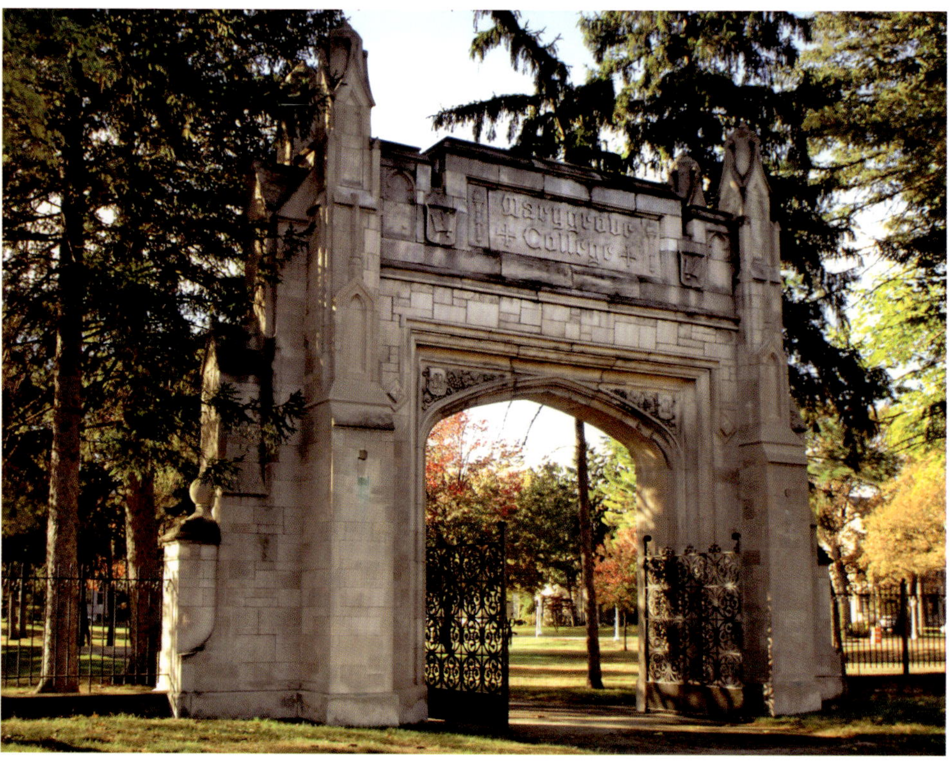

Always independent and progressive, Marygrove deepened its roots in Detroit more than most over the past few decades. Instead of following the great exodus to safer, suburban communities, it embraced the changing community that surrounds it and aimed to address its needs. To me, the diversity of the student population demonstrates the real possibility of racial harmony. - NR

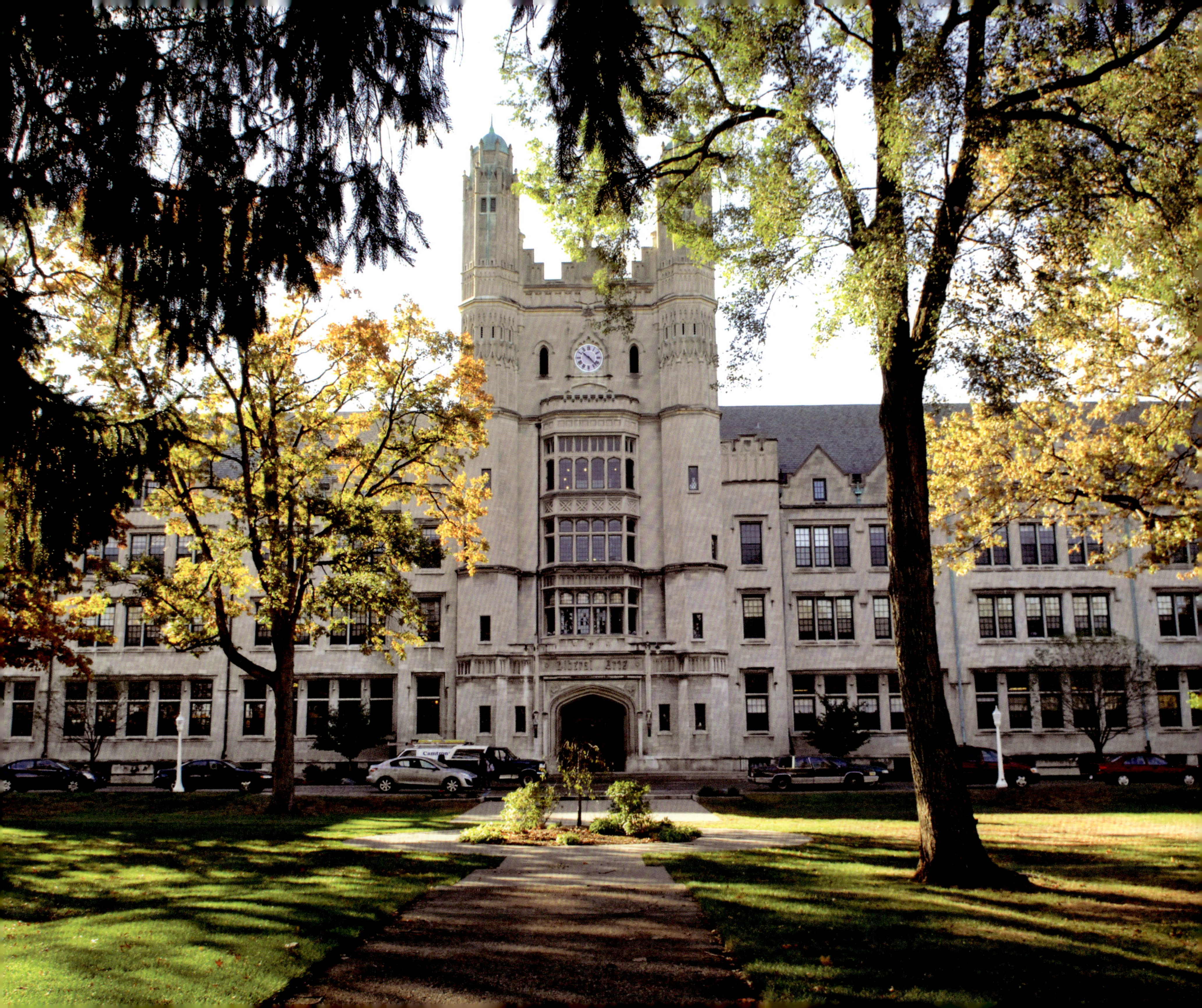

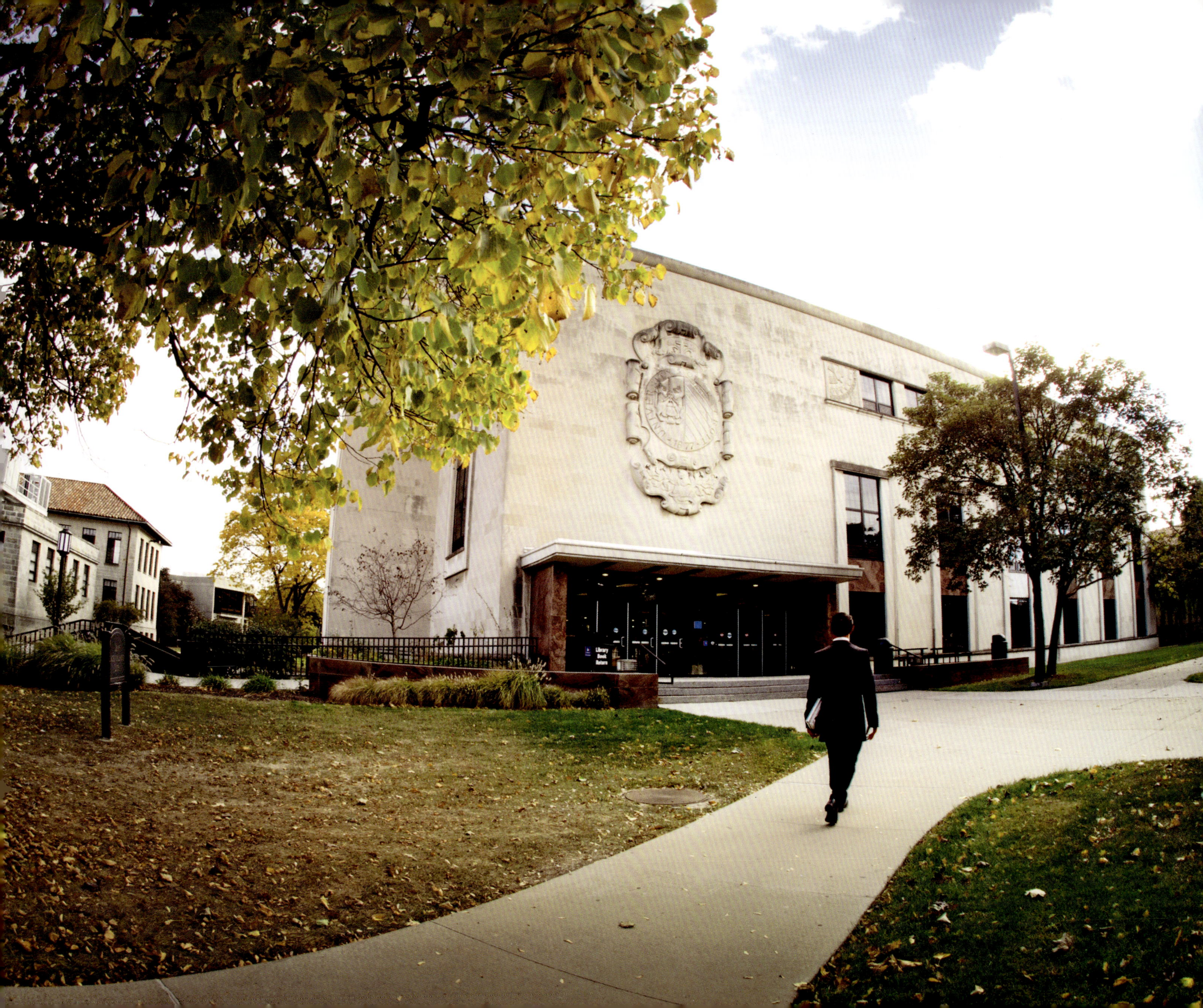
Library
Book
Return

UNIVERSITY OF DETROIT MERCY

4001 W. McNichols Ave., Detroit, 48221
www.udmercy.edu

The largest Roman Catholic university in Michigan and ranked in the top tier of Midwestern universities, the University of Detroit Mercy has been educating students since its formation by the Jesuits in 1877. Spread over three campuses across Detroit, its main campus is located at McNichols and Livernois. Renowned for its Law, Architecture and Dentistry Schools, it offers more than a hundred academic degrees and programs of study. Despite its small student population, UDM has an extensive sports history. The Titan football team played from 1896 to 1964, winning a national championship with a 9-0 record in 1929. UDM is known best for its basketball heritage: a Titan All Star Alumni team would include NBA greats Dave Debusschere, Spencer Haywood, John Long, Terry Tyler, Terry Duerod, Earl Cureton and Willie Green, coached by Dick Vitale.

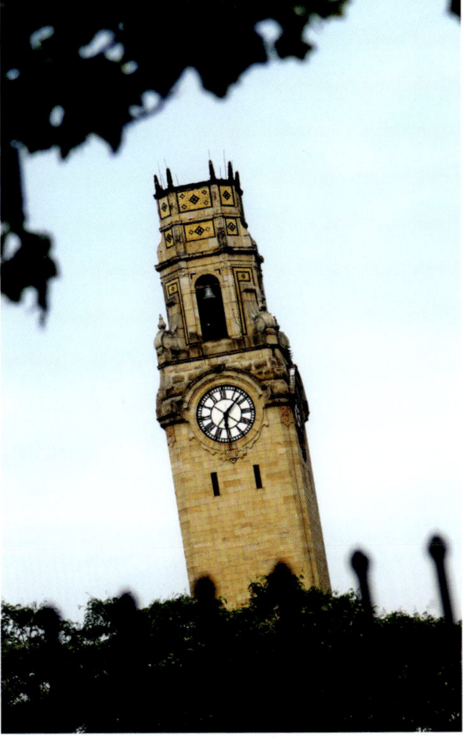

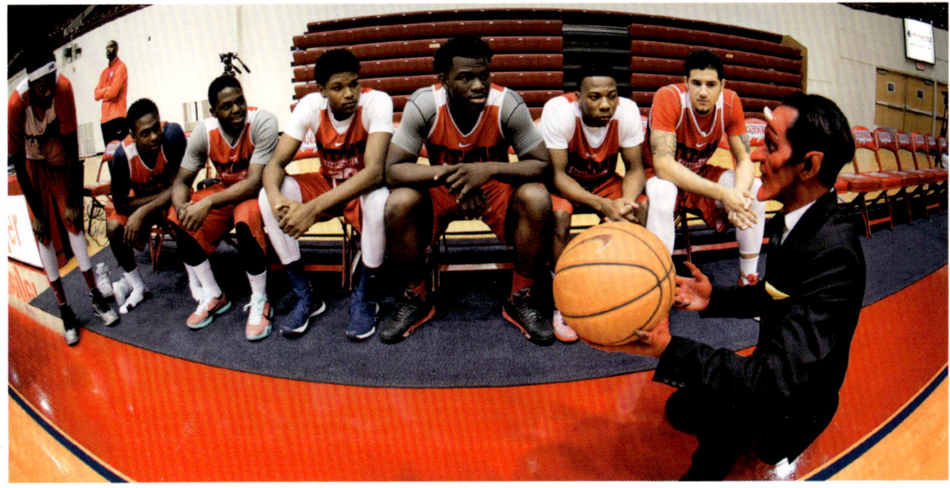

Dominating the McNichols main campus, the UDM Clock Tower can be seen for miles. It gives the campus an old-world ambience and inspires higher learning. With only 5,600 students, UDM has an intimate and friendly atmosphere. When it comes to college basketball, I would put up an all-time starting five from U of D Mercy's basketball team against any other school and I bet we'd win. - NR

WAYNE STATE UNIVERSITY

42 W. Warren Ave., Detroit, 48202
www.wayne.edu

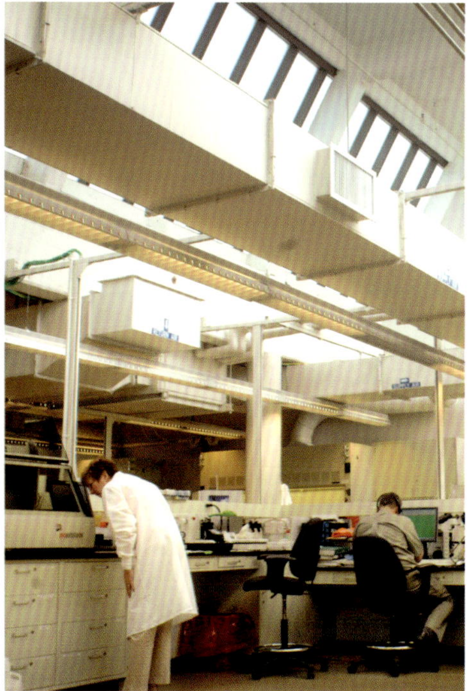

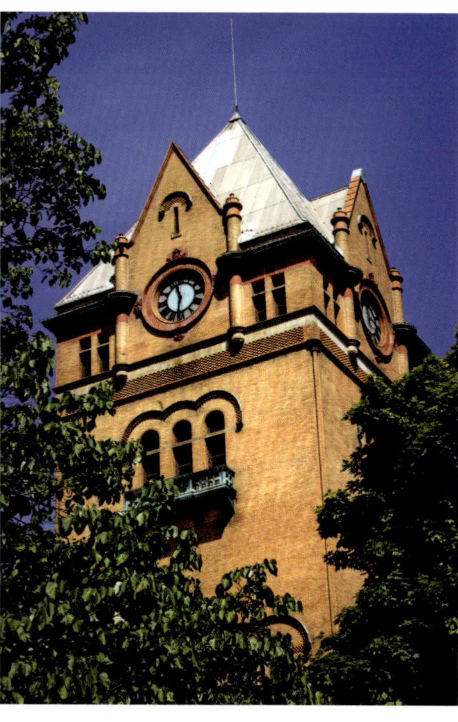

Wayne State University is the third largest public university in Michigan with 28,000 students. Founded in 1868 as the Detroit Medical College, it combined with other schools, officially becoming Wayne State University in 1934. As a major urban university, WSU has a diverse student population and is ranked as one of the nation's top research universities, renowned for its contributions to the sciences. The main campus anchors Detroit's Midtown neighborhood and the western end of the Cultural Center, home to Detroit's major arts and cultural institutions.

On the north end of the Cass Corridor (as I still call it), WSU attracts students who, in my opinion, are more rebellious and free-thinking than average. Maybe it's from the edginess and urban environment that surrounds it. Bolstering this narrative, during the tumultuous Vietnam era, WSU was a bastion of revolutionary thinking led by Fifth Estate founder Harvey Ovshinsky, John Sinclair, the White Panthers, and the MC5. - NR

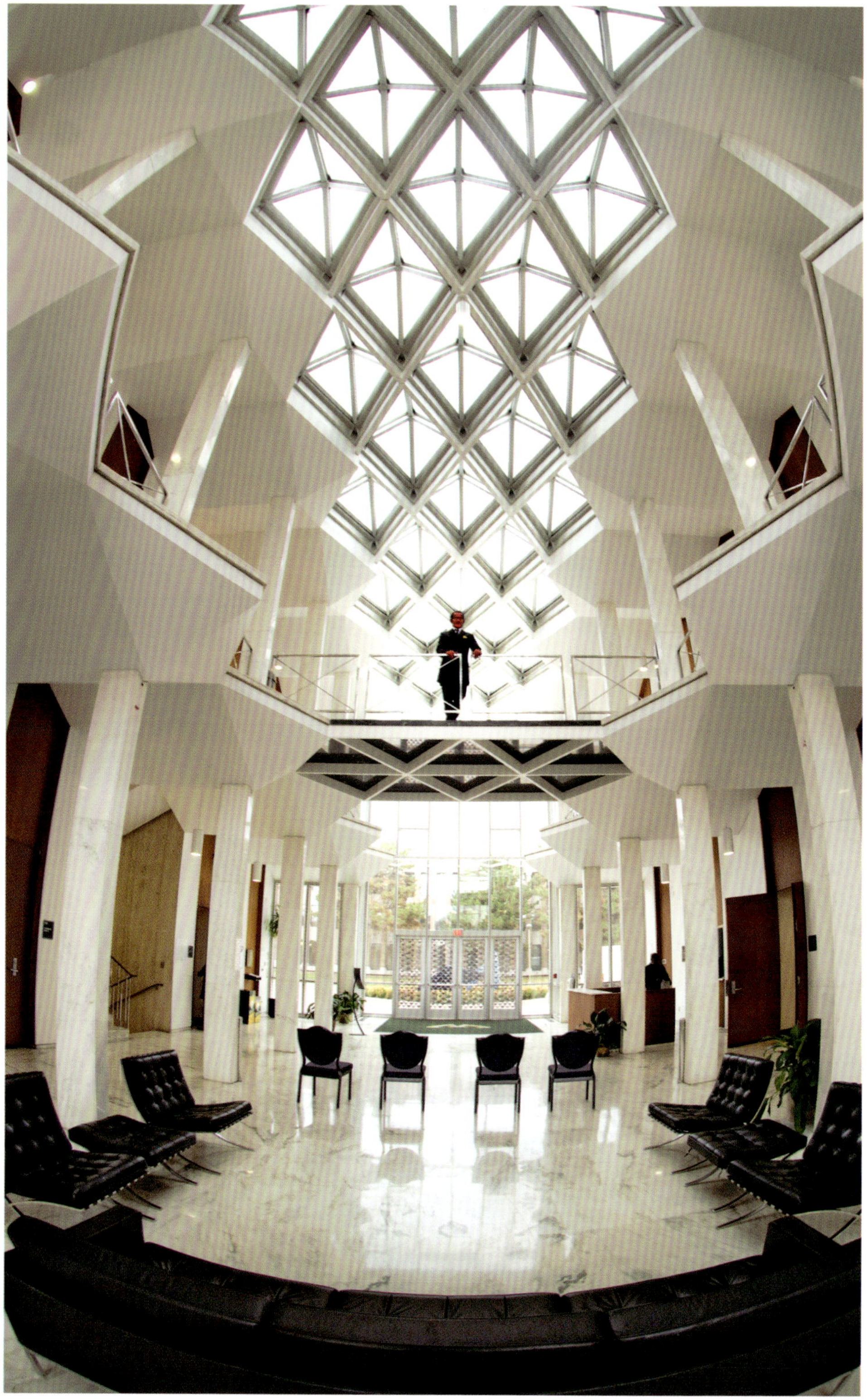

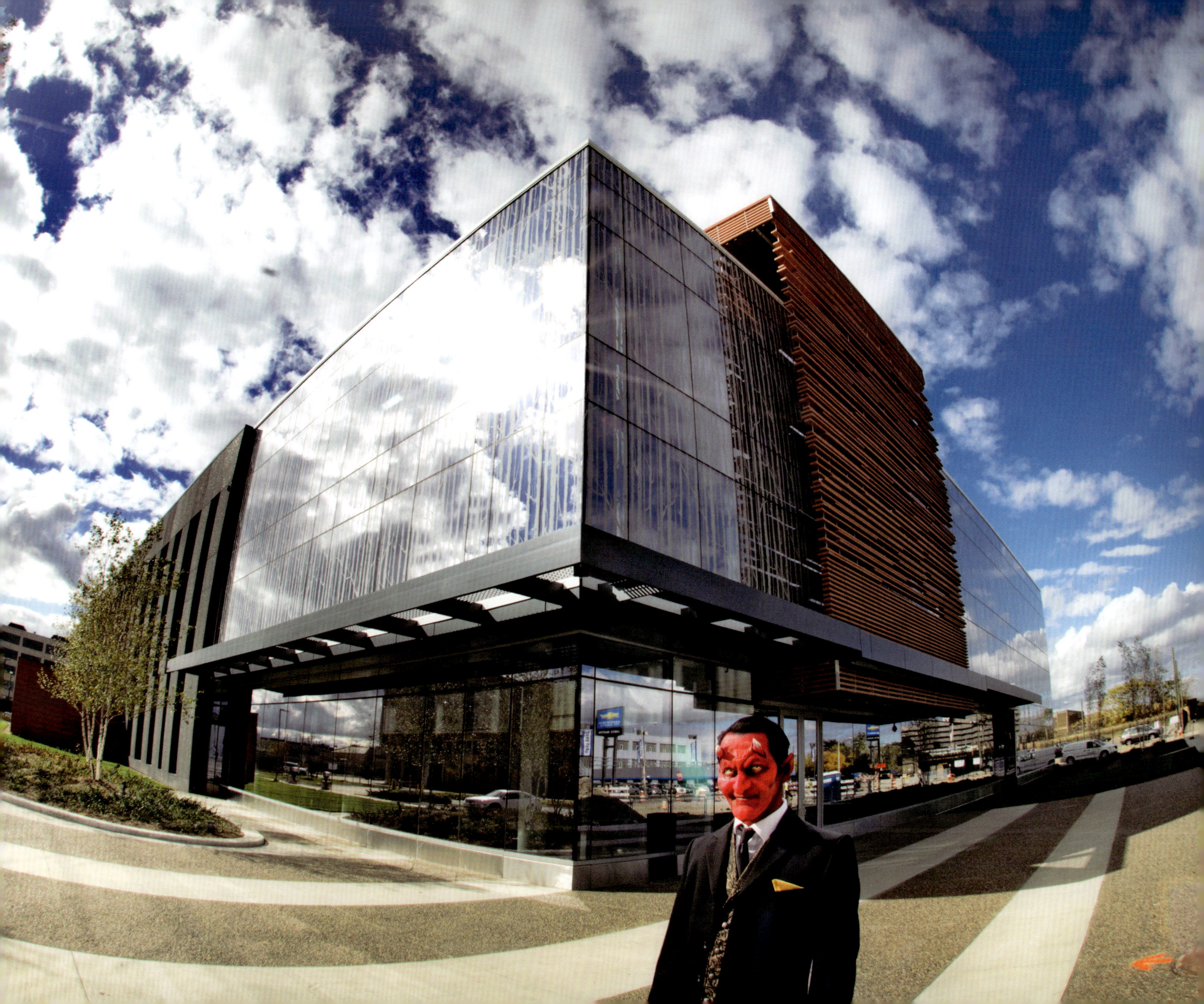

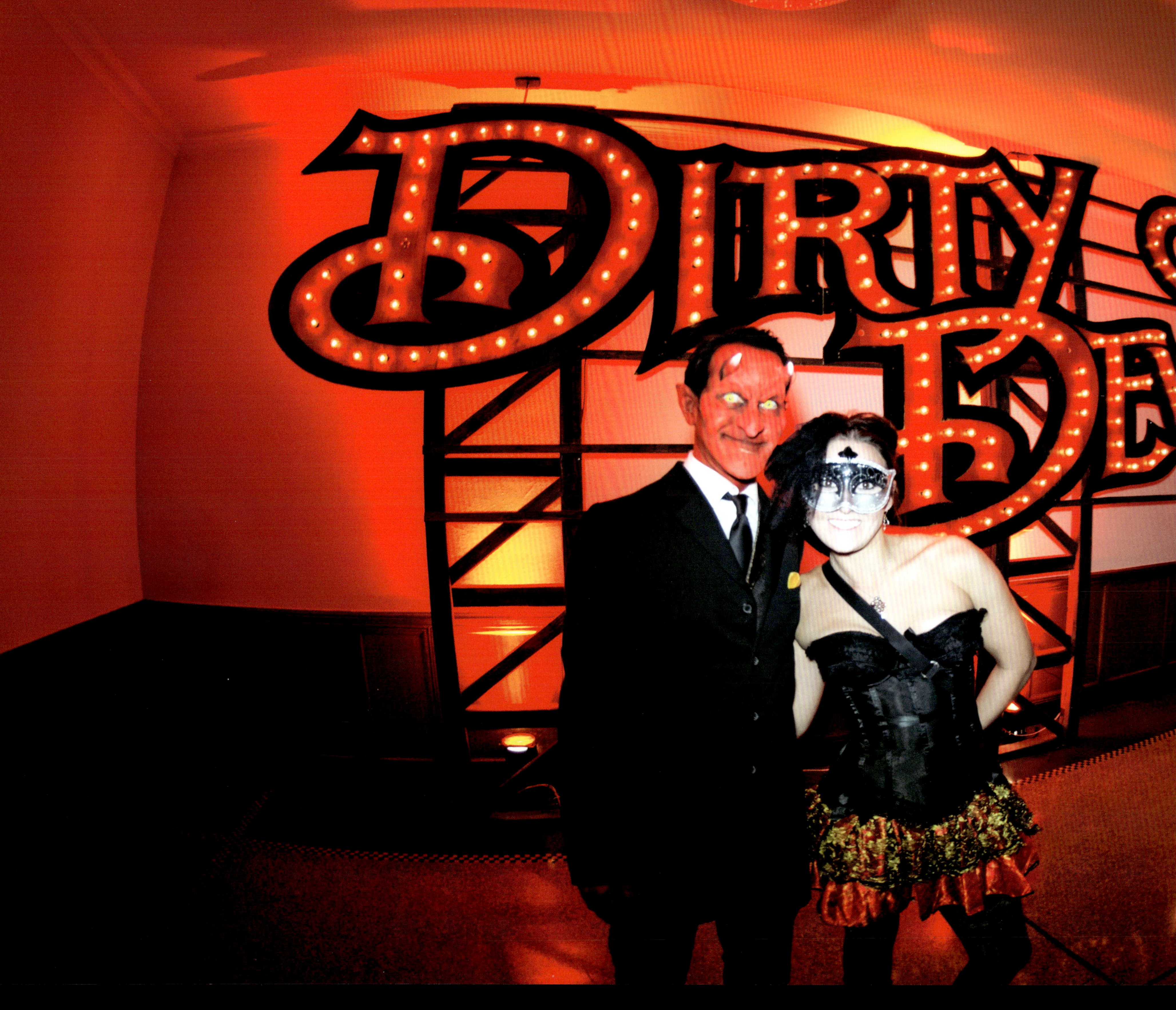
DIRTY

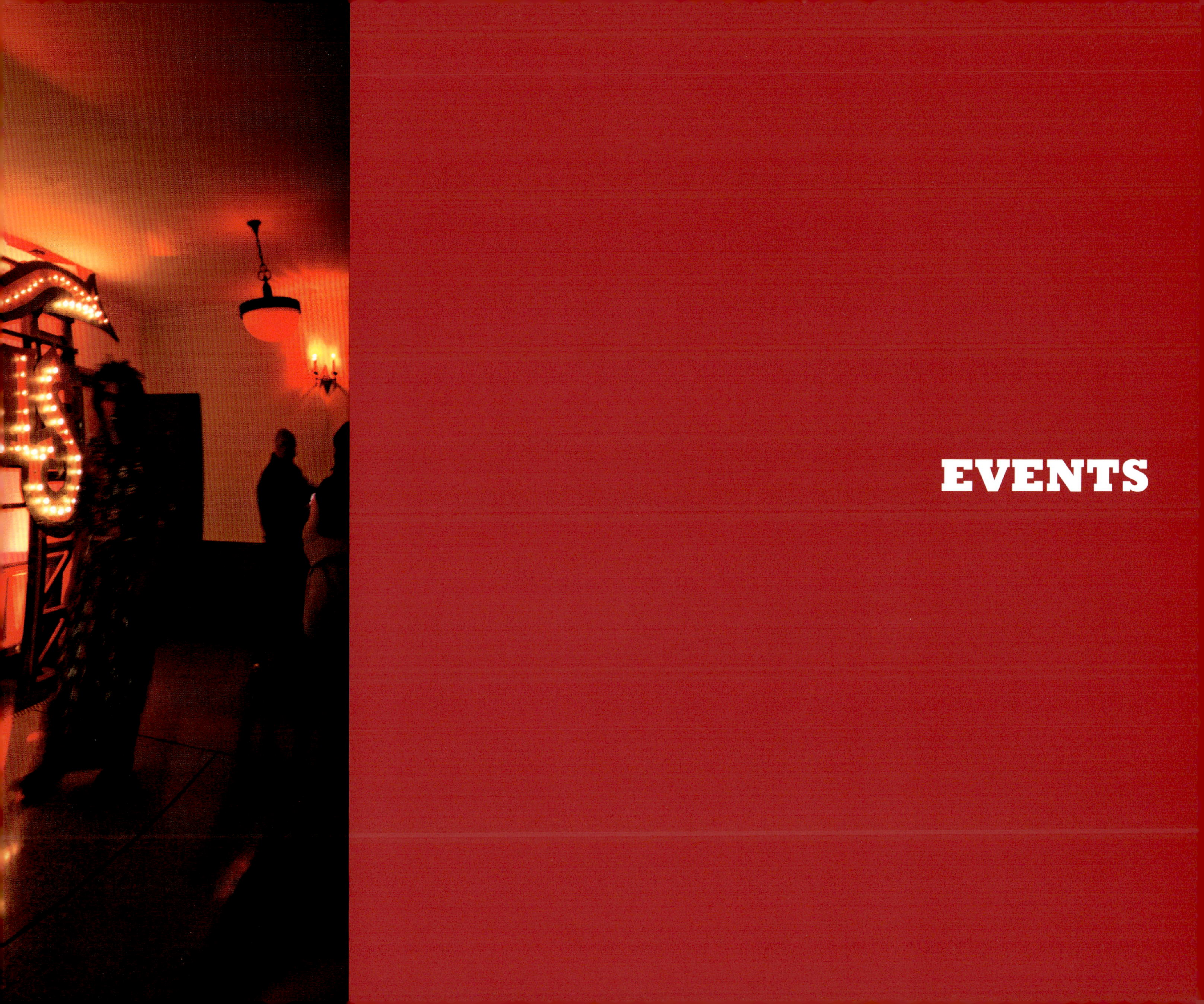

EVENTS

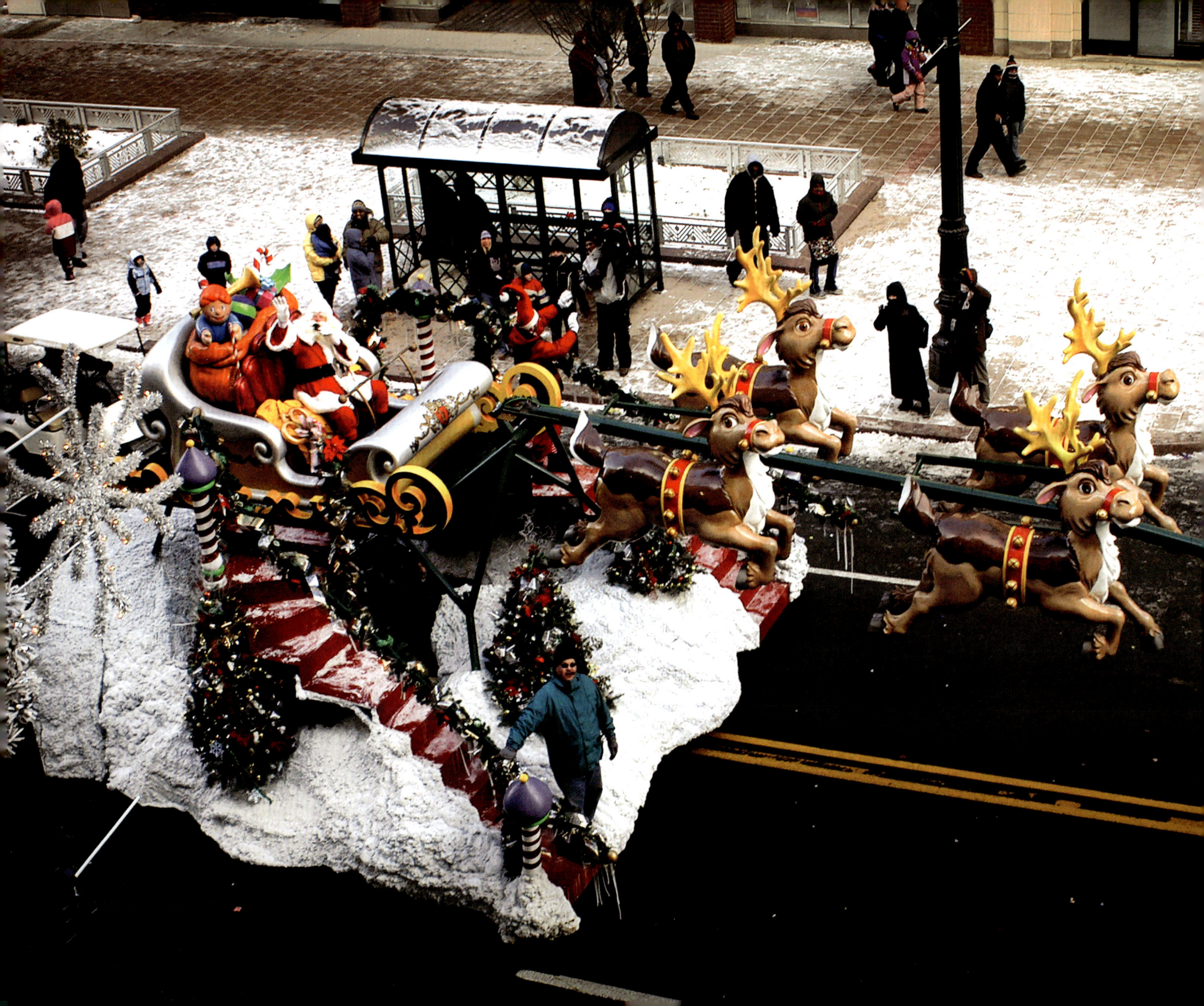

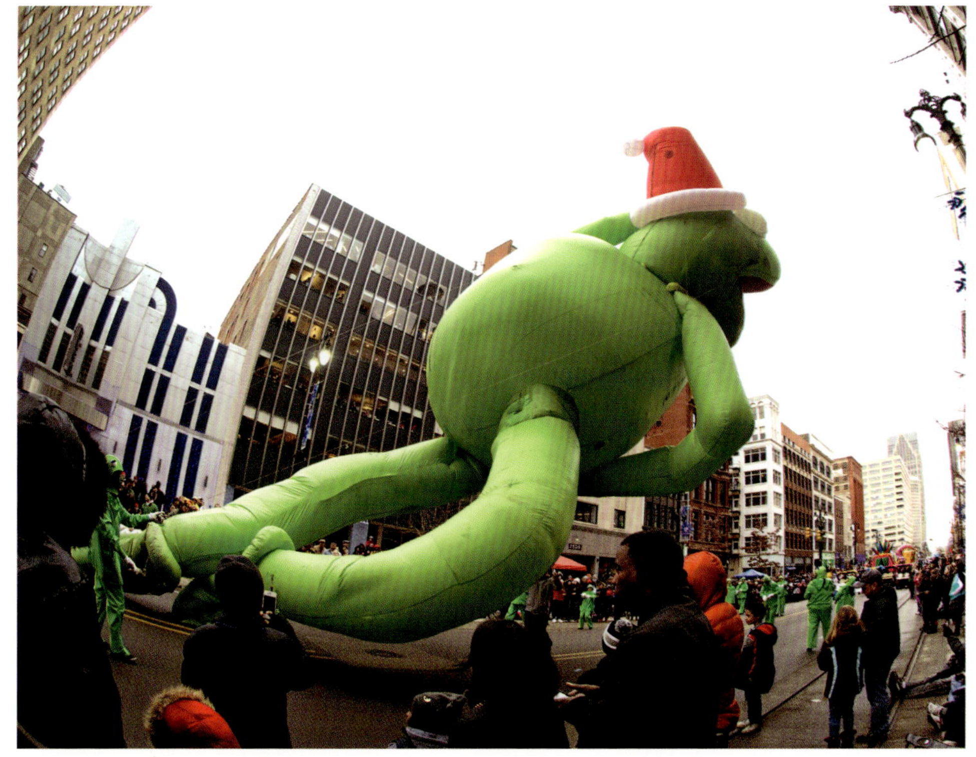

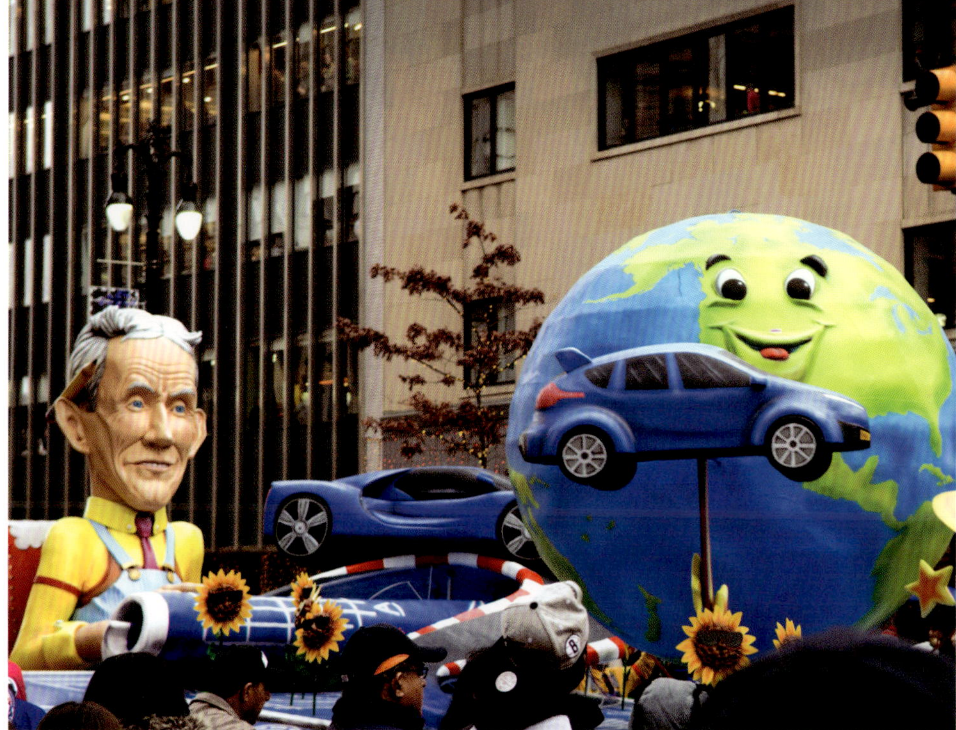

AMERICA'S THANKSGIVING PARADE

Woodward Ave., Detroit, 48226
www.theparade.org

The oldest Thanksgiving Day parade in the United States, sharing the title with Macy's, began in 1924. The parade has marched down Woodward Ave. ever since, delighting children and their parents, ushering in the arrival of Santa Claus. Floats, balloons, and marching bands entertain more than one million parade goers each year. Unique to Detroit, and hometown favorites, are the large papier-mâché heads of celebrities created in Viareggio, Italy. First broadcast on radio in 1931, the parade has been nationally televised since 1959. Since 1982, the Parade Company has produced the parade, sponsored by Art Van, continuing the great tradition.

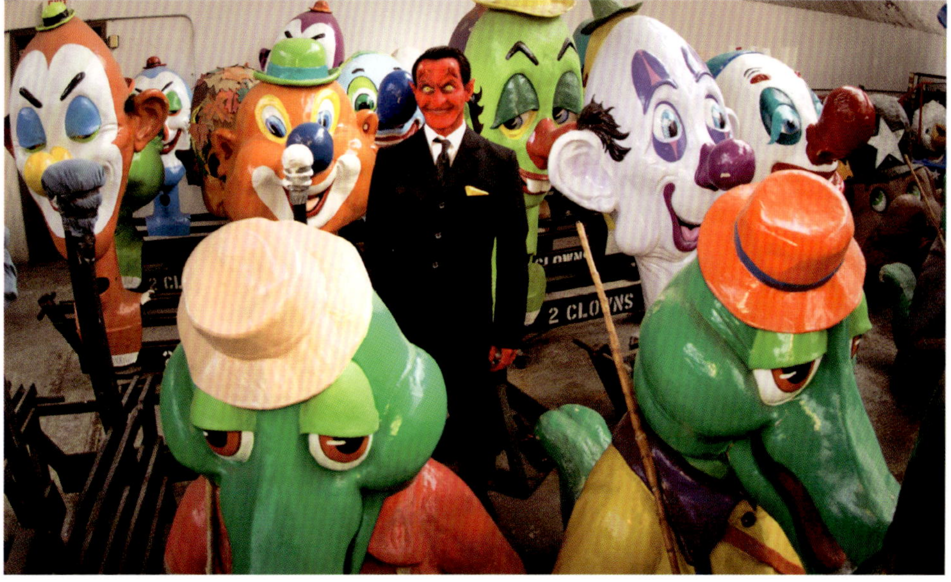

Thanksgiving Day marks another year for two very Detroit traditions. Thousands of families gather in the morning, anticipating the arrival of Santa in the nation's oldest Thanksgiving parade, and every year I wait in guarded anticipation that one of the famed Detroit celebrity heads will be a representation of me. After the parade, I walk down to Ford Field to watch the Detroit Lions host their annual Thanksgiving Day football game, a tradition that began with their first season in 1934. - NR

BLESSING OF THE LOWRIDERS

St. Anne Church, 1000 St. Anne St., Detroit, 48216

Since the late 1990s, a group of Southwest Detroiters have gathered together on a Sunday after the Cinco de Mayo parade to have a Catholic priest bless their lowrider cars. In 1997, Victor Villalobos joined a local club called the Royalty Car and Bicycle Club. Made up of young Latinos interested in bikes and lowrider cars, the group was stereotyped as a gang by the neighborhood. Misunderstood and feared within their own community, the group, persuaded by Victor, sought out a Catholic priest from St. Anne's Church, who blessed the first collection of bikes after mass. As the congregation became familiar with the club members, the fears and stereotypes disappeared. The Blessing of the Lowriders is hosted at a different location each year in Southwest Detroit, accompanied by music, break dancers, and car aficionados. It has come to symbolize the start of the lowrider season.

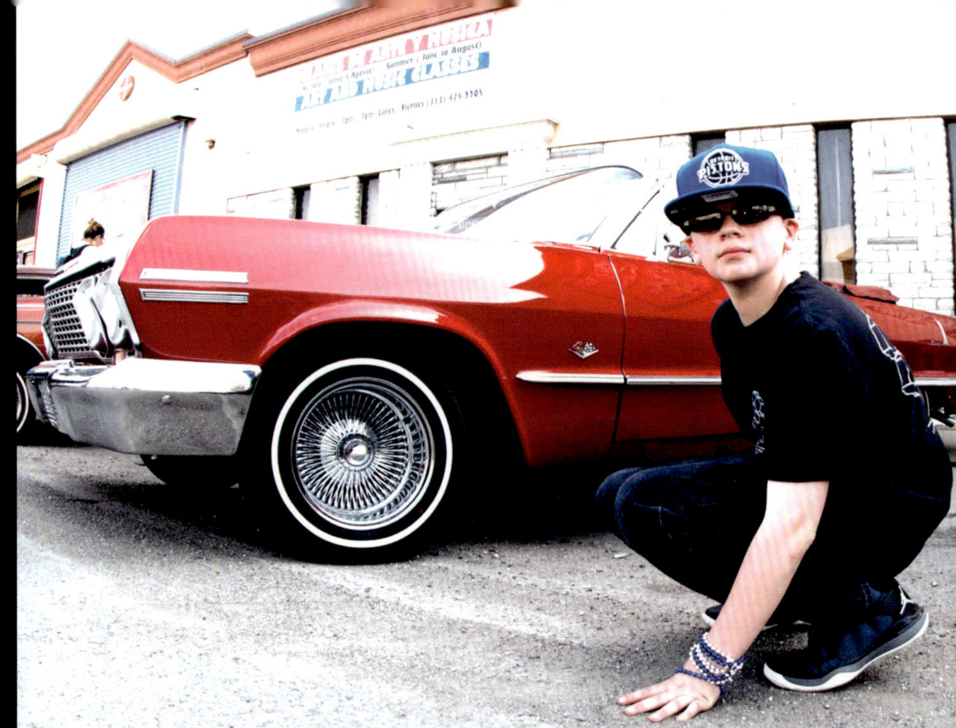

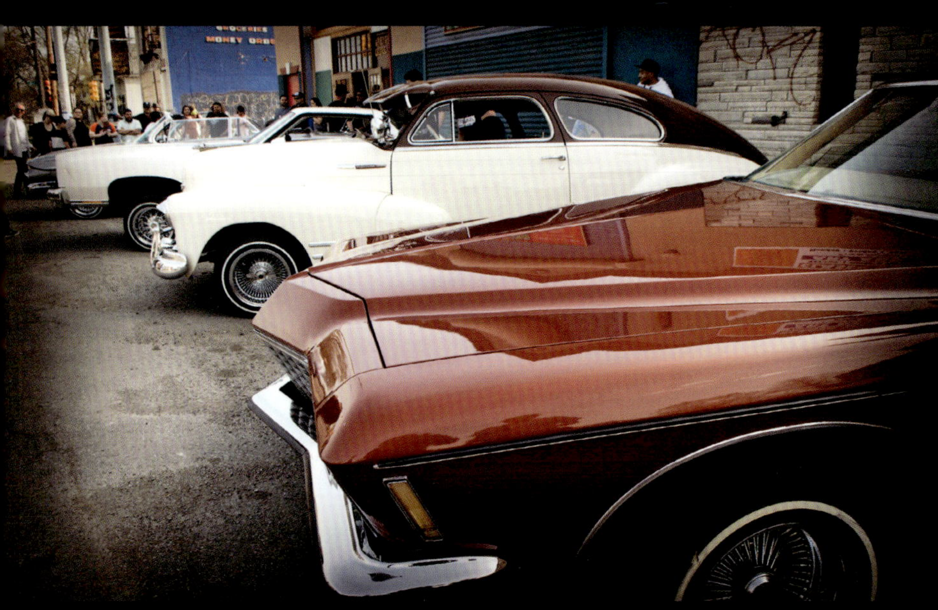

Cinco de Mayo in Southwest Detroit is a day-long party. One event I never want to miss is the Blessing of the Lowriders. Low key and off the radar, members of the local car clubs gather at rotating locations, showing off their personalized hot rods and seeking blessings from a Catholic priest. - NR

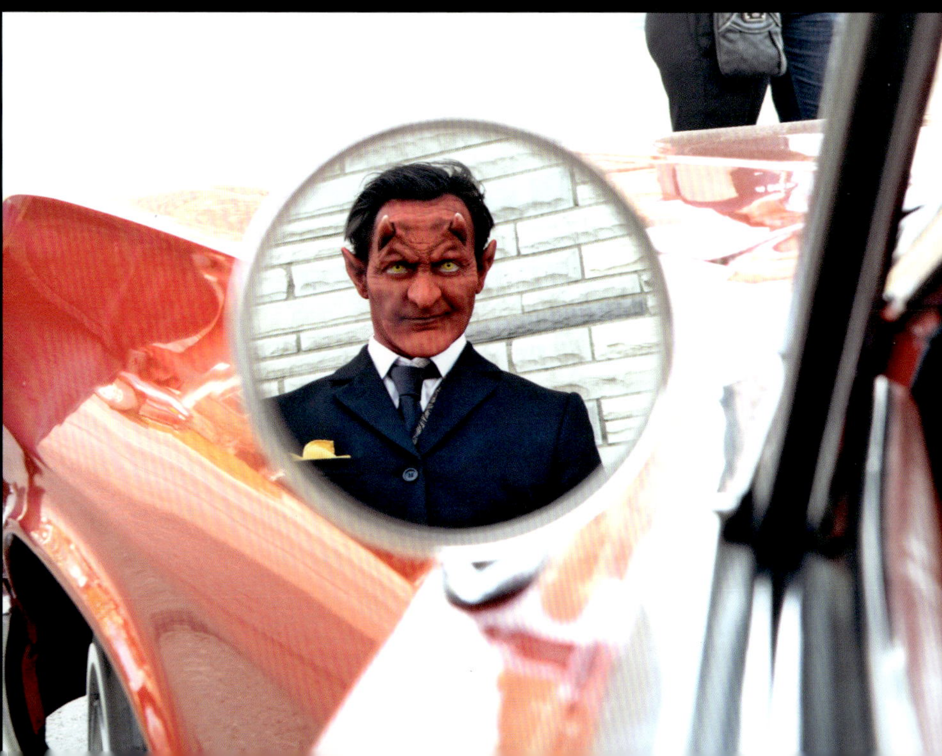

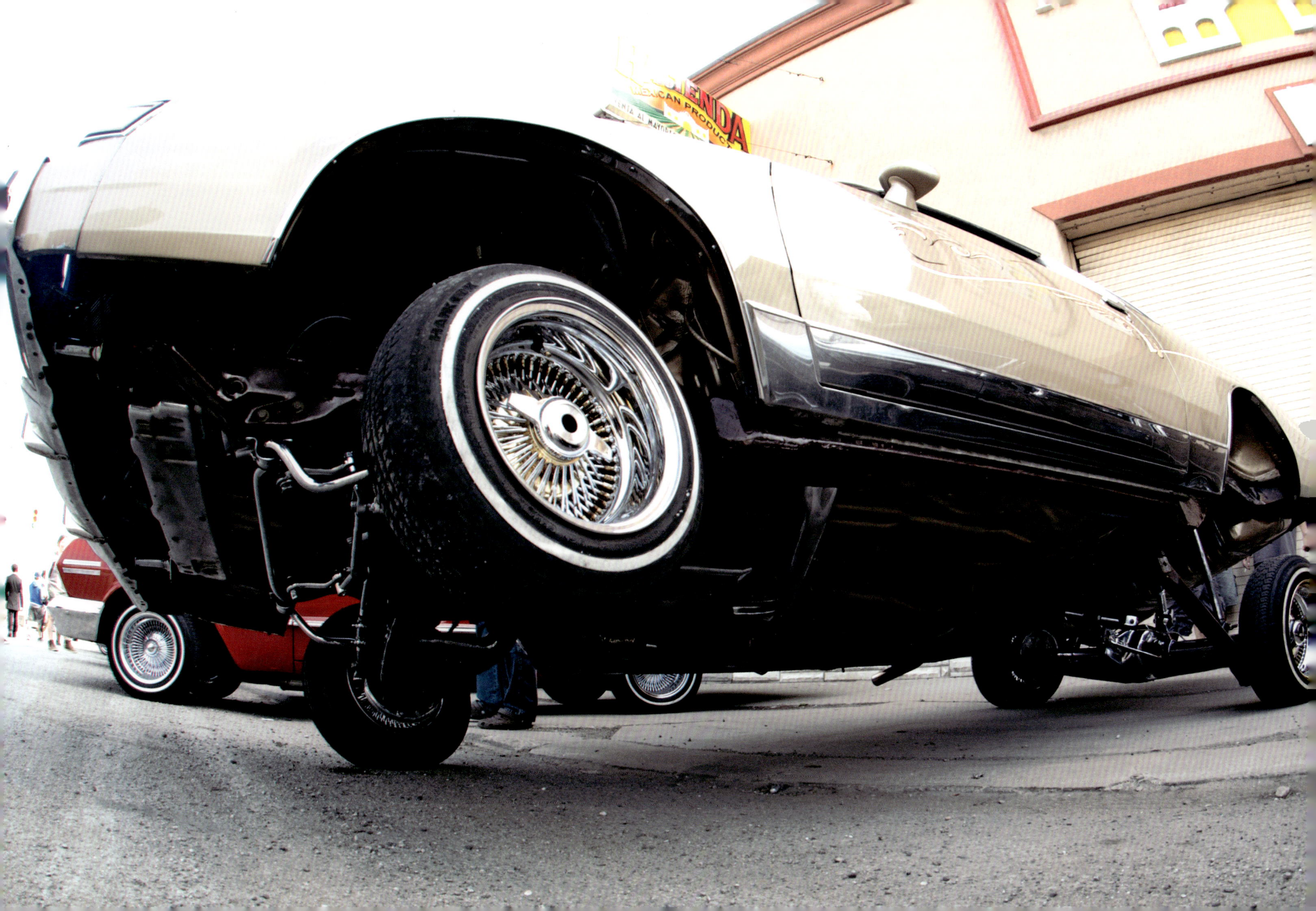

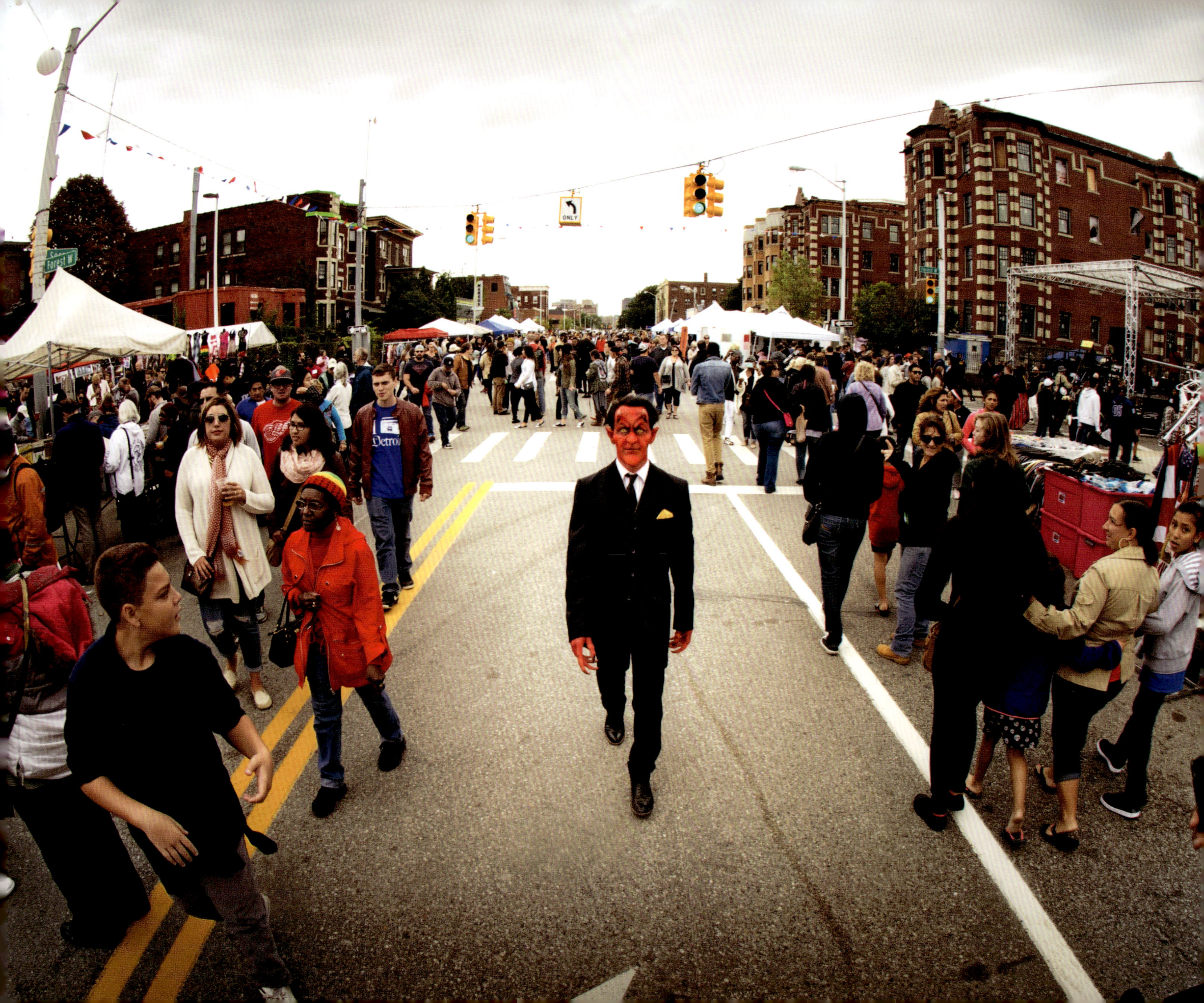
Forest W
ONLY

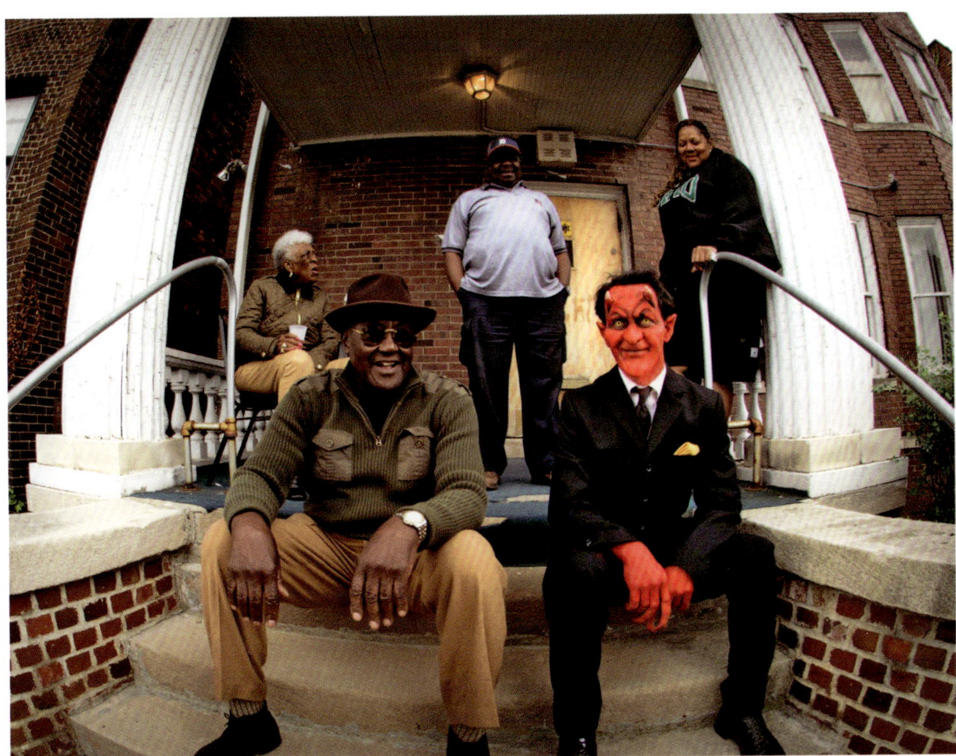

DALLY IN THE ALLEY

Forest Ave. Alley, Detroit, 48202
www.dallyinthealley.com

The largest community festival in Detroit is held annually on the Saturday after Labor Day. In the shadow of Wayne State University, the Cass Corridor has always been Detroit's alternative neighborhood. With cheap rent and its proximity to WSU, artists and musicians imprinted the area with an inspirational and rebellious attitude. The heyday came during the 1960s and 70s as notable contributors included the MC5 and John Sinclair, Cass Corridor artists, *Creem* magazine, and the *Fifth Estate* newspaper. The alley between Second and Third Streets and Hancock and Forest has been home to the "Dally" since it began in 1977. Conceived originally as a neighborhood party, it evolved over the years. As its popularity has grown, so has its footprint, which has expanded into nearby streets. Local bands play on four stages while artists and vendors sell their wares in booths lining the streets.

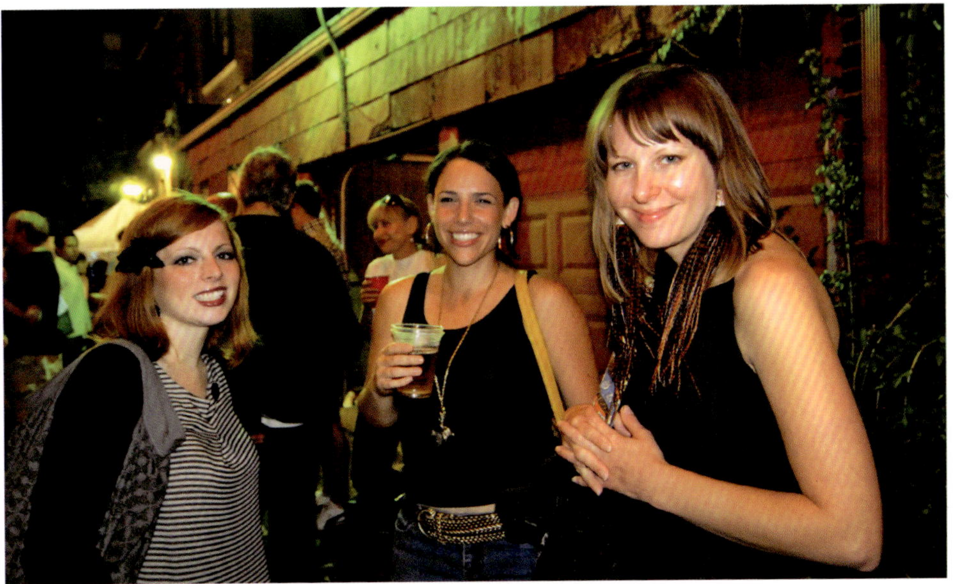

This is what Detroit is all about. Gather a bunch of nonconformists, musicians, and artists, find a neighborhood alley, and toss in a few kegs of beer. The result: the greatest street party ever. - NR

DETROIT GRAND PRIX

Belle Isle, Detroit, 48207
www.detroitgp.com

As the Motor City and the Automobile Capital of the World, Detroit would be expected to host an auto race. The Detroit Belle Isle Grand Prix is just the latest chapter in open-wheeled racing. From the 1920s to the 50s, AAA held the Detroit 100 at the State Fairgrounds. During the 1980s, a Formula One World Championship race weaved its way through the streets of downtown. CART replaced the international race and after three years moved to Belle Isle until 2001. Famed Indy driver and owner Roger Penske revived the IndyCar Series in 2006 and since 2012, Detroit is the only city to award points on both racing days.

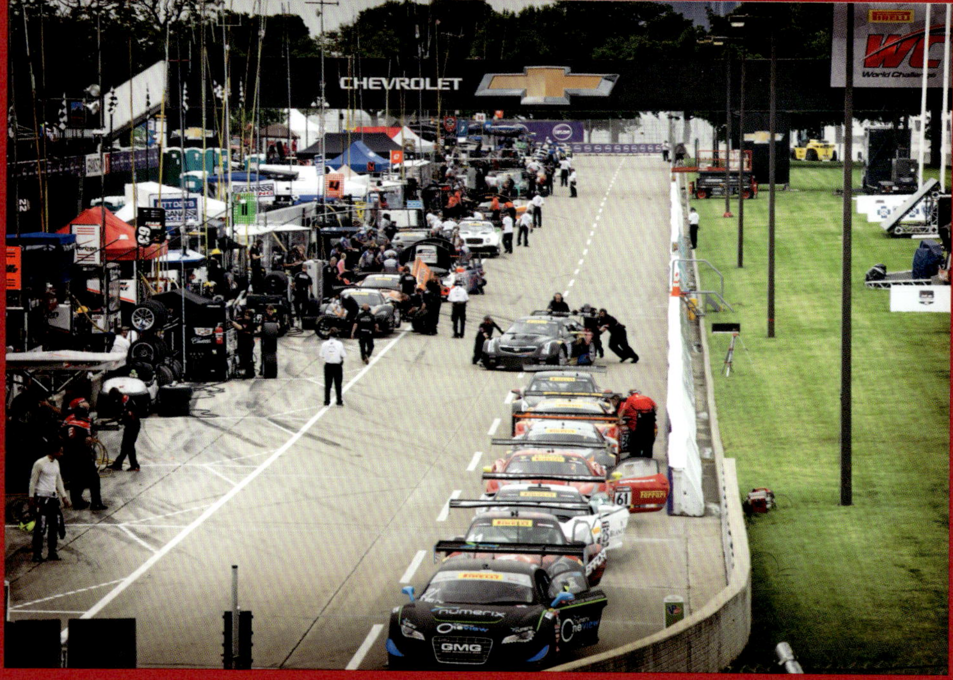

If you could describe Detroit's passion in two words, what would they be? If you asked me, I'd say "fast cars." Henry Ford's famous "Red Devil," named after you know who, set a land speed record in 1904, and ever since we have been building, racing, and enjoying faster and faster cars. - NR

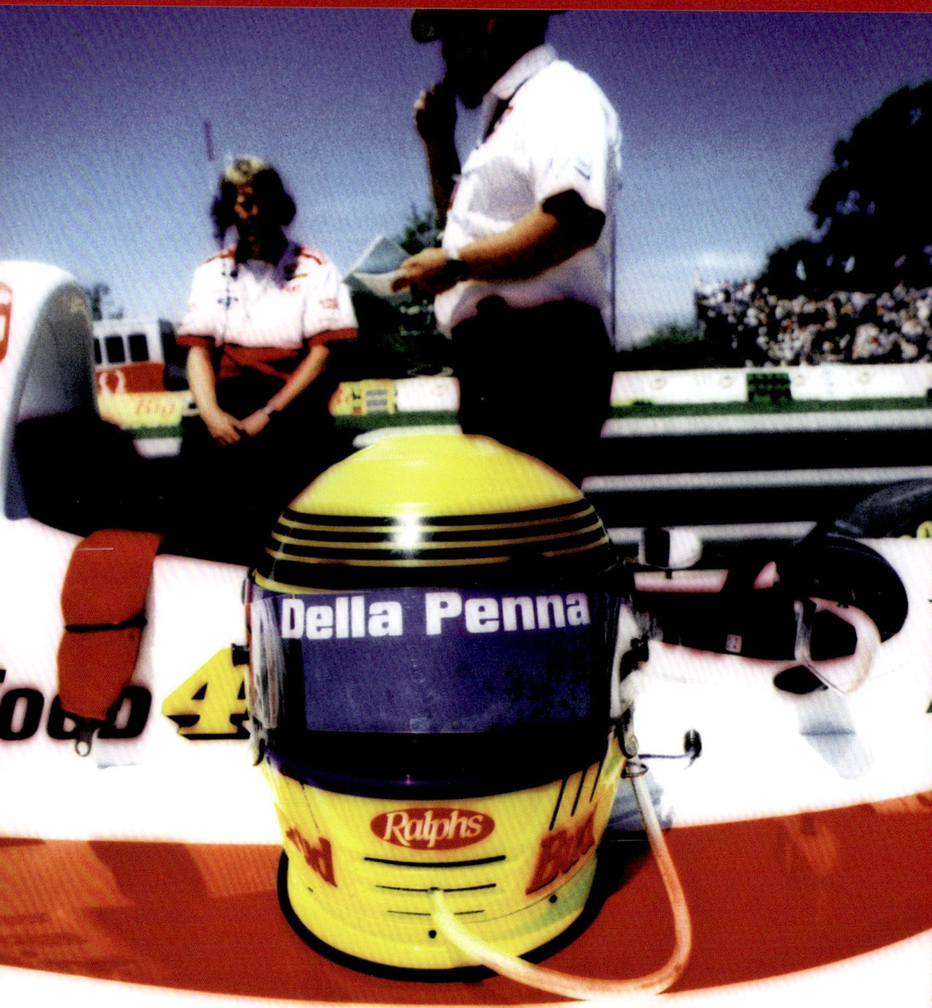

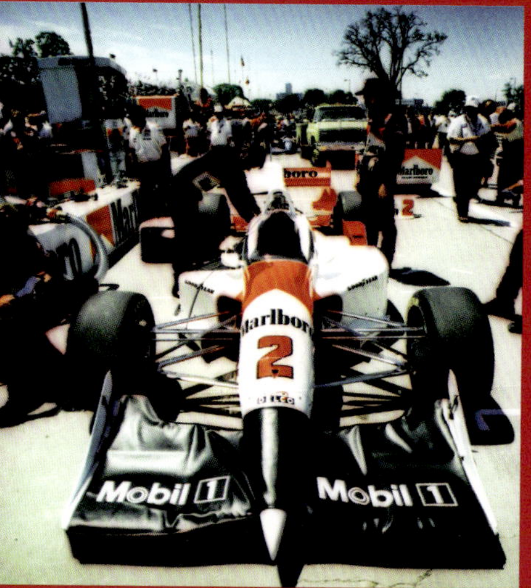

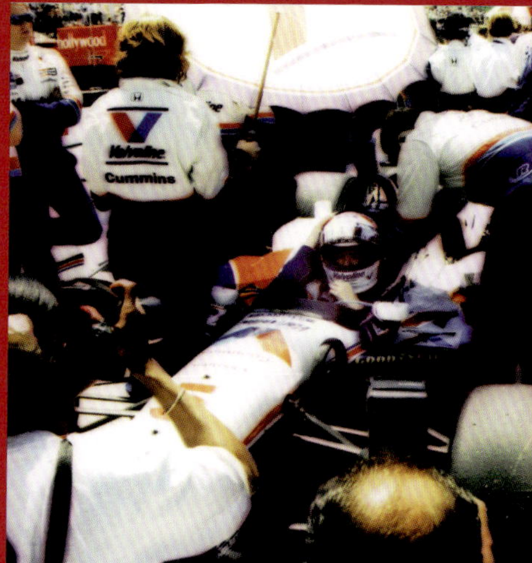

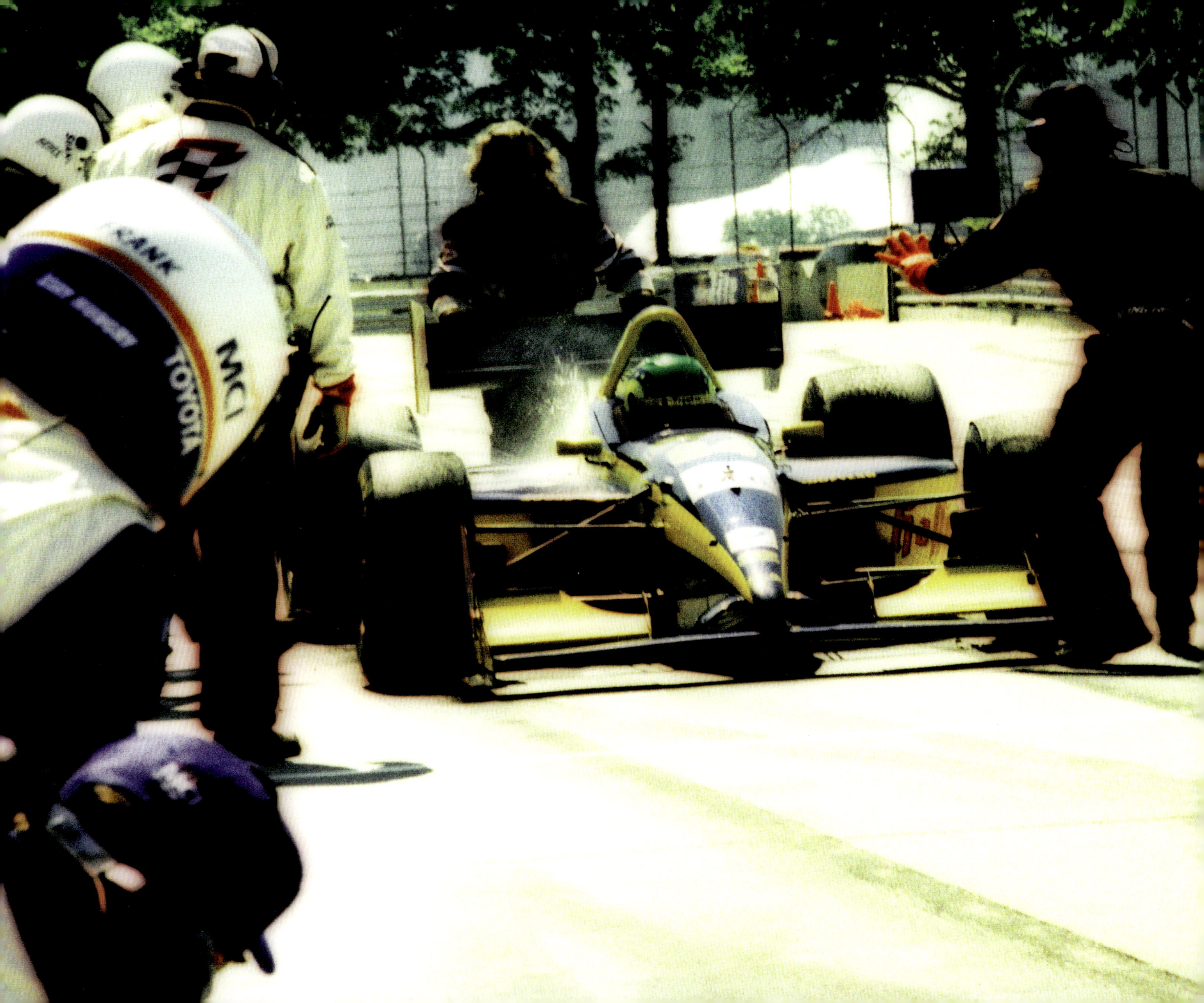
MCI
TOYOTA

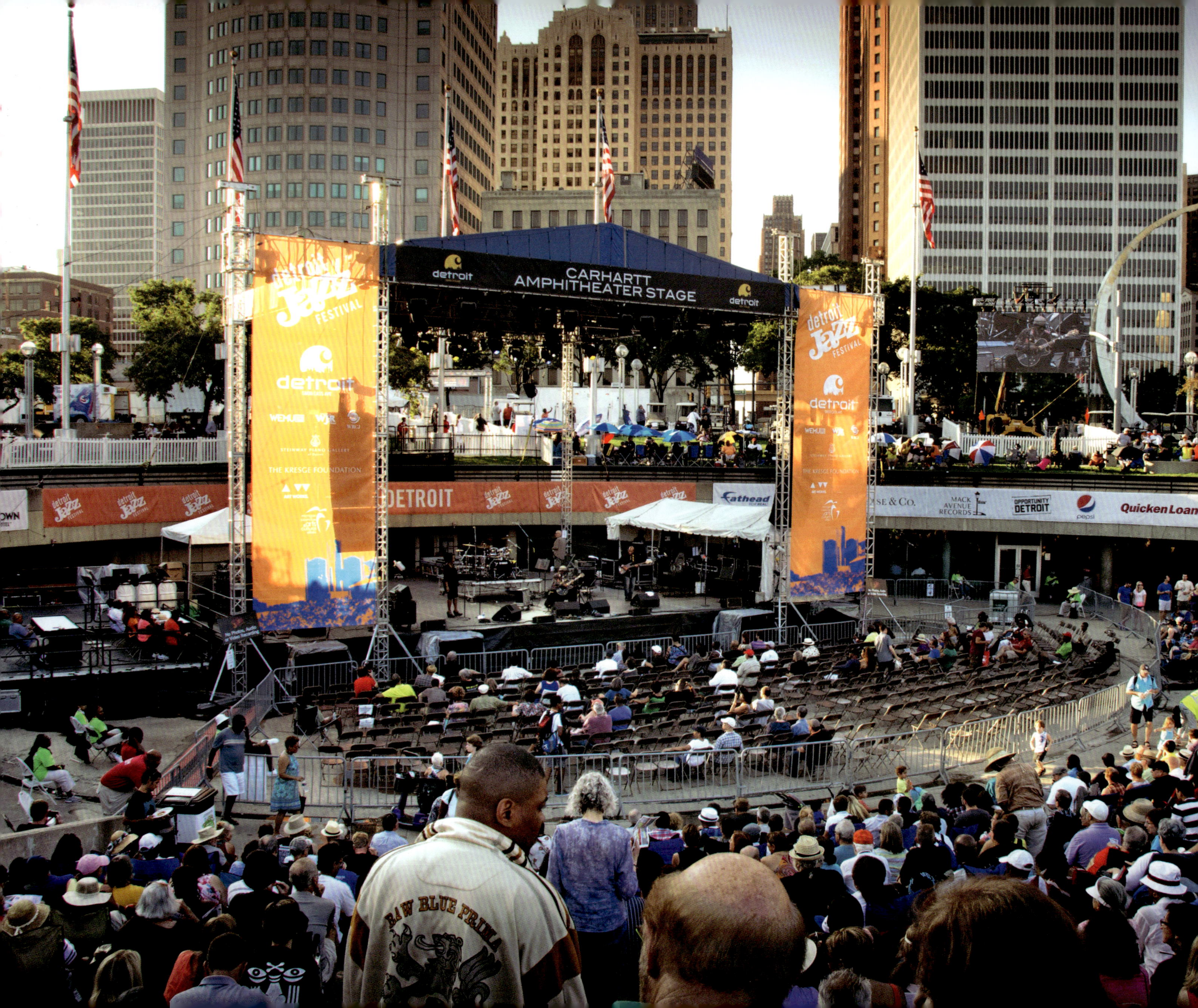

CARHARTT
AMPHITHEATER STAGE
detroit
detroit Jazz FESTIVAL
THE KRESGE FOUNDATION
DETROIT
Fathead
MACK AVENUE RECORDS
OPPORTUNITY DETROIT
pepsi
Quicken Loans

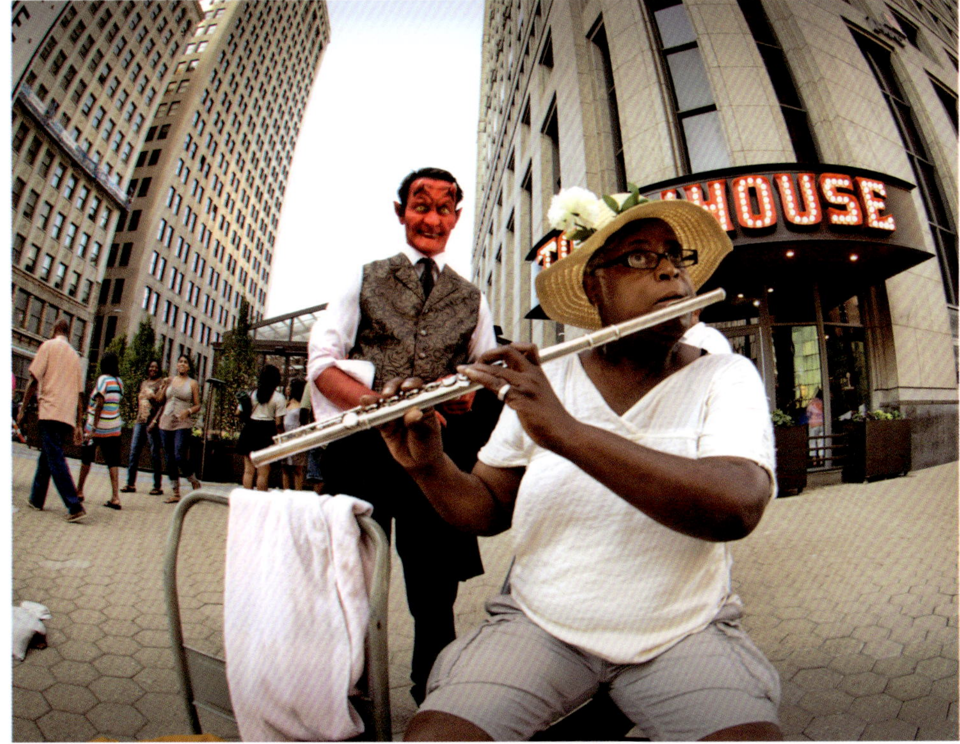

DETROIT JAZZ FESTIVAL

Hart Plaza and Campus Martius, Detroit, 48226
www.detroitjazzfest.com

One of the premier jazz festivals in the world is held every Labor Day weekend in downtown Detroit. Founded in 1980 in partnership with the prestigious Montreux International Jazz Festival, the Montreux-Detroit Jazz Festival, as it was known for its first 11 years, quickly earned a world-class reputation. Through the recent support of Mack Avenue Records and Gretchen Valade, the Detroit Jazz Fest, the world's largest free jazz festival, has expanded its lineup, offering multiple stages and more then 100 acts.

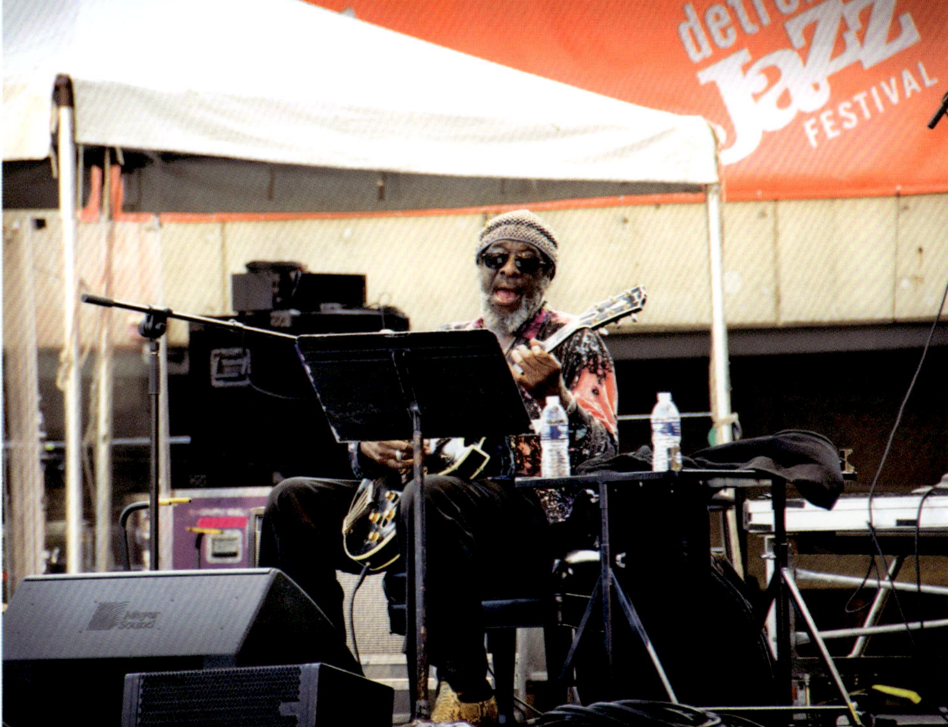

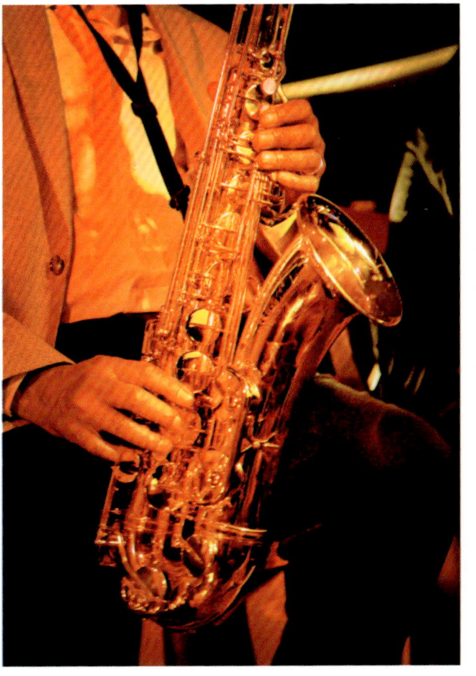

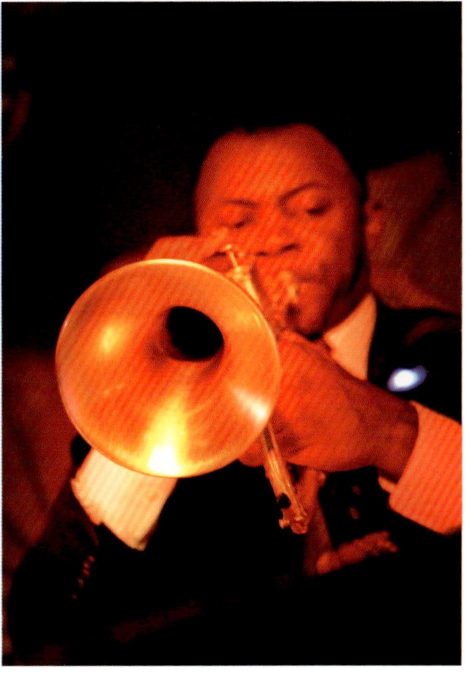

No surprise here. Of course Detroit would host a world-class jazz festival. Our musical heritage knows no bounds. Building on that legacy during the Jazz Age, Paradise Valley and Black Bottom speakeasies became lively venues for the new sound. With their discerning musical tastes, Detroit audiences embraced the jazz sound while an endless list of local musicians achieved international recognition. - NR

DIRTY SHOW

Russell Industrial Center, 1600 Clay St., Detroit, 48211
www.dirtydetroit.com

Brainchild of demented artist and general miscreant Jerry Vile, the Dirty Show has exhibited salacious and scatological art since 1999. Accompanied by former staffers and friends of defunct *Orbit Magazine*, Vile built an art empire on the temptation, fascination, and exploitation of sex. Paintings, photographs, and sculptures illustrate and interpret all varieties of sexual behavior. Recurring every Valentine's Day, the annual show includes striptease artists, cage dancers and burlesque performances. Most consider audience participation mandatory for the event and wear outfits as racy as the art on the walls.

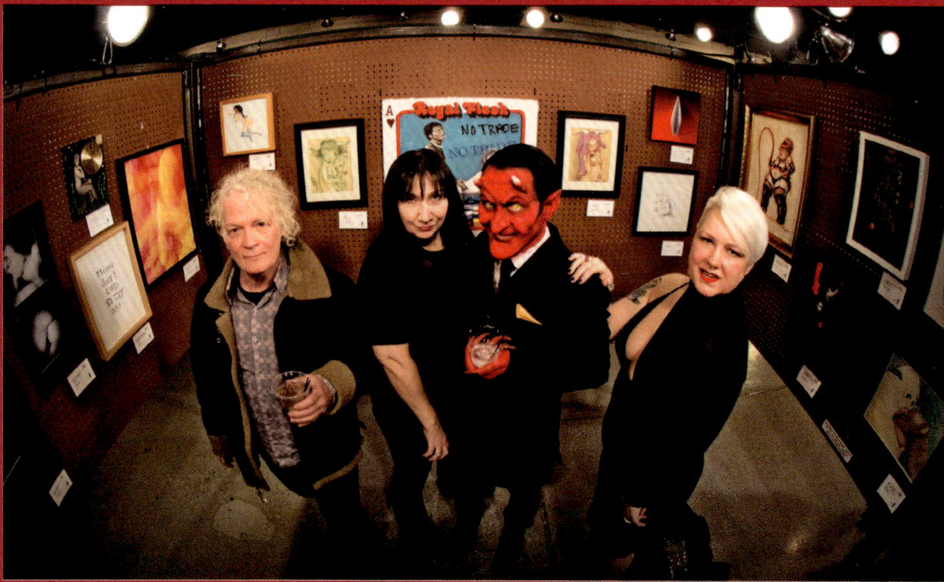

There are some things that are acceptable, there are some things that are considered regionally popular, and then there are things that can only happen in Detroit. Although the Dirty Show was conceived by Detroit's greatest huckster and showman, Jerry Vile, it is the demented and perverse masses who call Detroit home who have made it such a success. I am impressed that after almost twenty years, Jerry continues to exhibit new and original depictions of genitalia. - NR

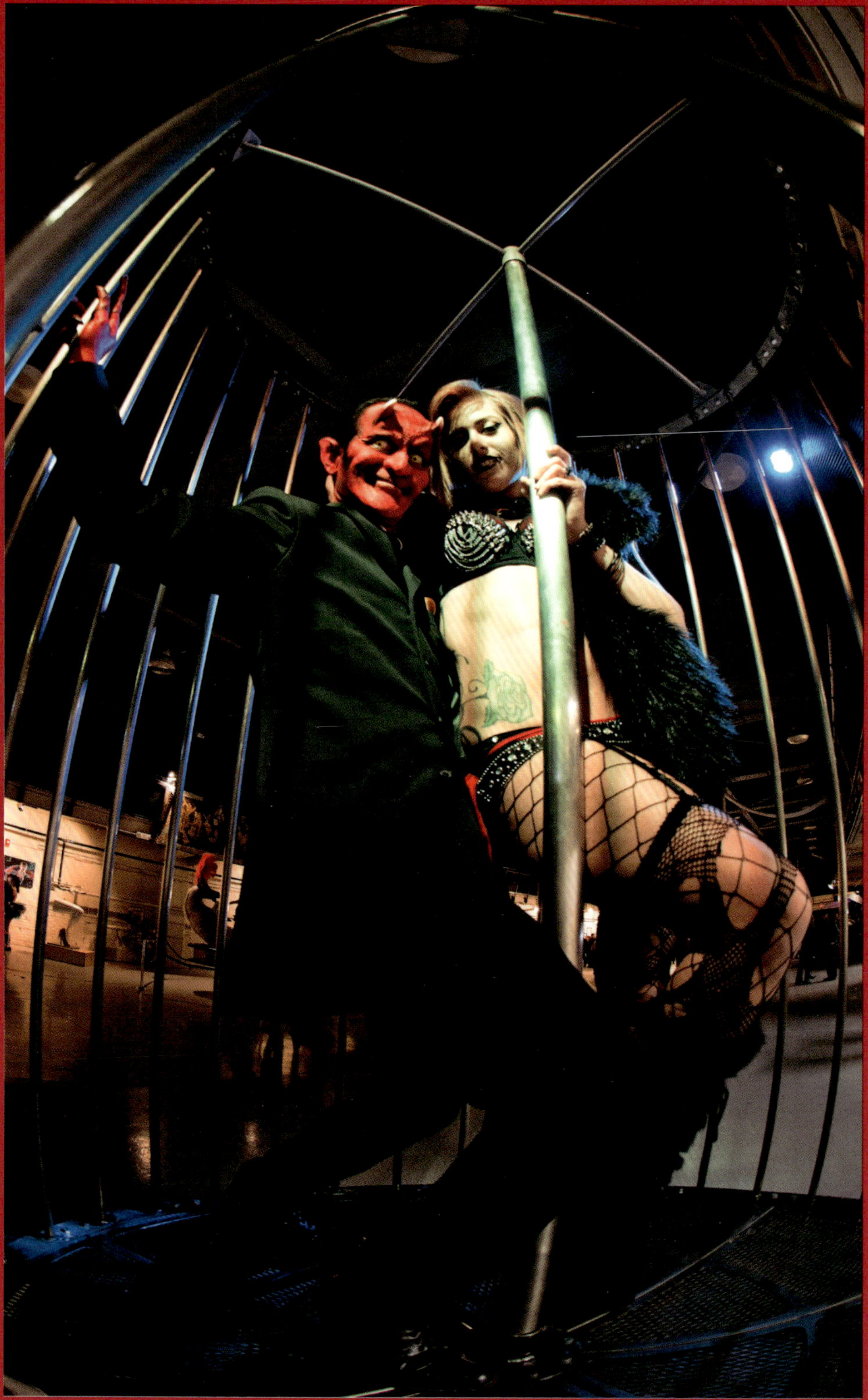

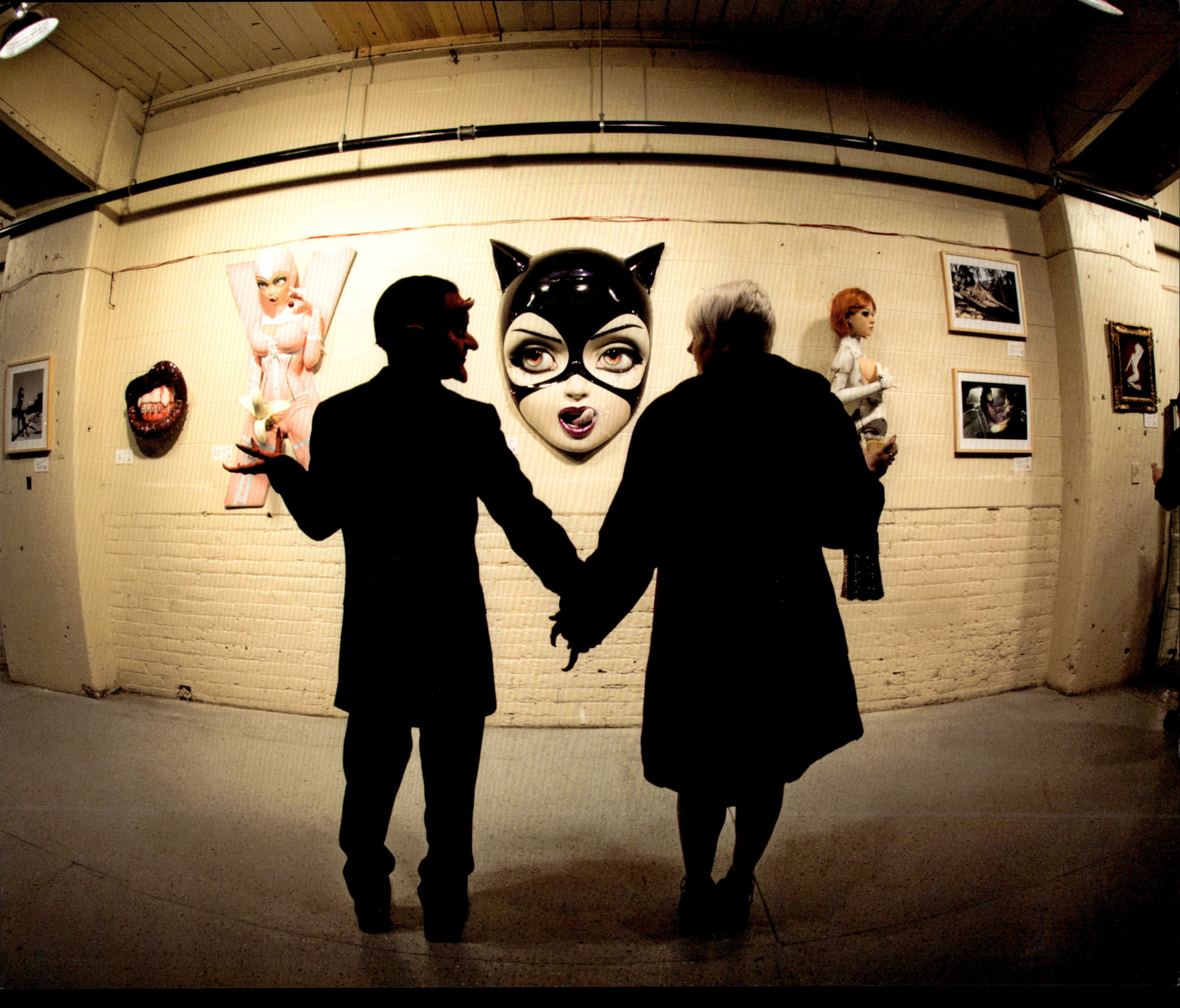

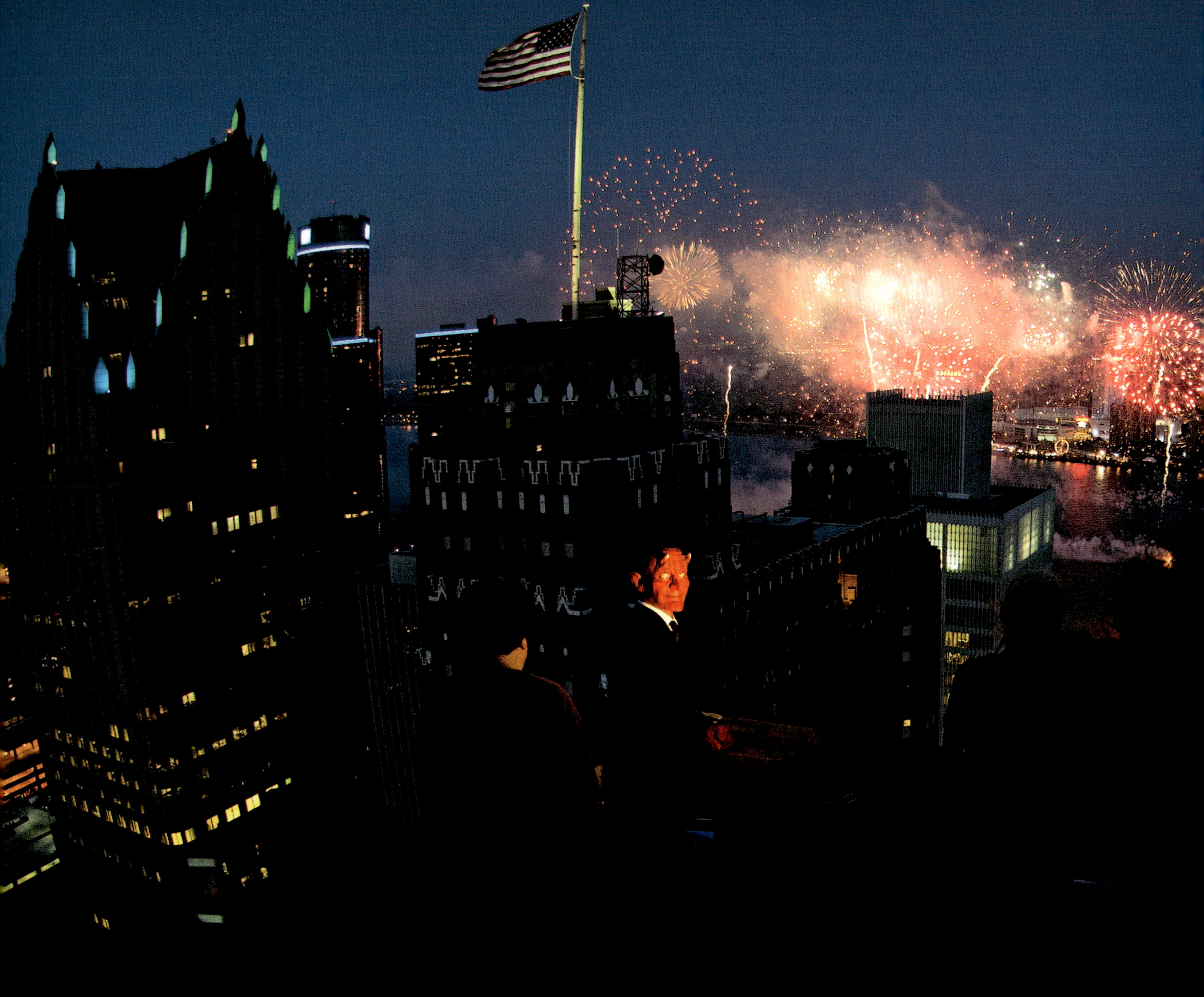

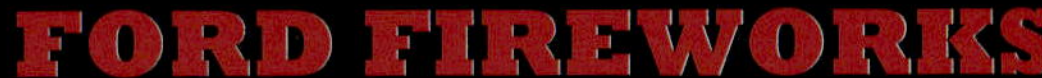

FORD FIREWORKS

Detroit River, Detroit, 48226
www.theparade.org

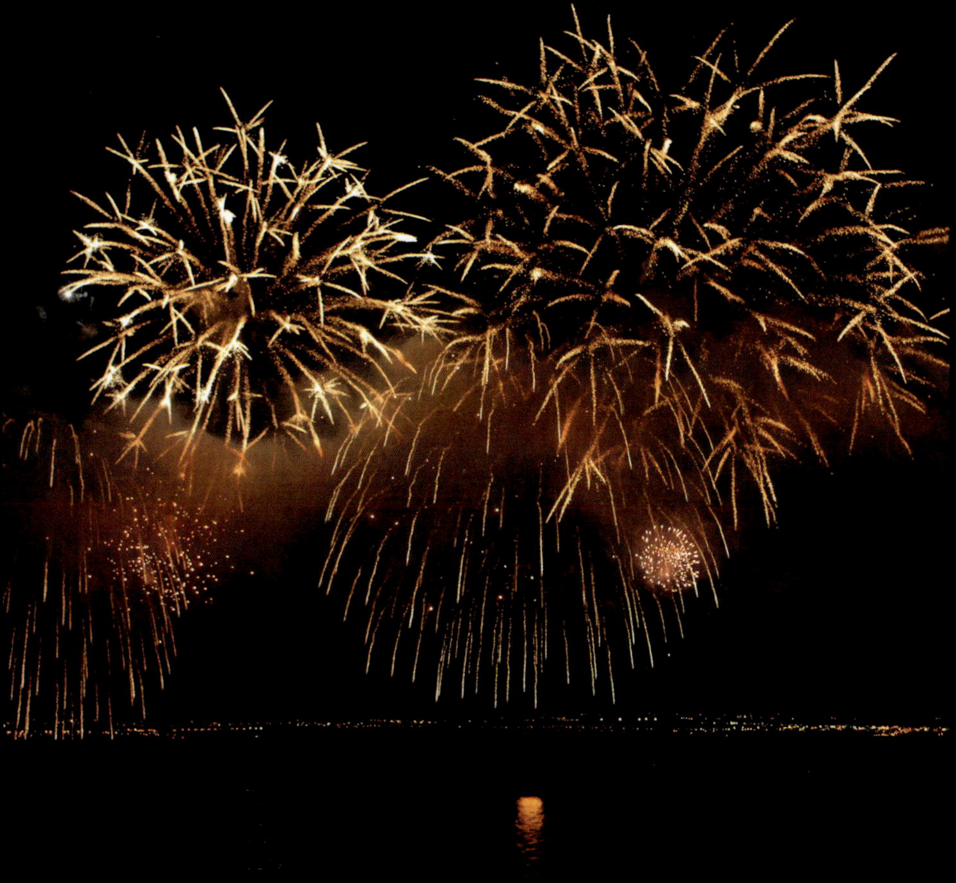

Usually held the last Monday of June, the Ford Fireworks are one of the world's largest fireworks displays. They serve as the highlight of the International Freedom Festival, now known as Summer Fest in Windsor and as River Days in Detroit. A million people, from both countries, line the shores of the Detroit River to watch the annual spectacle. The International Freedom Festival began in 1959, in recognition of the United States' Independence Day, on the Fourth of July, and Canada's Independence Day, on July 1st. Throughout the weeks-long event, entertainment, music, and a carnival offer something for all ages to enjoy.

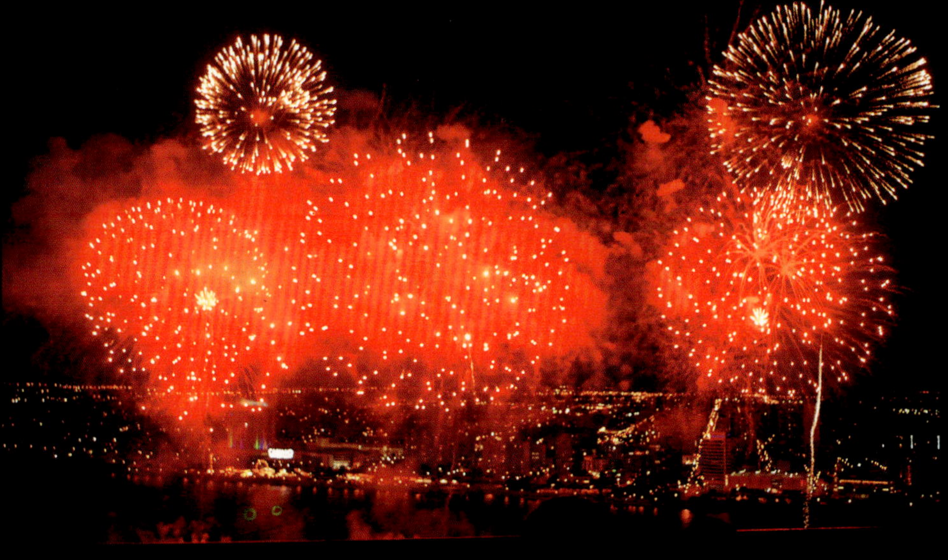

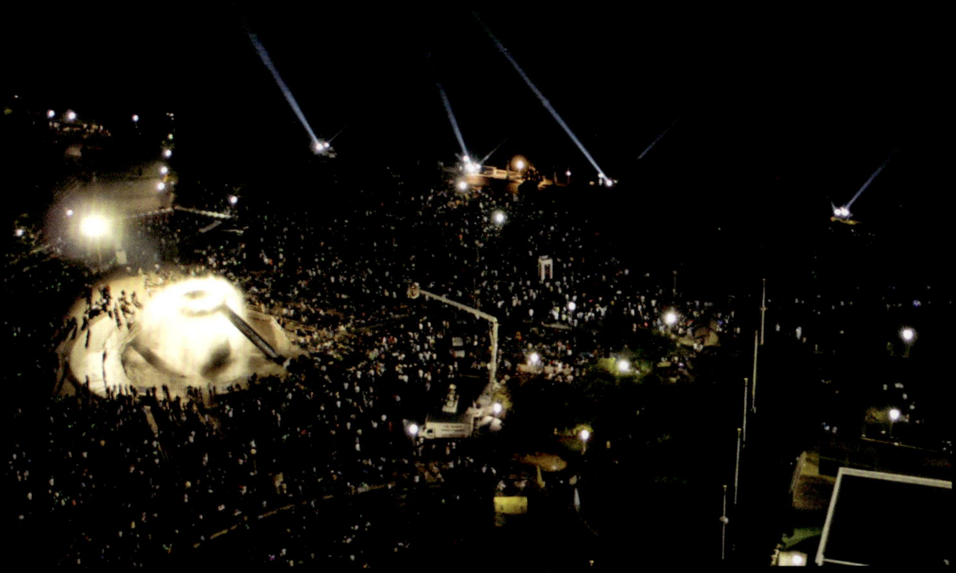

Although I have spent more time on Detroit's side of the river, I consider myself a resident of both shores. I have witnessed the French, the British, Americans, and Canadians fight over territory that was once the Indians' ancestral homeland. It is inspiring to see the United States and Canada, who were formerly adversaries, become close allies. Nowhere is that more visible then the shared celebration of both countries' independence from Britain. - NR

GOLD CUP HYDROPLANE RACES

Detroit River, Belle Isle, Detroit, 48207
www.detroitboatraces.com

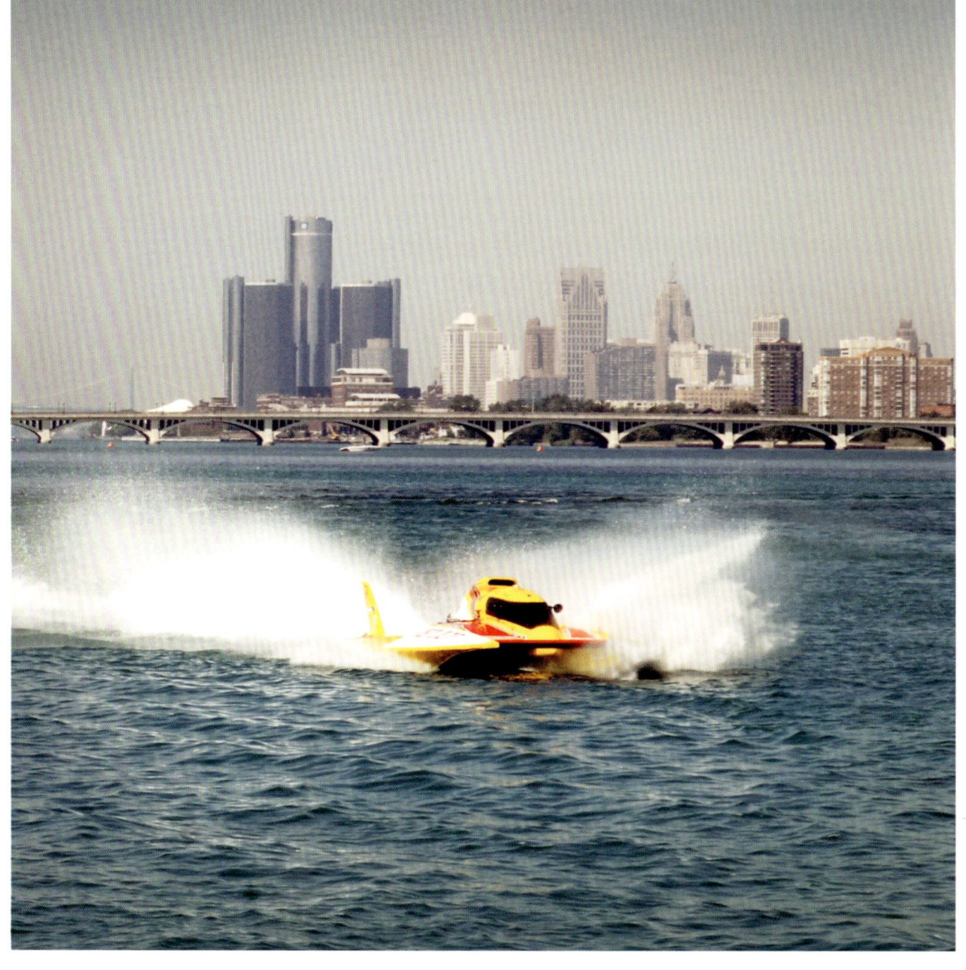

The Gold Cup is the oldest active trophy in motorsports. First awarded in 1904, it rotated between locations until 1990. *Miss Detroit*, designed by Chris Columbus Smith, a Detroiter and founder of Chris Craft, and piloted by Jack Beebe and John "Freckles" Milot, won the first Cup for Detroit in 1915. The next year, Detroit held its first Gold Cup race. During the 1920s, Detroiter Gar Wood was the first to win five Cups in a row and is regarded as one of the greatest hydroplane pilots ever. More Gold Cup races have been held on the Detroit River than any other course as Detroit celebrated its 100th anniversary, in 2016, again as host.

The Motor City is not only about cars; we have been innovators and leaders in boats too. The first outboard motor was designed by Detroiter, Cameron Waterman, in 1905, and famed racing boat company Chris Craft was headquartered just north of Detroit on Lake St. Clair. Our love affair with motors and speed compel us to compete, and our history in hydroplane racing proves we can win.

- NR

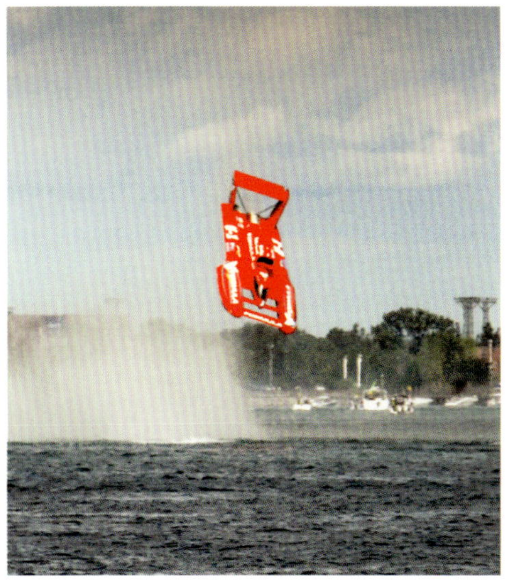

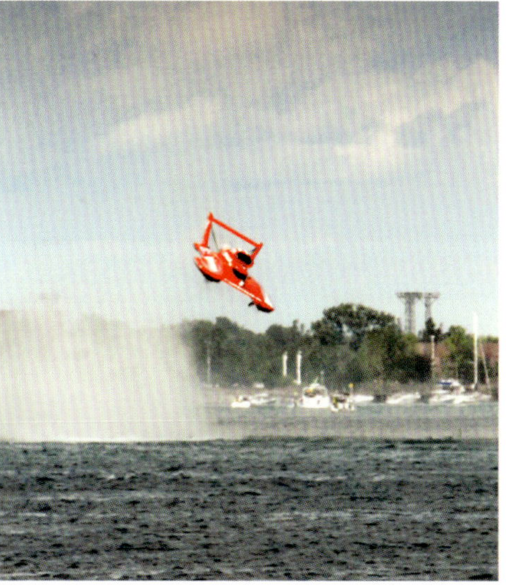

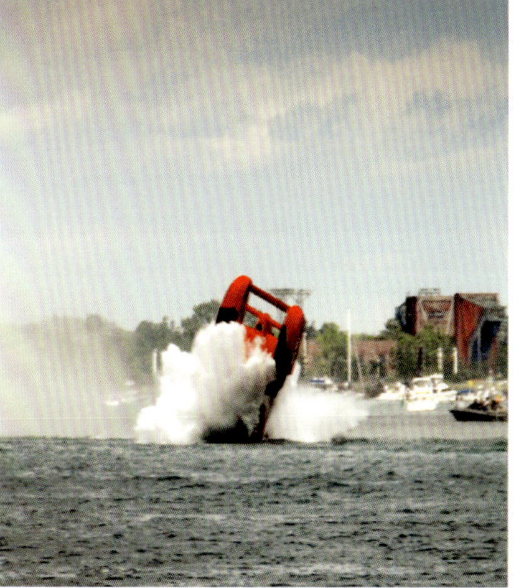

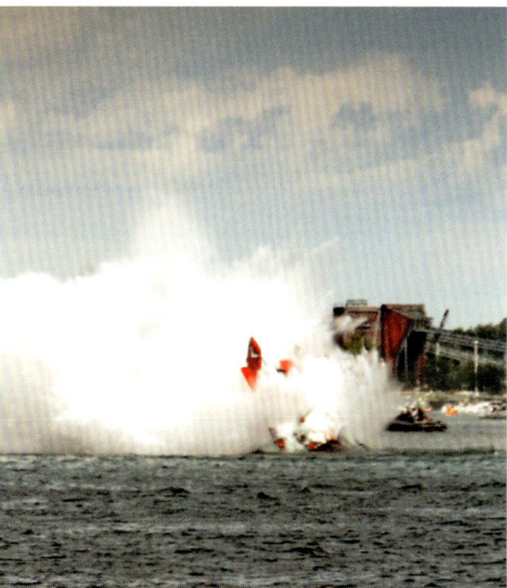

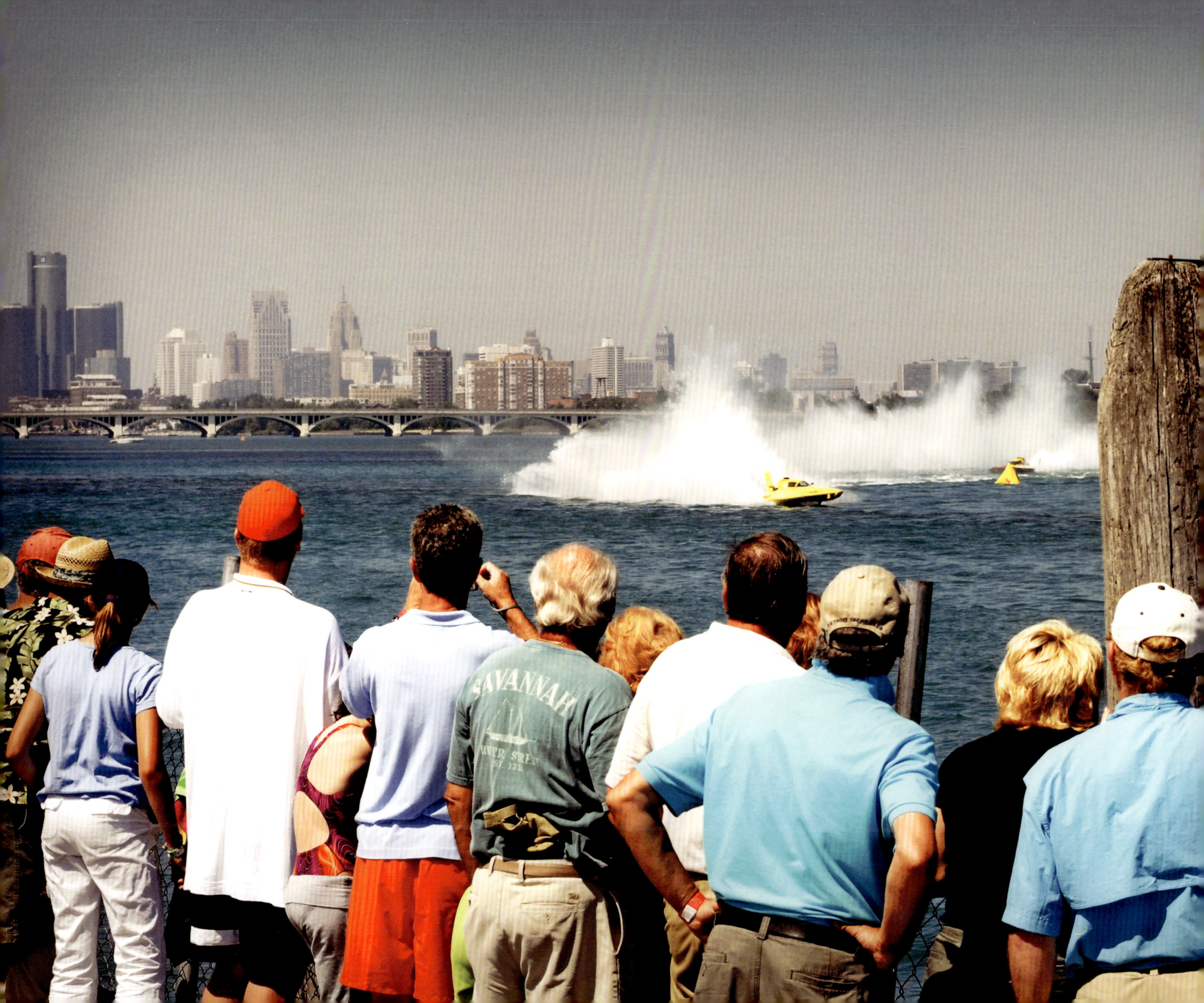
SAVANNAH

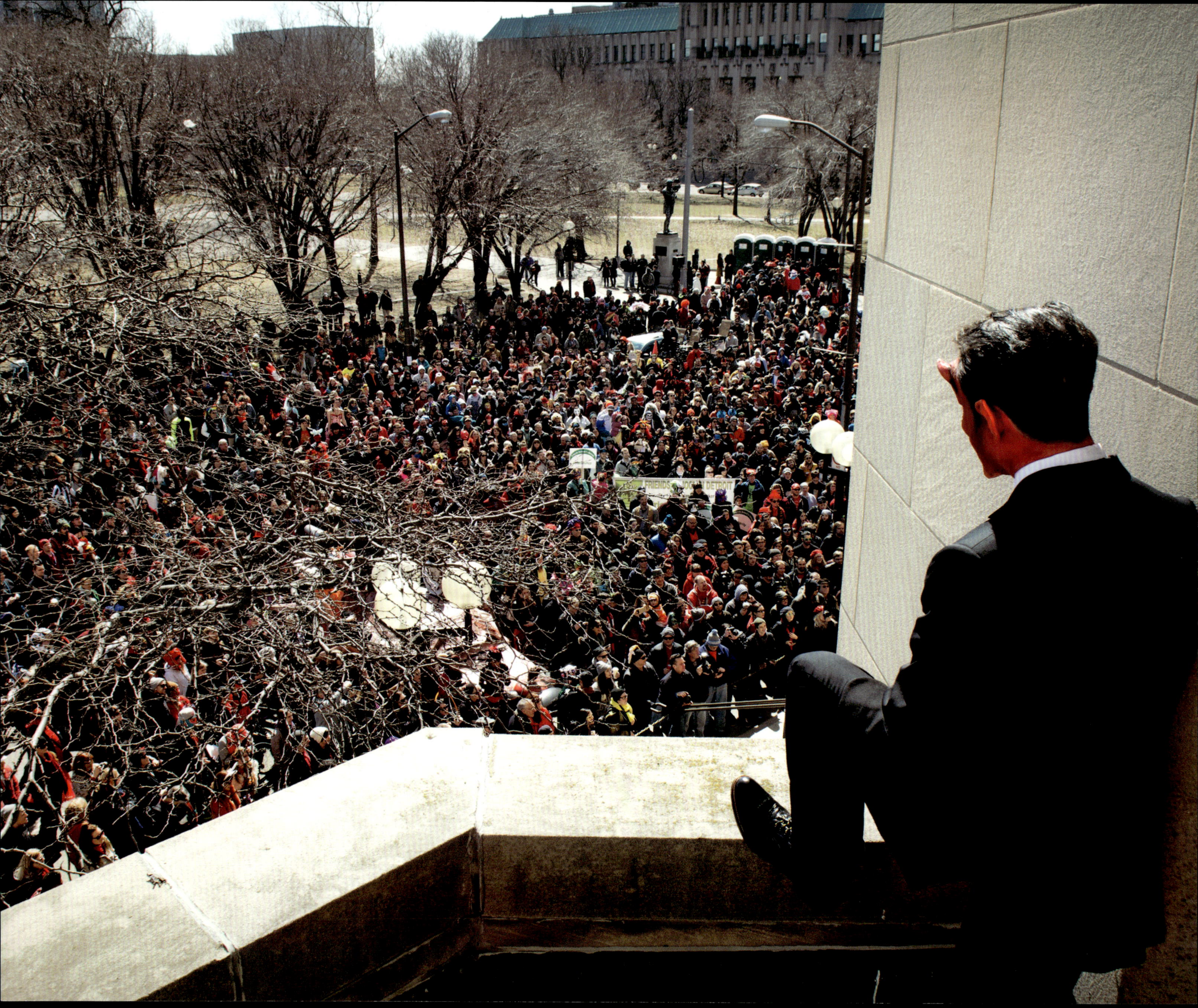
FRIENDS
DETROIT

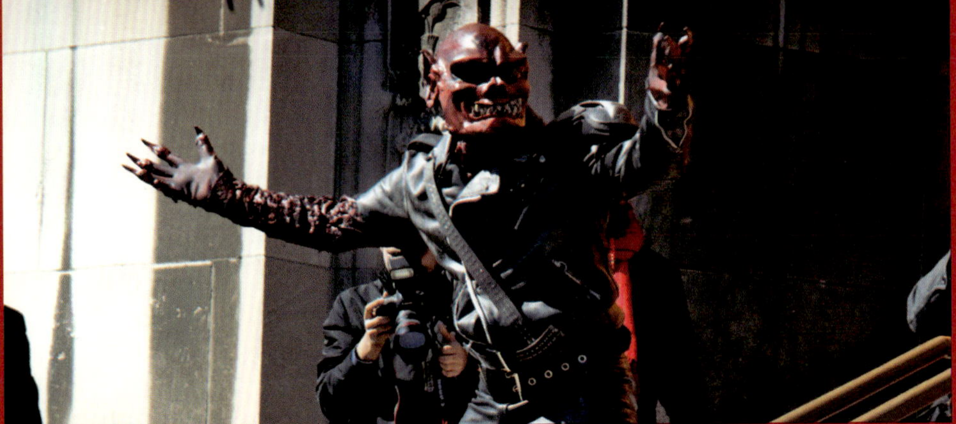

MARCHE DU NAIN ROUGE

Second Ave. and Temple St., Detroit, 48201
www.marchedunainrouge.com

Promoting the mistaken notion that the Nain Rouge is responsible for all that is wrong in Detroit, the Marche du Nain Rouge, a Mardi Gras-inspired parade, has been held every year since 2010 on the Sunday after the Vernal Equinox, with floats and participants dressed in costumes. After arriving on the steps of the famed Masonic Temple in Cass Park, an imposter appears representing the Nain Rouge and exhorts them to leave town or accept his domination of Detroit. Based on 18th century folklore myths about the Nain Rouge, the parade perpetuates the misconception of who the Nain Rouge truly is.

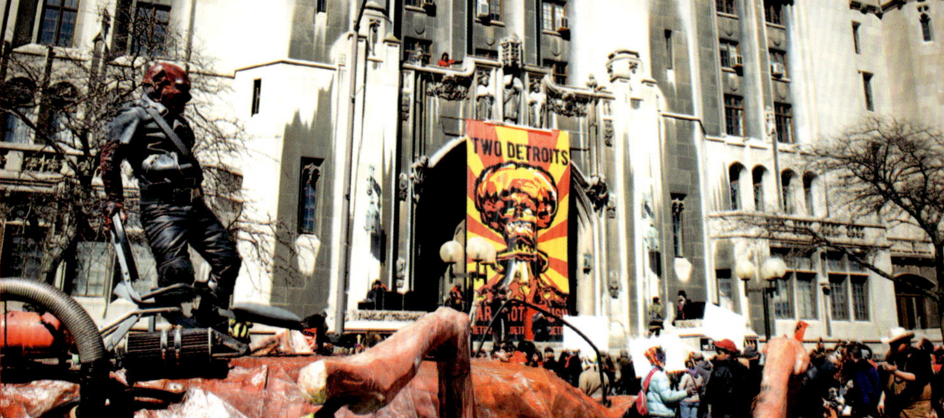

An insult to my character, the Marche du Nain Rouge is actually really fun to watch. All those poor chilly bastards complaining about their problems and blaming me. This has been a constant throughout my life in Detroit. As an outsider who doesn't need to parade his successes in your face, I'm an easy target when things get rough. Understand this: I love this town. I love the people. Only now am I trying to tell my story. - NR

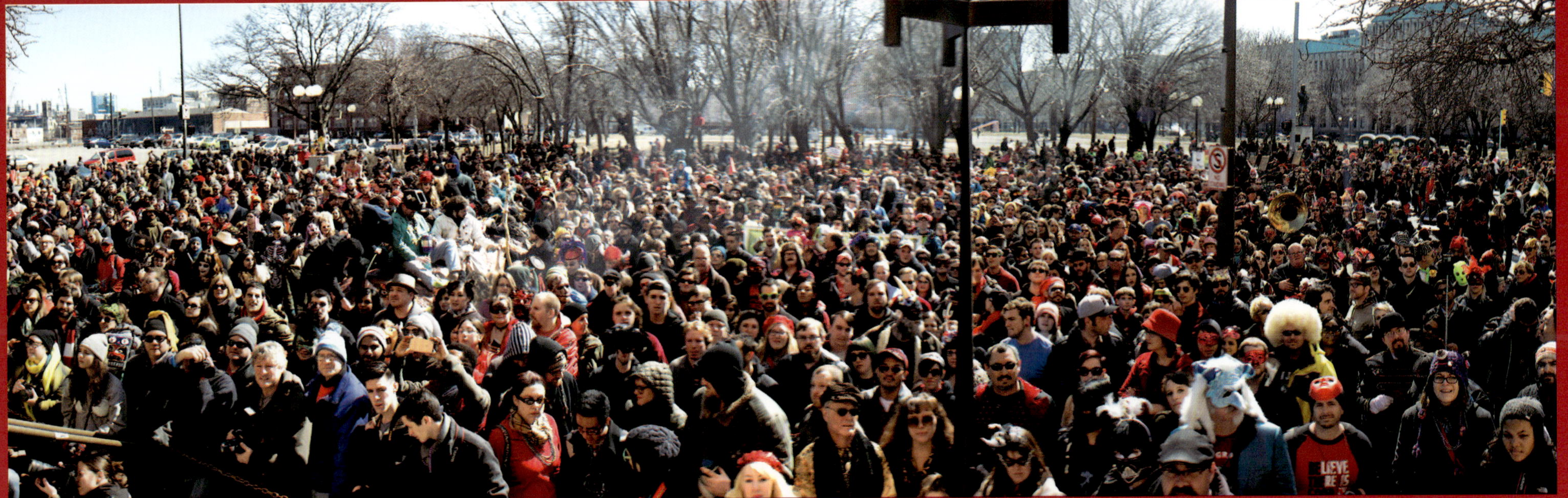

MOVEMENT ELECTRONIC MUSIC FEST

Hart Plaza, Detroit, 48226
www.movement.us

Led by Derrick May, Juan Atkins, and Kevin Saunderson, among many others, Techno music was born in Detroit in the late 1980s and went on to attain international popularity. The first Detroit Electronic Music Festival was held at Hart Plaza in 2000. Visitors and Techno fans from around the world came to Detroit to celebrate the music and congregate in the city that created it. Over the years, the Movement Festival, as it was renamed, has become one of the top electronic music festivals, attended by thousands of fans, who turn the entire city into a giant rave for the Memorial Day weekend.

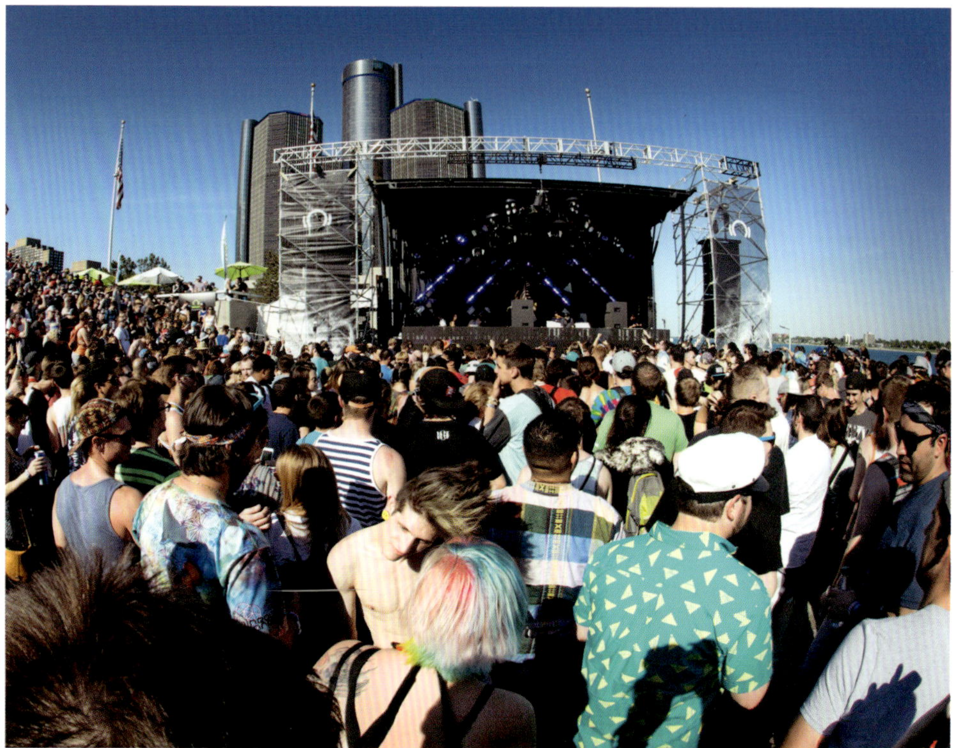

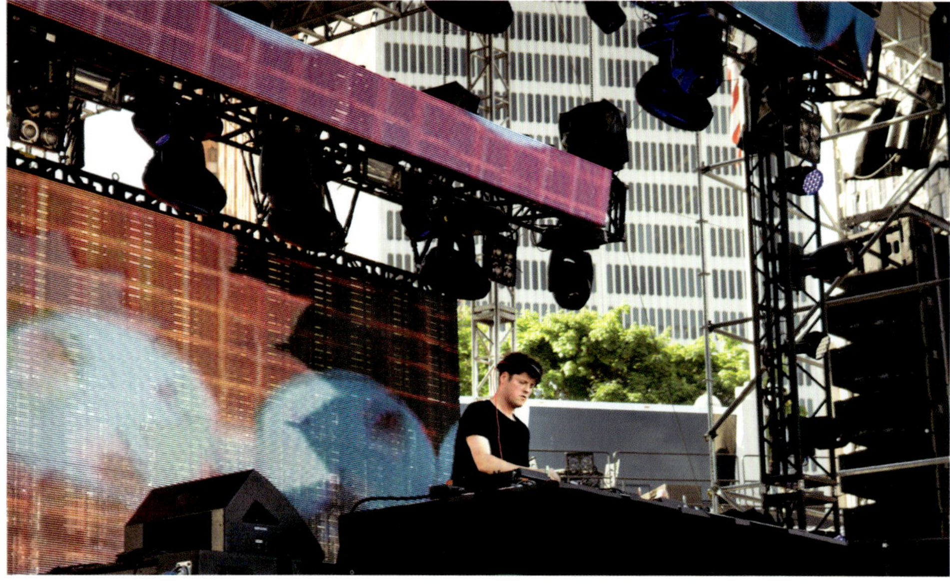

A few innovative DJs began a movement and turned it into a new music genre. From its beginnings in clubs in Detroit, Techno exploded onto the scene in Europe. I hung around with Derrick during this time and thought he was gifted. I just never expected that it would take off the way it did. Detroit does it again. - NR

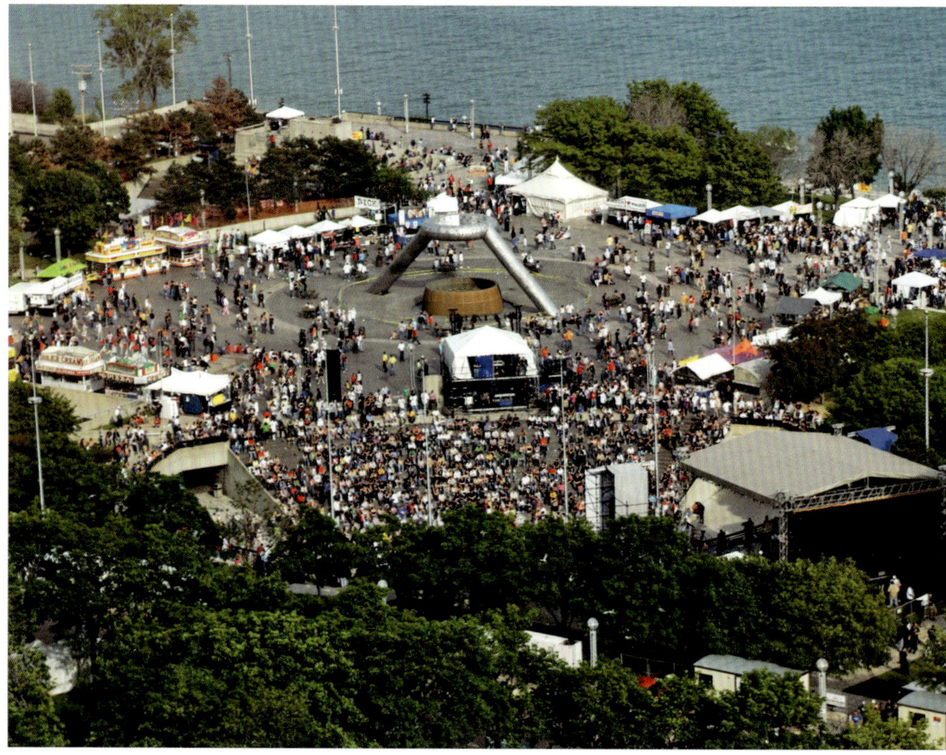

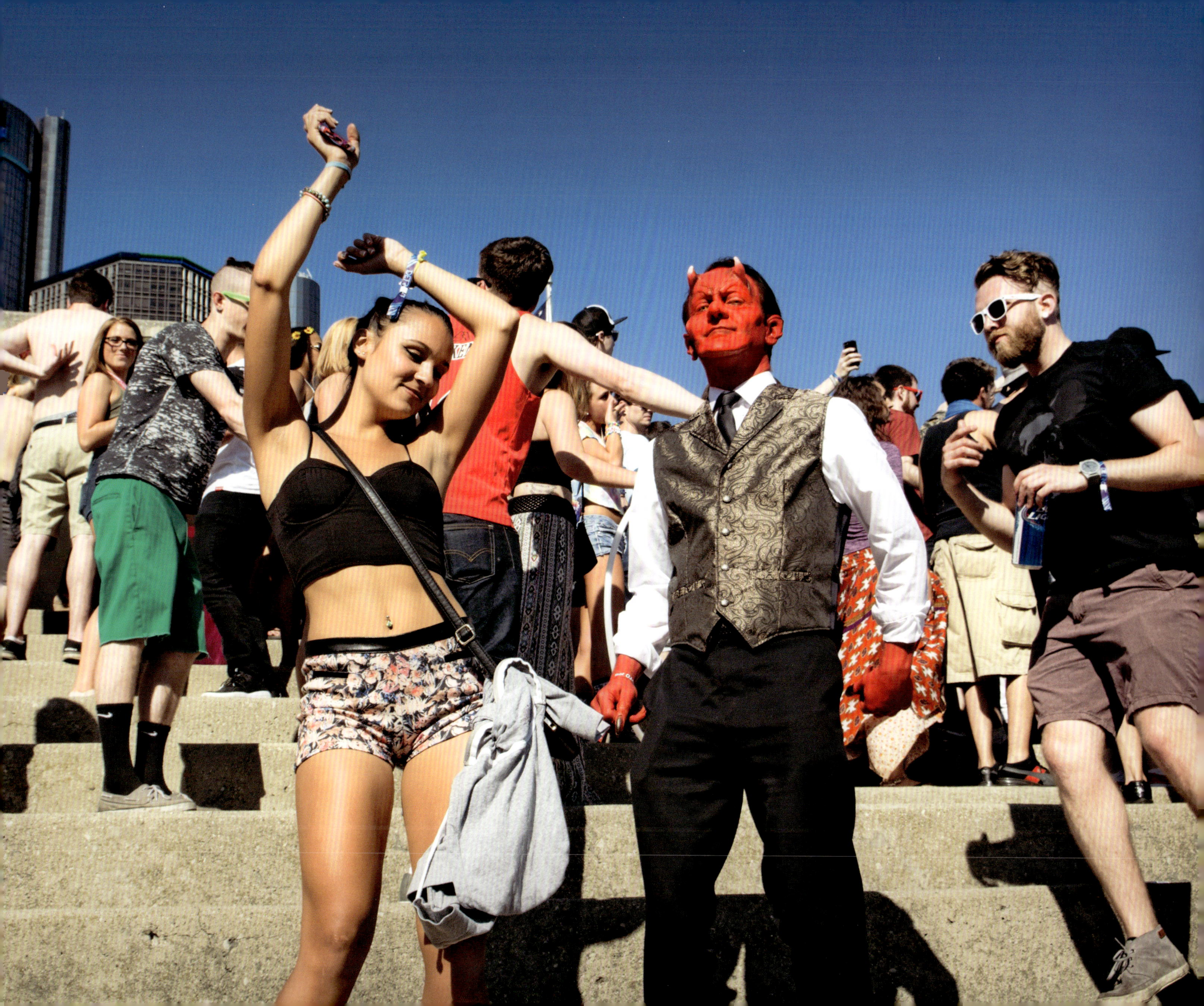

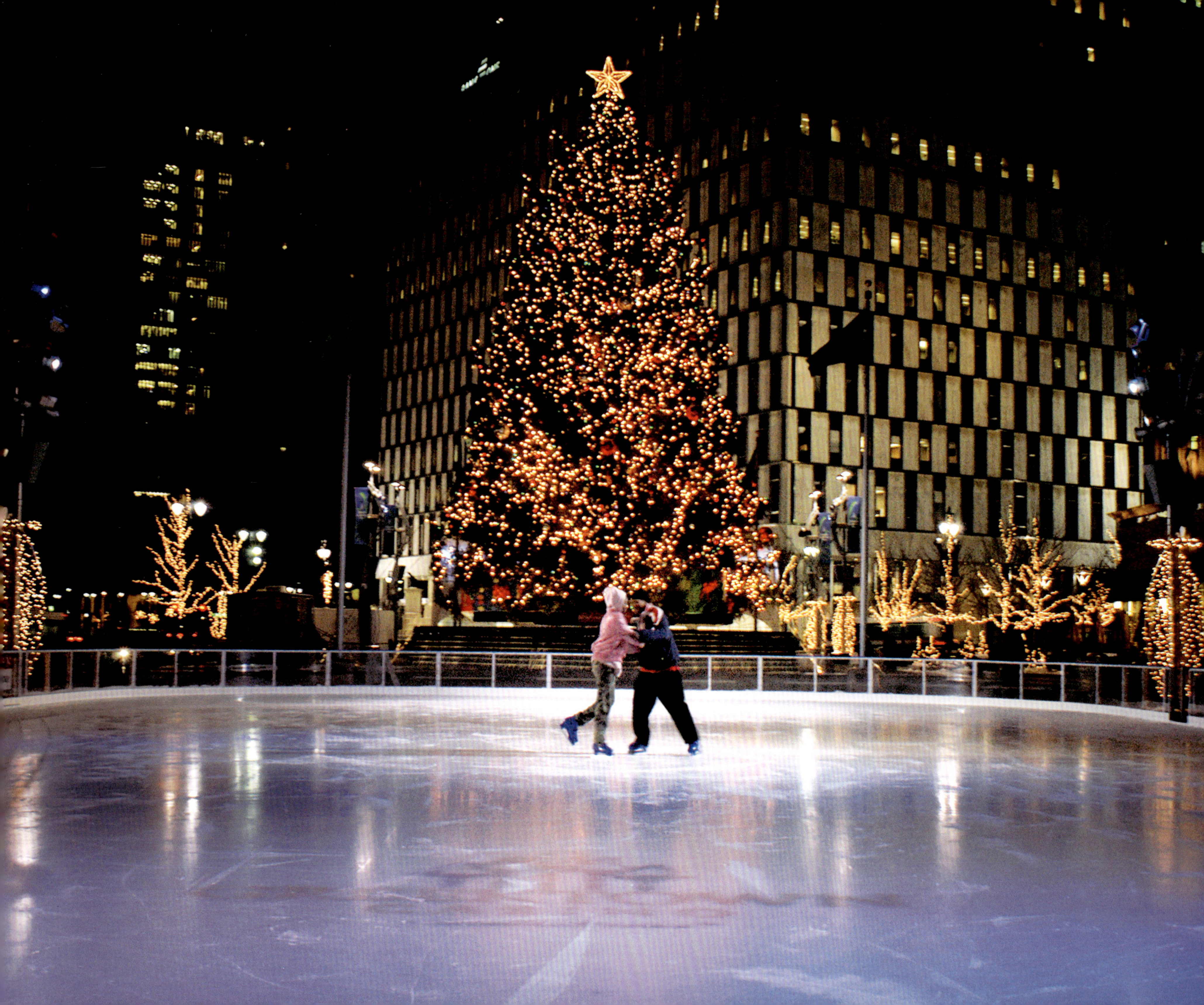

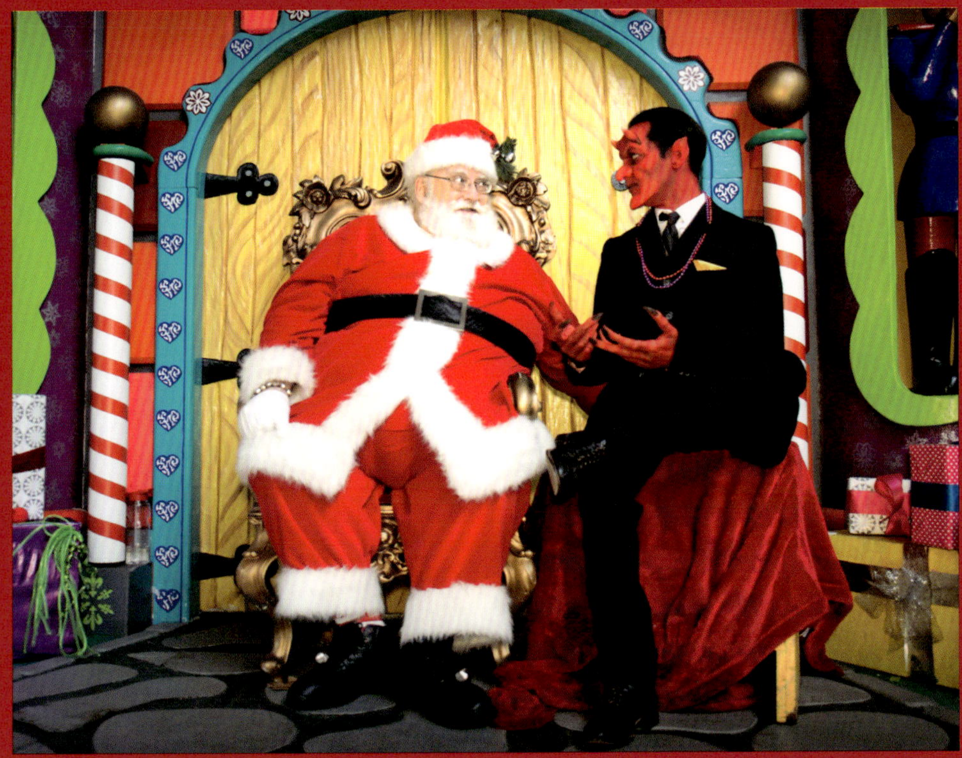

NOEL NIGHT/CHRISTMAS IN DETROIT

Cultural Center, 5200 Woodward Ave., Detroit, 48202
Campus Martius, Detroit, 48226
www.midtowndetroitinc.org/events/noel-night/noel-night

The Monday before Thanksgiving, the official Christmas tree lighting is held in Campus Martius Park, marking the start of the holiday season. Thousands gather to sing Christmas carols and count down to the lighting of the tree while skaters, surrounded by the tall buildings bathed in Christmas colors, enjoy the skating rink set beneath the tree. Since 1973, the Cultural Center has hosted Noel Night, an annual holiday festival featuring artists, musicians, and Christmas-themed events including a visit with Santa, at more than 60 venues in Midtown, centered around Woodward Avenue between the Main Library and the Institute of Arts.

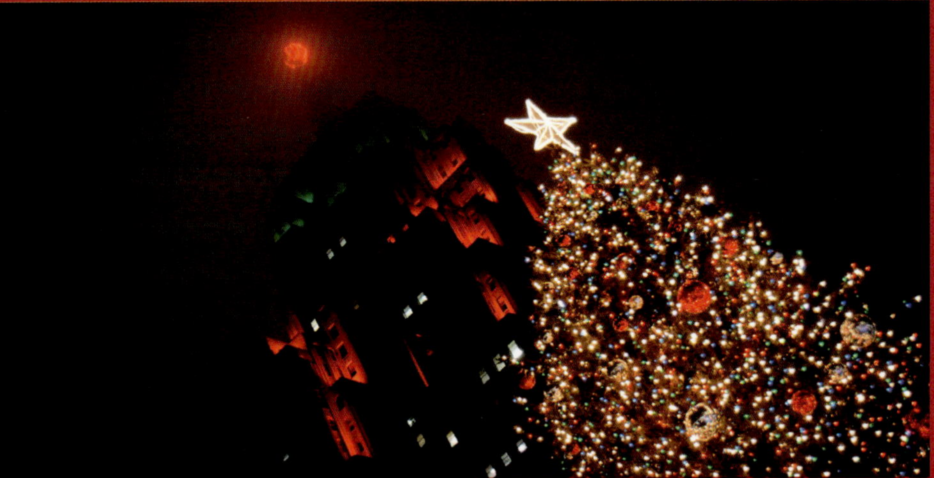

Folks have gathered together in the city center during winter for centuries. The start of the holiday season, the Christmas Tree lighting has become a grand celebration. Downtown buildings are lit in Christmas red and green. Farther uptown, and a few weeks later, Noel Night has become another family holiday tradition. Weaving my way through the crowds to see Santa Claus, buying a few presents, then drinking hot cider and singing the old carols on Woodward, I really feel the Christmas spirit. - NR

NORTH AMERICAN INTERNATIONAL AUTO SHOW

Cobo Center, Detroit, 48226
www.naias.com

The North American International Auto Show is hosted every January at Cobo Center. Since its conception in 1987, the NAIAS has exemplified Detroit's prominence within the auto industry. Recognized worldwide as one of the most influential and important shows, the NAIAS draws thousands of the best designers and industry insiders, debuting industry innovations, and showcasing the most important concept cars from the hometown Big 3, General Motors, Ford, and Chrysler, as well as other international automakers.

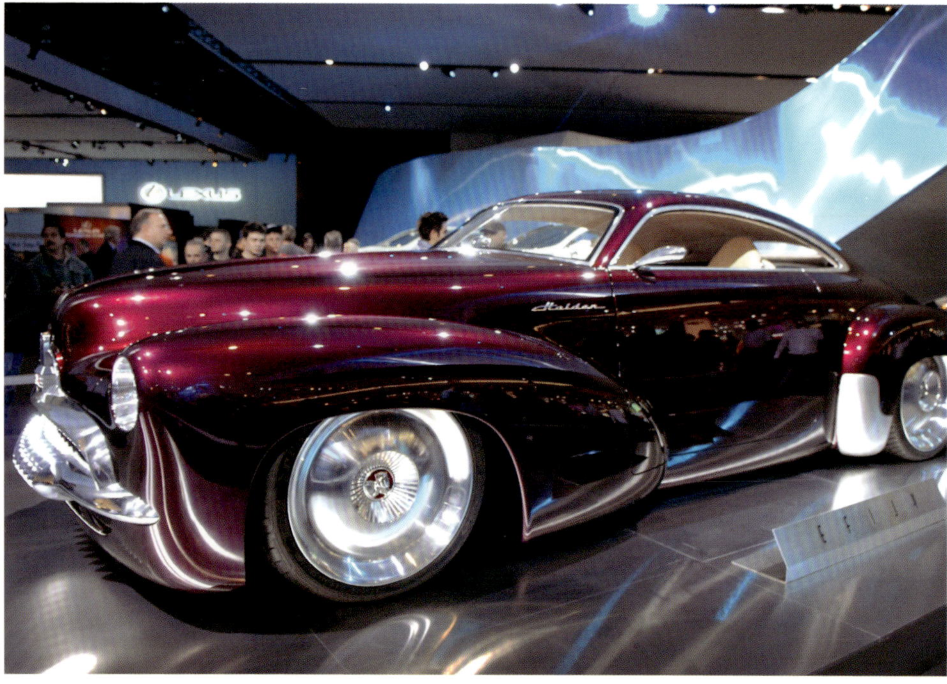

As the Automotive Capital of the World, Detroit should be expected to host the greatest annual exhibition of new cars and technology. Debuting concept cars that showcase new innovations and introducing next year's models, the NAIAS is a weeks-long party celebrating Detroit's major export. - NR

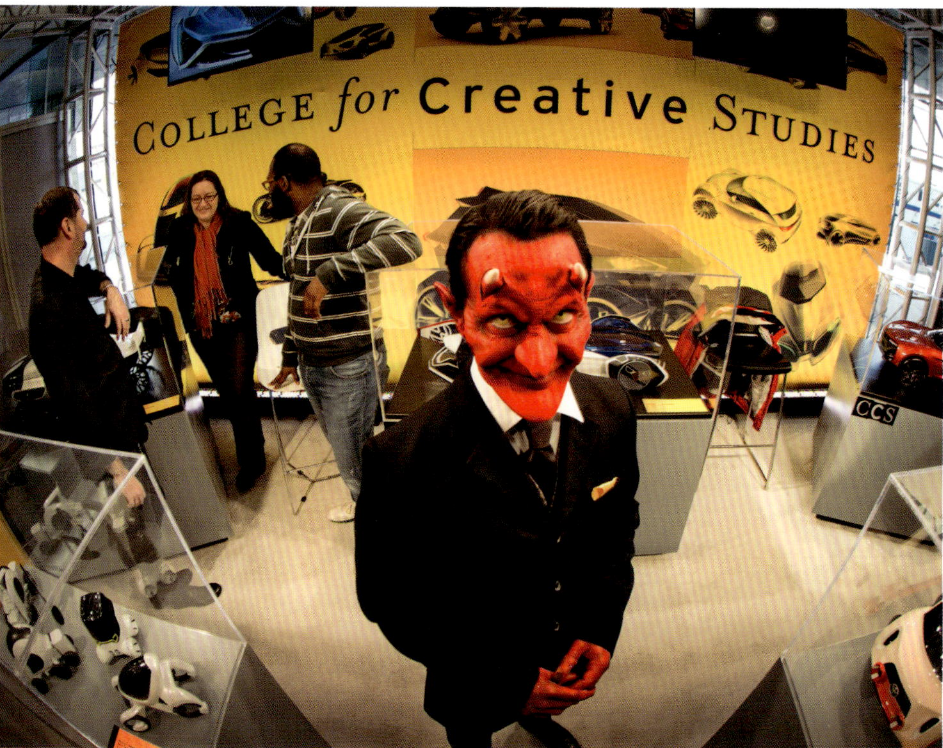

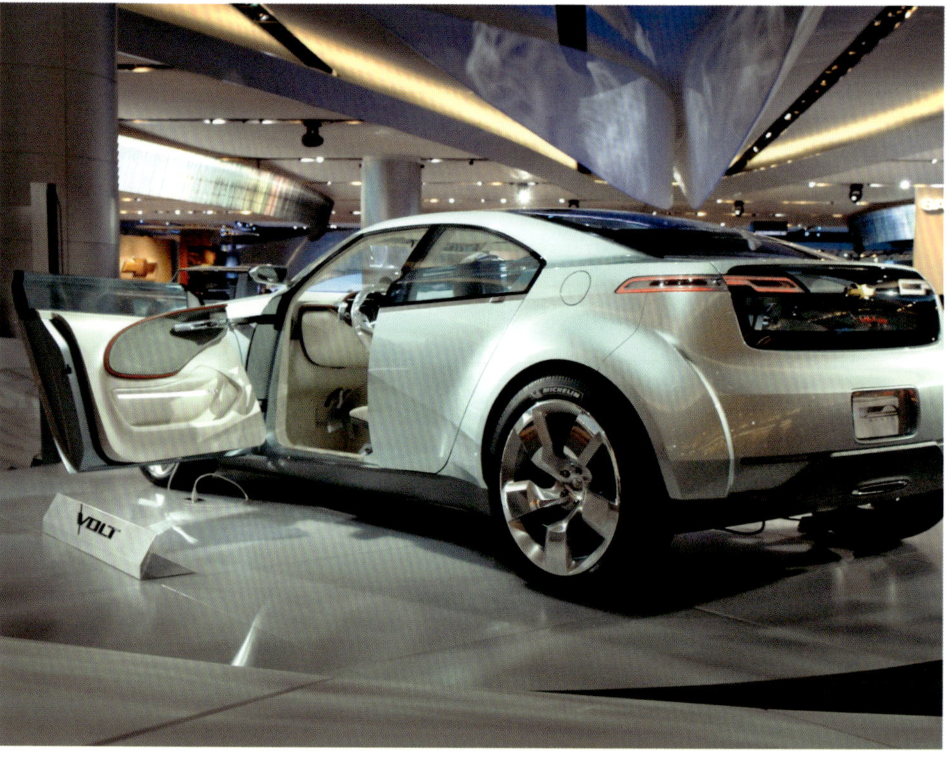

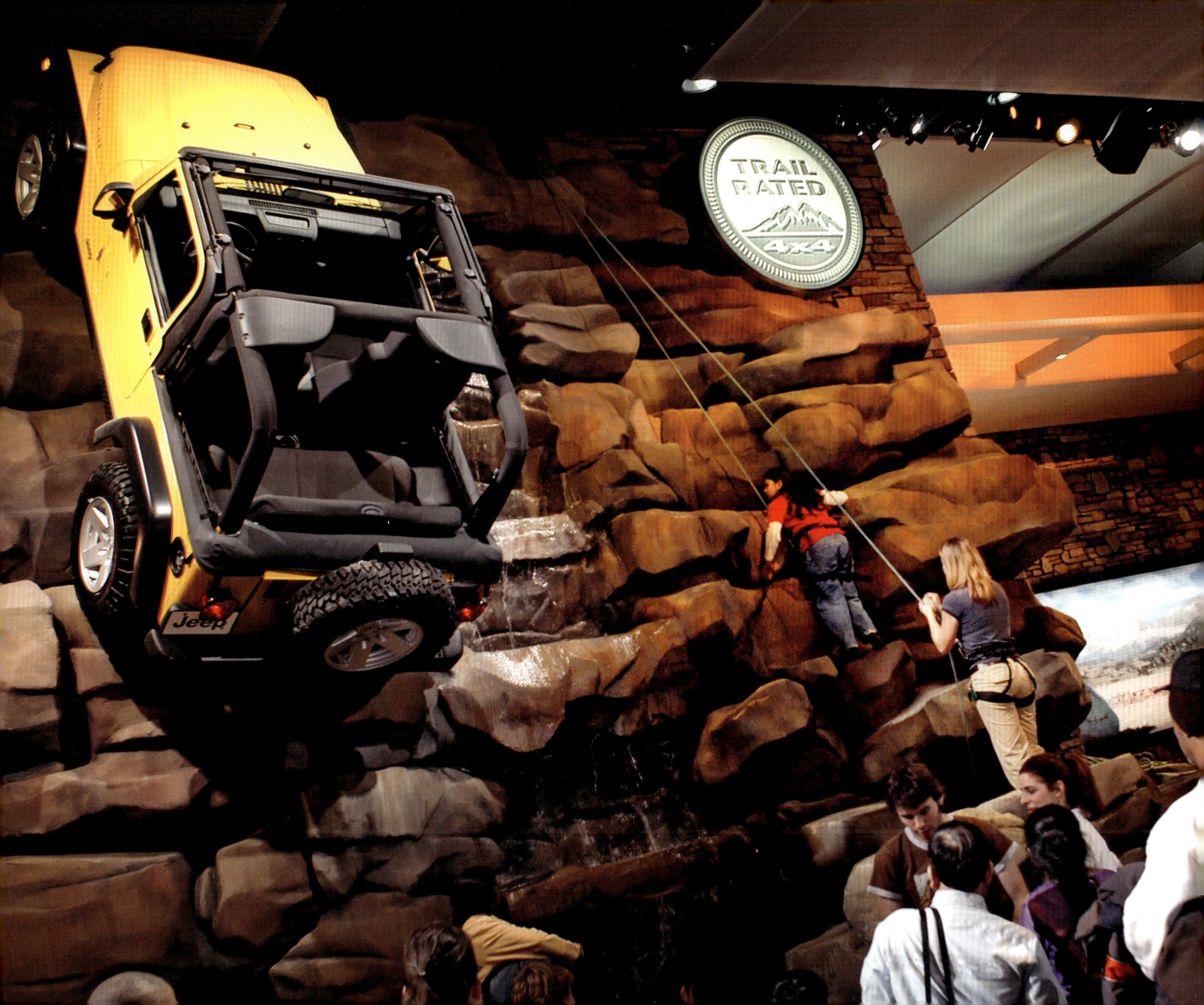
TRAIL RATED
4x4
Jeep

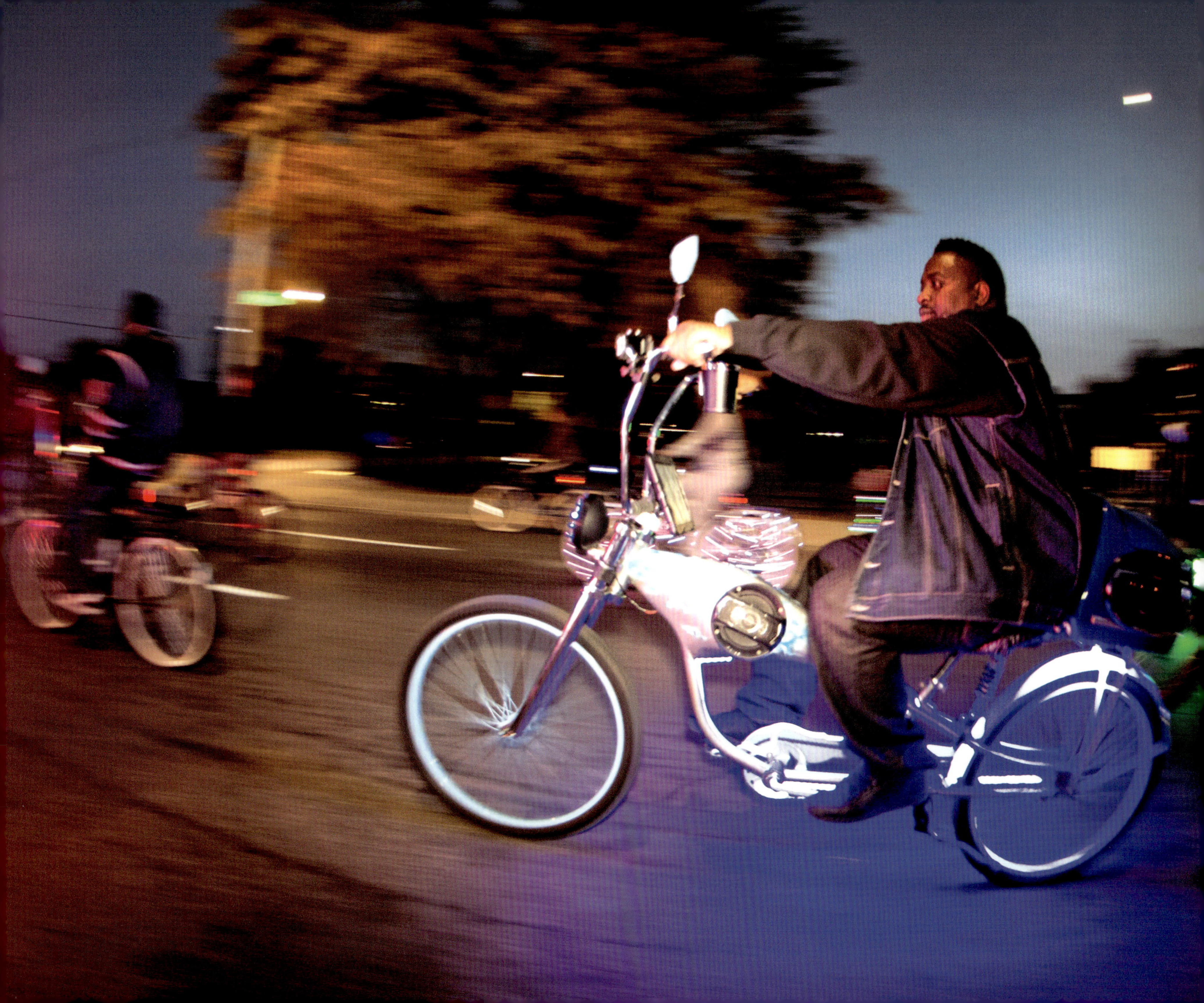

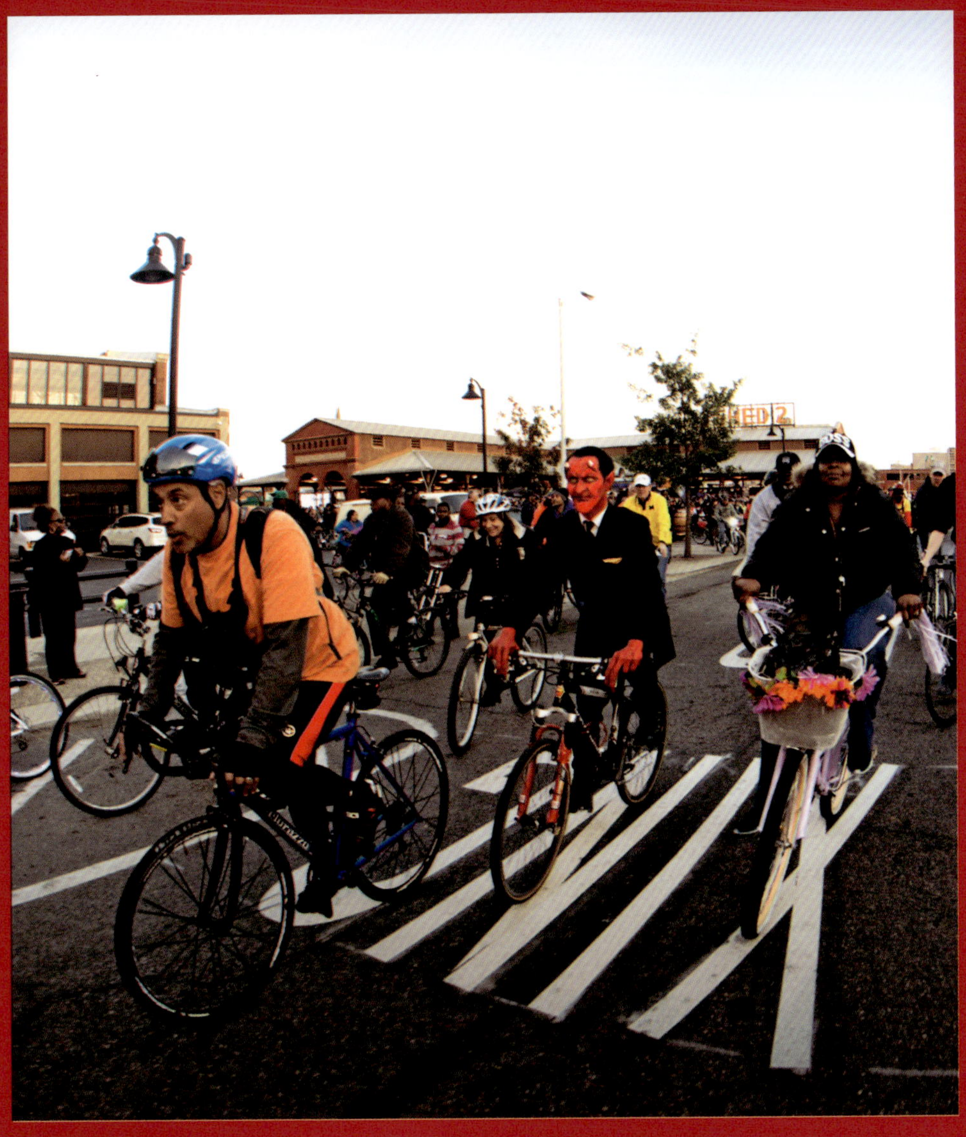

SLOW ROLL

Slow Roll Detroit
www.slowroll.bike

Mixing the popularity of bike riding with the novelty of cruising Detroit's wide streets, Slow Roll has evolved into a weekly party on wheels. It draws thousands of bike enthusiasts, amateurs, pros, locals, and tourists every Monday in the spring, summer and fall to explore the city. Started by a couple friends who wanted to ride together, it has exploded into a mile-long cavalcade.

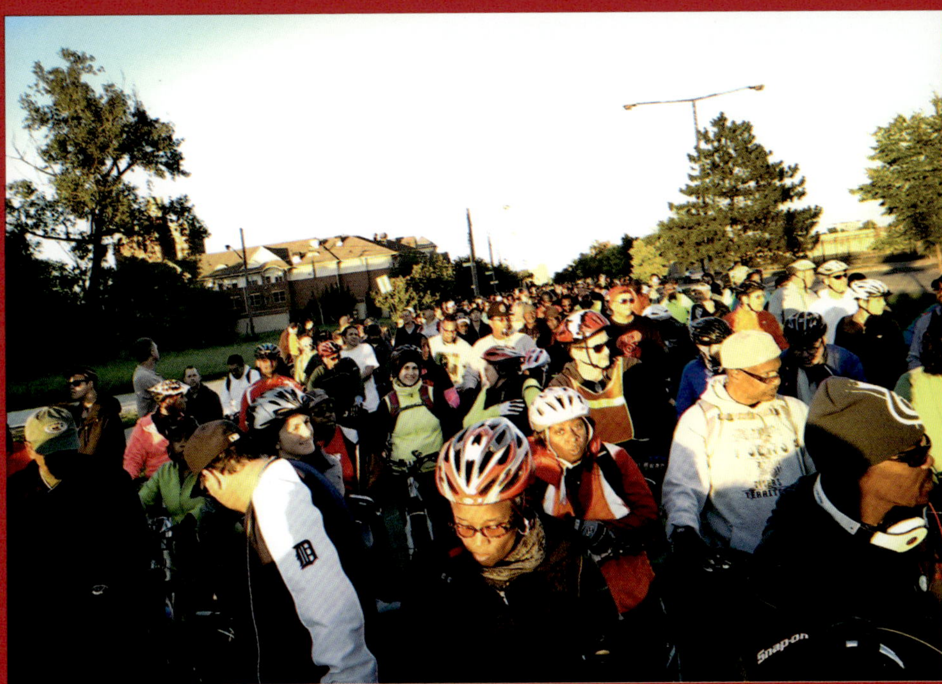

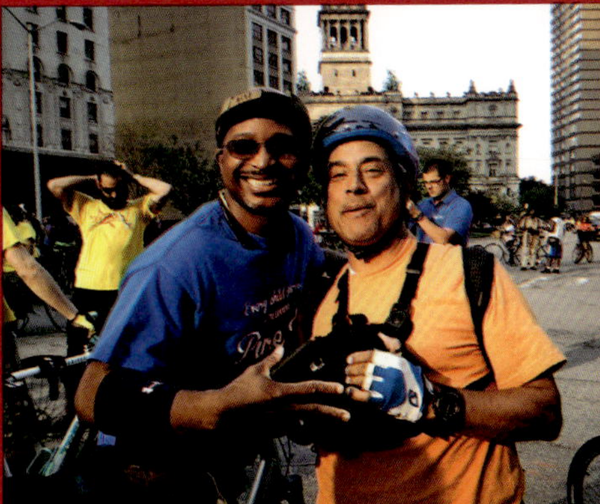

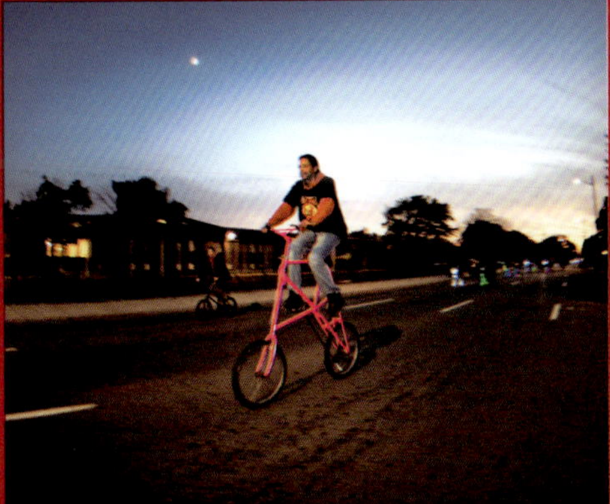

I met Jason Hall and Mike MacKool years ago while I was aimlessly riding my bike through the city. They invited me to ride along with them that night. After our ride, we decided that we would go out the next week, inviting more friends to ride with us. In turn, those friends invited more friends, who invited their friends, and so on...

- NR

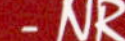

THEATRE BIZARRE

Masonic Temple, 500 Temple Ave., Detroit, 48201
www.theatrebizarre.com

The greatest Halloween party ever originated in the imaginative minds of John Dunivant and his cohorts. Theatre Bizarre is a masquerade ball and carnival sideshow. Guests are entertained by hundreds of Burlesque dancers, circus sideshow performers, illusionists, bands, and fire performers. It is an interactive audience-driven experience only Detroit could create.

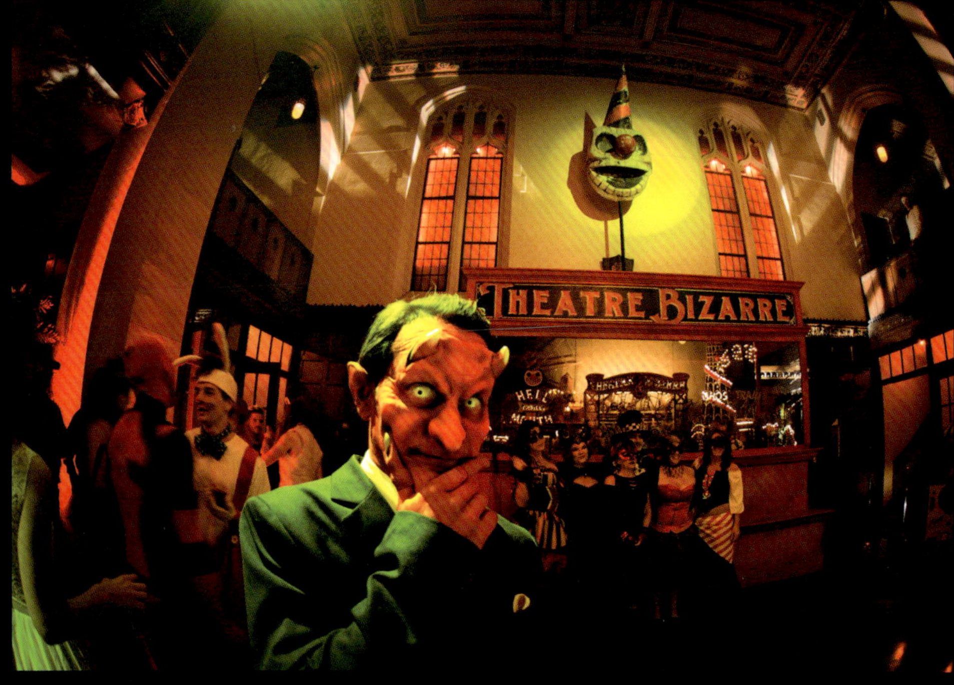

The only time of year when I truly fit in. Guests are required to come in costume, and some spend the whole year preparing, becoming as fascinating as the hosts and performers. Floors are divided into themes, which change annually. With more than a hundred performers, and a guest list reaching thousands, there is always something unexpected about to happen. - NR

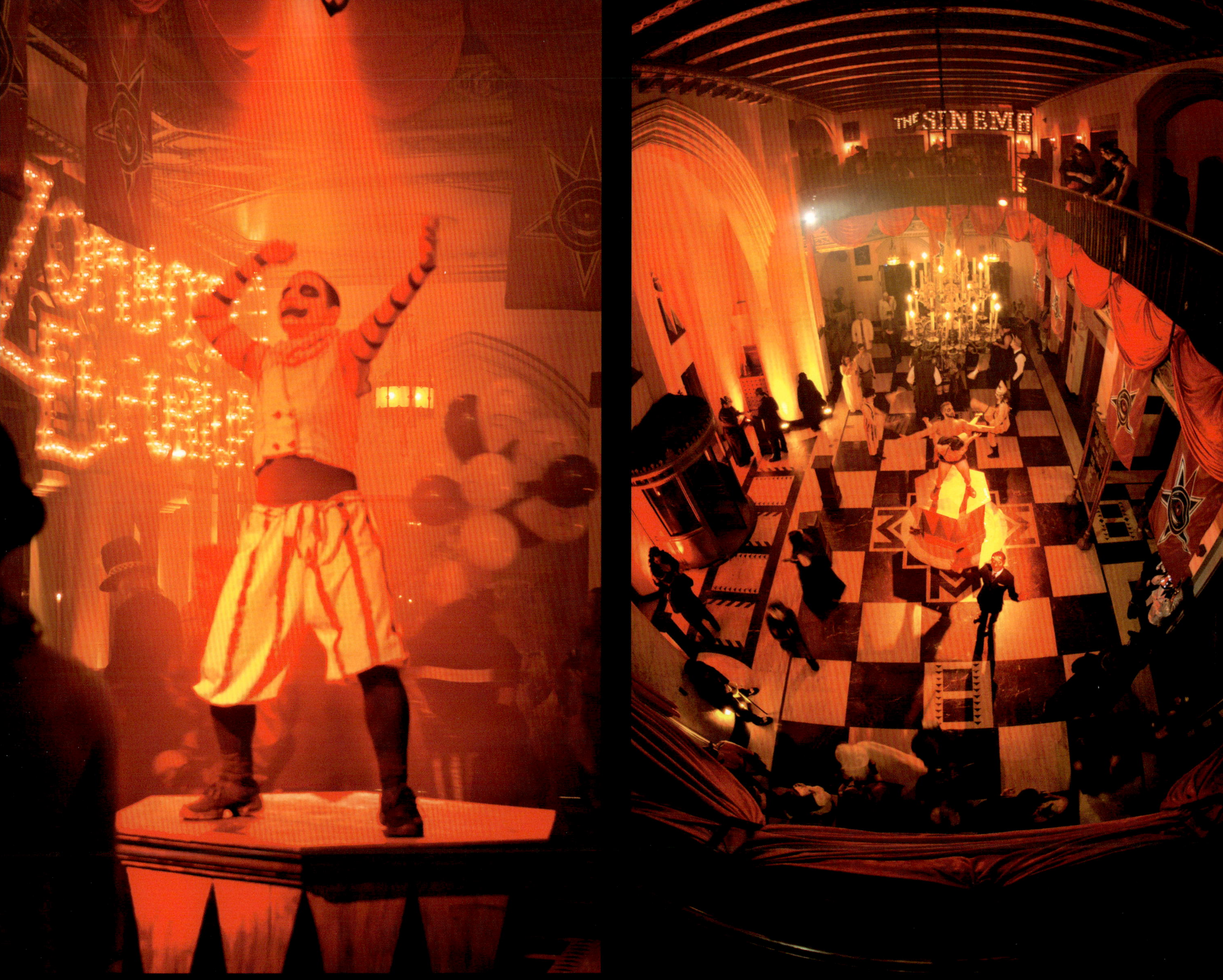
THE SINEMA

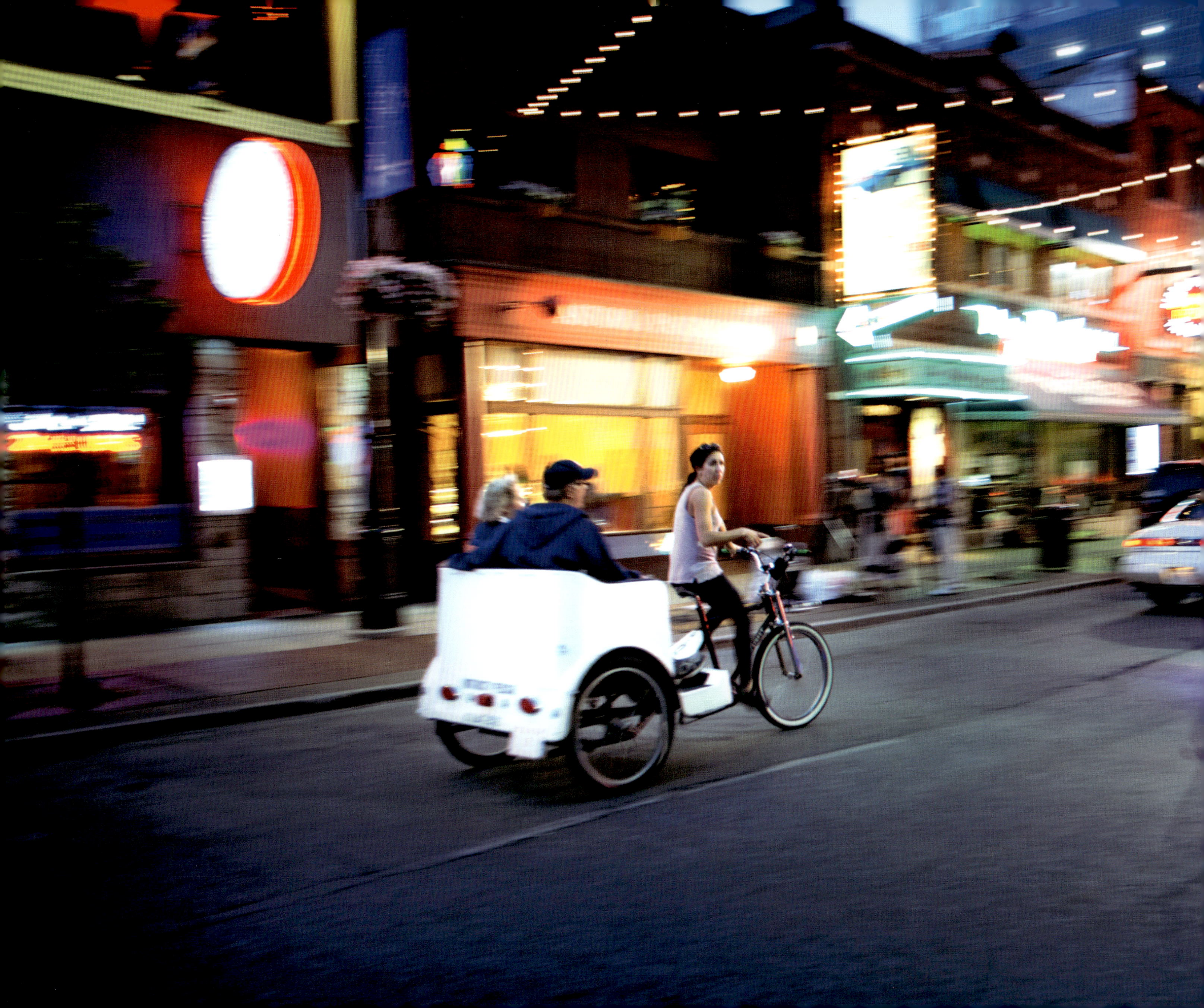

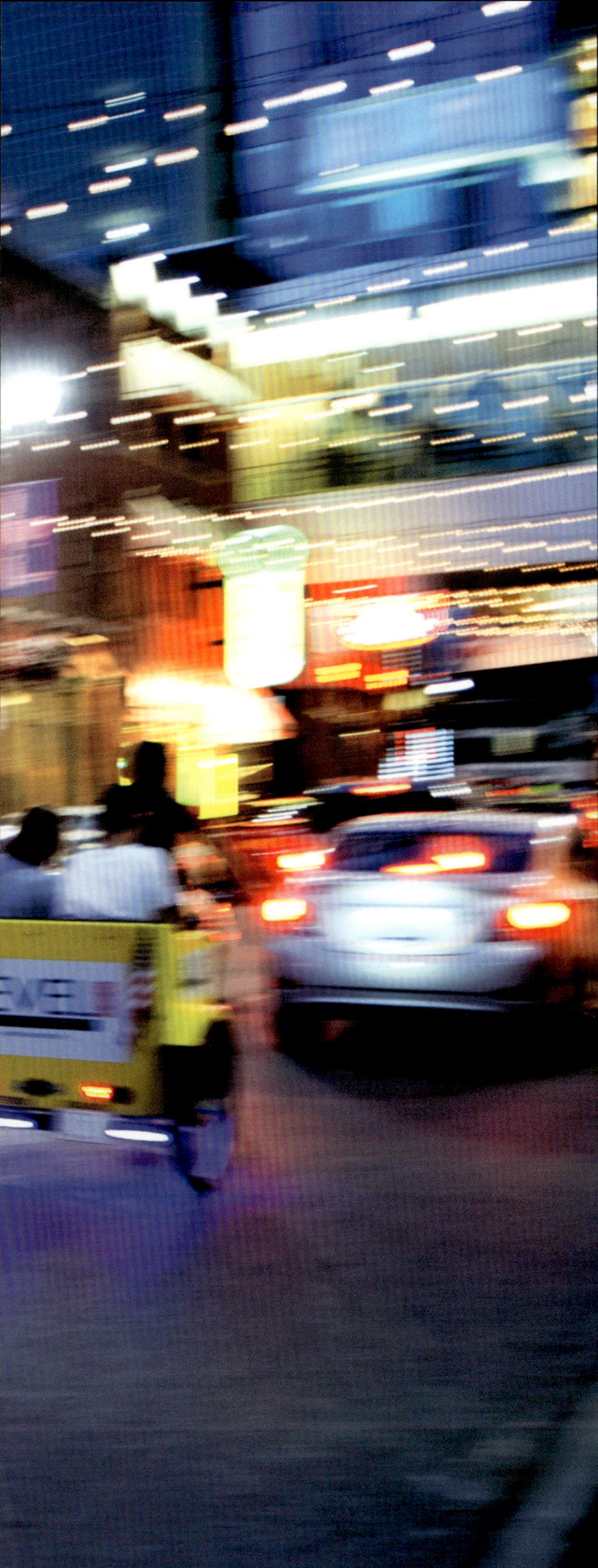

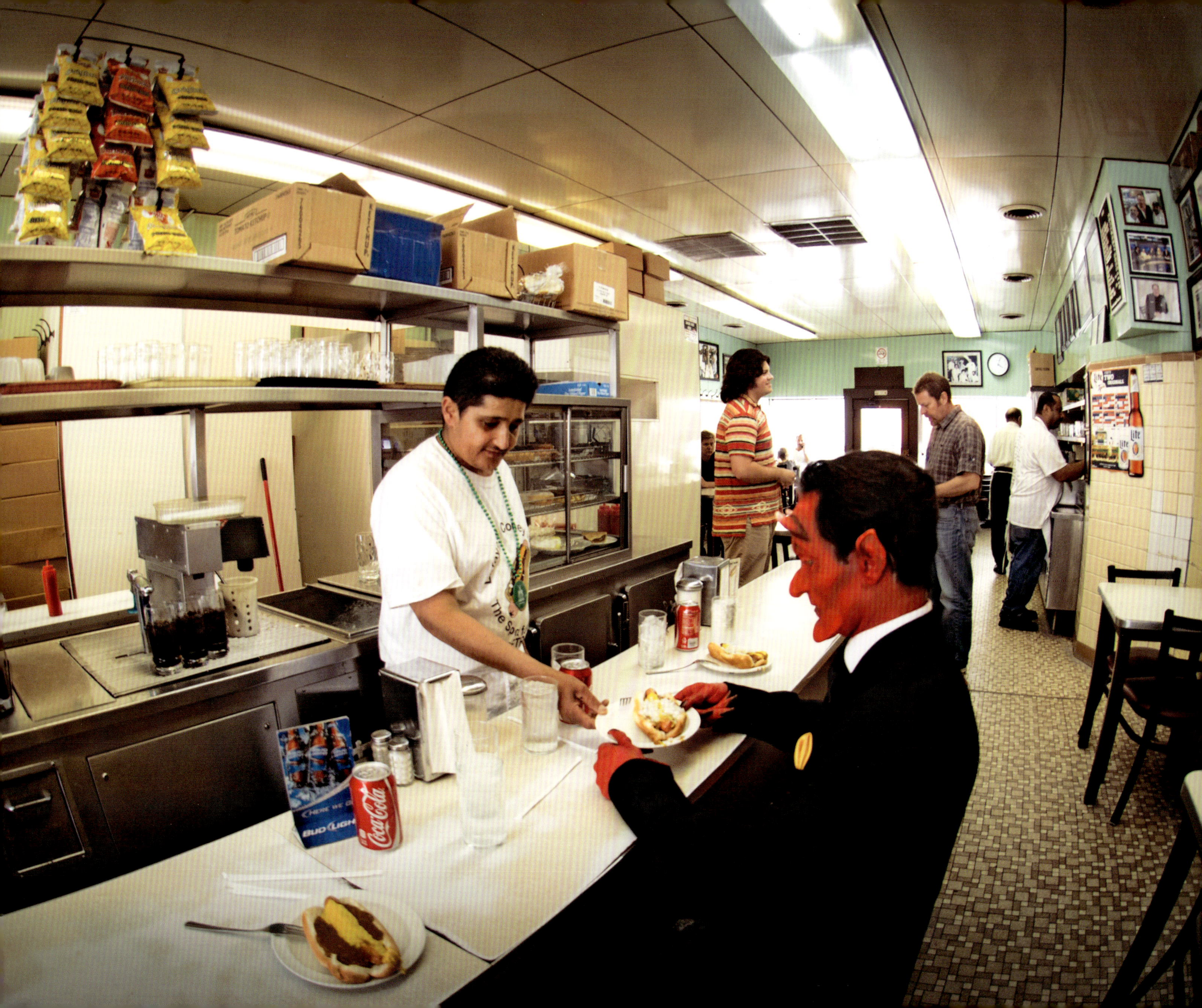
Coca-Cola

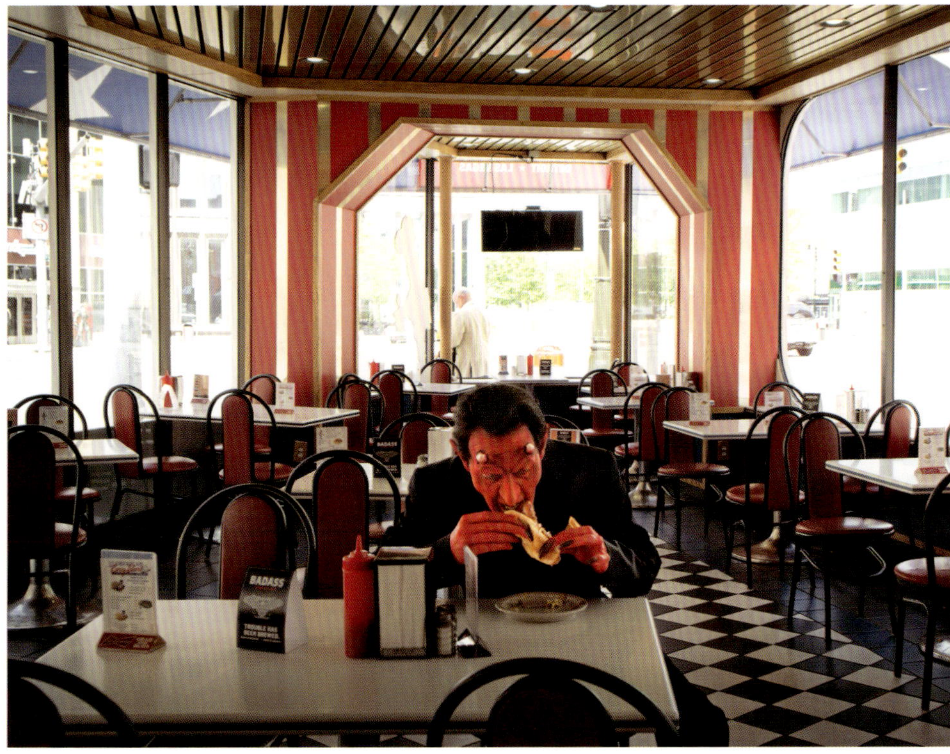

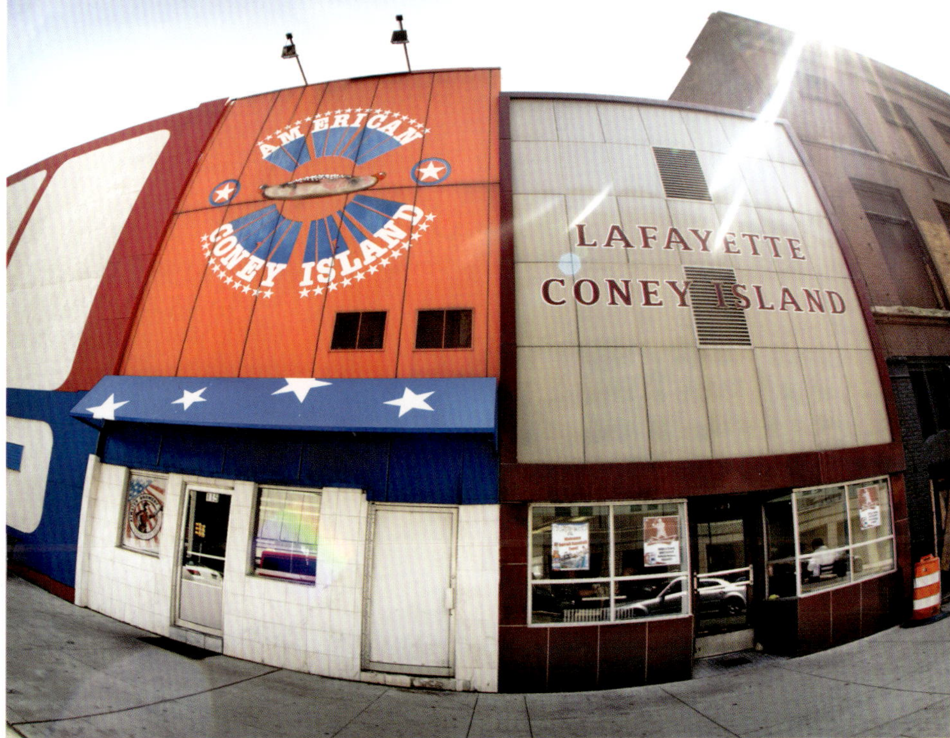

CONEY ISLANDS

American Coney Island
114 W. Lafayette Blvd., Detroit, 48226
www.americanconeyisland.com

Lafayette Coney Island
118 W. Lafayette Blvd., Detroit, 48226

Rivals for over a century, and originally owned by the same family, American Coney Island and Lafayette Coney Island have become famous Detroit institutions. Greek immigrant brothers Gus and Bill Keros were inspired by the chili dogs at New York's Coney Island. In Detroit, a Coney Island is a hot dog covered in chili, onions and mustard. As simple as that sounds, legions of Detroiters are divided over which restaurant is the best.

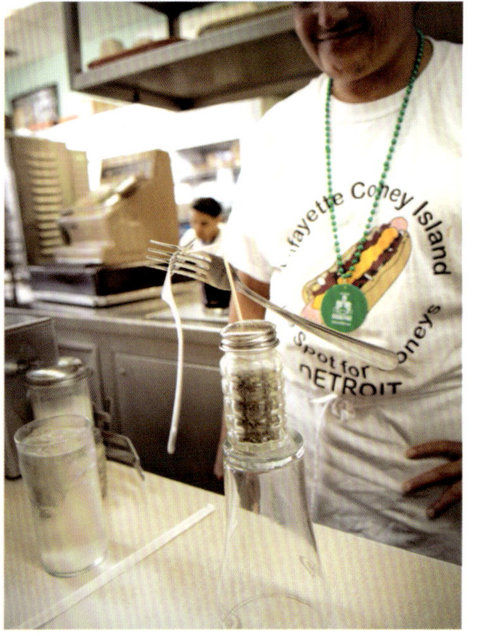

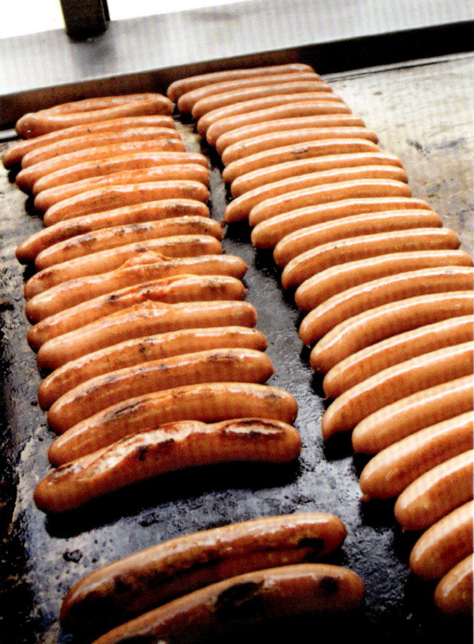

Who would think a family fight would divide a city? Who can believe that countless Detroiters swear allegiance to one and dismiss the other as inferior, thus fueling this family dispute? Me, I refuse to take sides, but I do find that these "Coney Islands" are the best chili dogs in the country. They taste even better late at night after barhopping. - NR

DIAMOND JACK'S

Rivard Plaza, 1340 Atwater St., Detroit, 48207
www.diamondjack.com

Boats and ferries have always operated up and down the lakes, connecting Detroit to Chicago, Buffalo, Cleveland, and beyond. Diamond Jack's comes from a long line of ferry services Detroiters have enjoyed over the years. Starting from Rivard Park, one of three boats – the *Diamond Jack*, the *Diamond Queen*, or the *Diamond Belle* – gives daily tours around Belle Isle to the Ambassador Bridge and back, providing passengers with great historical insights and footnotes for almost every place on either side of the river.

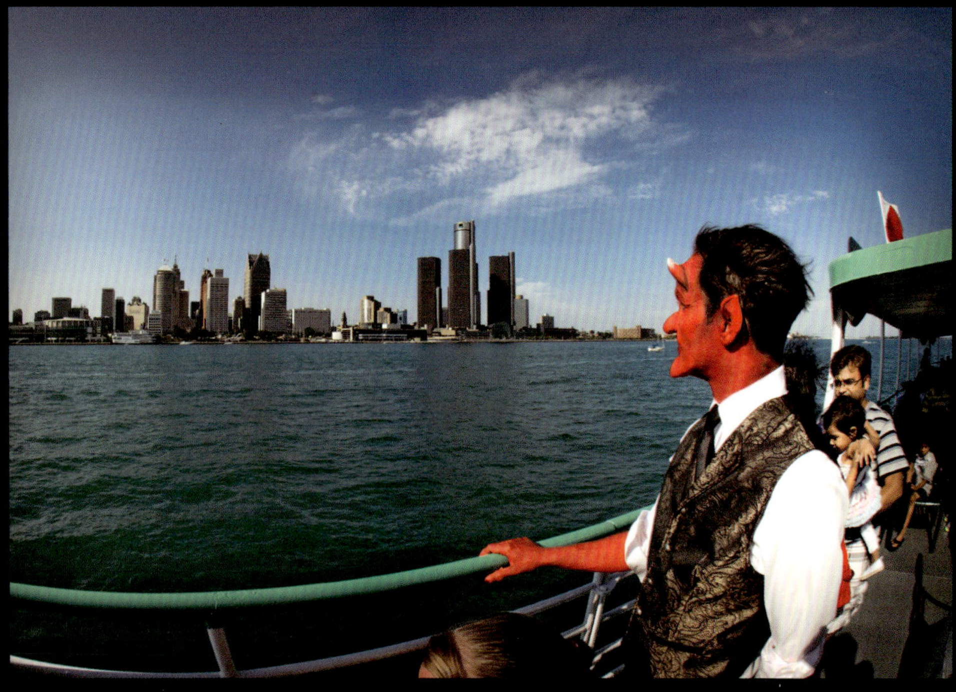

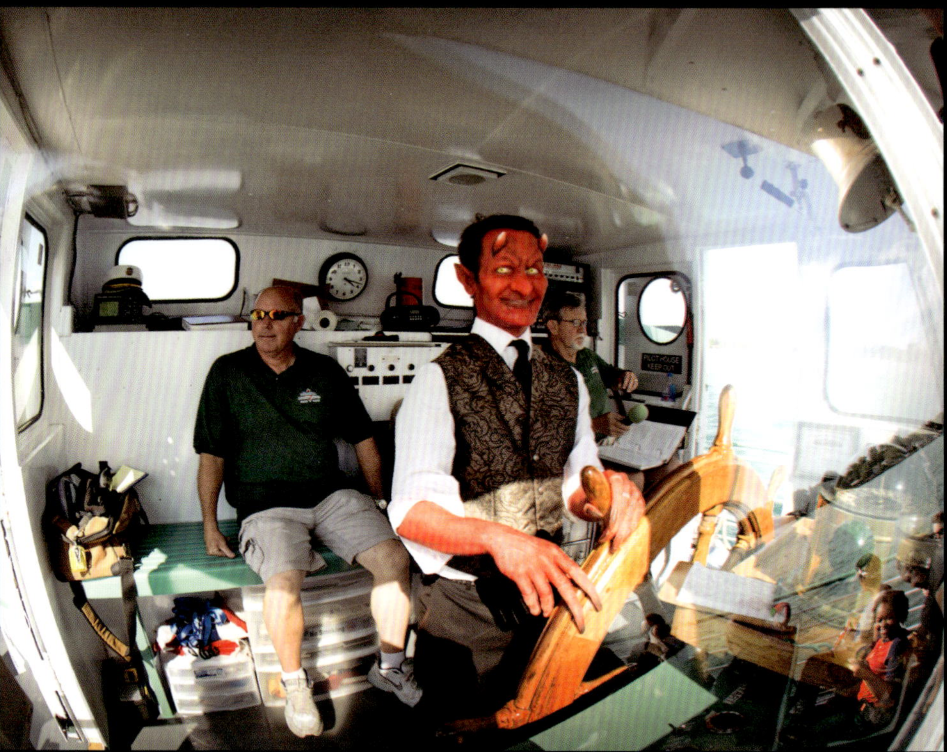

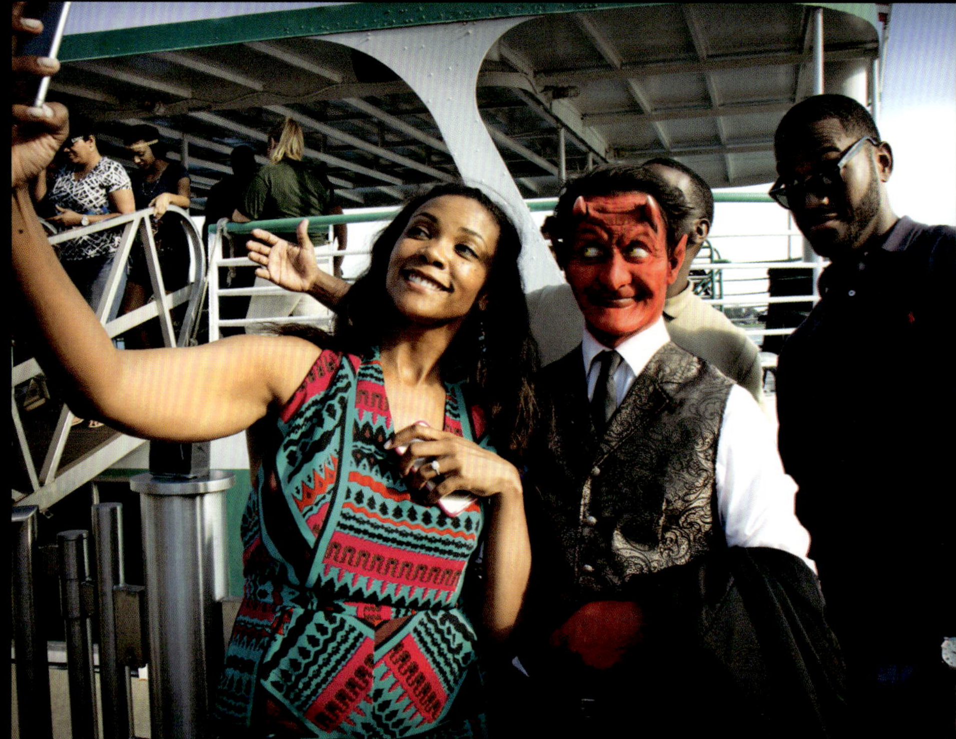

For almost 100 years, one of the best boat trips was on either the St. Claire or the Columbia to Bob-lo Island. These boats took us on an extraordinary adventure, dancing, sightseeing, and meeting new loves during the hours-long ride. Diamond Jack's is about as close as you'll get to that memory, and if you're lucky, you'll be a passenger when I'm the pilot. - NR

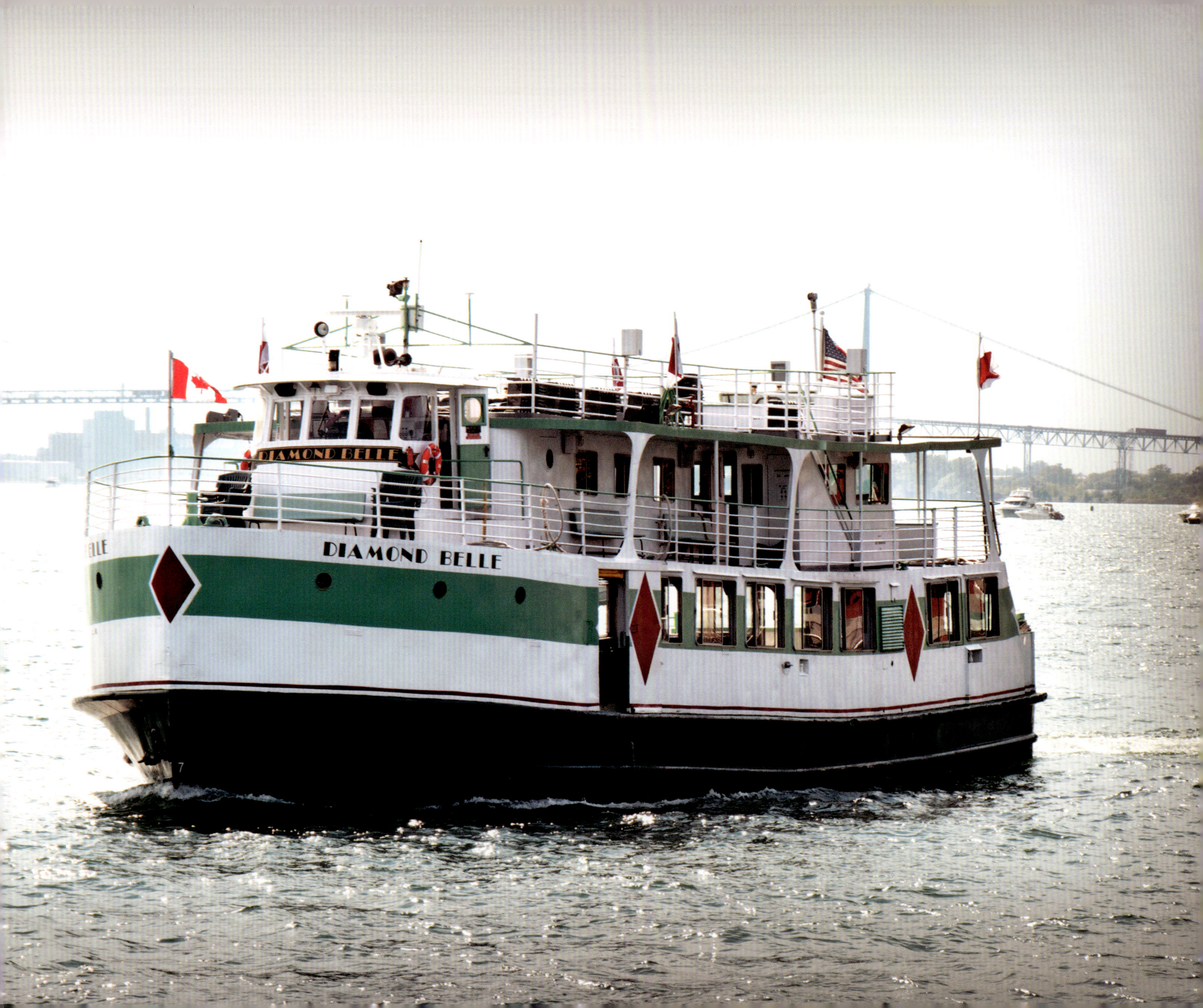
DIAMOND BELLE
DIAMOND BELLE

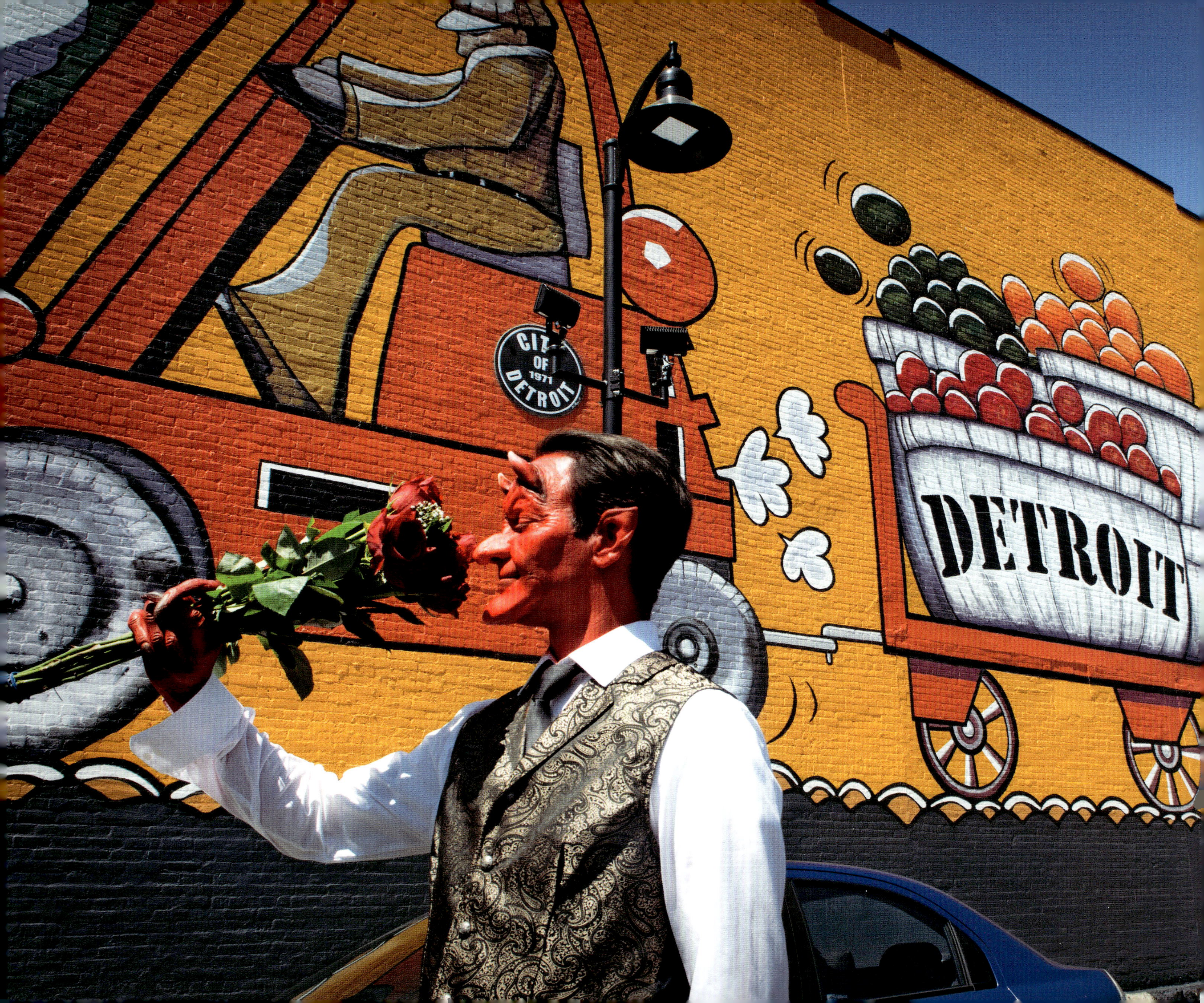
CITY OF DETROIT
1971
DETROIT

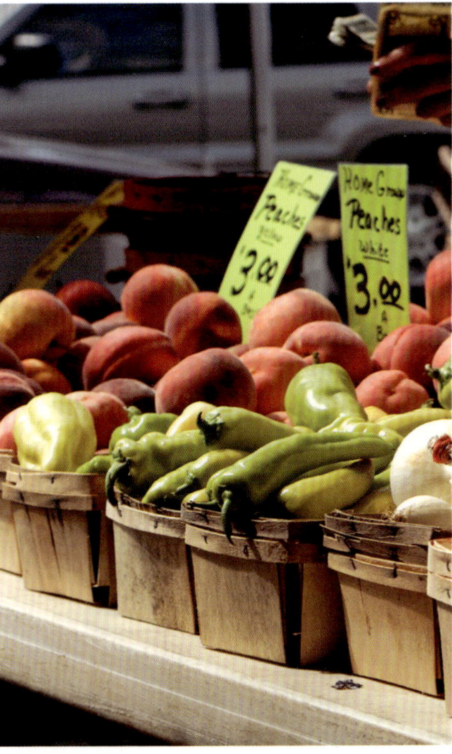

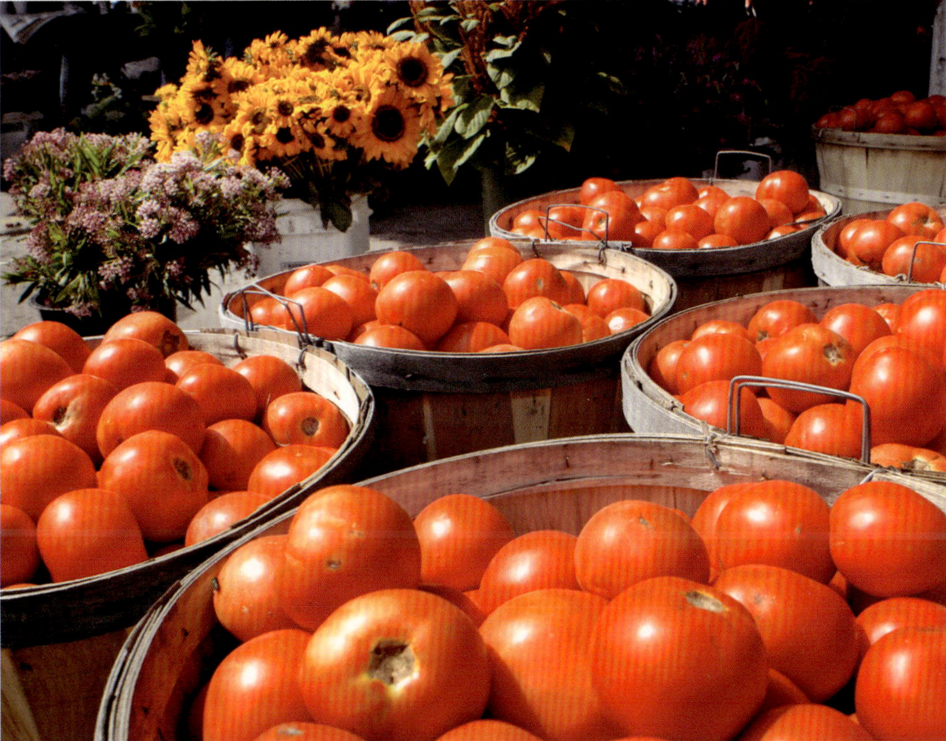

EASTERN MARKET

Eastern Market Corp., 2934 Russell St., Detroit, 48207
www.easternmarket.com

Covering 43 acres, Eastern Market is the largest historic public market in the United States. Since the 1850s, farmers have offered fresh produce to the locals who come by the tens of thousands on any given Saturday. Along with recently added organic and locally grown options, the market has expanded its hours, responding to growing attendance. The popular Flower Day is a local spring ritual as Detroiters celebrate the return of summer. Internationally known graffiti artists have transformed the surrounding buildings with incredible murals.

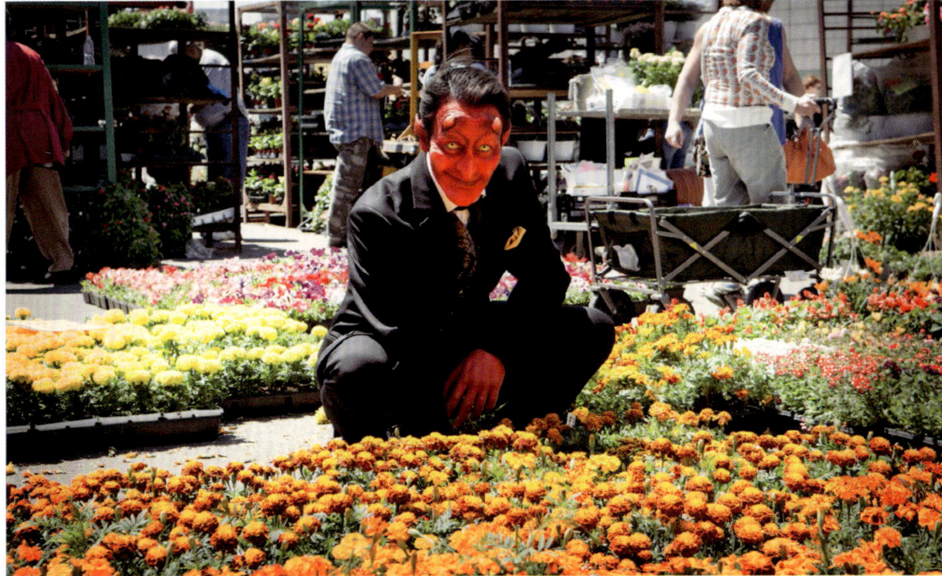

My Saturday morning ritual begins and ends at Eastern Market. I stop at my favorite stalls. Farmers I have met over the years – maple syrup from Clare Mi., the honey guy, the organic veggie gal –know just what I want. I go to DeVries for cheese, Germack for coffee, and after all of that shopping, I head to Supino for a slice of pizza. One of the bonuses is bumping into friends following the same ritual. - NR

GREEKTOWN

Monroe St., between Brush St. and St. Antoine St., Detroit, 48207

As Greek immigrants arrived to Detroit during the heyday of the 1920s, they settled on Monroe Street, the heart of Greektown. Open air cafes line the street as diners relax, enjoying the summer breeze as shouts of "Opa" are heard as flames rise from plates of saganaki.

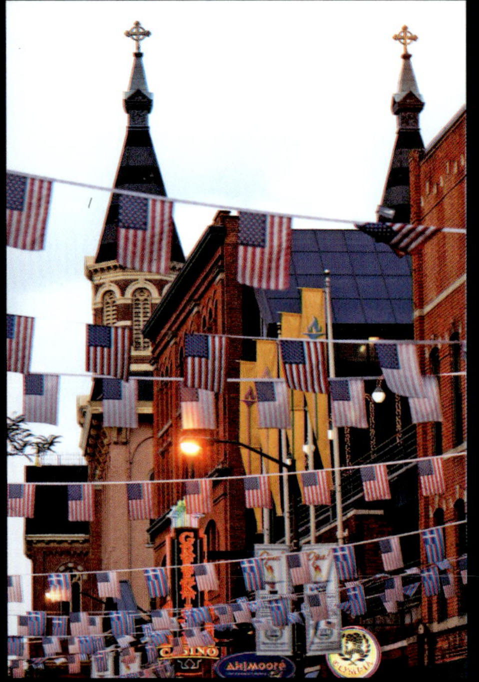

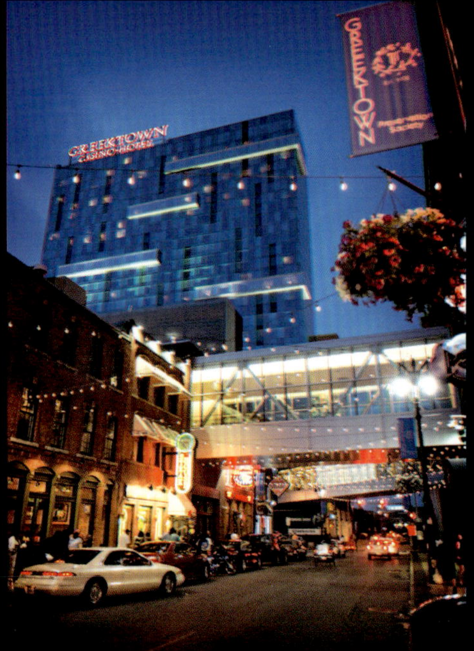

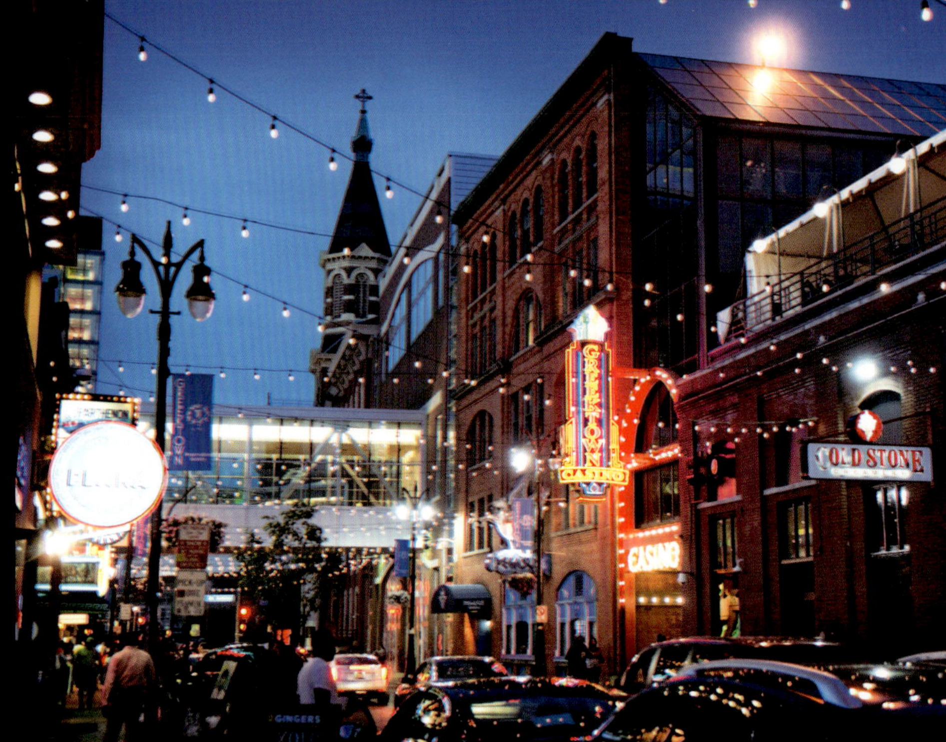

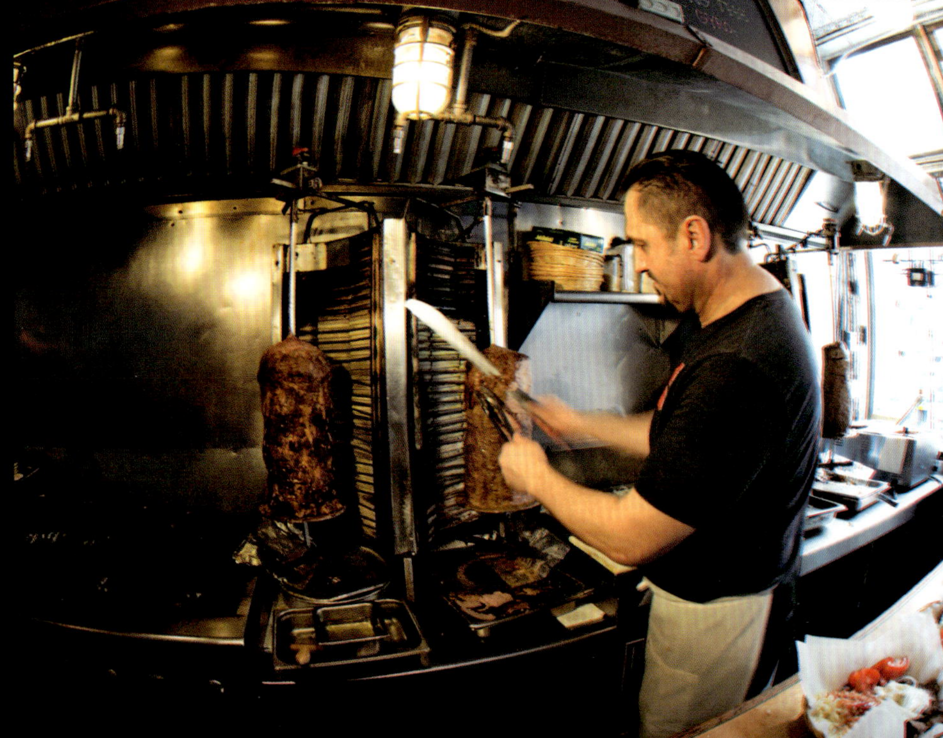

On one of the busiest areas downtown, Greektown has been a popular destination for generations. Family-owned restaurants offer Greek food and flare when serving Saganaki, or flaming cheese. I remember spending time in the old coffee shops. While old men drank Greek coffees and talked, I'd play pinball for hours. - NR

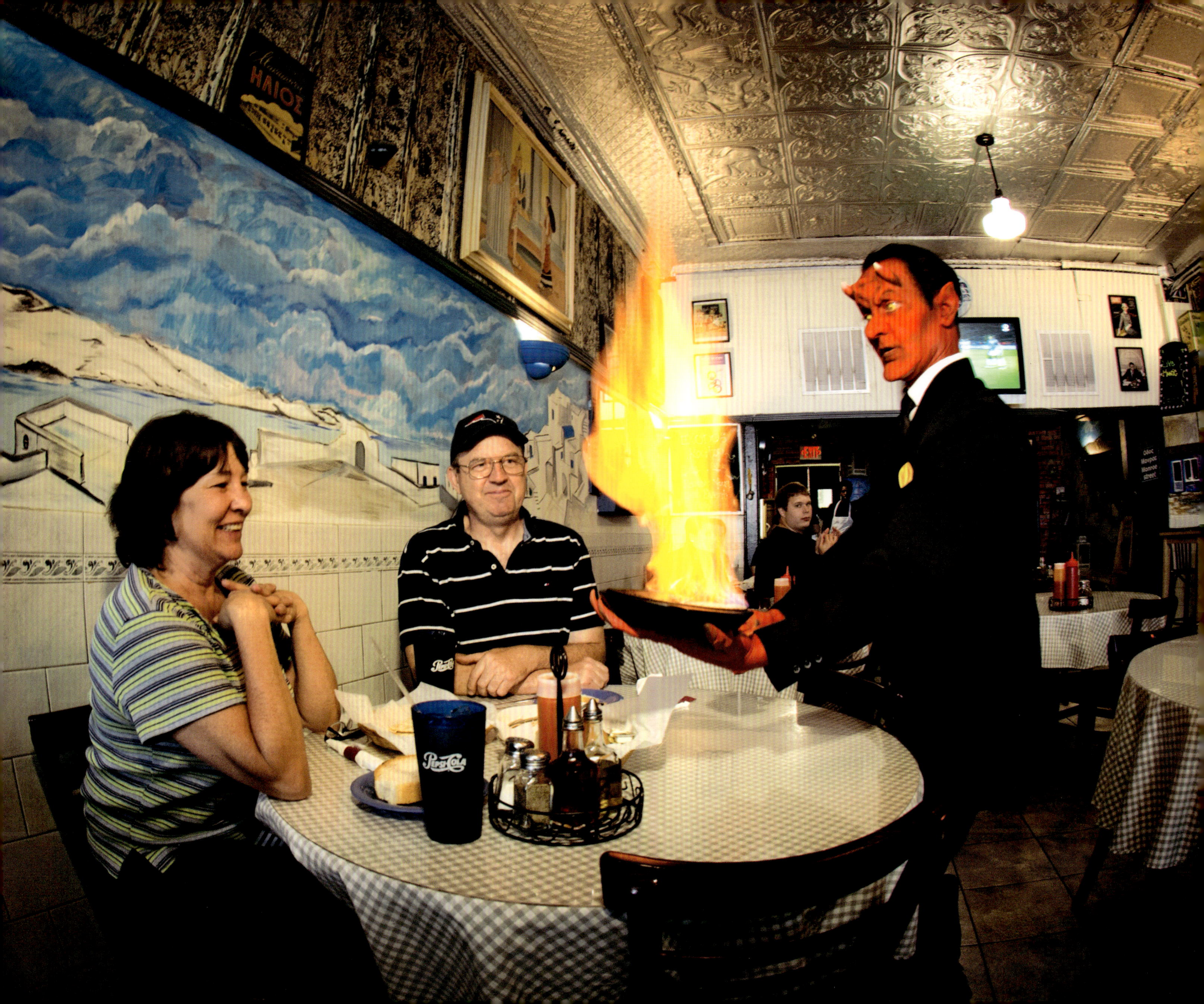

ΗΛΙΟΣ
EXIT
Pepsi-Cola

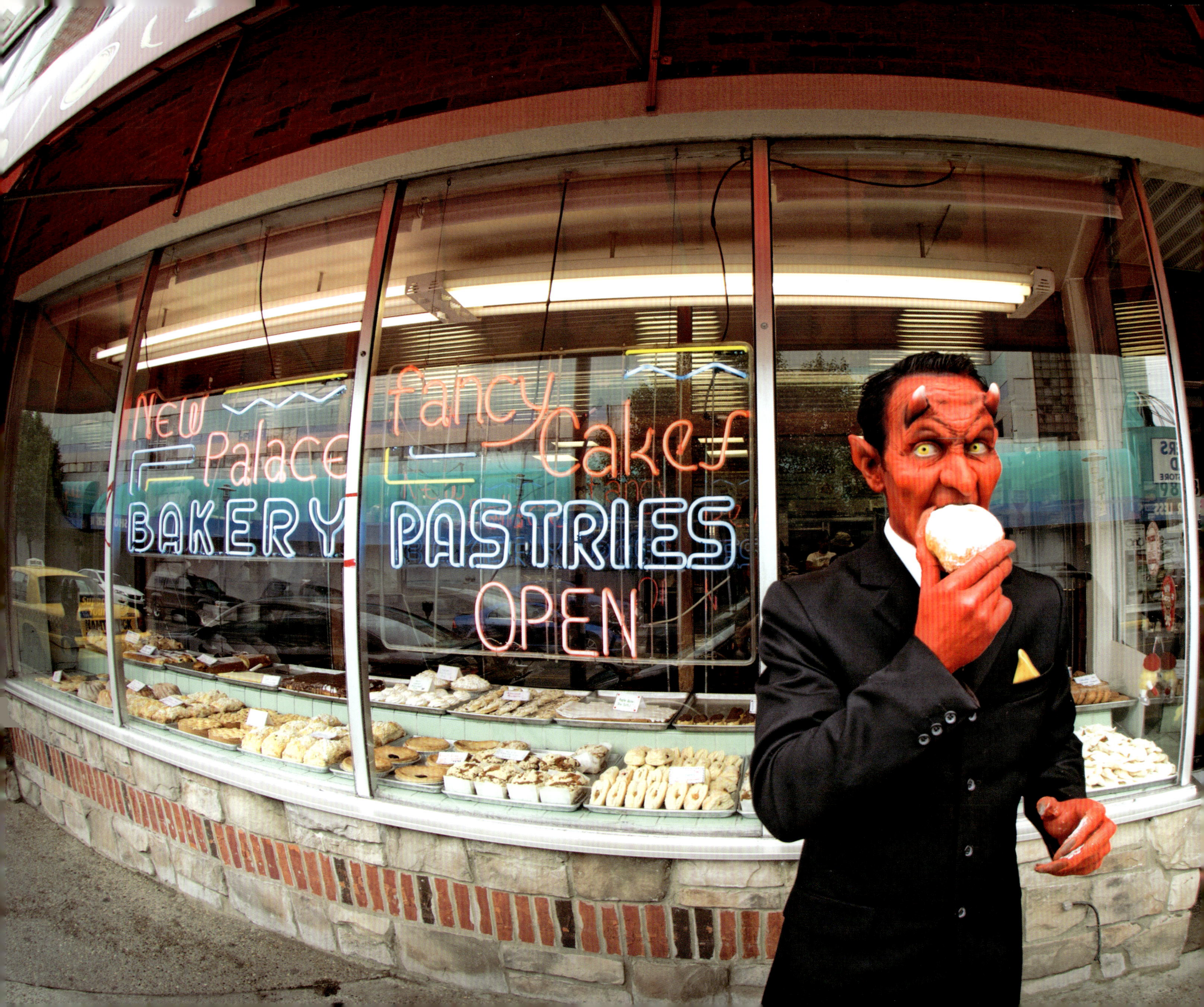
New Palace
BAKERY
fancy Cakes
PASTRIES
OPEN

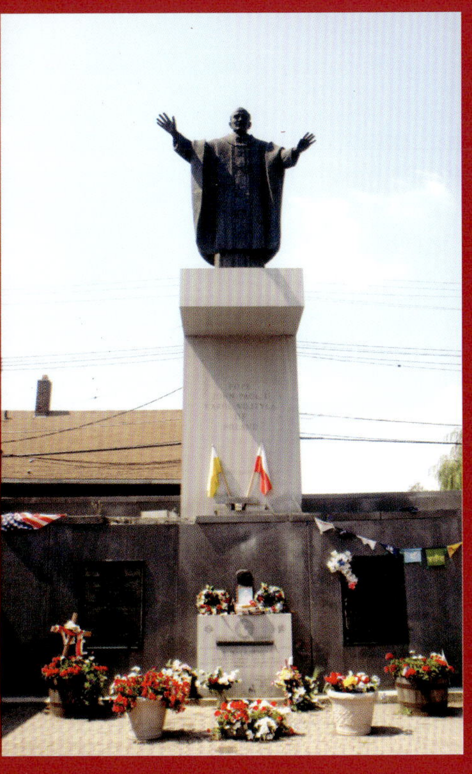

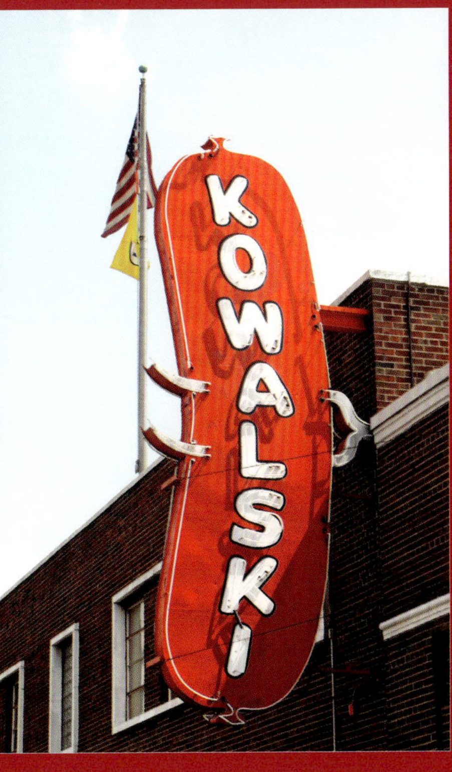

HAMTRAMCK/POLETOWN

Jos Campau Ave., Hamtramck, 48212
www.hamtramck.us

As Detroit's auto industry exploded in the early 20th century, immigrants arrived in overwhelming numbers for manufacturing-job opportunities and better lives. In 1914, the Dodge Brothers opened their factory and offices in a small enclave surrounded by Detroit called Hamtramck and hired mostly Eastern Europeans and Poles, who settled here and in the adjoining Poletown neighborhood in Detroit, forming one of the most diverse communities in Michigan, with more than two dozen different languages spoken. Recent immigrants from Bangladesh, Yemen, Albania, and Bosnia have established a large presence here.

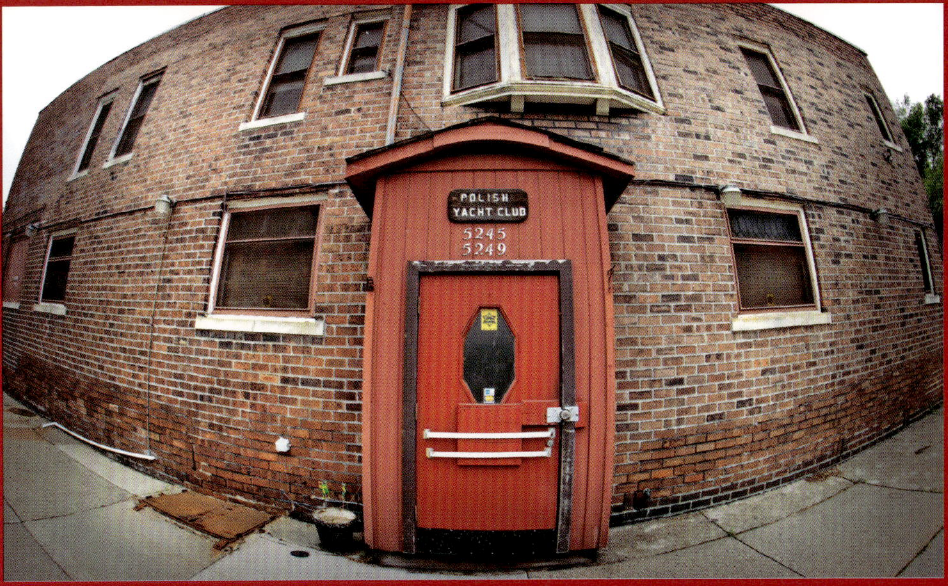

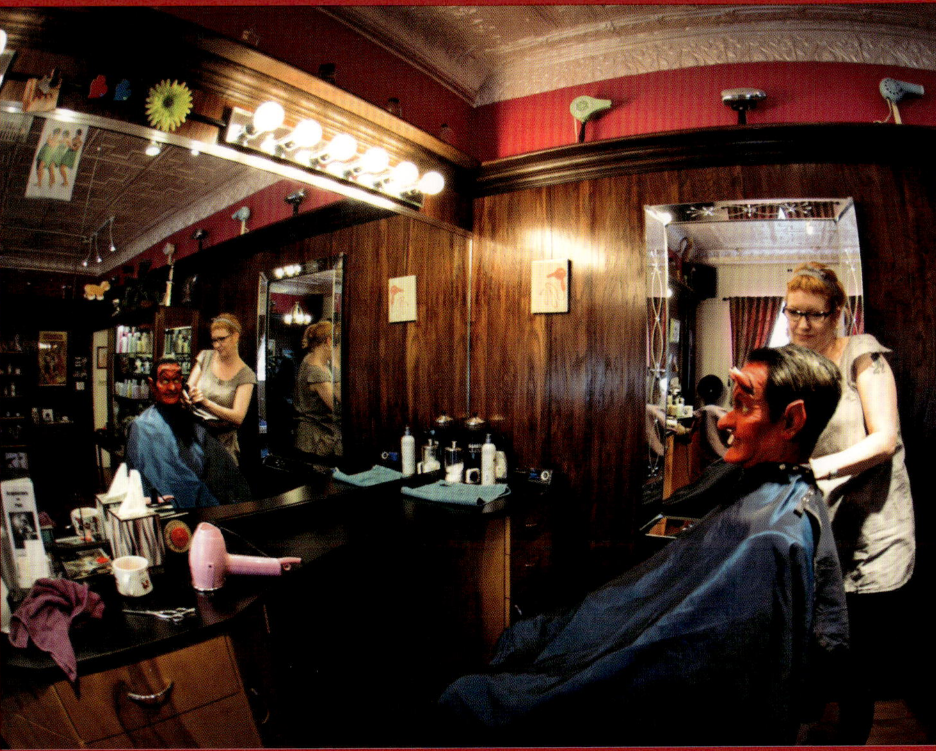

Poletown and Hamtramck were centers for Polish and Ukrainian first generation immigrants. Poletown was all but lost when a new auto plant was built destroying the neighborhood, and Hamtramck has diversified with new immigrant populations from Yemen, Bangladesh, India and Albania. Every Fat Tuesday before Lent, the bakeries are packed as people devour paczkis. One of my favorite hangouts is the Polish Yacht Club in Poletown, surrounded by dozens of empty blocks, and nowhere near water. - NR

JOHN K. KING USED & RARE BOOKS

901 W. Lafayette Blvd., Detroit, 48226
www.kingbooksdetroit.com

With more than one million books under one roof, John King has been described by *Salon* magazine as having "one of the largest and strangest collections in North America." The main building is a maze of fully stocked, functional shelves filling four floors, but if you ask, you can visit the rare book room, which is classically done with massive oak wall shelves and offers a more subdued energy.

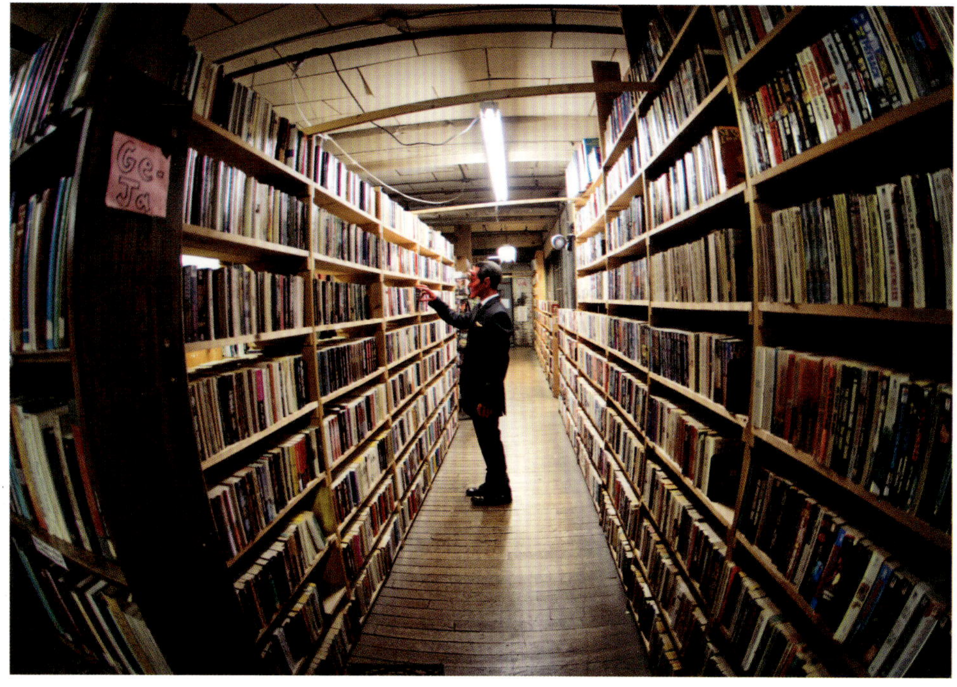

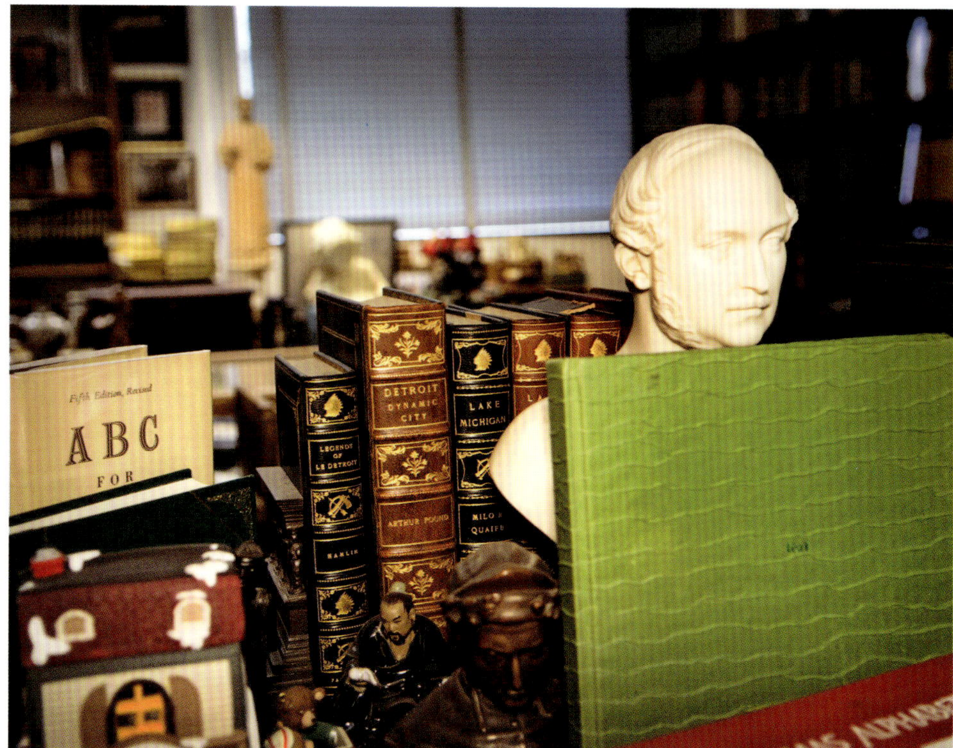

John King Books is a book lover's dream. Rows upon rows, stacks and stacks of books fill every available space. I recommend at least a half a day for exploring. The Rare Book Room is amazing (and orderly too). - NR

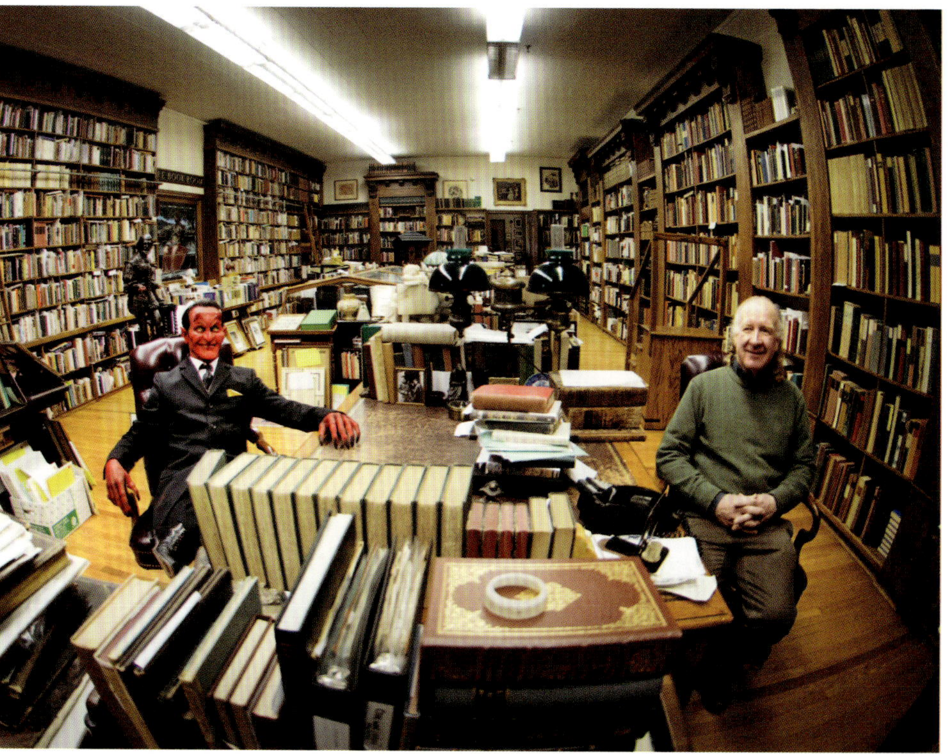

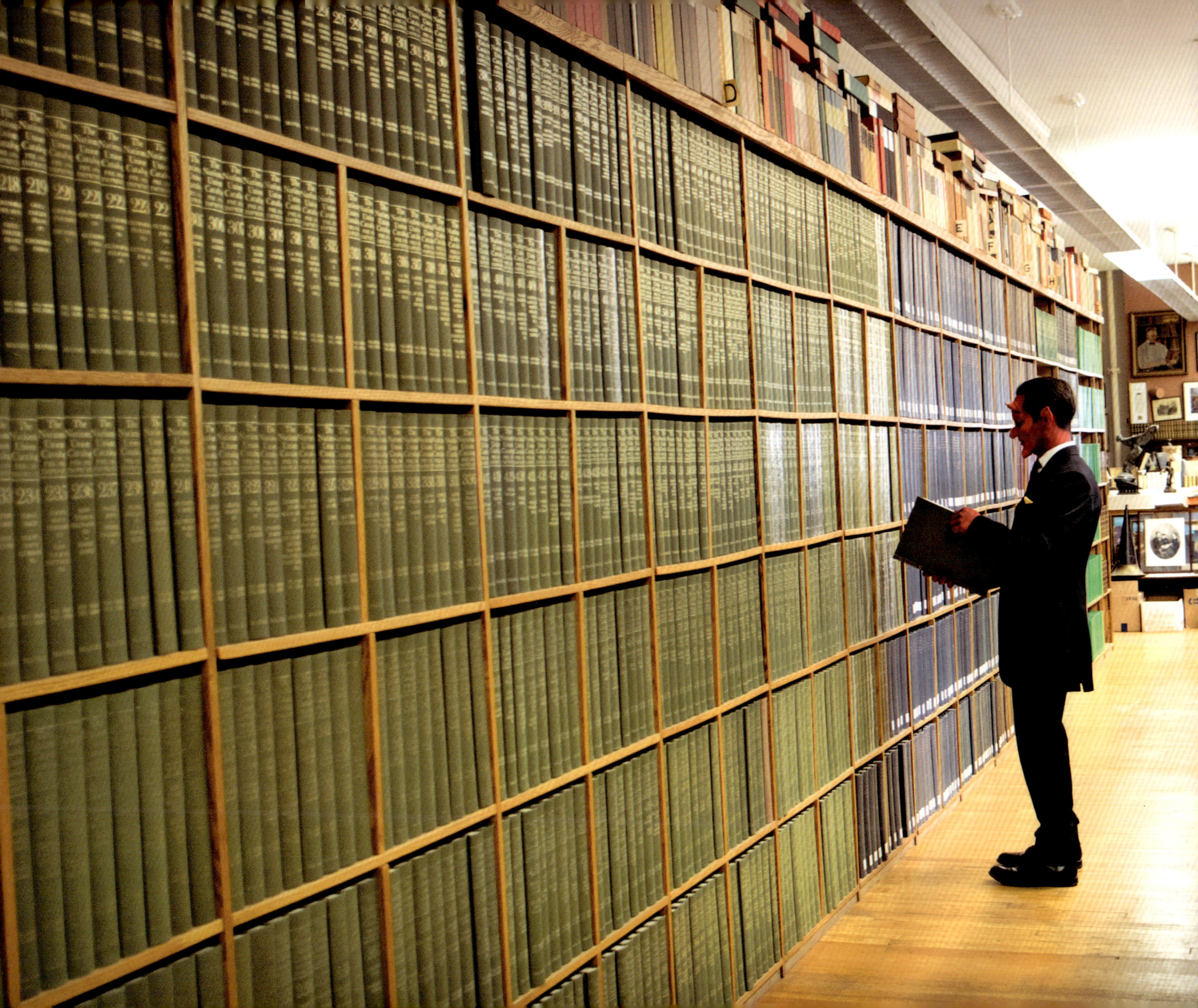

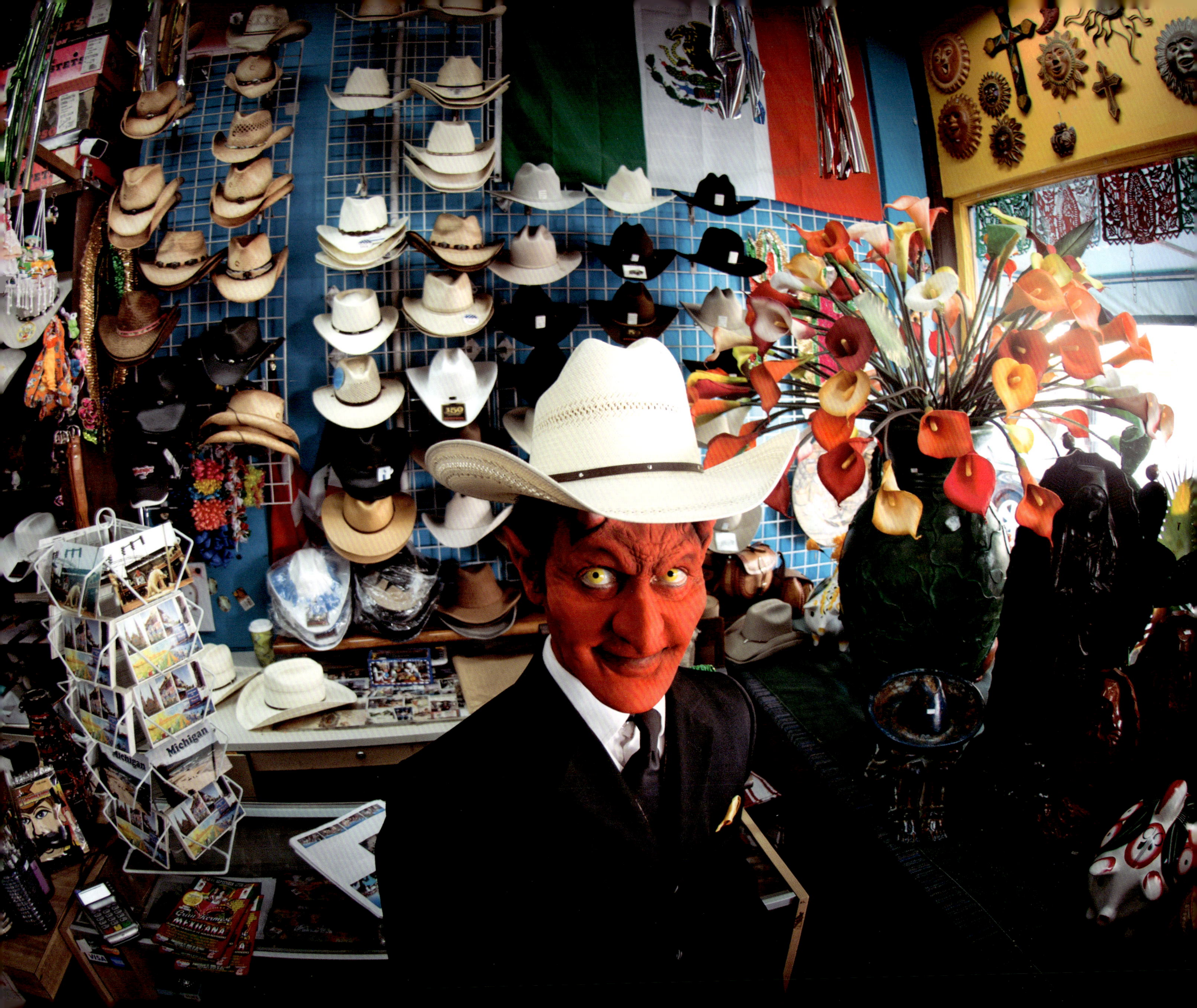
Michigan
Michigan
MEXICANA

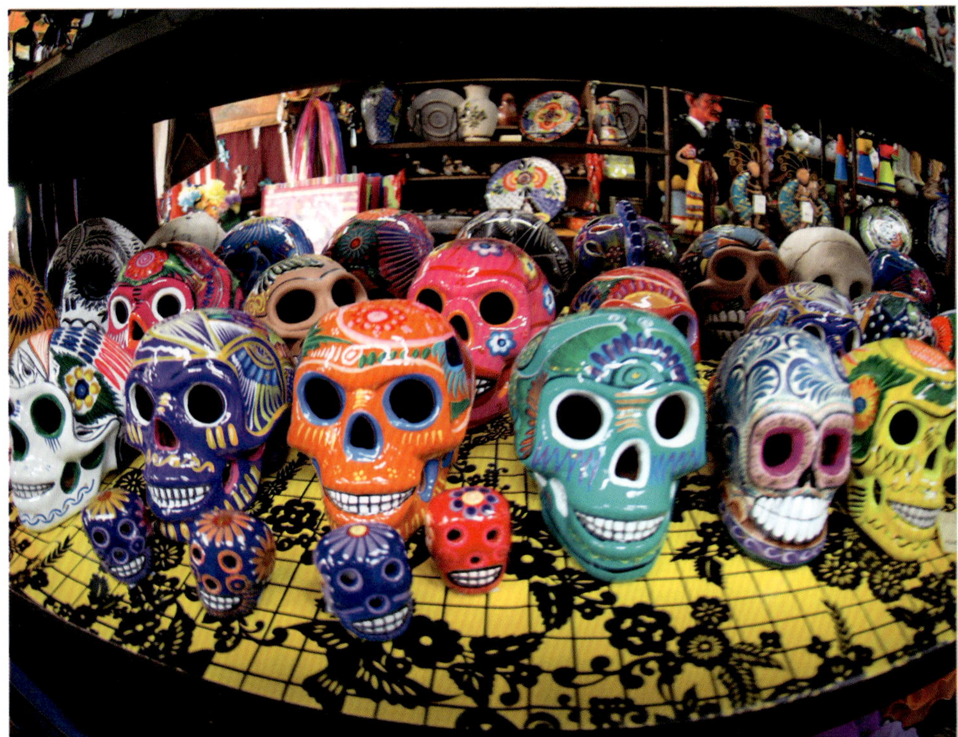

MEXICANTOWN

Bagley Ave., Between 23rd St. and 24th St., Detroit, 48216
www.savorsouthwest.org

As Mexican and Latino immigrants began arriving and settling in southwest Detroit in the 1920s, a vibrant community took shape. Originally located around Bagley Avenue, or "La Bagley," as it once was known, it was the heart of Mexicantown. As the Latino population has grown throughout the years, much of southwest Detroit has seen an increase in density, remaining a vibrant, dynamic neighborhood.

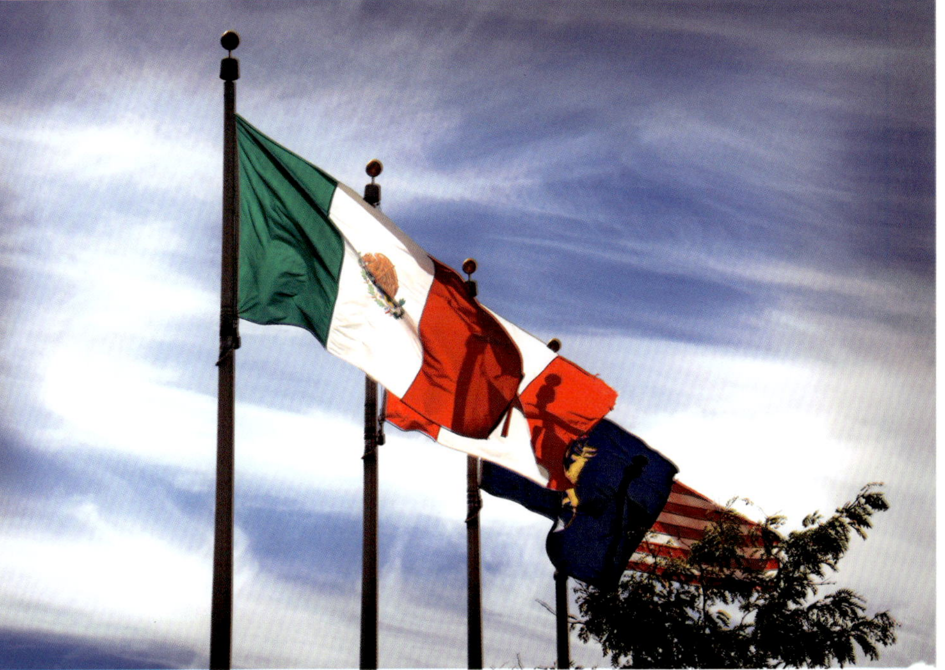

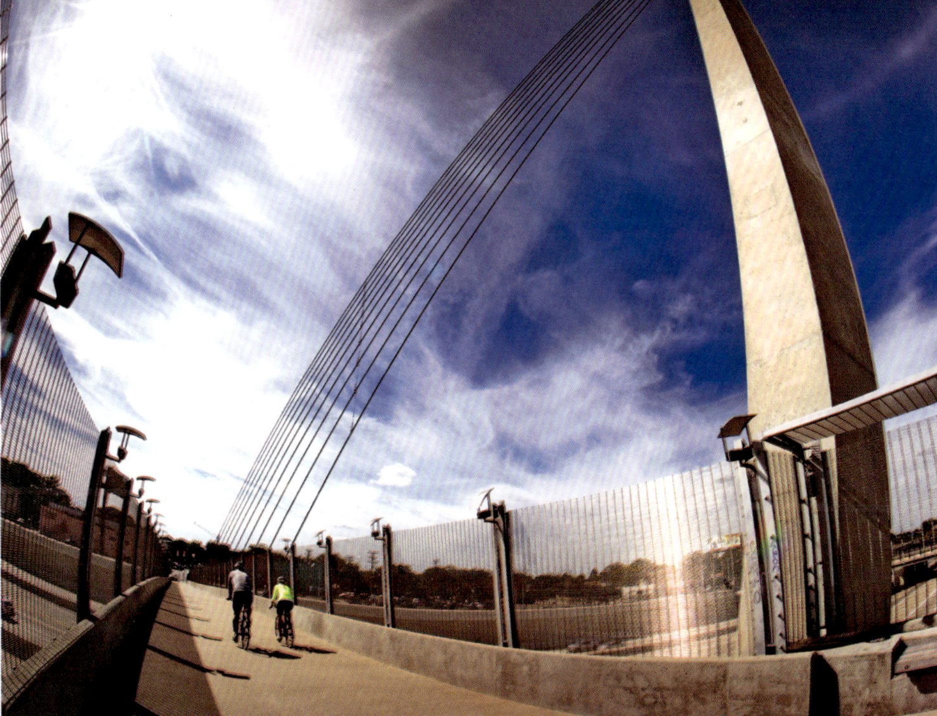

Still centered on "La Bagley", Mexicantown has become more than the few original blocks. As Detroit was losing population, Southwest Detroit was the only neighborhood that grew with a steady stream of Mexican and Central American immigrants. I have found many great restaurants and shops have expanded along Vernor Avenue.
- NR

OLD MIAMI

3930 Cass Ave., Detroit, 48201

After the Vietnam War, Danny Overstreet bought a bar in the Cass corridor so he and his veteran buddies could have a place of their own. Over the years, vets from all over the country have donated memorabilia to the bar. The walls became covered with patches and photos from the war as the bar grew into an important hangout for those who served. Unknown to most first-timers, in the back of the building is the greatest backyard respite in all of Detroit with a koi fish pond, an outdoor stage and, sometimes, BBQ.

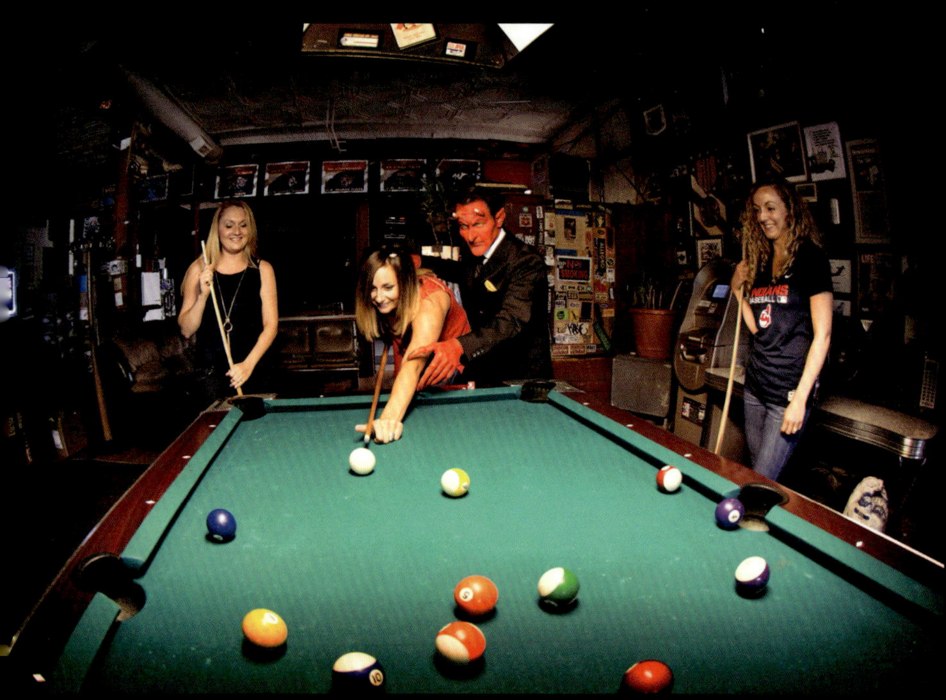

One of my favorite hangouts, the Old Miami is a true Detroit bar: kinda dirty, kinda rough, in the heart of the Cass Corridor, and populated with a bunch of eccentric regulars. I have been friends with the owner Danny for years. His generosity is displayed every Thanksgiving and Christmas, when he prepares a feast for those not uniting with family, and his respect for vets is legendary. - NR

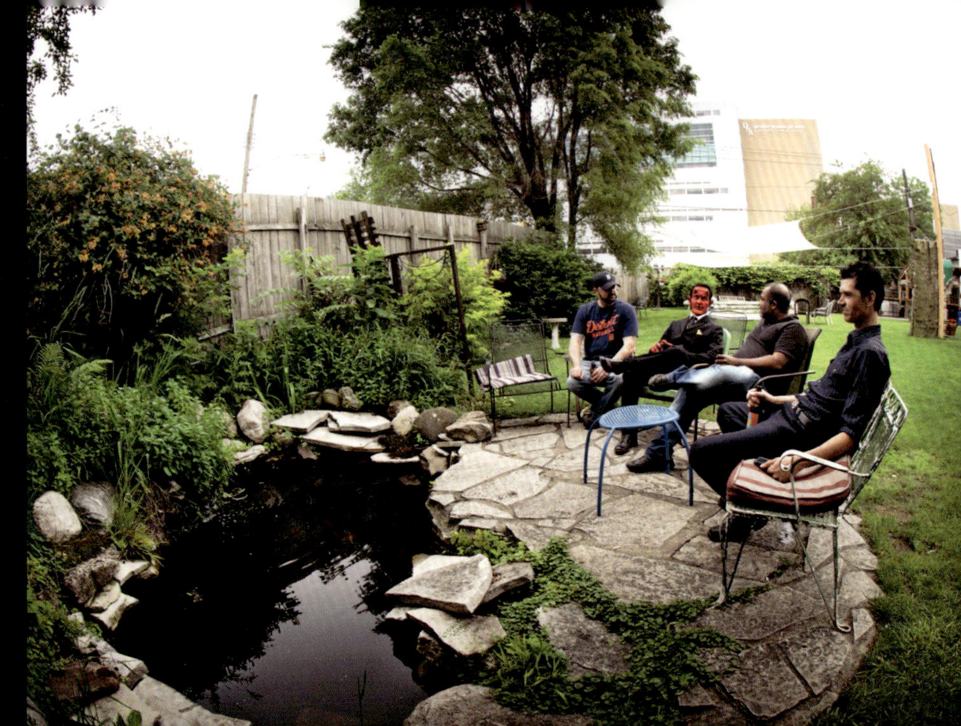

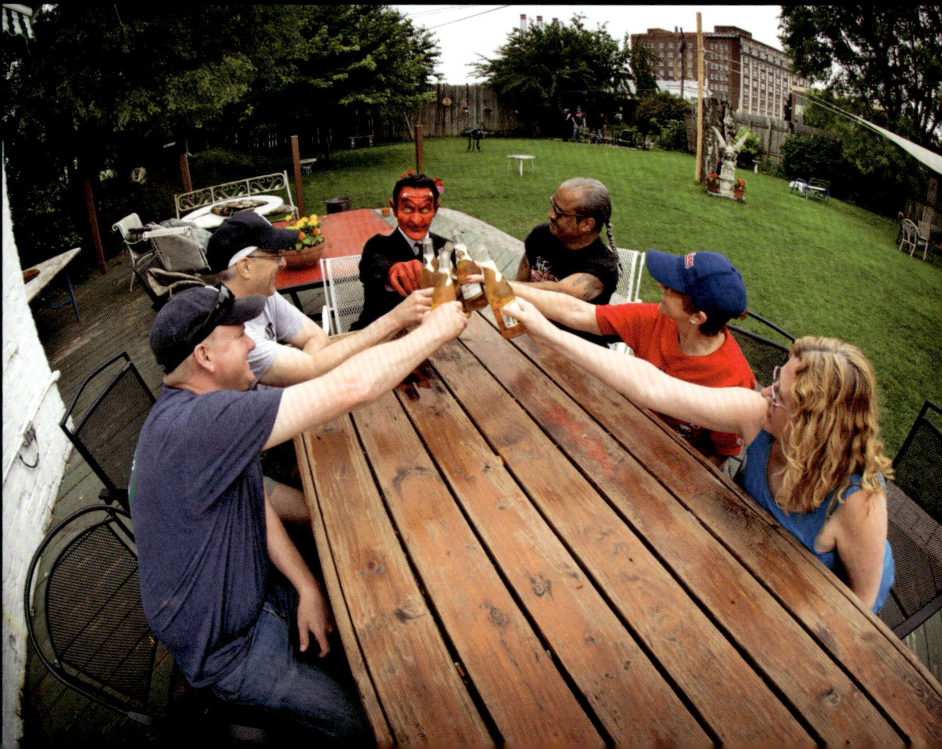

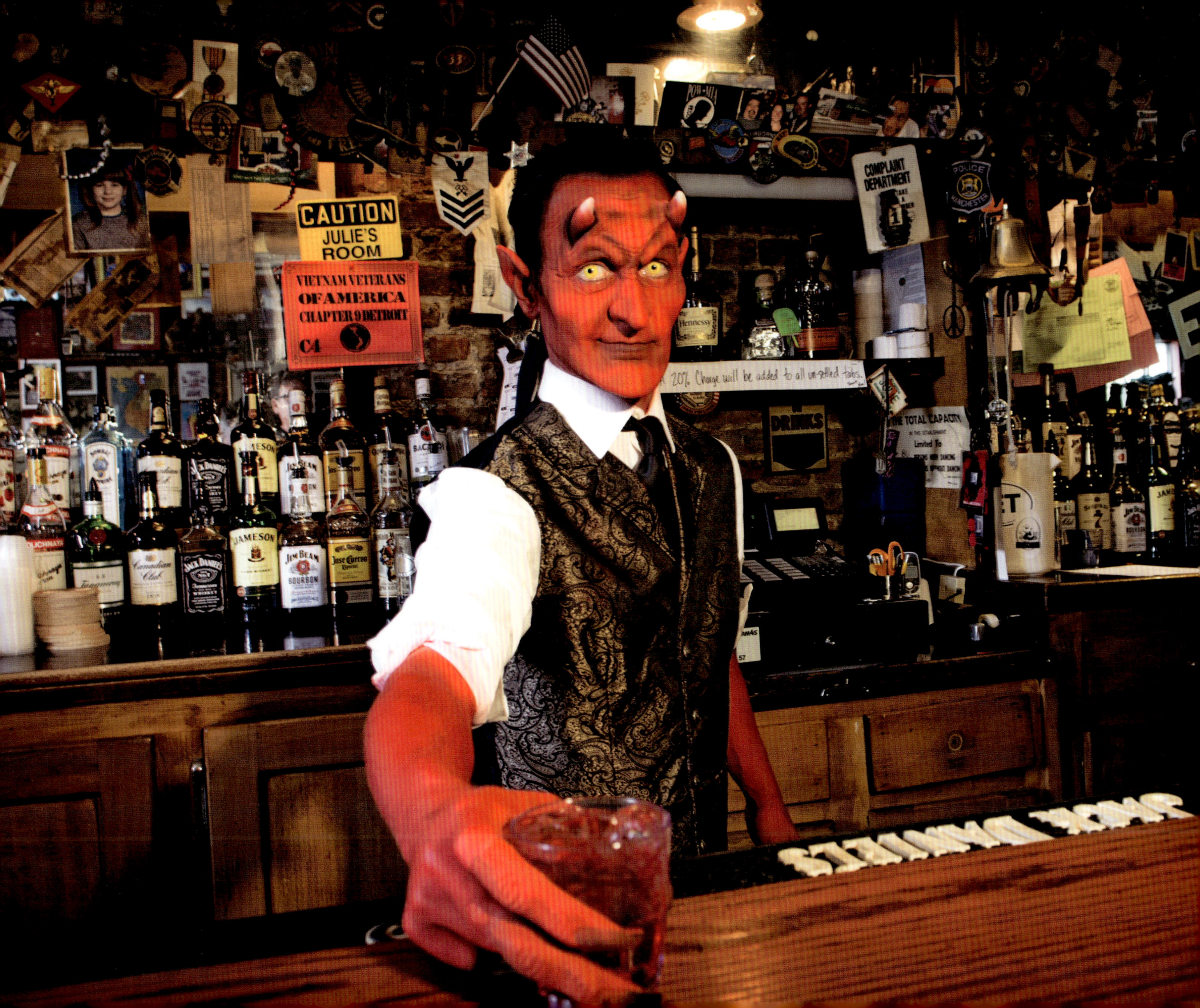
CAUTION
JULIE'S
ROOM
VIETNAM VETERANS
OF AMERICA
CHAPTER 9 DETROIT
C4
COMPLAINT
DEPARTMENT
POLICE
MANCHESTER
POW-MIA
20% Charge will be added to all un-settled tabs.
DRINKS
THE TOTAL CAPACITY
Limited To
Hennessy
JAMESON
JIM BEAM
BOURBON
Jose Cuervo
Canadian Club
JACK DANIEL'S
Tanqueray

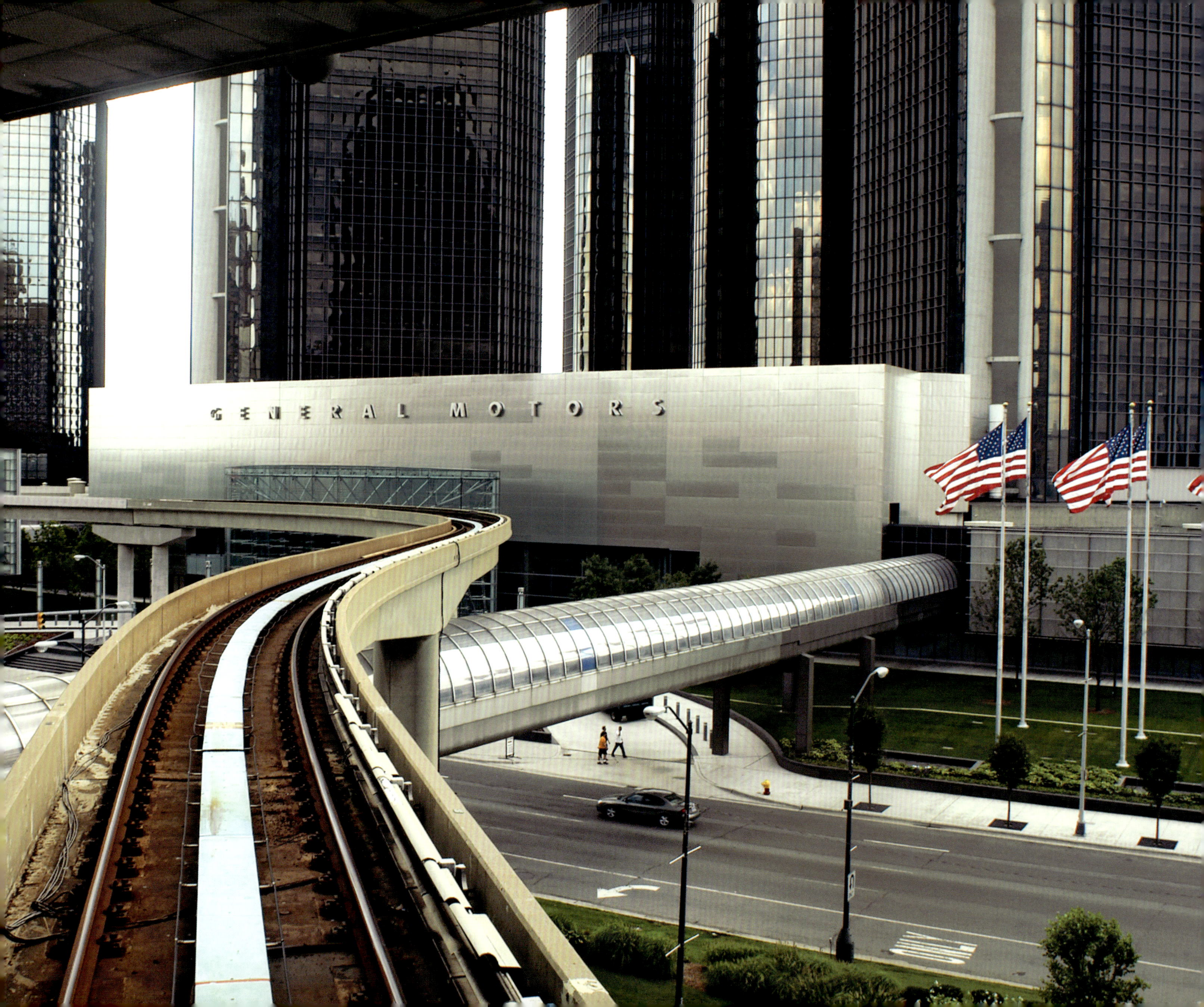
GENERAL MOTORS

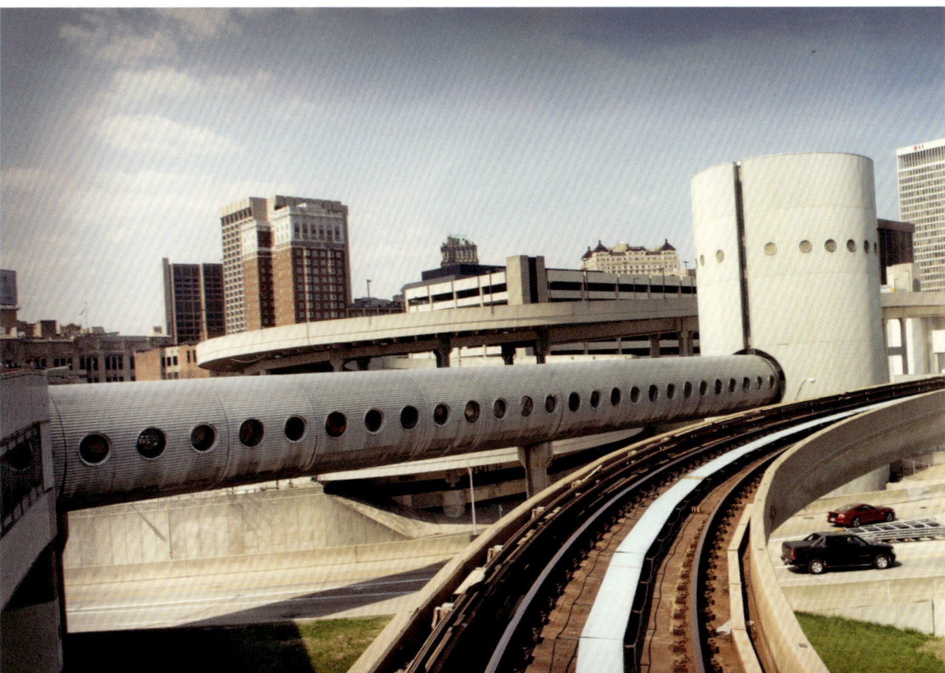

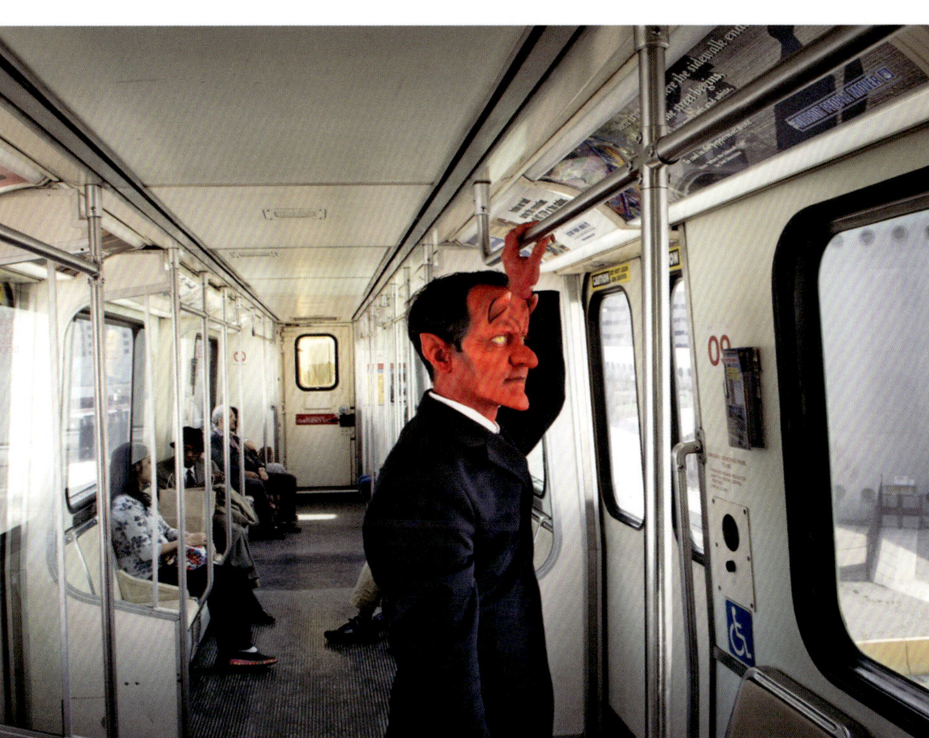

PEOPLE MOVER

Central Business District, Detroit, 48226
www.thepeoplemover.com

Detroit's light rail line, the People Mover debuted in 1987 after decades of planning. Circling downtown, the driverless cars travel a 2.8-mile track in about 15 minutes, connecting with 13 stops, each decorated with original artworks designed specifically for each station. Originally intended to expand into a regional transit system, it continues to serve the downtown core.

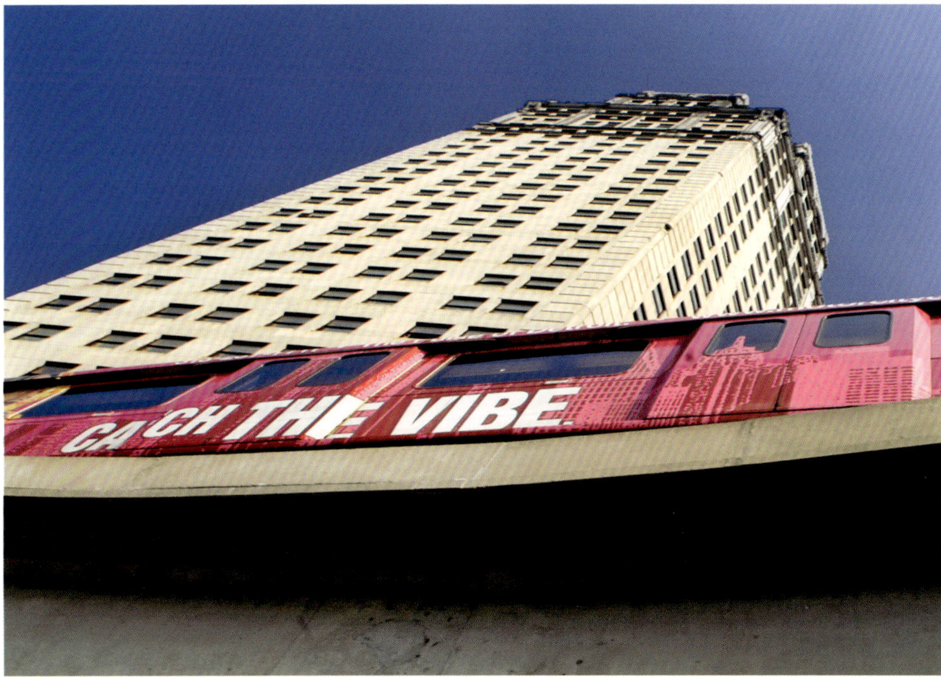

Circling the downtown core, the People Mover is more amusement ride than transportation. In a town too dependent on cars, Detroiters will famously drive a block to the store instead of walking. Built at a time when the streets were devoid of traffic, the People Mover only seemed useful during the auto show or a hockey game. With parking now at a premium and downtown repopulating, it's not so easy to park anywhere you want. I expect it will finally get the respect it's due in the coming years. - NR

REDFORD THEATRE

17360 Lahser Rd., Detroit, 48212
www.redfordtheatre.com

One of the last remaining neighborhood theaters in Detroit, the Redford Theatre has endured decades of socioeconomic changes. Initially designed in 1931 with a Japanese motif, it was painted over in battleship grey during World War II. The Redford is one of only forty theaters that has its original pipe organ, still maintained by the Motor City Theatre Organ Society. After decades of volunteer work, the original extravagant Japanese-inspired interior has been restored. On weekends, the Redford screens a variety of silent films with organ accompaniment, Hollywood classics, or 3D film festivals.

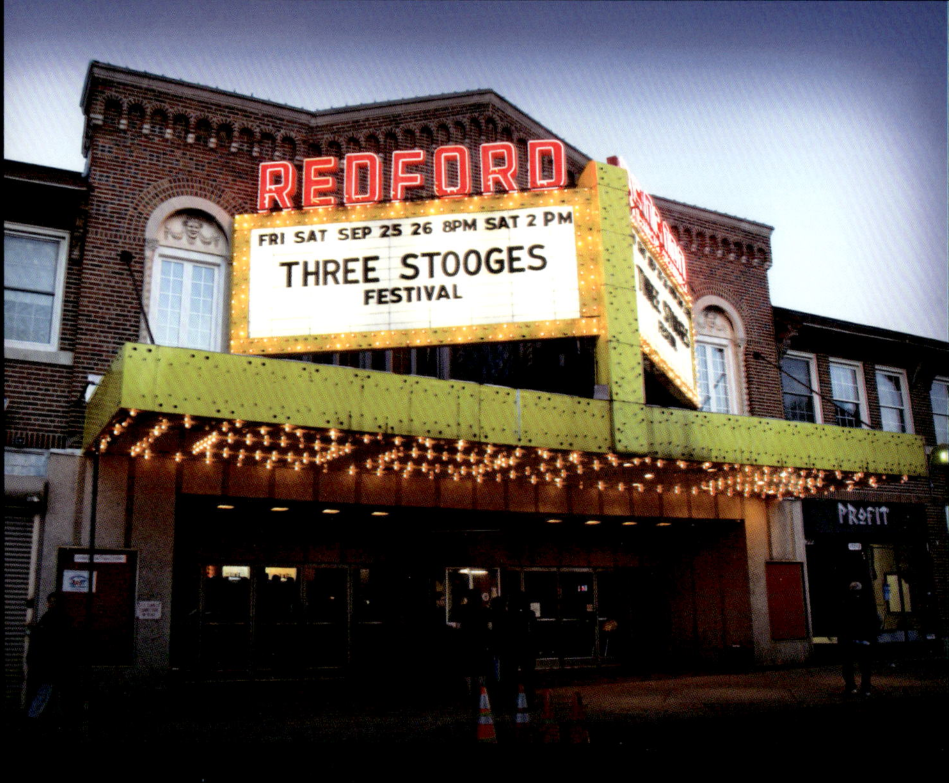

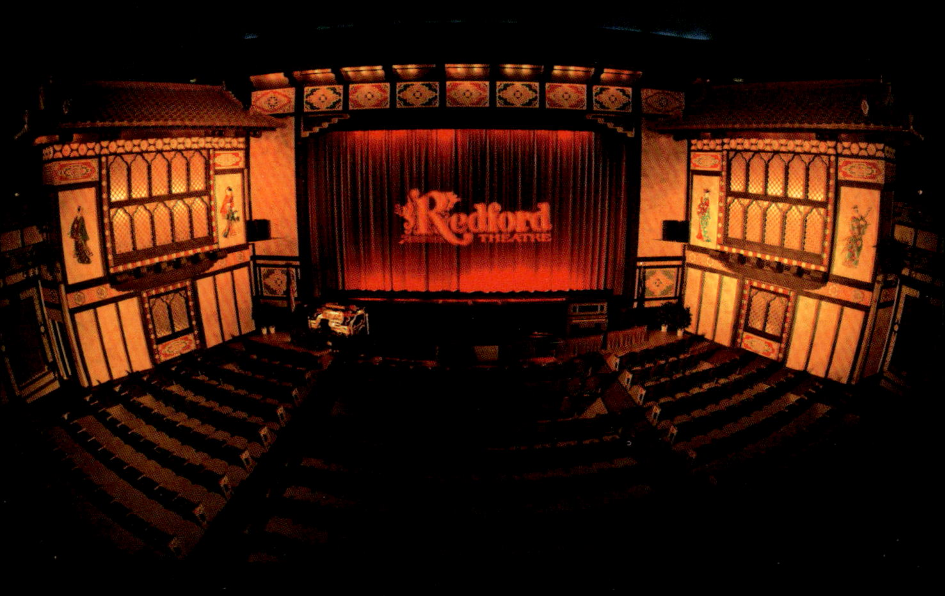

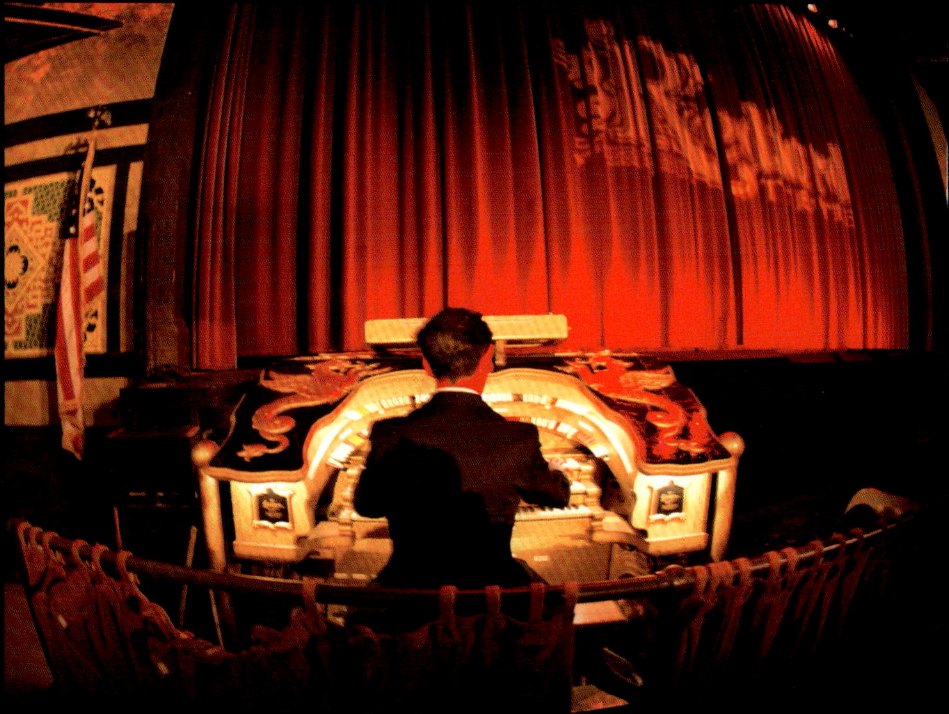

On the northwest side of town, the Redford Theatre is one of the coolest theatres around the metro area. Silent movies are shown accompanied by an organist, and sometime it'll be me. Maintained by a dedicated group of film lovers and volunteers, the Redford is one of the examples of hard work paying off for the rest of us. - NR

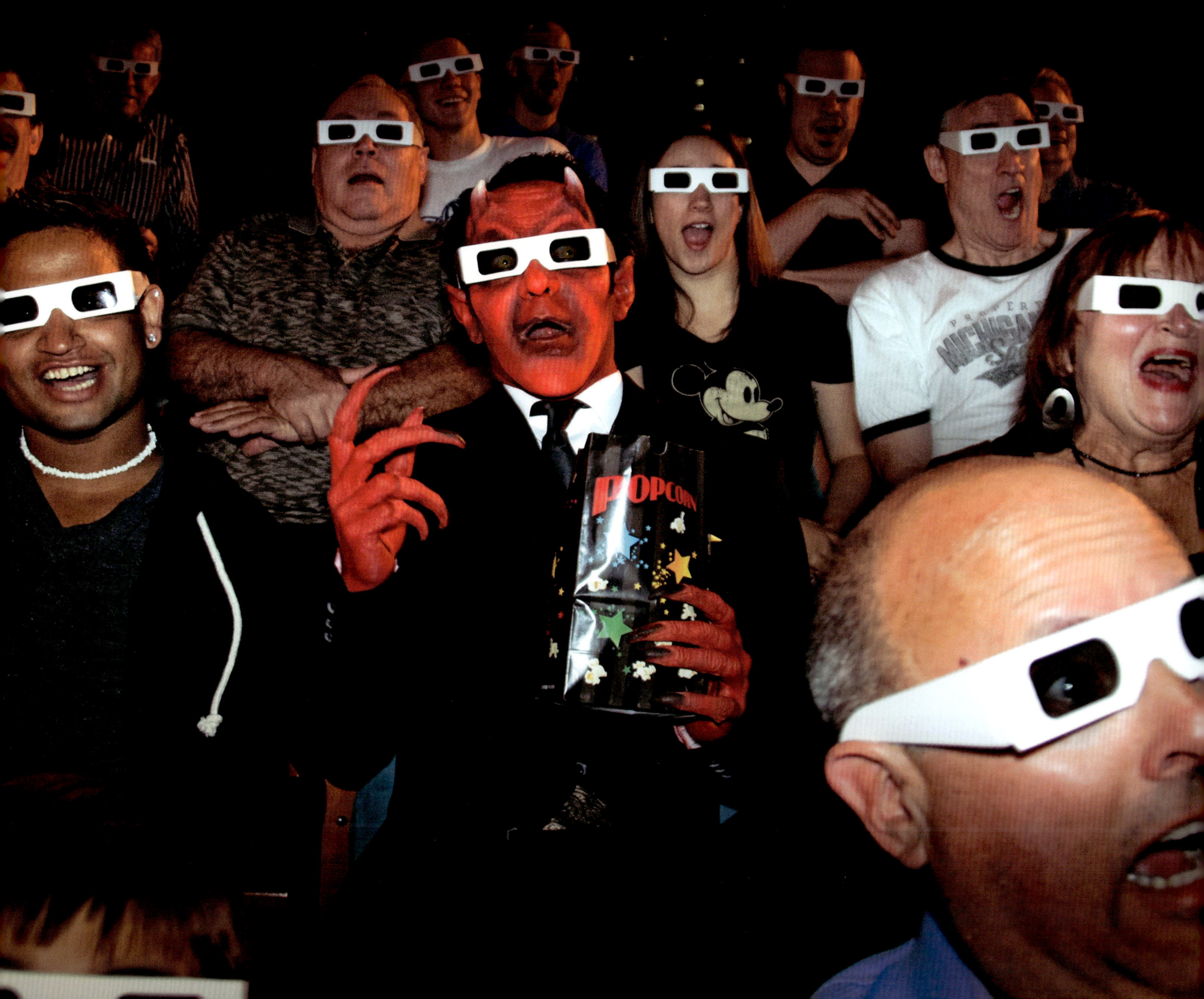
POPCORN

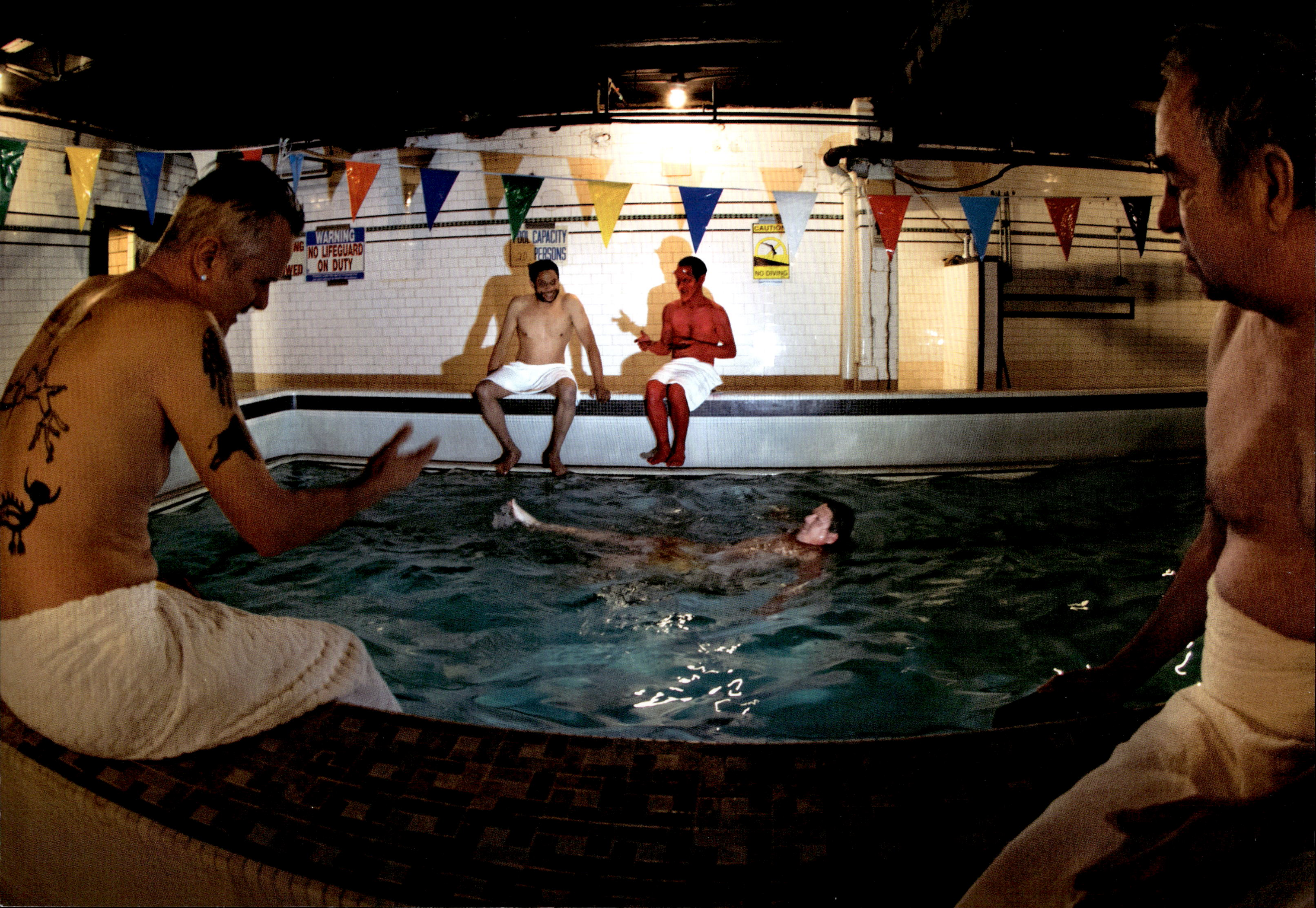
WARNING
NO LIFEGUARD
ON DUTY
CAUTION
NO DIVING

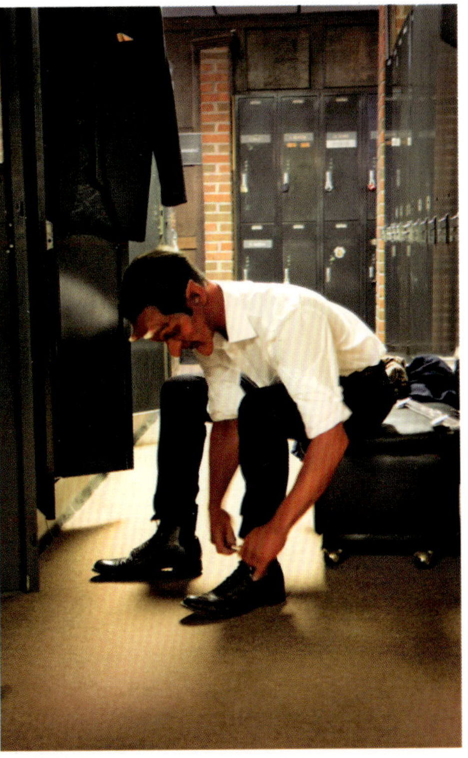

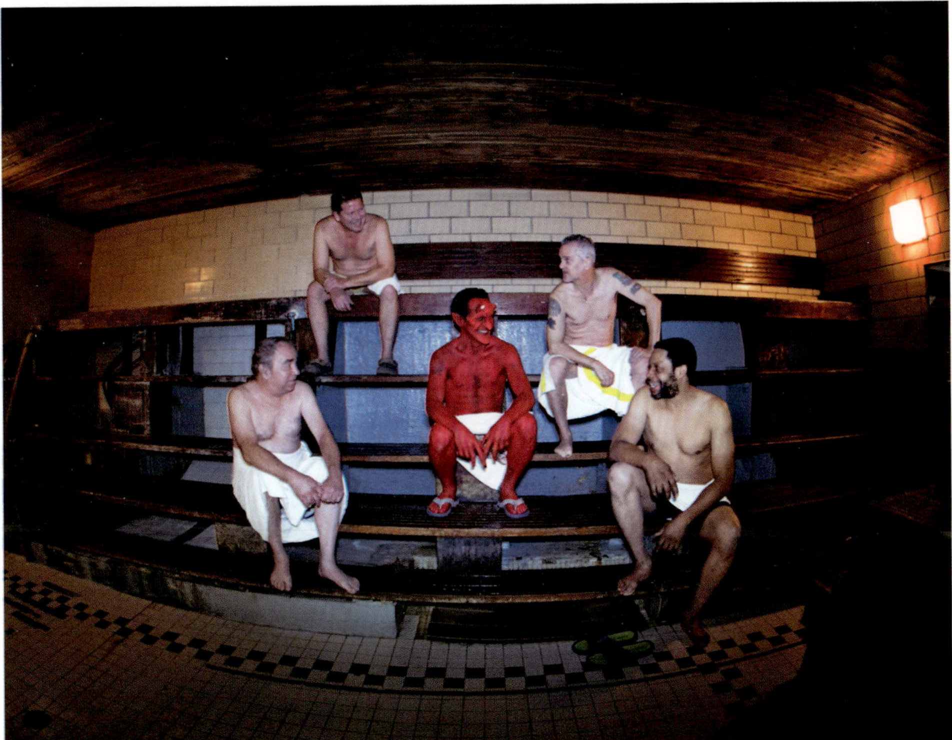

THE SCHVITZ RUSSIAN BANYA CLUB

82950 Oakland Ave., Detroit, 48211
www.banyaclub.com/schvitz

Since 1930, the Schvitz has been synonymous with steam baths in Detroit. As the grandest and last remaining bathhouse on Oakland Avenue, the Schvitz continues to offer patrons a place to relax and commiserate while enjoying the Old World traditions of Eastern Europe. Originally frequented by Jewish immigrants and members of the notorious Purple Gang, the Schvitz is one of the few remaining "banyas" in the United States. Keeping alive the practices of centuries old Russian bathhouses, it offers men- and women-only nights, and on the weekends, it hosts a raucous couples' night, where the more adventurous assemble.

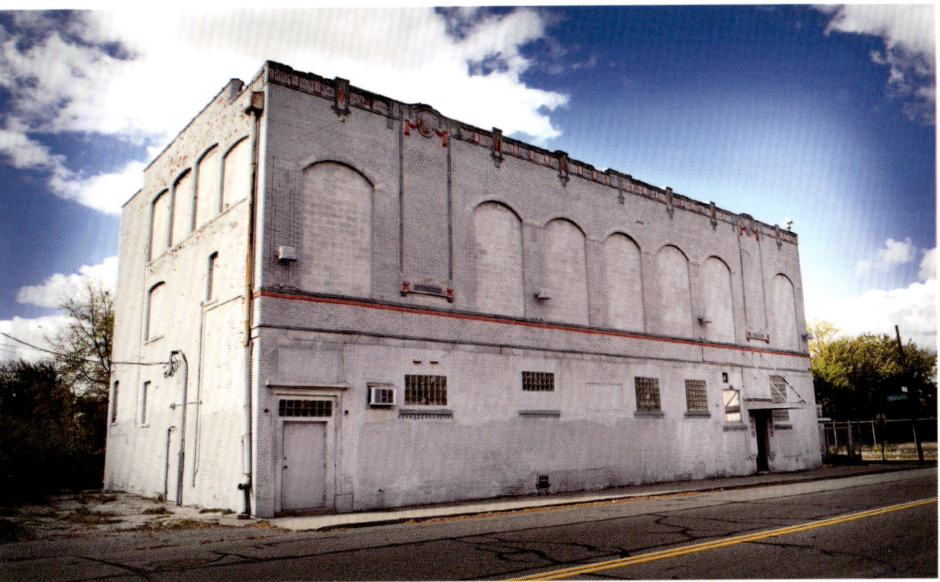

After decades of use, the Schvitz is a bit worn on the inside and downright frightening on the outside. Painted a dull grey, with no signage, the Schvitz seems determined to scare you away. Don't be so quick to judge. Entering on the pool level, unchanged since it opened, you get hit with a sense of history, then you relax and take a hot steam. - NR

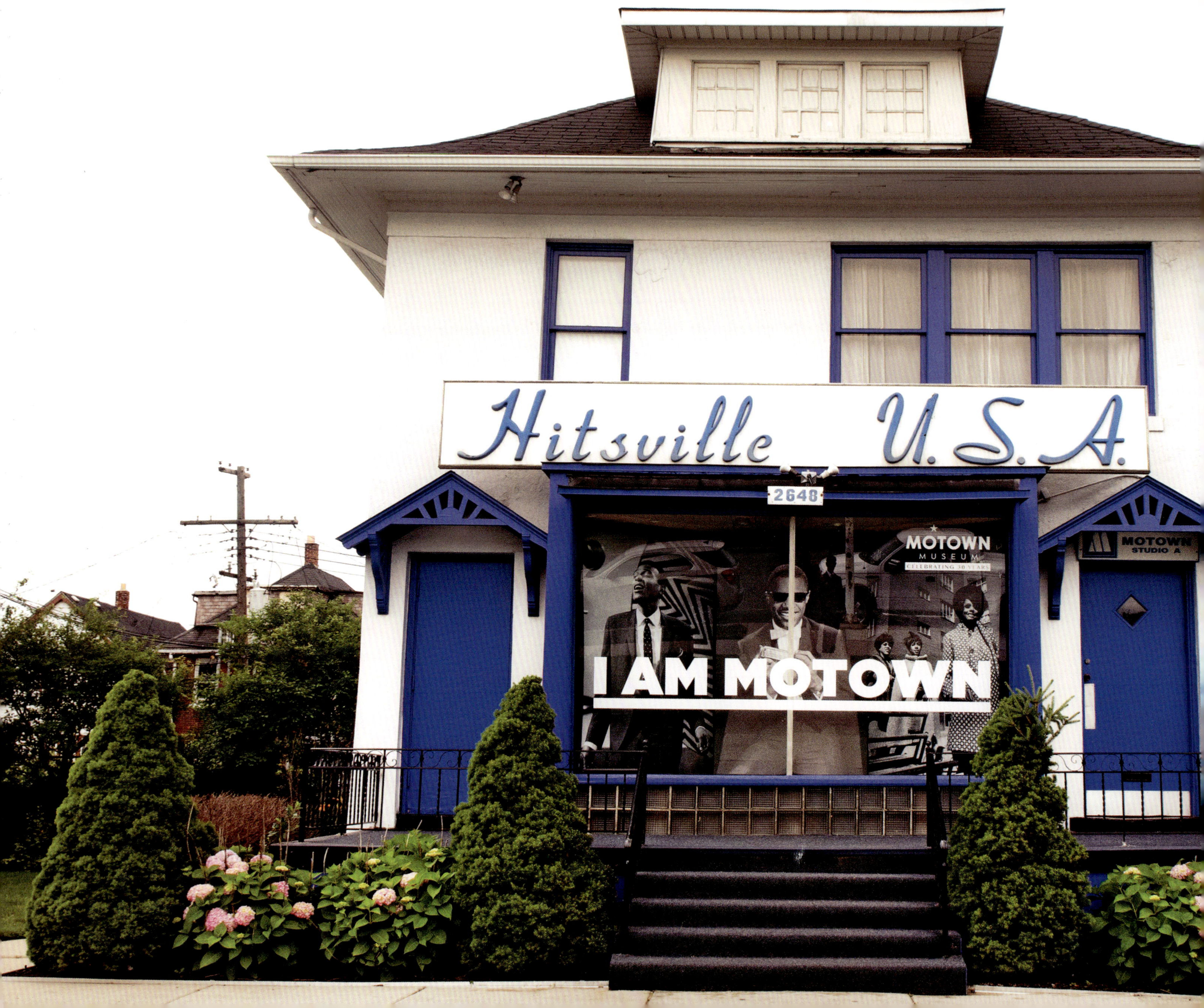
Hitsville U.S.A.
2648
MOTOWN
MUSEUM
CELEBRATING 30 YEARS
I AM MOTOWN
MOTOWN
STUDIO A

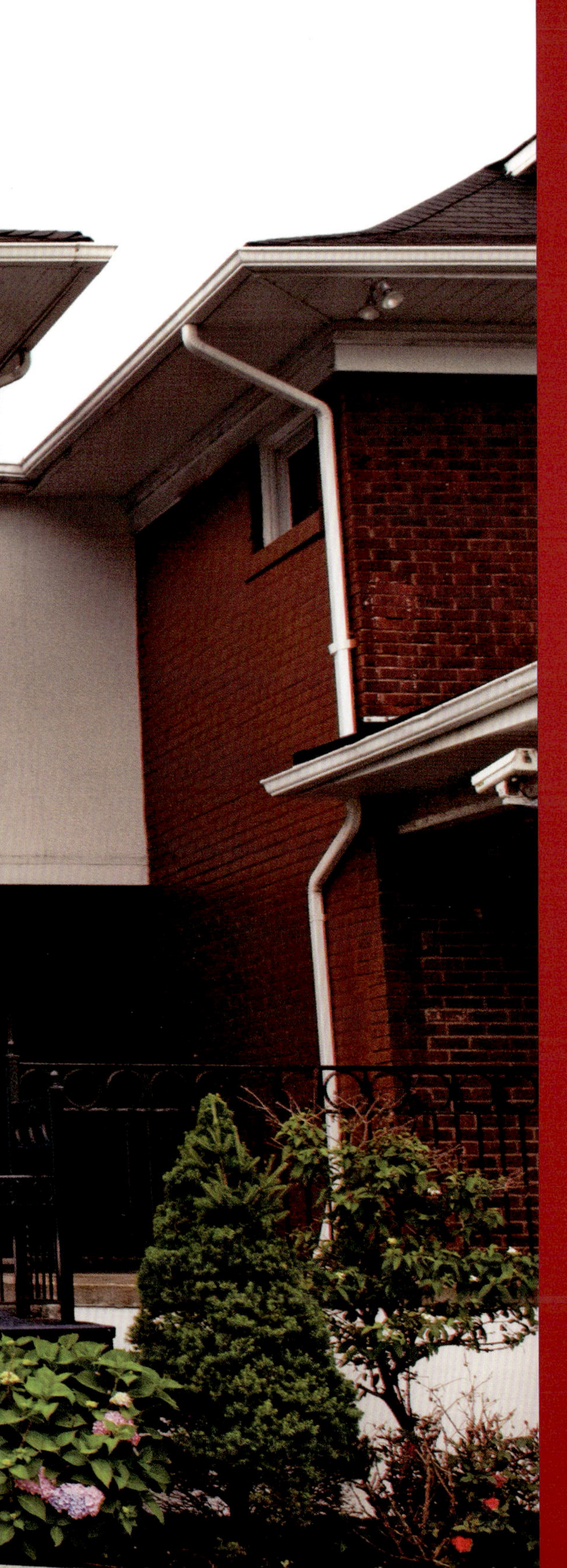

HISTORY & NATURE

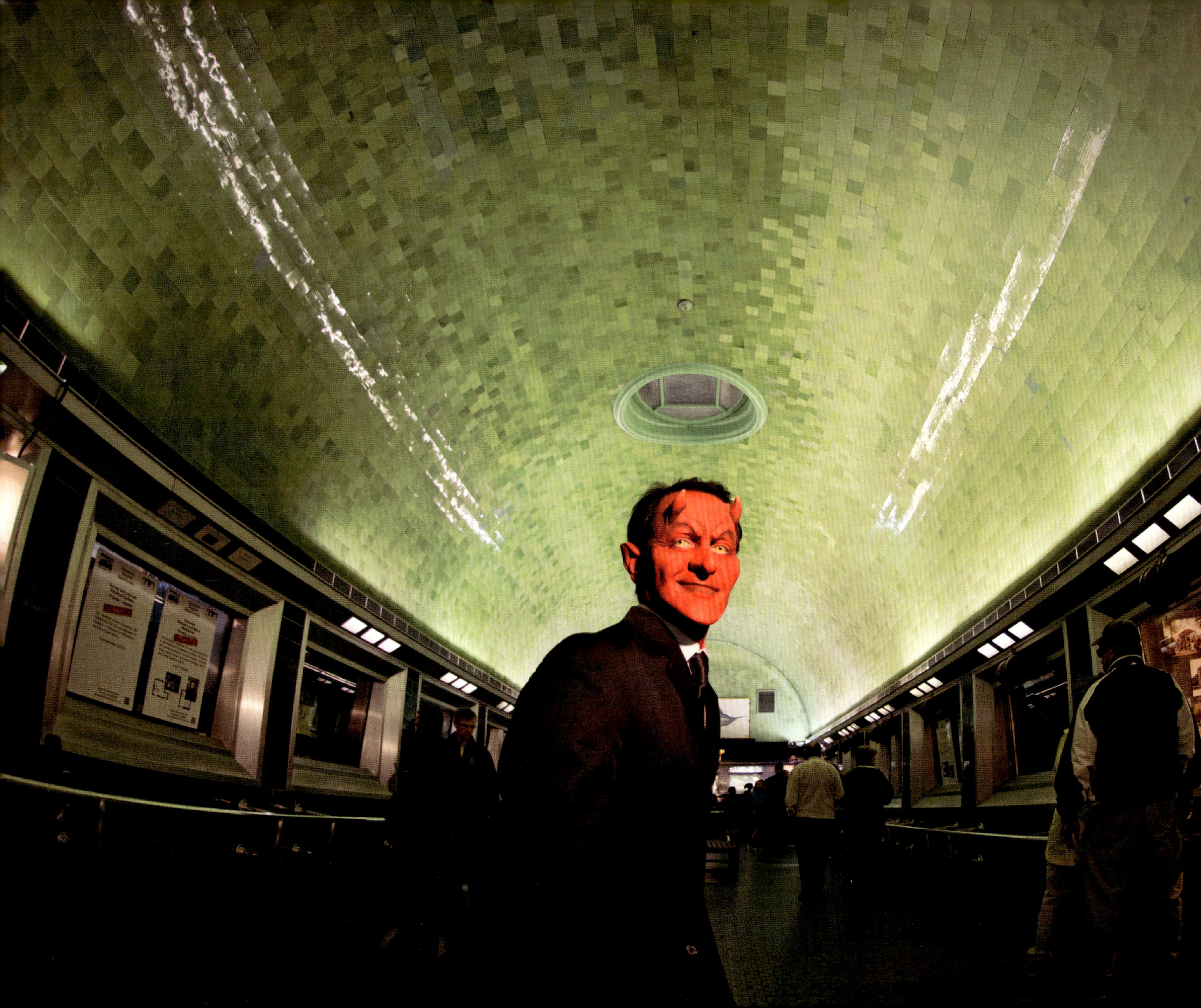

BELLE ISLE AQUARIUM

900 Inselruhe Ave., Detroit, 48207
www.detroitaquarium.weebly.com

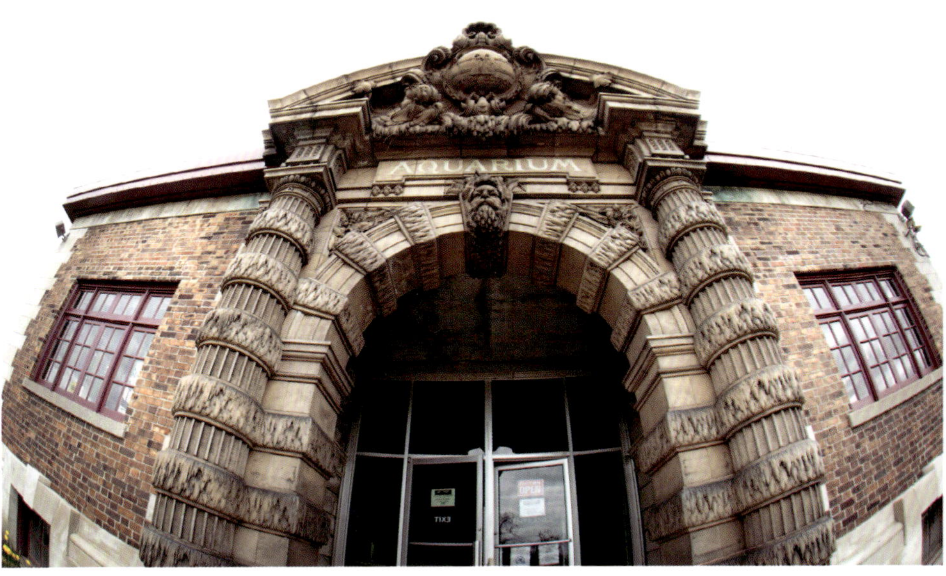

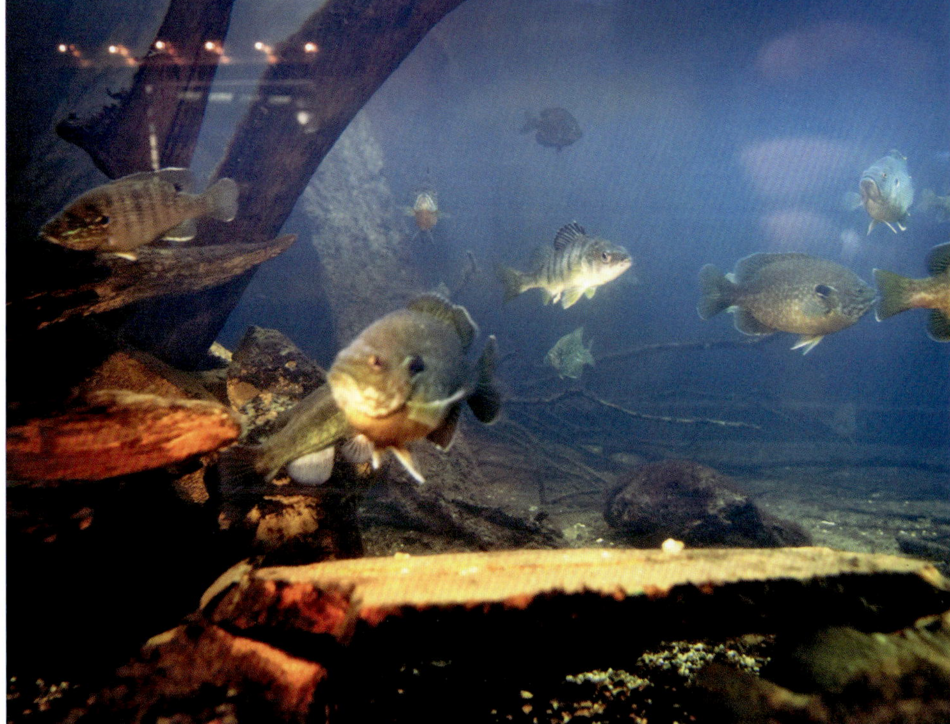

Designed by famed local architect Albert Kahn, the Belle Isle Aquarium opened in 1904, becoming the first in the United States, the world's third largest, and the finest ever seen. Upon opening, the exhibits overwhelmingly showcased Great Lakes freshwater fish with a few tanks dedicated to salt water species. A little known fact: the basement served as a speakeasy during Prohibition. The tanks were then reused for species too large for the original exhibits. Following Detroit's financial collapse, the Aquarium was forced to close. Beloved by the public and with a grass roots effort, the Aquarium has reopened, operated by a volunteer group.

I remember back in the day, the most fascinating exhibit was an electric eel in a tank with a string of lights. As the eel touched the extended wires, the lights would flash with an electric charge. It was captivating as the crowd stood anticipating the next burst. Detroit's fortunate to have dedicated folks like those who have reopened this wonder so new generations can form vivid memories of it like mine. - NR

ANNA SCRIPPS WHITCOMB CONSERVATORY

7000 Inselruhe Ave., Detroit, 48207
www.belleisleconservancy.org

The oldest continually operated conservatory in America, the Anna Scripps Whitcomb Conservatory opened alongside the Aquarium in 1904 and was later renamed for a patron. In the 1950s, Anna Scripps assembled one of the world's largest orchid collections. Many of the orchids came from Britain and were saved during World War II. The surrounding rose-lined gardens highlight Detroit native and sculptor Marshall Frederick's first commission, *Leaping Gazelle*, one of his most reproduced works. The Conservatory is supported by 20 greenhouses containing its many varieties of plants.

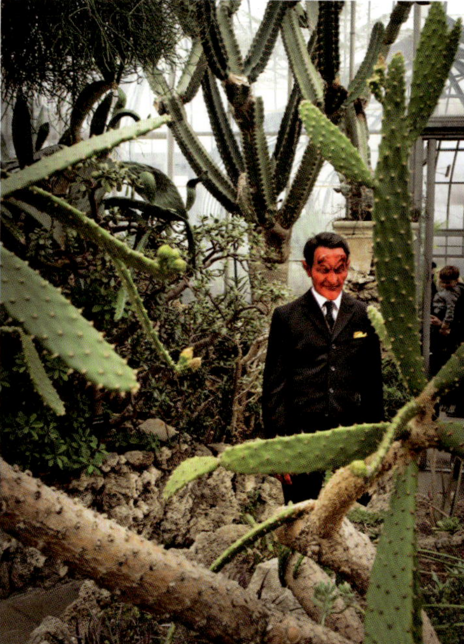

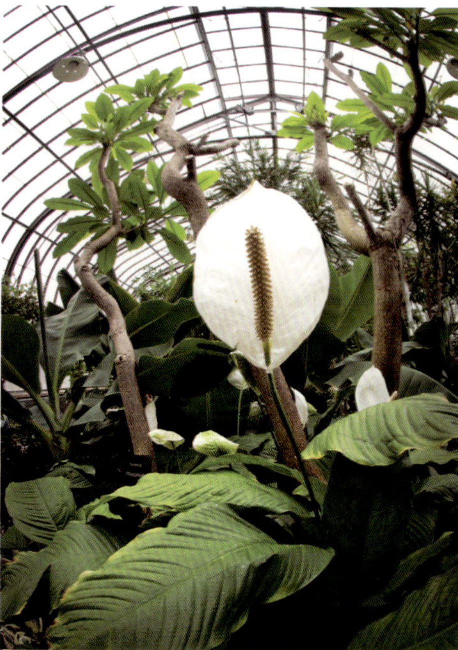

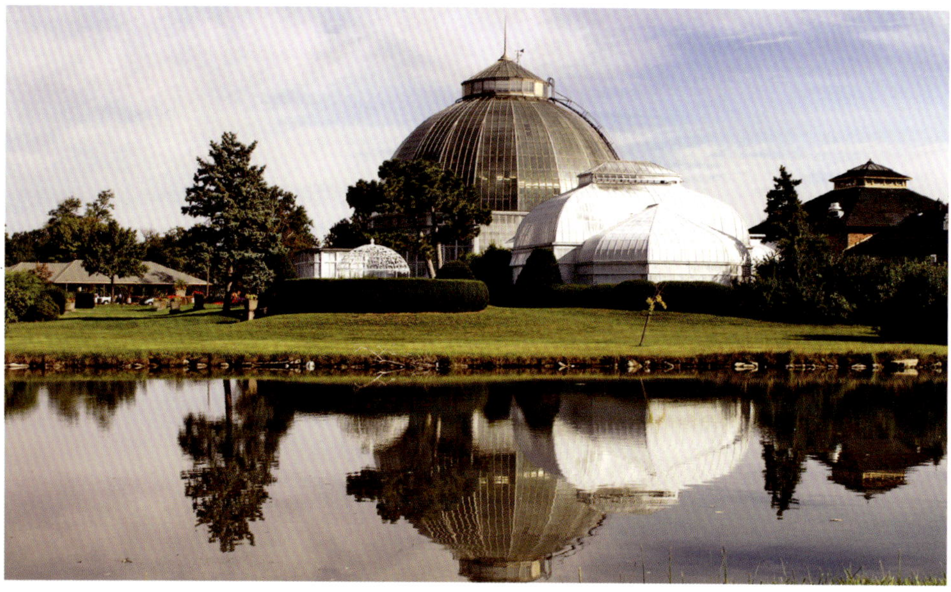

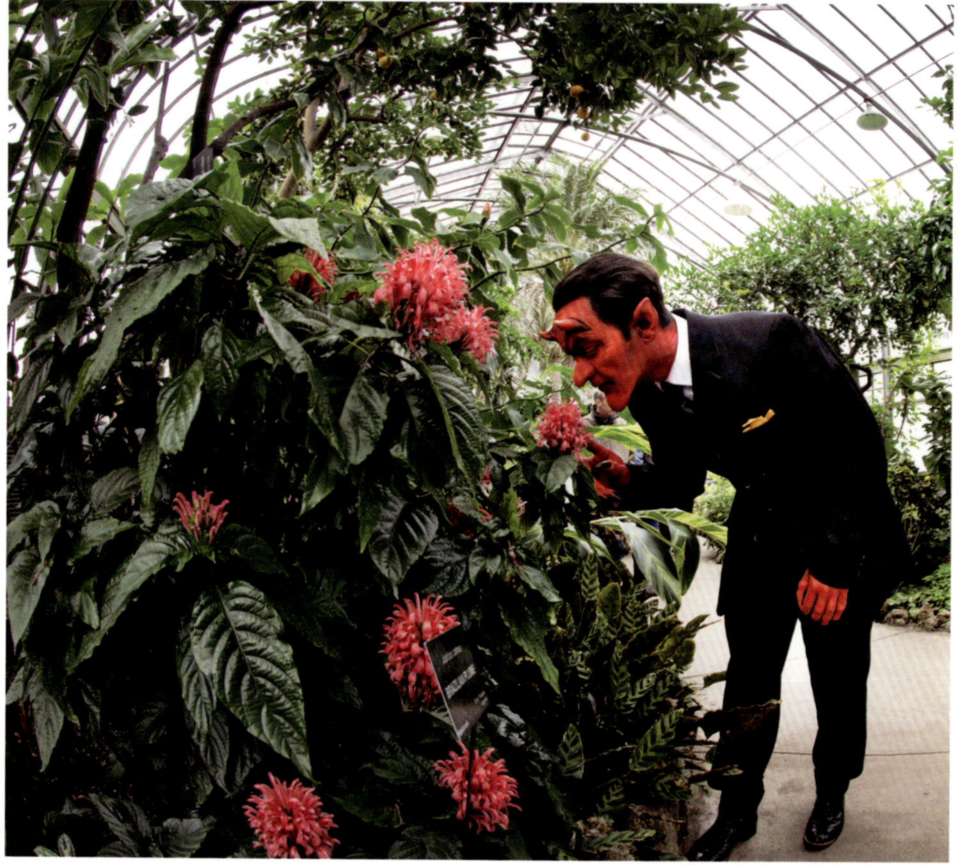

This essential place allows me to survive through another February in Detroit. A visit to the Conservatory helps remind me that the icy temperatures, grey snow, and equally grey skies will succumb eventually to spring. Always warm, green, and flowering, the Conservatory reinvigorates the mind. It is always striking to my senses when walking from the moist air in the Fern House to the dry heat in the Cactus House. - NR

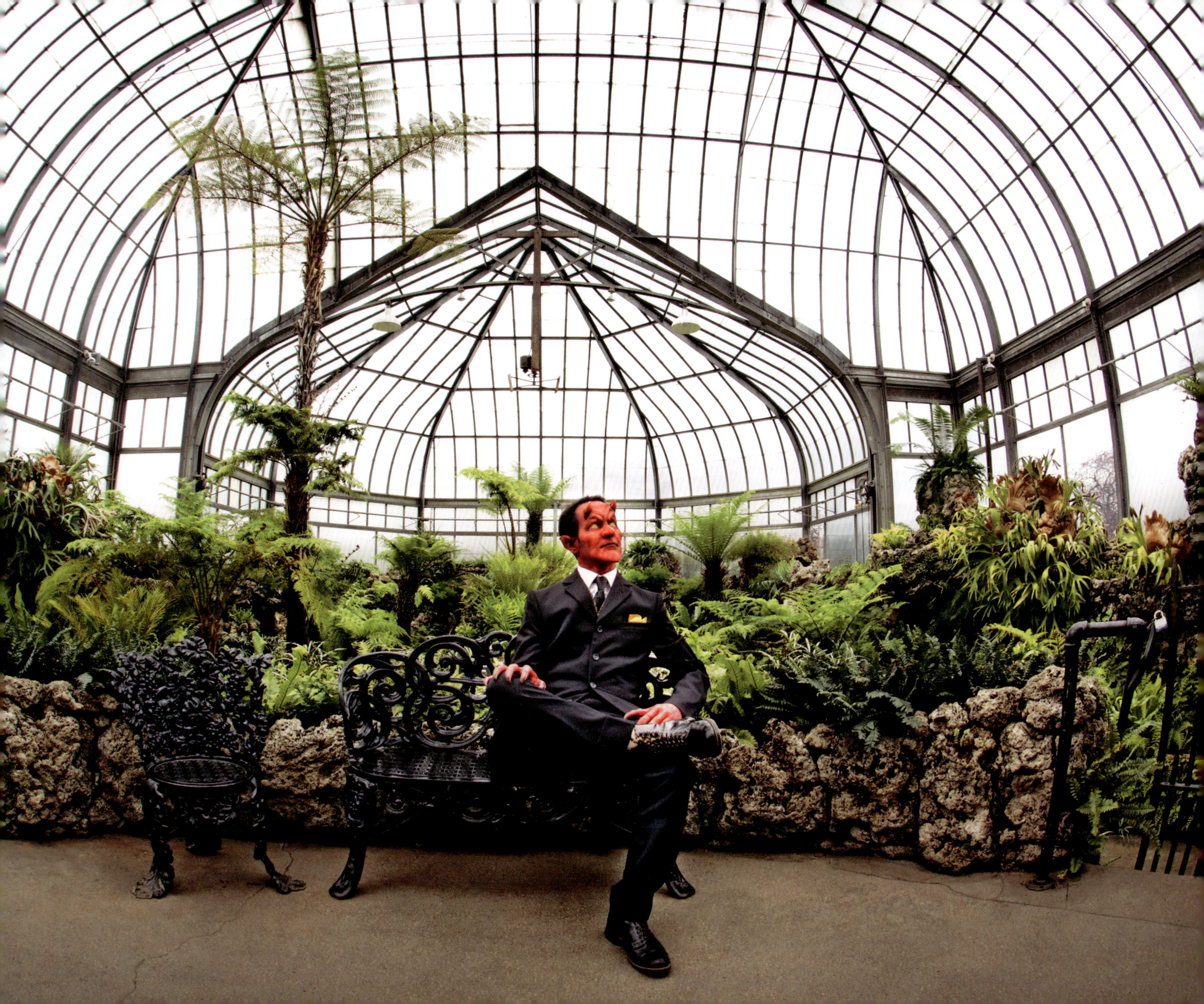

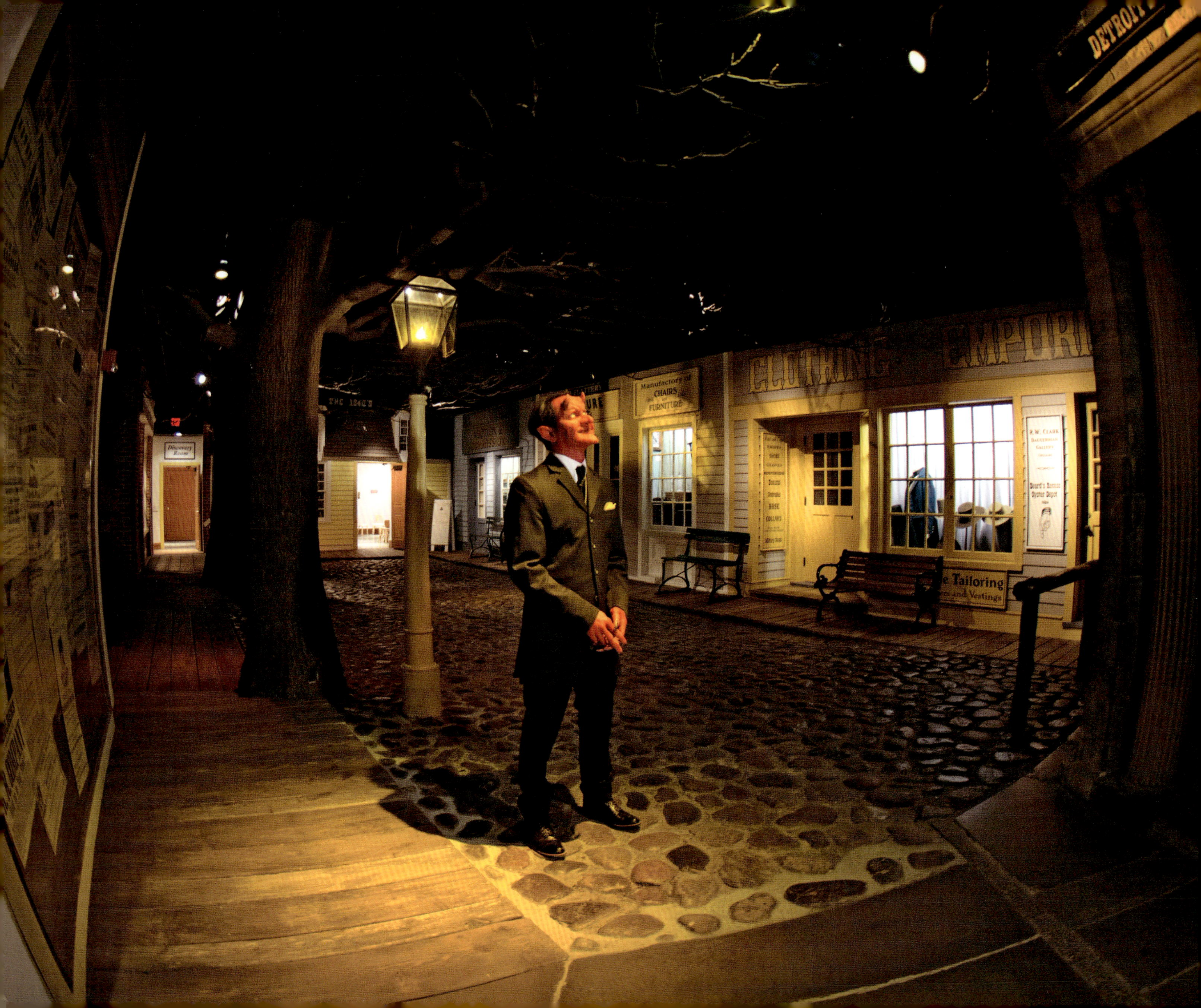
Discovery Room
Manufactory of CHAIRS and FURNITURE
CLOTHING
R.W. CLARK
Tailoring

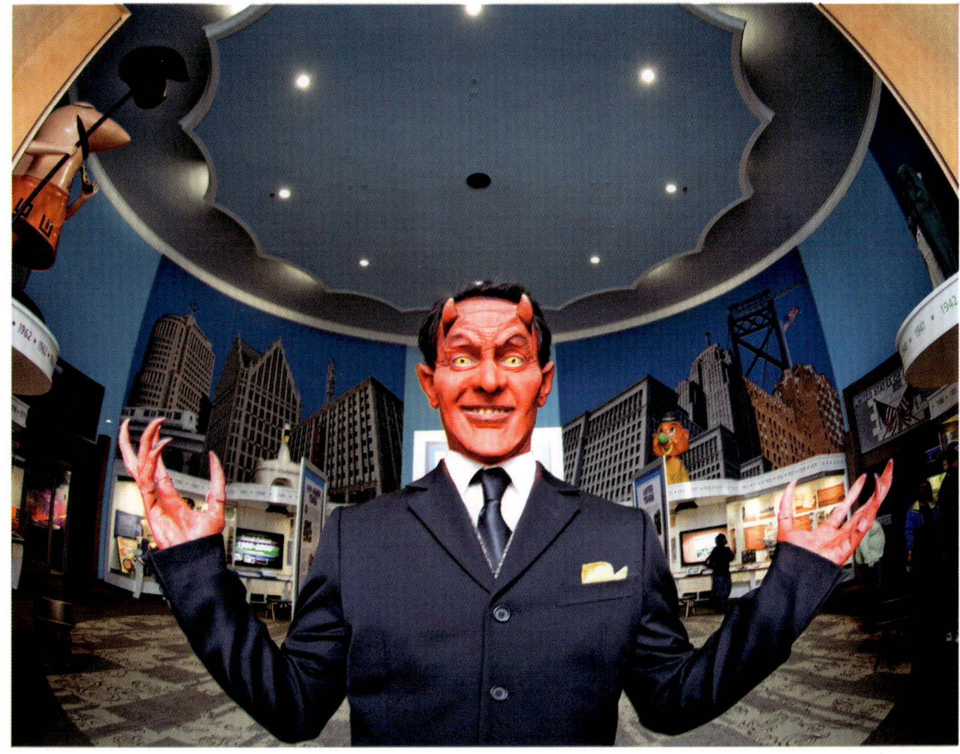

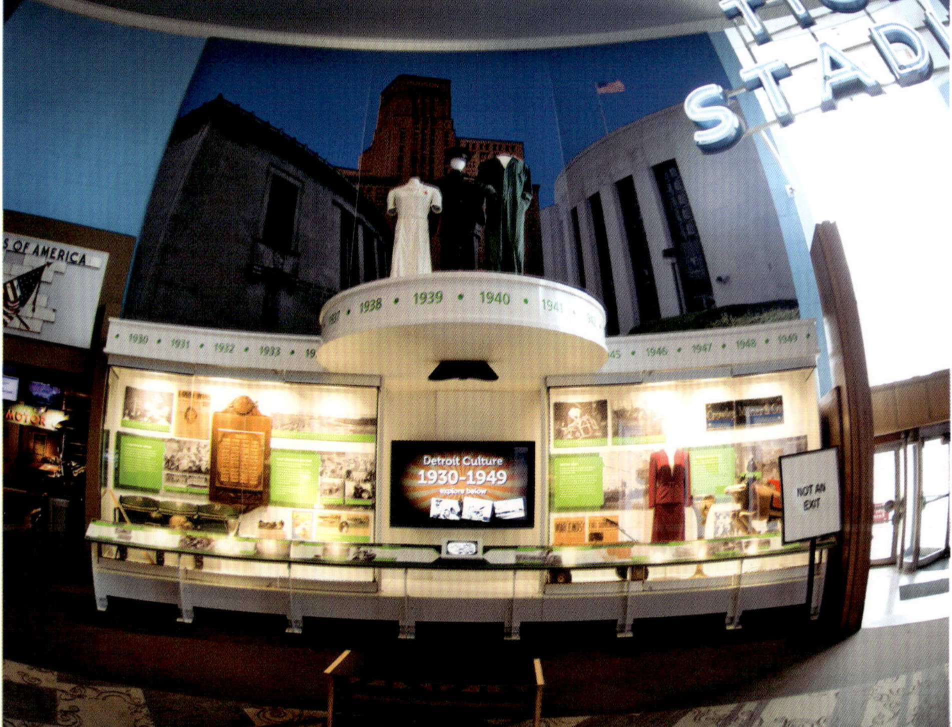

DETROIT HISTORICAL MUSEUM

5401 Woodward Ave., Detroit, 48202
www.detroithistorical.org

Dedicated on the 250 anniversary of Detroit's founding, the museum promotes the city's historical achievements and contributions to the world. The Detroit Historical Society began in 1921 to preserve and display the city's history. Exhibits include the Streets of Detroit, a collection of old shops and street styles from previous centuries; the Motor City Exhibition, which examines Detroit's development into the Automotive Capital of the World; and the Kid Rock Music Lab, which celebrates Detroit's influence in the music industry. Ever-changing exhibits continue to keep the museum fresh while exploring important moments in Detroit's history.

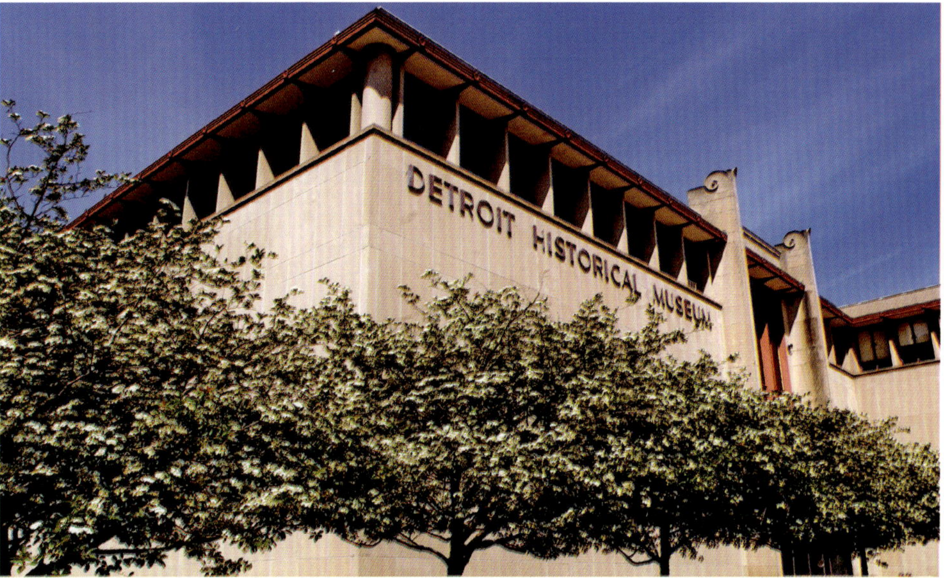

This museum is like a personal scrap book of my life in Detroit. It covers everything from the arrival of Cadillac to recent albums by Kid Rock and all the inspiring moments in between. The automobile exhibit always amazes me. Detroit had so many auto companies in the beginning and one by one they disappeared or were swallowed up by another company. The Streets of Detroit is like a walk back through time, while just around the corner, I'll stop and play with the model trains from the Glancy train collection. - NR

DETROIT ZOO

8450 W. 10 Mile Rd., Royal Oak, 48067
www.detroitzoo.org

Just two miles north of the city, the Detroit Zoo was the first zoo in the country to use cageless exhibits. With more than 280 species on 125 acres, the zoo has been educating and entertaining visitors since 1928. One of the highlights is the miniature railroad that transports riders from the zoo entrance to the far end of the park. Major exhibits include the Arctic Ring of Life featuring polar bears, the Great Apes of Harambee, the Butterfly Garden and the new Polk Penguin Conservation Center. Managed by the Detroit Zoological Society, the Zoo offers an extensive variety of animals connecting visitors with the greater world.

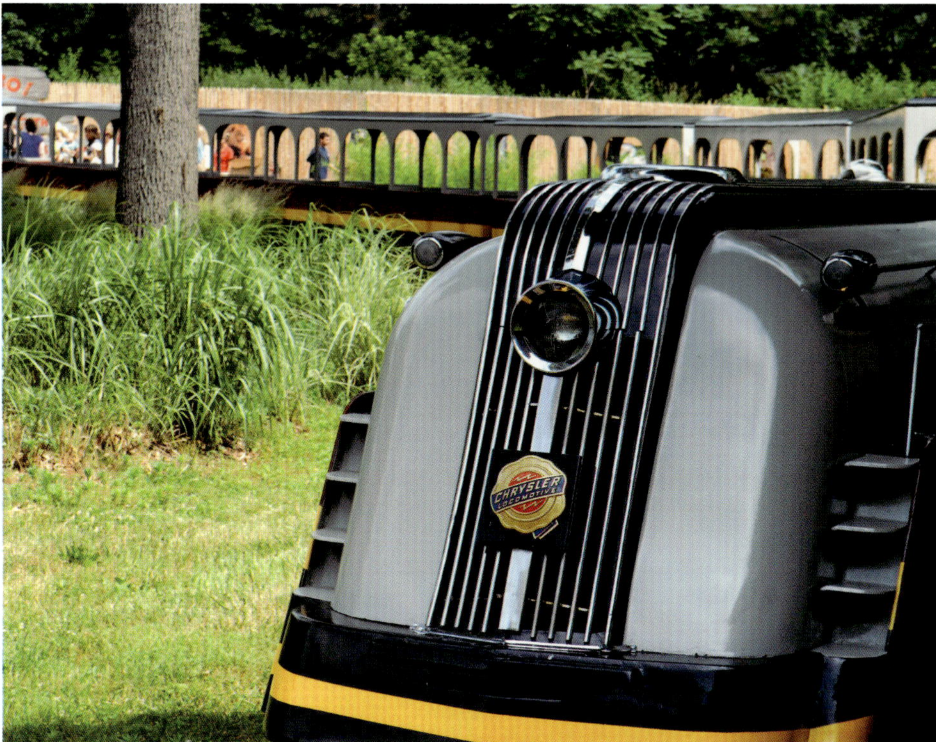

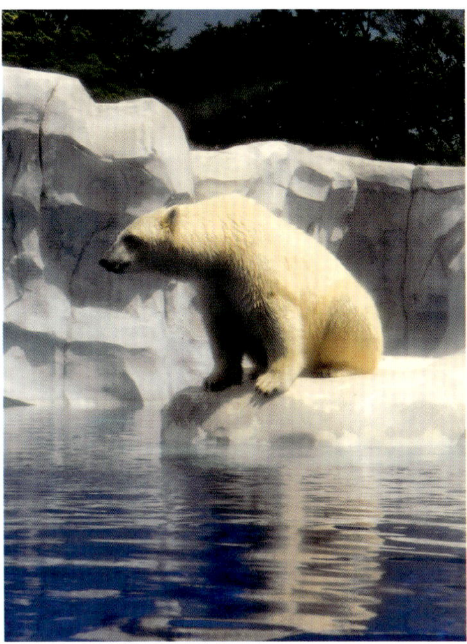

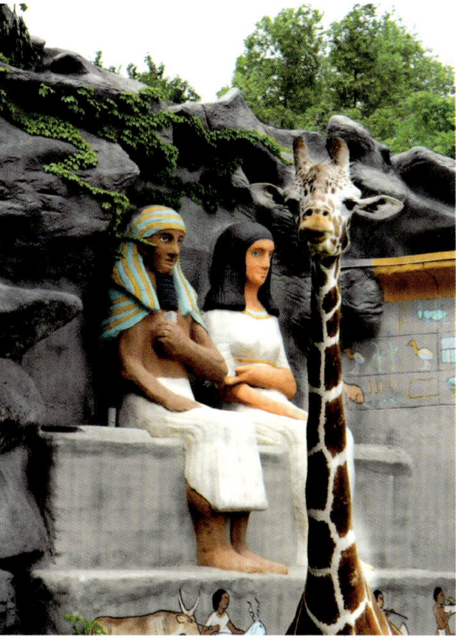

The Detroit Zoo is notable for designing exhibits where the animals move about freely. Whenever I visit, I have to take the train to the Africa station. I pretend I've arrived onto the African savannah, encountering so many different species of animals roaming unhindered by a cage or bars. By the time I get back to the entrance, I have crossed five continents and enjoyed a lovely lunch. - NR

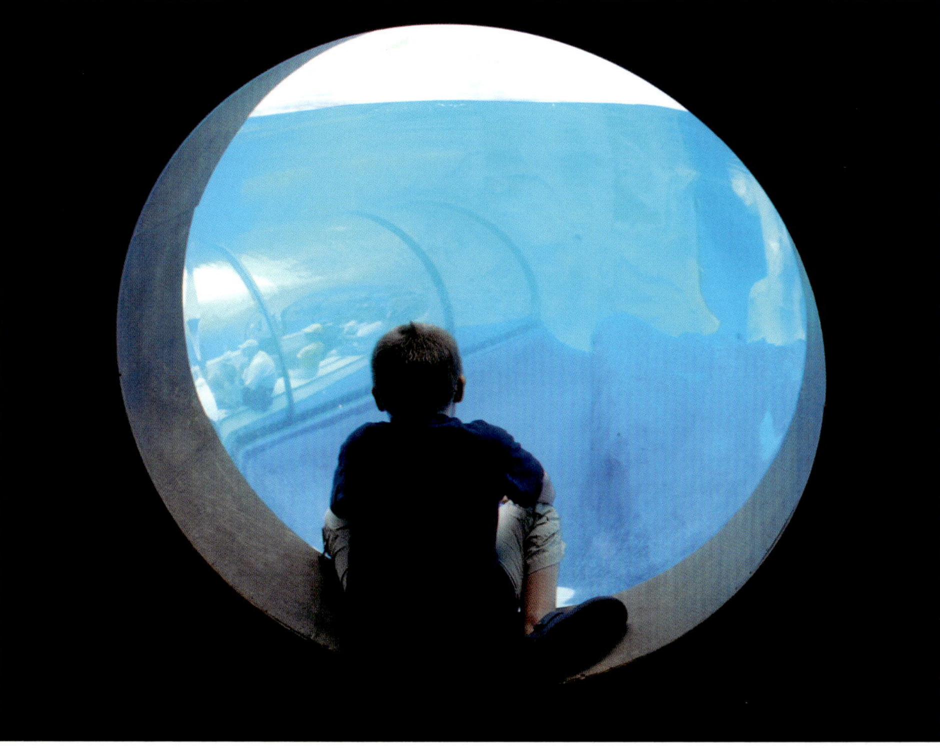

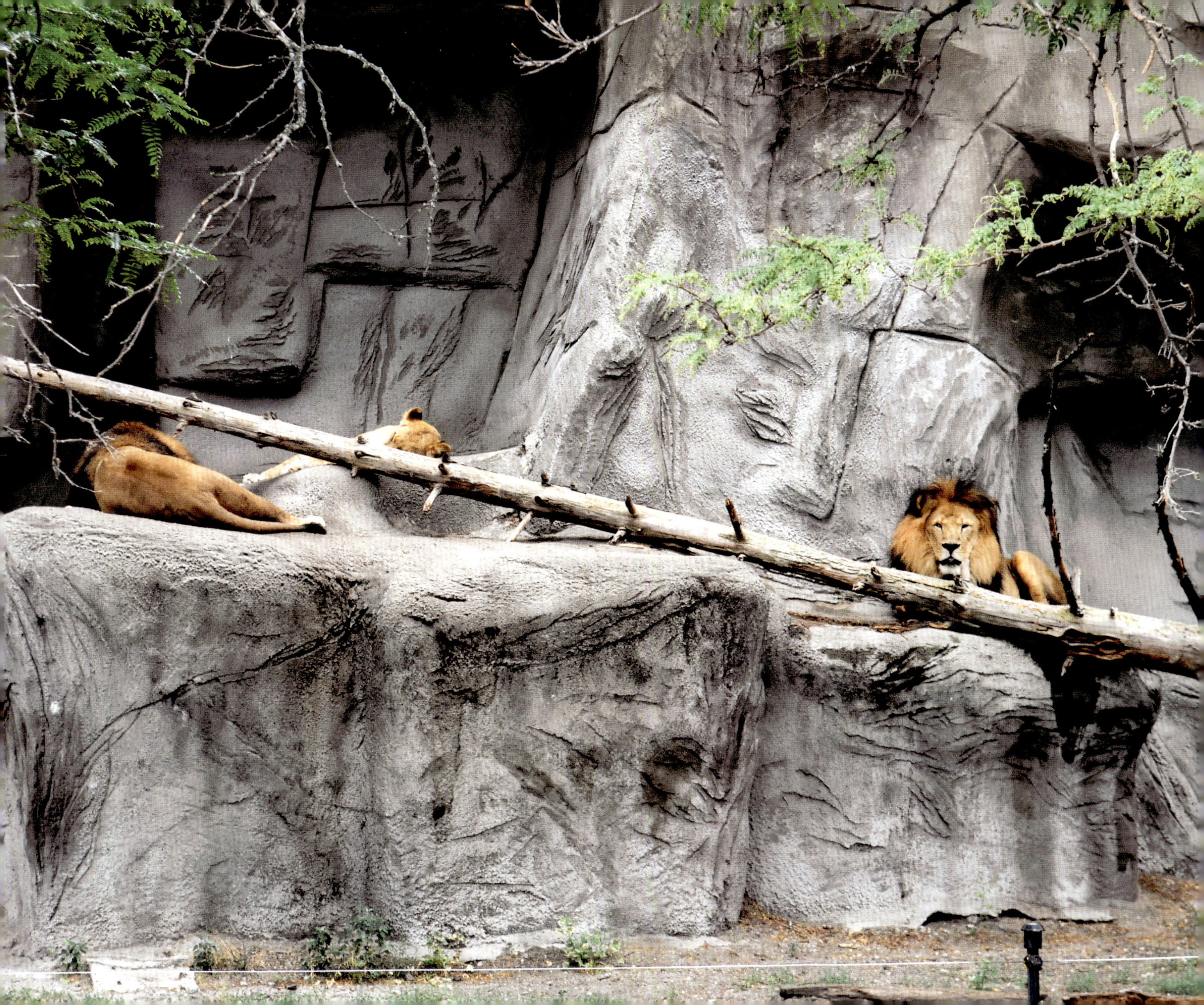

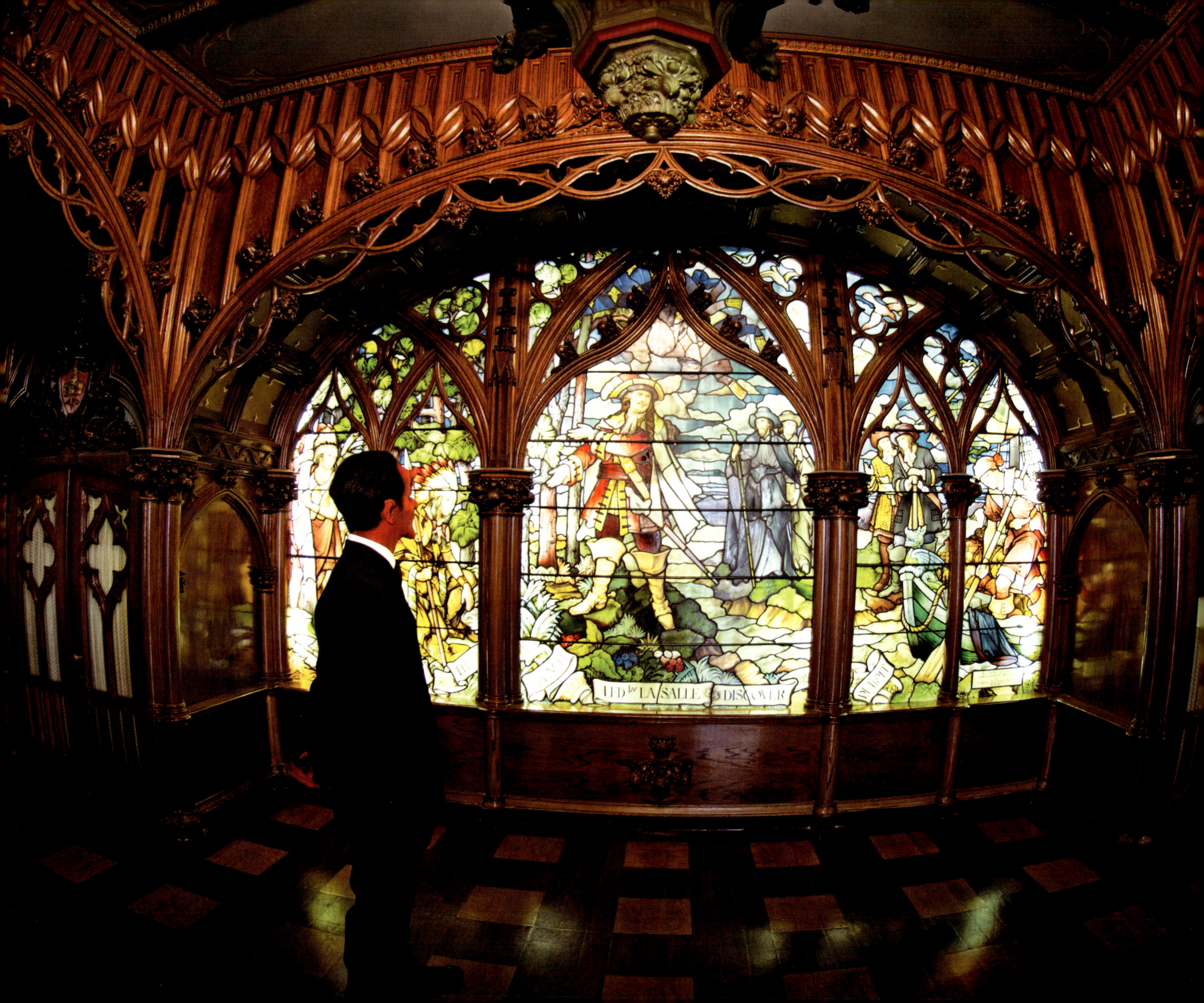
LED by LA SALLE DISCOVER

DOSSIN GREAT LAKES MUSEUM

100 The Strand St., Detroit, 48207
www.detroithistorical.org/dossin-great-lakes-museum

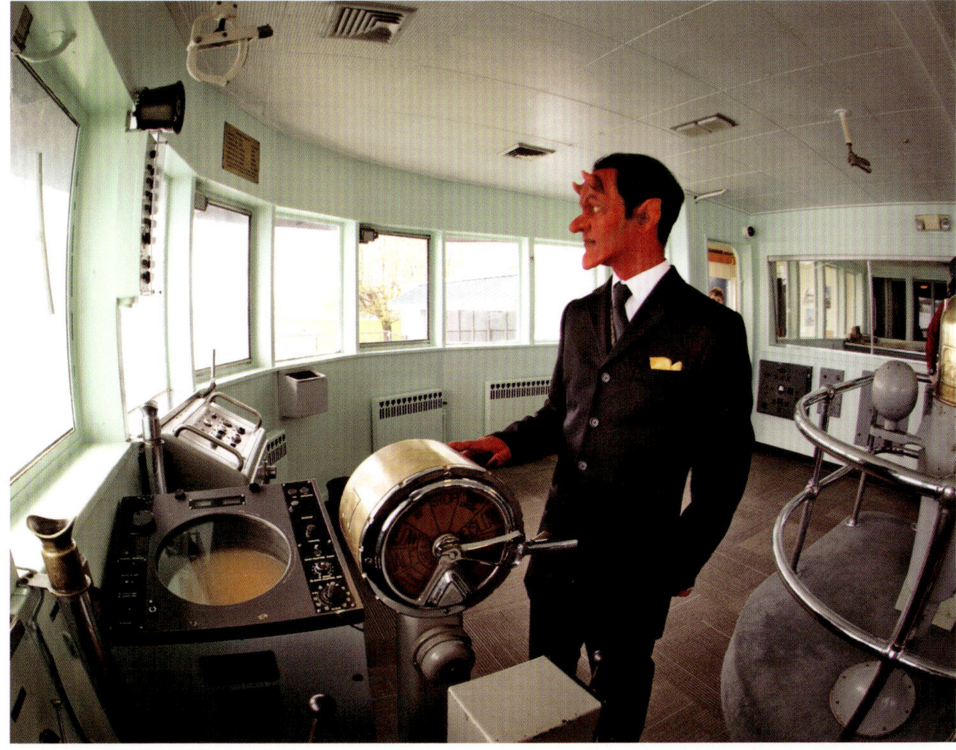

Detroit's maritime museum celebrates the rich history of the city's contributions to Great Lakes shipping. Upon entry, visitors find themselves in the smoking lounge of the *SS City of Detroit III* and are transported to the golden age of passenger travel. Exhibits illustrate the development of shipping and trade on the Detroit River. The museum is known for one of the largest collections of scale model ships in the world. From the original *SS William Clay Ford* Pilot House, guests can experience the duties of a Great Lakes freighter crew. The famous hydroplane racing boat, *Miss Pepsi*, the first boat to qualify for a race at a speed of over 100 miles an hour, is also on display.

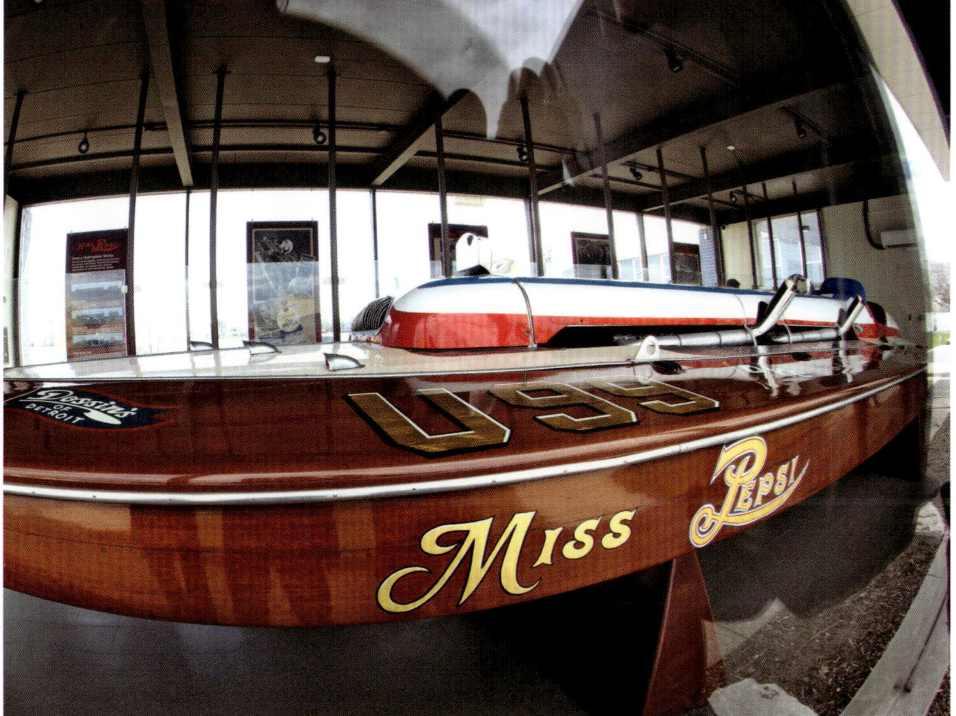

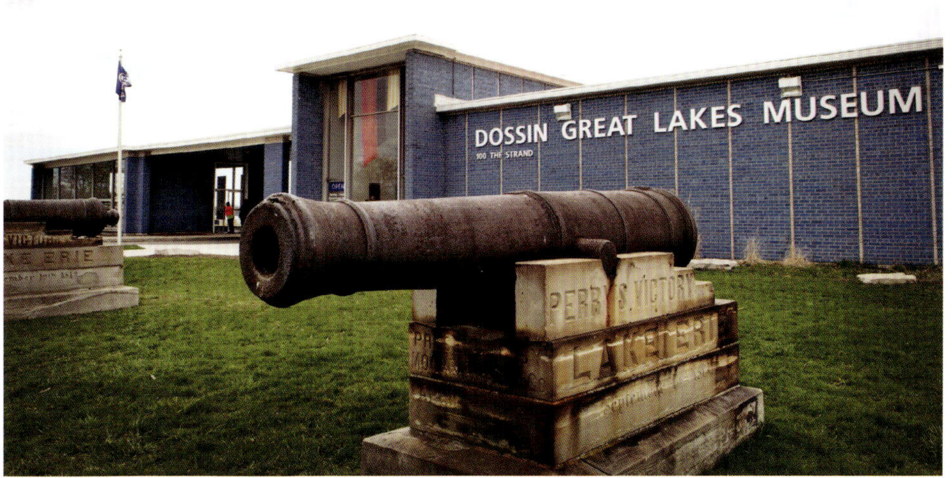

Displaying the rich history of shipping, the Dossin takes me back in time to the days when the river was the only efficient way to transport goods or people. The riverfront used to be riddled with docks and ships of all sorts. Sumptuously detailed ferries would bring passengers up from Buffalo, continuing on to Chicago. All of these memories are on display here. - NR

FORD PIQUETTE AVENUE PLANT

461 Piquette Ave., Detroit, 48202
www.fordpiquetteavenueplant.org

Located in the famous Milwaukee Junction, a center of early automotive innovations, Henry Ford's first factory opened in 1904. In 1908, he produced the first Model T here before moving production to Highland Park in 1910. Through his experiences and experiments in automation here, he created the first moving assembly line, transforming the industry. Today, there are versions of Dodge Bros., Hupmobile, and Studebaker vehicles on the assembly floors, as well as multiple Model T variations, trucks and trailers. The volunteers are all unpaid lovers of the history of the automobile who helped save the building from the neglect that has befallen too many of Detroit's other historic buildings.

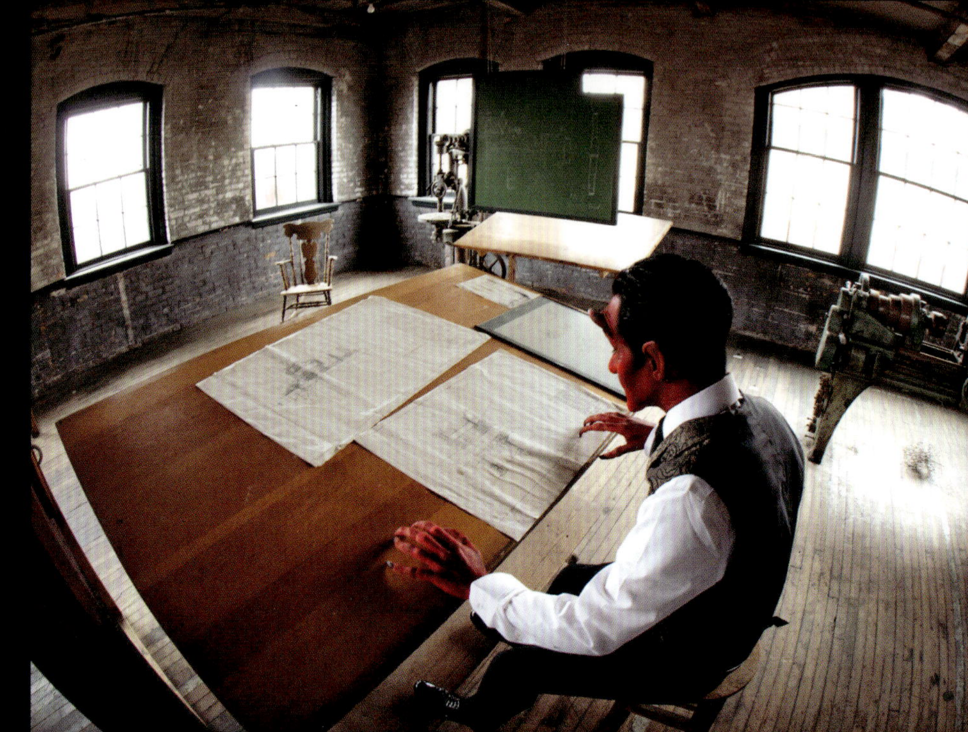

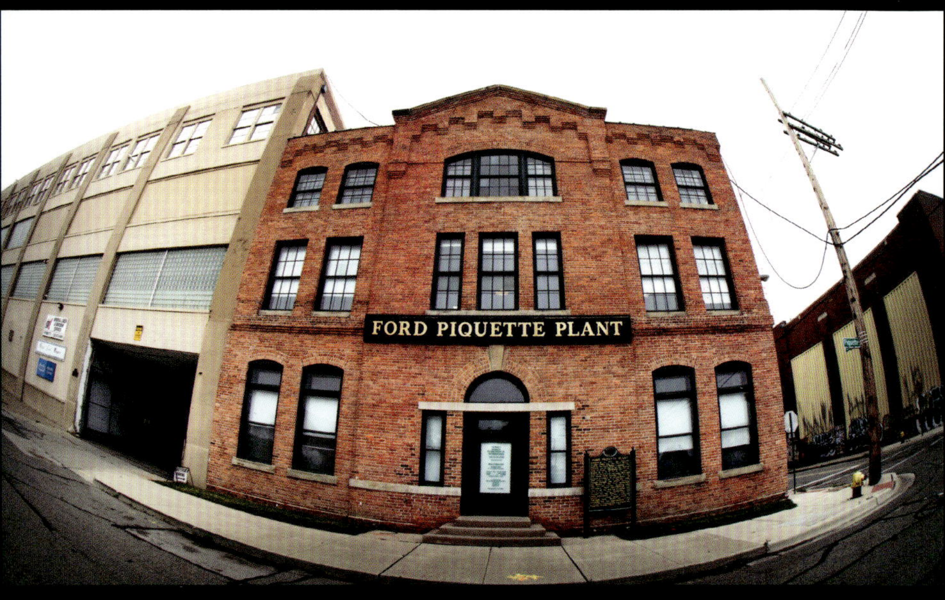

Milwaukee Junction, named for a nearby railroad junction, teemed with fledgling auto manufacturers when Ford opened his factory on Piquette Avenue. After a few successes and multiple failures, he designed his first Model T here. His famous line, "you can get it in any color as long as it's black," held true for most folks but not me. Henry gave me a shiny red one which is still displayed here. - NR

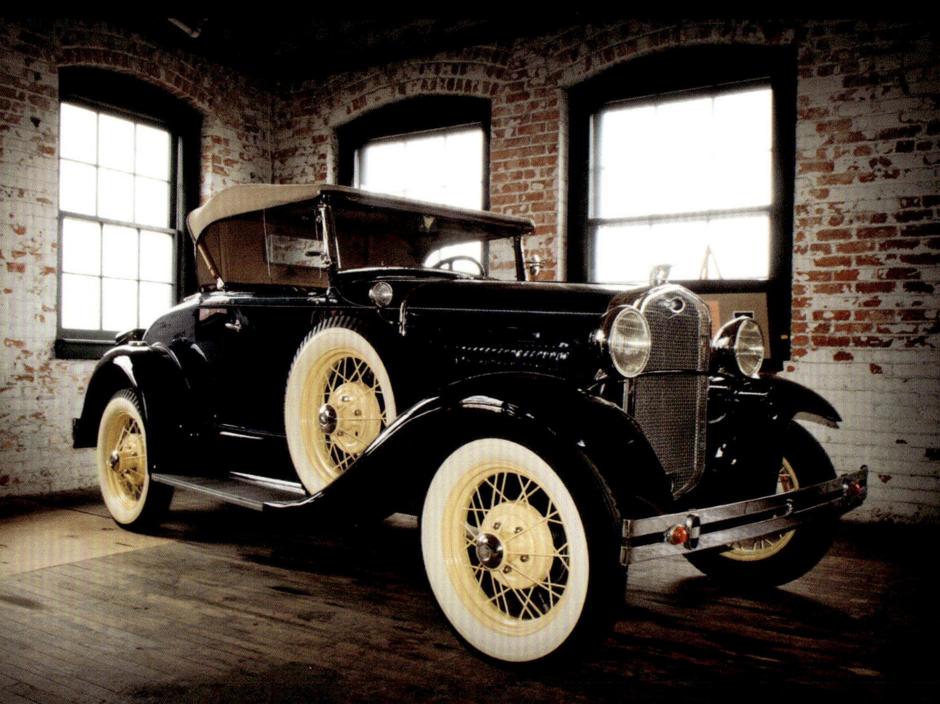

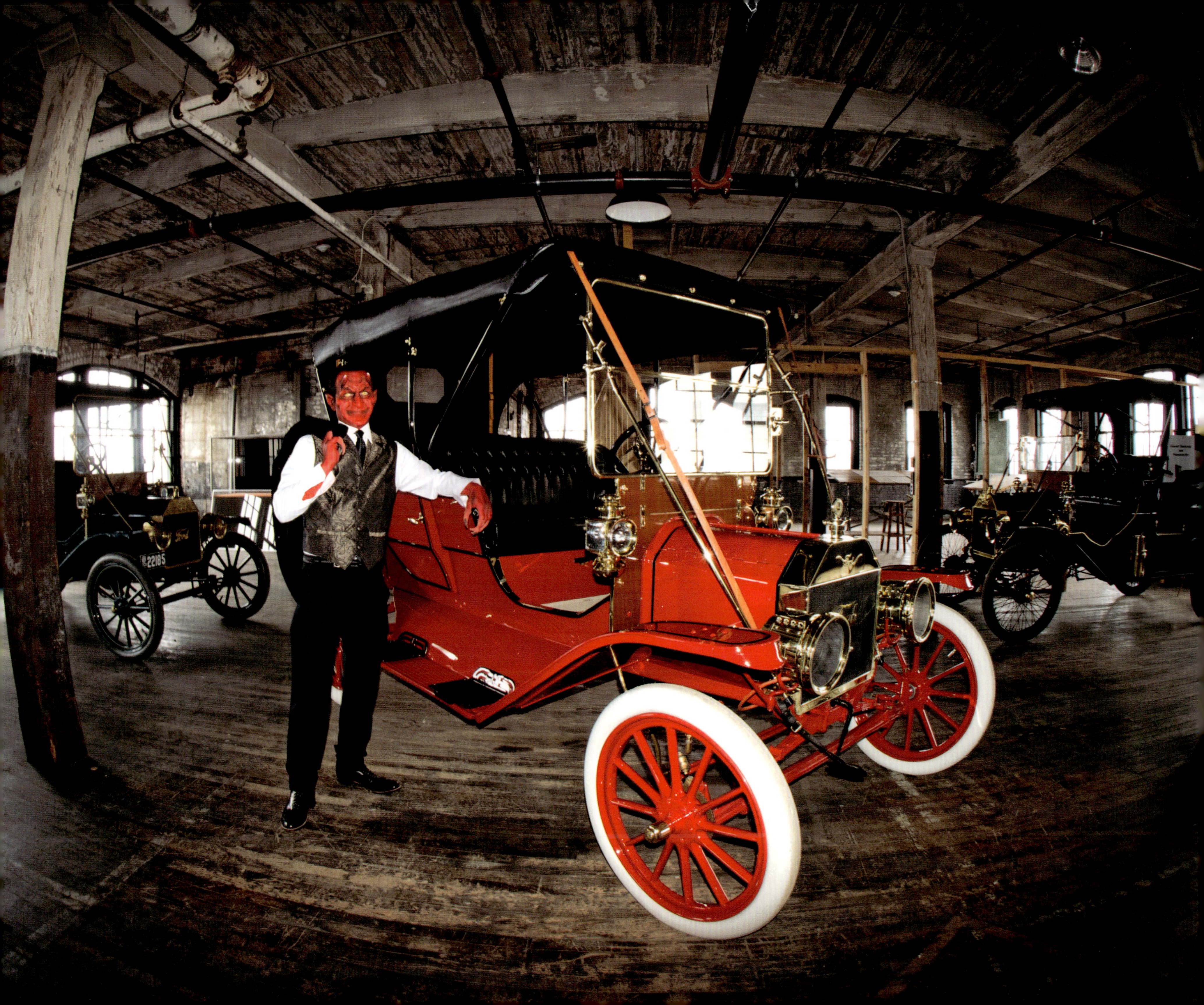
22185

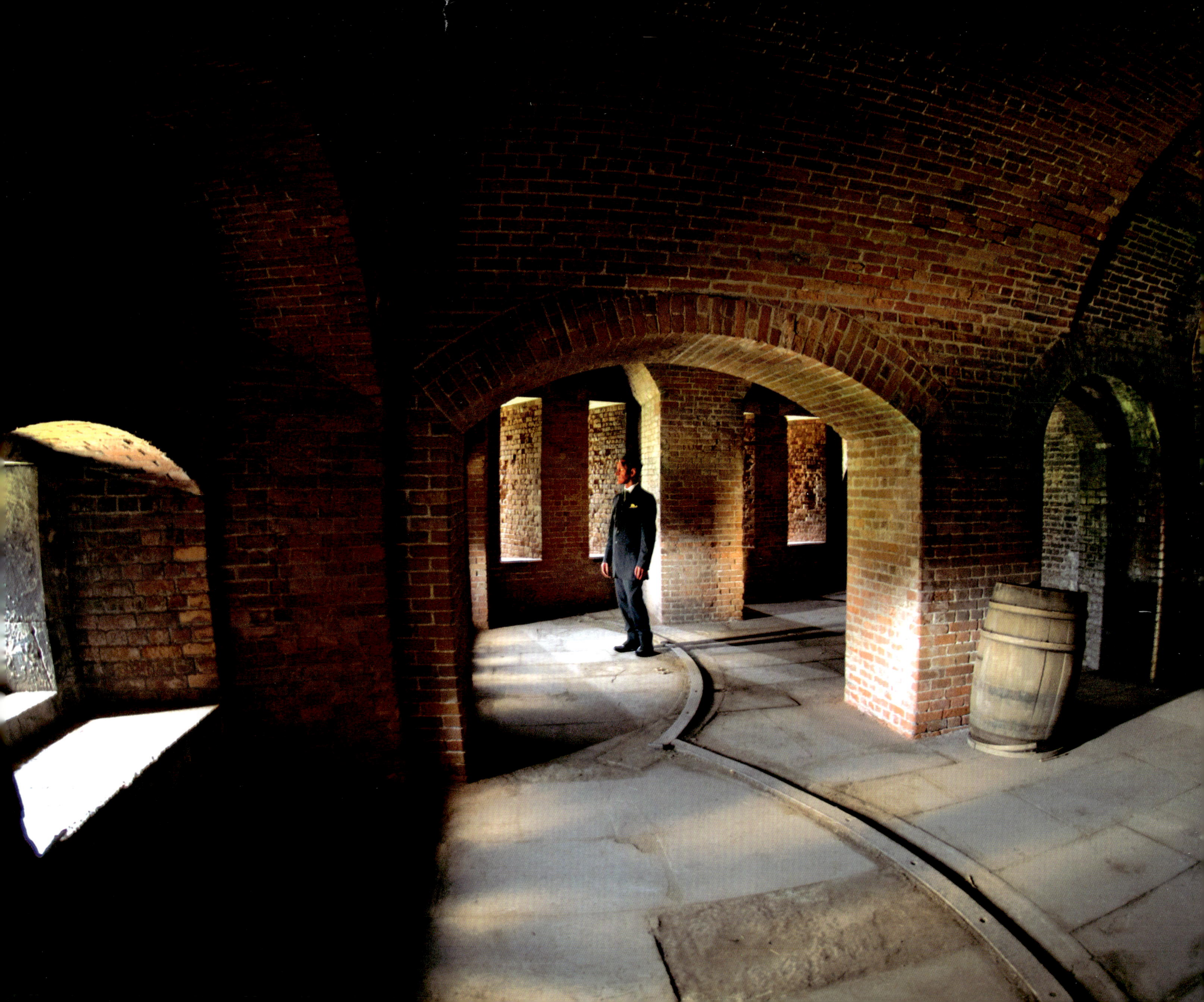

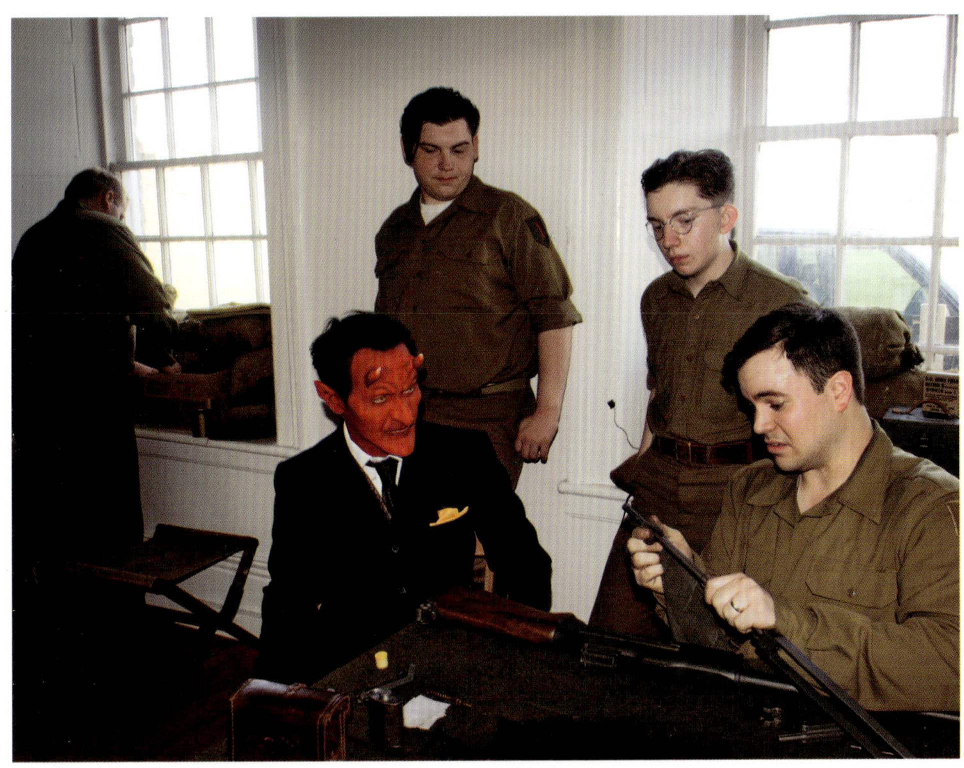

FORT WAYNE

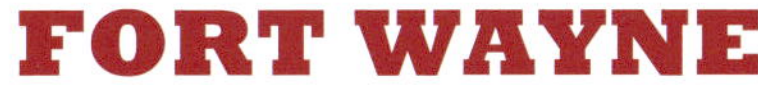

6325 W. Jefferson Ave., Detroit, 48209
www.historicfortwaynecoalition.com

Having been captured by the British in the War of 1812, Detroit was reoccupied by the Americans in 1815. Realizing the importance of controlling the river, and to secure the northern border, Americans began building Fort Wayne in 1842 and completed it in 1851. By this time and before any cannons were installed, peace with the British rendered the fort unnecessary. British sympathies for the South during the Civil War renewed fears and the fort was reinforced. During the two World Wars, it was used as a Motor Supply Depot, sending every single tank, truck, and jeep, to the fronts. The Red Ball Express, the famed African American transport drivers, trained here. Decommissioned in the early 1970s, the fort has become a historical site while the grounds host youth soccer games and festivals.

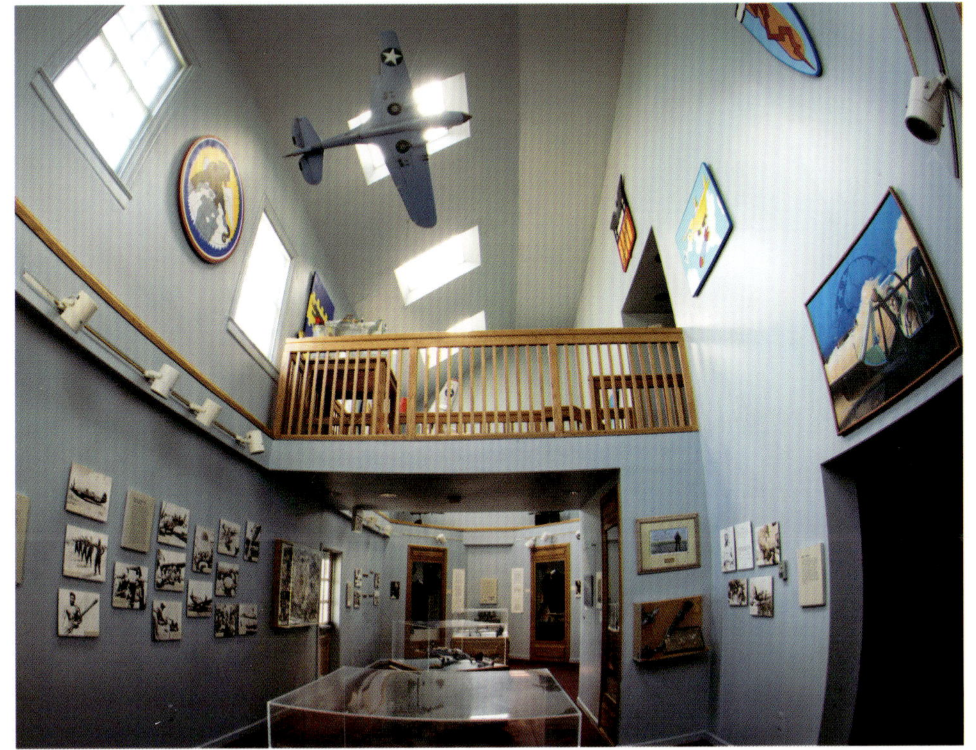

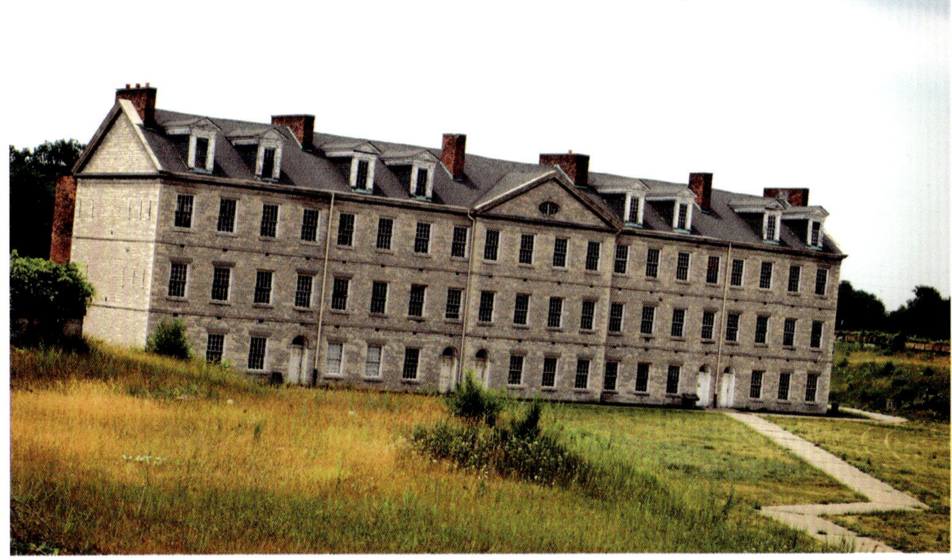

Unoccupied after its completion, and largely ignored, Fort Wayne became a great last stop on the Underground Railroad. We would house the freed slaves in the unfinished barracks and feed and clothe them until it was safe to cross the river to freedom in Canada. Later, in 1921, Ransom Olds debuted the first ride-on mower here. I got a kick riding that thing around and cutting the acres of grass surrounding the fort. - NR

MICHIGAN SCIENCE CENTER

5020 John R St., Detroit, 48202
www.mi-sci.org

The Michigan Science Center, founded in 1970, is located within Detroit's Cultural Center. Offering hands-on experiments designed to educate as well as entertain, the Science Center is a popular destination for young children. In addition to the three floors of exhibition space, there are also live demonstrations with audience participation, an IMAX Theatre, and the Digital Dome Planetarium.

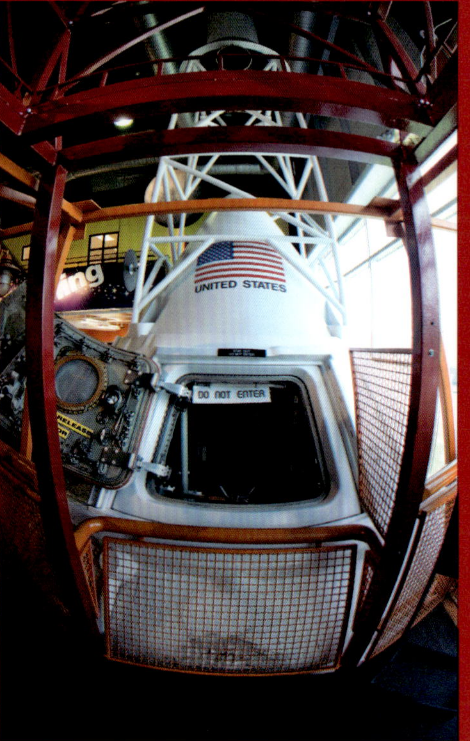

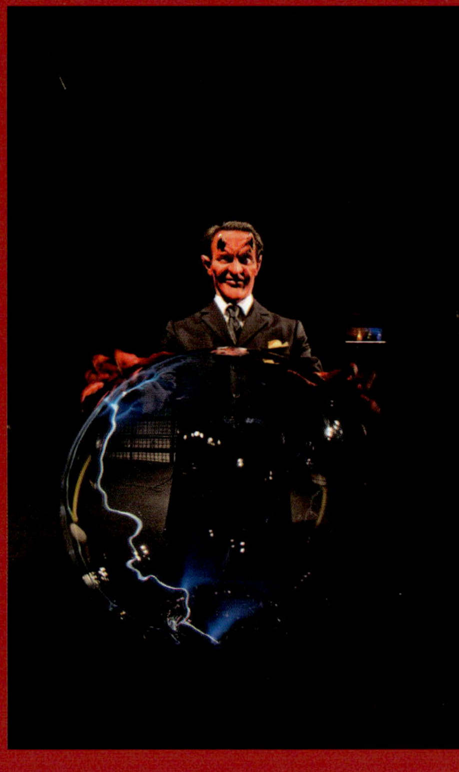

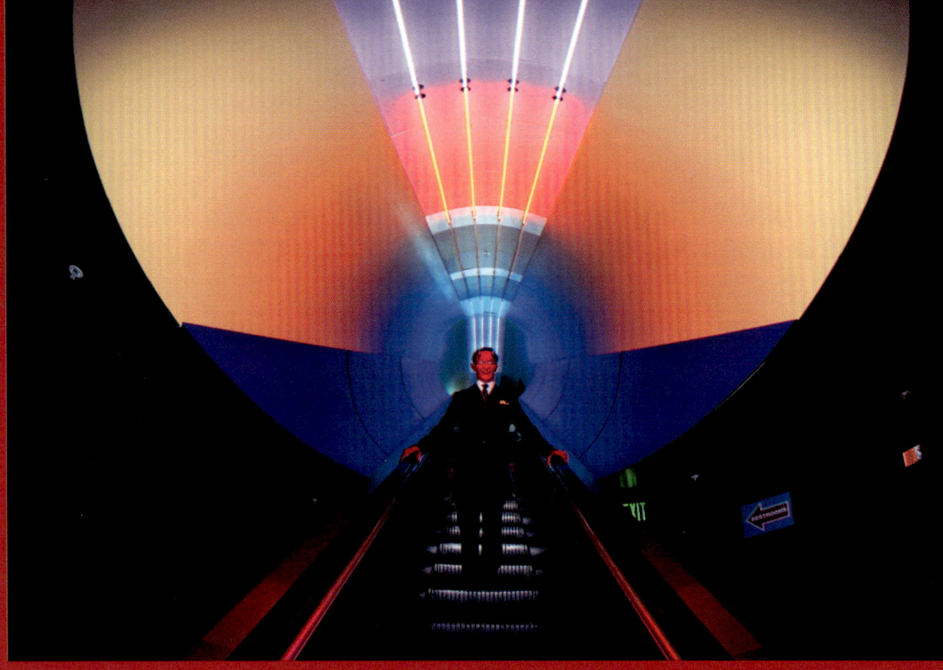

Asking questions, and figuring out how to find answers, leads to innovations and inventions, and this place encourages all that. Here, young children are exposed to the laws of nature, physics, and experimentation. As a volunteer, I try to make learning fun with simple experiments that illustrate the principles of science. - NR

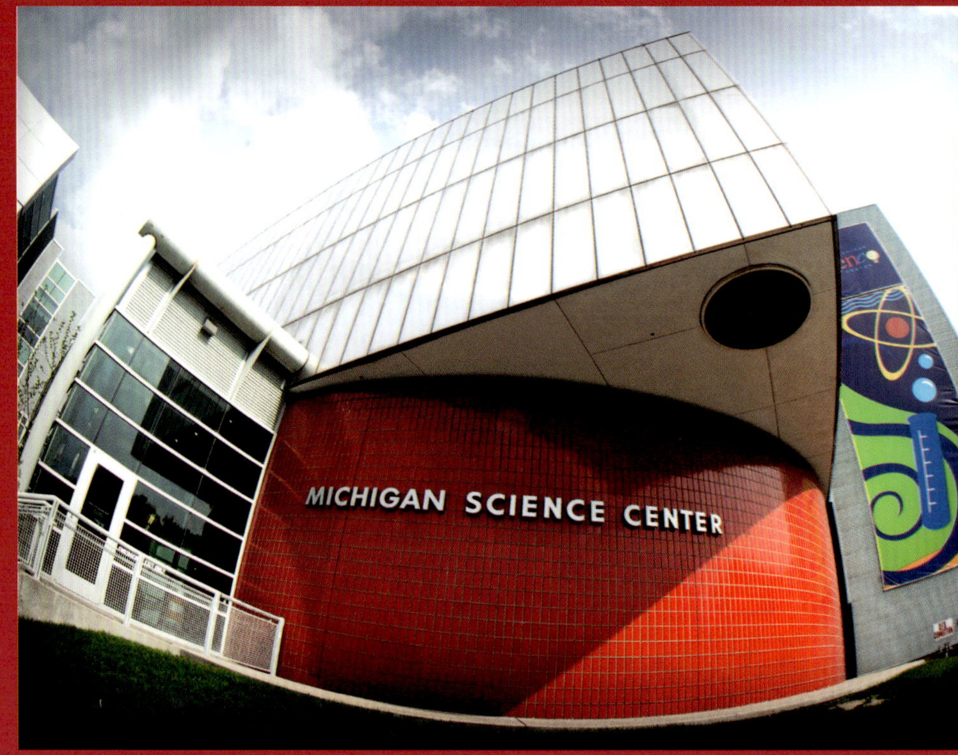

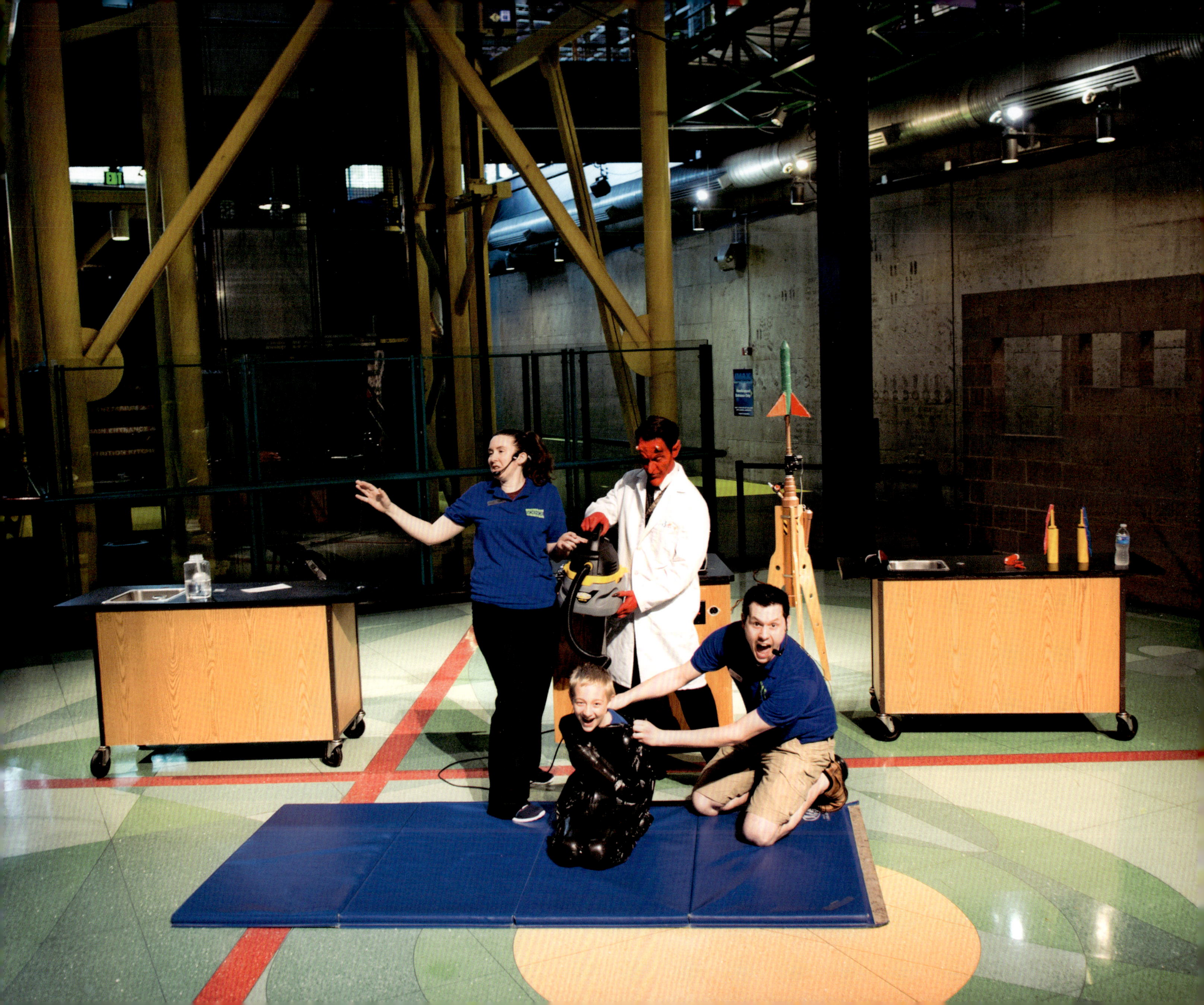

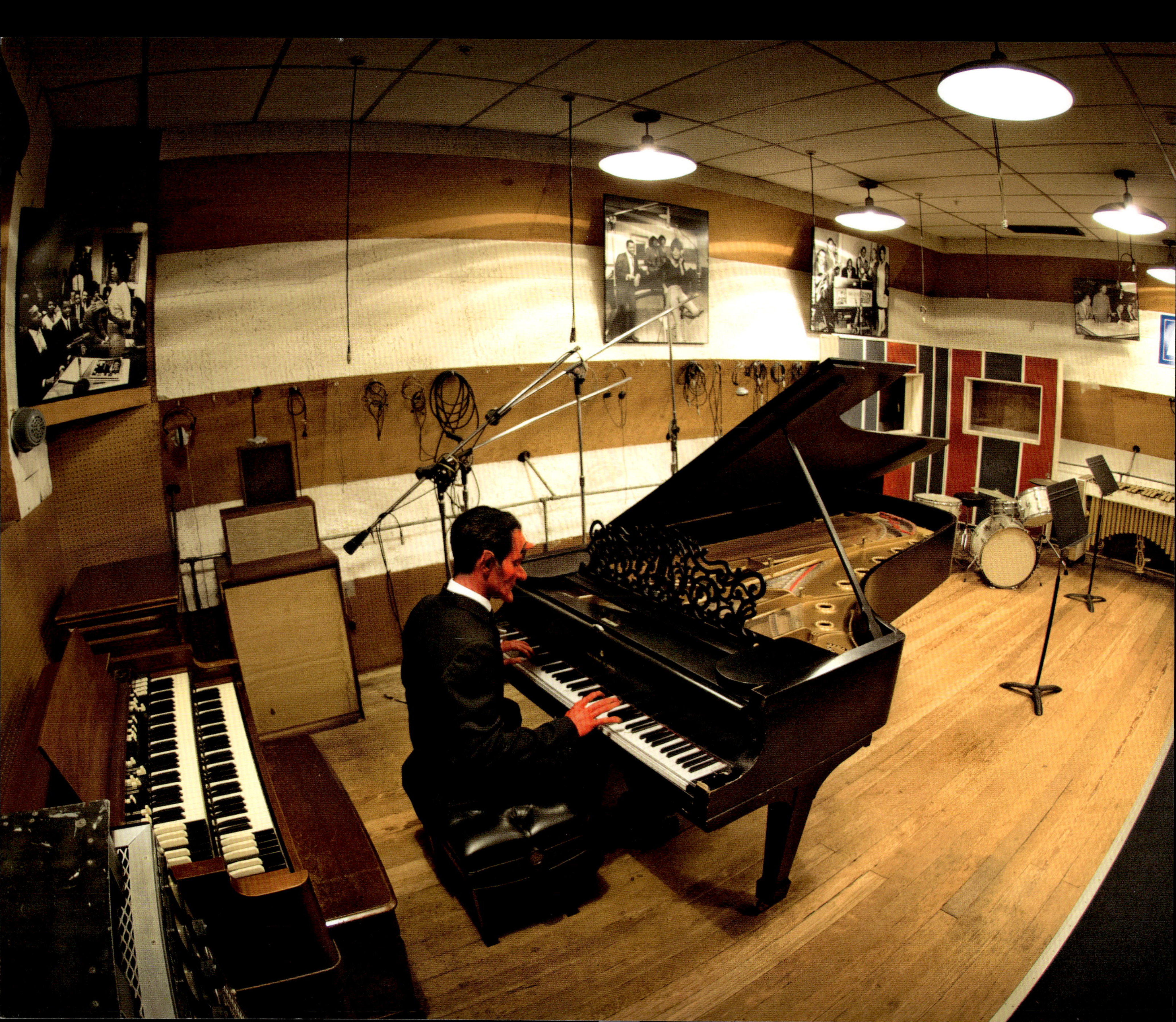

MOTOWN MUSEUM

2648 W. Grand Blvd., Detroit, 48208
www.motownmuseum.org

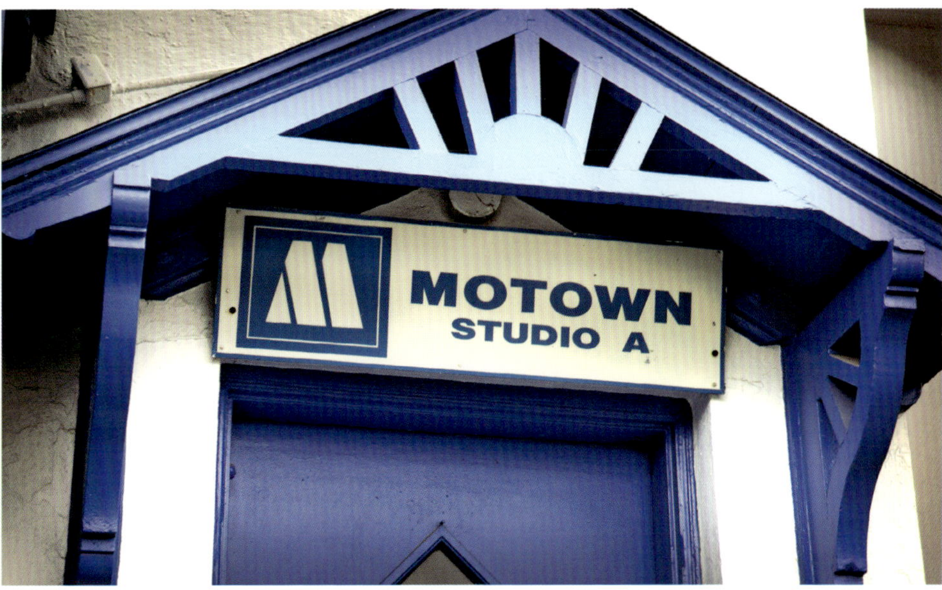

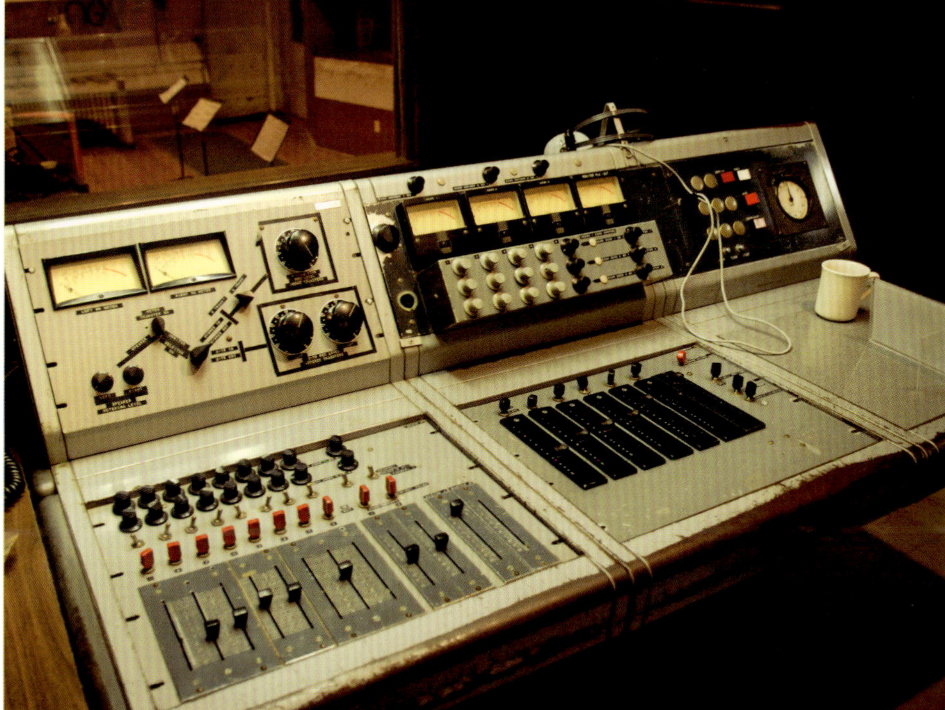

Hitsville USA, opened in a West Grand Blvd. home in 1959 by Berry Gordy, became the largest minority-owned record company in the world. Motown dominated the R&B charts throughout the 1960s and 70s becoming young America's soundtrack at the time. The number of artists who began their careers here is too long to list but includes Smokey Robinson, Marvin Gaye, Stevie Wonder, Michael Jackson, and Diana Ross. The Funk Brothers, the studio band, are credited for creating the legendary "Motown sound." The highlight of the museum tour is the famed Studio A, unchanged from its time as the greatest studio in the world.

The pinnacle of Detroit's musical contribution to the world, the "Motown Sound," grew out of a small basement studio on West Grand Blvd. Looking at it now, you might find it hard to believe that such a small and unremarkable room would have produced so many memorable songs. I sat in on some recording sessions myself, though you'll never see me credited in liner notes. Famous musicians and visitors from around the world come to pay homage, touring this modest home turned hit machine. - NR

ROUGE RIVER

www.therouge.org

If you travel up the Rouge River from Zug Island, you can see the remnants of the factories from Detroit's glorious automotive past. Passing the entrance to the vast salt mines that lay beneath Detroit, Great Lakes freighters still bring in raw materials and Ford keeps assembling vehicles. Covering over 127 miles and three tributaries, the river extends into Birmingham and Troy, through West Bloomfield and into Canton. The Rouge River is a part of our regional neighborhood, crossing through multiple suburban cities and towns, blessing us with its abundance of fish and wildlife, while offering us a glimpse at both the natural landscape and the industrial might of Detroit.

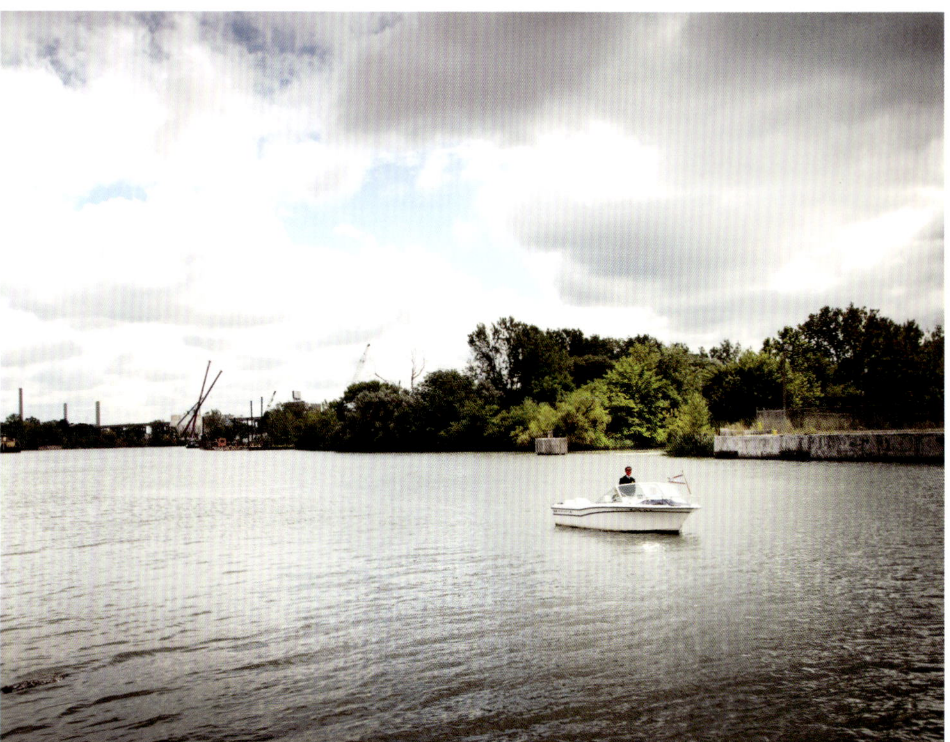

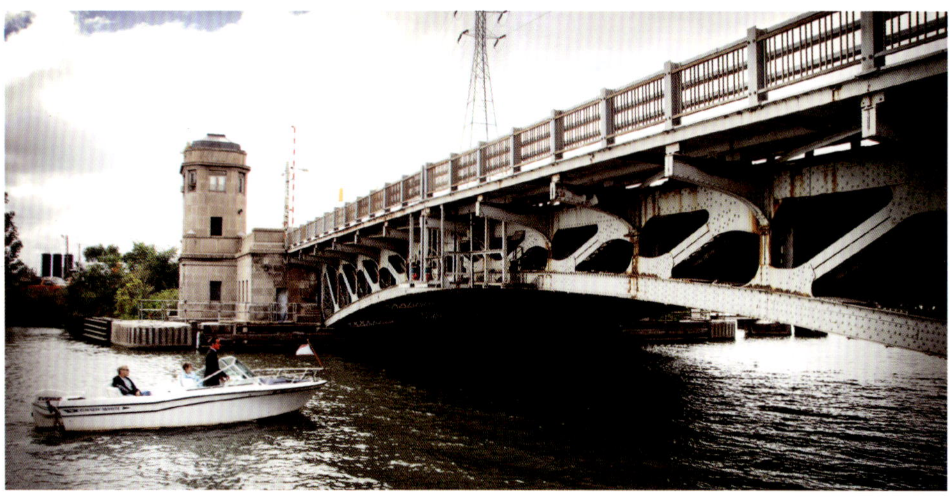

The River Rouge was one of my favorite places before industry took over. As much as industry has transformed the lower Rouge, the river remains mostly tranquil and devoid of people. The freighters are less frequent, and rarely do folks venture up here in pleasure boats, which suits me just fine. I can come and enjoy myself without interruption, passing under the many drawbridges crossing the river, so low that there are only inches to spare, while trains pass overhead. Even though the banks are still lined with industry or reminders of it, the world seems to slow down here, and I'm grateful for it. - NR

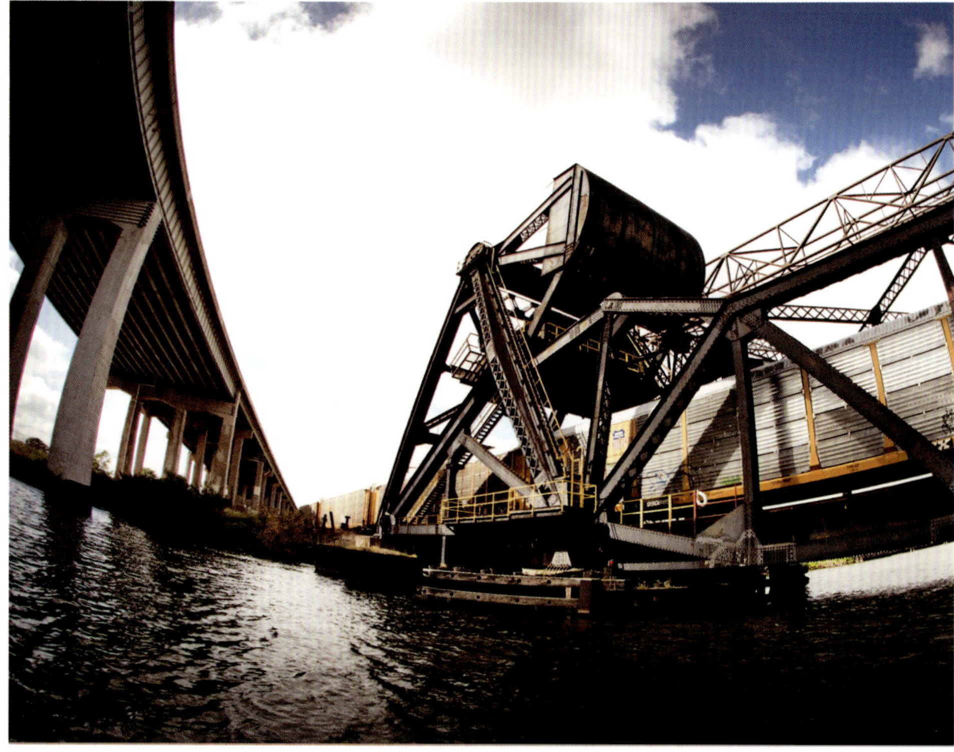

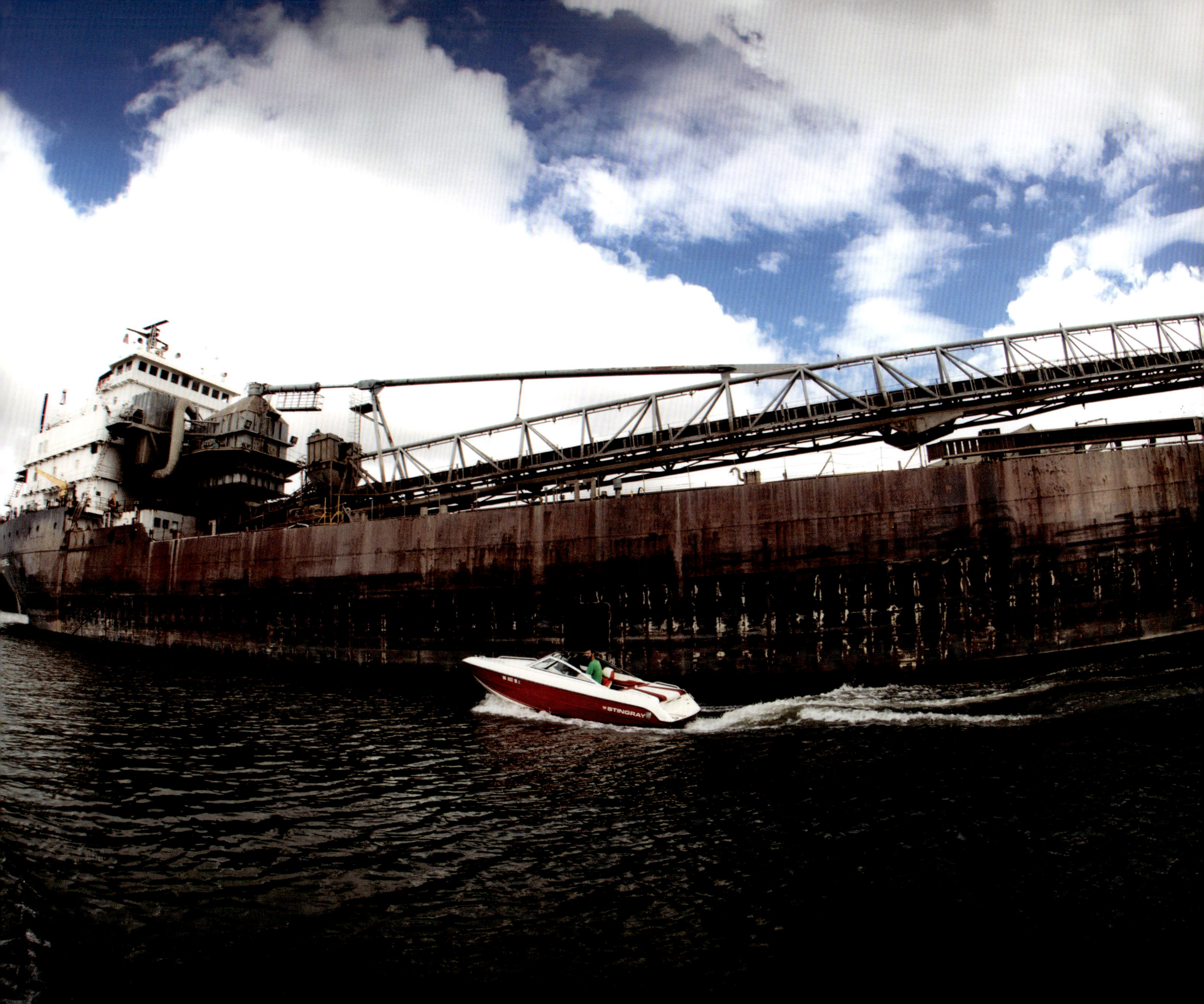
STINGRAY

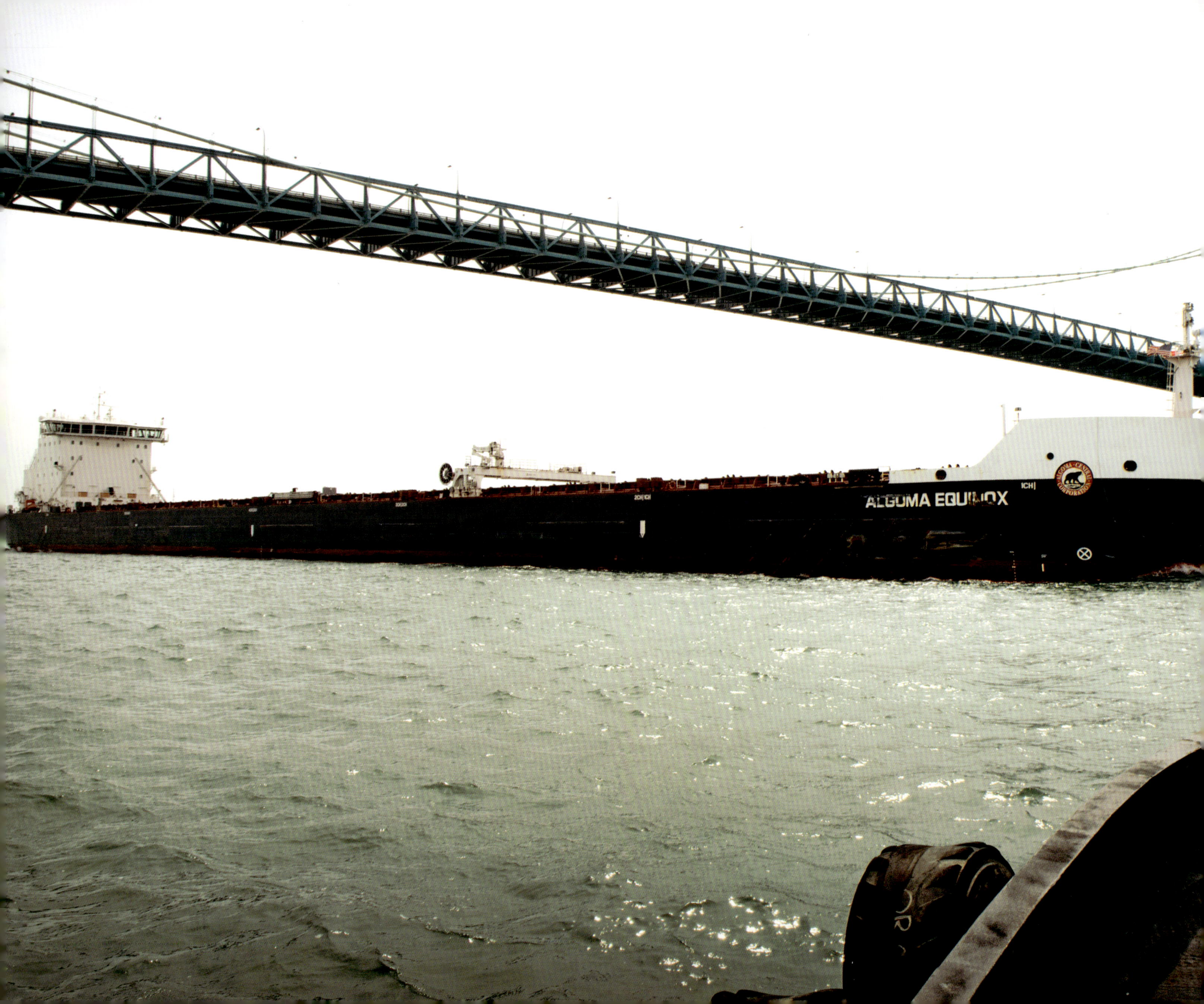
ALGOMA EQUINOX

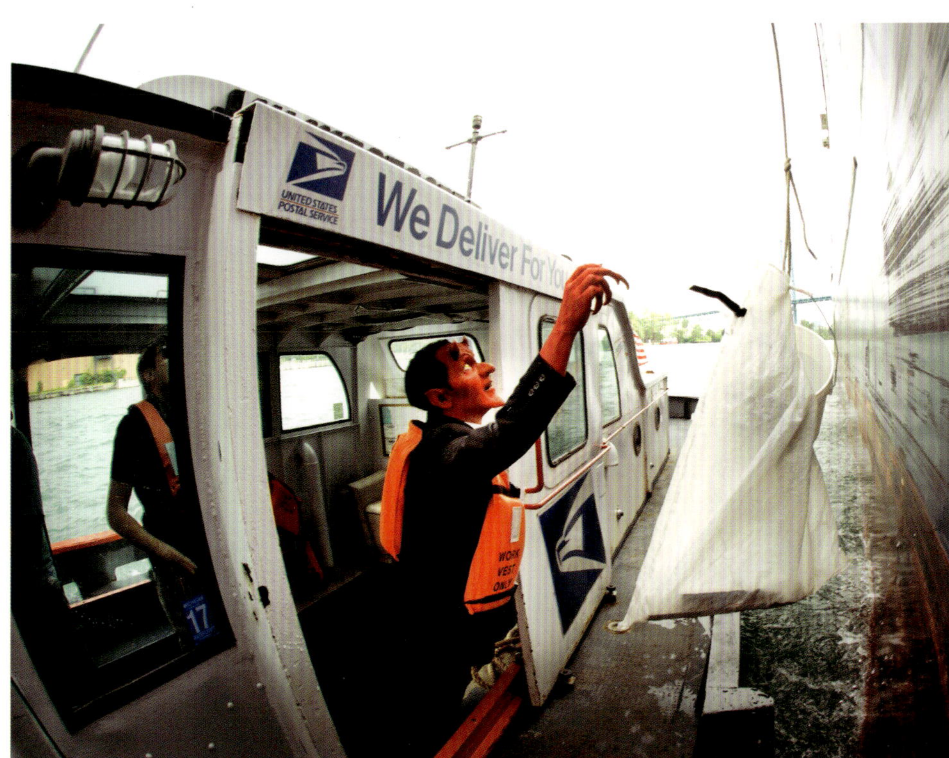

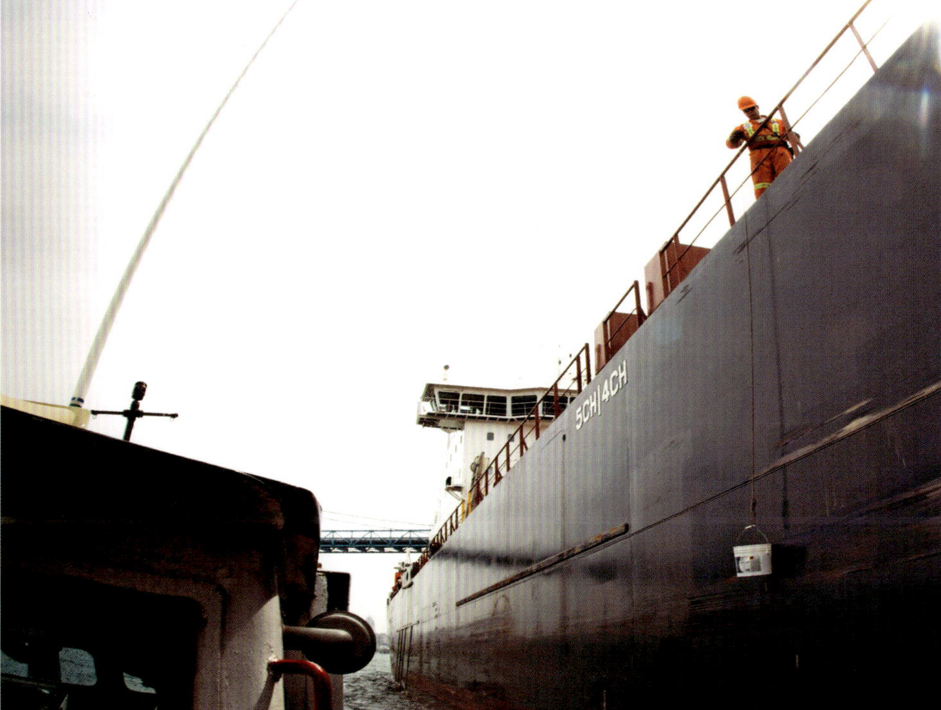

JW WESTCOTT

12 24th St., Detroit, 48222
www.jwwestcott.com

The *JW Westcott II* is just the latest boat to service the many freighters which pass through Detroit. Founded in 1874 by James Westcott and still family owned, the Westcott Company began transmitting destination and dock information to passing vessels by placing a notecard in a bucket that was then hoisted up by rope. The crews soon adopted his phrase "mail in the pail," which is still in use to this day. Over time, requests poured in from sailors who were isolated on their freighters for months. Letters from loved ones and packages of all sizes were mailed to the *JW Westcott* for delivery as the boats passed. In 1948, while handling almost 1 million pieces of mail each year, the U.S. Postal Service assigned the *JW Westcott* the world's first floating postal code. Anyone can send a letter; all you need is the following: *Vessel Name, Marine Post Office, Detroit, Michigan, 48222*. The package will wait until the ship has made it to town.

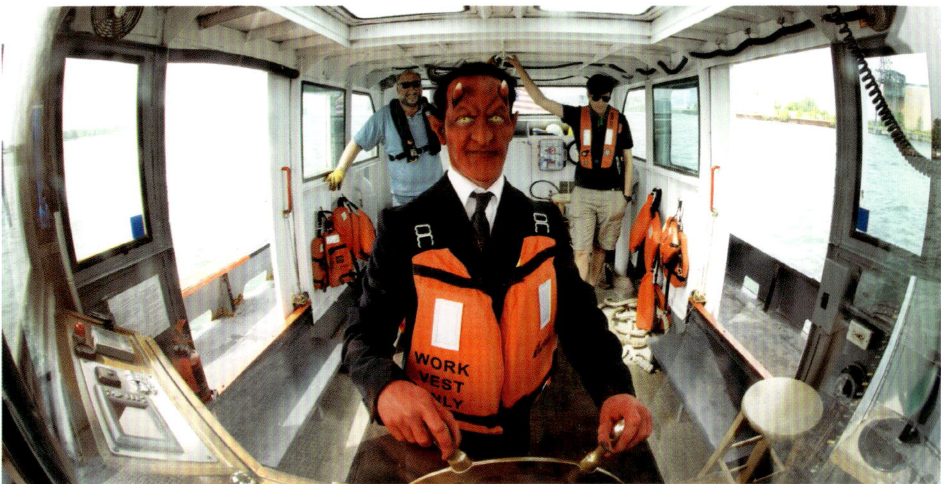

Being on the river is one of my favorite pastimes. Whenever I get bored, I drop down to Riverside Park and stop in on my old friends. I have known the Westcotts for a very long time, beginning with James. Over the years, I have helped deliver some strange items, including refrigerators, televisions, bicycles, gym equipment, and even pets. Some crazy bastards even ordered a set of golf clubs to use on their ship's deck. - NR

CHARLES WRIGHT AFRICAN AMERICAN MUSEUM

251 E. Warren Ave., Detroit, 48202
thewright.org

Being in a largely African-American city, you should expect a museum dedicated to the African-American experience. Dr. Charles Wright had that dream in 1965 when he founded the museum. It is home to the Blanche Coggin Underground Railroad Collection, the Harriet Tubman Museum Collection, the Coleman A. Young Collection, and the Sheffield Collection, a series of documents about the labor movement in Detroit. The permanent exhibit, And Still We Rise, is a powerful testament to those taken from Africa to the slave plantations of the South and to their descendants who faced racism in the northern cities. The museum is a great reminder of the struggles that African Americans experienced and the successes they have achieved.

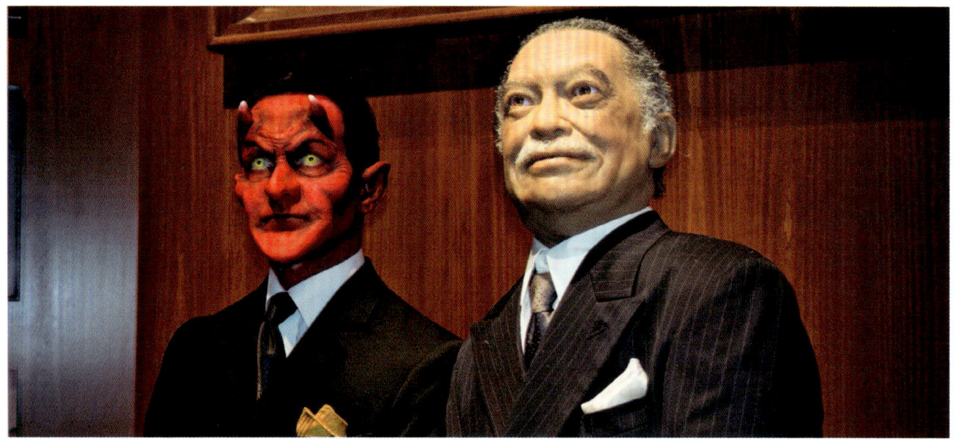

There is an ugly truth in the history of African-Americans living in a very segregated Detroit. Generally, they were ignored and isolated, allowed only a few neighborhoods to live in without fear or prejudice. When the Chrysler Freeway was constructed, it basically eradicated the center of the African-American community around Hastings Street. Consequently, African-Americans began moving into all-white neighborhoods that either resisted or saw its residents flee to the suburbs. In reaction, and to educate Detroiters and visitors alike about the African-American community's contributions to the city's development and culture, Dr. Charles Wright established a museum in his doctor's office. Later, this fantastic building was built to perpetuate his mission. - NR

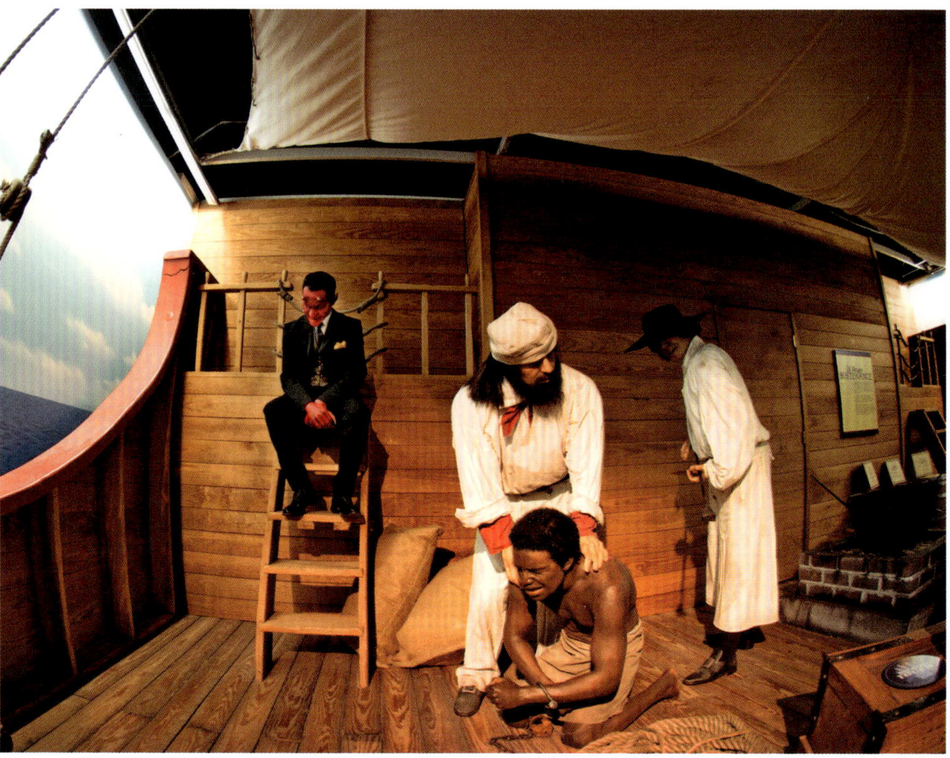

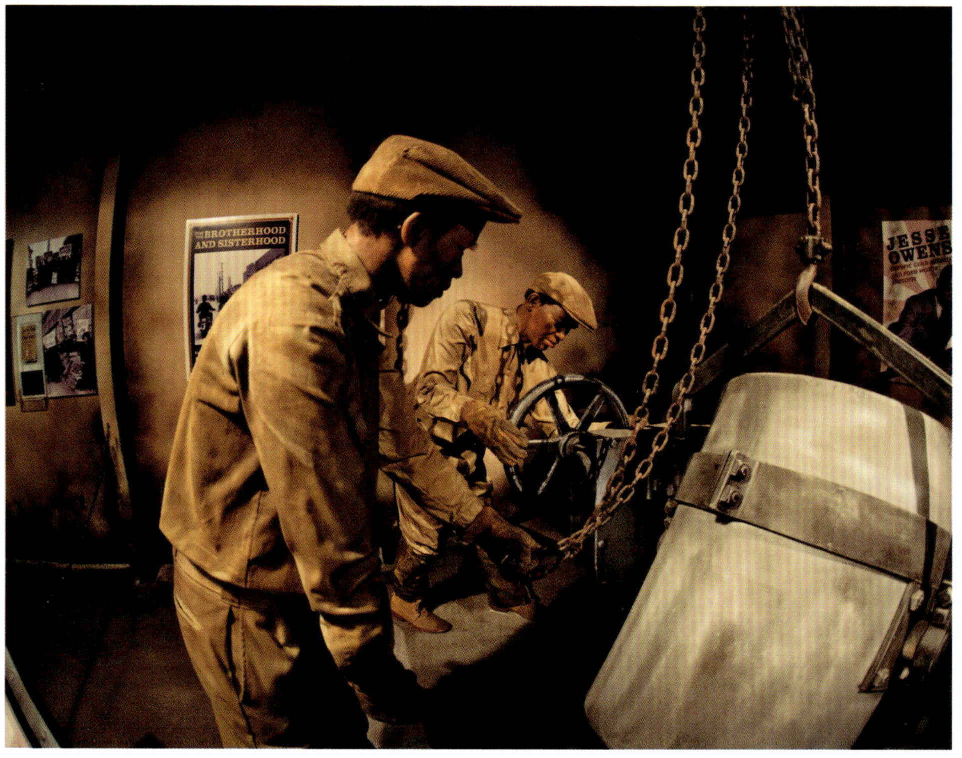

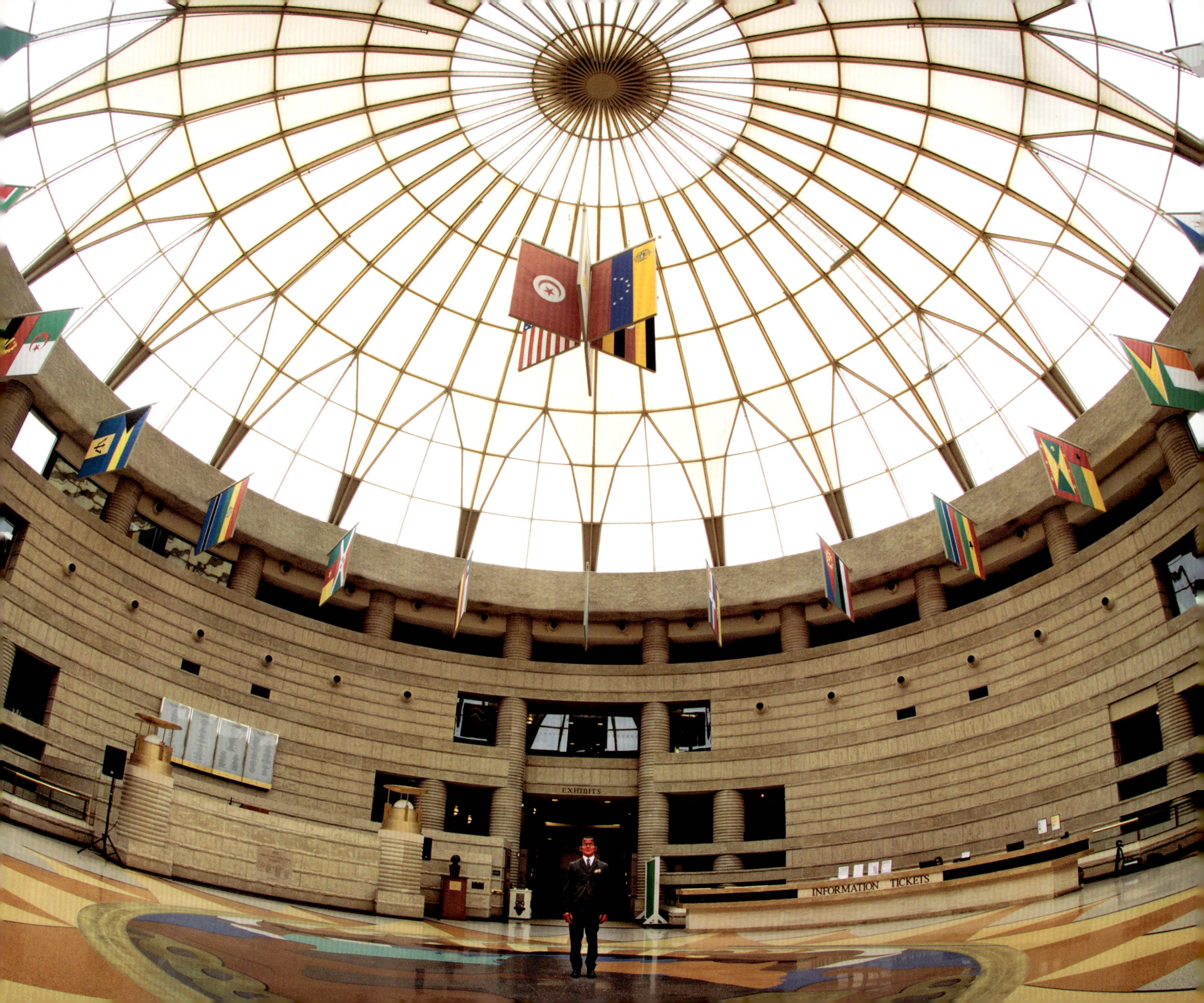
EXHIBITS
INFORMATION
TICKETS

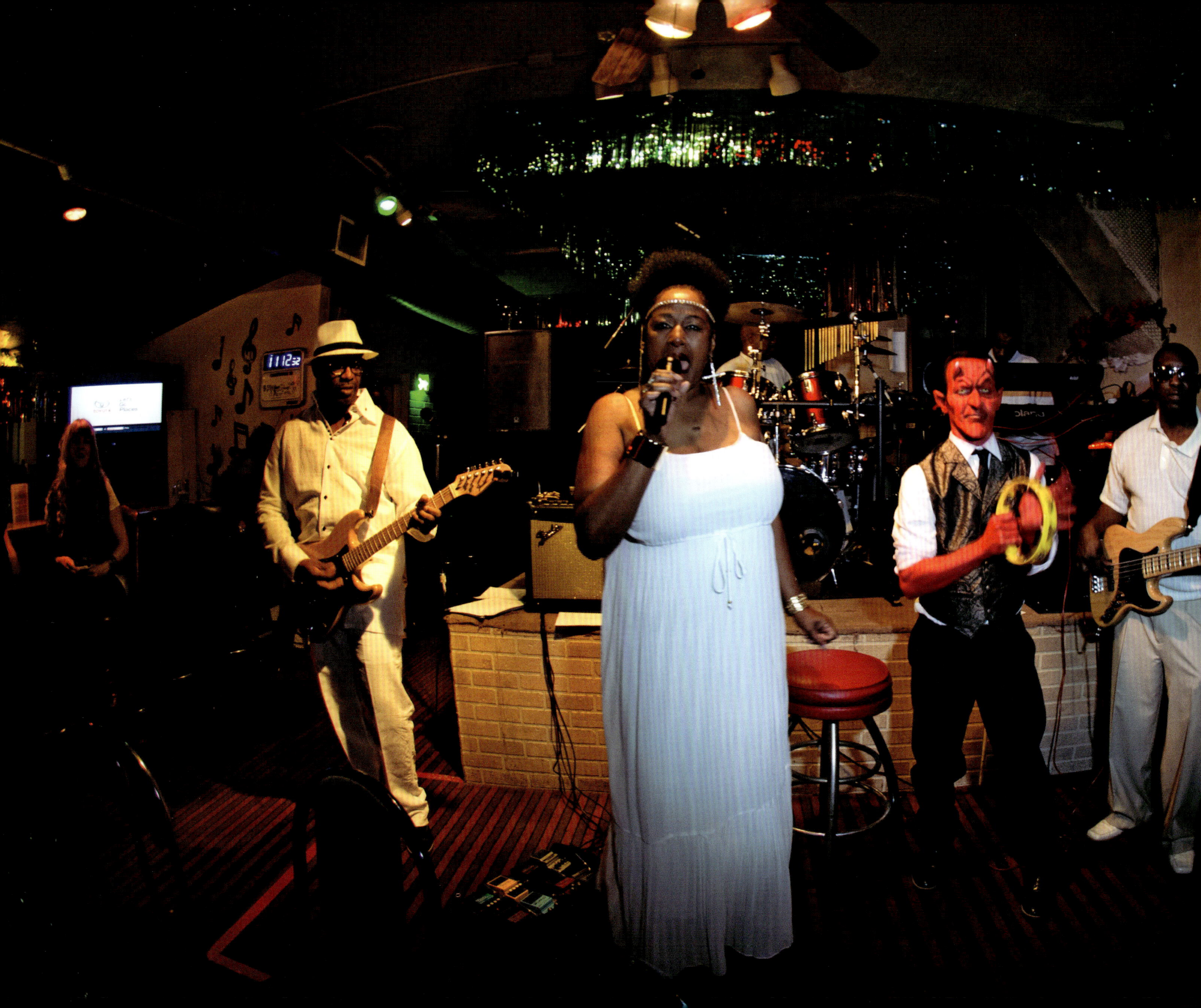

MUSIC VENUES & THEATRES

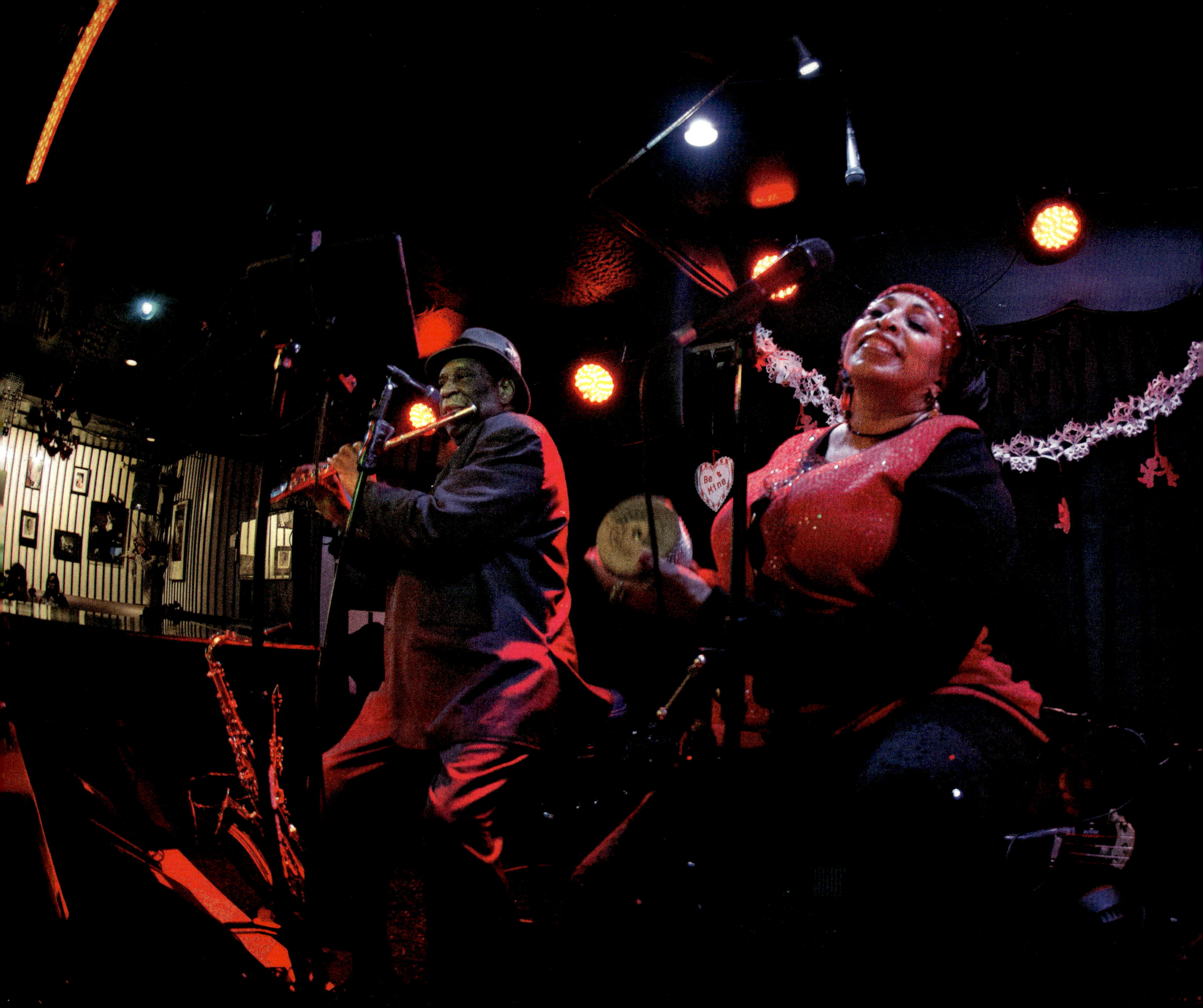
Be Mine

BAKER'S KEYBOARD LOUNGE

20510 Livernois Ave., Detroit, 48221
www.theofficialbakerskeyboardlounge.com

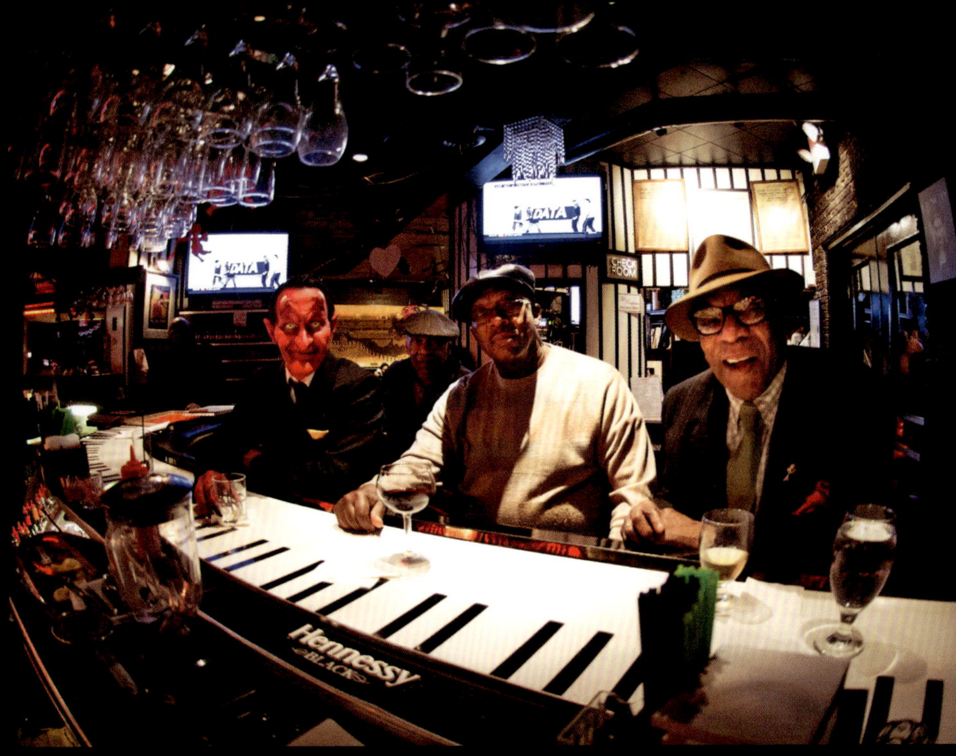

The world's longest-operating jazz club, the famous Baker's Keyboard Lounge has been showcasing jazz music since 1934. Its signature art deco design features a winding piano-shaped bar with a keyboard-patterned top. With excellent acoustics, and noted for its intimacy between musician and audience, Baker's has showcased many of the greats in jazz history. Ella Fitzgerald, Louis Armstrong, John Coltrane, Cab Calloway, Oscar Peterson, and Miles Davis are just a few of the illustrious musicians who have taken the stage. Detroit-bred Earl Klugh credits his teenage visits with fostering his career.

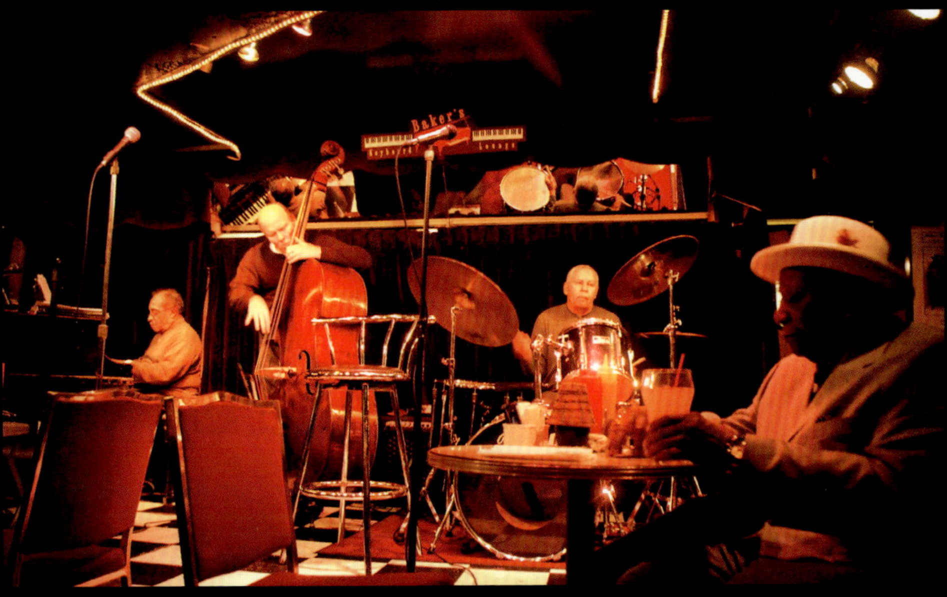

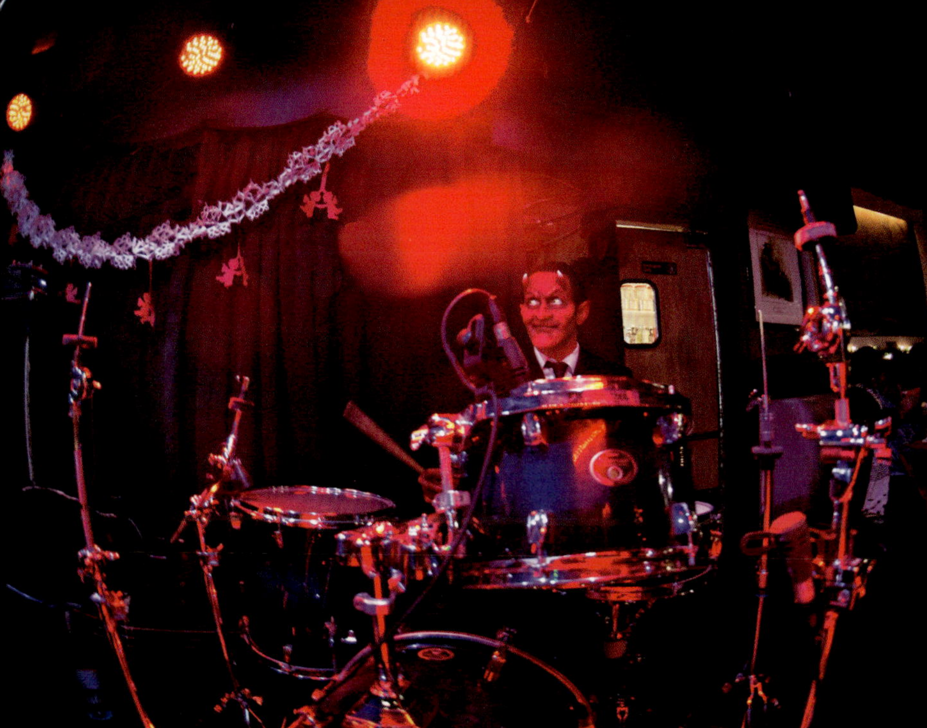

In one of my favorite parts of town, on the old Avenue of Fashion and just south of famed 8 Mile Road, is the hottest spot for jazz in the country. I'm pretty much a regular here. When I'm not sitting in on a session, I come out for the best damn karaoke around. Happy hour is wall to wall and the tunes are classics belted out by my neighbors. - NR

COMMUNITY THEATRES

Park Players, 18445 Scarsdale St., Detroit, 48223
www.parkplayers.org

Detroit Repertory Theatre, 13103 Woodrow Wilson St., Detroit, 48238
www.detroitreptheatre.com

Matrix Theatre, 2730 Bagley Ave., Detroit, 48216
www.matrixtheatre.org

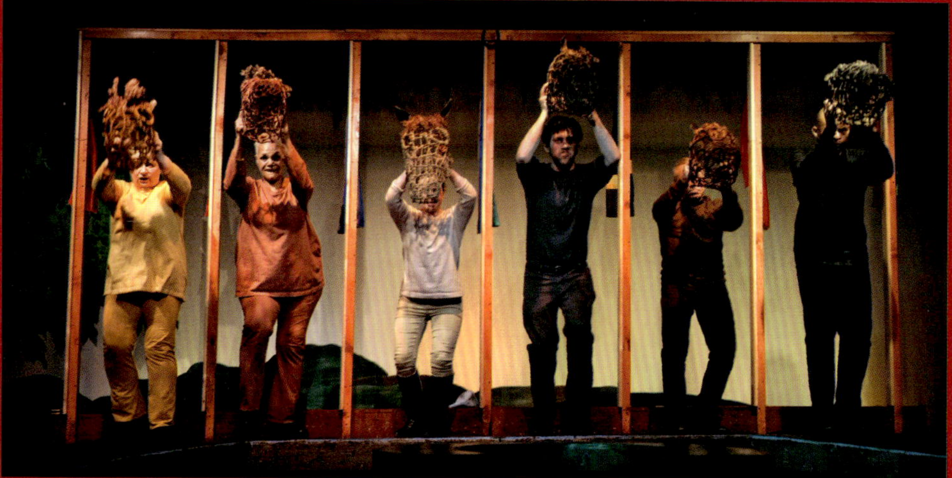

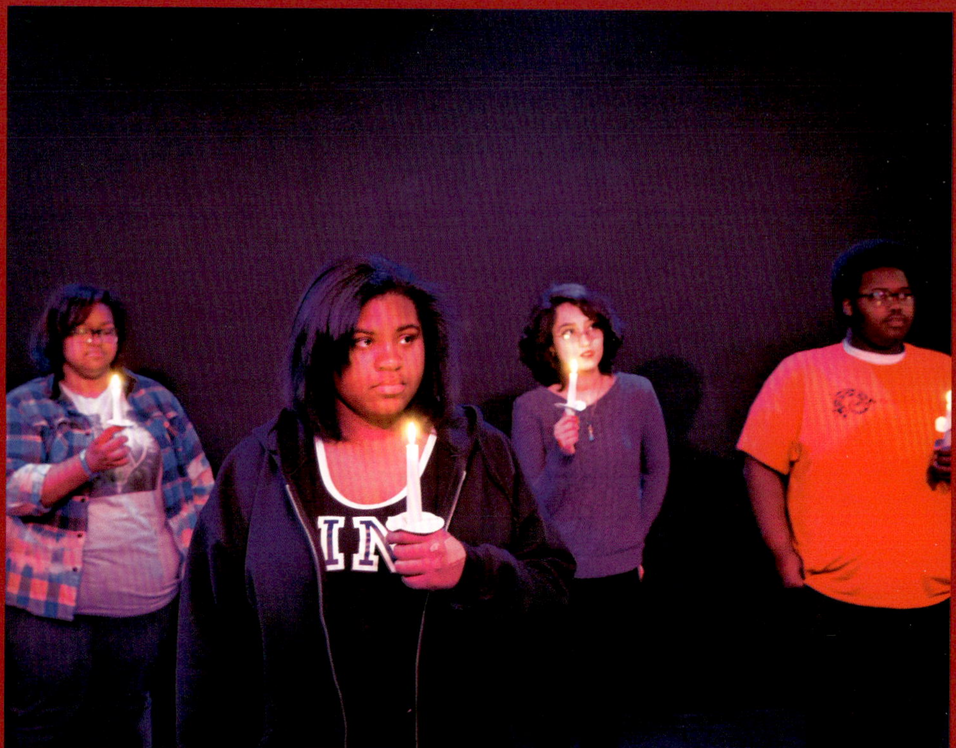

Live theatre has always been a part of the fabric of Detroit. The oldest amateur community theatre group, the Park Players, formed in the 1950s in the North Rosedale Park neighborhood. Launched in 1991, the award-winning Matrix Theatre focuses primarily on community issues and local partnerships. The famous Detroit Repertory Theater is the oldest alternative professional theatre in Michigan. Since 1957, the Rep has pioneered efforts in community involvement, interracial casting, and artistic diversity while maintaining quality performances in one of Detroit's most devastated neighborhoods.

Performing is in our DNA. Whether it's music, comedy, or theatre, Detroit performing artists such as George C. Scott, Lily Tomlin, Della Reese, Keegan-Michael Key, and Gilda Radner, to name just a few, got their starts in Detroit before establishing themselves on Broadway and in film and television. These venues offer us thespians a chance to hone our acting chops and blow people's minds. - NR

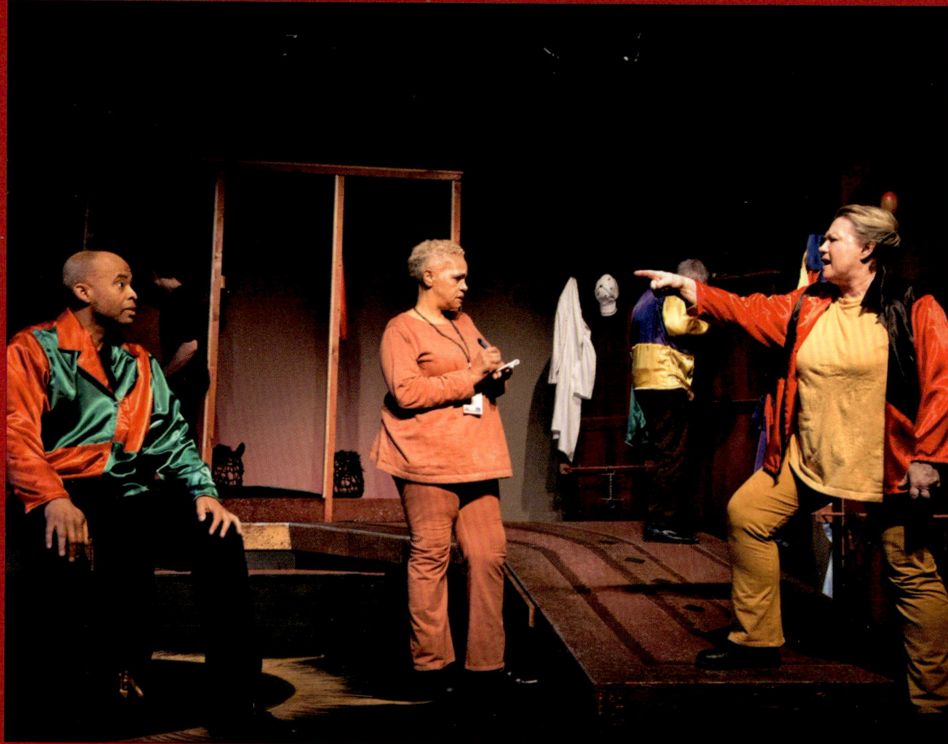

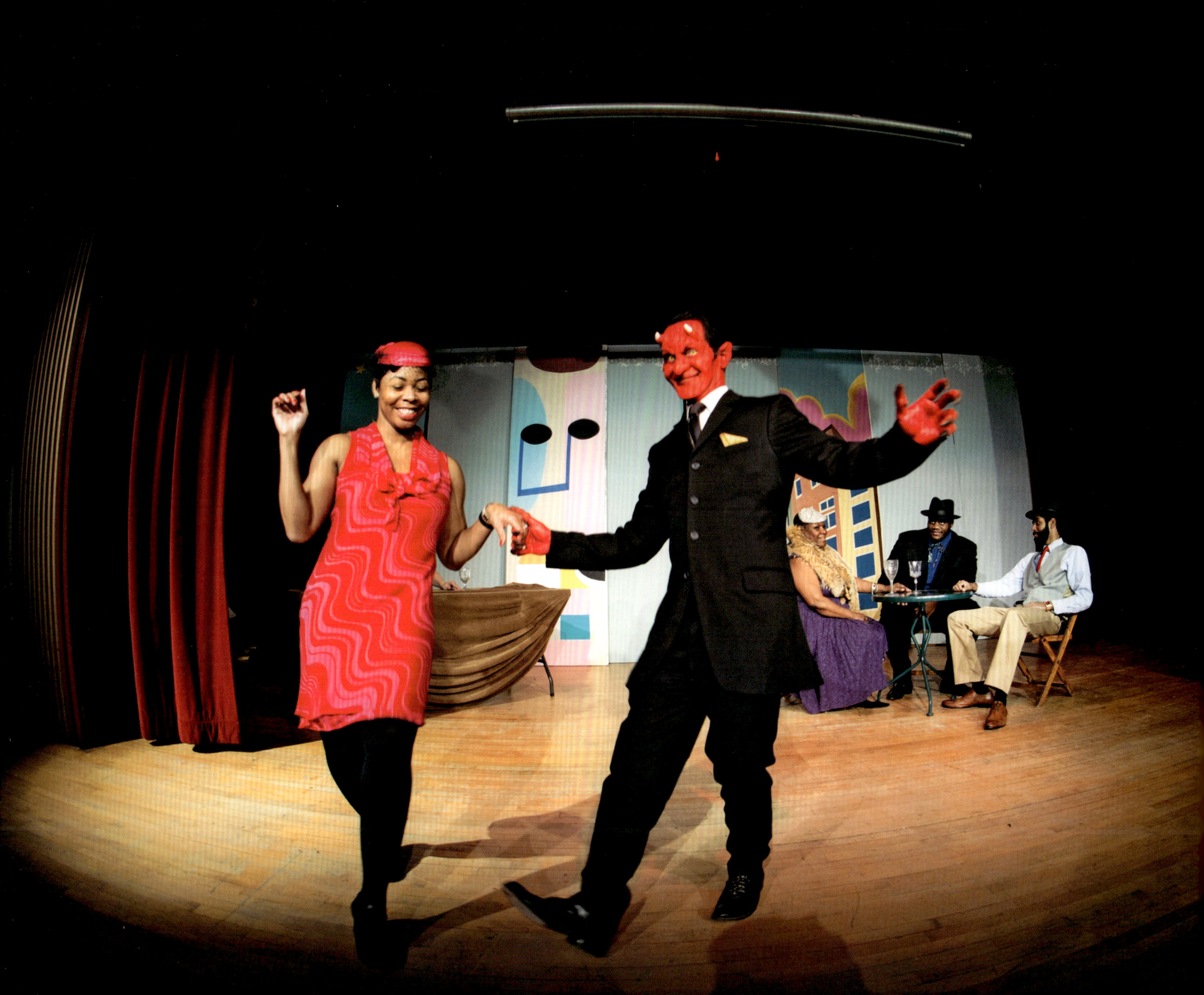

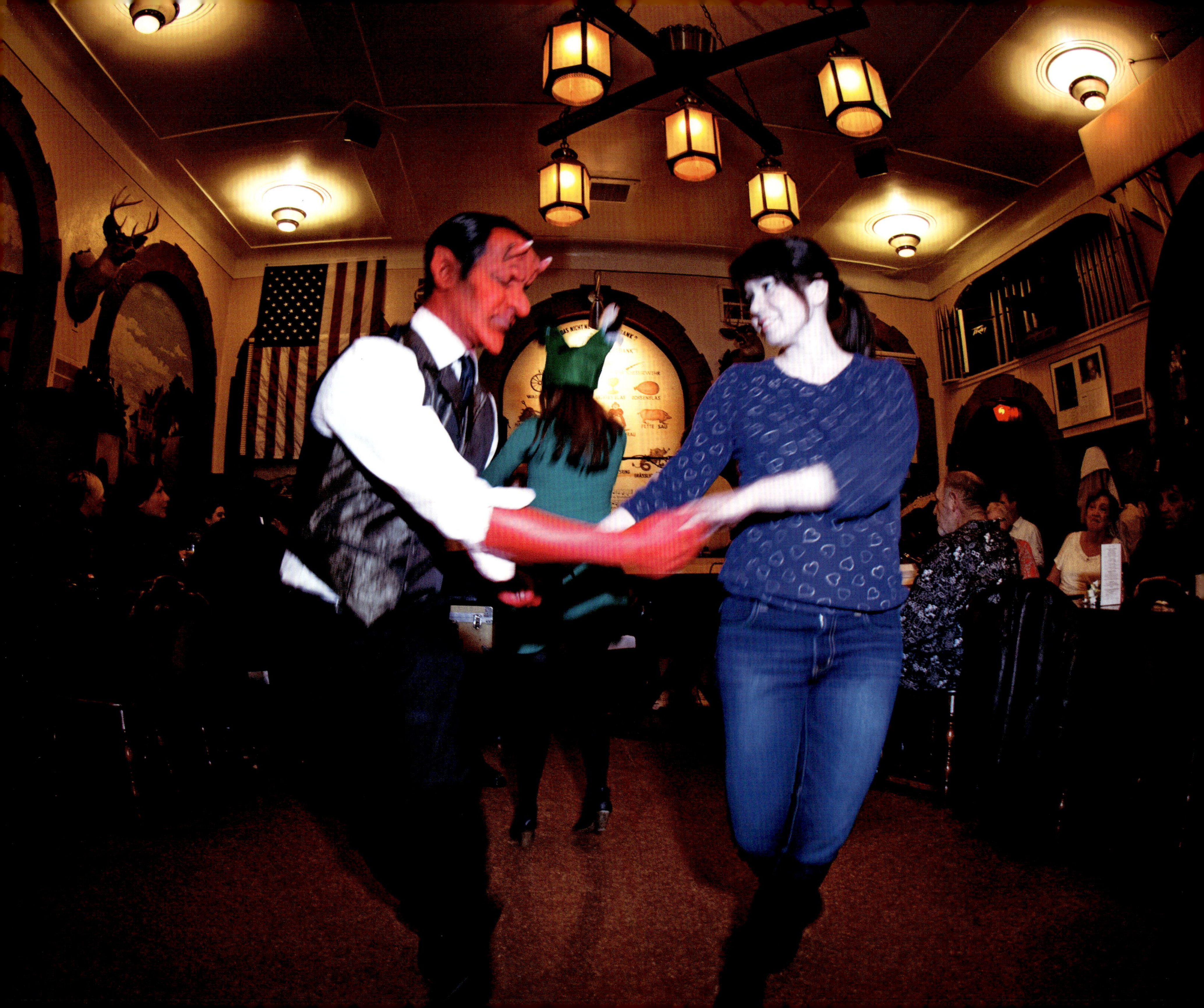

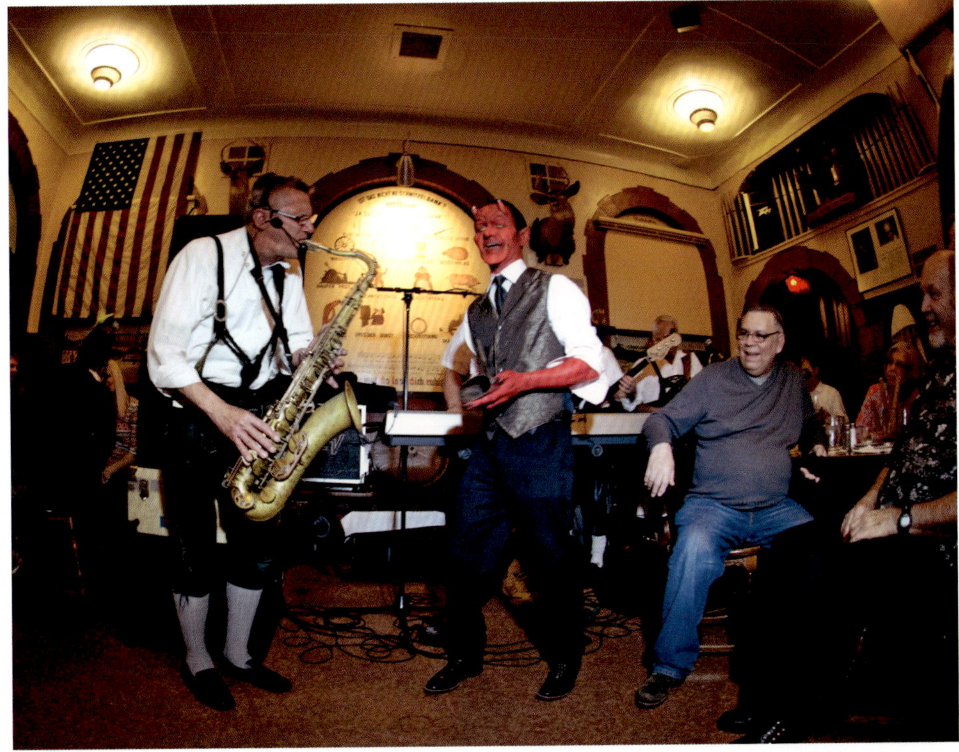

THE DAKOTA INN RATHSKELLER

17324 John R St., Detroit, 48203
www.dakota-inn.com

Karl Kurz is the third generation host of this family-owned German beer hall, which has served guests, beer drinkers, and polka lovers since 1933. The interior was designed by his grandfather, Karl, to resemble the beer halls he remembered frequenting in his youth in Bavaria. Karl's restaurant serves authentic German food and beers. Guests are encouraged to sing along to traditional beer hall standards or get up and dance to an oompah band or polka. The Dakota Inn's Oktoberfest celebration rivals any of the great beer halls of Germany.

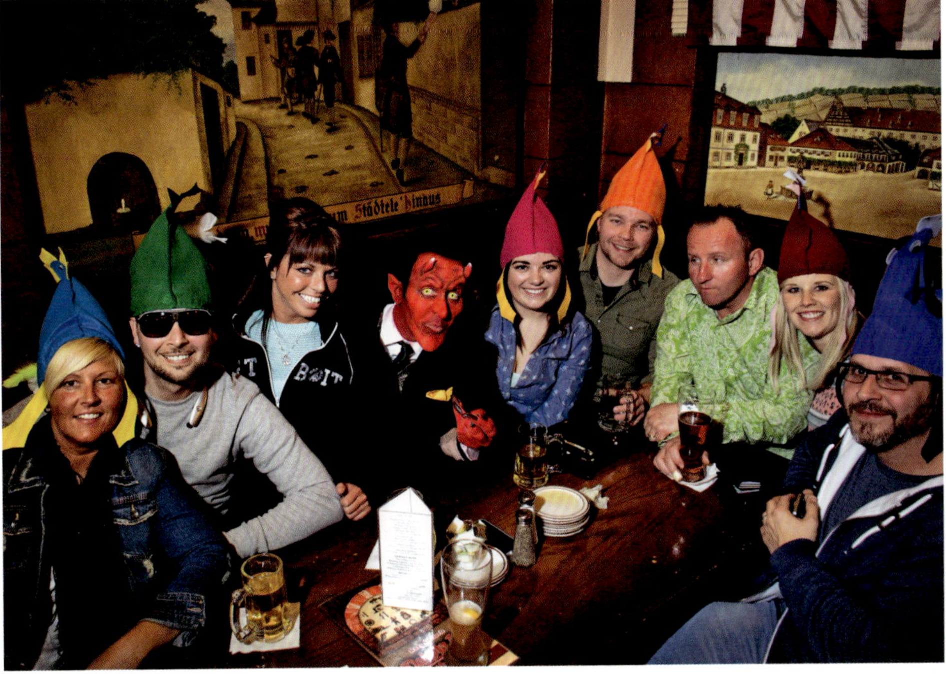

For a time, every neighborhood had a distinctive immigrant bar where first generations would gather, eat, drink, sing, and dance. During Oktoberfest, this place is packed with descendants of Detroit's early German settlers. These folks are probably no more German than I am, but damned if we don't have fun singing and dancing to the old folk songs from across the pond. - NR

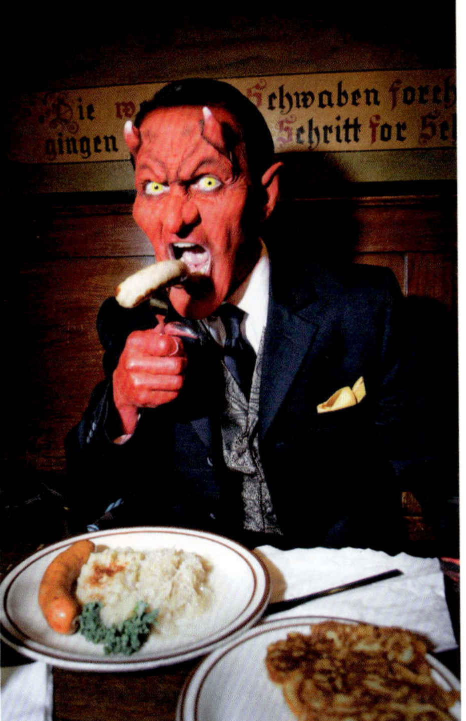

DETROIT SYMPHONY ORCHESTRA

3711 Woodward Ave., Detroit, 48201
www.dso.org

The fourth oldest orchestra in the United States, the DSO has been performing since 1887. In 1918, Ossip Gabrilowitsch became musical director. A close friend of Mahler and Rachmaninoff, he demanded a new performance space and Orchestra Hall became home until 1939. The world's first radio broadcast of a symphony orchestra concert was performed by the DSO in 1922. During the 1940s, after the DSO left, Orchestra Hall became the Paradise Theater and hosted great African American artists and jazz performers including Count Bassie and Duke Ellington. After the Paradise Theater closed in 1951, the hall was abandoned for 20 years until Paul Ganson, a DSO bassoonist, initiated the movement to renovate it. Noted for its excellent acoustics, it has been fully restored with an additional performance space, the Music Box.

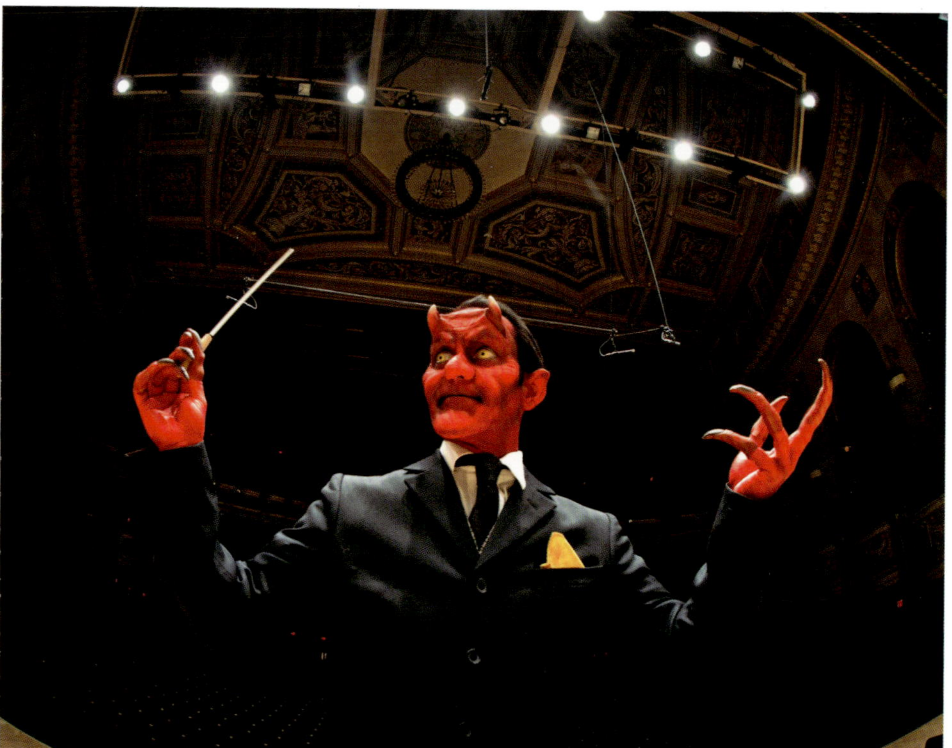

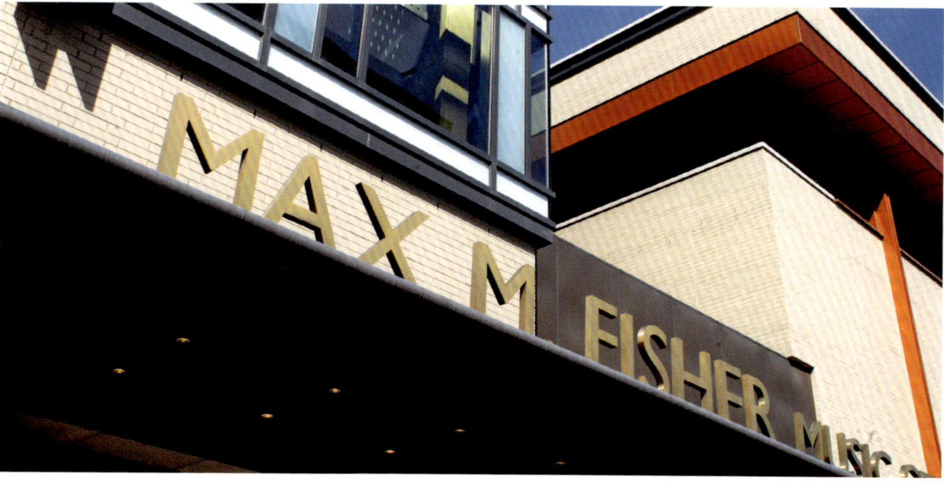

One of the perks of knowing everyone here for so long is that I occasionally am invited to conduct. I usually choose something from "The Planets" or a Mozart tune but I've been known to mix it up a bit. I met Paul when I directed a Mahler piece in the early 70s. I told him how great the acoustics were at Orchestra Hall and we set out to return the DSO back to its original home. After we accomplished that feat, the place expanded beyond my expectations.
- NR

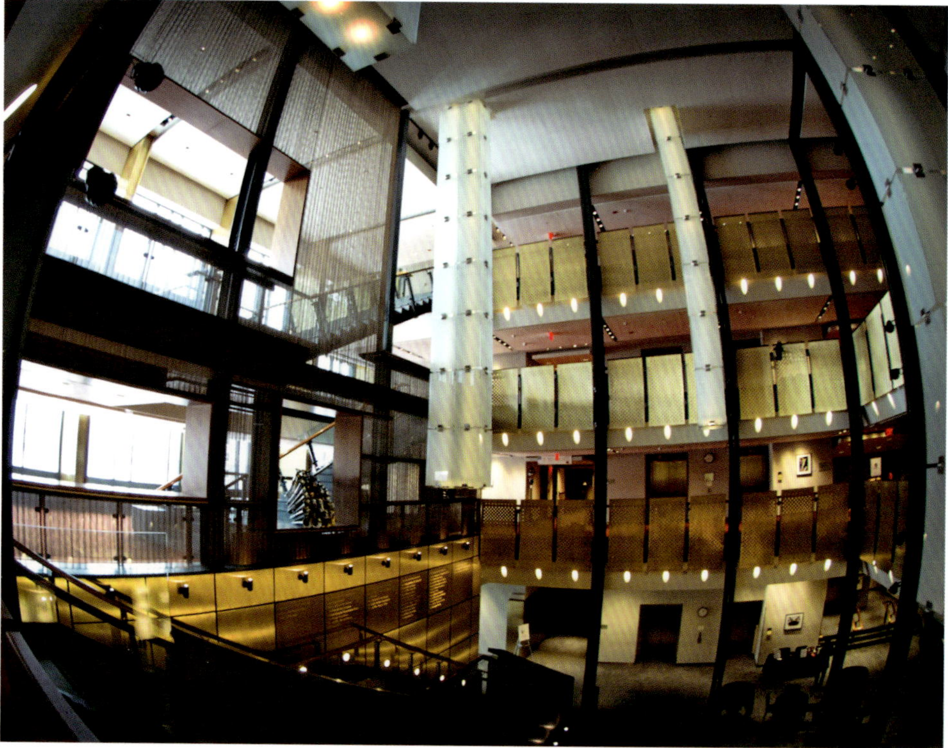

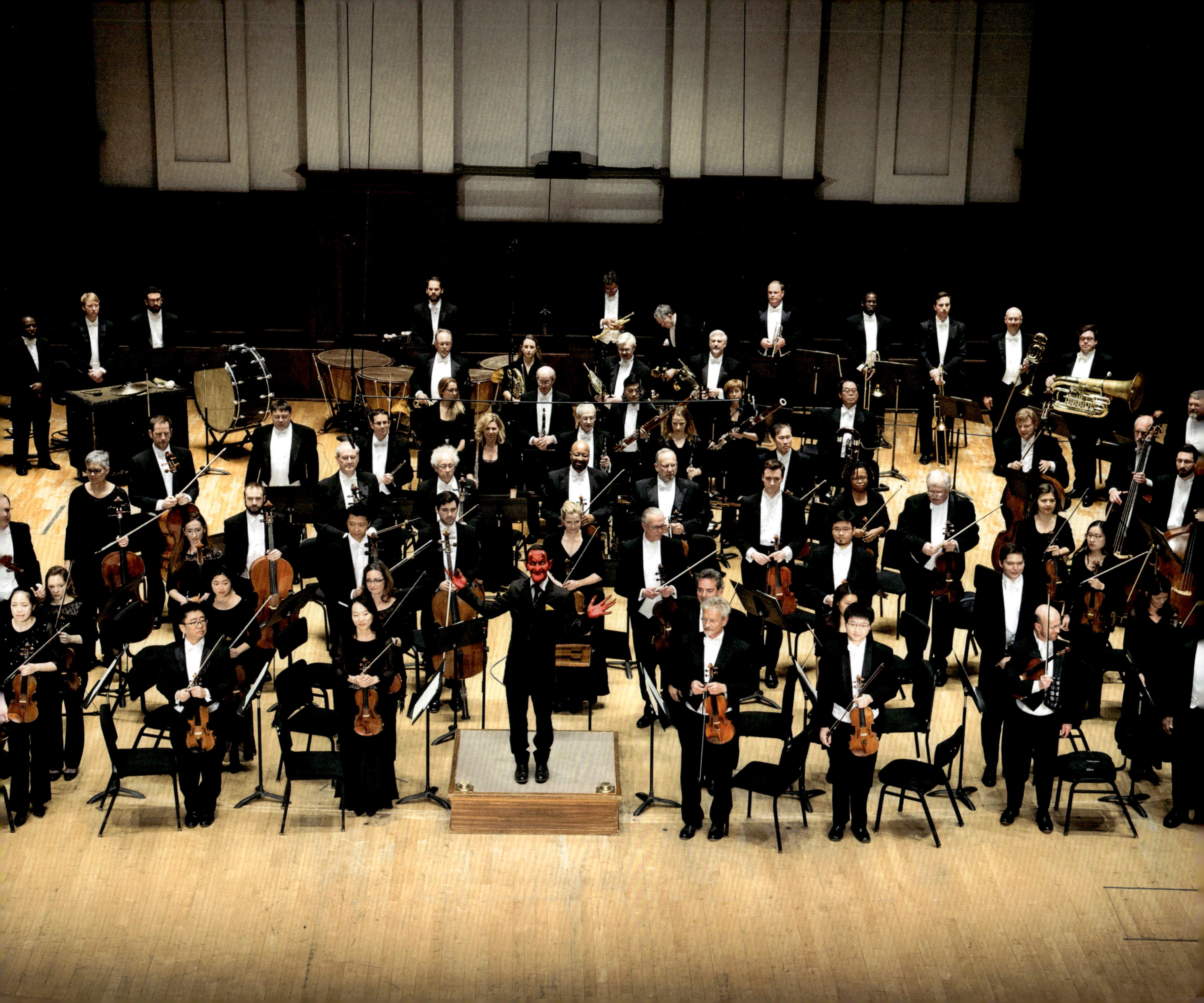

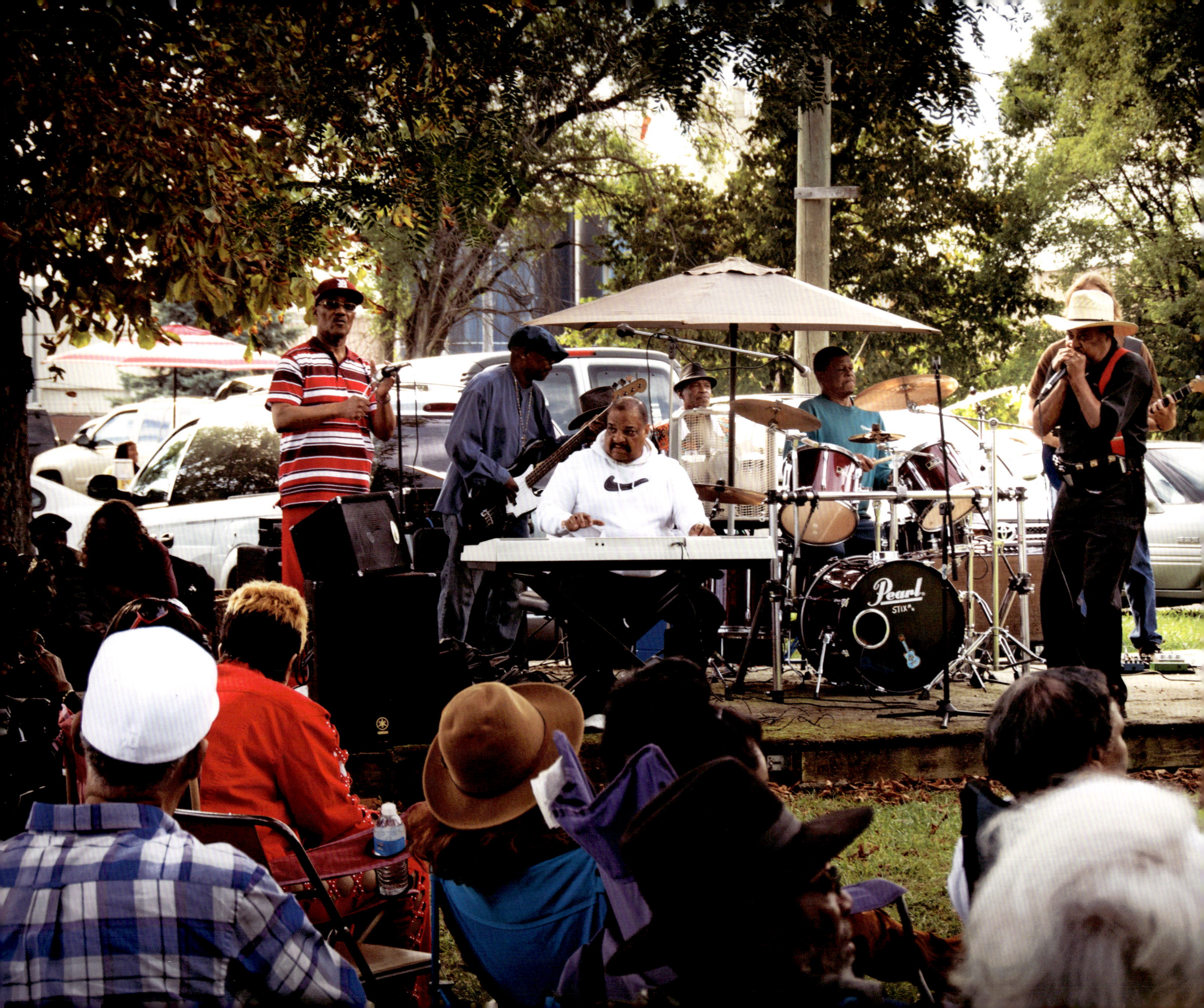
Pearl
STIX

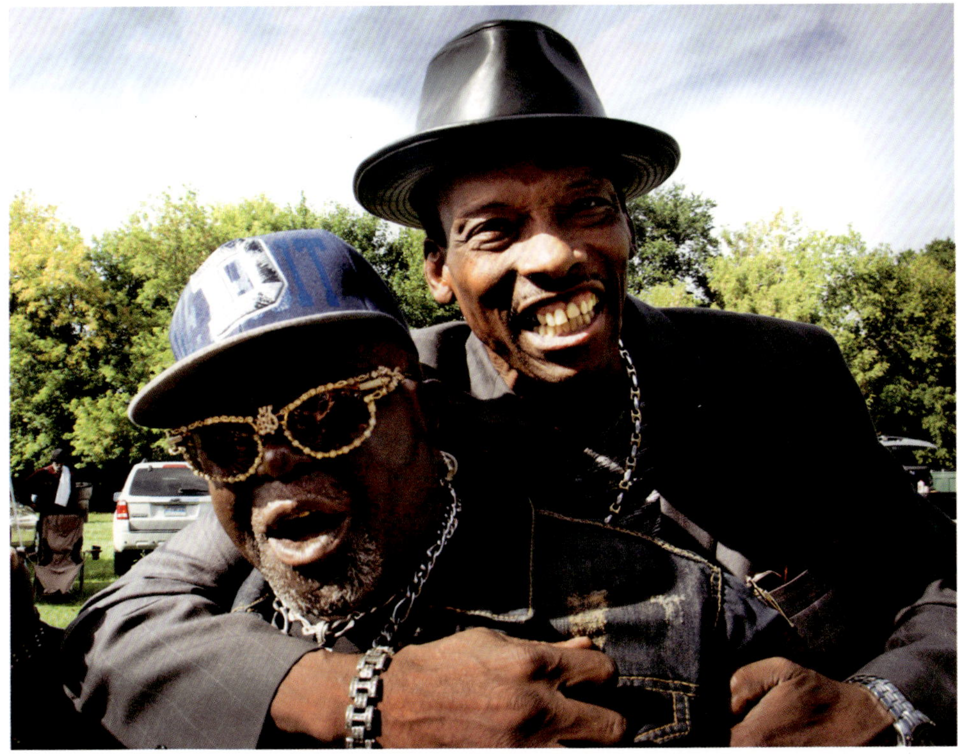

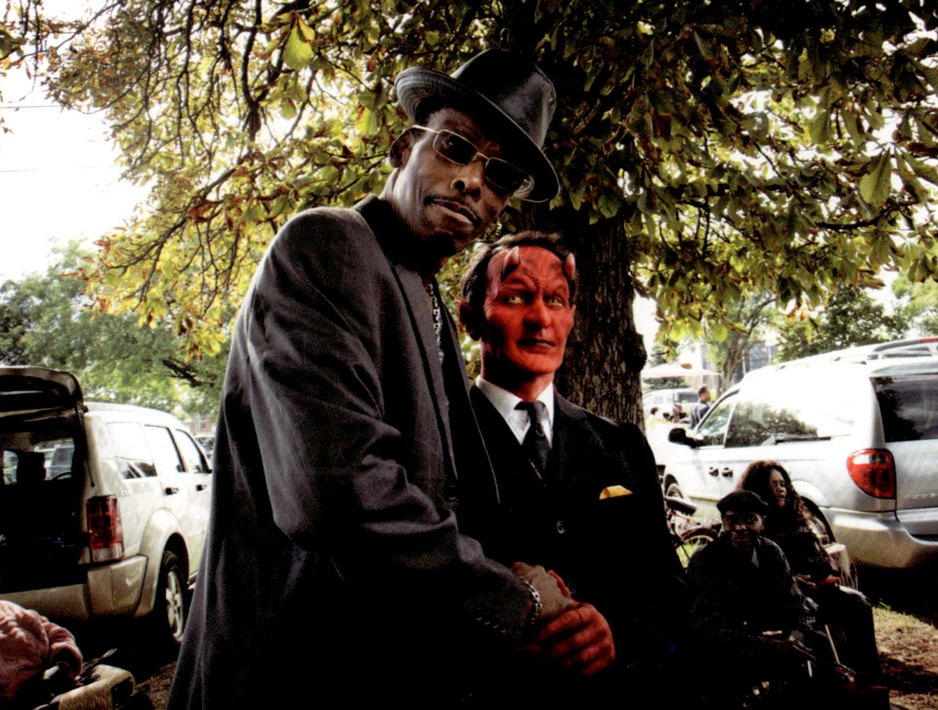

JOHN'S CARPET HOUSE

2133 Frederick St., Detroit, 48211
www.johnscarpethouse.com

A summer outdoor party, Detroit style. Blues drummer John Estes began John's Carpet Blues in the 1980s on the eastside in a small shed next to his home for the neighbors to get together to enjoy the blues. He lined the walls with carpet for better acoustics and soon local musicians began playing every weekend. After John's passing, "Big Pete" continued the shows. After John's house burned down, the shows moved across the street to an empty lot. The concerts are free but donations are encouraged to help mow the field and clear the trash. A few BBQ grills offer up food while it's BYOB for the audience.

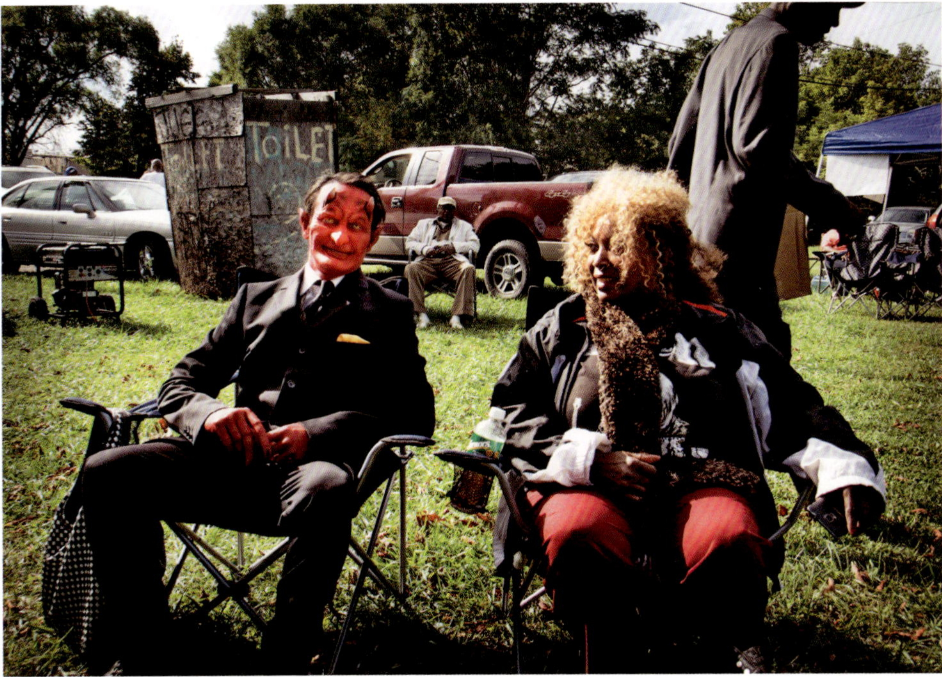

I could try to list all the musical talent here, but that would take too long. Some people have it, but most don't. If you call Detroit home, then you already have it. All summer long, my neighbors and my friends gather up after church and throw down one of the best picnic jams around. With a roster of rotating musicians keeping the beats, folks set up on lawn chairs and in the backs of cars to spend another Sunday as Big Pete's guests. - NR

MICHIGAN OPERA THEATRE

1526 Broadway St., Detroit, 48226
www.michiganopera.org

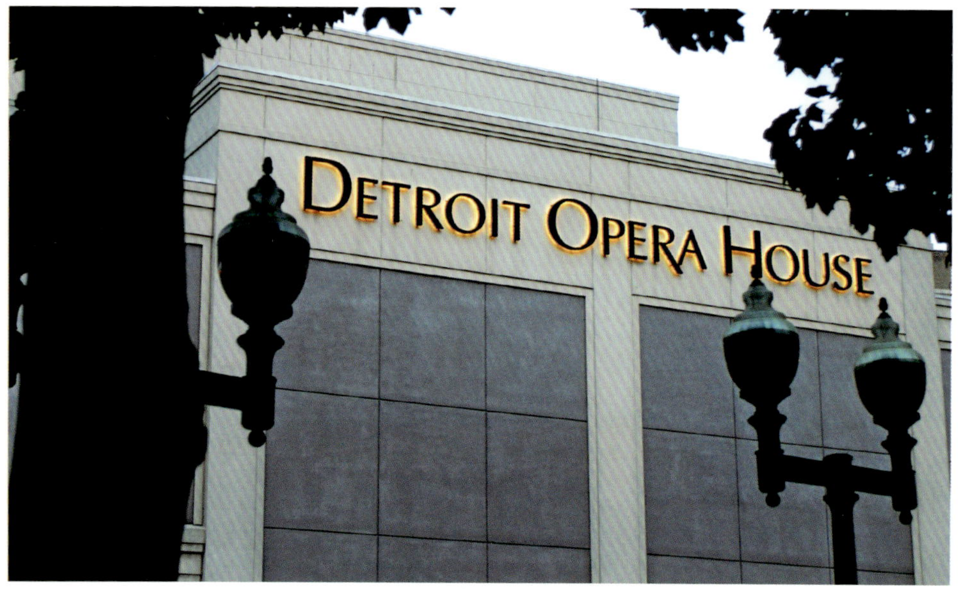

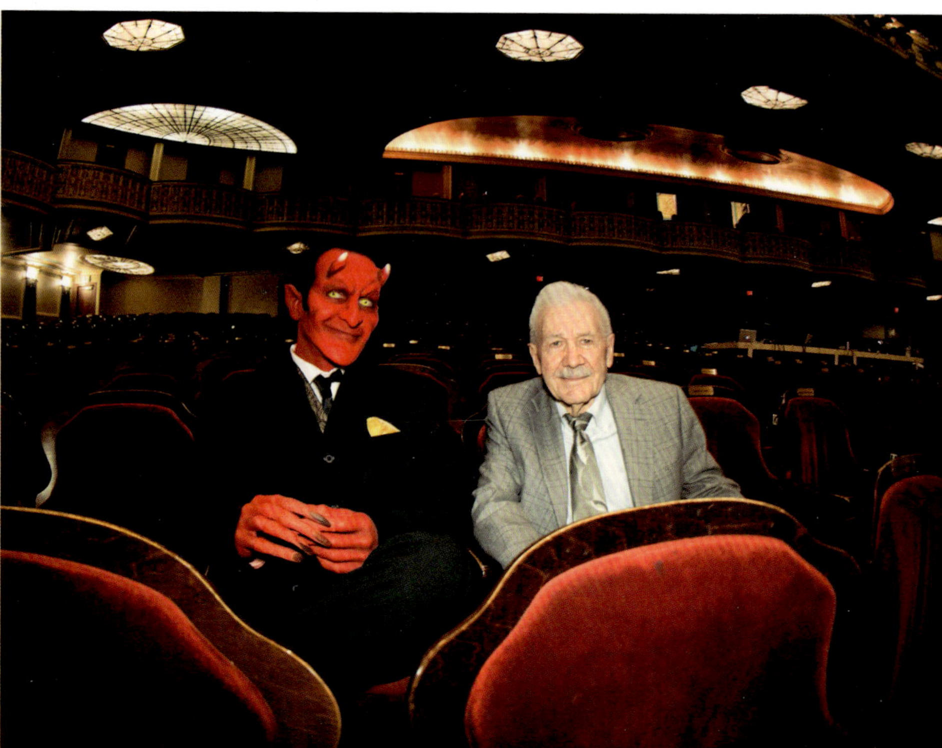

Founder and General Director David DiChiera has led the Michigan Opera Theatre since 1963, returning opera as an art form to Detroit. The MOT has become an important and popular opera company, establishing an international reputation for staging rarely performed operas. In 2005, it debuted the world premiere of Margaret Garner, based on Toni Morrison's novel Beloved. It established its home, the Detroit Opera House, in the former Capital Theatre in 2000. The MOT presents four operas a year in their original languages and hosts touring dance companies and offers educational programs, dance programs, and workshops for children.

I met David at Oakland University well before the MOT was formed. He always spoke of his desire for Detroit to have its own opera company and opera house. Since then, through our mutual love for opera, we became good friends. Propelled by his determination and leadership, the Michigan Opera Theatre has grown into a world class company. With almost any new production, he invites me to sit in on the final rehearsals, seeking my opinion or approval. - NR

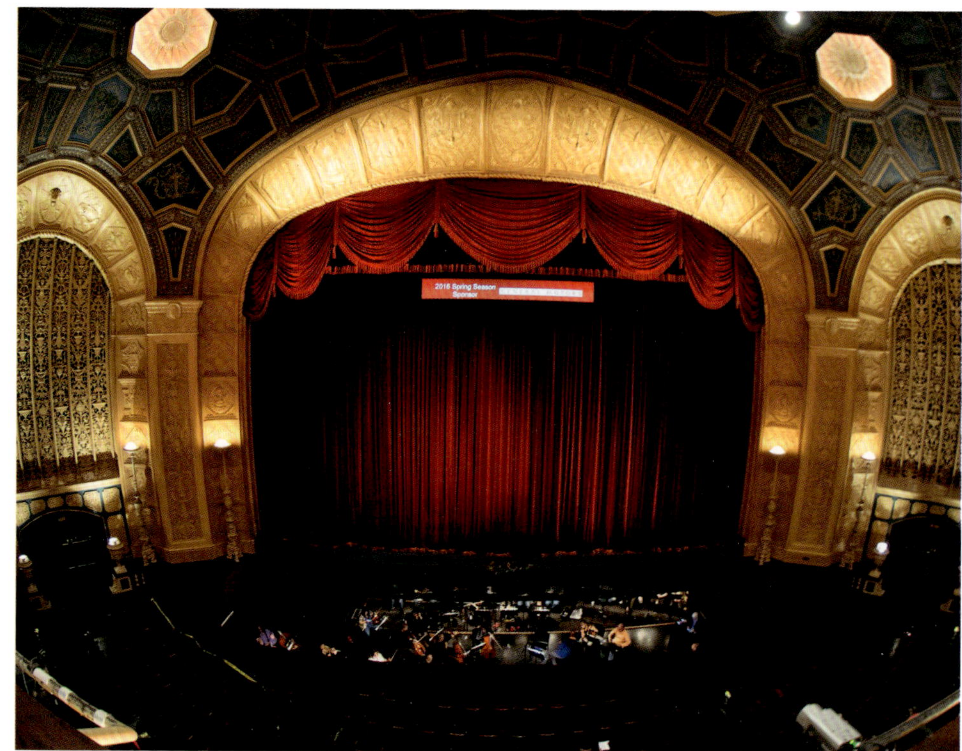

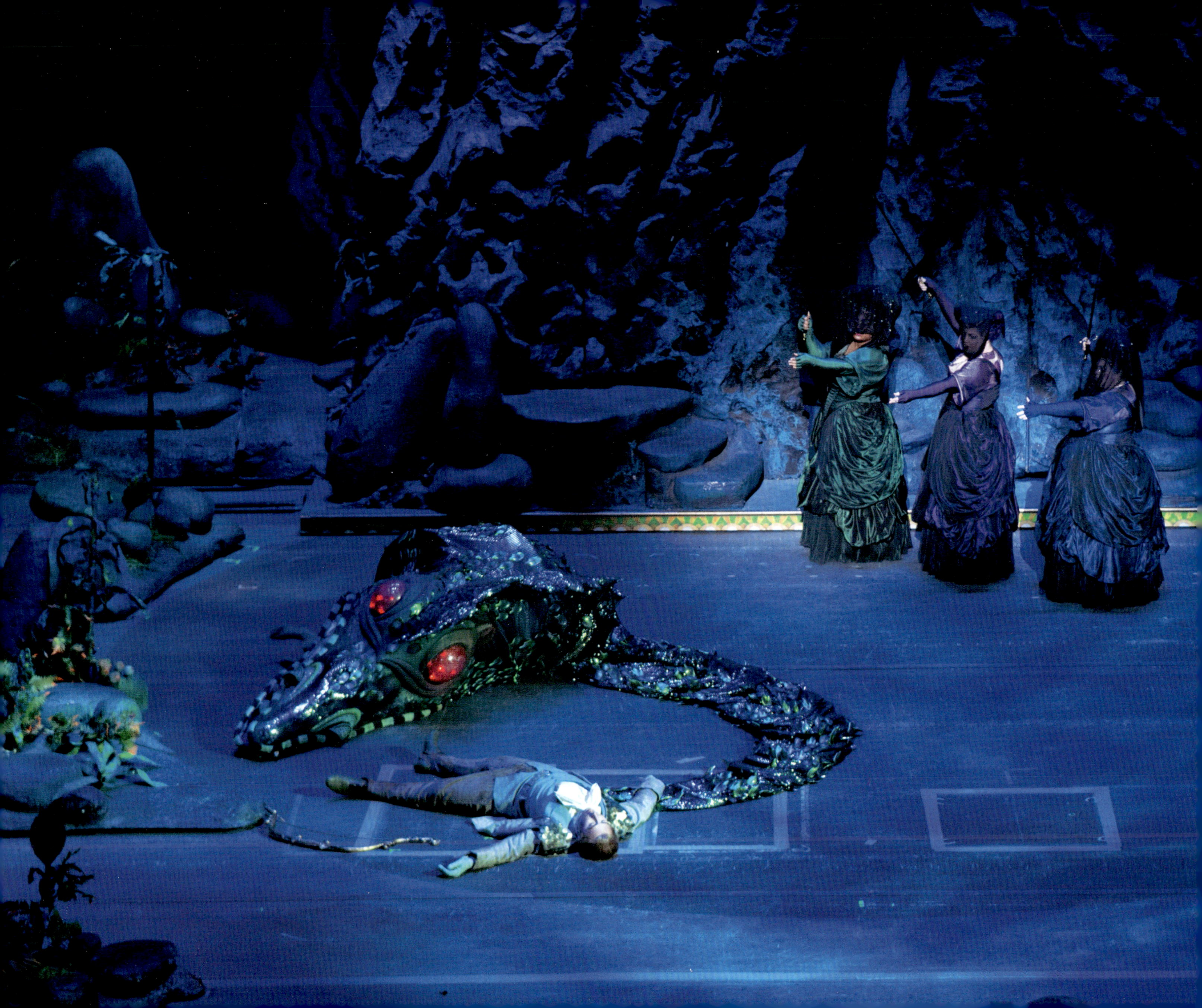

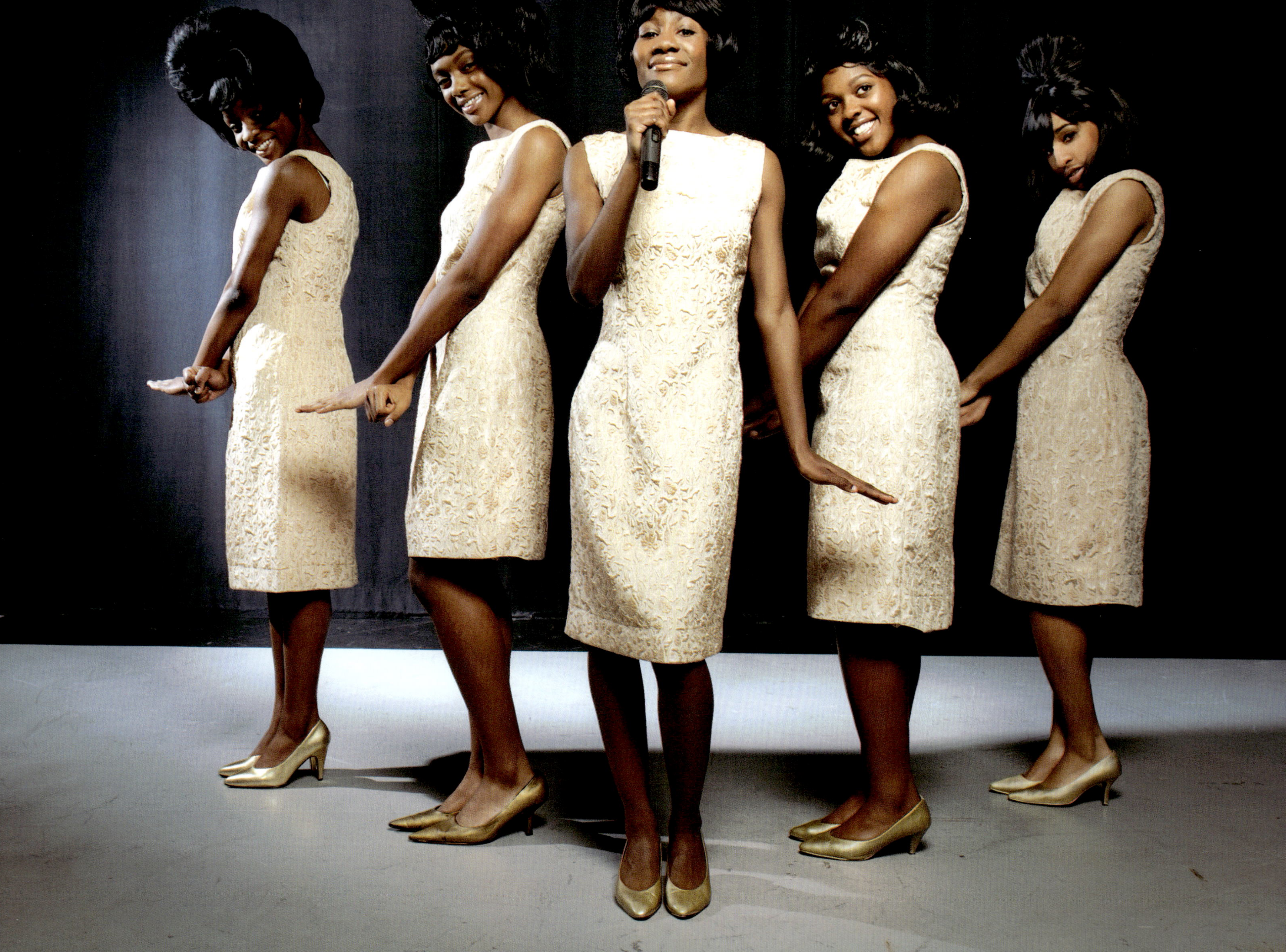

MOSAIC YOUTH THEATRE

2251 Antietam Ave., Detroit, 48207
www.mosaicdetroit.org

Critically acclaimed and internationally recognized as a leader in music and theatre arts education, Mosaic Youth Theatre was formed in 1992 by Rick Sperling in response to the severe cuts in public school arts funding. Mosaic's all-teen theatre and vocal music performances have toured Africa, Asia, Europe, Canada, and 25 states throughout the United States, including performances at the White House, the Kennedy Center, Carnegie Hall and the Apollo Theater. Mosaic has performed as an opening act for Aretha Franklin, Pete Seeger, Al Green, John Legend, and the Temptations and has won national awards from the President's Committee on the Arts and Humanities and the National Endowment for the Arts, as well as two gold and two silver medals at the 2014 World Choir Games in Latvia. Mosaic has ongoing partnerships with the Public Theater in New York and the Stratford Shakespeare Festival in Ontario. Since its founding, more than 95% of Mosaic performers have graduated from high school and gone on to college.

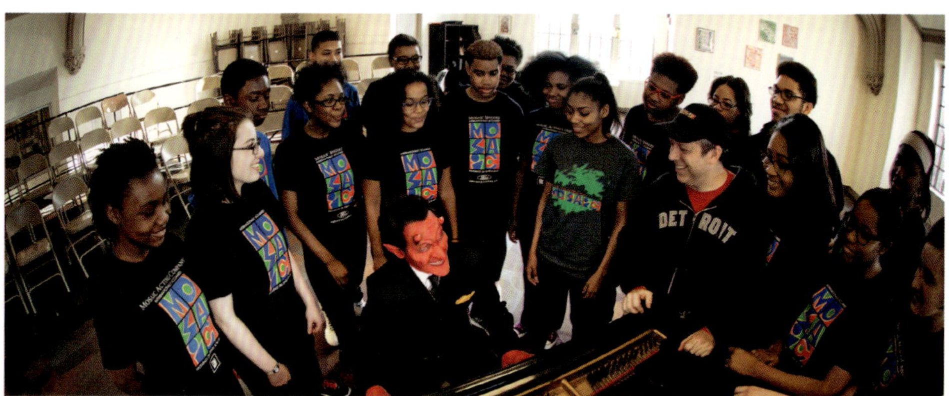

A few decades ago, when I was a player with the Attic Theatre in Greektown, I met Rick Sperling, a fledgling actor. We held an open casting call for young actors for a new play we were staging. The response was overwhelming: more than three hundred students auditioned for four roles. I told Rick that he'd make his mark in the world with teaching, not acting. He wasn't a half bad actor, at least that's what I told him, but he was a hell of a gifted leader. Recognizing the amazing talent here, and fulfilling a huge need by educating young performers, Rick has developed Mosaic into one of the premier student ensembles in the country. - NR

RAVEN LOUNGE

5145 Chene St., Detroit, 48211
www.theravenloungeandrestaurant.com

Before starting Motown, Berry Gordy used to sell Polaroids to the Raven clientele, and Jackie Wilson began his career here. Legends like Aretha Franklin, Smokey Robinson and Martha Reeves have played and hosted shows here, and local blues musicians bring the house down every weekend. Owner Tommy Stephens greets you at the door, welcoming you like a regular even if it's your first time. As Detroit's oldest blues bar, and one of the last live blues venues, the Raven is a testament to the great neighborhood music venues which once populated the city.

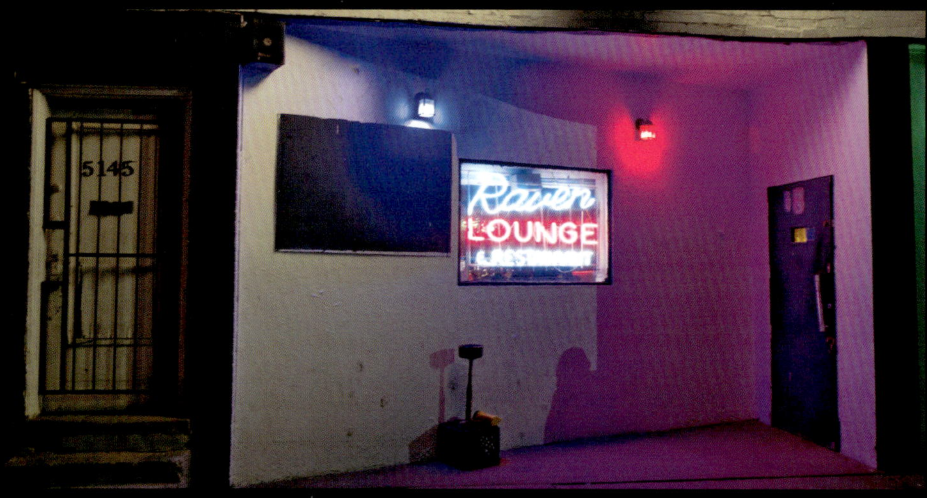

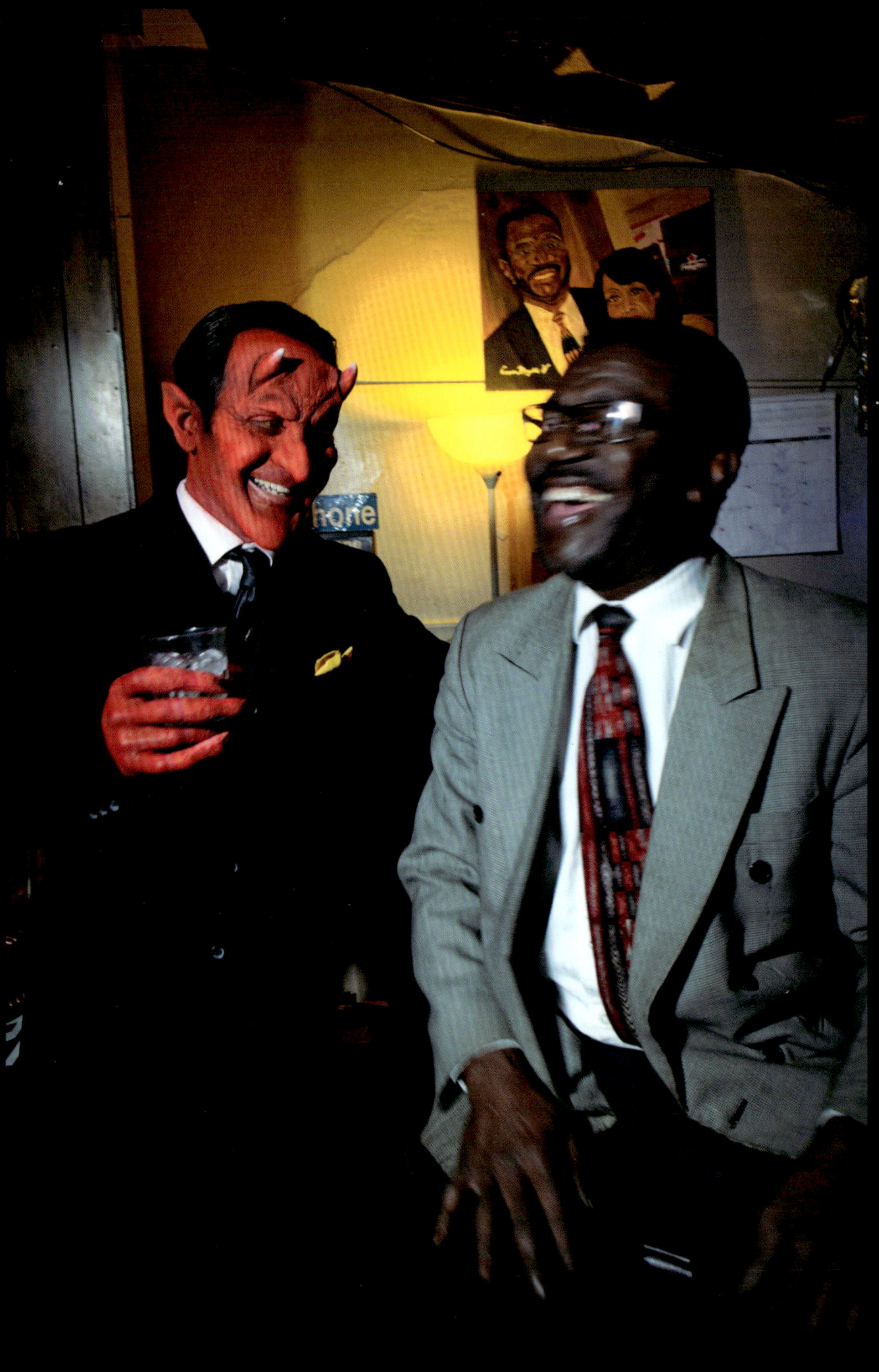

I stumbled into the Raven decades ago when young Tommy worked the door. On stage, Jackie Wilson, "Mr. Excitement," had the audience mesmerized. I have been a regular ever since. A few years back, I brought a group of friends to celebrate a mate's bachelor party. I asked the band if they would give him a brief shout out. They responded with a resounding "No." I was told to get a chair and set it in the center of the room instead. The singer, who could've been the young man's mother with a few more years tacked on, called him up and sat him down. For the next 20 minutes, she gave one of the best performances I've ever seen, belting out to the women in the audience to keep their hands off her man as she gave him an unforgettable lap dance. - NR

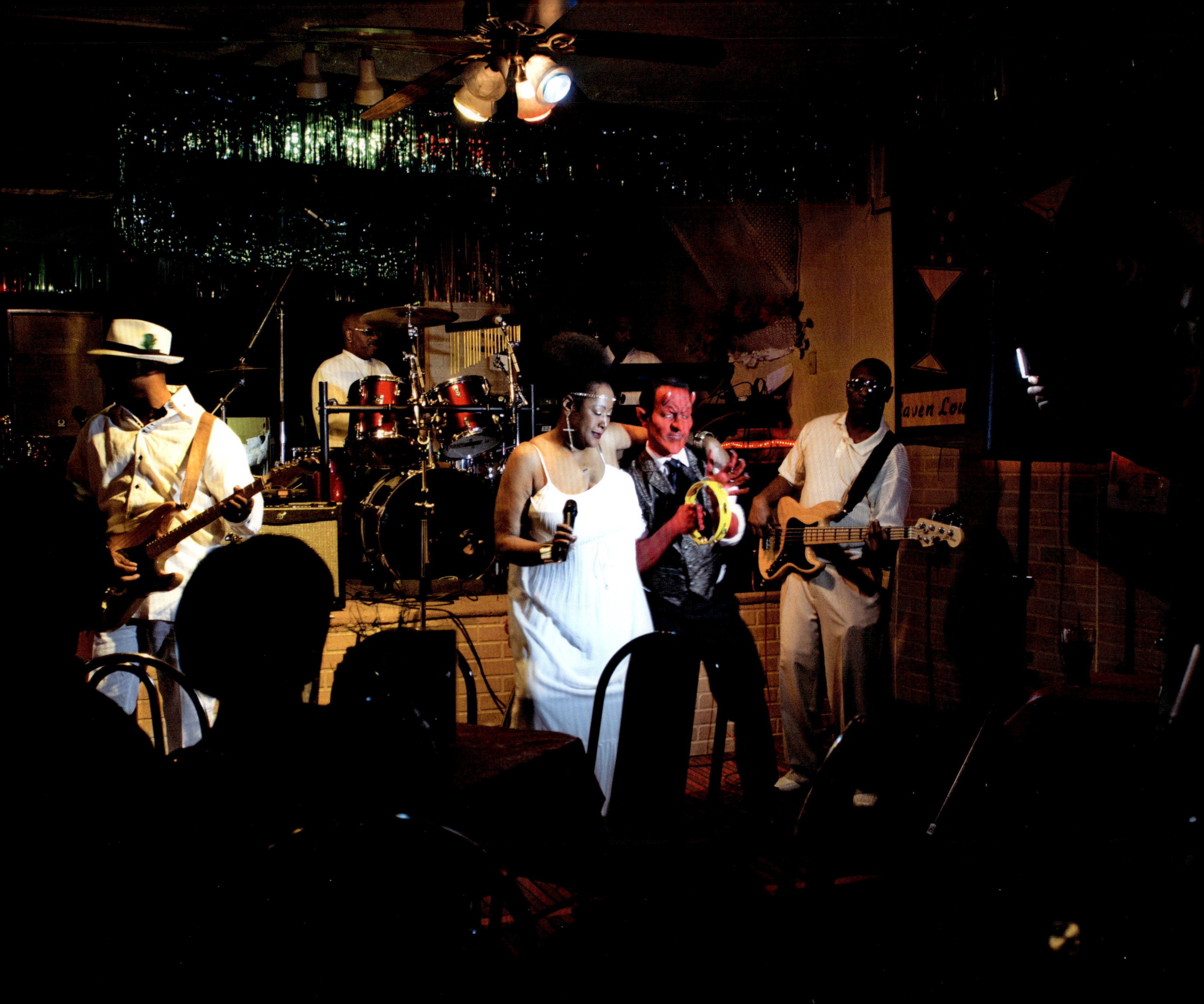

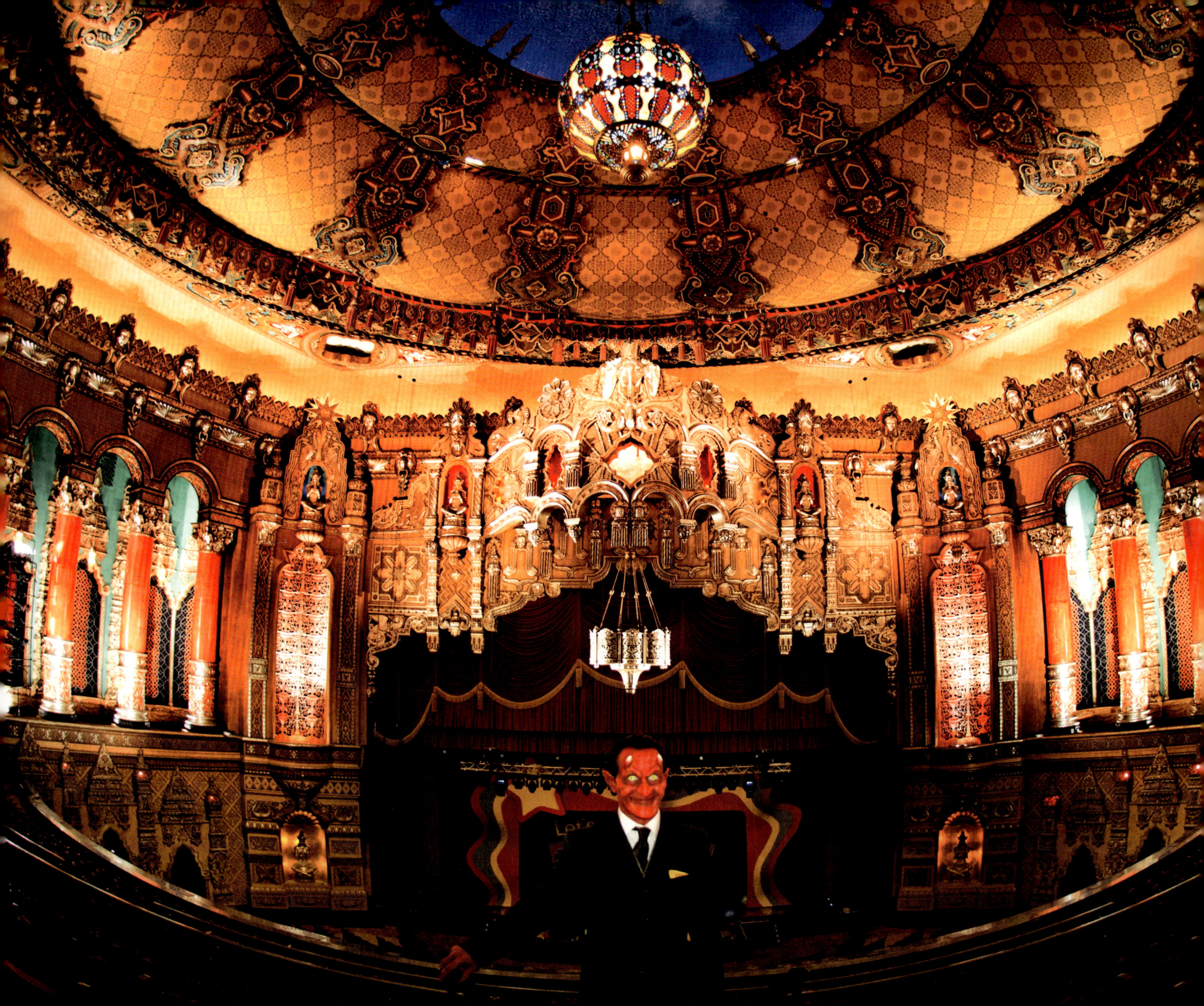

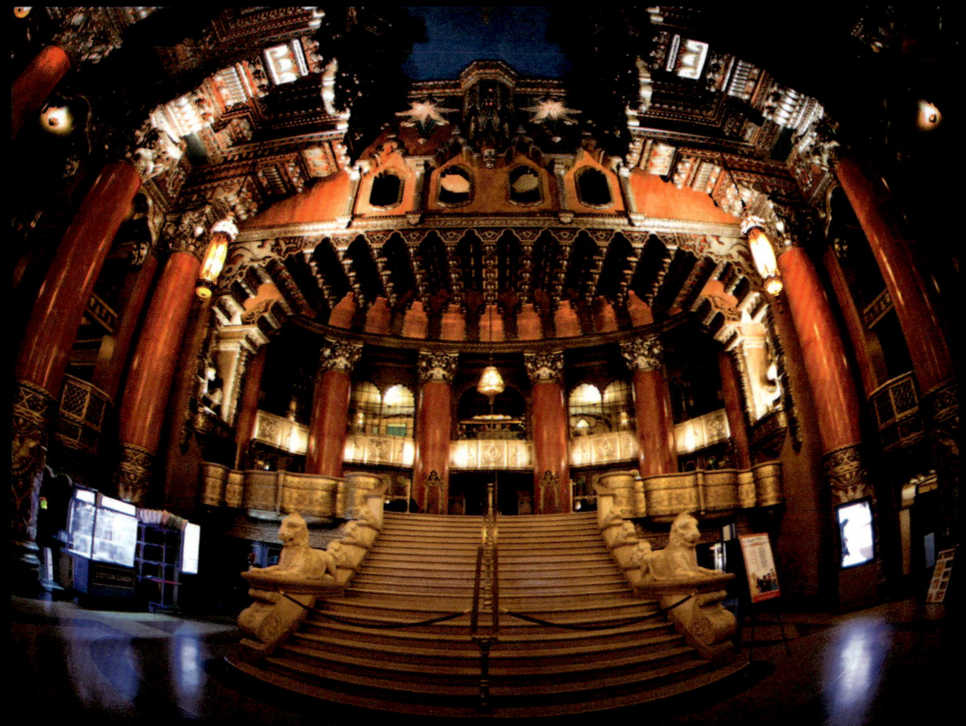

THEATRE DISTRICT

Fox Theatre, 2211 Woodward Ave., Detroit, 48201
www.foxtheatredetroit.com

Music Hall, 350 Madison St., Detroit, 48226
www.musichall.org

Gem Theatre & Century Theatre, 333 Madison St., Detroit, 48226
www.gemcolonyevents.com

The Fox Theatre is the largest and grandest of the former Fox movie palaces. Its lavish red and gold interior blends Persian, Indian, and Chinese motifs. One of many extravagantly decorated movie theaters that ringed Grand Circus Park, it survived the changing tastes of audiences, becoming a live performance space. Gifted to Detroit by Matilda Wilson, widow of John Dodge, the Music Hall focuses on alternative performances emphasizing dance, theatre, and music. The Gem and Century Theatres offer smaller, more intimate experiences in cabaret-style seating arrangements. Saved from demolition when a new sport stadium was built, they were moved five blocks to their present location in 1997.

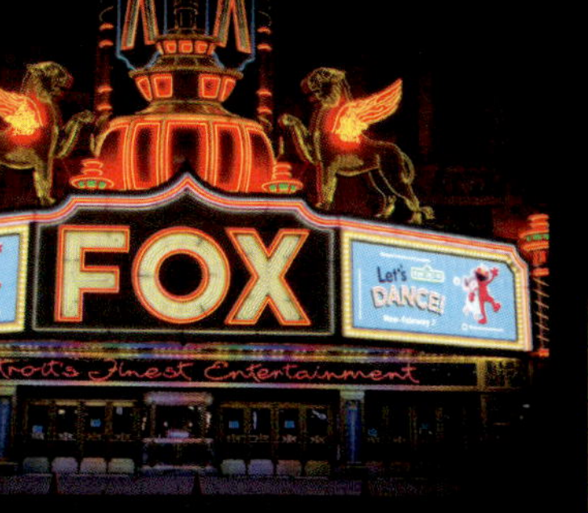

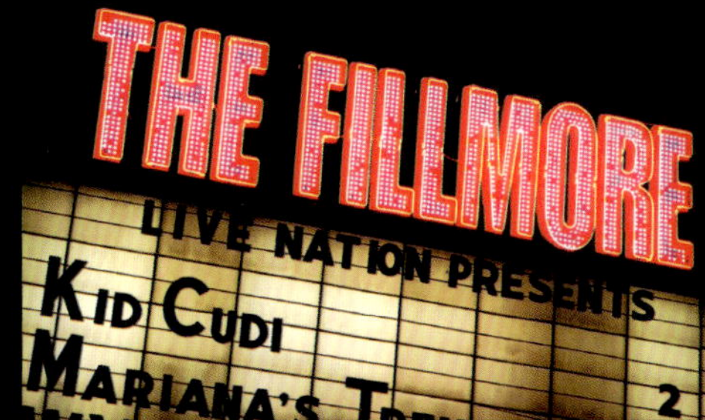

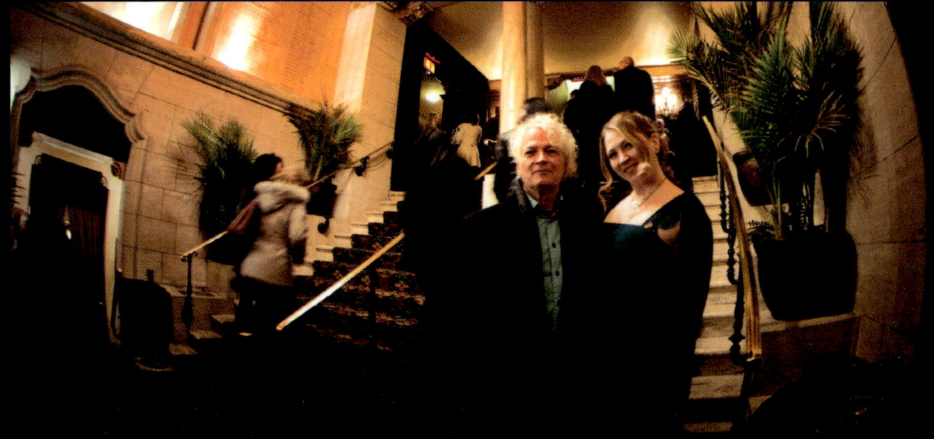

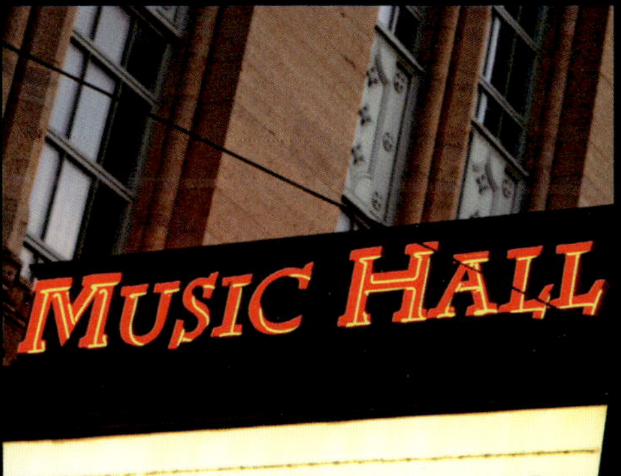

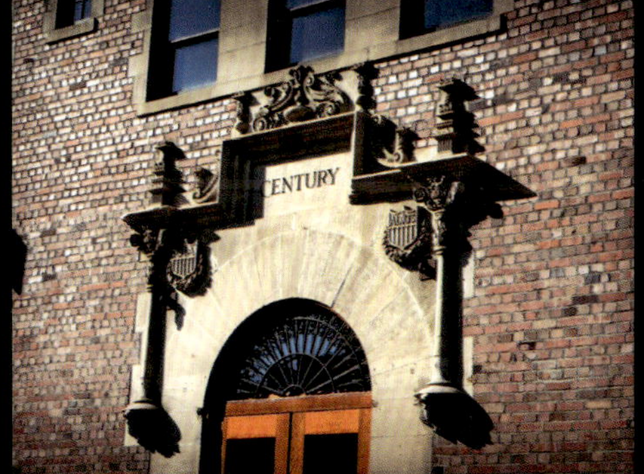

Entering the Fox Theatre, you are immediately overwhelmed by its detailing. Shimmering gold trim accents everything, and the lavish décor sometimes upstages the performers. One of many venues off Grand Circus Park, the Fox, with 5,600 seats, hosts national shows, while next door the Fillmore offers rock and roll. I prefer the variety at the Music Hall, where you can catch theatre, dance jazz, or damn near anything that is unconventional. - NR

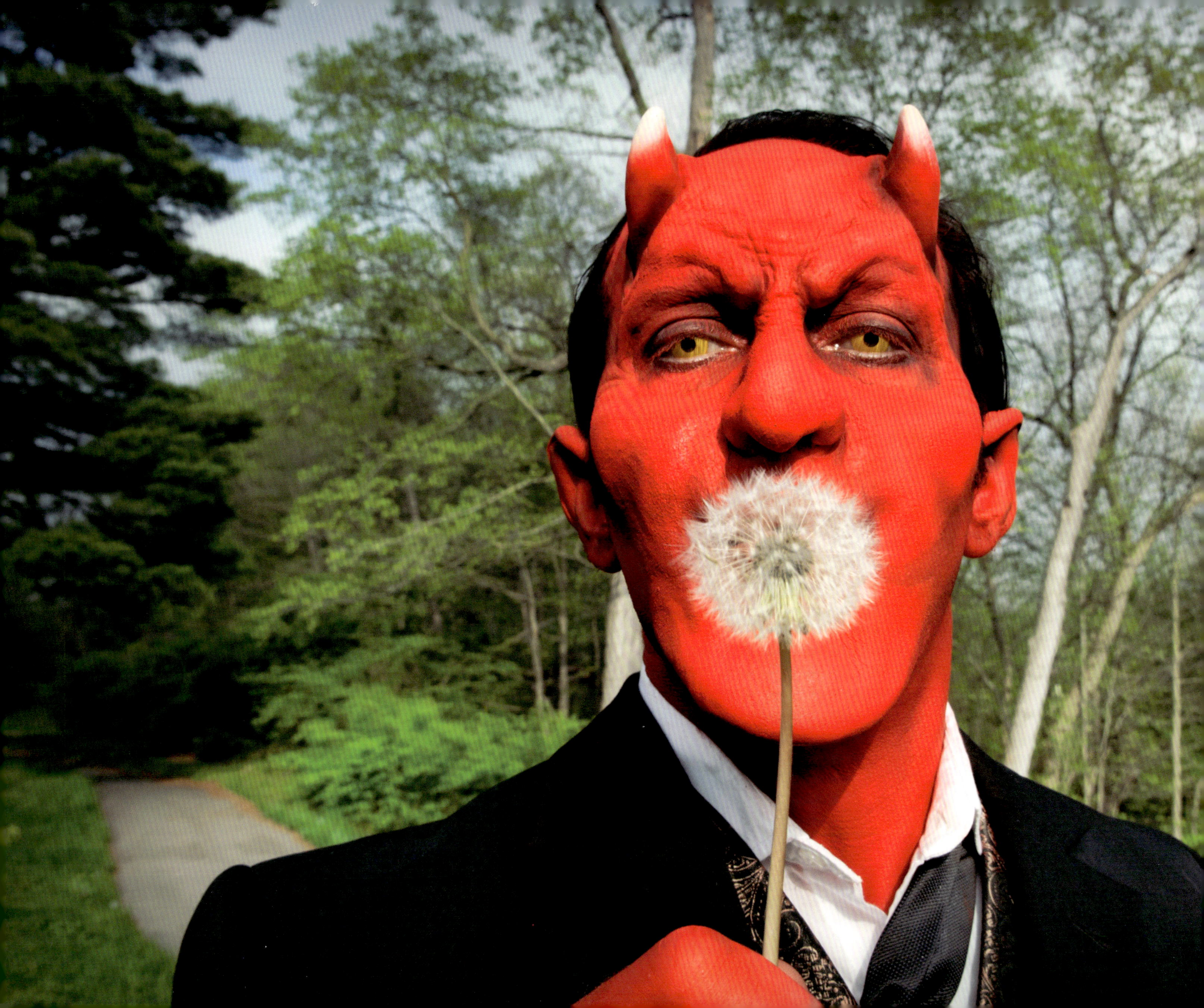

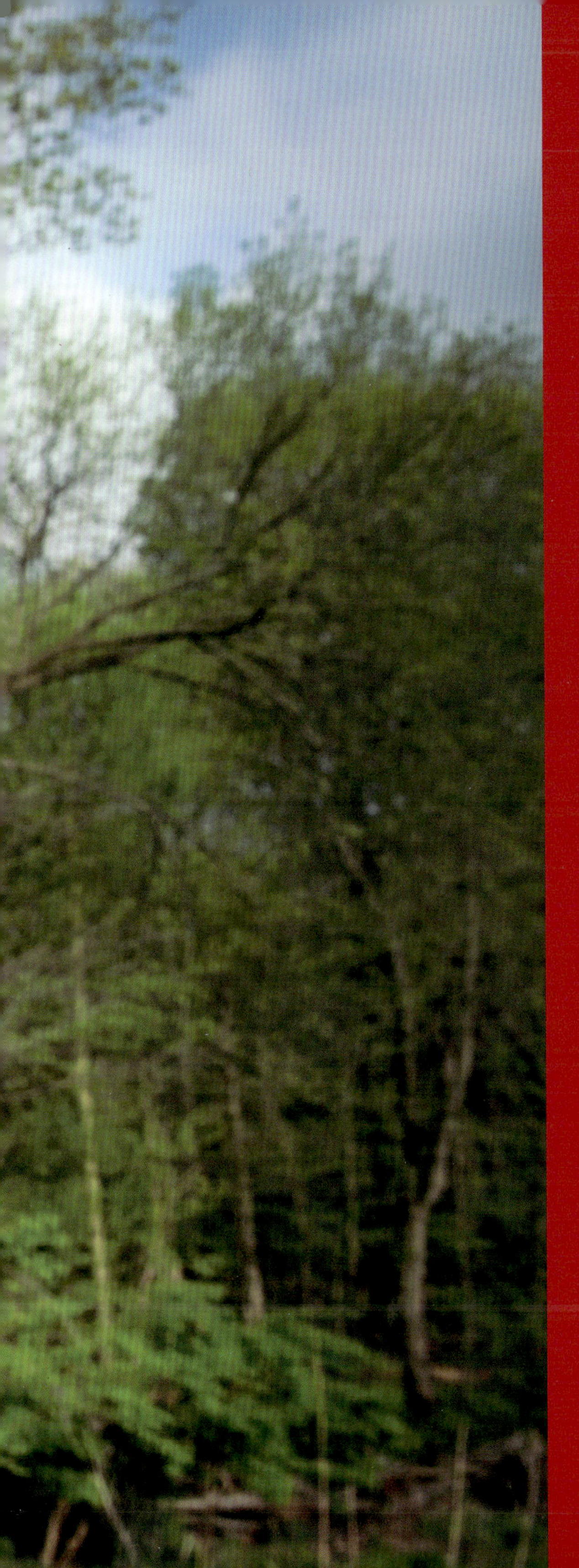

PARKS

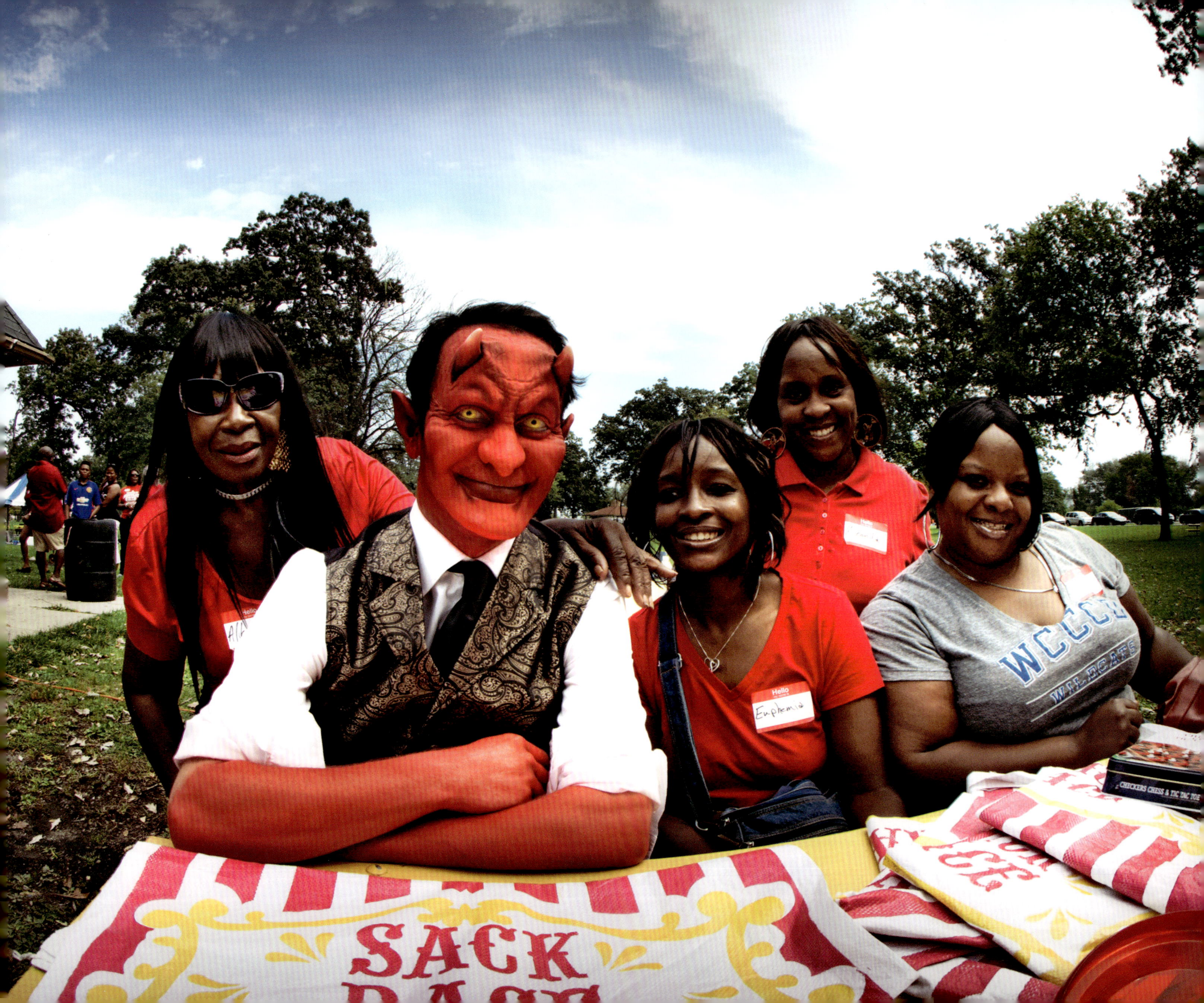
Hello
Euphemia
WILDCATS
CHECKERS CHESS & TIC TAC TOE
SACK

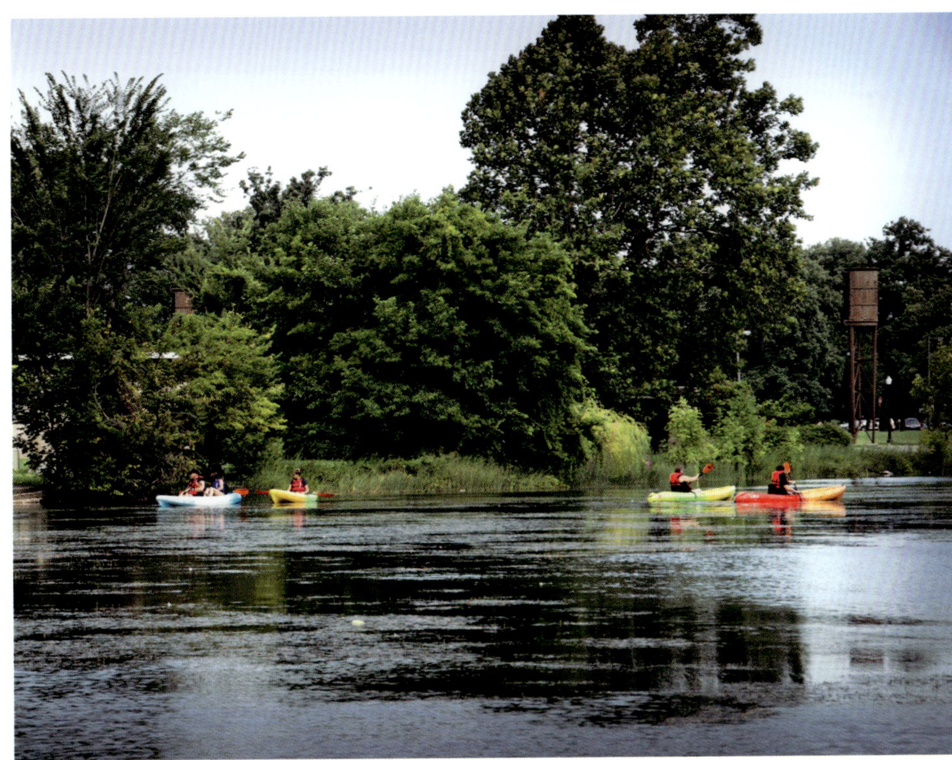

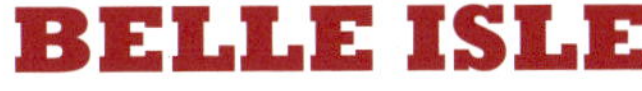

BELLE ISLE

E. Jefferson Ave. and E. Grand Blvd., Detroit, 48214
Open 5am to 10pm, everyday
www.belleisleconservancy.org

The largest municipal island park in the United States, Belle Isle was designed by Frederick Law Olmsted and named after Lewis Cass's daughter Isabelle. It is, unquestionably, Detroit's backyard. Summer family reunions and week-end BBQs fill the Victorian-era pavilions while bicyclists and runners circle the island. Swimmers enjoy the crisp clean water at the only beach in Detroit as others seek the solitude of the acres of hiking trails on the undisturbed east end.

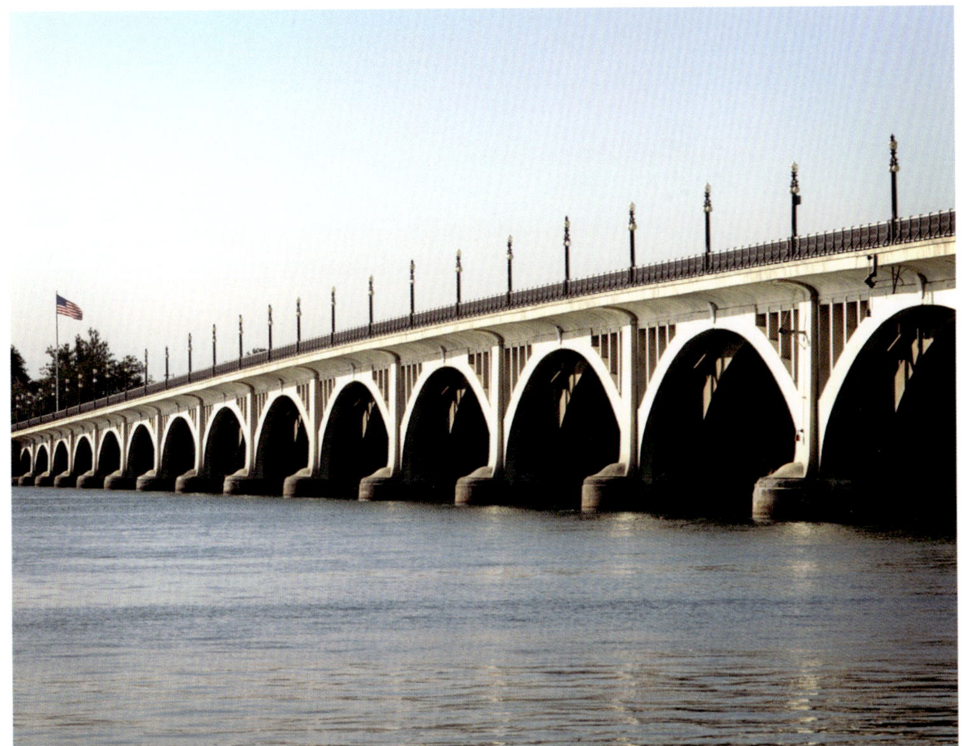

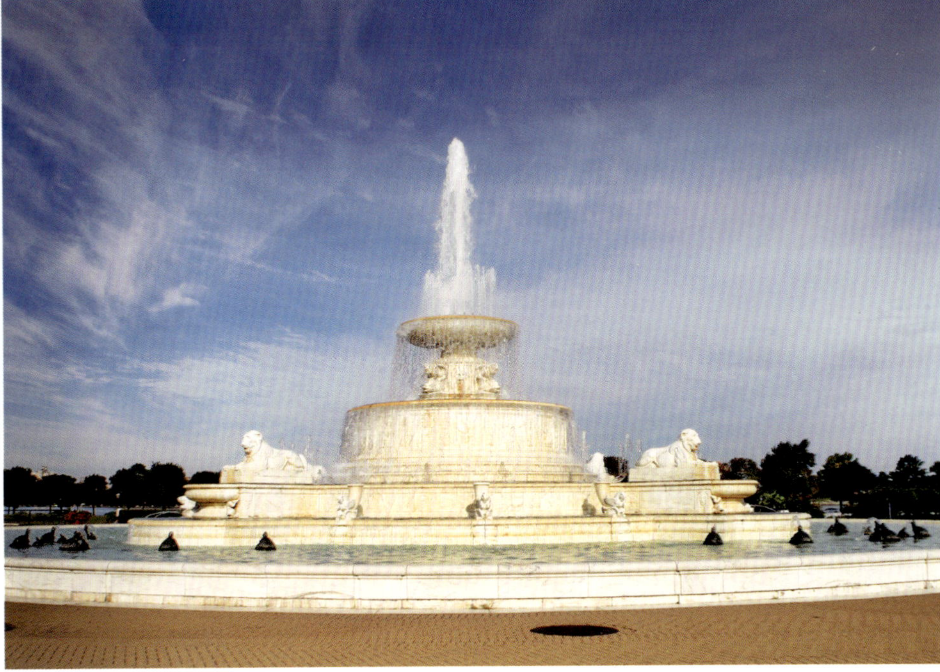

Considered the jewel of Detroit, Belle Isle is Detroit's playground, offering something for everyone. On a summer weekend, it seems like the entire city has left home to visit the island. Every Sunday, it seems there are at least a couple dozen family reunions, birthday parties or family get-togethers celebrating under picnic shelters with the music hopping, kids playing, and the BBQ smoking. - NR

CAMPUS MARTIUS

800 Woodward Ave., Detroit, 48226
www.campusmartiuspark.org

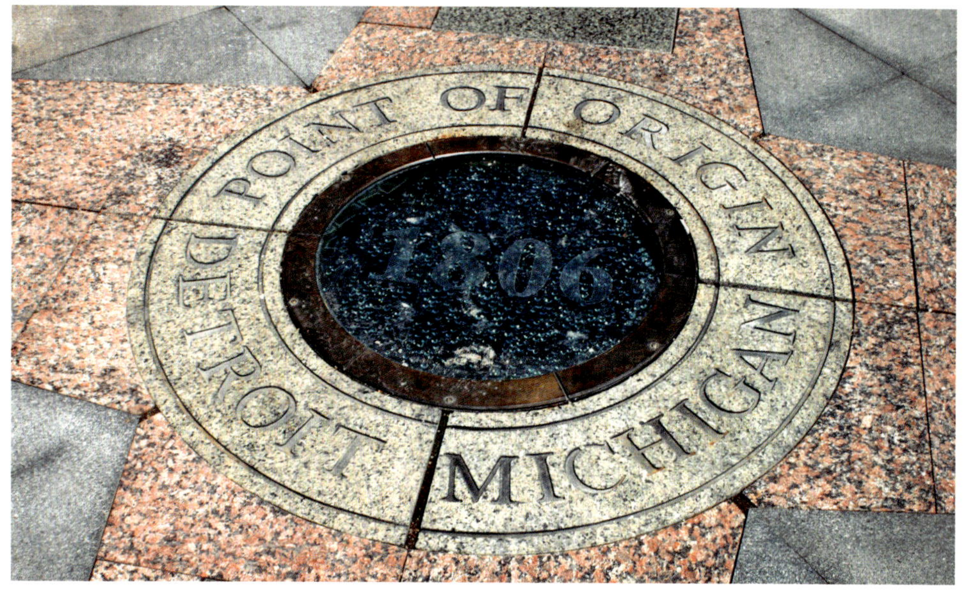

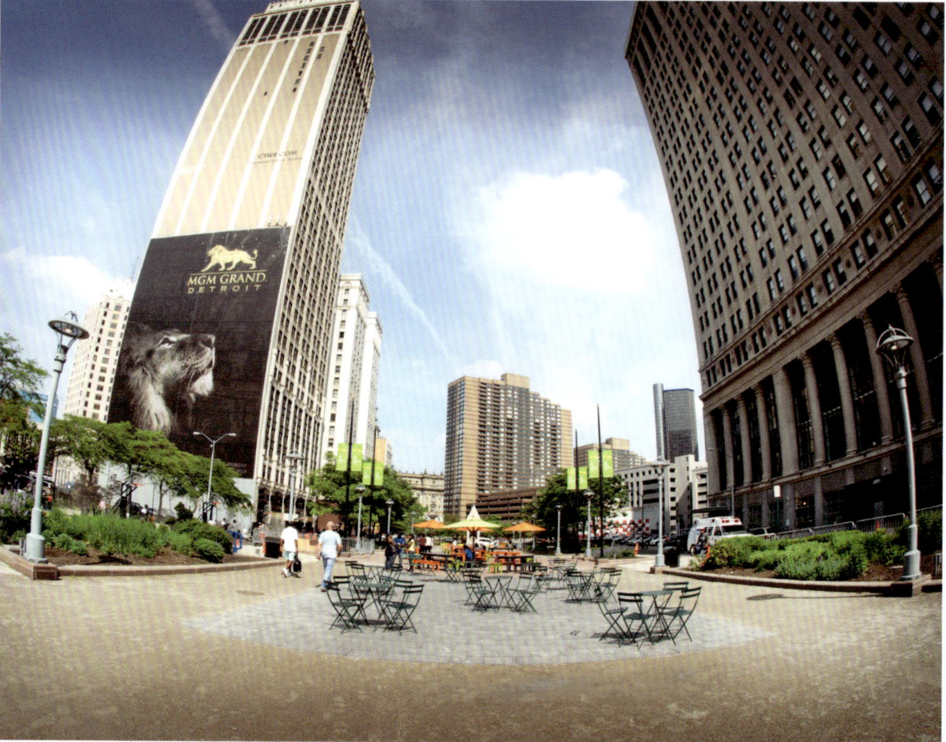

Campus Martius, Latin for *Field of Mars*, has always been the center of the city. Originally used as a marshaling and drilling area for the military starting in 1788, it became a popular gathering place for all sorts of activities. In the center of the park is the original survey stone, the Point of Origin, placed by Judge Woodward after the Great Fire of 1805, establishing the roads and boundaries for most of the state. The infamous 8 Mile Road is exactly eight miles north of here. The park is a year-round gathering place, hosting summer activities winter ice skating, and holiday festivities such as the Christmas tree and Menorah lighting and a New Year's celebration.

The newest version of Campus Martius, dedicated on the 300th anniversary of its founding, is by far the best. Lunchtime is fun time. Office workers pour out from their cubicles and catch some summer rays, noshing on the offerings from the many food trucks, or playing pickup basketball in Cadillac Square. In winter, the park changes things up, offering ice skating and the annual Winter Blast Festival.
- NR

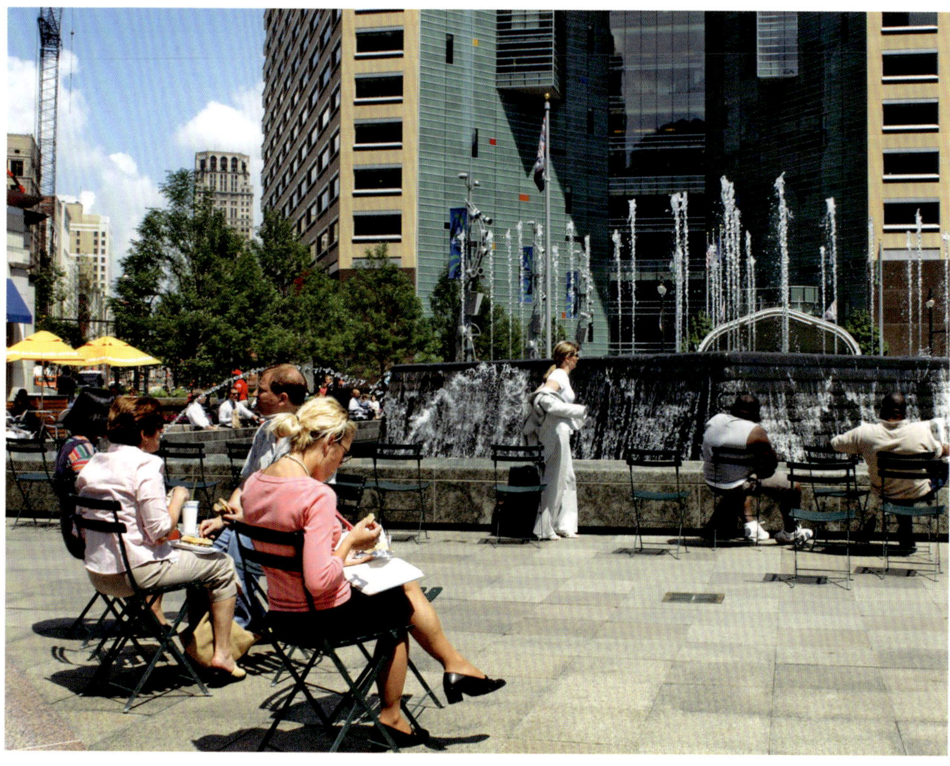

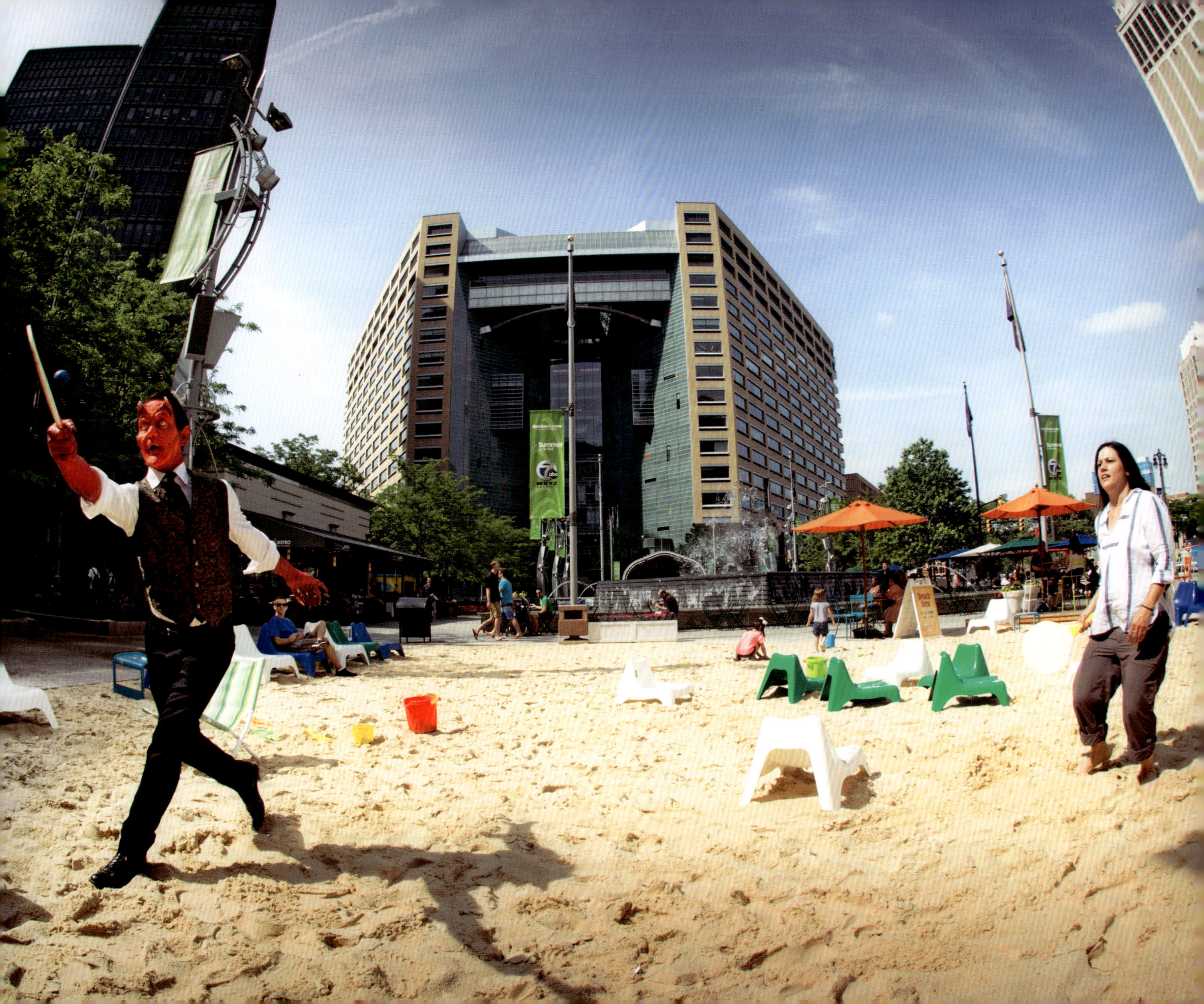
Summer
7 abc
WXYZ

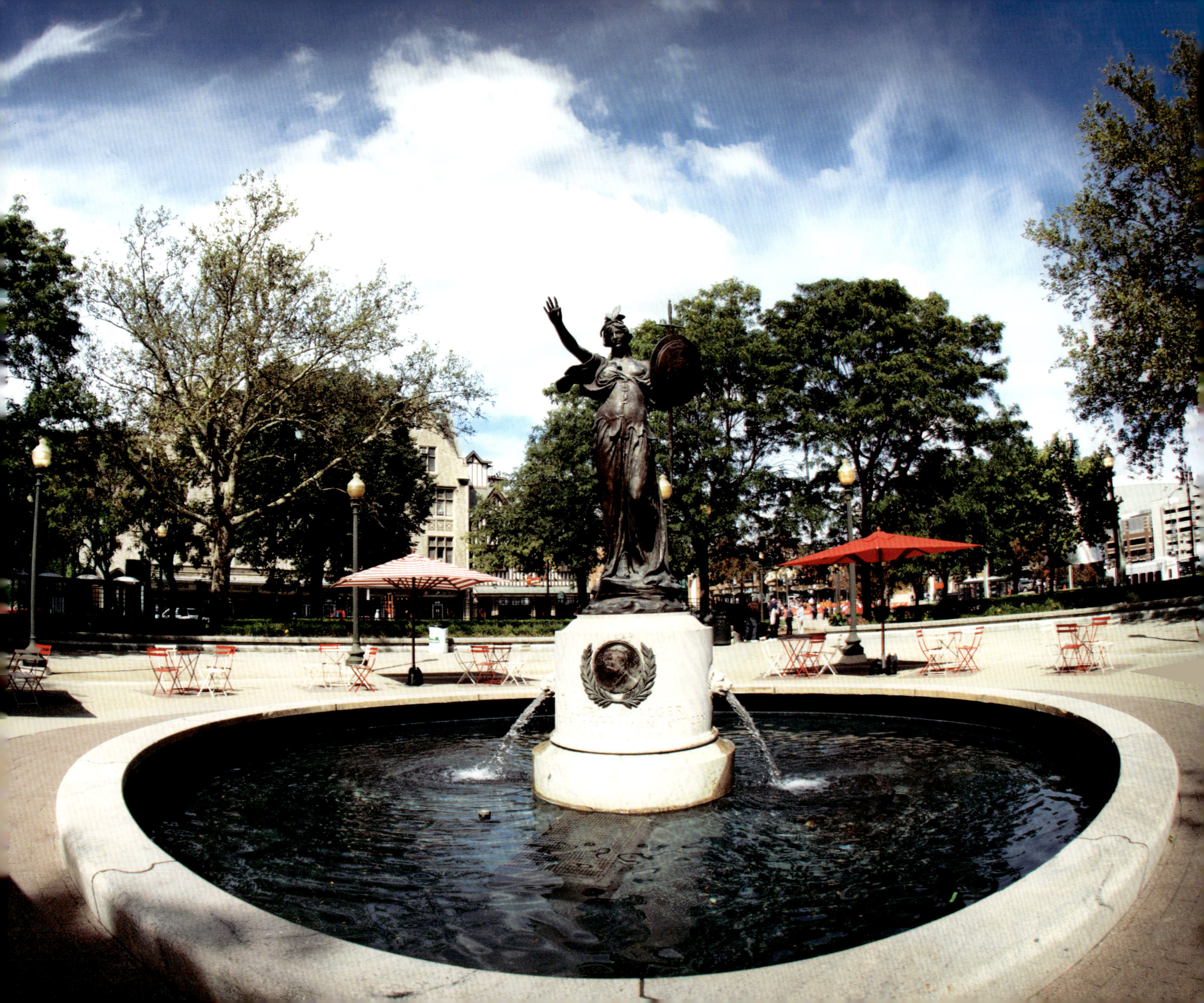

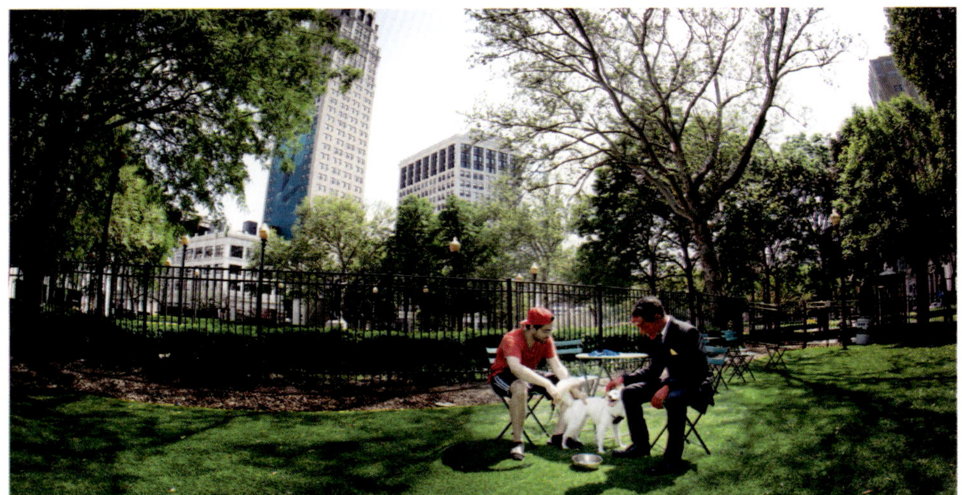

GRAND CIRCUS PARK

Woodward Ave. and Adams St., Detroit, 48226

The unusual street design of downtown Detroit, inspired by Pierre Charles L'Enfant's plan of Washington DC, is never more evident than at Grand Circus Park. After the Great Fire of 1805, Judge Augustus Brevoort Woodward designed a new street map for the city. Grand Circus Park became the only circular plaza as the streets were laid out based on interconnecting equilateral triangles. Deemed overly complicated, the plan was eventually abandoned, leaving only half a wheel. Grand Circus Park anchors the north end of downtown as the two "Davids" – the David Whitney building and the David Broderick building – act as sentries upon entering the central business district.

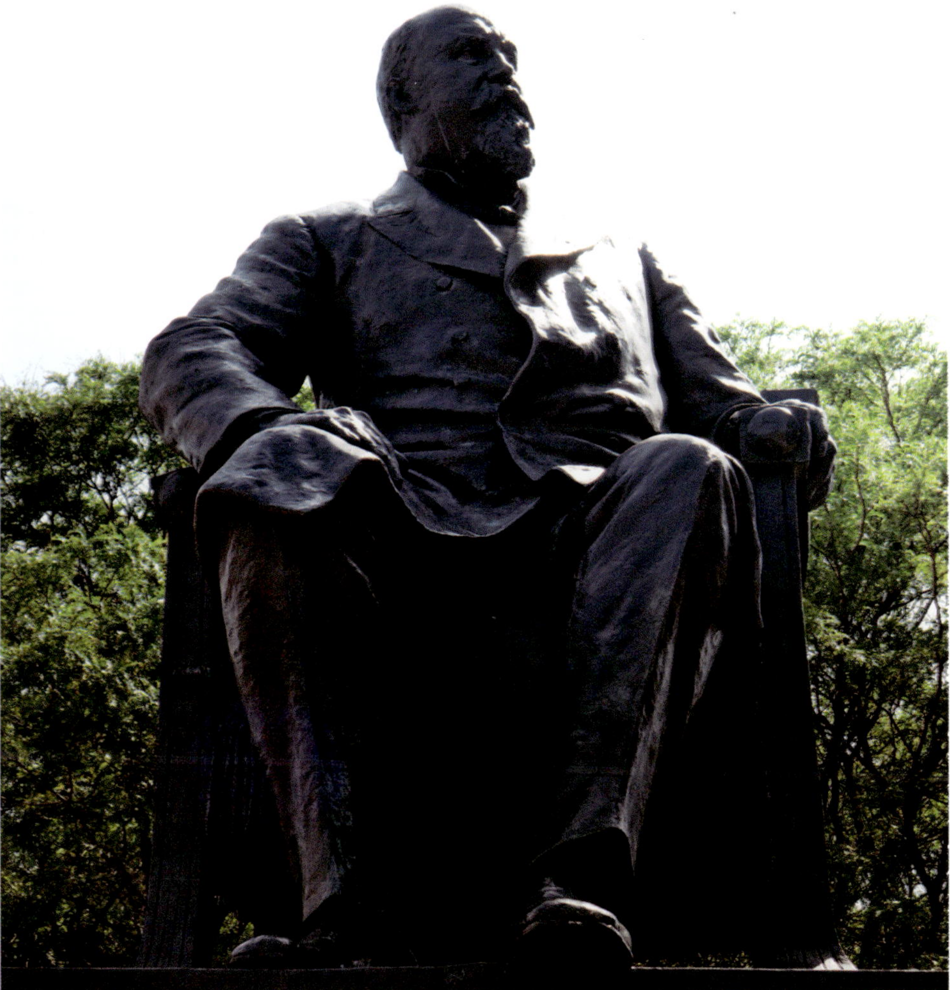

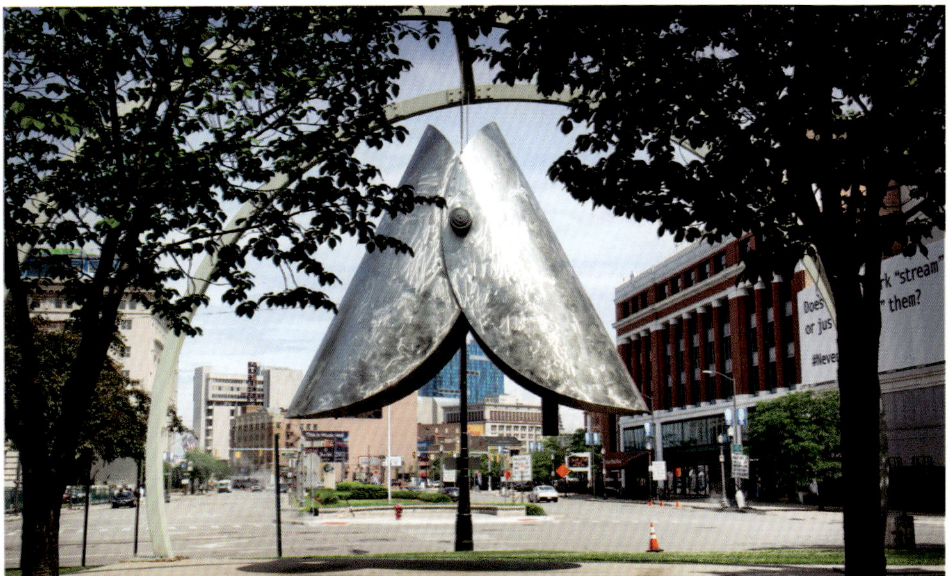

Uniquely designed as a half circle, Grand Circus Park is actually my favorite city park. As the nearby office towers have been converted to apartments, the park has developed a neighborly ambience. I run in to familiar faces at the dog park or under one of the umbrellas near the Alger fountain as I catch up on my social media posts. The Millennium Bell, or "Giant Fish Head," as I call it, was designed by my good friends Chris Turner and Matt Blake. Matt passed away a few years ago, and gazing up at the Bell recalls all the good times we had together. - NR

HARMONIE PARK

311 E. Grand River Ave., Detroit, 48226

One of two small pocket parks created by the new street design after the Fire of 1805, Harmonie Park has always been the center of immigrant life. During the 1840s, the park and surrounding neighborhood was a destination for Germans emigrants. In the early 20th century, it became known as Paradise Valley, a segregated enclave where black visitors and entertainers felt comfortable and welcomed. Entertainers such as Ella Fitzgerald, Duke Ellington, and Count Basie played in the nearby clubs and stayed in the hotels.

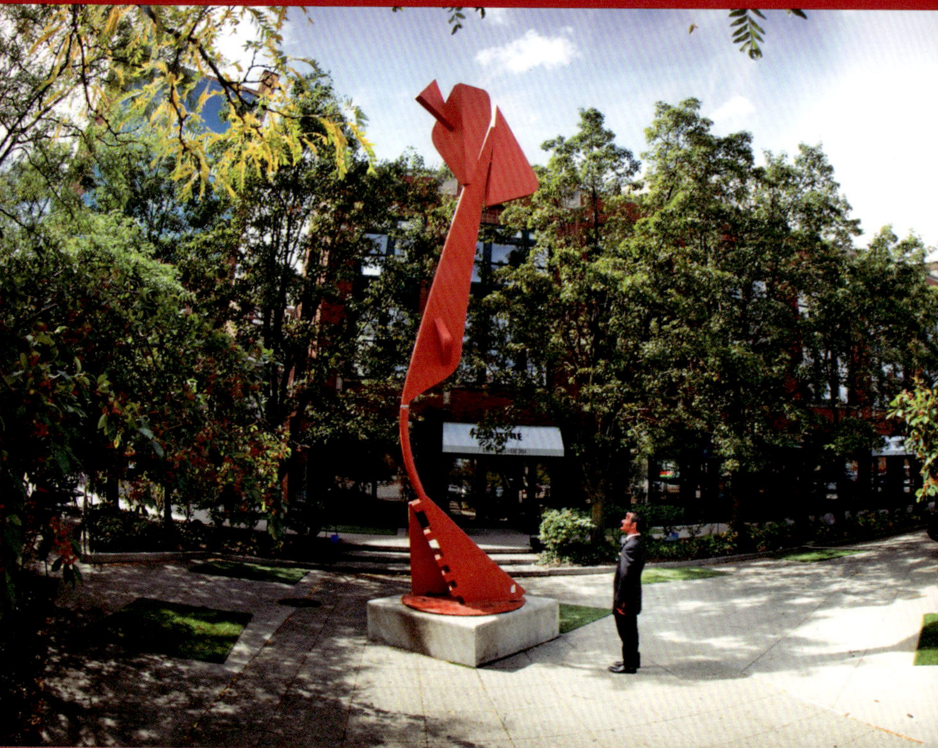

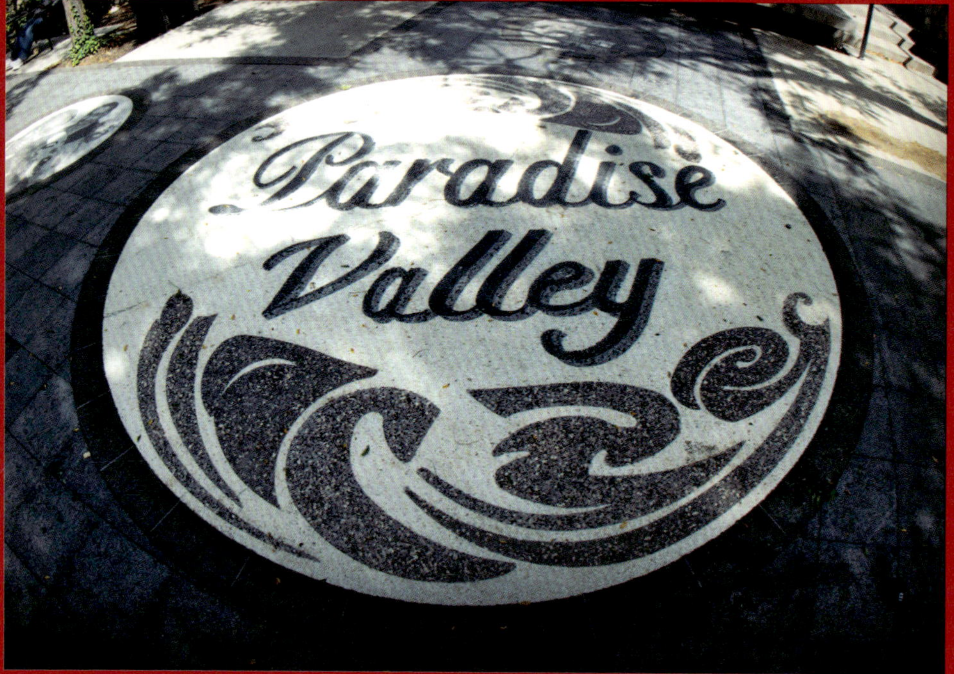

Thanks to the complicated layout of the city, Harmonie Park is a sliver of serenity within downtown. On a pleasant day, I'll take my lunch and sit under the trees or check out the latest art installation. Its intimate size and configuration reminds me of the public squares in European cities. Capitol Park, it's counterpart on the west side, and once home to the State Capitol, offers a similar respite. - NR

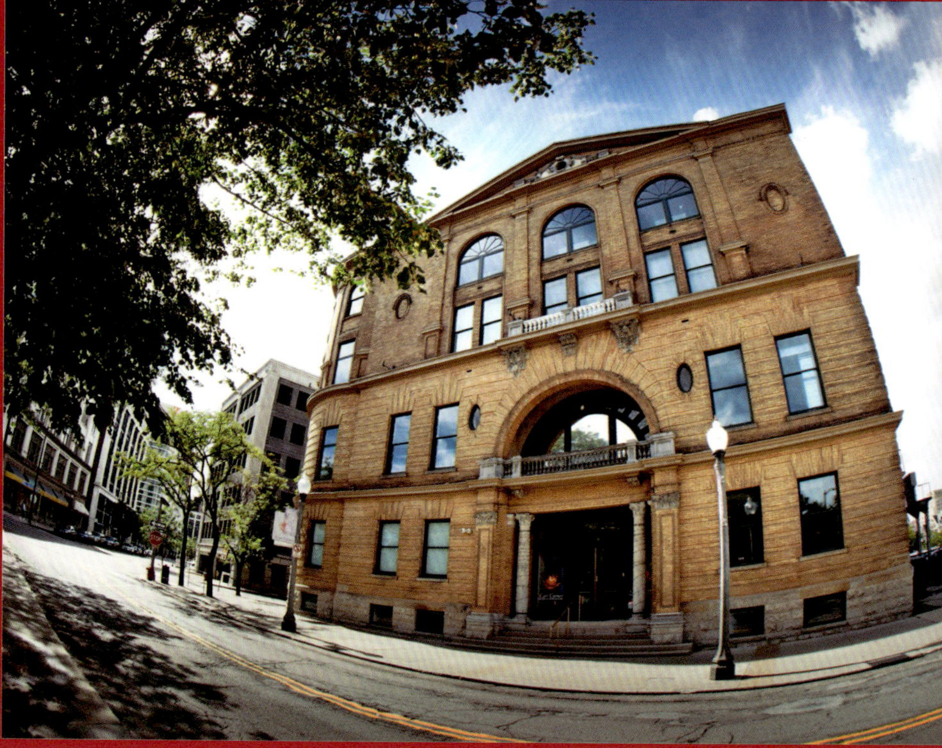

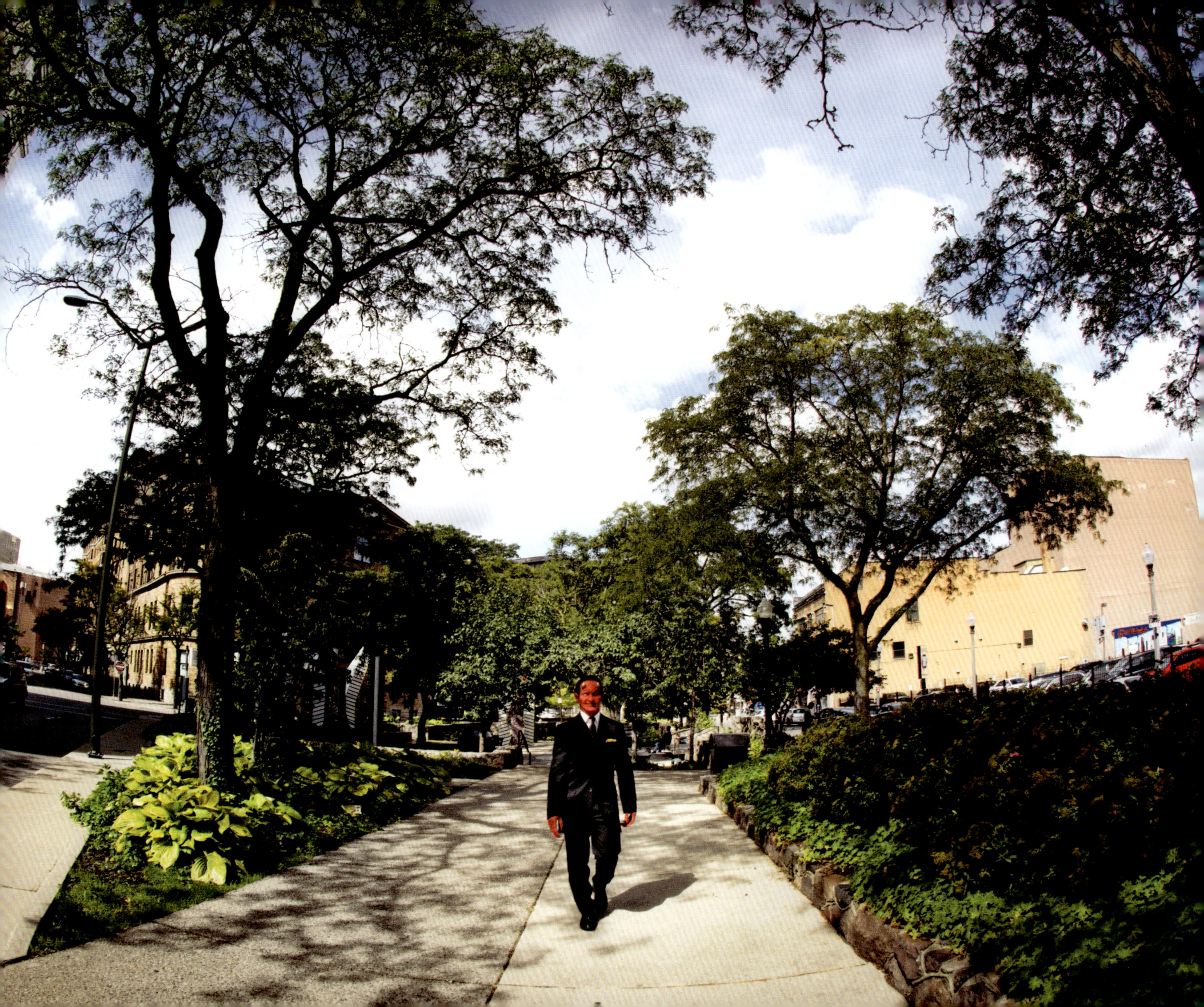

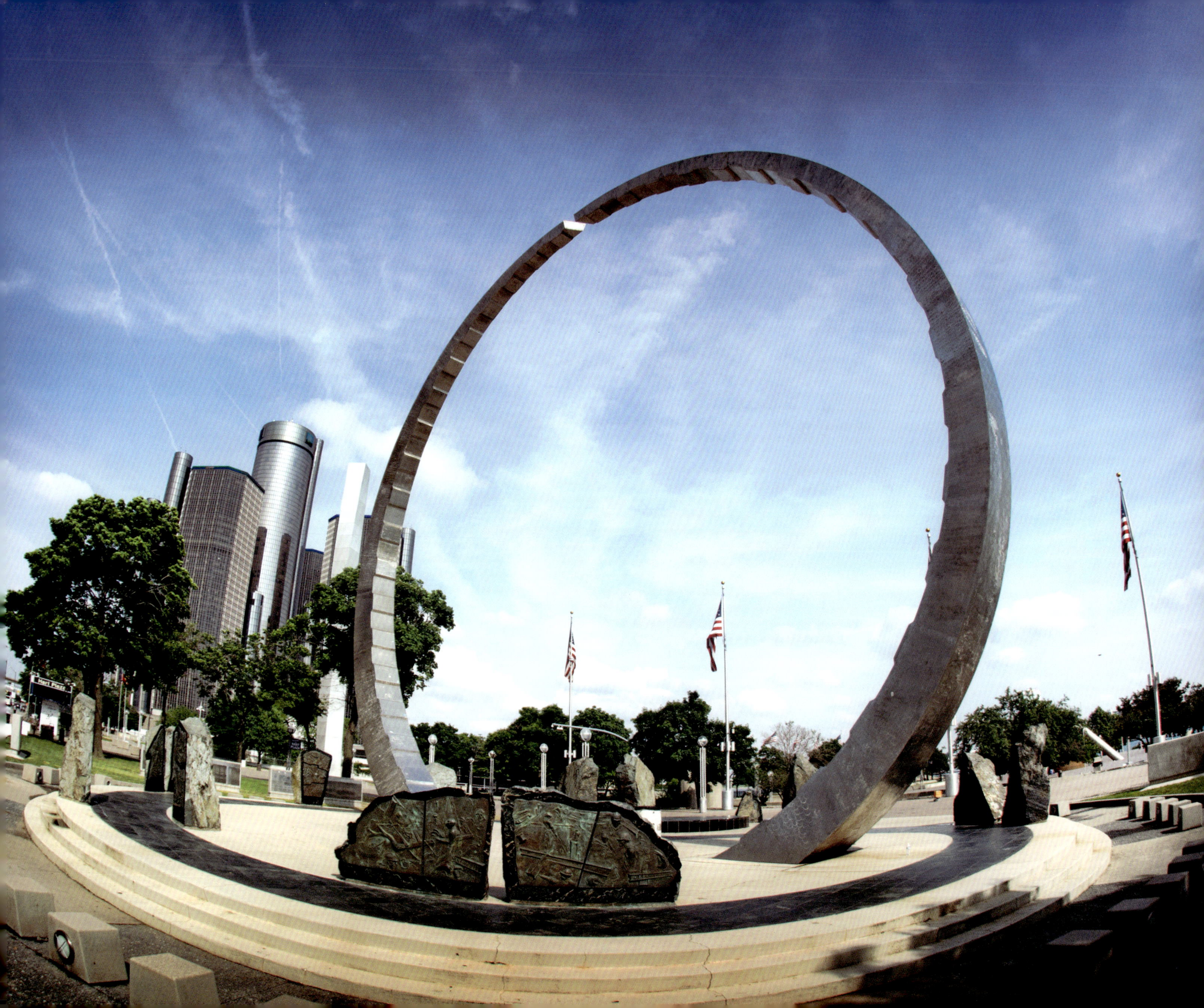
Hart Plaza

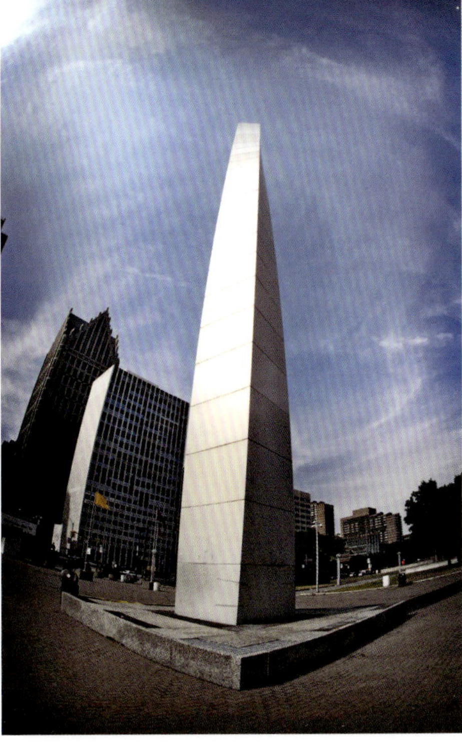

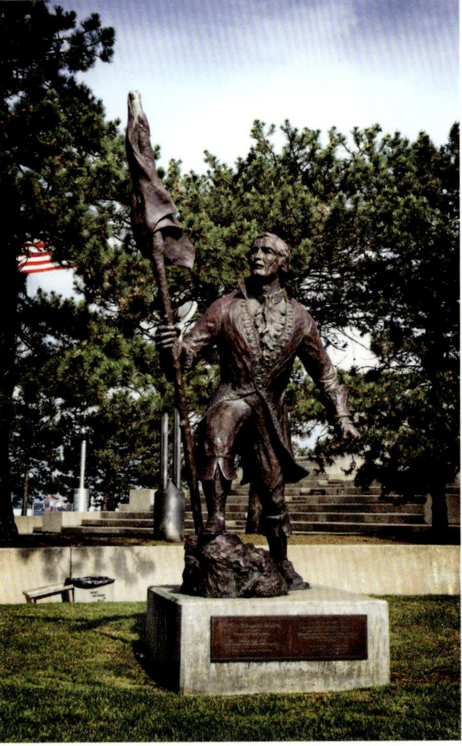

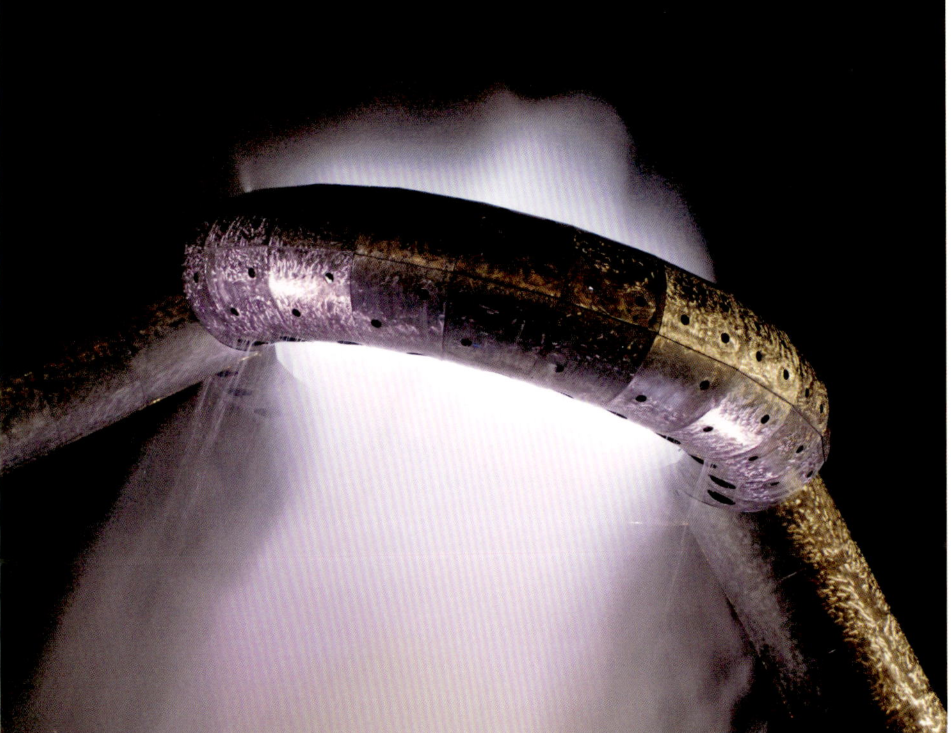

HART PLAZA

1 Hart Plaza, Detroit, 48226
www.detroitriverfront.org

On July 24, 1701, Antoine de la Mothe Cadillac and a small band of French settlers and trappers came ashore at this spot, founding Detroit and establishing a French presence and greater expansion into the Great Lakes. As a strategic and favorable location along the river, Detroit grew from a small outpost of fur traders to an internationally recognized city. Designed by Isamu Noguchi, Hart Plaza opened in 1975, fulfilling a decades-long plan to open the industrial waterfront to recreation. Dominating the center of the park is the modernistic Dodge Fountain. At the river's edge, The Gateway to Freedom International Monument represents the struggles of African Americans to escape slavery and celebrates the successes of Underground Railroad. The Detroit sculpture represents a group of slaves longing to be free, while in Windsor, a former slave raises his arms celebrating his emancipation. Detroit was the last stop for many escaping to freedom in Canada.

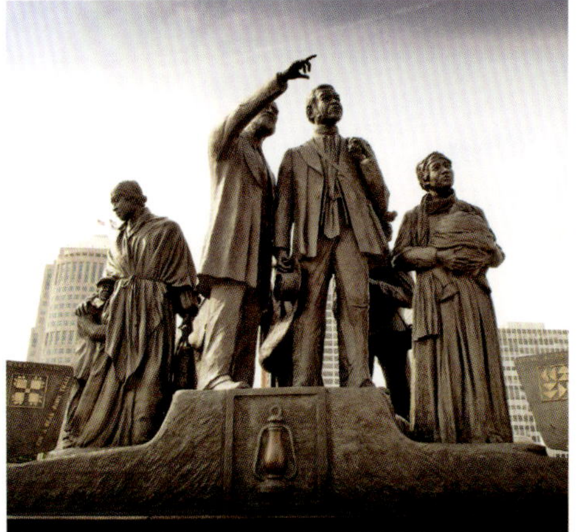

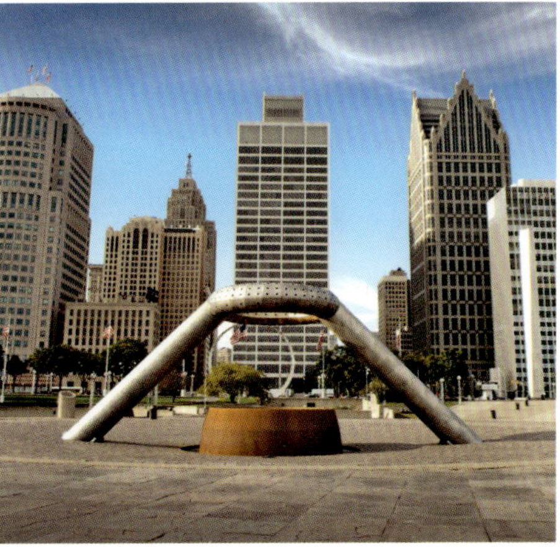

On a steamy July day in 1701, my life changed when a few canoes pulled up onto what is now Hart Plaza. Led by the notorious Antoine de la Mothe Cadillac, the trappers and missionaries were a scruffy, smelly bunch, not having bathed in weeks and stuck in those small canoes. Taking over my home, they founded the city of Detroit. Hart Plaza returned the river to the public by again making it the gateway to the city. - NR

PALMER PARK

9021 Woodward Ave., Detroit, 48203
www.peopleforpalmerpark.org

Senator Thomas Witherell Palmer donated the park bearing his name in 1893, insisting that the virgin forest be preserved as a natural habitat for all to enjoy. Having withstood development, it is the largest remaining forest in the city. Lush hiking trails traverse the woodland, giving visitors the sense of nature's serenity within the city. For the more energetic, golf, tennis, baseball, basketball, chess, and a splash pad offer residents recreation and relaxation.

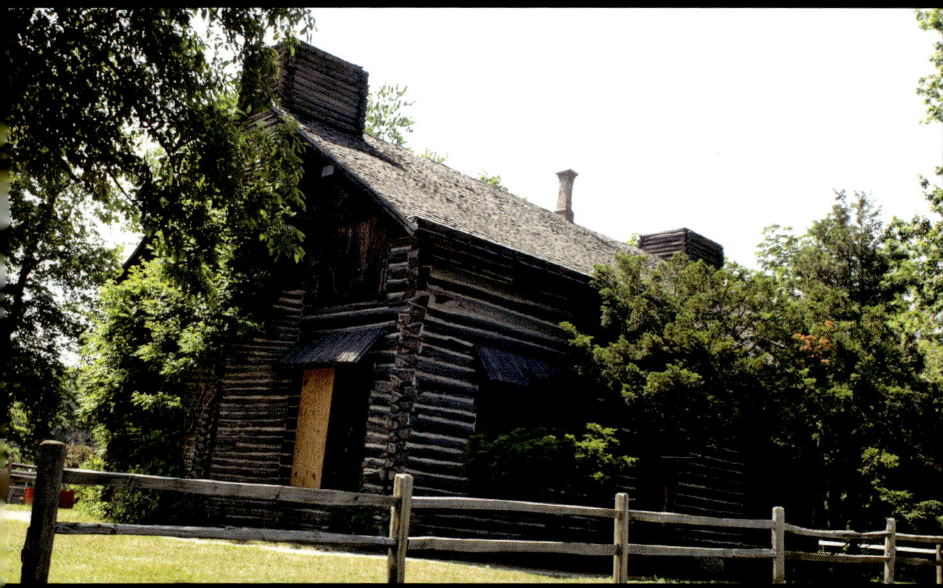

As the Palmers grew weary of city life, I encouraged them to build the log cabin or 1887's "Font Hill Log House" overlooking Lake Francis, named after Lizzie's mother. Knowing I was an admirer of the river, the Palmers built a small lighthouse that stands over the man-made lake. Surrounded by these 296 acres of pristine forest, Lizzie wanted to live a simpler life as in earlier days. During the summers, the Palmers and I, their frequent guest, would relax on the porch of the cabin or walk the many trails through the park that visitors enjoy today. I continue to spend a lot of time hiking and biking the trails that the Senator and I used for horseback riding.

- NR

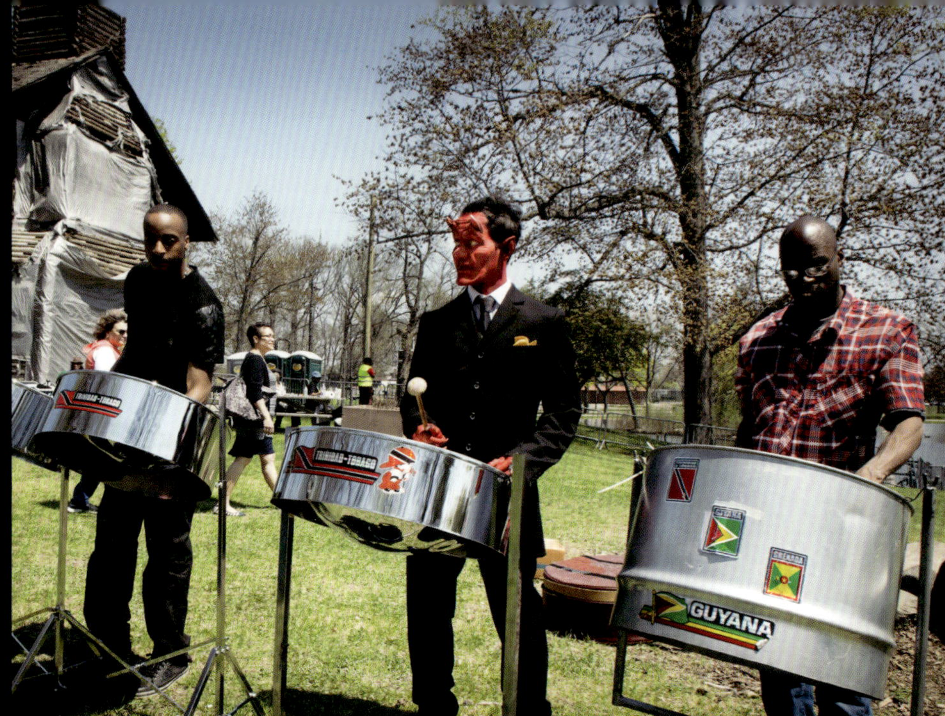

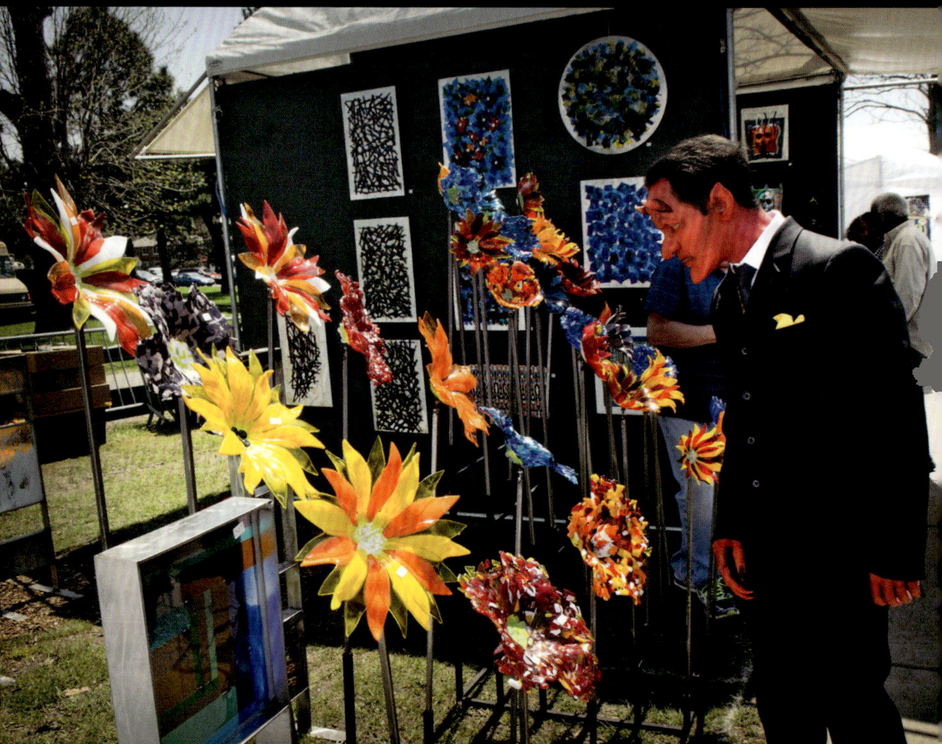

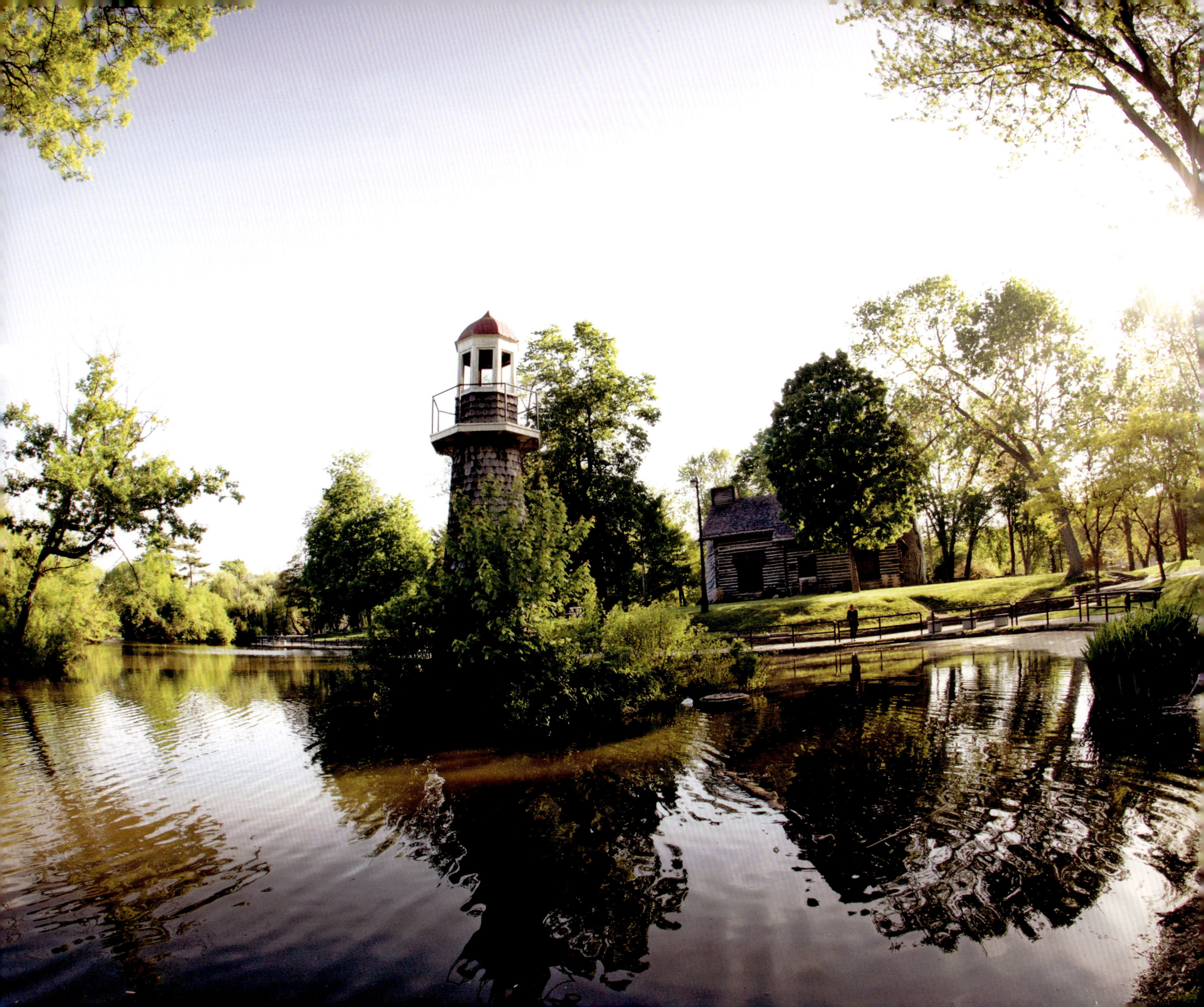

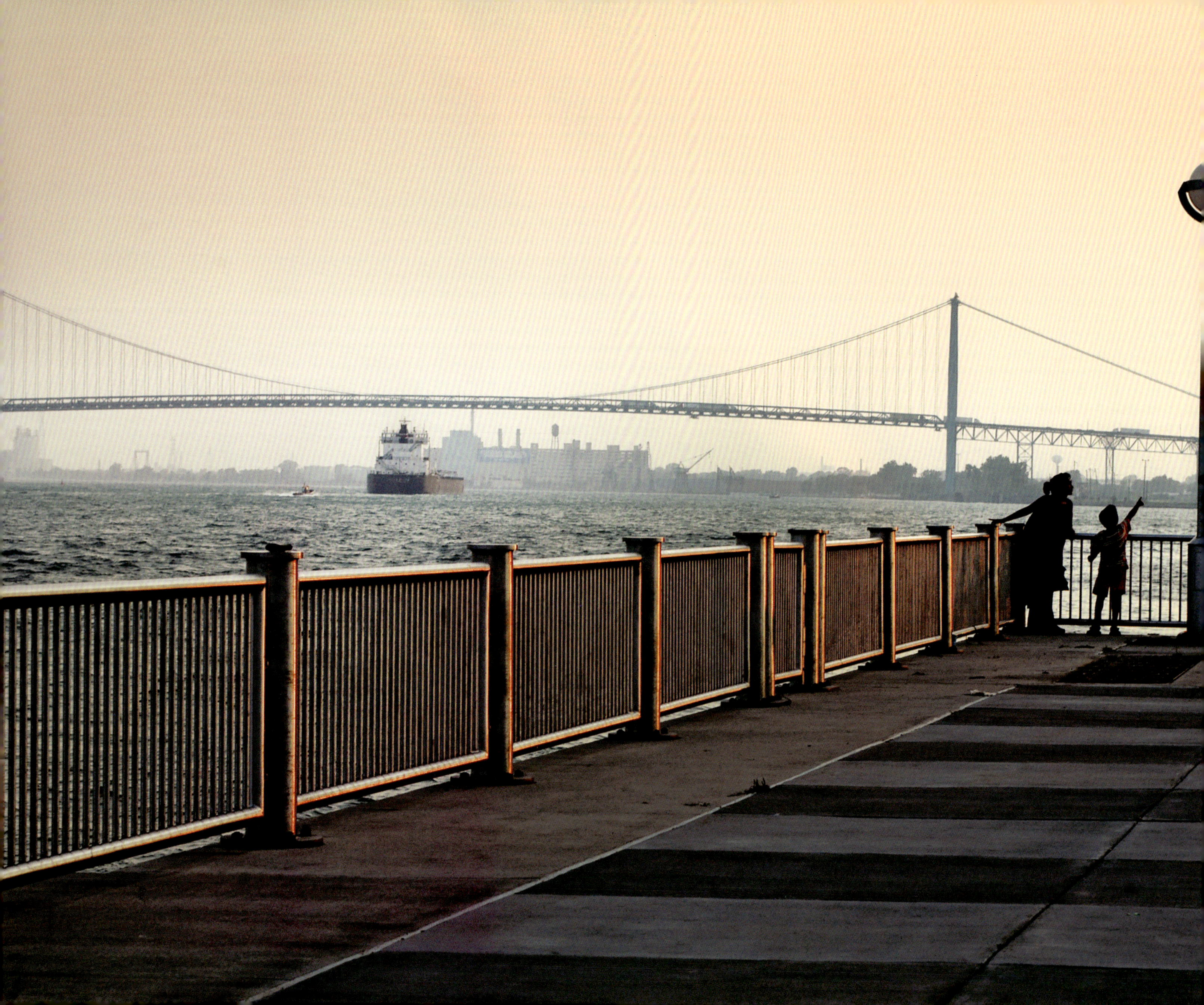

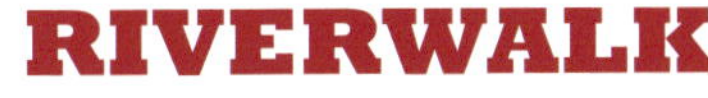

RIVERWALK

Rivard Plaza, 1340 Atwater St., Detroit, 48226
www.detroitriverfront.org

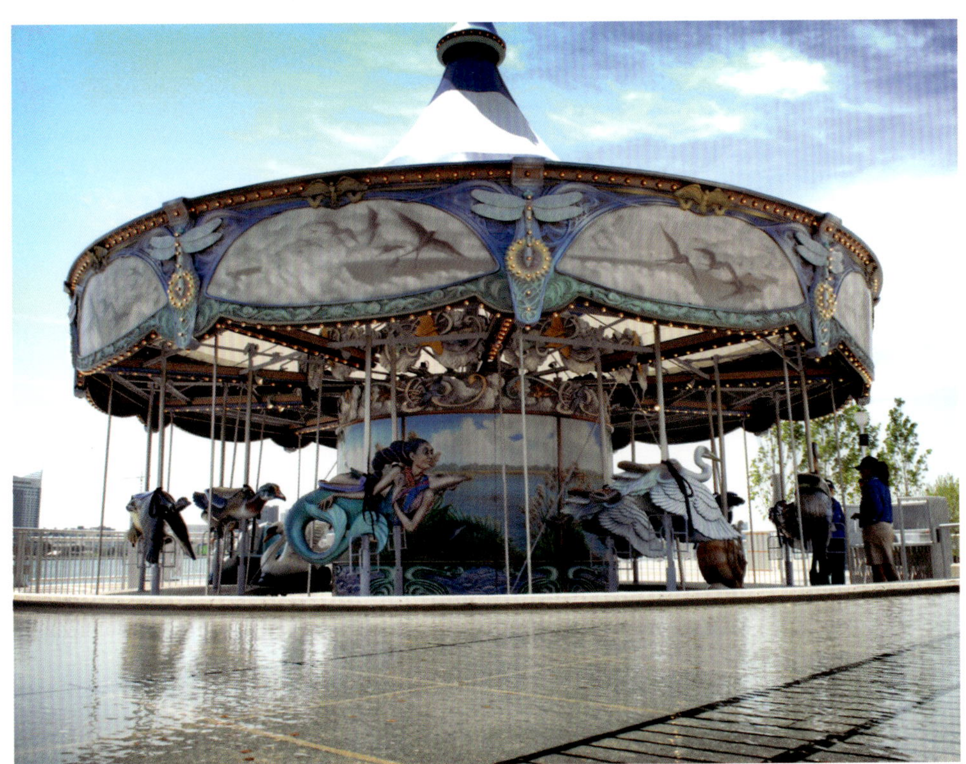

Originally named "Rivière du Détroit" by the French settlers, the Detroit River begins at Lake St. Clair and extends 24 miles to Lake Erie. As Detroit's industry expanded, the river was vital as an economic thoroughfare. Foundries and dry docks converged along the river, turning pristine shoreline into an industrial muddle of warehouses and factories expelling the effluence of production and polluting the river and riverbank. After years of planning, the RiverWalk has returned river access to the public, creating a greenway linking Belle Isle to the Ambassador Bridge. At Rivard Place, bike rentals and merry go round rides are available, while Mt. Elliott Park offers a splash pad for youngsters. The Outdoor Adventure Center entertains and educates kids about the ecology of the region, and Milliken State Park has reestablished a natural wetland environment.

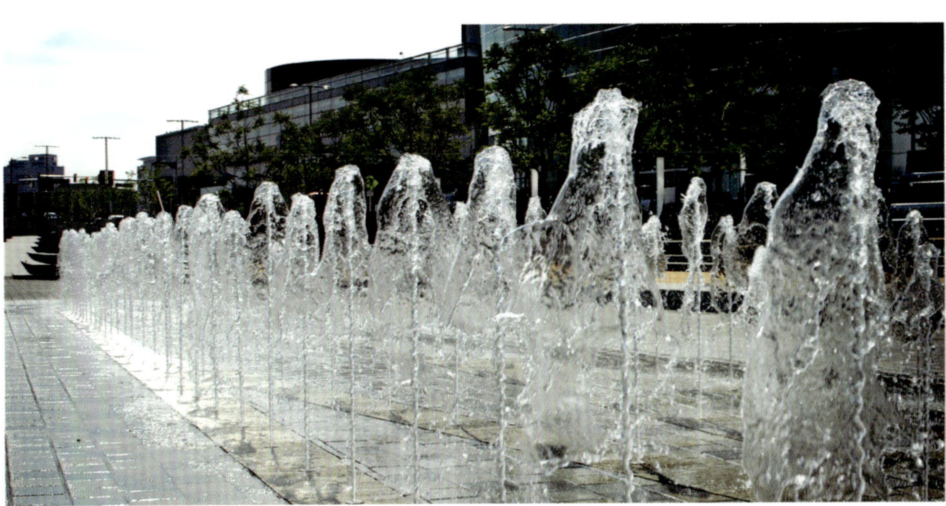

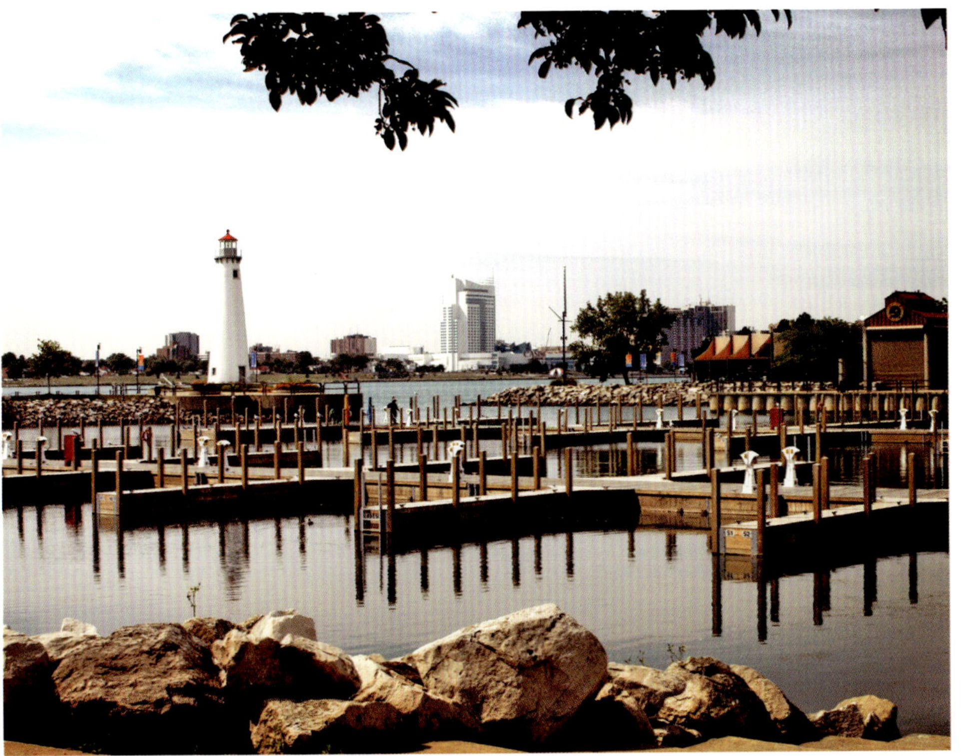

For years, I looked across the river to Windsor envying their riverfront walkways and parks. On the Detroit side, you could walk for blocks without ever seeing the river. Fortunately, with the RiverWalk the waterfront has again become an integral part of our daily life, reconnecting Detroit with the river that has meant so much to our history. - NR

ROUGE PARK

West Outer Drive, Detroit, 48228
www.rougepark.org

Buffalo Soldiers Heritage Center
21800 Joy Rd., Detroit, 48239

Off West Outer Drive on the west side of Detroit is Rouge Park, at 11,181 acres, Detroit's largest. The Rouge River flows more than two miles through the park, which also contains a Donald Ross-designed 18-hole golf course, the Alex Jefferson Model Airplane Field, 14 ball fields, 11 tennis courts, and eight miles of bicycle trails. Brennan Pools, designed by Albert Kahn, hosted the 1956 U.S. Olympic Trials. The Buffalo Soldiers Heritage Center occupies an old stable, offering children horse rides and history lessons about the contributions of black soldiers.

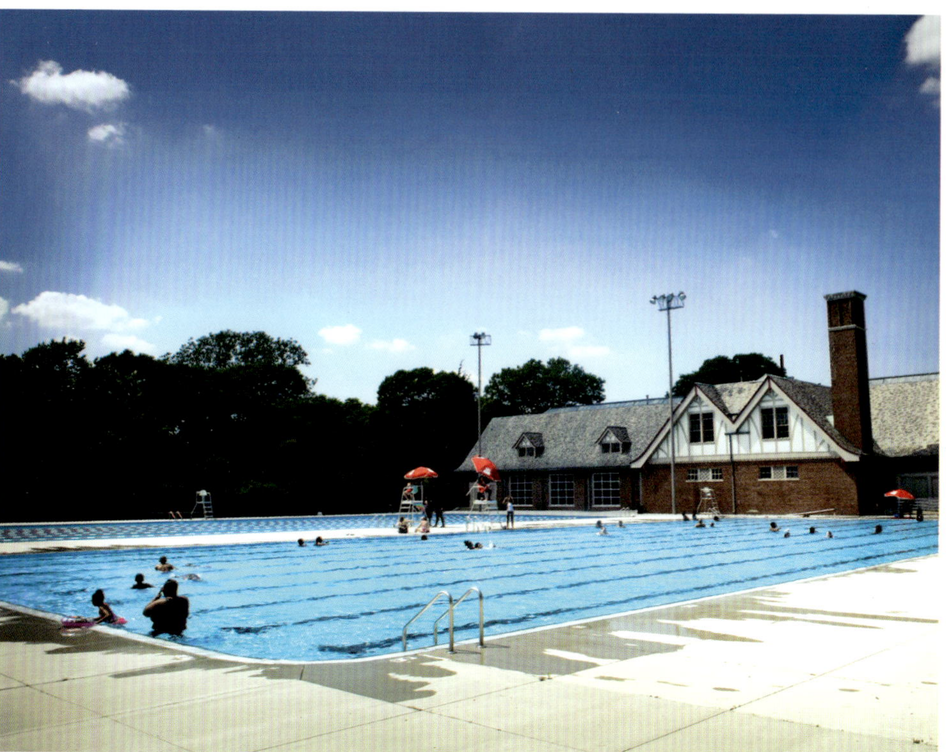

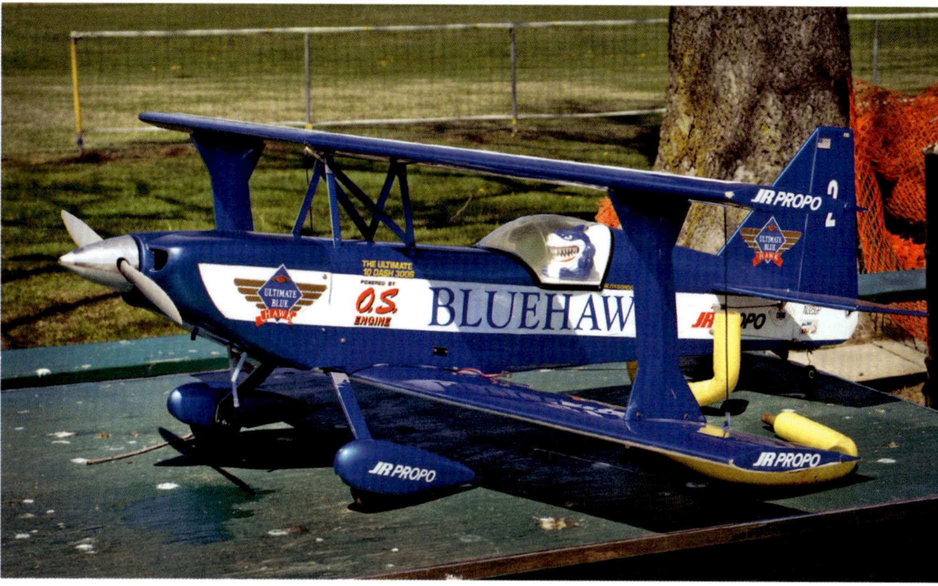

The largest and least developed park in the city, Rouge Park has one thing the rest don't: the Rouge River. The Rouge River flows 127 miles from northwestern Wayne county and southern Oakland county through Detroit into the Detroit River. Here, wetlands and forest line the riverbanks while nature trails allow visitors to get closer to the natural wildlife. City dwellers need these sorts of verdant refuges. I know I do anyway. - NR

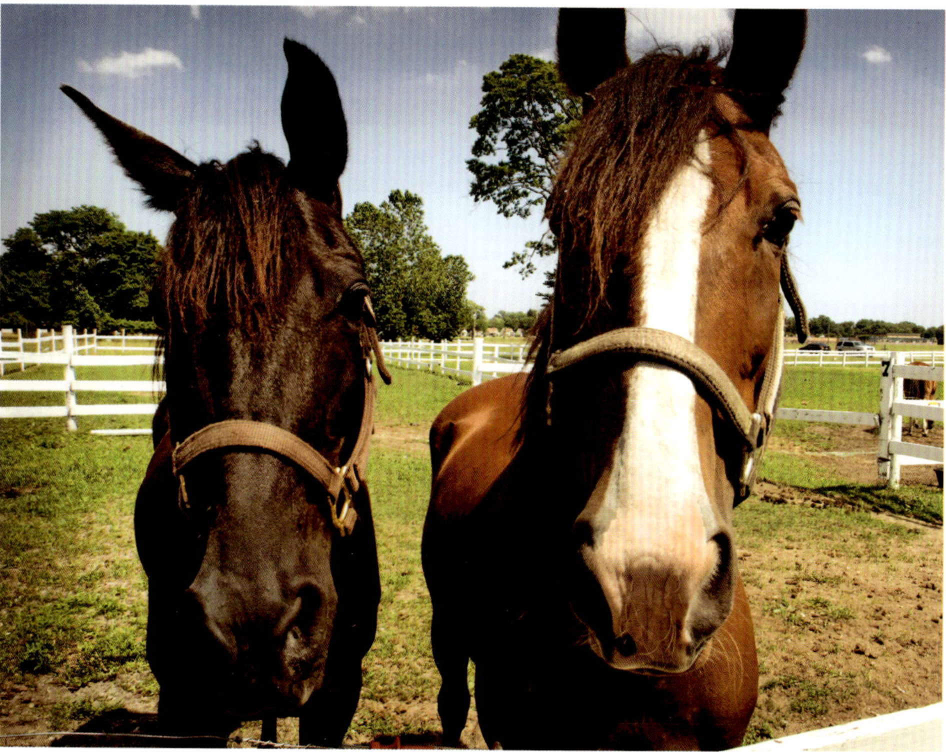

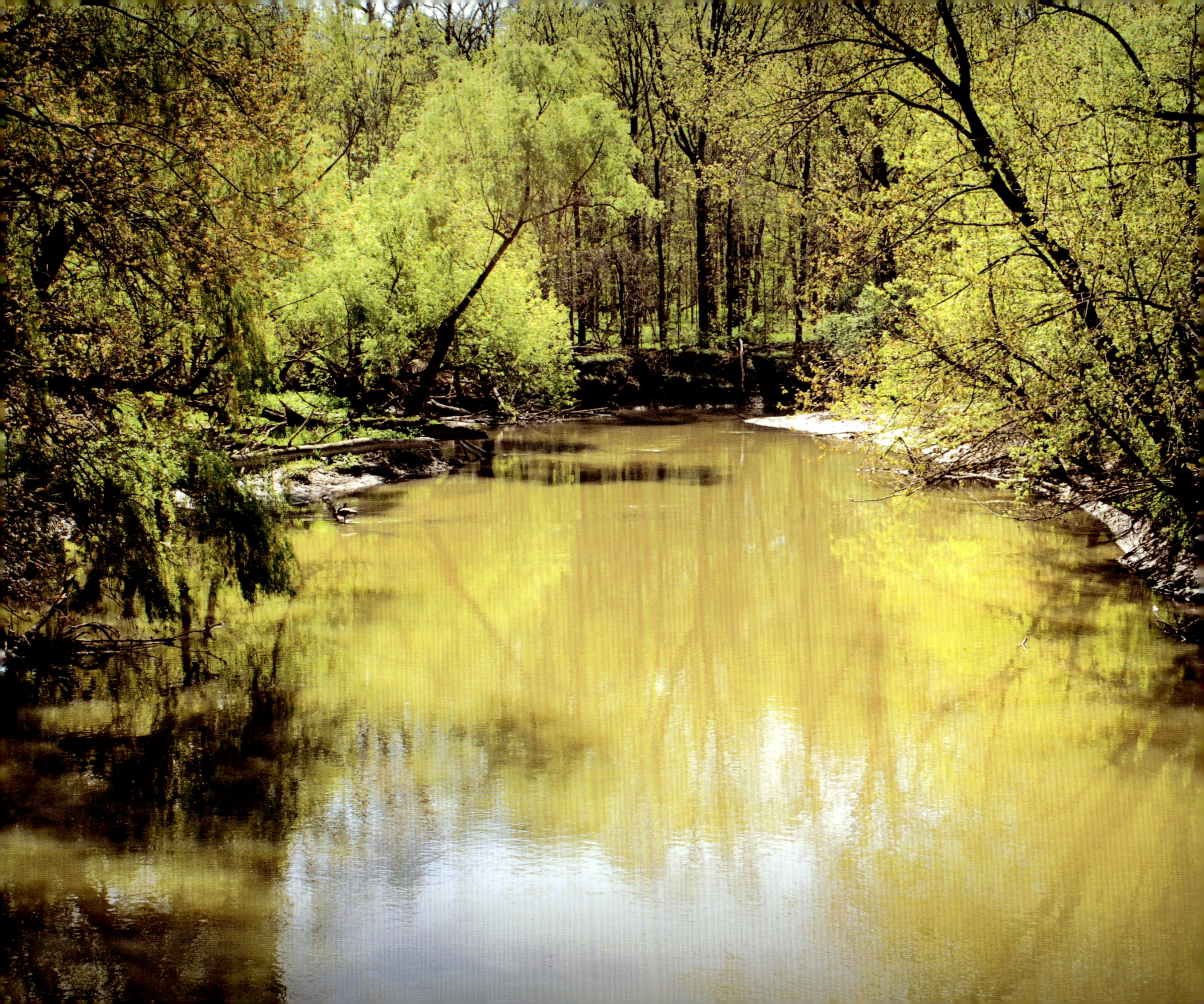

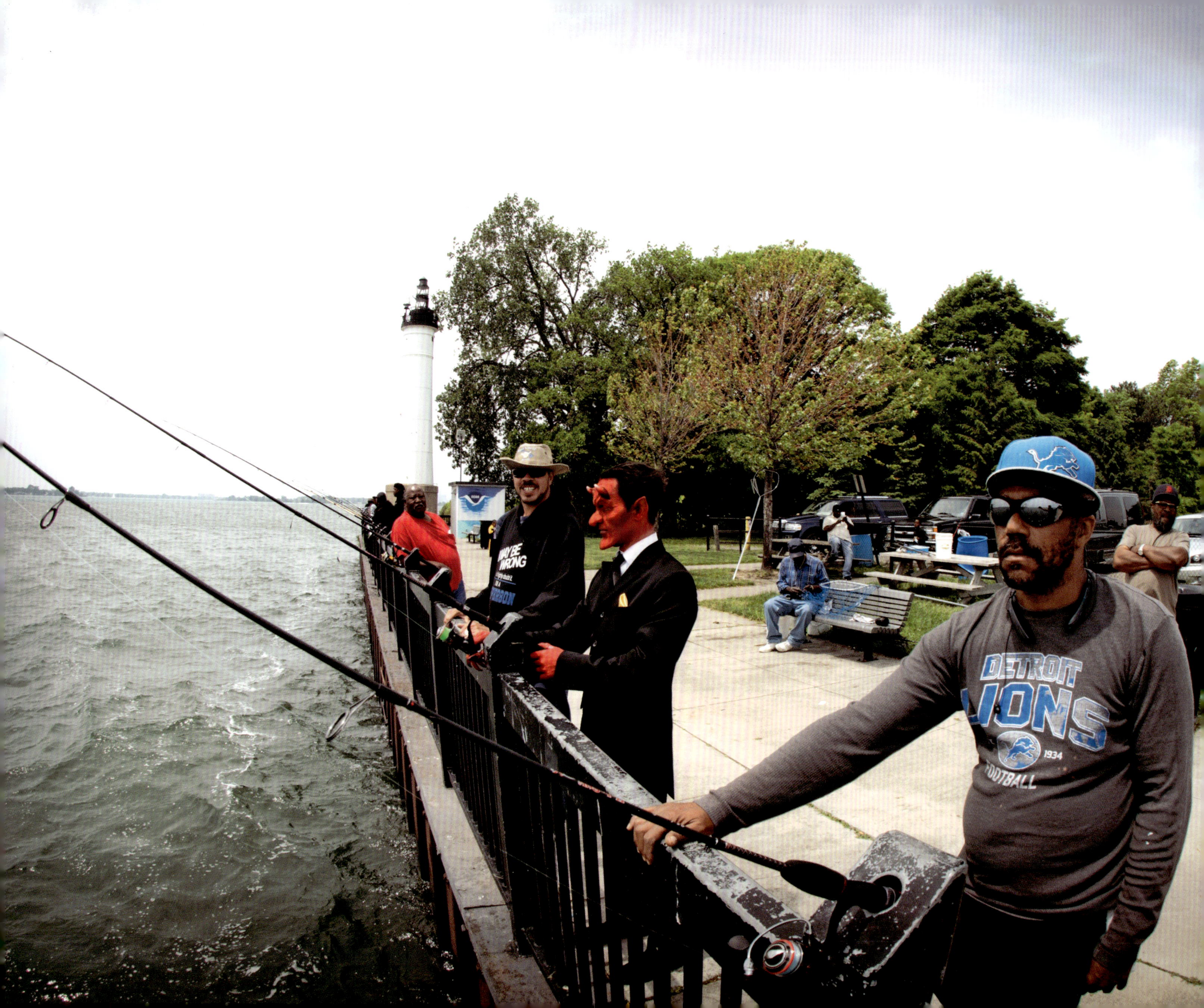
WRONG
DETROIT
LIONS
1934

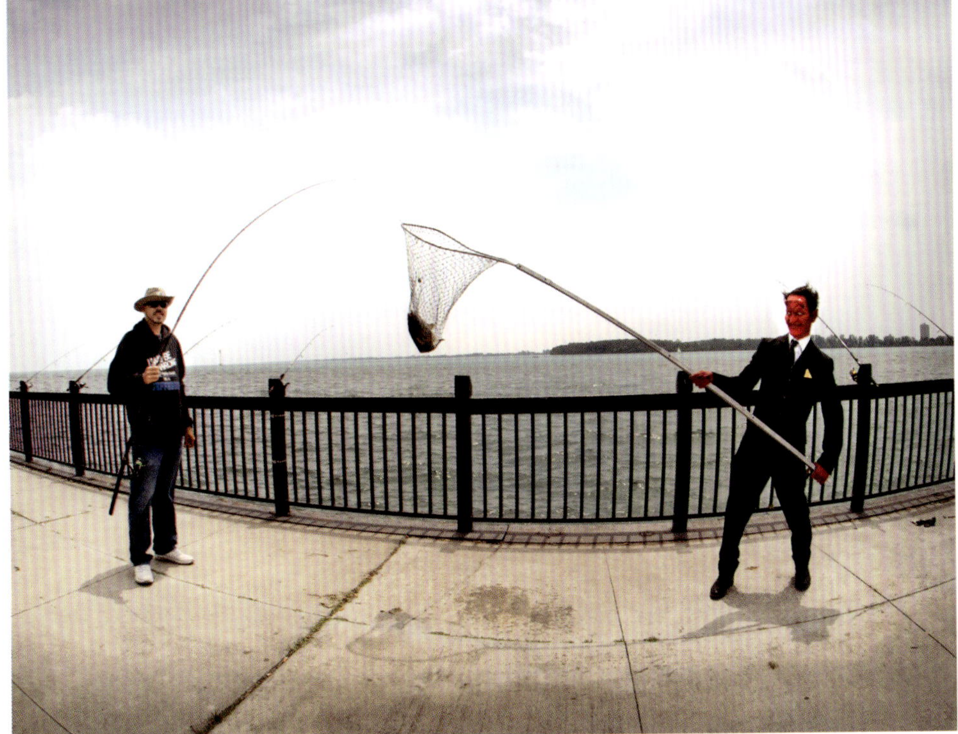

WINDMILL POINT

Alter Rd. and Riverside Blvd., Detroit, 48215

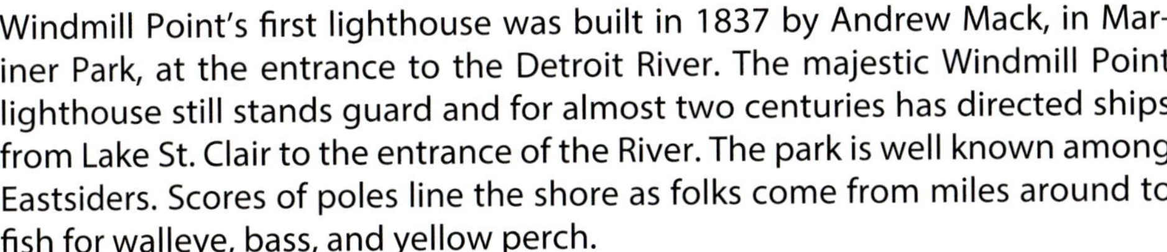

Windmill Point's first lighthouse was built in 1837 by Andrew Mack, in Mariner Park, at the entrance to the Detroit River. The majestic Windmill Point lighthouse still stands guard and for almost two centuries has directed ships from Lake St. Clair to the entrance of the River. The park is well known among Eastsiders. Scores of poles line the shore as folks come from miles around to fish for walleye, bass, and yellow perch.

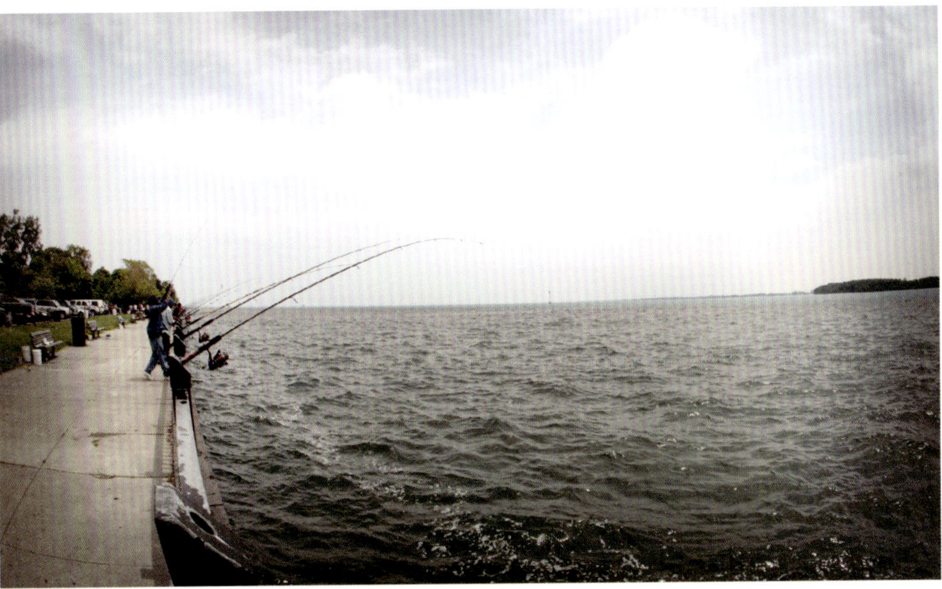

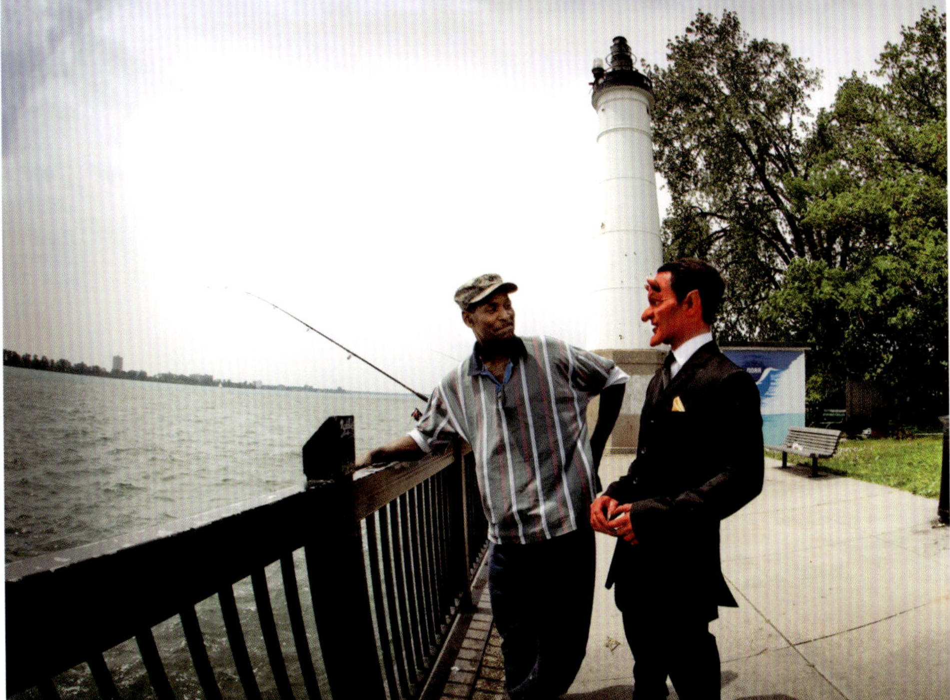

Alter Road, which leads you to the park, is the physical and psychological divide between Detroit and the Grosse Pointes. The dramatic chasm between suburban wealth and exclusivity on one side and the decades of urban decay and abandonment on Detroit's eastside creates a startling reminder of the differences of class and race. Despite this, folks still come for the fishing and camaraderie, ignoring the economic partition as best they can. I usually make my way here early in the morning to stand in the shadow of the lighthouse just as the sun rises over Lake St. Clair, greeting others who are out for an early catch. This serene area helps me relax and remember that the world is a much more forgiving place than the divisions we create would suggest. - NR

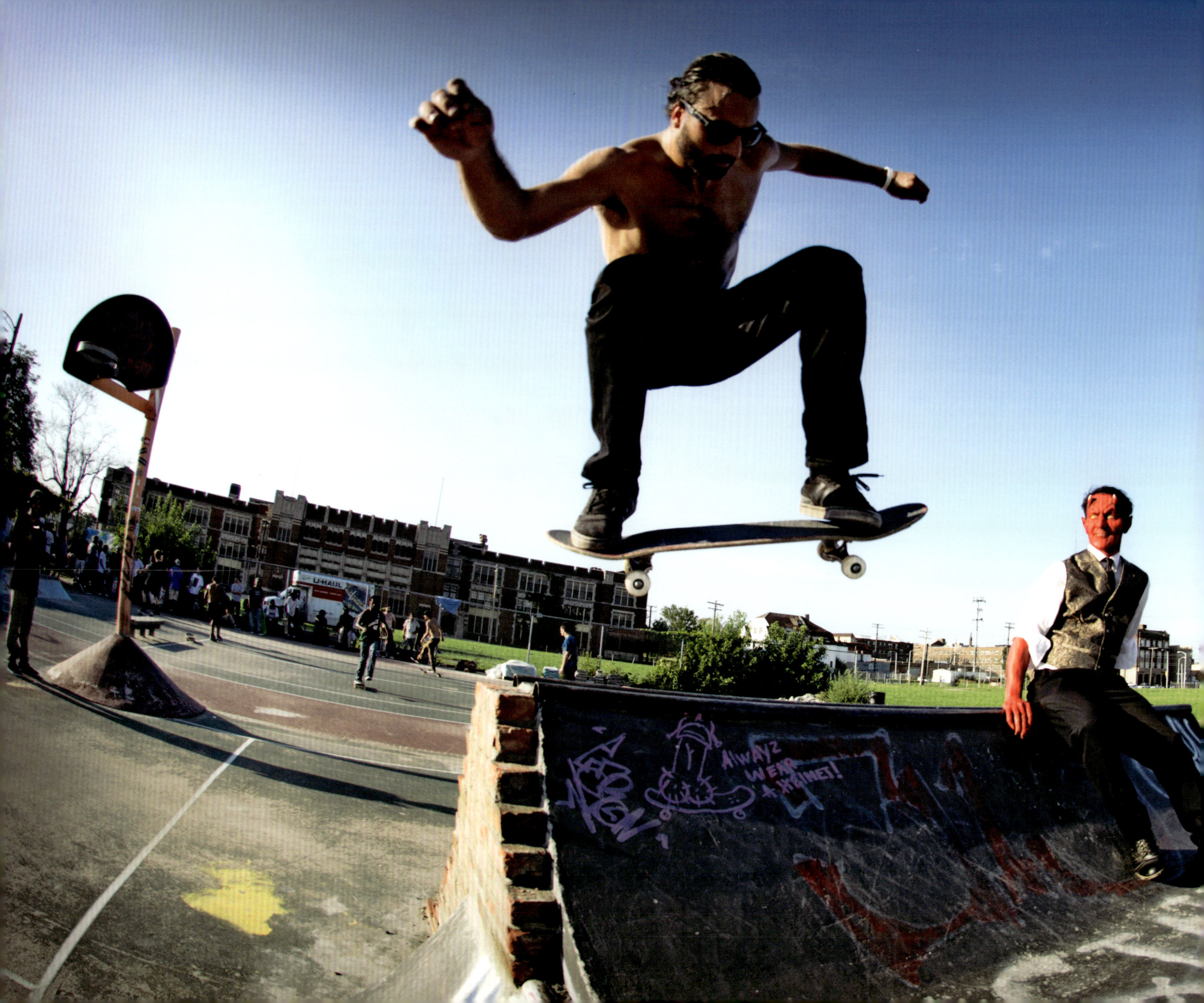
U-HAUL
ALWAYZ
WEAR

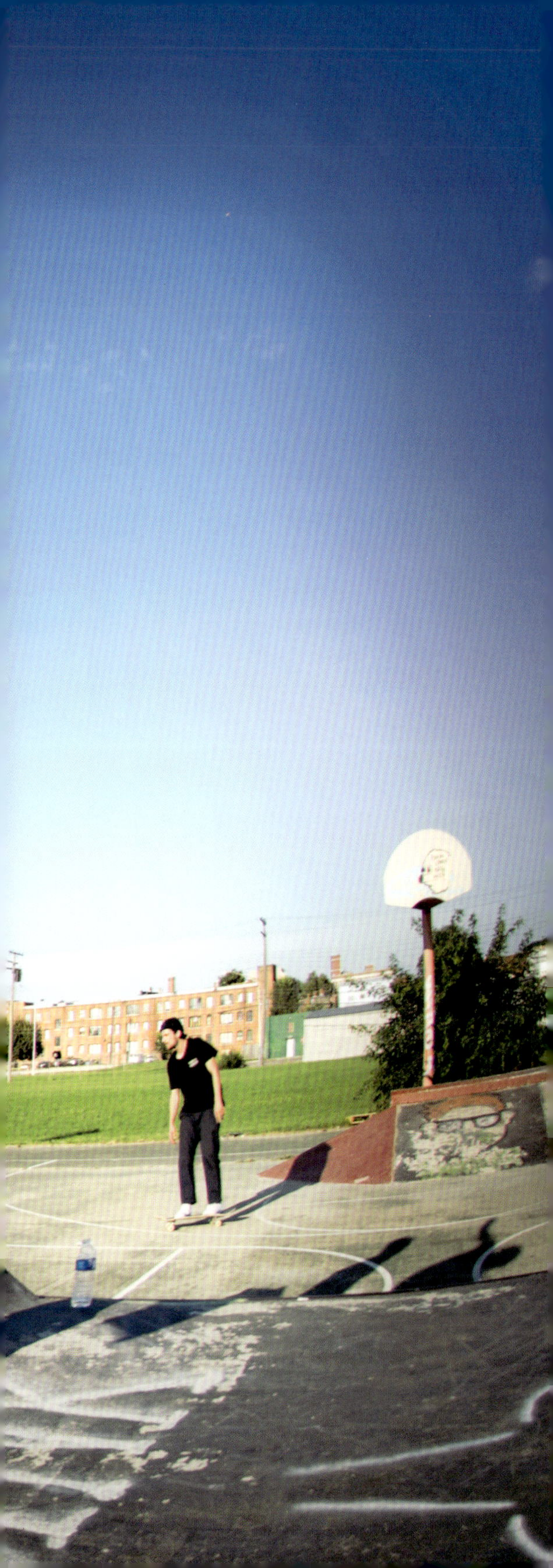

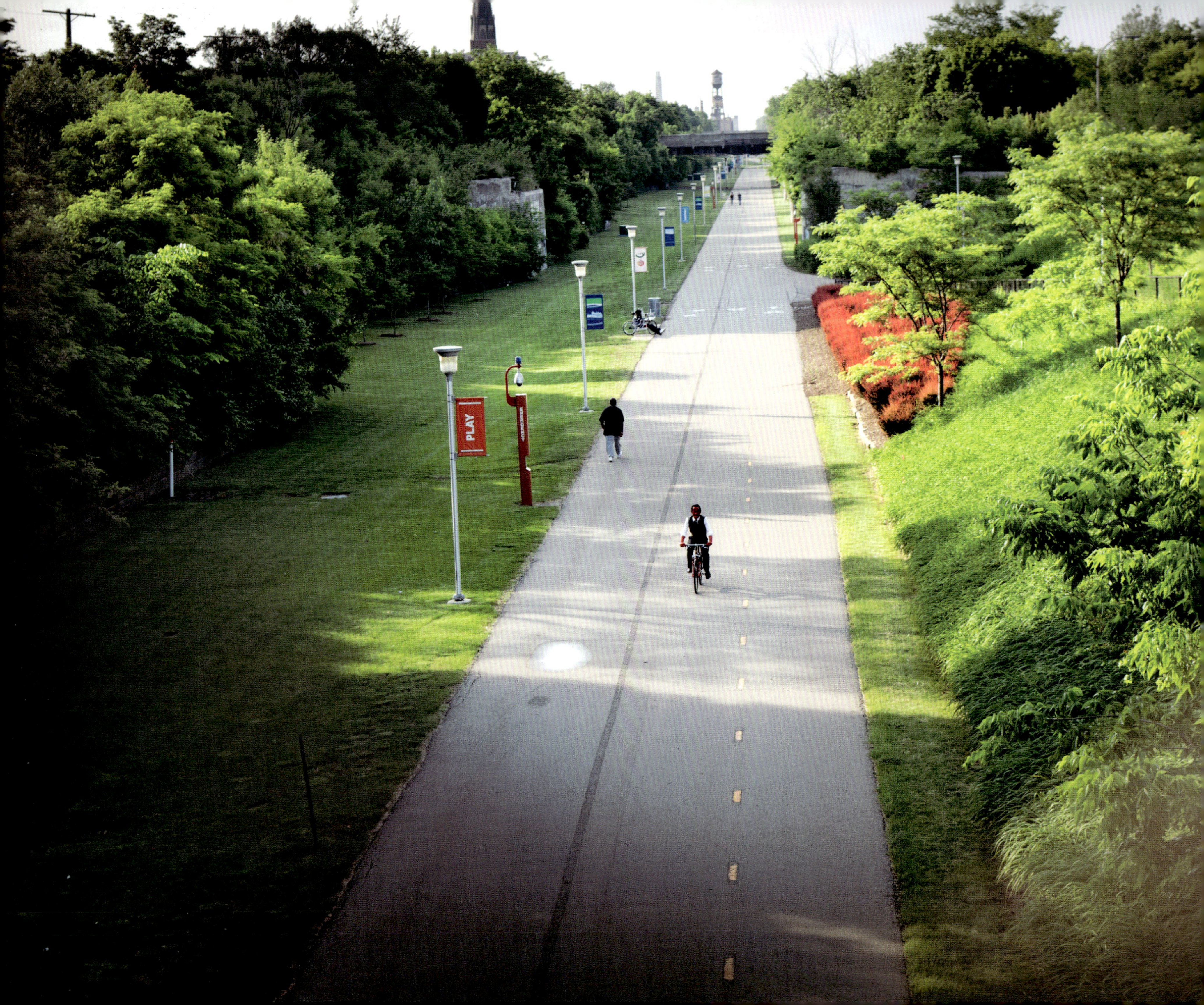
PLAY

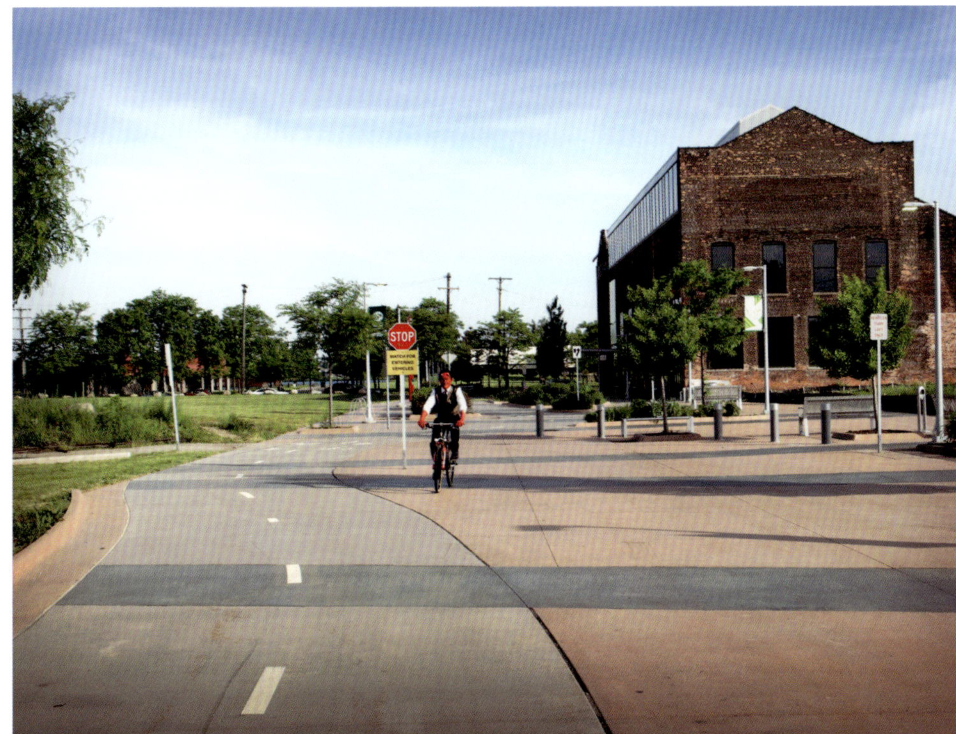

DEQUINDRE CUT

Eastern Market to Riverwalk, Detroit, 48207
www.detroitriverfront.org/riverfront/dequindre-cut/dequindre-cut

Transforming a former train line, the Dequindre Cut connects Eastern Market to the Riverfront and Belle Isle on an trail designed for recreation and exploration. Situated below street level, the trail is surrounded by hills of green, embracing nature and concealing the chaotic traffic above. Murals cover the concrete bridge abutments and overpasses. Enjoyed by joggers, bikers and folks just out for a stroll, it has become one of Detroit's favorite destinations.

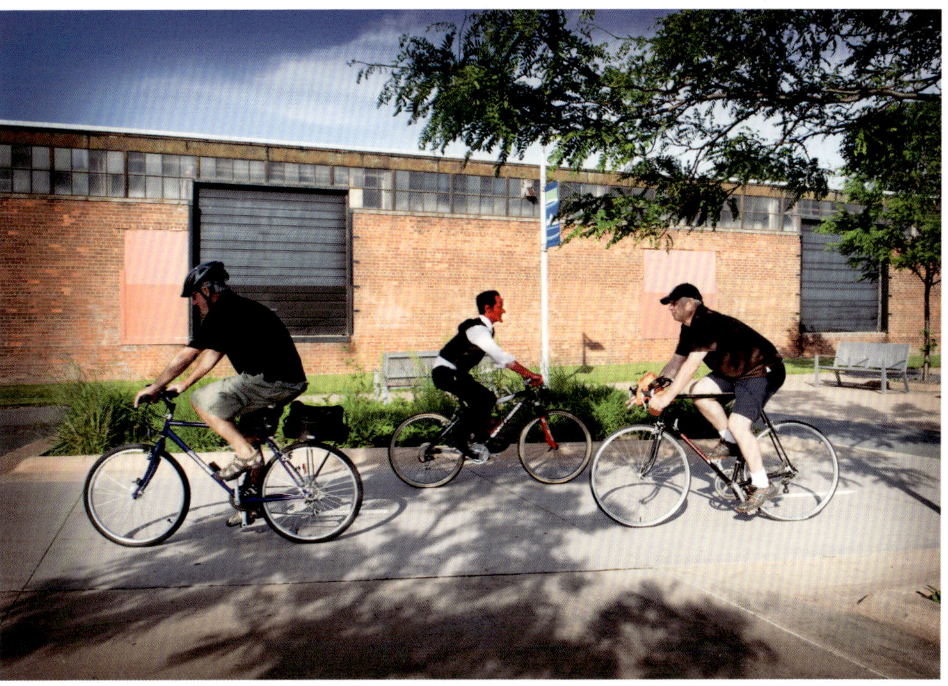

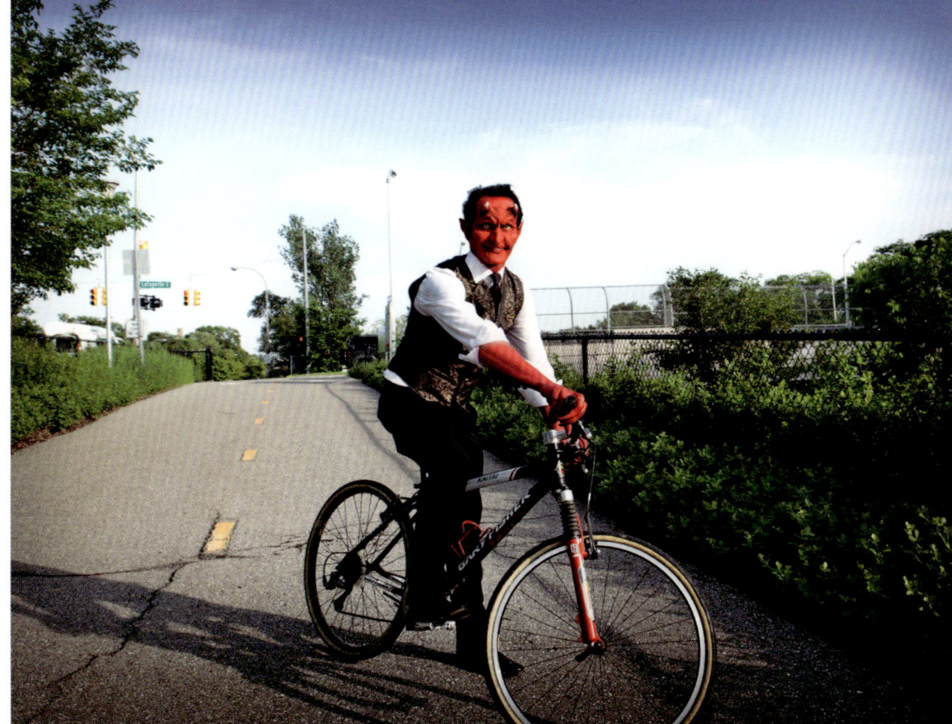

Reuse. One of the best illustrations of reuse is the Dequindre Cut, part of a master plan for bike lanes and trails. Where there once were railroad tracks, I can now ride my bike from the Eastern Market to the river without dodging traffic. The city has finally embraced alternative travel methods on streets and greenways.
- NR

DETROIT DERBY GIRLS

Masonic Temple, 500 Temple St., Detroit, 48201
www.detroitderbygirls.com

Inspired by earlier incarnations, the Detroit Derby Girls in 2005 formed a flat-track roller derby league comprising five teams: the D-Funk All Stars, the Devil's Night Dames, the Detroit Pistoffs, the Pistolwhippers, and the Grand Prix Madonnas. They also have three interleague teams, an A class team, a B class team, and a pick up team. In 2009, they finished third in the WFTDA National Championships. Drew Barrymore's film *Whip It* was shot in Detroit using many of the teams in the production. The season is September to May at the Masonic Temple.

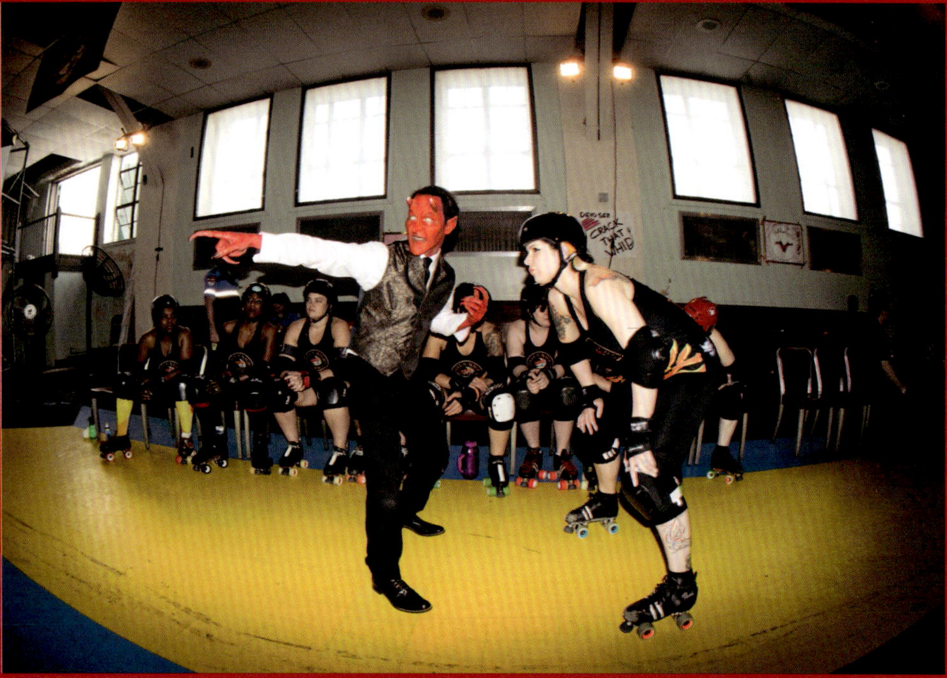

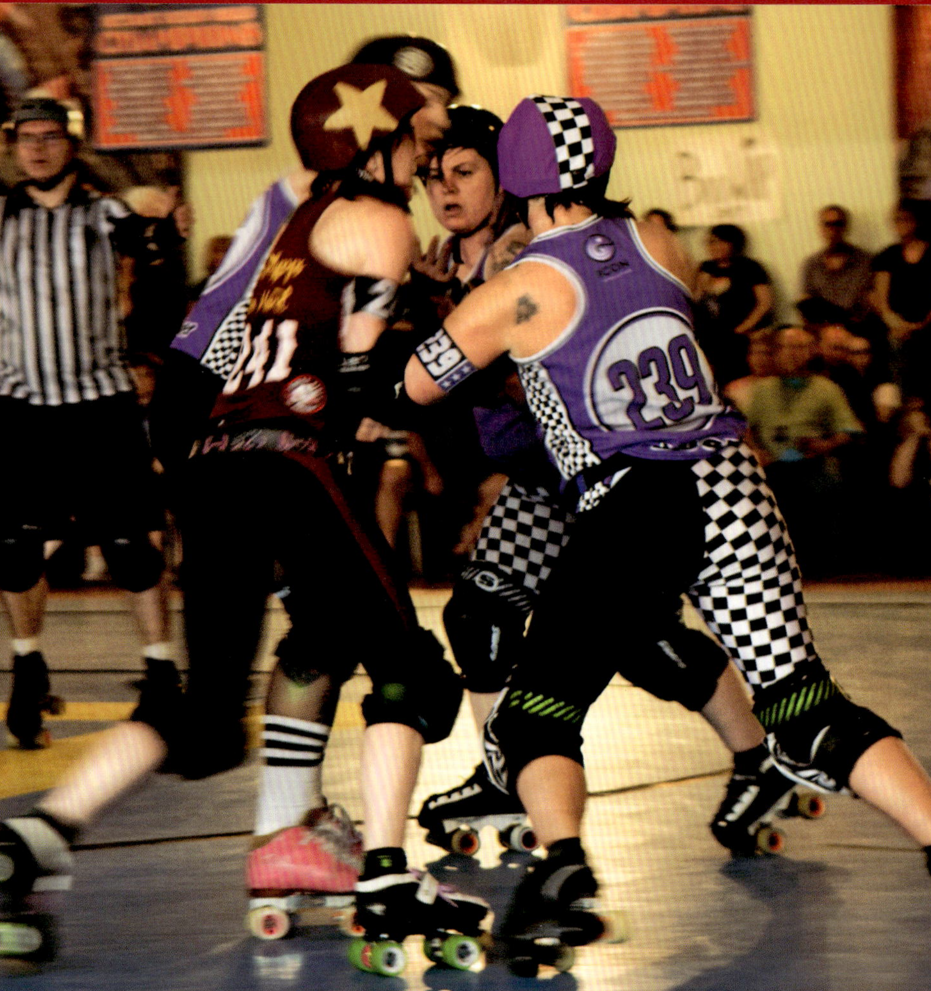

Derby Girls act all sweet and friendly off the track but they need an outlet to express their inner feelings. Toughness and hardness are common traits in Detroit, but these ladies are especially ferocious on roller skates. When I was asked to coach one of the teams, I was too intimidated to say no. - NR

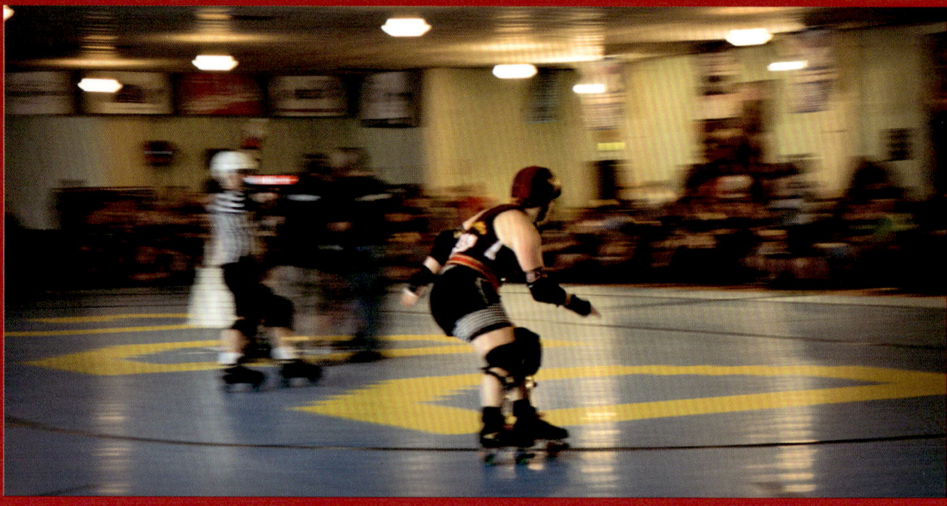

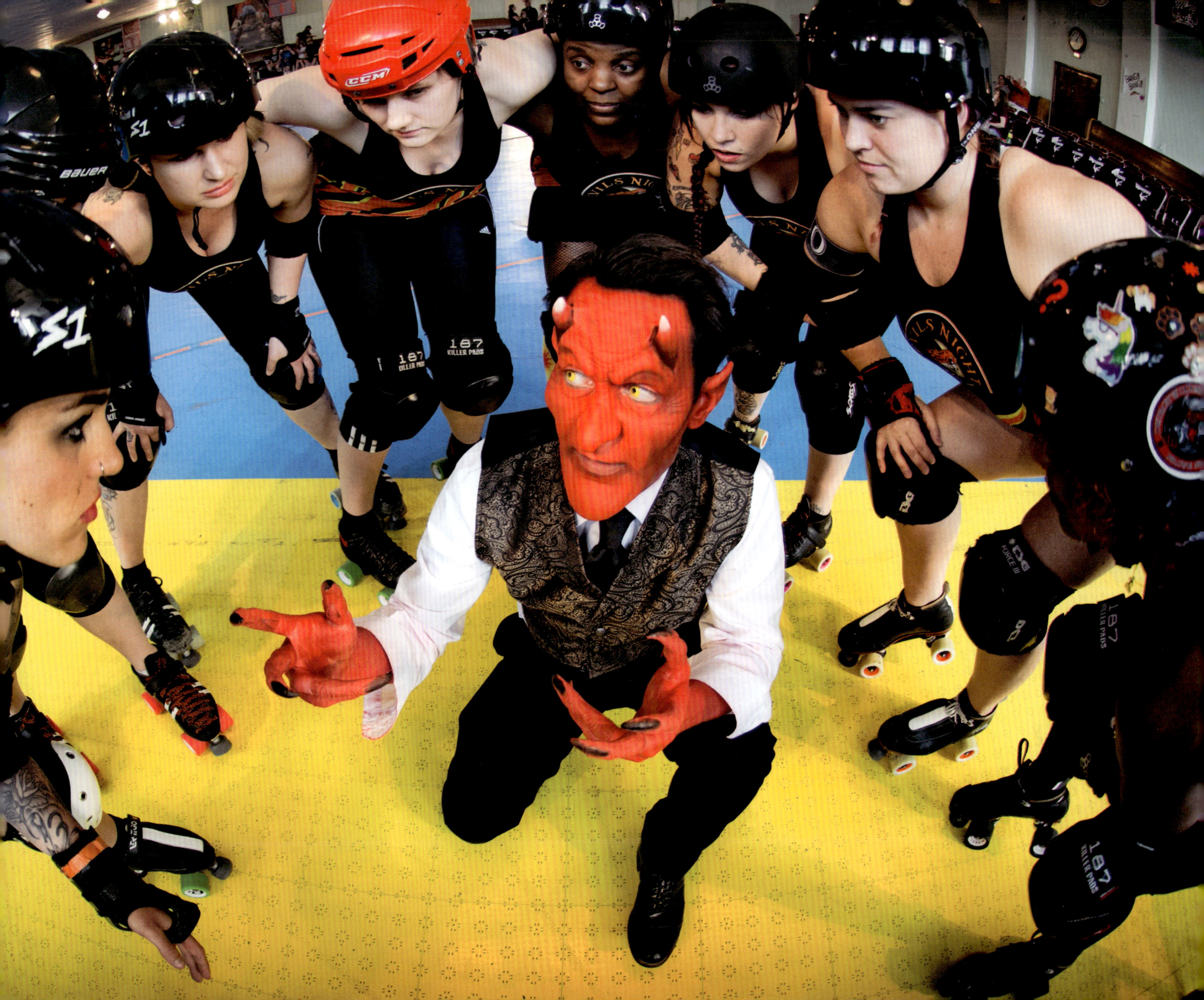
CCM
S1
BAUER
187
KILLER PADS

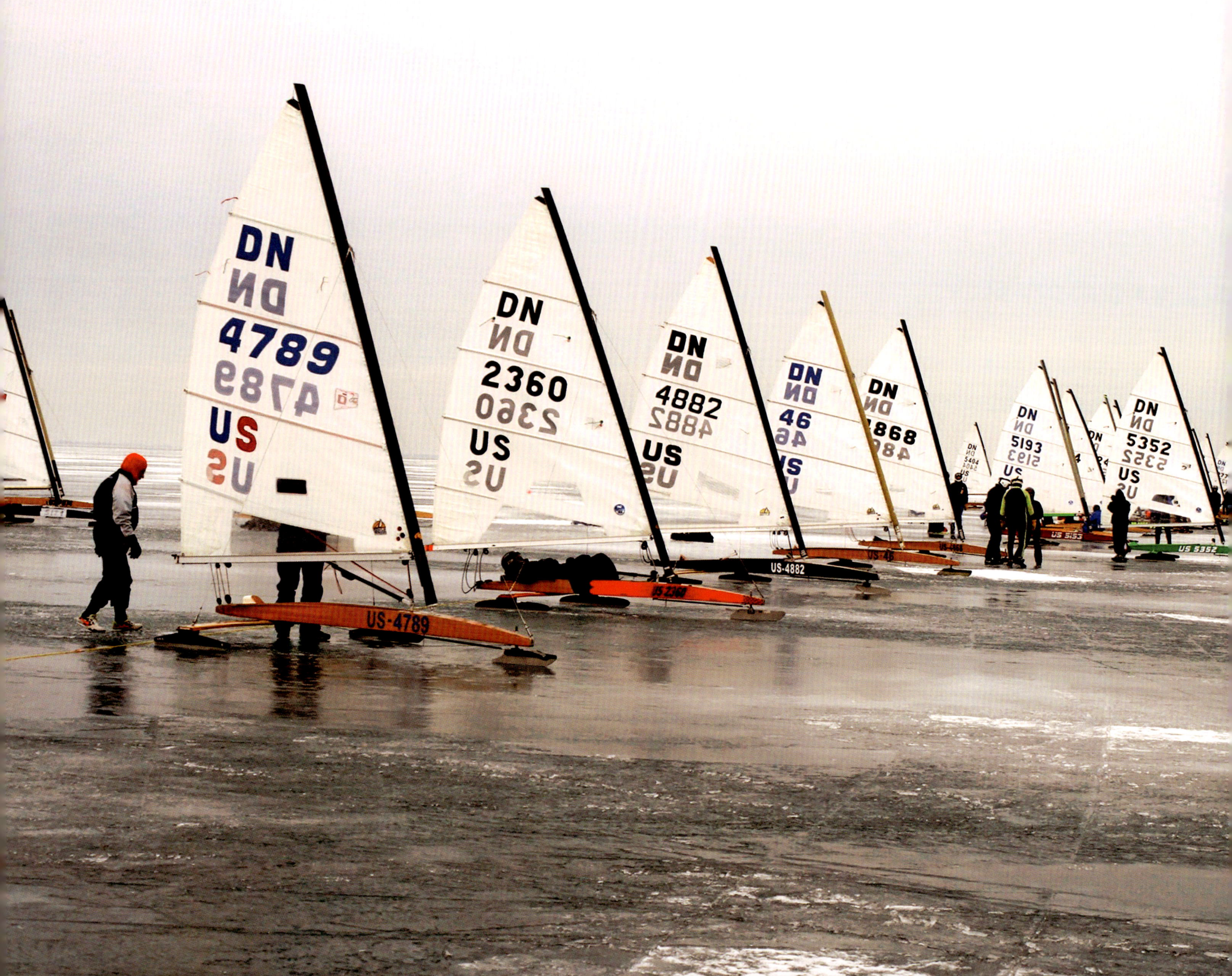

DN
4789
US
US-4789
DN
2360
US
DN
4882
US
US-4882
DN
46
DN
5193
DN
5352
US
US 5352

DN CLASS - ICE BOAT RACING

na.idniyra.org

An ice boat resembles a sail boat but is fitted with three blades designed to skate across the ice. At 12 feet long with a cross plank and a 16 foot mast, it is designed to carry one person at speeds up to 65 miles per hour. Known around the world, the DN class of ice boats is also the most popular. Originating in Detroit in 1936, the "DN" denotes the *Detroit News*, whose employees designed the first boat. DN boats are raced predominantly in the northern US, Canada, northern Europe, and Scandinavia, with a World Championship hosted in alternating years between Europe and North America.

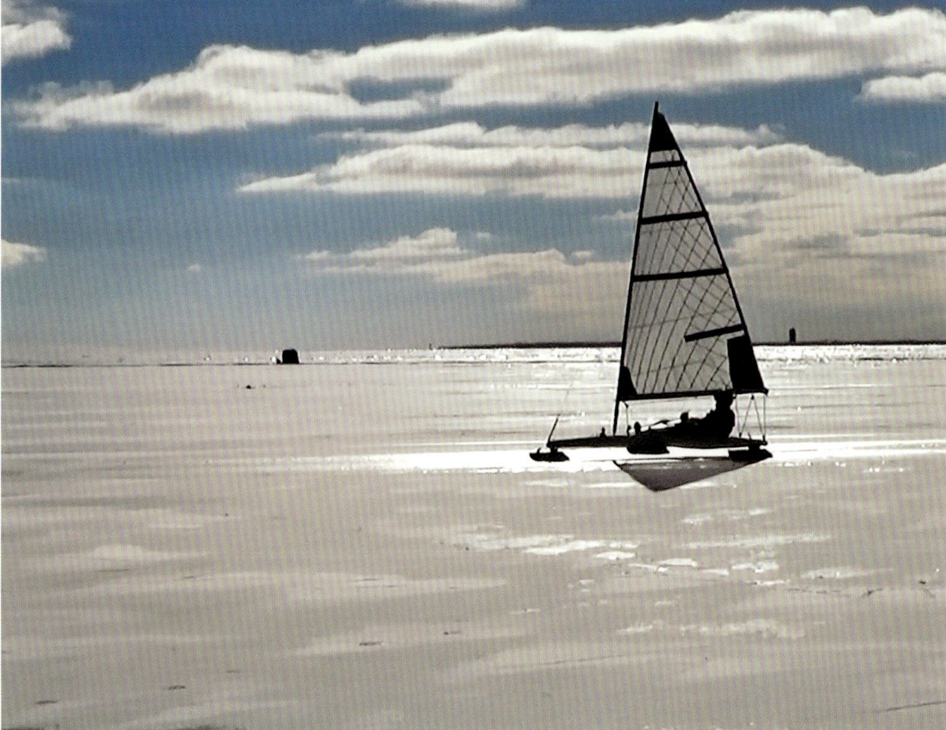

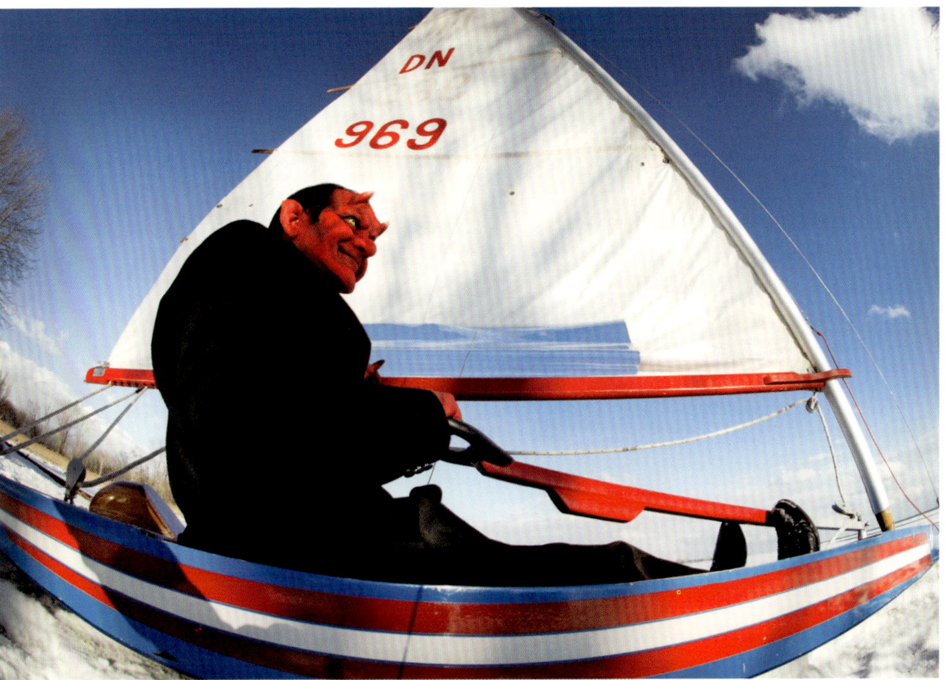

When winter comes and freezes Lake St. Clair and the river, Detroiters are unfazed, trading in their sailboats for an all-together different craft. DN boats are lightweight and easy to assemble. Fierce winter winds push you across the glass-like ice at incredible speeds. - NR

DOWNTOWN BOXING

6445 E. Vernor Hwy., Detroit, 48207
www.downtownyouthboxing.org

Kronk Boxing Gym
9520 Mettetal St., Detroit, 48227
www.kronkboxingteam.com

Detroit has a rich history of boxing champions. With the dominating punches of Joe Louis, the swift feet of Sugar Ray Robinson, the strategies of trainer Emanuel Steward, and the stable of talent at Kronk Boxing, Detroiters have impacted the sport for generations. Continuing in that tradition, Downtown Boxing Gym was created in 2007 by Khali Sweeney, who was responding to the loss of friends to the streets. His answer – using the self-determination of boxing to guide inner city kids to control their destinies – became a success story. For those lucky enough to be accepted, there is a six-month waiting list. They are provided with tutors and mentoring before stepping into the ring, resulting in a 100% graduation rate.

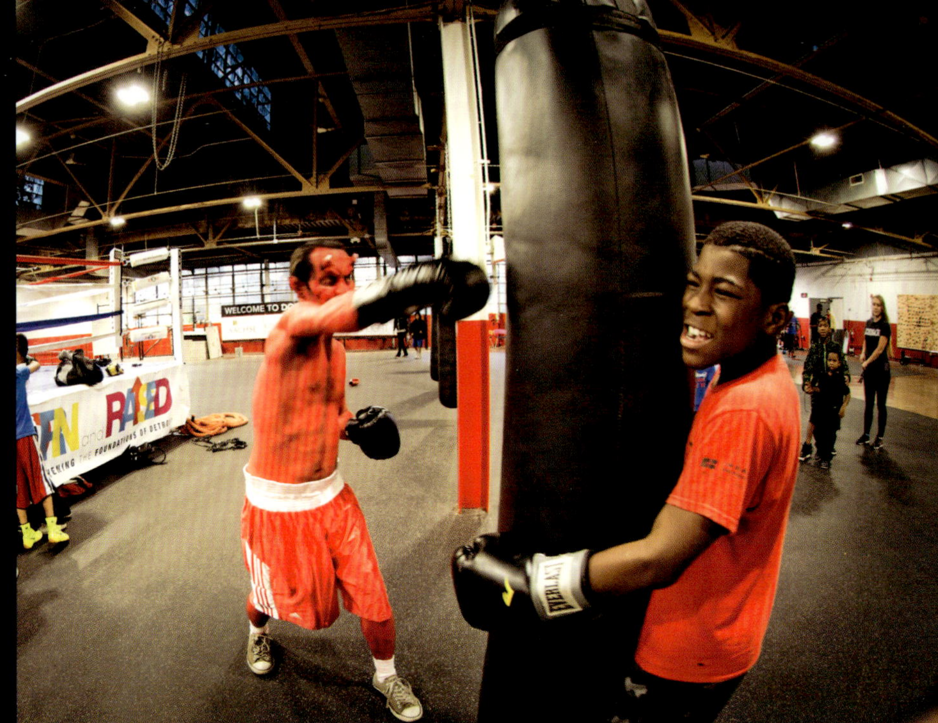

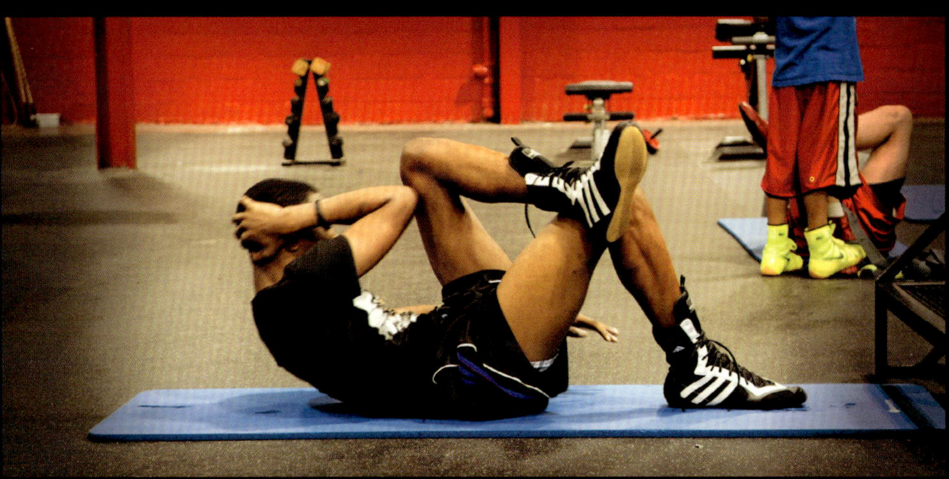

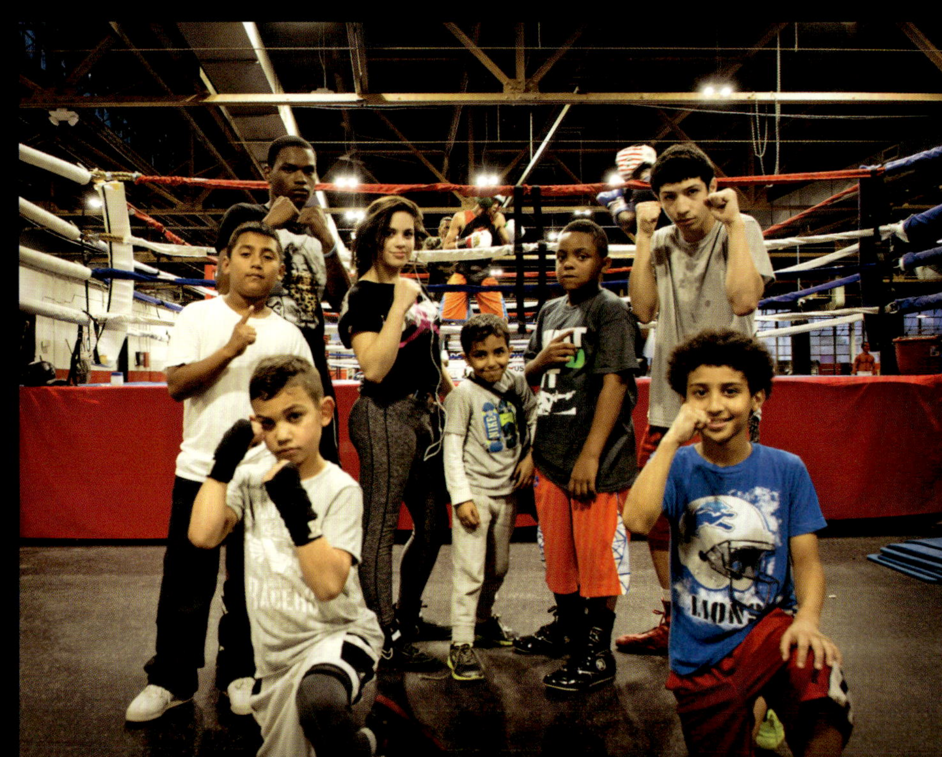

As a blue collar town where manufacturing jobs require a lot of hard labor, perhaps it's only natural that Detroit produced so many boxing champions. I've thrown some punches at the Downtown Boxing Gym, but the place is really notable for its after-school program for youngsters, which has been lauded for its approach in getting kids to complete their education. Coming off the streets of Detroit, the kids at Downtown Boxing already have the drive and desire, but here they must earn their way into the ring by succeeding in school.

- NR

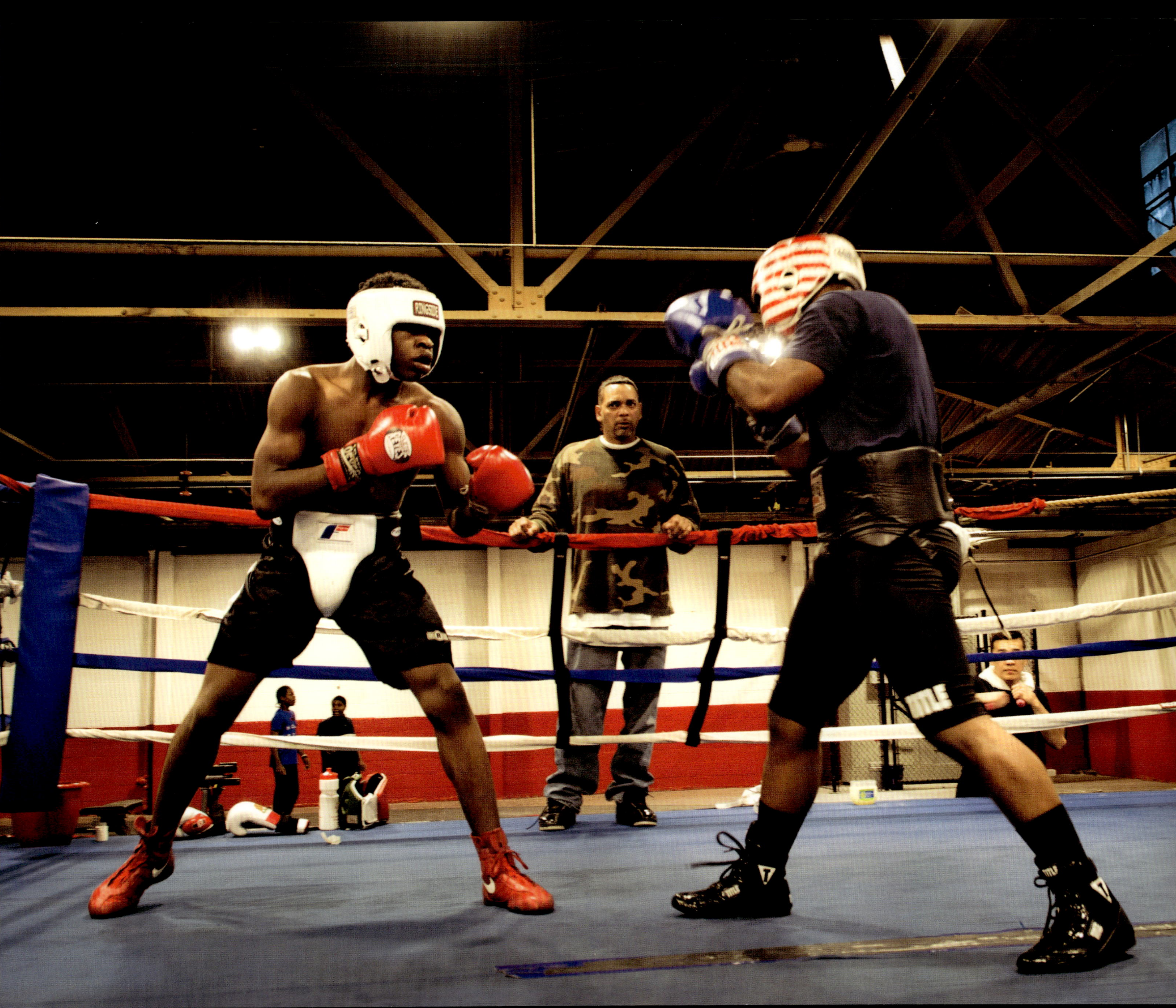
RINGSIDE

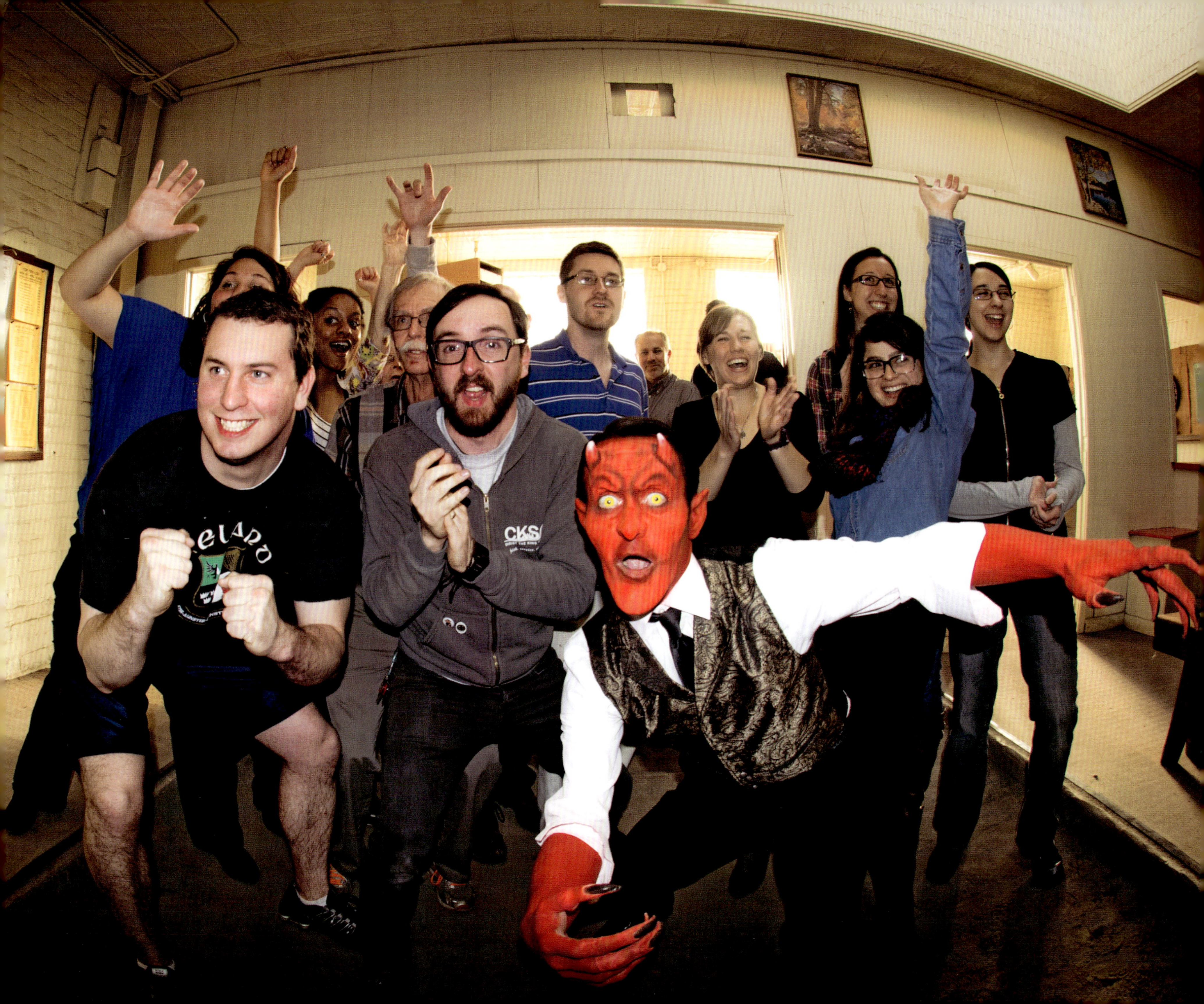

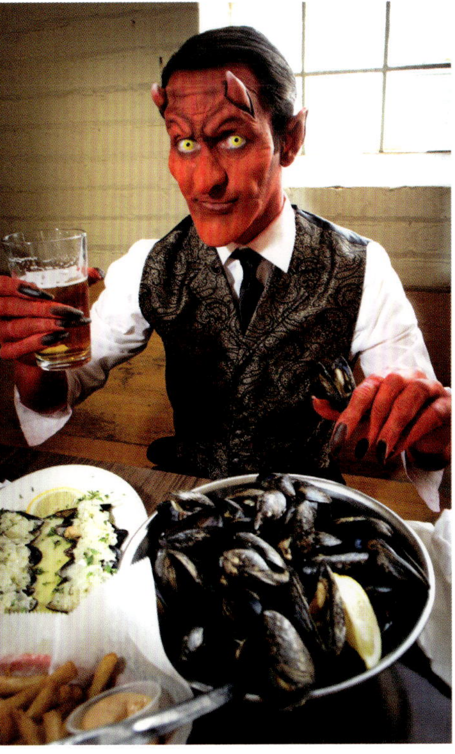

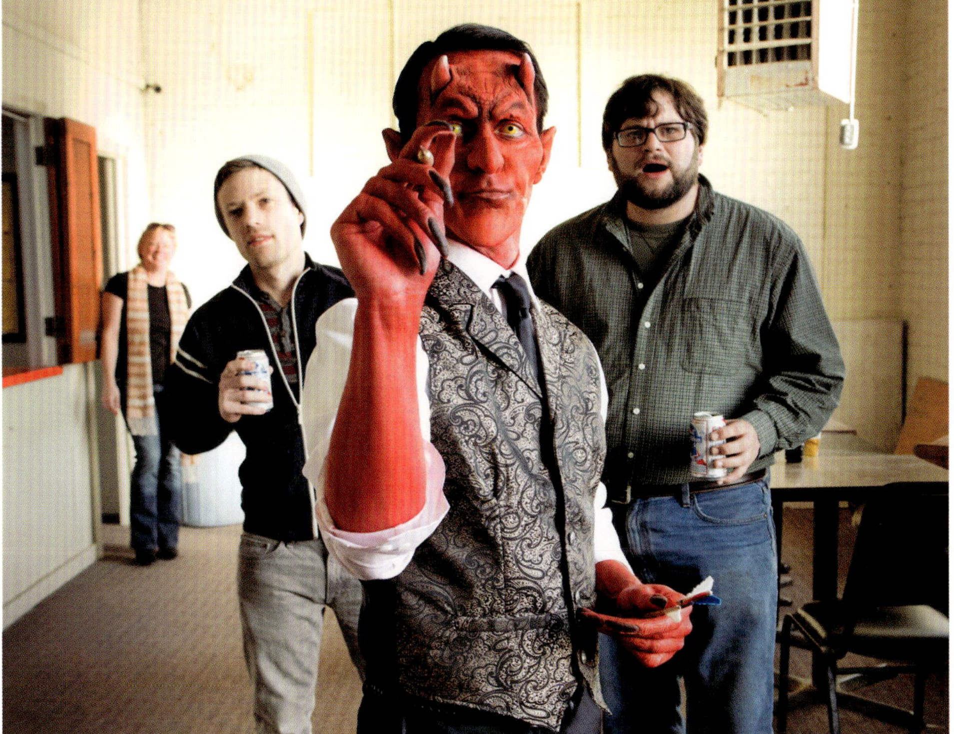

FEATHER BOWLING

Cadieux Café, 4300 Cadieux Rd., Detroit, 48224
www.cadieuxcafe.com

Feather bowling is the Flemish version of bocce or horseshoes. Players roll large wheels, simulating wheels of cheese, from one end of the court to the other, trying to get the wheel closest to a single feather planted in the dirt. The Cadieux Café, an eastside favorite, was established as a speakeasy during Prohibition, becoming a social center for Flemish immigrants. It is the only place in the United States to offer feather bowling, continuing the Flemish tradition (though the game is rarely played in Belgium anymore). The Cadieux is also renowned for its mussels and fries, Belgium's national dish.

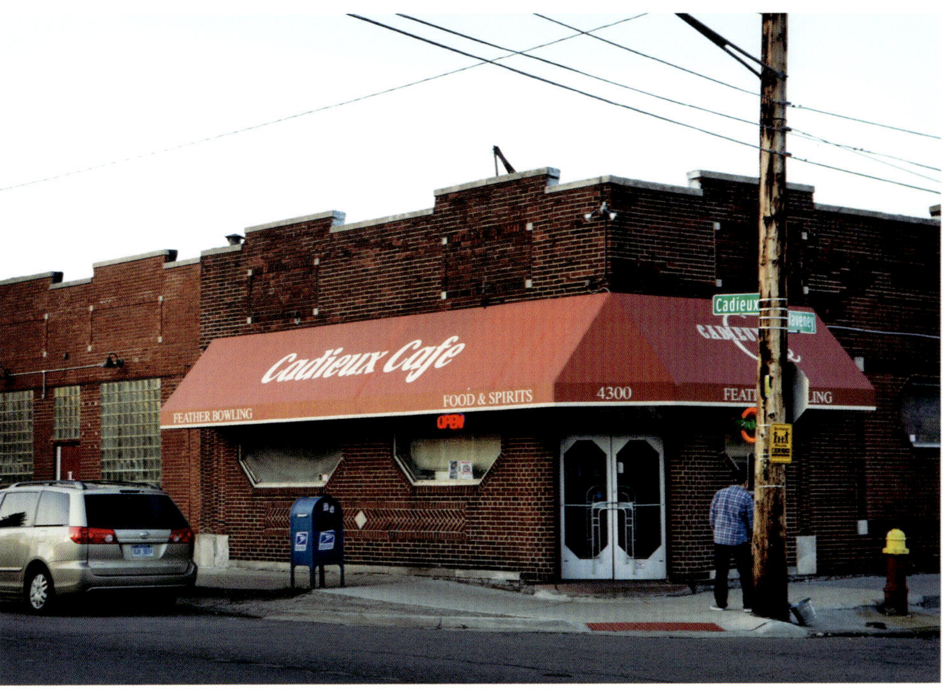

The Flemish are a strange bunch. Feather bowling had to be invented by some cheesemakers who were either drunk or bored. I've been on a number of winning tournament teams but have been banned, labeled a ringer, due to my mastery of the game. I continue to play recreationally at the Cadieux Café, but I come here more for the awesome mussels and beers than to compete. - NR

FOWLING

3901 Christopher St., Detroit, 48211
www.fowlingwarehouse.com

Detroiter Chris Hutt and a few buddies accidently created Fowling in 2000 while they were tailgating at the Indy 500. After setting up a mini bowling alley, they took time out to play catch with a football. An errant throw ignited an idea to create an entirely new game combining the pins from bowling and replacing the ball with a football. As Fowling tournaments expanded the popularity of the sport, a permanent home for it was finally established in 2014.

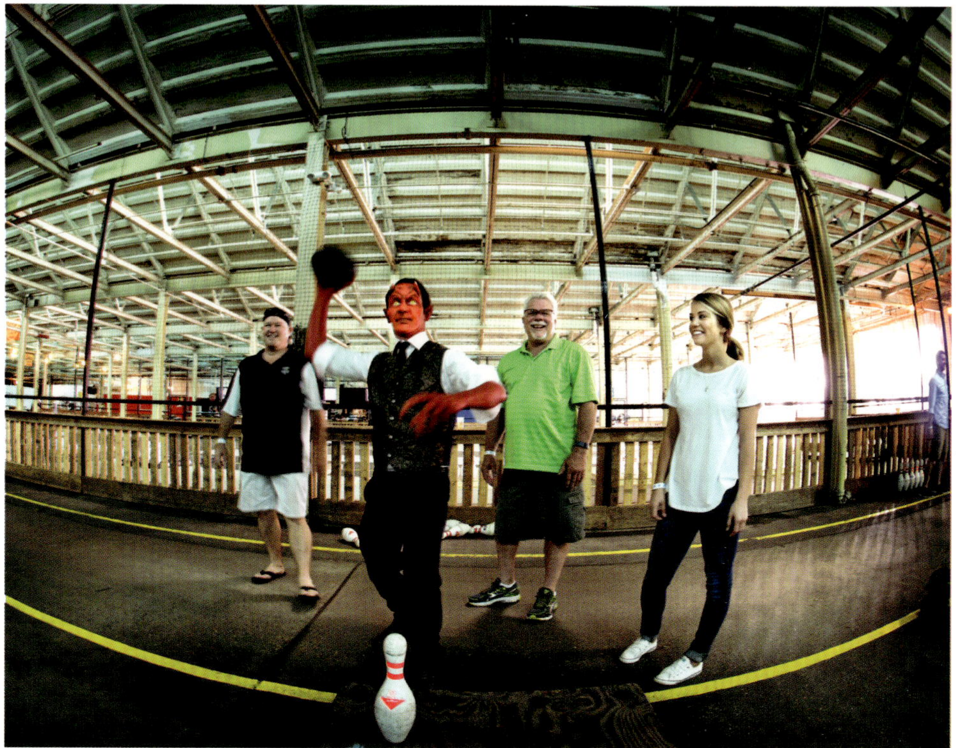

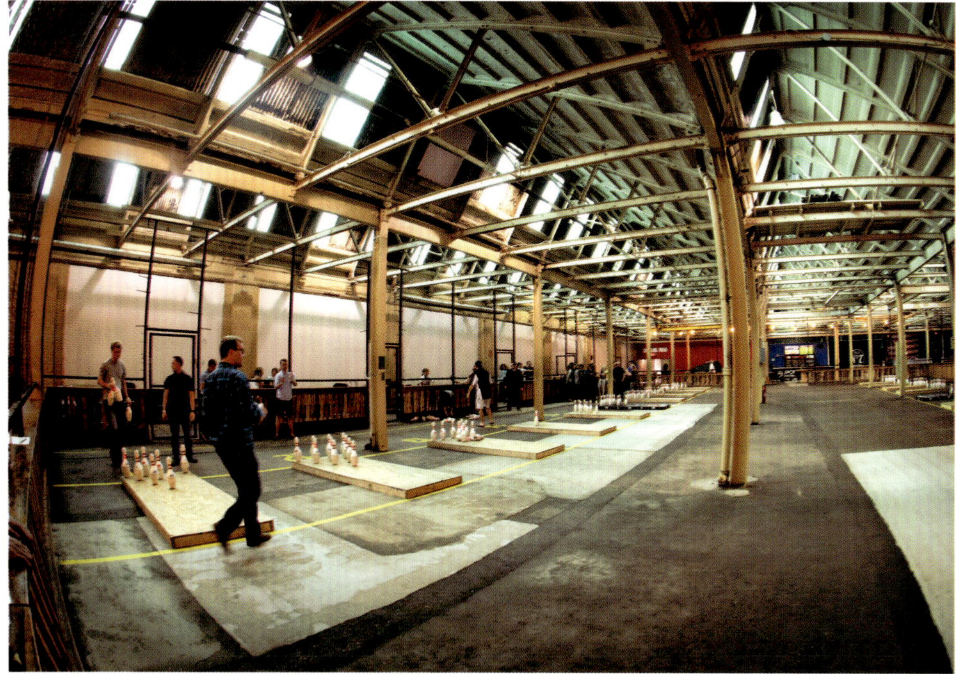

Driven to compete in almost anything, Detroiters sometimes invent crazy alternatives to existing sports. An odd hybrid that pairs well with beer-drinking, fowling is one of those that actually grew a following. - NR

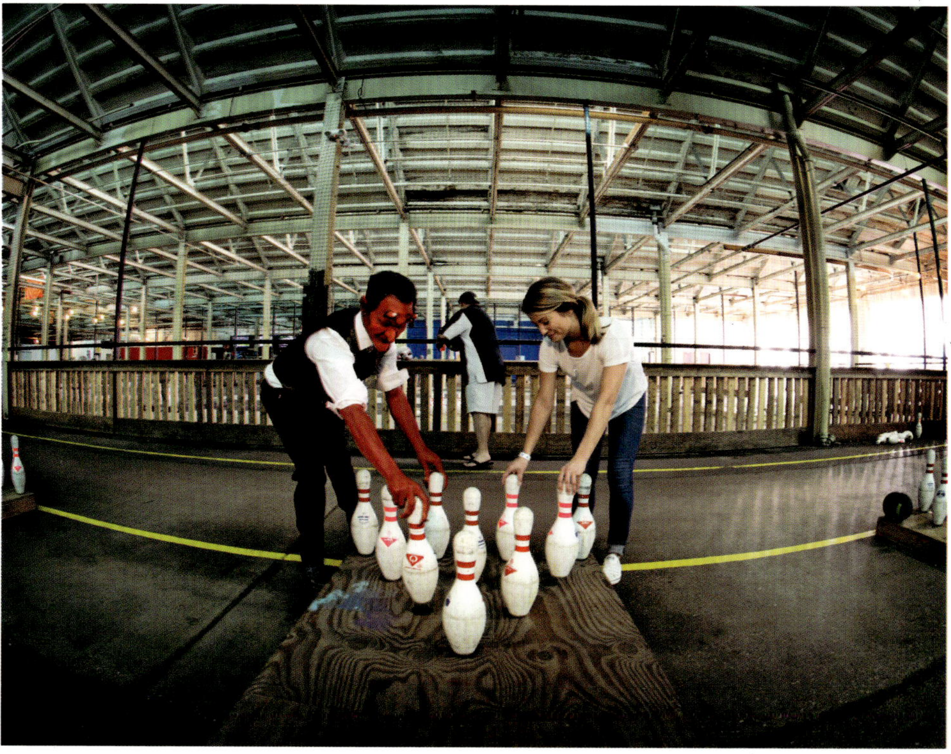

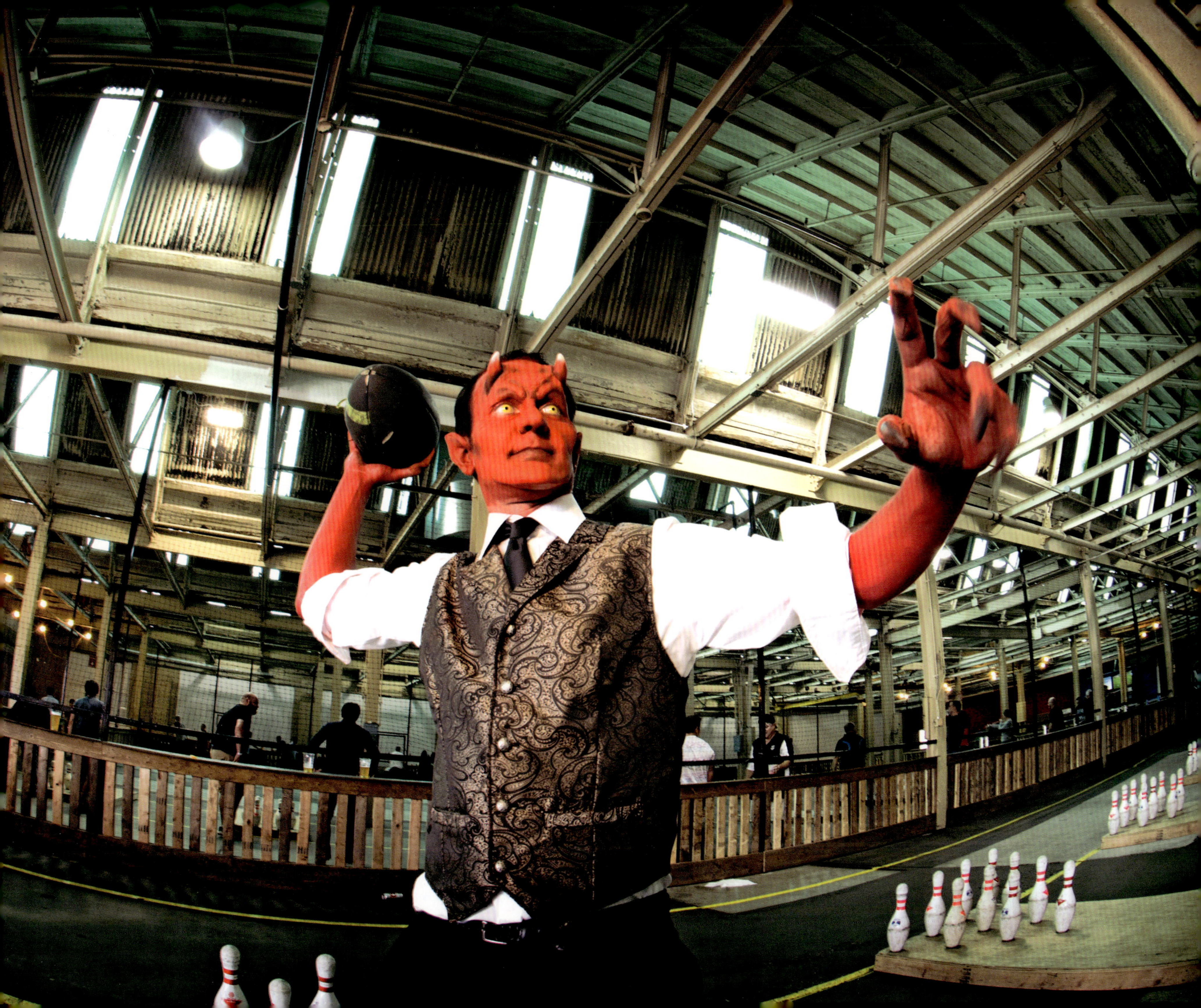

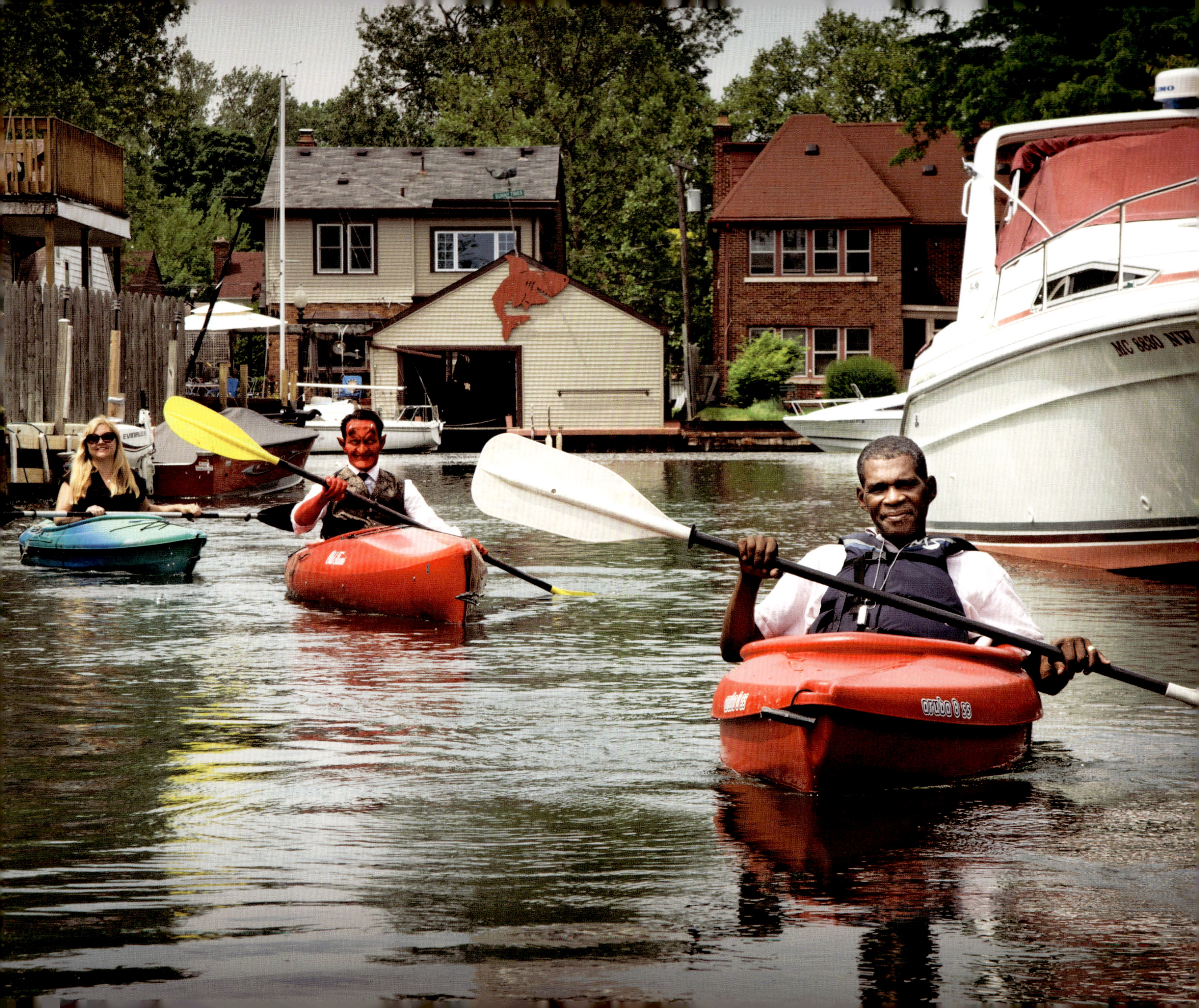
MC 8880 NW
aruba 8 ss
EVINRUDE

FOX CREEK CANALS

Harbor Island, Detroit, 48215

Recognizing the value of prime riverfront, the canals of Jefferson Chalmers, and chiefly Harbor and Klenk Islands, were developed in 1918. Offering access for recreational boating, the canals connected the new residences to the Detroit River. Utilizing the canals' convenience and seclusion, the canals became a favorite destination used by rumrunners smuggling in alcohol from Canada during Prohibition. Lined with boat houses and situated along two large parks, the canals remain one of Detroit's hidden treasures.

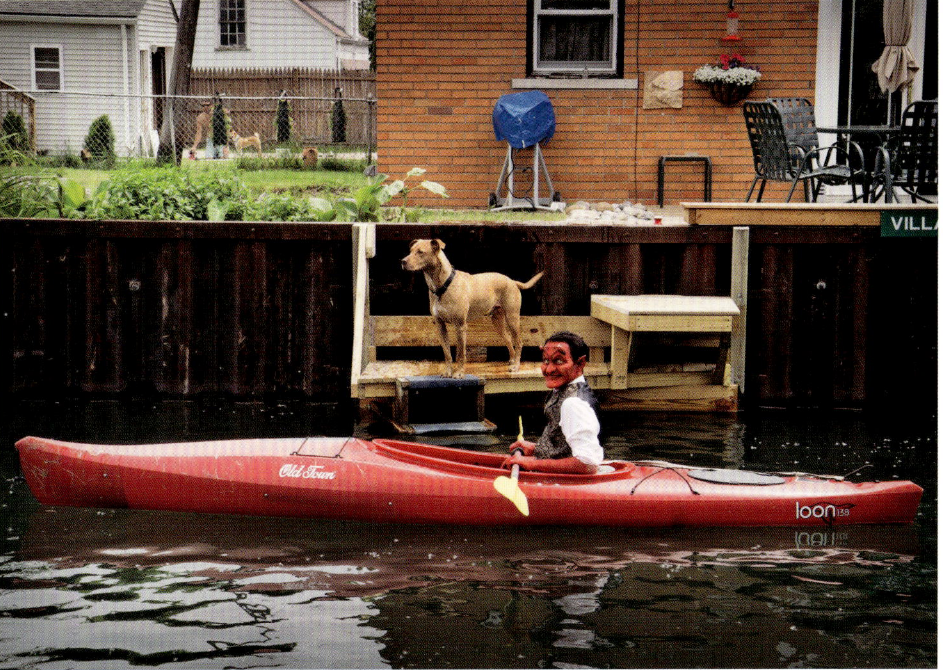

One of my best friends, Eric, and his wife, Buffy, own a home on the canals. They invited me to give kayaking a try a few years back. The calm and steady waters in the canals make it easy for a novice like me. In this tight, friendly community, we pass friends and neighbors grilling or gardening in their backyards. One neighbor even installed a diving board in his, right over the water. - NR

GARDEN BOWL

4120 Woodward Ave., Detroit, 48201
www.majesticdetroit.com/garden-bowl-detroit

Since 1913, balls have been striking pins at the nation's oldest continuously operating bowling alley, the Garden Bowl. In 1912, the Detroit Bowling Association was formed, followed in 1918 by the Detroit Women's Bowling Association. The game's popularity exploded. By 1941, the city had 89 bowling alleys, and one in seven Detroiters bowled, making the city the "bowling capital of the world." In 1960, there were 35 bowling alleys within two miles of the Garden Bowl. Now, the Garden Bowl is one of only two remaining in the city.

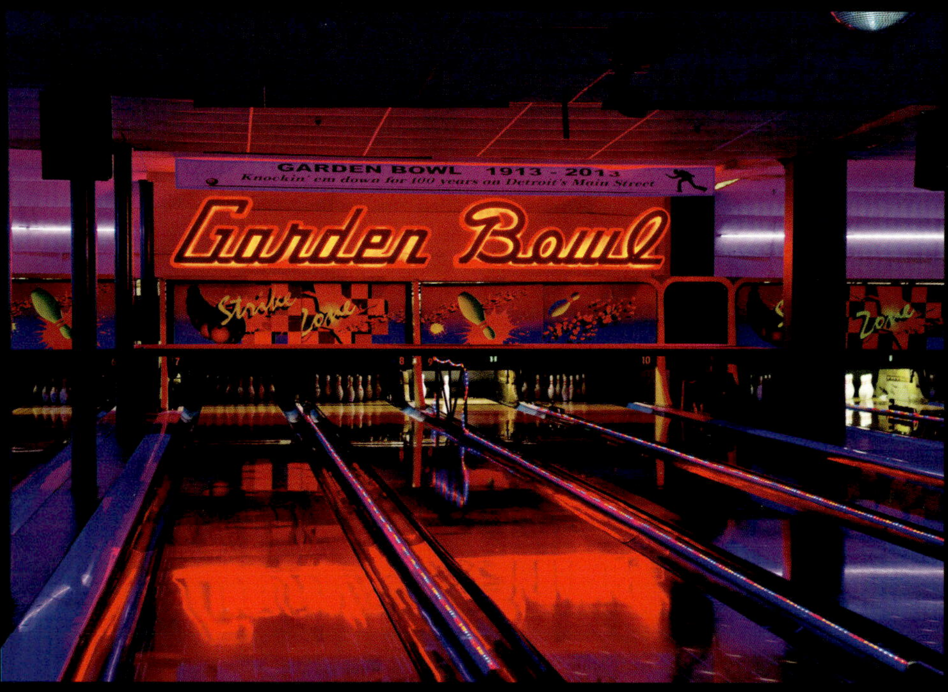

Family owned since 1946, the Garden Bowl is part of the Majestic Theatre Complex, led by Papa Joe Zainea and his sons, Dave and Joey. Still offering amateur and league play during the days, the Garden Bowl becomes the popular Rock & Bowl at night, adding smoke machines, black lights, and a DJ spinning music. - NR

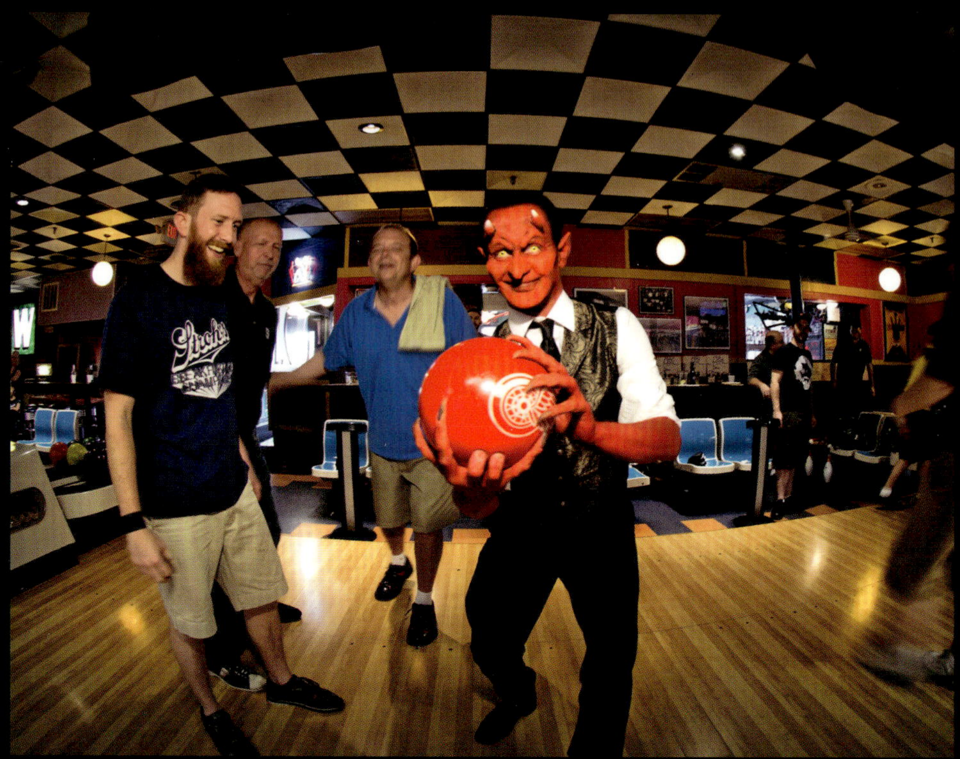

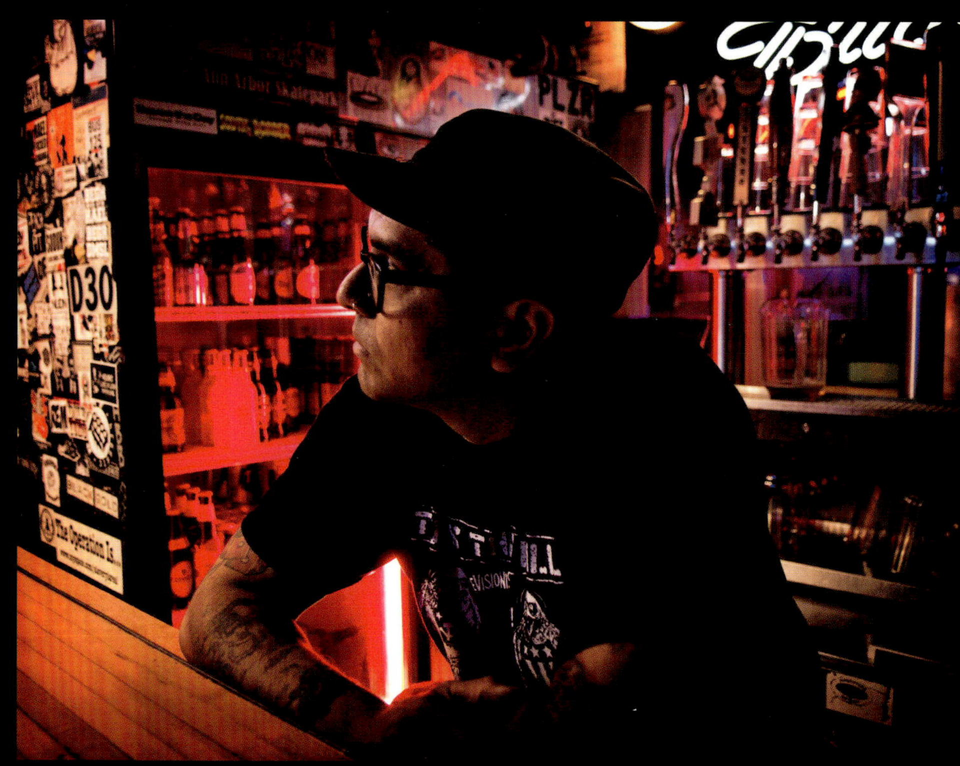

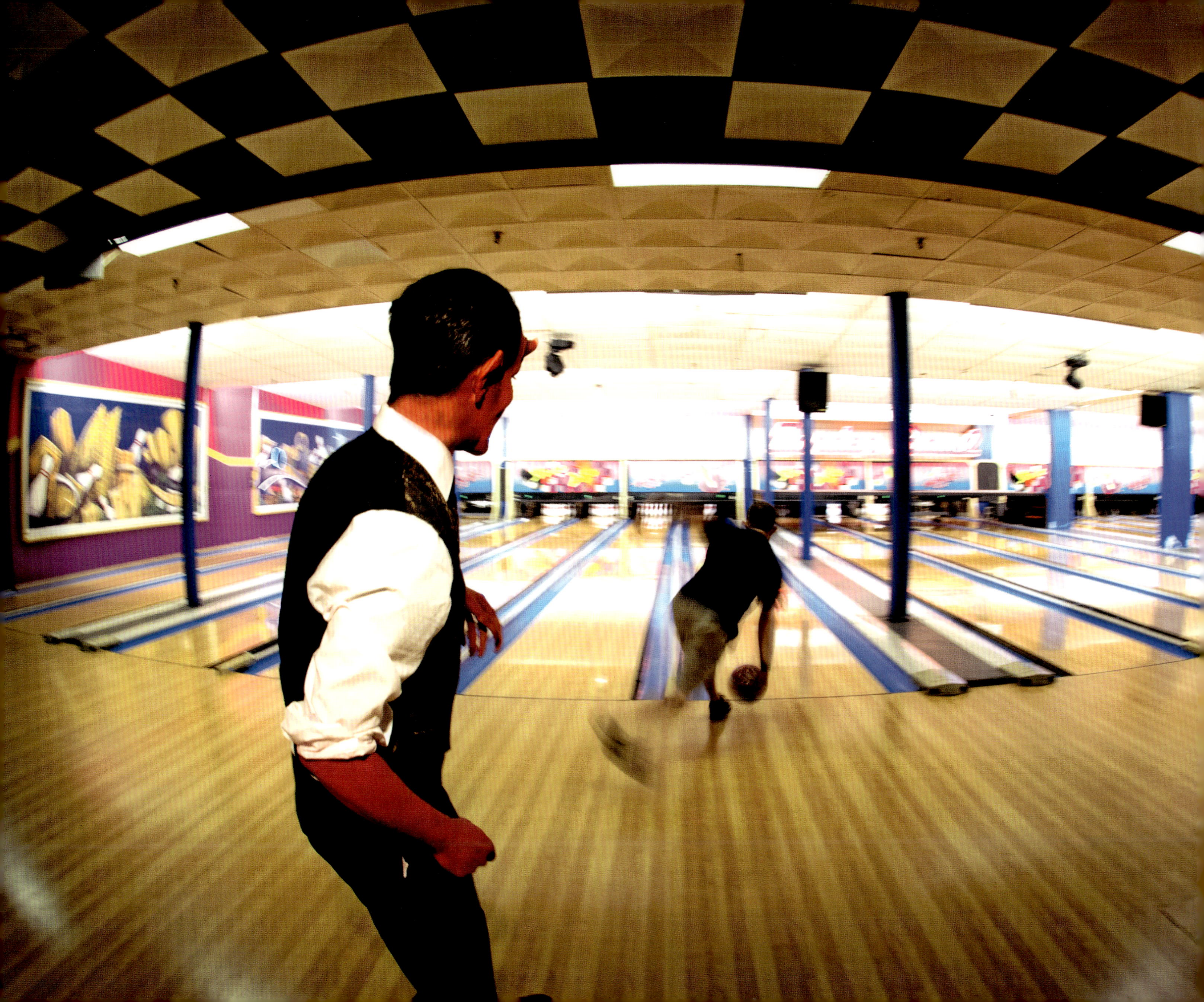

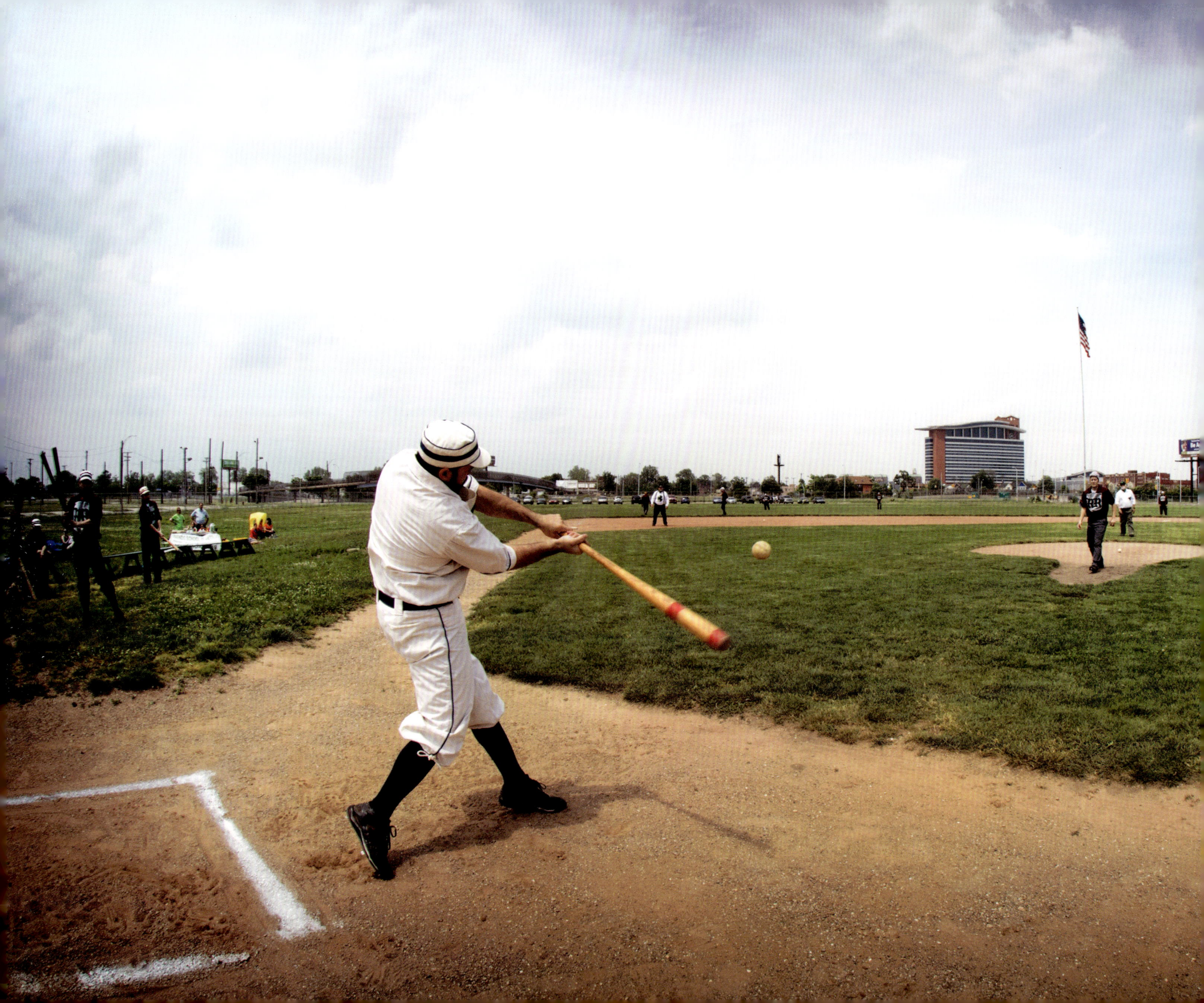

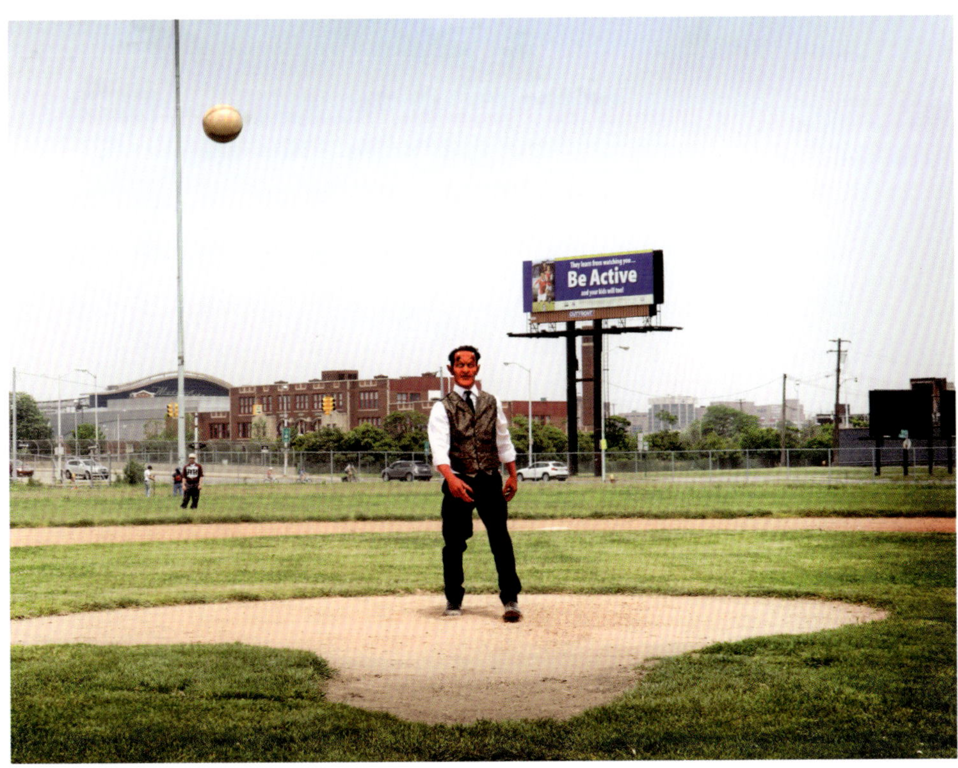

NAVIN FIELD GROUNDS CREW/OLD TIME BASEBALL

2121 Trumbull Ave., Detroit, 48216
www.navinfieldgroundscrew.blogspot.com

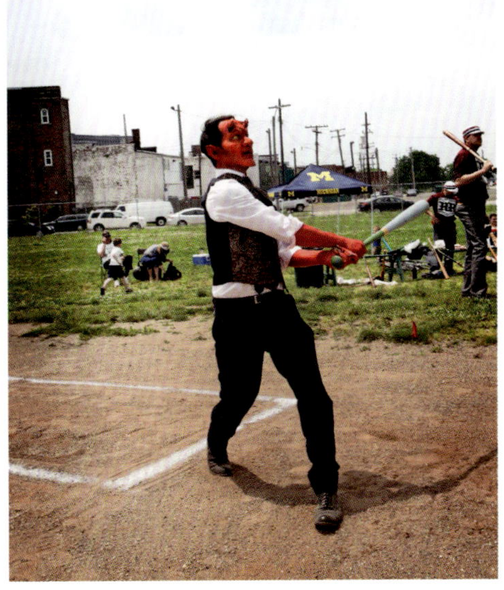

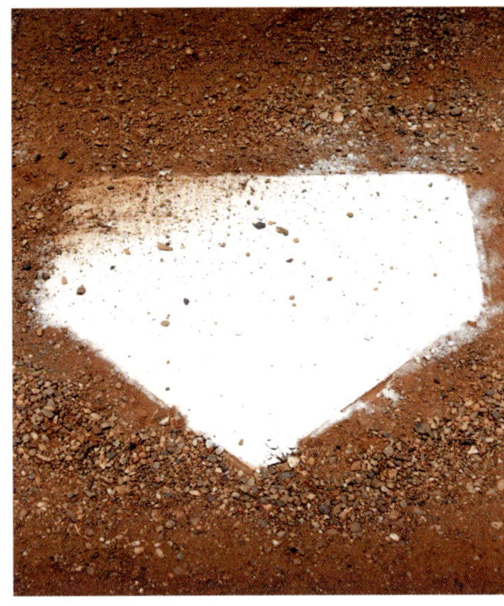

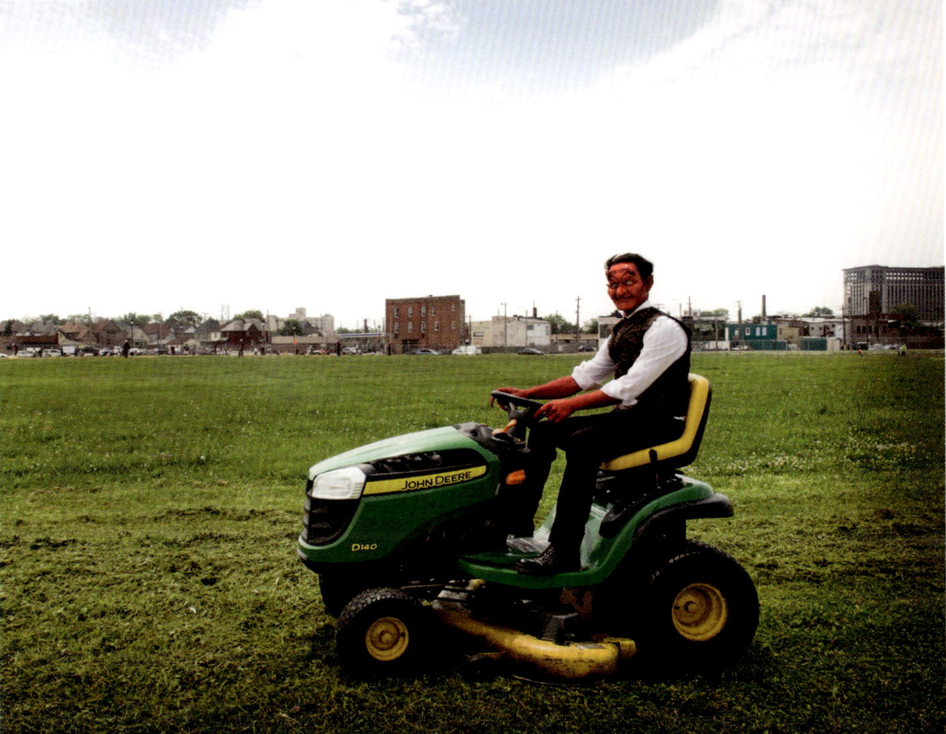

Dedicated to preserving the history and field of the former home to the Detroit Tigers, the Navin Field Grounds Crew became the champions of the former Tiger Stadium. Losing the battle to save a portion of the original stands, they convinced the city to maintain the original playing field, saving the original grounds so future ballplayers can run the same bases as Ty Cobb, Willie Horton, and Charlie Gerhinger. The Crew volunteered their time and money to maintain the field for neighborhood pickup games, vintage baseball teams, and anyone else who wanted to remember the great baseball moments that occurred at the "Corner" for almost a century.

Like most Detroiters, I was heartbroken when they tore down the old ballpark. For a while, the original stands and dugouts of Navin Field were all that remained. Pleas from the Navin Field Grounds Crew to preserve the grass, the last remnant, for pick-up games or little league teams fell on deaf ears, but through our efforts, the original field design will remain, renamed after Tiger great and friend, Willie Horton, maintained by the Detroit Police Athletic League for little league teams. - NR

THE WIG SKATEBOARD PARK

3550 John C. Lodge Fwy., Detroit, 48201
www.communitypush.org

On the grounds of the former Bruce Wigle Recreation Center, a group of skateboarders began transforming the old basketball courts into a skate park. Community Push was soon organized, representing the interests of the local skateboard community and focusing on a long-term plan to develop a "green" skate park. In the interim, the Wig was conceived. It immediately was recognized by skate magazines, pro teams, and tourists. Growing more popular, the Wig continues to expand.

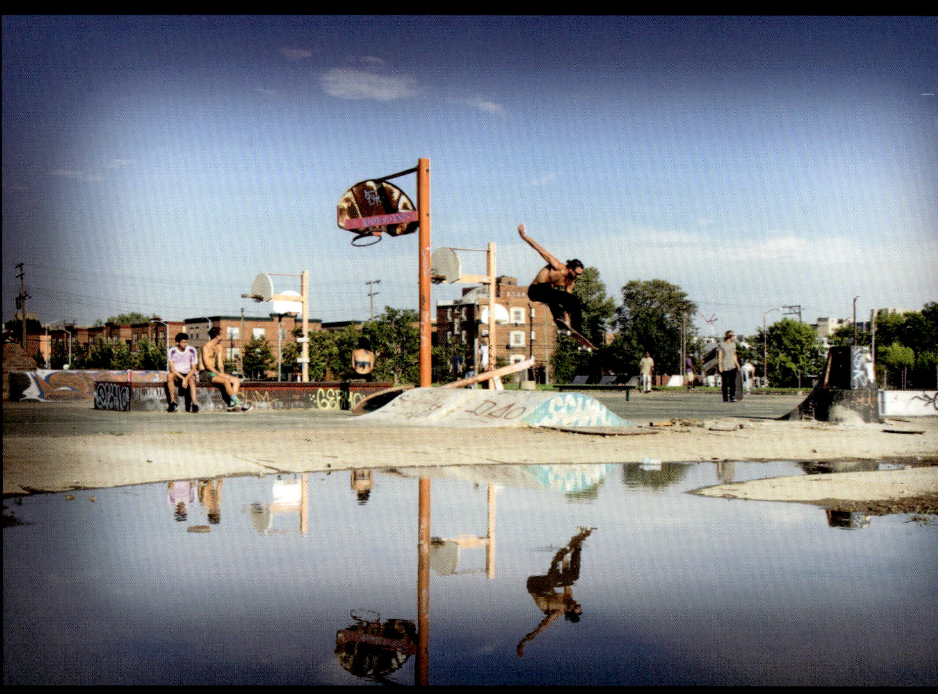

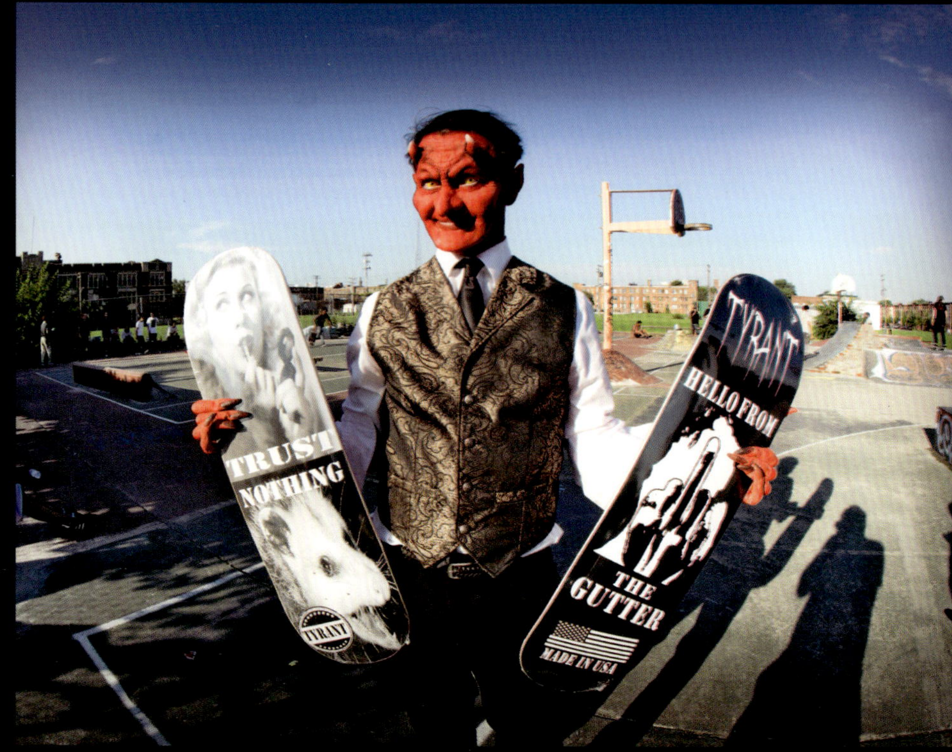

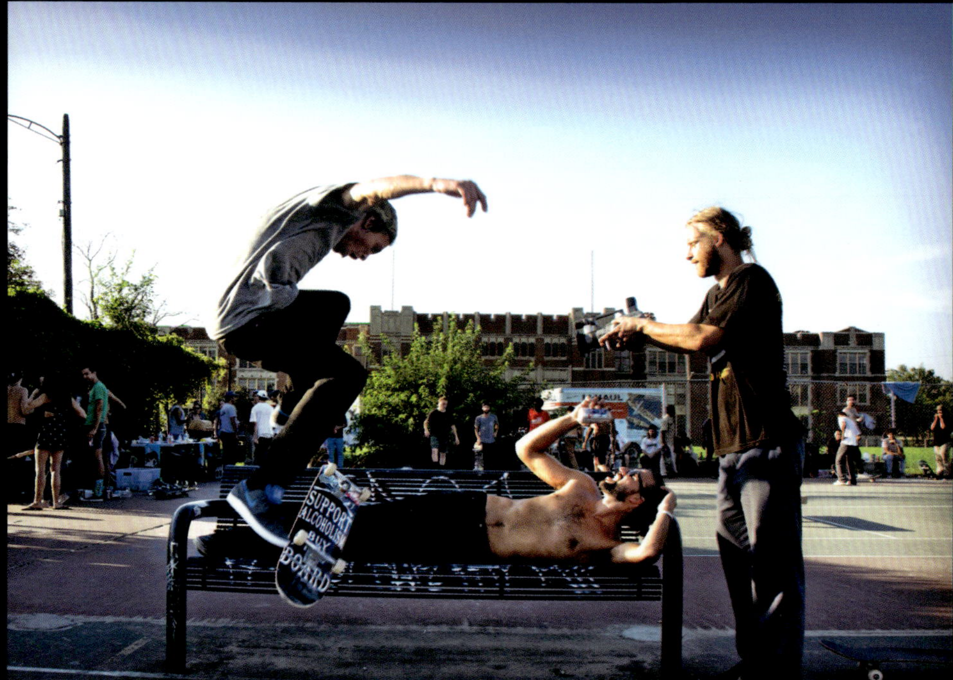

Skateboarders always have a hard time finding places to skate. Taking advantage of an abandoned rec center, we started designing a local skate park where we could go without getting hassled. Within two years, assisted by more than 100 volunteers, we created an iconic and nationally recognized park. - NR

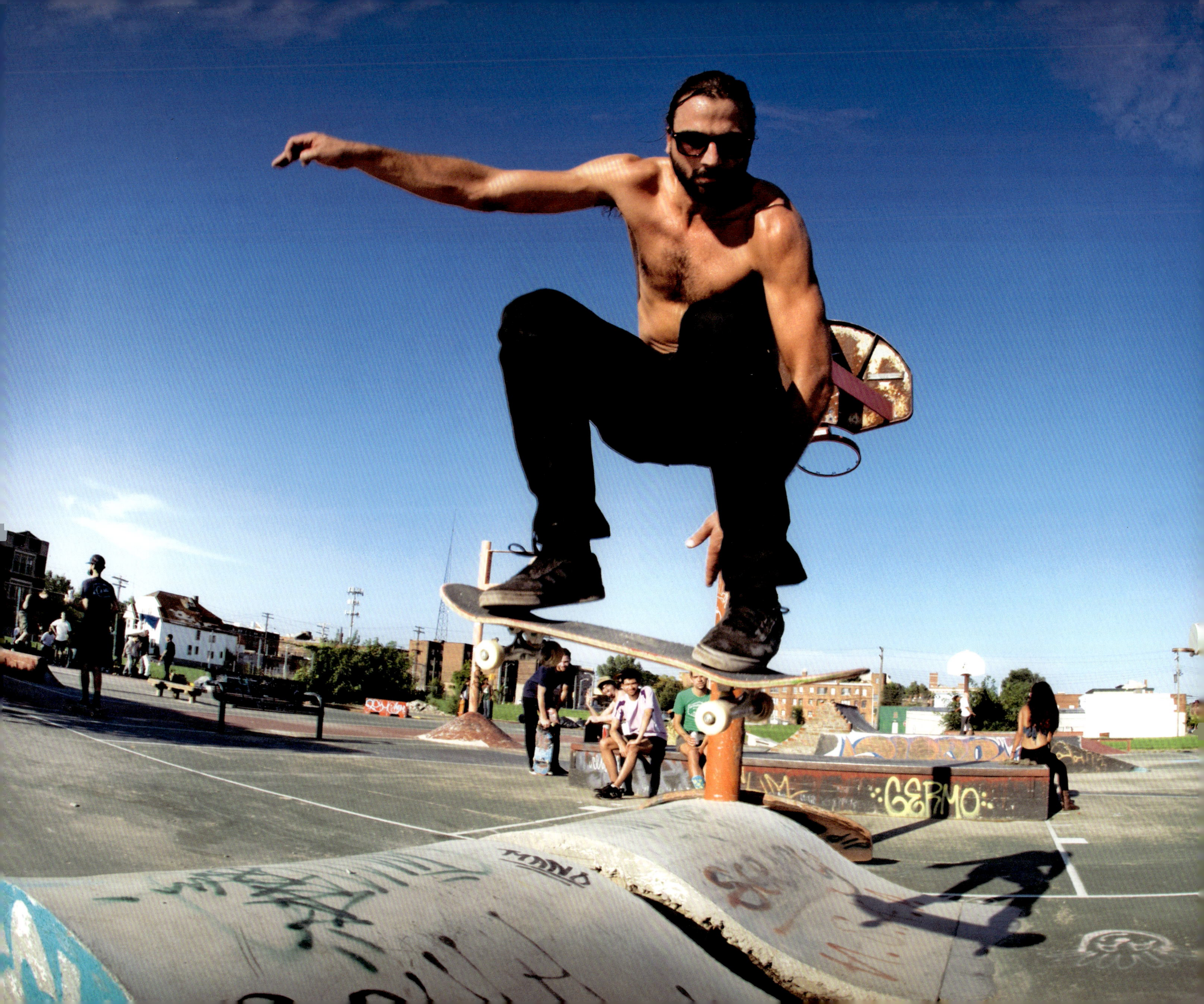
GERMO

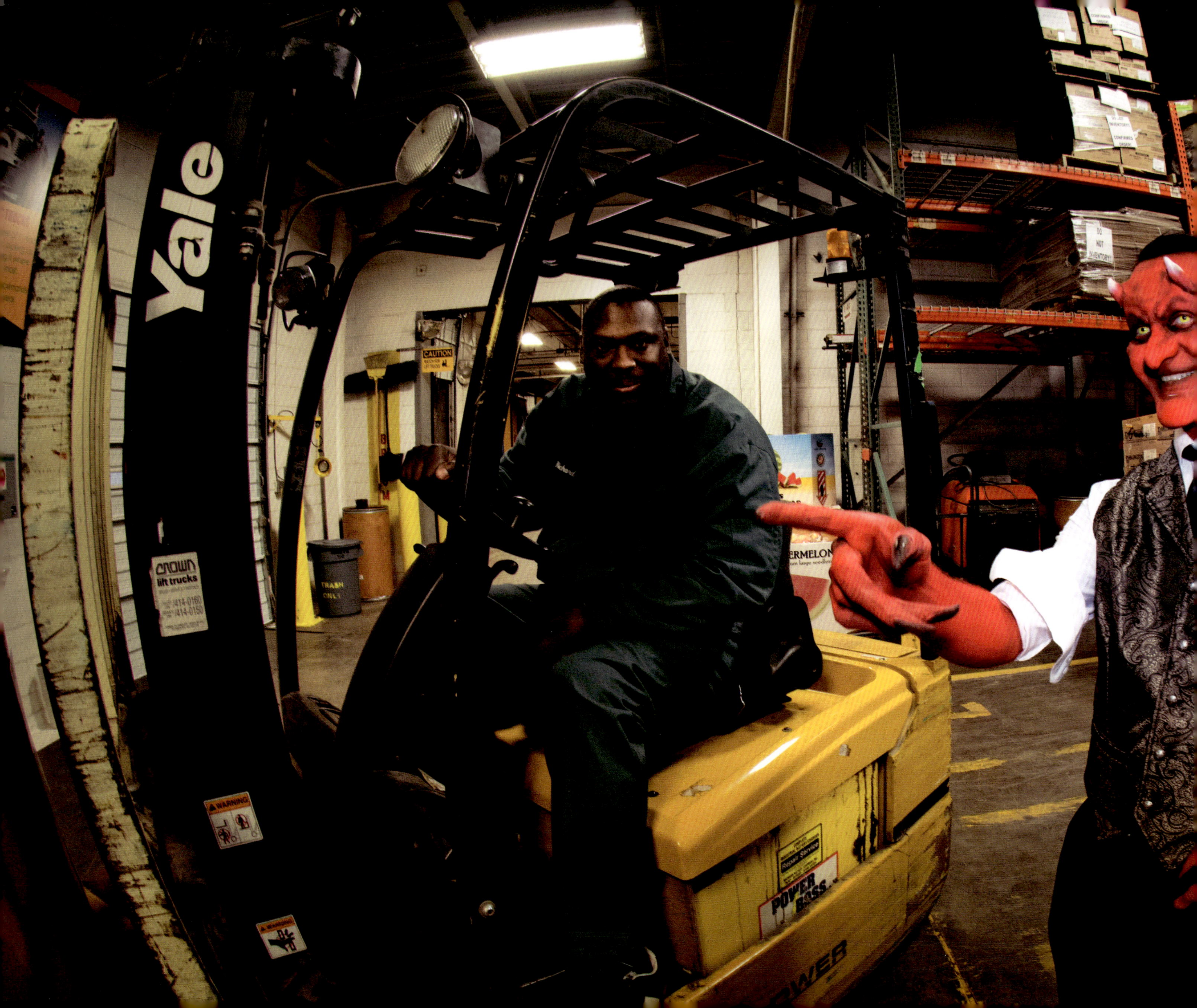

Yale
CROWN
lift trucks
CAUTION
TRASH
ONLY
DO NOT INVENTORY!
WARNING
POWER BOSS

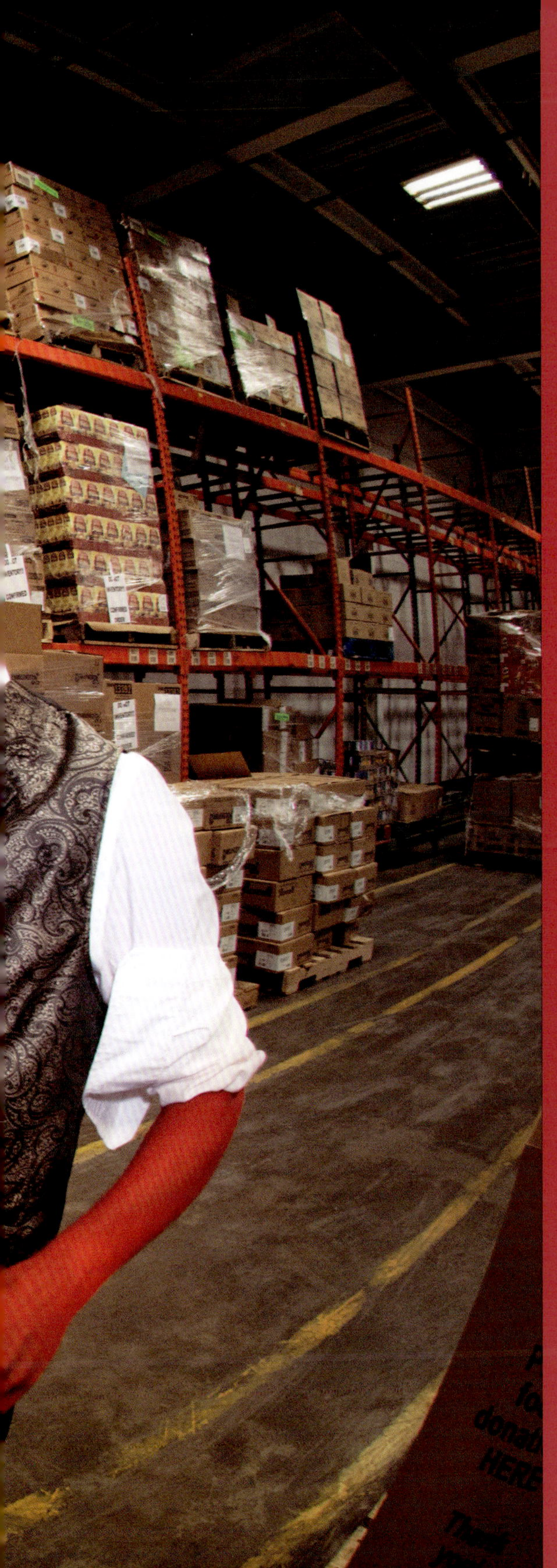

VOLUNTEERING

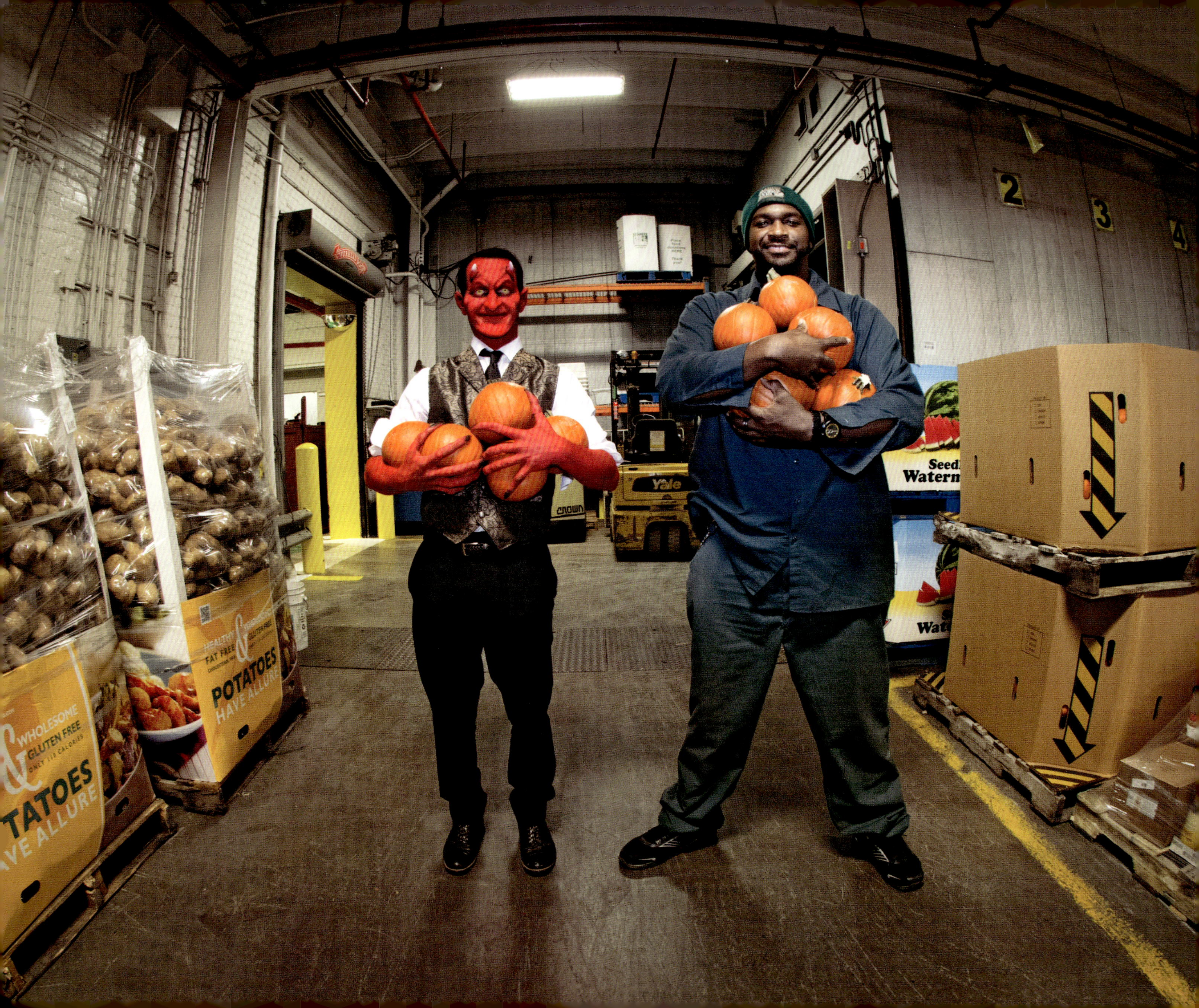
FAT FREE
POTATOES
HAVE ALLURE
WHOLESOME
GLUTEN FREE
Yale
CROWN
2
3
4

GLEANERS COMMUNITY FOOD BANK

2131 Beaufait St., Detroit, 48207
www.gcfb.org

Through the inspiration of Gene Gonya, and the determination of supporters in the community, a simple idea led to the creation of one of the first food banks in the United States, Gleaners Community Food Bank, formed in 1977. Dedicated to serving the neediest in their most trying times, Gleaners recognized that food waste from grocery stores, farmers, and distributors could be salvaged to feed those less fortunate. Every year, Gleaners' 48,000 volunteers distribute 20 million pounds of food to hungry families throughout the Detroit area.

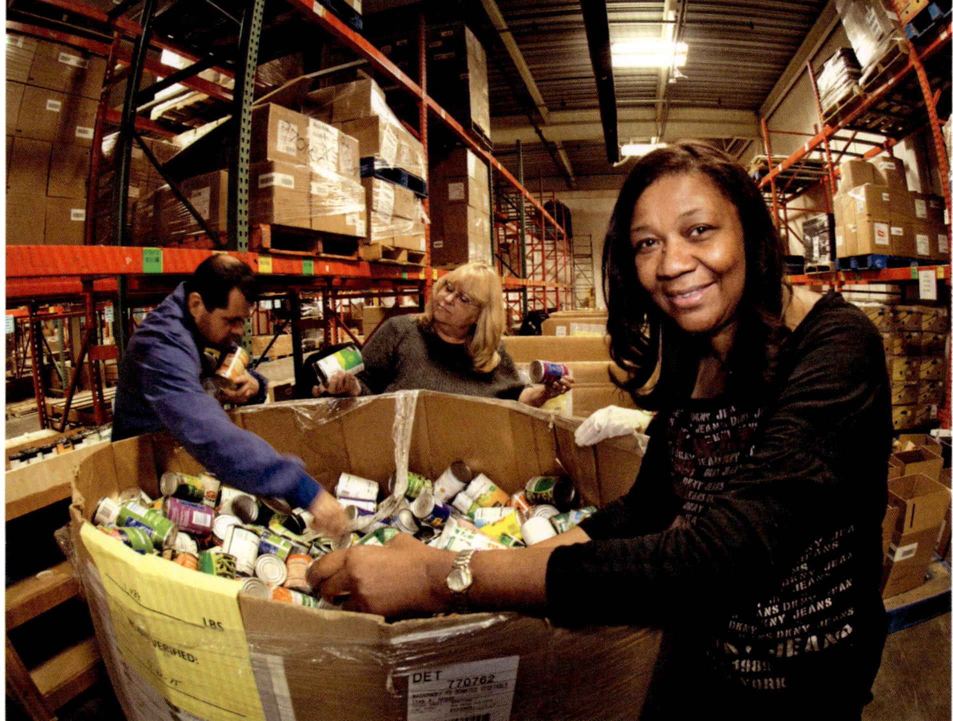

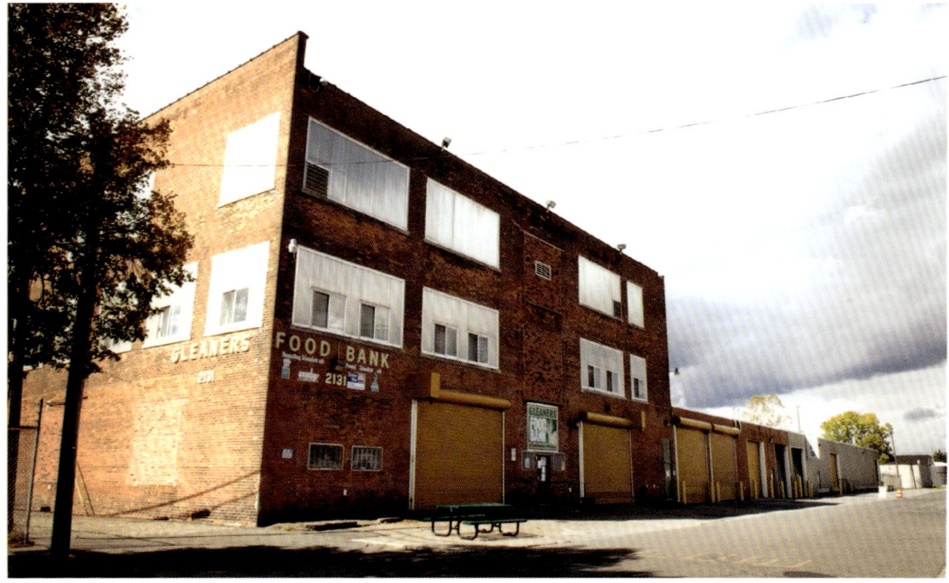

Wasting food in a city where a lot of people go hungry would be a damn dirty shame. Recognizing that, the good folks at Gleaners step in to collect food that otherwise would be thrown away and provide food packages to thousands of impoverished families. Resourceful Detroiters helping out where help is needed – you can't beat it.

- NR

GREENING OF DETROIT

1418 Michigan Ave., Detroit, 48216
www.greeningofdetroit.org

Detroit was once known as the "City of Trees." Every residential street was covered with a tree-lined canopy offering shade, coolness, and beauty. Between 1950 and 1980, more than 500,000 trees were lost to Dutch Elm disease and attrition. Founded in 1989 by Elizabeth Gordon Sachs, the Greening of Detroit was determined to reforest the city and return the lush canopies to the neighborhoods. Since it began, 89,000 trees have been planted. Recognizing the importance of neighborhood involvement, Greening of Detroit has initiated programs to employ Detroit's youth during the summers and an adult workforce training program for the unemployed.

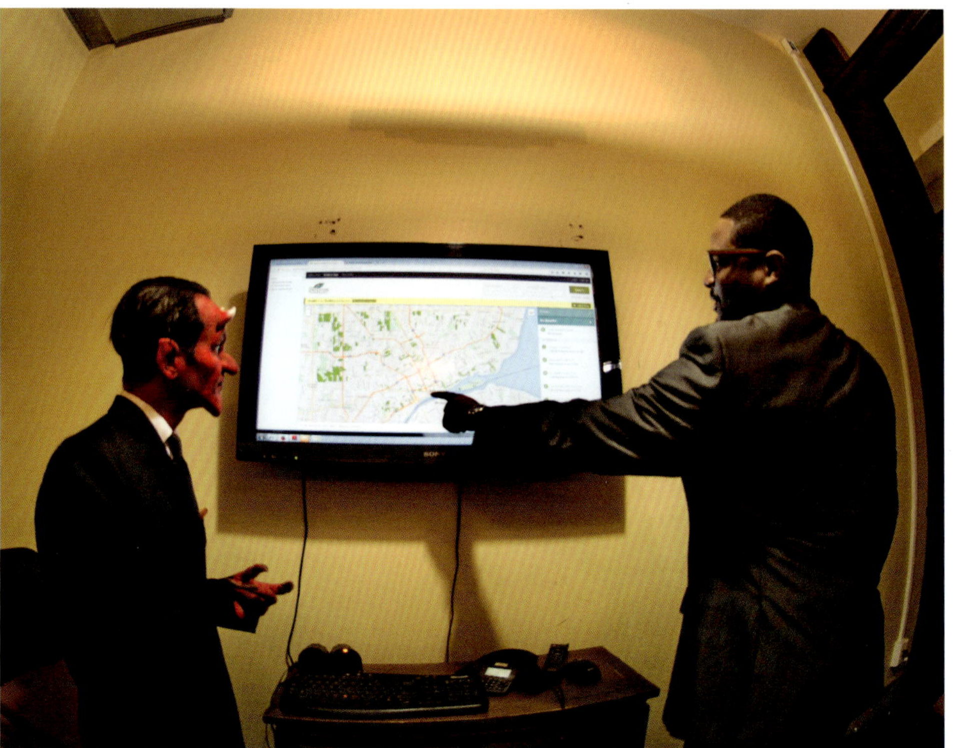

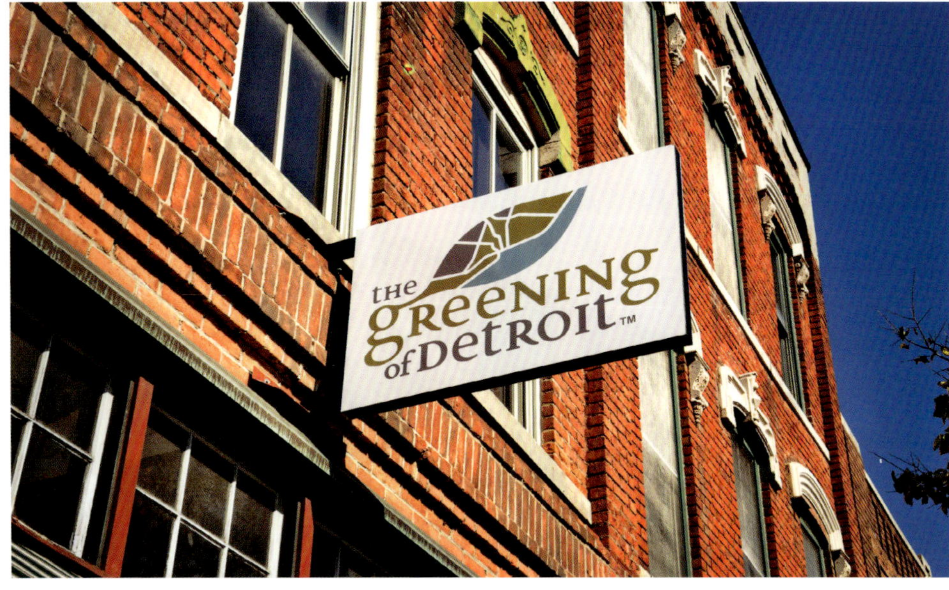

When, decades ago, canopies of Elm trees shaded Detroit's streets in summer and offered vibrant bursts of orange in fall, they really made the city something to see. Then again, planting so many trees from a single species turned out to be rather silly, as the devastation wrought by Dutch Elm disease showed. Now, my friends with Greening of Detroit help neighborhoods replace the trees with a better understanding of the ecology. - NR

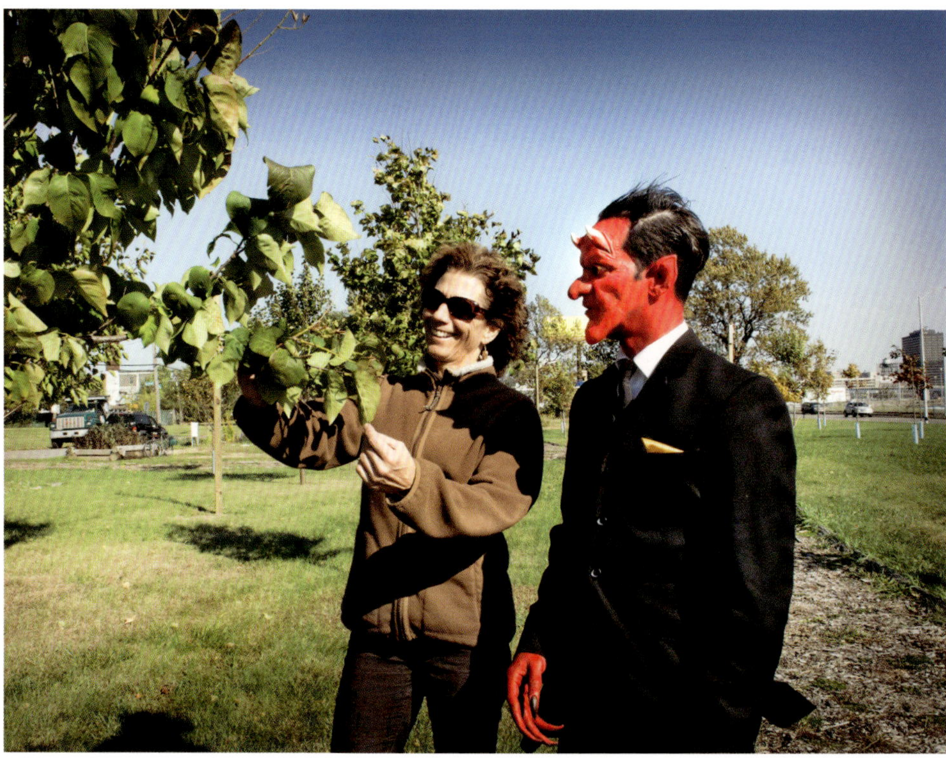

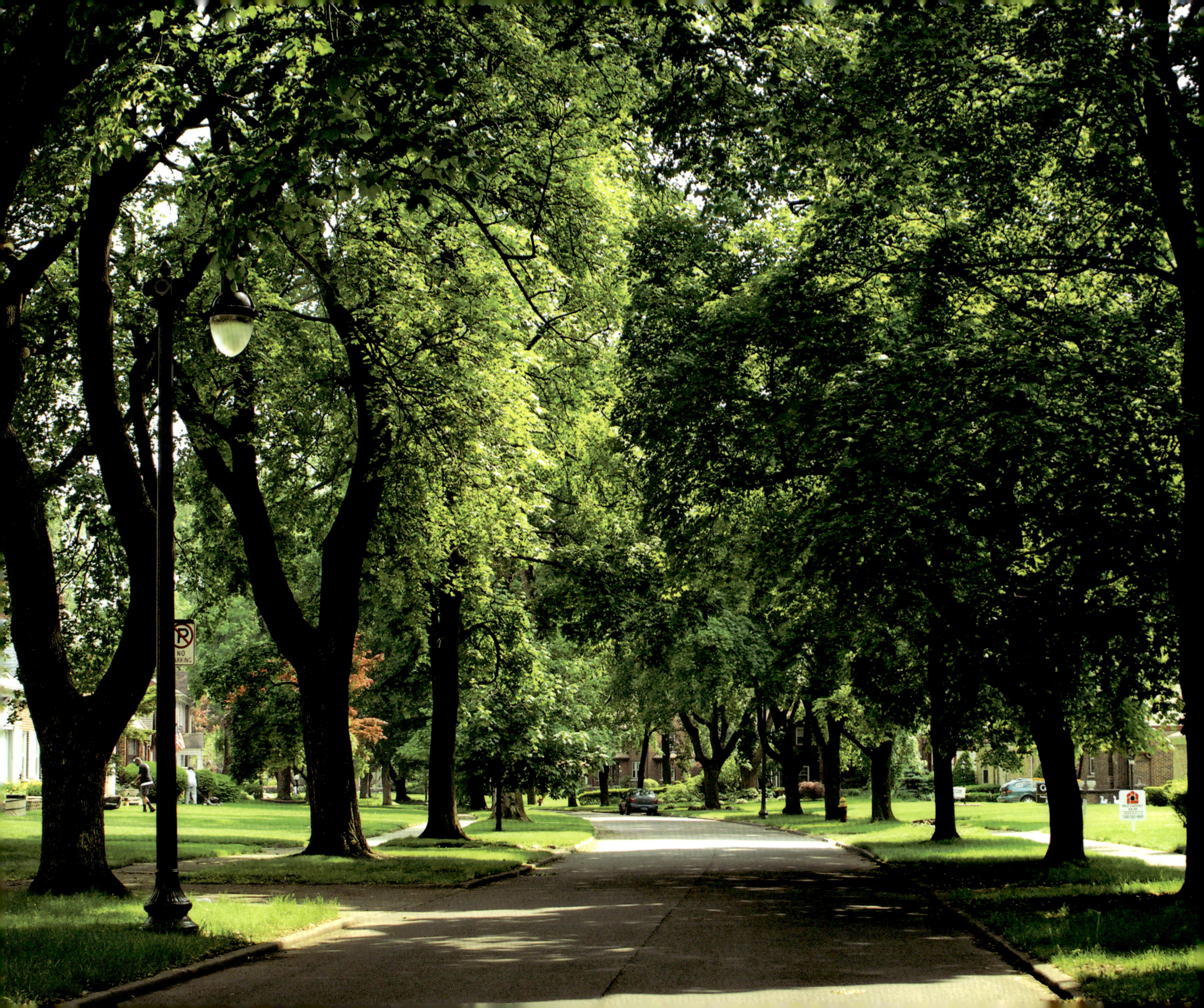
NO

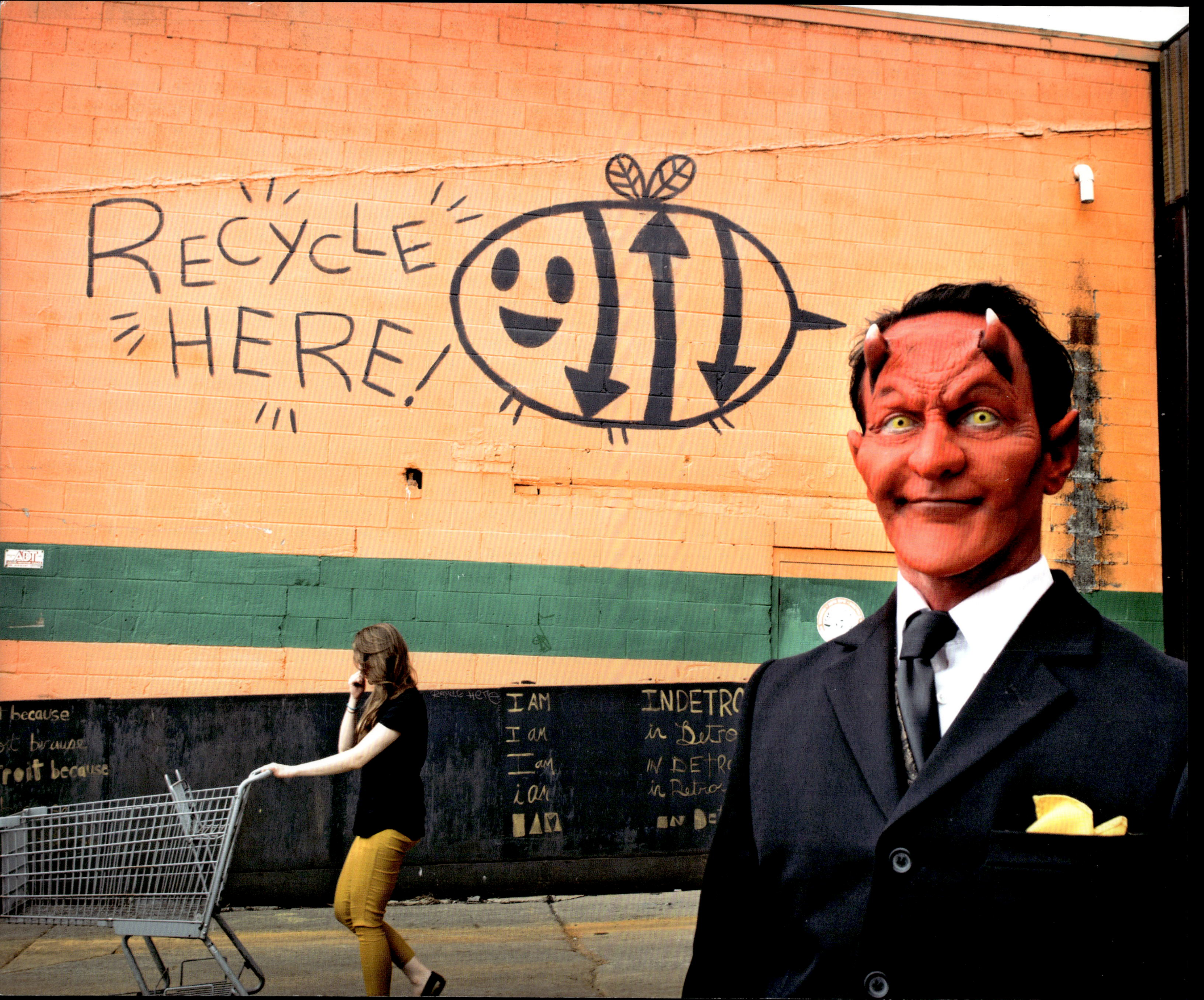
RECYCLE HERE!
because
I AM
I am

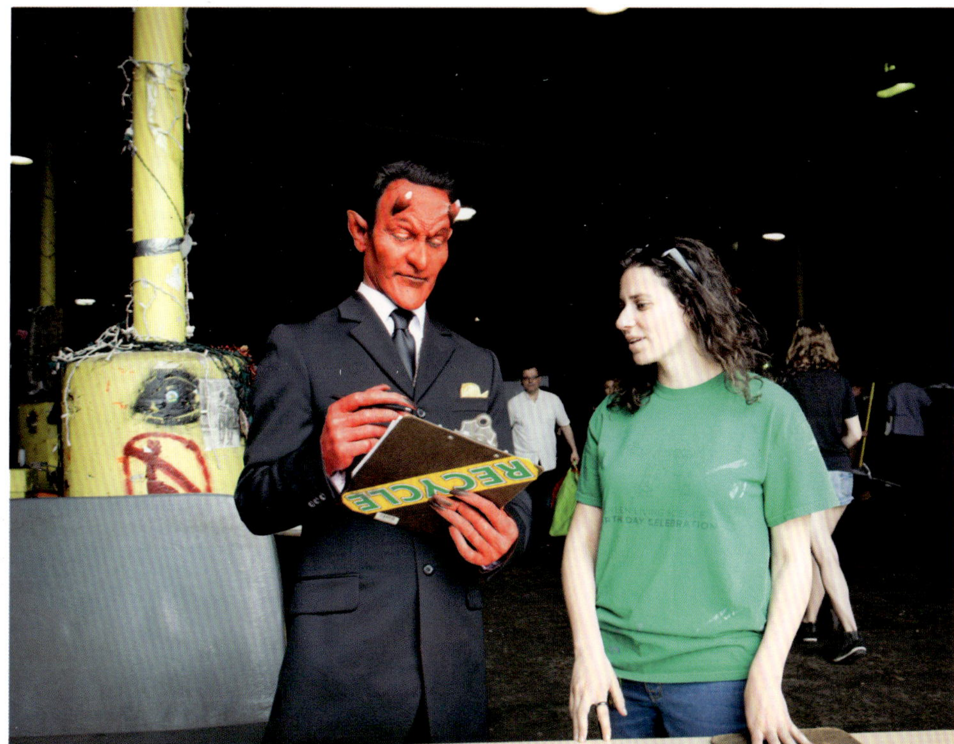

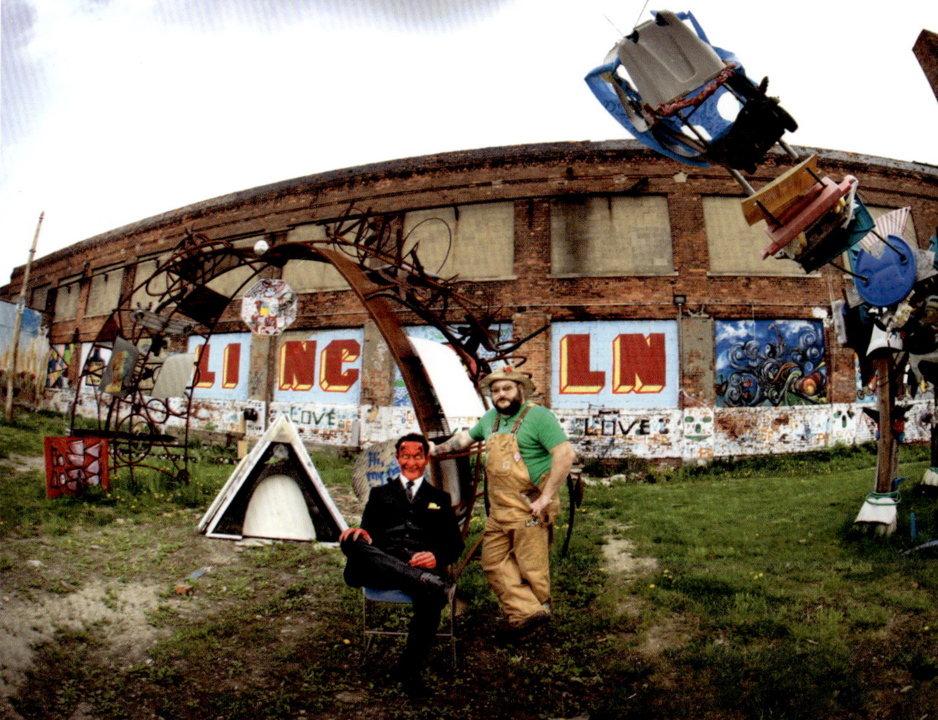

RECYCLE HERE!

1331 Holden St., Detroit, 48202
www.recyclehere.net

Addressing the lack of recycling options for city residents, Recycle Here began its first city wide program in 2005. Starting as a grassroots neighborhood event, the program expanded and is now fully funded and partnered with the city. The Detroit Public Schools' Recycling Program teaches students and their families the benefits of recycling and how they can make changes in their daily lives to reduce their impact on the environment. The main location on Holden Street sponsors the nearby Lincoln Art Park, using found material to create works of sculpture.

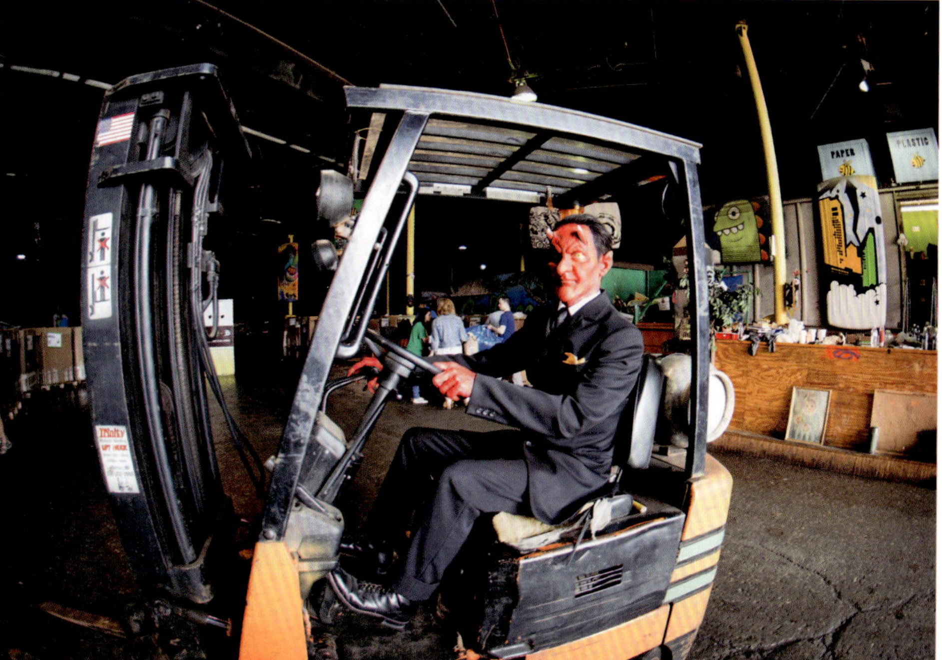

Finding inspiration in garbage, these crazy fuckers are always up to something. Establishing the Lincoln Street Art Park with help from local artists, this outfit's leader, Matt Naimi, has become Detroit's most famous garbage man. - NR

URBAN FARMS

Michigan Urban Farming Initiative
www.miufi.org

Keep Growing Detroit
www.detroitagriculture.net

Capuchin Soup Kitchen - Earthworks Urban Farm
www.cskdetroit.org/earthworks

New and trendy in certain parts of the country, urban farming is an old idea to Detroit. During the depression of 1893, the urban population faced a food crisis. In response, Mayor Hazen S. Pingree requested that all empty lots be converted into vegetable gardens, earning himself the nickname "Potato Patch." Following the recent movement towards local and organic farming, and with a abundance of abandoned property, urban farmers have seized the moment, reusing the empty lots, educating neighbors, and creating markets for a produce-starved city.

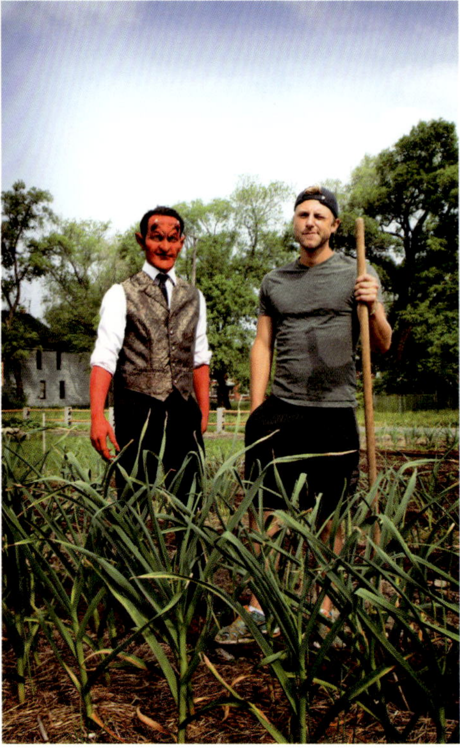

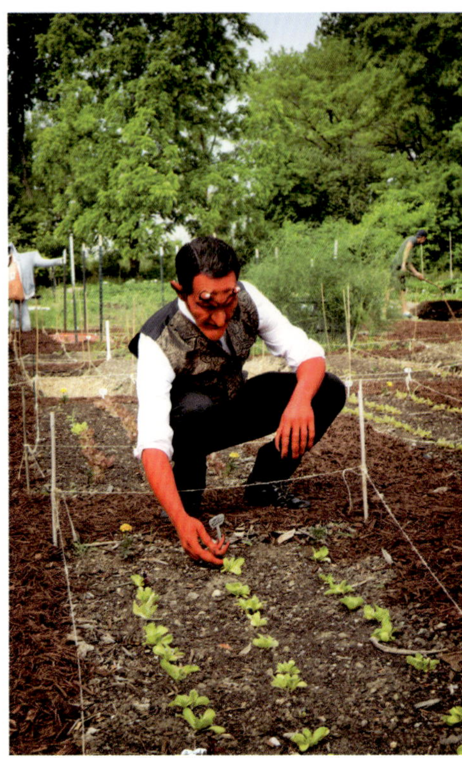

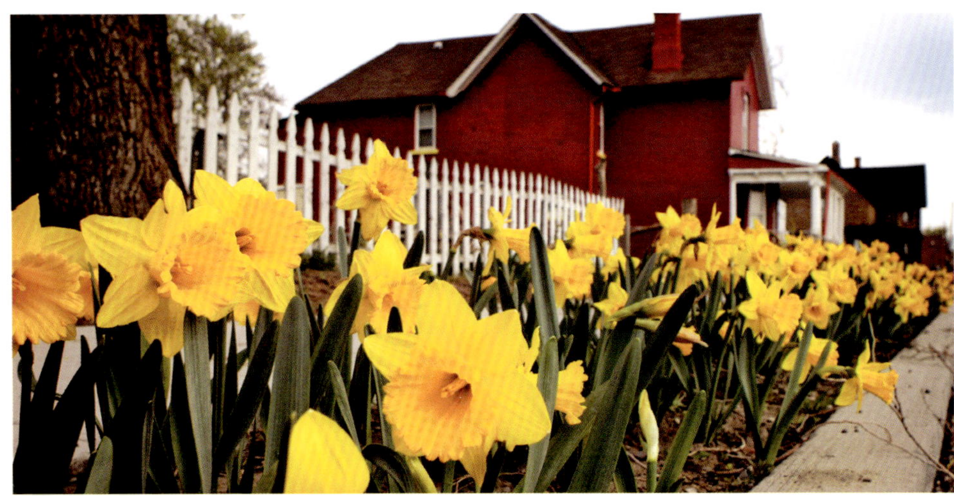

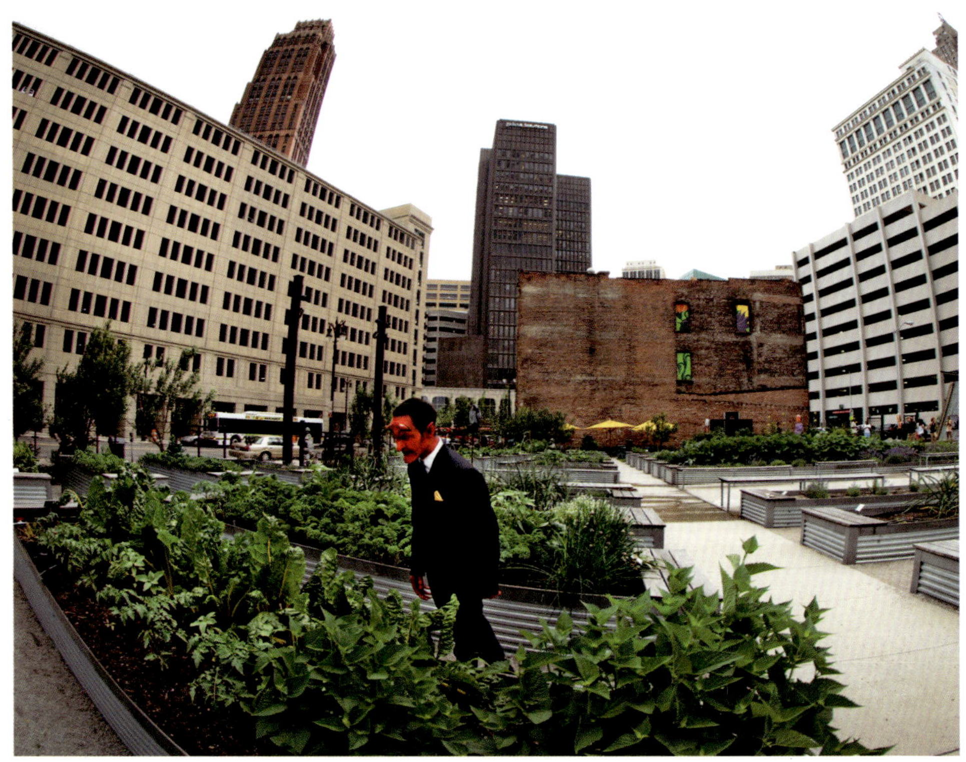

Detroiters have been farming from the city's very beginnings, whether tilling the long ribbon farms French settlers plotted along the river, taking advantage of the rich soil that gave Black Bottom its name (and helping the Ferry Seed Company to become the largest seed supplier in the world), or planting vegetable gardens when unemployment hit 40% in the 1890s. Unfortunately, we've got a lot of empty space around Detroit nowadays, but my resourceful fellow Detroiters are doing what they've always done: doing what they've got to do to survive. - NR

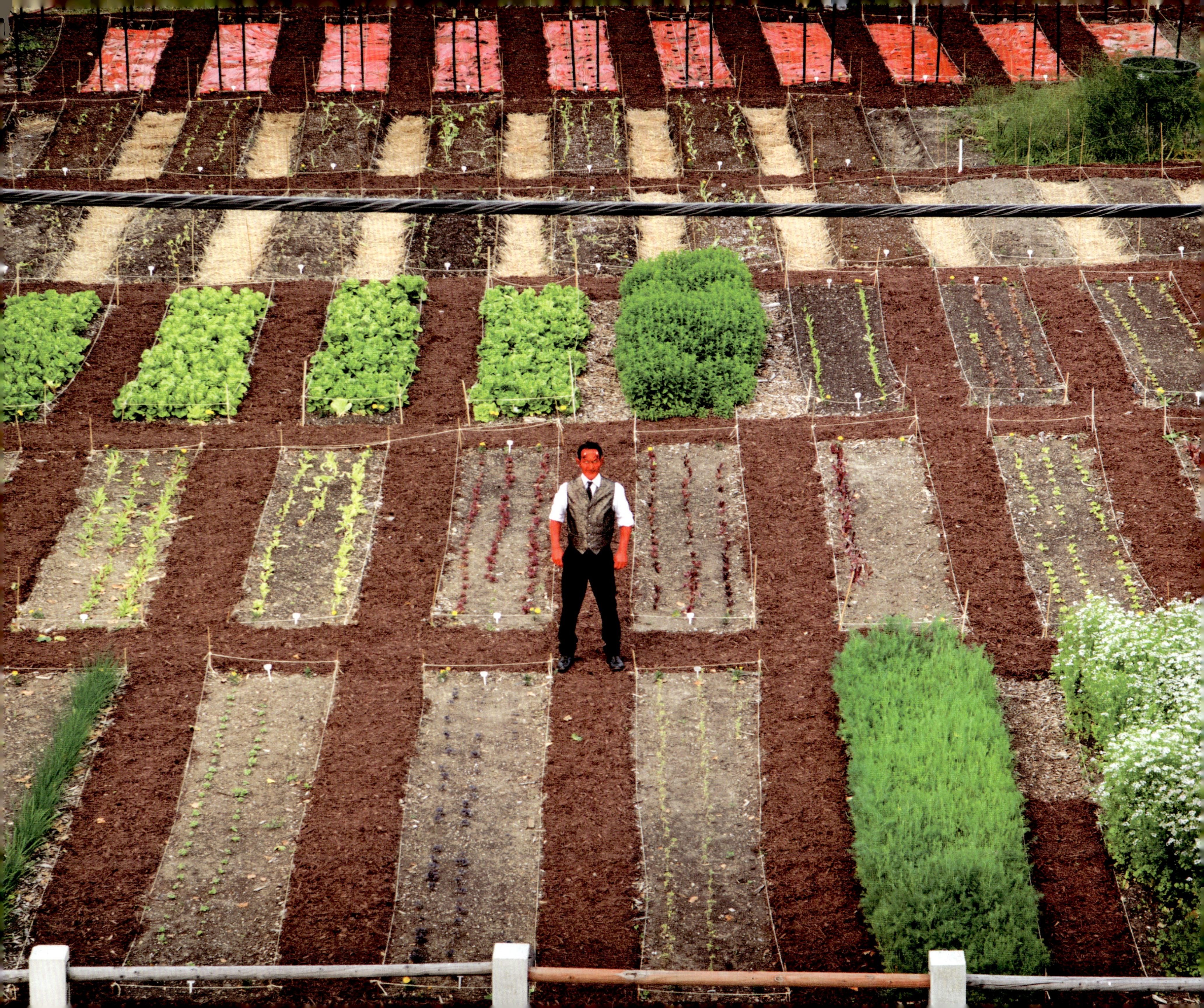

Biographies

Dave Krieger

A Detroit native, Dave Krieger has been a photographer, music video director, and movie producer. Having worked in Paris, LA, and NYC, he returned to Detroit for family. His brother-in-law says he is the "most successful unemployed person he knows." His underwear was once signed by Andy Warhol on TV. He appeared in a Madonna lookalike contest with his brother and best friend. His work is buried in a box, part of the permanent collection at the Detroit Institute of Arts.

www.kriegerphoto.com

Andrea O'Donnell

Andrea O'Donnell has been creating beauty in various forms for decades. Growing up in her mother's beauty salon, Andrea naturally gravitated toward the world of makeup and beauty. She spent her formative teen years selling sex toys at Noir Leather and graduated with her cosmetology license in 1988 at the age of 18. Andrea's knack of blending the traditional with the not-so-traditional in the world of art and makeup stems from her belief that to be happy and successful in life, you always do what you love and love what you do!

Andy Wainio

Andrew Wainio was raised in the woods of the upper peninsula of Michigan. After being left for dead by his parents, he received a bachelor of arts degree from the University of Michigan. He moved to Rochester, New York, where he stole an MFA from RIT. Tricked into being the Nain Rouge, Andy was abused and berated until he would no longer perform his duties.

Special Thanks and Recognition

Without the encouragement and assistance of these folks, this book would still just be another one of my undeveloped ideas.

I'd like to begin by thanking my mother for encouraging my brother and me to pursue the stupid idea that being artists would be financially rewarding. Despite her damning MS, she pushed us to be creative, taking my brother early in his life to art classes at Cranbrook and indulging any idiotic request I had. Unable to walk, she would drop me at age nine at the DIA, where I would wander for hours looking at the collection, or leave me downtown on some street corner, where I would sketch buildings, dreaming of becoming an architect or city planner.

Thanks to my father for showing us Detroit and telling us its history while trying to find something for us to do on the cheap every other weekend. His commitment to teaching in Highland Park was inspiring, and he taught us the importance of diversity of race, class, and thought.

Thanks to my brother who has been my best friend over the years. His artistic abilities far surpass anything I ever attempted.

Thanks to my sons, Jackson and Dylan for being the best and most artistic thing I have ever created.

Andy Wainio, as the Nain Rouge, was abused for over a year with my demanding schedule changes and total disrespect. He has endured despite wanting to quit after the first day.

Andrea O'Donnell deserves praise for her excellent work in creating our rendition of the Nain Rouge. I don't know what this would look like without her skills in SFX makeup. A special thanks goes to her assistants, Melissa Drogmiller, who was always there for us when Andrea didn't want to do it, and Angela Brown.

Aku Lahti became an essential support for Andy as I beat him up psychologically to the point where he wouldn't do it without Aku there.

John Rodwan sifted through incoherent and run-on sentences and tried to correct massive mistake after mistake.

Brent Bacher lent me the tools to achieve the look I wanted. Without him, everything would look worse than it already does.

Special thanks to Kiersten Armstrong and Mike Warlow at KMW studio publishing for their insane trust in me and for their guidance, design and inspiration to keep going.